Indiana-Born Major
League Baseball Players

Indiana-Born Major League Baseball Players

A Biographical Dictionary, 1871–2014

PETE CAVA

McFarland & Company, Inc., Publishers
Jefferson, North Carolina

LIBRARY OF CONGRESS CATALOGUING-IN-PUBLICATION DATA

Cava, Pete.
Indiana-born major league baseball players :
a biographical dictionary, 1871–2014 / Pete Cava.
    p.   cm.
Includes bibliographical references and index.

ISBN 978-0-7864-9901-4 (softcover : acid free paper) ♾
ISBN 978-1-4766-2270-5 (ebook)

1. Baseball players—Indiana—Biography—Dictionaries.   2. Baseball players—United States—Biography—Dictionaries.   3. Baseball—United States—History.   I. Title.

GV865.A1C325 2015   796.3570922—dc23   [B]   2015027846

BRITISH LIBRARY CATALOGUING DATA ARE AVAILABLE

© 2015 Pete Cava. All rights reserved

No part of this book may be reproduced or transmitted in any form or by any means, electronic or mechanical, including photocopying or recording, or by any information storage and retrieval system, without permission in writing from the publisher.

On the cover: (top, left to right) Mordecai Brown, Max Carey, Billy Herman and Chuck Klein; (bottom, left to right) Sam Rice, Edd Roush, Amos Rusie and Sam Thompson

Printed in the United States of America

*McFarland & Company, Inc., Publishers
Box 611, Jefferson, North Carolina 28640
www.mcfarlandpub.com*

For my parents,
Bud (1916–2001) and Adele,
who placed great value on a well-rounded education.
They didn't discourage me when I announced my intent
to play for the New York Yankees.
Instead, they suggested having a backup plan.
I appreciated their wisdom when opposing pitchers began throwing curves.

For Dan O'Brien,
whose friendship, encouragement, advice and
incredible research skills are invaluable assets.
Rube, you're my pick for Most Valuable Player.

And in memory of Paul Sandin (1950–2012),
a teammate, friend and colleague whose vision
helped launch this project.

Ad maiorem Dei gloriam

Contents

Acknowledgments ix
Introduction 1

The Players 3

Bibliography 227
Index 243

Acknowledgments

I want to thank my reviewer, proofreader, roommate and best friend, Molly Mehagan Cava, who suffers from the double affliction of rooting for the Cubs and marriage to a writer.

Also, special thanks to Dr. Peter Bjarkman, a friend and mentor; the Society for American Baseball Research, its chapters in Indianapolis, South Bend and Fort Wayne, and SABR's Biographical Research Committee; and to libraries and librarians throughout Indiana and many other states, especially the Indiana State Library, the Indianapolis/Marion County Public Library, the Greenwood Library, and the National Baseball Hall of Fame Library.

I owe a huge debt of gratitude to the membership of the Indiana Writers' Workshop, present and past: David Ballard, Teri Barnett, John Clair, June McCarty Clair, Steve Heininger, Sylvia Hyde, Mark Lee, Tony Perona, Cheryl Shore, Steve Wynalda, Kathleen Schuckel Andrews, Bob Chenoweth, Reid Duffy, Dan Fenton, Nancy Frenzel, Jay Hill, Andy Horning, Joyce Jensen, Kathy Nappier, Kitty Smock, and the late Pat Watson Grande and Lucy Schilling.

Also, my thanks to Mike Ahern, Richard Akers, Tom Akins, Esther Alexander, Bill Allee, Marc Allen, Neil Amdur, Rich Andriole, Vicki Armstrong, Jerry Baker, Larry Baldassaro, Dr. Warrick Barrett, Hal Bateman, Chad Bates, Mason Bell, Rick Bell, Steve Bell, Cyndi Pote Bennett, Maudine Bennum, Lou Bergonzi, Dick Beverage, Bob Beyke, Dave Bohmer, Ray Boomhower, Brian Bosma, Wally Brant, Brent Brown, Cal Burleson, Rob Butcher, Bill Carle, Curt Cassell, Ollan Cassell, Dick Cassin, Andy Cava, Nancy Cava, Mike Chappell, Gene Cherry, Larry Cohen, Dick Contos, JJ Cooper, Jerry Cosby, J.L. Craney, Linda Craney, Pat Craviso, Kit Crissey, Cheri Daniels, Scott Davis, Bob Dellinger, Dr. Susan Dellinger, Dick Denny, Garry Donna, Jerry Duhamell, Jim Dunaway, Mark Durr, Les East, Charles Eberhardt, Darlene Eberhardt, Morris Eckhouse, Matt Eddy, Bill Eidson, Dr. John Ellis, Sheryn Ellis, Ed Esposito, John R. Esposito, Mary Esposito, Ed Evans, Paul Feinman, Nate Flannery, Will Flemming, Noel Fliss, Kurt Freudenthal, Cappy Gagnon, Tony Giacobbe, Jean Gieseking, Steve Gietschier, John Ginter, Nate Goldstein, Dr. Dave Goss, Susan Gray, Bob Gregory, Bill Haber, Chris Hansen, Bill Hardy, Jerry Harkness, Tim Harms, Roger Hawks, Dr. Jim Hennegan, Steve Herman, Blake Hibler, Dan Hickling, Bill Hickman, Charlie Holdaway, Ed Holdaway, Steve Holdaway, Jim Holsapple, Barry Horn, Ray Howard, Tom Hudson, Rick Huhn, Greg Ingle, Brian Jackson, John Jackson, Don Jellison, Chris Jensen, Rob Jensen, Cliff Johnson, Dave Johnson, Gary Johnson, Jan Johnson, Ludwig Johnson, Sherm Johnson, Dr. Ron Johnston, Alan Katchen, Adrian Katschke, Jack Kavanagh, Howard Kellman, Kim Kemerly, Russ Kemmerer, Alex Kirby, Steve Krah, Francis Lafferty, Bob Lamey, Joe Larr, Judy Larr, Ralph Leonard, Jane Leavy, Len Levin, Chuck Licari, Hank Lowenkron, Michael Lunsford, W.C. Madden, Richard Malatzky, Rich Maloney, Greg Mark, Mike Marot, Marty Martinez, Bill McAfee, Mike McCormick, Andy McCue, Dick McGowan, Jim McGrath, Pat McKee, Glen McMicken, Martha Mead, Karla Mehagan, Robin Miller, Sandy Miller, Tom Miller, Gary Mitchem, Mike Mullen, Julie Moralez, Pat Moran, Peter Morris, Mark Morrow, David Morton, Rick Morwick, Ray Nemec, Nat Newell, Beth Day Nolan, Connor O'Gara, Gary O'Neal, Tim Paramore, Danny Peary, Rich Perelman, James

Acknowledgments

Perkins, Jr., Dave Pishkur, Bobby Plapinger, Michael Pointer, Bill Potter, Wanda Rusie Potts, Nelson Price, Sherry Quack, Joe "Huck" Quigley, Greg Rakestraw, Manny Randhawa, Dale Ratermann, Phil Richards, Jon Richardson, Tony Rinier, Garner Roberts, Matt Roberts, Chris Robinson, Cliff Robinson, Nathan Rode, Kim Rogers, Bert Rosenthal, Harold Rosenthal, Brian Ross, Andy Rubin, Jeff Rubin, Rodger Ruddick, Barbara Rush, Paul Rush, Loretta Rusie, Michael Salmon, Jay Sanford, Rich Sauveur, Gabriel Schecter, Tom Schieber, Chuck Schisla, Art Schott, Bruce Schumacher, Max Schumacher, Matt Segal, Mike Shannon, John Shaughnessy, Roseann Silnes, Dr. Bob Simmermon, Chuck Skow, Donna Skow, John Skurkay, Brian Smith, Myla Smith, Tracy Smith, Jack Snyder, Bill Snyder, Mark Springer, Don Steffens, Trey Strecker, Geri Strecker, Lori Ames Stuart, Al Stupp, Trish Sullivan, Tom Surber, Carol Swenson, Mike Takaha, Bruce Tenen, Milt Thompson, Rich Torres, Chuck Traylor, Dean Treanor, Eddy Tridle, Jerry Varnau, Tomas Vera, Phil Wade, Dan Walker, Mark Walpole, Gennie Watts, Paul White, Courtney Whitehead, Morris Wildey, Jason Wille, Jack Willier, Phil B. Wilson, Mike Wolinsky, David Woods, John Yost, John Zajc and all the Hoosier-born big leaguers and their family members who provided information for this project.

A small village provided assistance during the research for this book. If I've omitted anyone, I apologize.

Introduction

Indiana has produced some of the game's greatest legends. Two dozen Indiana-born players wore major league uniforms in 2014, including three managers. With many organizations scouring the state for talent, more are on the way. Ten native Hoosiers are members of the National Baseball Hall of Fame (Three-Finger Brown, Max Carey, Billy Herman, Chuck Klein, Sam Rice, Edd Roush, Amos Rusie, Sam Thompson, Negro Leagues legend Oscar Charleston and former commissioner Ford Frick). That's six more than Michigan has produced (KiKi Cuyler, Charlie Gehringer, Hal Newhouser, John Smoltz). There are solid arguments that at least two more Hoosiers (Gil Hodges and Tommy John) deserve plaques in Cooperstown.

Rabid baseball fans include Indiana legends from other sports. As a youngster, Knute Rockne yearned to follow in the footsteps of Three-Finger Brown and Rube Waddell. John Wooden's favorite sport wasn't basketball but baseball. Piggy Lambert and Tony Hinkle were also college baseball coaches, and Bobby Knight's close friends include Johnny Bench, Tony LaRussa and Jim Leyland, as well as the late Sparky Anderson and Ted Williams. In high school, NBA legend Oscar Robertson pitched for the Crispus Attucks baseball team. Joe Sexson, a member of the Indiana Basketball Hall of Fame, was a star outfielder–first baseman at Arsenal Tech and later for Purdue. Another Boilermaker first sacker was Terry Dischinger (a 1960 Olympic basketball gold medalist and NBA star), who played for a Babe Ruth League national championship team from Terre Haute. NFL quarterback Bob Griese was a star shortstop in high school who played in an American Legion national baseball tournament alongside Don Mattingly's older brother Jerry. Larry Bird—an avid Cubs fan—played his final game for Indiana State not on a court but on a diamond. Fuzzy Zoeller of PGA fame is a big fan, and bowling legend Mike Aulby owns an extensive collection of baseball cards. Former Indianapolis Colts executive Bill Polian, spotted in the stands during a Play Ball Indiana contest, admitted his No. 1 sport is baseball.

Plenty of Hoosiers in other walks of life are baseball fanatics, too. Former governor Joe Kernan, who caught for Notre Dame's baseball team, was once part-owner of the Midwest League's South Bend Silver Hawks. Long before his tenure as Butler University president, the late Bobby Fong spent his boyhood cheering for Mickey Mantle and the New York Yankees. Jerry Harkness, a popular Indianapolis sportscaster and businessmen after his days as an Indiana Pacer, grew up rooting for the Brooklyn Dodgers and Jackie Robinson. Dave Letterman, rarely seen around Manhattan without a baseball cap, is a big fan. The man who wrote the music for "Take Me Out to the Ballgame," Albert Von Tilzer, was born in Indianapolis.

As Casey Stengel used to say, you could look it up. And in this book, you'll find each of the 364 Indiana natives who have played baseball at the big-league level. These men turned many American youngsters into lifelong baseball fans, myself included.

The Players

ADAMS, Charles Benjamin ("Babe")
Born: May 18, 1882, Tipton. **Died:** July 27, 1968, Silver Spring, Maryland.
Height: 5'11". **Weight:** 185. **Batted:** left. **Threw:** right.
Debut: April 18, 1906. **Final game:** August 11, 1926.
Positions, teams, years: pitcher, St. Louis (NL) 1906, Pittsburgh (NL) 1907, 1909–1916, 1918–26.
Games: 482. **Innings pitched**: 2,995.1. **Won/lost:** 194–140. **Earned run average:** 2.76.

One of the all-time great control pitchers, **Babe Adams** was baseball's first rookie World Series star. At the age of 16 Adams moved with his family from Indiana to St. Louis. Within a few years, he went to live on a farm in the northwest Missouri town of Mount Moriah, where he starred in high school and sandlot ball. "The baseball fever which I had brought with me from Indiana got worse," he told the *Washington Post* years later. "Oh, I had it bad. I used to practice curves with potatoes, stones, or any old thing I could get my hands on."

In 1905 Adams began his professional career with Parsons, Kan., of the independent Missouri Valley League. The St. Louis Cardinals purchased his contract, and he opened the 1906 season in St. Louis. He started and lost his only appearance and was soon back in the minors, this time with Denver (Western). His 23 wins topped the league in 1907, and Pittsburgh obtained him late in the year. He lost his only two decisions with the Pirates and spent all of 1908 with Louisville (American Association), where he went 22–12 and walked just 40 batters in 312 innings. It was there that the darkly handsome Adams earned his nickname. Whenever he pitched, female admirers in the stands would call, "Oh, you babe!"

Back in Pittsburgh for 1909, Adams went 12–3 with a 1.11 ERA for the pennant-winning Pirates. Pittsburgh's pitching staff included six veteran pitchers, all 20-game winners during their careers. But for the first game of the World Series against the favored Tigers, Pirates manager Fred Clarke's starting pitcher was Adams, a 27-year-old rookie. Adams won, and beat Detroit again in Games Five and Seven to become the first pitcher to win three times in a seven-game Series. Adams limited Ty Cobb to one hit in 11 at-bats and posted an ERA of 1.33, emerging as the Fall Classic's first rookie star. The next first-year man to win the seventh game of a World Series was John Lackey of the Angels in 2002.

Adams developed into one of Pittsburgh's top pitchers, winning 22 games in 1911 and 21 in 1913. He was the Opening Day starter for the Pirates in 1911, 1913–14, and again in 1920–21. His seven shutouts led the NL in 1911. In 1914 Adams pitched all 21 innings of a game against the Giants without allowing a single walk. The Pirates released him in 1916 due to a sore shoulder. In 1917 Adams joined St. Joseph, Mo. (Western), where his shoulder problems disappeared and he won 20 games. He moved up to Kansas City (American Association) in 1918, posting 14 wins. America was mobilizing that year for World War I, and by midsummer the 36-year-old Adams was a valuable commodity: a quality pitcher exempt from military service. Late in the season he joined the Pirates for a third time.

In 1919 and 1920 Adams was once again one of baseball's best pitchers, winning 17 games in both seasons. He led the NL in shutouts for a second time in 1920, with eight. He issued just 18 bases on balls that year, still the Major League record for the fewest walks allowed by a pitcher with 250 or more innings. In 1921, as the NL's oldest player at 39, his .737 won-loss percentage was the best in the league. At age 41 in 1923 he won 13 games. "I cannot explain my lasting much longer than many other pitchers on any other theory than this," he told reporters that June. "I always take things easy, and I never worry."

Adams was around for the Pirates' next World Series appearance in 1925, but this time he pitched only one inning of relief. Considered a kind of good-luck charm, Adams returned in 1926. His big league career ended abruptly that August. By that season, former Pittsburgh manager Fred Clarke had become a team stockholder. Clarke was in uniform on the bench during games, second-guessing the moves of manager Bill McKechnie. The situation created a rift between Clarke and several players who were sympathetic to McKechnie. Asked for an opinion, Adams said a manager should be able to do his job without interference. Soon after, in a show of support for Clarke, the Pirates released Adams and two other players. "I am 18 years in baseball without ever opening my mouth," observed Adams, "and then when I answer a question, I find myself chucked off the club."

In 1927 Adams pitched for minor league teams in Johnstown, Pa., of the Mid-Atlantic League (where he started the year as player-manager) and in Springfield, Mo. (Western Association). Throughout his career he had invested in farmland, and by 1928 he left baseball for good and returned to his farm in Mount Moriah. In 1958 he moved to Silver Spring, Md. He spent his final years there with his wife Blanche, whom he'd married prior to the start of that memorable 1909 season. After his death, Adams' ashes were buried in Mount Moriah, where a monument in his honor was erected in the town square. In 2002 the Missouri General Assembly renamed a portion of U.S. 136 the Babe Adams Highway.

AKERS, Albert Earl ("Jerry," "Al")

Born: November 1, 1887, Shelbyville. **Died:** May 15, 1979, Bay Pines, Florida.
Height: 5'11". **Weight:** 175. **Batted:** right. **Threw:** right.
Debut: May 4, 1912. **Final game:** May 25, 1912.
Positions, teams, years: pitcher, Washington (AL) 1912.
Games: 5. **Innings pitched:** 20.1. **Won/Lost:** 1–1. **Earned run average:** 4.87.

Blond-haired **Jerry Akers**, the son of a judge, grew up in Quincy, Ill., and graduated from Quincy High School. In 1905 he starred for the Quincy Reserves, an independent team. The side-arm pitcher began his professional career at age 18 in 1906 with Jacksonville, Ill. (Kitty). He went 15–15 for Jacksonville in 1907, but quit baseball after the season to work for a paper company.

In 1908 Akers returned to Jacksonville (by now in the Central Association) for one start. He had a 10–12 record there in 1909 and began the 1910 season with Kearney (Nebraska State). He finished the 1910 campaign in Dubuque, Iowa (Three-I). After a 19–12 record in 1911 for Dubuque, he joined the Washington Senators for the 1912 season. He was the winning pitcher in his first big league game, hurling six and two-thirds innings of relief in an 8–7 triumph over the Boston Red Sox. The loser, Ed Cicotte, later pitched for the Chicago White Sox and was banned from baseball for his role in the 1919 World Series scandal.

Akers appeared in just four more games. At the end of May, Washington sent him and two other players to Montreal (International) for first baseman Chick Gandil, another future Black Sox player. Akers finished the year with Rochester, N.Y. (International). He was out of organized baseball again in 1913, but he was back with Peoria, Ill. (Three-I) in 1914 and Fort Worth (Texas) in 1915.

A World War I veteran, Akers managed a clothing store in Columbus, Ohio, before retiring to Tampa, Fla., in 1953. After losing his left leg due to occlusive arterial disease, he died from a heart ailment at age 91.

ALDRIDGE, Victor Eddington ("The Hoosier Schoolmaster")

Indiana Baseball Hall of Fame, 2007.
Born: October 25, 1893, Indian Springs. **Died:** April 17, 1973, Terre Haute.
Height: 5'9". **Weight:** 175. **Batted:** right. **Threw:** right.
Debut: April 15, 1917. **Final game:** August 29, 1928.
Positions, teams, years: pitcher, Chicago (NL) 1917–

18, 1922–24, Pittsburgh (NL) 1925–27, New York (NL) 1928.
Games: 248. **Innings pitched:** 1,600.2. **Won/Lost:** 97–80. **Earned run average:** 3.76.

Vic Aldridge, a curveball pitcher who starred in the 1925 World Series, grew up in the Martin County hamlet of Cale and attended nearby Trinity Springs High School. He played baseball for the now-defunct Central Normal College in Danville, Ind., and also for club teams like the Peru Greys and the Logansport Ottos. As part of his college curriculum he taught school, which led to his nickname (*The Hoosier Schoolmaster*, Edward Eggleston's 1871 novel, was about a young teacher in pre–Civil War Indiana).

Aldridge left college after three years. "My success as a pitcher on the school team attracted the attention of various baseball men," he told *Baseball Magazine*, "and I was offered an opportunity with Indianapolis in 1915." That season he pitched for Indianapolis (American Association), Denver (Western) and Erie, Pa. (Central), compiling a 21–12 record. With Indianapolis for all of 1916, he went 16–14 with a 2.39 ERA and won a 3–0 no-hitter against Columbus on Sept. 2.

The Cubs bought Aldridge's contract after the season and he spent all of 1917 in Chicago. When the U.S. entered World War I in 1918, he joined the navy after just three games. Discharged as a chief petty officer, Aldridge returned to baseball in 1919. The Cubs sent him to Los Angeles (Pacific Coast), where he went 15–10, 18–15 and 20–10 between 1919 and 1921. His 2.16 ERA in '21 led the PCL. Back with Chicago for 1922, Aldridge logged three consecutive solid campaigns as a member of the Cubs starting rotation.

After winning 16 games in both 1922 and 1923 and 15 in 1924, Aldridge was part of a six-player trade with Pittsburgh. The Pirates, with five reliable starting pitchers, won the 1925 pennant. Aldridge went 15–7 and started the second game of the World Series, beating Washington 3–2. Down three games to one, the Pirates again sent Aldridge to the mound for Game Five. He came through again with a complete-game 6–3 victory. The seventh game was rained out and, when play resumed, he started against Walter Johnson. Both pitchers were looking for a third Series win. Aldridge didn't get past the first inning, retiring only one of the six batters he faced and departing with a 4–0 deficit. But the Pirates rallied in the bottom of the eighth for a 9–7 triumph that clinched the Series.

Over his next two seasons Aldridge went 10–13 in 1926 (when he was Pittsburgh's Opening Day starter) and 15–10 in 1927. The Pirates won another pennant in 1927, and he was started and lost the second game of the World Series against the powerful New York Yankees. He was a holdout in 1928, and that February the Pirates traded him to the Giants for pitcher Burleigh Grimes. While Grimes won 25 games for Pittsburgh, Aldridge won four, lost seven, and drifted back into the minor leagues. His baseball career ended in 1931 with Newark, N.J. (International).

Aldridge's mechanics were once described as "a halting, milk wagon–like delivery." But one rival hitter, Hall of Famer Rogers Hornsby, said Aldridge was one of the three best curveball pitchers he'd ever seen. Aldridge entered Voorhees School of Law after leaving baseball and earned a degree in 1937. He was admitted to the bar and served in the Indiana State Legislature from 1937 to 1948. In 2007 he was inducted posthumously into the Indiana Baseball Hall of Fame.

ALLENSWORTH, Jermaine LaMont
Born: January 11, 1972, Anderson. **Lives:** Bloomington, Illinois.
Height: 6'0". **Weight:** 178. **Batted:** right. **Threw:** right.
Debut: July 23, 1996. **Final game:** May 29, 1999.
Positions, teams, years: outfield, Pittsburgh (NL) 1996–98, Kansas City (AL) 1998, New York (NL) 1998–99.
Games: 342. **At-bats:** 1,031. **Home runs:** 15. **Average:** .260.

A speedy outfielder, **Jermaine Allensworth** starred in baseball at Madison Heights High School in Anderson, where he was a starting guard on the basketball team and averaged 190 in bowling. The California Angels selected Allensworth in the 15th round of the 1990 draft, but he opted instead to attend Purdue. An All–Big 10 selection as a sophomore and junior, he was a supplemental first-round draft pick (34th overall) by the Pittsburgh Pirates in 1993.

Allensworth broke in that summer with Welland, N.Y. (New York–Pennsylvania). Two years later he was one step away from the majors at Calgary, Alberta (Pacific Coast), where he batted .316 in 51 contests. In July 1996 he was batting .330 for Calgary and was leading the PCL with 77 runs when he joined the Pirates. He hit .262 in 61 games and opened the 1997 season as Pittsburgh's starting center fielder. "He is very intelligent and recognizes things a lot sooner than other guys," said Pirates hitting coach Lloyd McClendon, another Indiana native.

On May 15, 1997, Allensworth suffered a fractured metacarpal bone in his left hand and was sidelined for a month. He struggled the rest of the year, finishing with a .255 average. In June 1998 he was hitting .309 after 69 games when the Pirates traded him to the Kansas City Royals. In August the New York Mets claimed him on waivers. After the 1999 season the Mets traded him to the Boston Red Sox.

Out of baseball in 2000 due to a rotator cuff injury, Allensworth spent 2001 and 2002 with minor league clubs in the Detroit Tigers and Atlanta Braves organizations. Allensworth went to Spring Training with the Indianapolis Indians (International) in 2003, but the parent Milwaukee Brewers released him before the start of the season. From 2004 through 2008 he played for independent Northern League teams in Joliet, Ill., Gary, Ind., and Schaumburg, Ill.

After retiring, Allensworth settled in Bloomington, Ill., where he coached youth league baseball and worked as a hitting instructor at Sports Enhancement Center.

ANDERSON, Robert Carl ("Andy," "The Hammond Hummer")

Born: September 19, 1935, East Chicago. **Lives:** Tulsa, Oklahoma.
Height: 6'4". **Weight:** 210. **Batted:** right. **Threw:** right.
Debut: July 31, 1957. **Final game:** September 25, 1963.
Positions, teams, years: pitcher, Chicago (NL) 1957–62, Detroit (AL) 1963.
Games: 246. **Innings pitched:** 840.2. **Won/Lost:** 36–46. **Earned run average:** 4.26.

Soon after graduation from Hammond High School, **Bob Anderson** passed up a scholarship offer from Western Michigan University to sign with the Chicago Cubs. He broke in with Cedar Rapids, Iowa (Three-I), in 1954 and pitched for Des Moines, Iowa (Western), in 1955. In 1956 he set a Pacific Coast League record with 70 relief appearances for the pennant-winning Los Angeles Angels, rated the seventh-best team in PCL history by historian Richard Beverage.

After spending parts of 1957 and 1958 with the Chicago Cubs, Anderson won a starting role in 1959. He was Chicago's Opening Day pitcher that season and posted a 12–13 record. The strapping blond was a central figure in an unusual play at Wrigley Field on June 30, 1959. With one out in the fourth inning, Anderson had a 3-1 count on Stan Musial of the Cardinals. His next pitch got past catcher Sammy Taylor and rolled to the backstop. Home plate umpire Vic Delmore called ball four, but Anderson and Taylor argued that the ball had ticked Musial's bat.

No one had called time, however, and while Anderson and Taylor jawed at Delmore, Musial took off for second base. Around the same time the ump was handing a new baseball to Anderson, Chicago third baseman Alvin Dark retrieved the original ball. Anderson spotted Musial and threw to second baseman Tony Taylor. When Anderson's throw sailed into center field, Musial took off for third, but he was tagged out by Cubs shortstop Ernie Banks, who'd taken a throw from Dark. After a lengthy discussion, Musial was declared out. The Cardinals played the game under protest, but dropped it after going on to win 4–1.

Anderson was the Cubs Opening Day starter again in 1960, when he went 9–11. He spent the next two years in the Chicago bullpen, going 7–10 in 1961 and 2–7 in 1962 with a total of 12 saves. After the 1962 season the Cubs shipped him to Detroit. Pitching almost exclusively in relief, he went 3–1 with a 3.30 earned run average for the Tigers. Detroit dealt him to the Kansas City Athletics in a five-player trade, and he started the 1964 season at Dallas (Pacific Coast). Bothered by arm trouble, he finished the season at Lewiston, Idaho (Northwest), and retired.

During off-seasons, Anderson attended Western Michigan and eventually earned a degree in business administration. He worked for Inland Steel until 1993, when he relocated to Tulsa, Okla.

ANDRES, Ernest Henry ("Junie")
Indiana Baseball Hall of Fame, 1999.
Born: January 11, 1918, Jeffersonville. **Died:** September 19, 2008, Bradenton, Florida.
Height: 6'1". **Weight:** 200. **Batted:** right. **Threw:** right.
Debut: April 16, 1946. **Final game:** May 16, 1946.
Positions, teams, years: third base, Boston (AL) 1946.
Games: 15. **At-bats:** 41. **Home runs:** 0. **Average:** .098.

Ernie Andres played two professional sports in the same city simultaneously. He had a brief big league fling, but enjoyed a long career as a college baseball coach.

A member of Jeffersonville High School's 1935 state runner-up basketball team, he was a two-sport star at Indiana University. In basketball he won All-American honors as a senior in 1938–39, setting a Big Ten record with 30 points in a game against Illinois. Twice he earned the Balfour Award as Indiana U.'s top athlete.

After graduation, Andres signed to play baseball for Louisville (American Association) and hit a home run in his first at-bat. An excellent fielder and a high-average hitter, he put in three solid seasons with Louisville. During the off-season he was a starting guard for the Indianapolis Kautskys of the National Professional Basketball League.

Andres joined the U.S. Navy in 1942 following America's entry into World War II. After playing for a service all-star team that included Bob Feller, he spent five months on a sub-chaser in the Aleutians. Discharged in 1945 with the rank of lieutenant, he rejoined the Kautskys for the 1945–46 season.

Andres opened the 1946 baseball campaign with the Red Sox and doubled in his first at-bat. He had only three more hits in his next 14 games, however, and was soon back in the minors.

During the 1946–47 basketball season, Andres served as player-coach for the Kautskys, and led the club to a second-place finish in the National Basketball League's Western Division. That summer he played baseball for Indianapolis (American Association) and led the Indians with 84 runs batted in.

Andres left pro sports in 1948 to join Indiana University's athletic department. For 11 years he served as an assistant to basketball coach Branch McCracken. He coached the Hoosiers' baseball squad for 25 seasons and three of his players—Sammy Esposito, Ron Keller and Bruce Miller—reached the Major Leagues.

Andres was elected to the Indiana Basketball Hall of Fame in 1975 and entered the Indiana Baseball Hall of Fame in 1999. He is the lone Indiana U. alum to play two sports professionally.

ARNDT, Harry John ("Feathers," "Chicken")
Born: February 12, 1879, South Bend. **Died:** March 24, 1921, South Bend.
Height: unknown. **Weight:** 165. **Batted:** right. **Threw:** right.
Debut: July 2, 1902. **Final game:** May 25, 1907.
Positions, teams, years: second base (94), outfield (82), third base (77), shortstop (6), first base (6), Detroit (AL) 1902, Baltimore (AL) 1902, St. Louis (NL) 1905–07.
Games: 271. **At-bats:** 985. **Home runs:** 6. **Average:** .248.

Harry Arndt was South Bend's first Major Leaguer. He was the manager and star first baseman for Battle Creek (Michigan State) in July 1902 when Detroit purchased his contract. Sold by the Tigers to the Baltimore Orioles, he returned to the minors after just ten games. He spent 1903 with Columbus and 1904 with Louisville, both in the American Association.

In 1905 Arndt failed a spring trial with the Cincinnati Reds. He jumped to Coatesville, Pa., of the outlaw Tri-State League, but later joined St. Louis and batted .243 in 113 games as the Cardinals' primary second baseman. His game-ending steal of home versus Pittsburgh on September 12 was the first of the modern era (since 1900).

Arndt switched to third base in 1906 and played briefly with St. Louis in 1907 before returning to the Tri-State League. He went back to South Bend in 1912 as player-manager of the local Central League franchise. He hit .302, but his club finished last in a 12-team league. He managed Ludington (Michigan State) for part of 1913.

The versatile Arndt saw big league action in the outfield and at all four infield positions. One minor league teammate described him as "an aggressive and heady ballplayer." Prior to the 1906 season, he and Major League catcher Lou Criger (also a native Hoosier) helped train Notre Dame's baseball team. Arndt died at 42 after a long battle with tuberculosis.

AYDELOTT, Jacob Stuart

Born: July 6, 1861, North Manchester. **Died:** October 22, 1926, Detroit, Michigan.
Height: 6'0". **Weight:** 180. **Batted:** left. **Threw:** right.
Debut: May 15, 1884. **Final game:** July 13, 1886.
Positions, teams, years: pitcher (14), outfield (1), Indianapolis (American Association) 1884, Philadelphia (American Association) 1886.
Games: 14. **Innings pitched:** 124. **Won/Lost:** 5–9. **Earned run average:** 4.79.
At-bats: 50. **Home runs:** 0. **Average:** .100.

When the first New Orleans professional baseball team took the field, **Jake Aydelott** was the starting pitcher. He joined New Orleans in 1887 when the Pelicans entered the Southern League after two previous major league seasons in the American Association, where he compiled a 5–7 record for the Indianapolis Hoosiers in 1884 and an 0–2 slate in 1886 for the Philadelphia Athletics.

The Pels' first exhibition game in the Crescent City took place February 24, 1887, against Cincinnati. Aydelott went all the way in a 10–3 loss to the big league club. On April 17, 1887, he started again on Opening Day for New Orleans and posted a 5–2 win over Mobile, Ala. Sidelined by typhoid fever for part of the summer, there were erroneous newspaper reports that he was back in Indiana and near death. "The press all over the country are circulating all kind of reports about our pitcher Aydelott [sic] dying with malaria, consumption, and a lot of other diseases," *The Sporting News* reported on July 2, 1887. "But he is up and all right and will be in the box soon again."

Aydelott left New Orleans before the season ended and was out of organized ball in 1888. He opened the 1889 campaign with Atlanta (Southern), and when the club disbanded he shifted to Charleston, S.C. After the Southern League broke up in June, he joined Evansville (Central-Interstate) as player-manager and won four of seven decisions. He gave up the managerial reins before the season ended, with Evansville mired in last place. He managed Bluffton (Indiana State) in 1890, and for part of the 1895 season he was manager of Jacksonville, Ill. (Western Association).

After leaving baseball, Aydelott lived in the Indiana towns of Xenia (now Converse), Marion and Cambridge City, working as a traveling salesman for a confectionery company and later as a laborer. He made his home in Columbus, Ohio, before relocating to Detroit after World War I.

BAKER, Kirtley ("Whitey")

Born: June 24, 1869, Aurora. **Died:** April 13, 1927, Covington, Kentucky.
Height: 5'9". **Weight:** 160. **Batted:** right. **Threw:** right.
Debut: May 7, 1890. **Final game:** June 14, 1899.
Positions, teams, years: pitcher (58), outfield (4), Pittsburgh (NL) 1890, Baltimore (NL) 1893–1894, Washington (NL) 1898–1899.
Games: 65. **Innings pitched:** 371. **Won/Lost:** 9–38. **Earned run average:** 6.28.
At-bats: 166. **Home runs:** 0. **Average:** .211.

Before entering professional baseball, fair-haired **Kirt Baker** starred for southeastern Indiana town teams in Aurora and Lawrenceburg. He was playing for the semi-pro Cincinnati Blue Licks when the Pittsburgh Alleghenies of the NL signed him for 1890. That season he had the dubious distinction of being the bellwether of the league's worst team. Pittsburgh finished last with a record of 23–113 and Baker won just three of 22 decisions. His 178 innings and 76 strikeouts led the pitching staff. Arm trouble sidelined him for the last two months of the season. Released in September, he returned to Aurora to play for the local team.

Baker joined Ottumwa, Iowa (Illinois-Iowa), in 1891 and in 1892 he starred for Chattanooga, Tenn. (Southern), as a pitcher-outfielder, winning 22 games. He returned to the majors with Baltimore in 1893 and spent two seasons shuttling between the Orioles and New Orleans (Southern). He languished in the minors until 1898, when he returned to the NL with Washington. He was 3–10 for the Nationals in parts of two seasons and finished his career with Springfield, Mass. (Eastern), in 1900.

As a big leaguer Baker played four games in the outfield, and in 1893 he batted .298. During his first year with Pittsburgh, his roommate was outfielder Billy Sunday. They remained close friends, even after Sunday retired to become a nationally renowned evangelist.

Baker settled in Lawrenceburg after leaving baseball and became a successful businessman. He worked for a buggy company before purchasing a soft drink and confectionery shop, and in 1919 he bought a grocery store. He died from a pulmonary embolism at age 57.

BALL, Arthur Clark

Born: April (date unknown) 1872, Madison. **Died:** December 26, 1915, Chicago, Illinois.
Height: unknown. **Weight:** 168. **Batted:** unknown. **Threw:** right.
Debut: August 1, 1894. **Final game:** October 15, 1898.
Positions, teams, years: third base (15), shortstop (14), second base (3), outfield (1), St. Louis (NL) 1894, Baltimore (NL) 1898.
Games: 33. **At-bats:** 84. **Home runs:** 0. **Average:** .190.

Artie Ball joined the St. Louis Browns in 1894 after spending most of the year with Memphis, Tenn. (Southern). En route to a 26–8 loss to the White Stockings at Chicago on August 1, 1894, St. Louis manager Doggie Miller made wholesale position changes in the Browns lineup. Ball replaced Tommy Dowd at second base and went 1-for-3 in his initial major league game.

Ball spent the next three seasons in the minors. In 1895 he played for Fort Wayne in the Western Inter-State League, which operated from May 2 to May 24. He was with Minneapolis from 1896 to 1898, helping the Millers to the 1896 Western League title. In June 1898 he went from Minneapolis to the Baltimore Orioles, where he backed up Hall of Famer John McGraw at third base and batted .185 in 32 games.

Returning to the minors, Ball played for Rock Island-Moline, Ill. (Western Association), and St. Paul, Minn. (Western), in 1899, and for Des Moines, Iowa (Western), in 1900. He settled in Chicago after leaving baseball and worked as a night watchman. He died there from cirrhosis of the liver, peritonitis and pulmonary tuberculosis at age 39.

BARKER, Alfred L.

Born: January 18, 1839, Lost Creek Township. **Died:** September 15, 1912, Rockford, Illinois.
Height: unknown. **Weight:** unknown. **Batted:** unknown. **Threw:** unknown.
Debut: June 1, 1871. **Final game:** June 1, 1871.
Positions, teams, years: outfield, Rockford (National Association) 1871.
Games: 1. **At-bats:** 4. **Home runs:** 0. **Average:** .250.

Before the advent of professional baseball, Civil War veteran **Al Barker** played for the Forest Citys team of Rockford, Ill, the only team that defeated the Washington Nationals during that club's 1867 tour of the Midwest. According to the *Rockford* (Ill.) *Morning Star*, Barker "was an unusually swift and accurate thrower, and played generally in the outfield and as change pitcher."

Barker was born in the Vigo County Township of Lost Creek near Terre Haute. His family left Indiana for Illinois in 1848 and settled in Rockford in 1853. During the War Between the States he served as a private in the 11th Illinois Infantry regiment and later as a lieutenant with the 74th Illinois.

After the war, Barker played for the Forest Citys Club town team. He was no longer a starting player by 1871, when the team joined baseball's first professional league, the National Association. He accompanied the team on a trip through the East that summer, seeing action mostly in exhibition games. On June 1 he played left field, batting eighth behind future Hall of Famer Cap Anson, in Rockford's regular-season contest with the Mutuals of New York at Brooklyn's Union Grounds. It was Barker's lone appearance in a professional game, and he became the first Indiana native to play in a major league contest.

Twenty-five years later, on April 13, 1896, Rockford hosted a game in honor of Harry Wright. Wright had organized the Cincinnati Red Stockings, the first pro team, and all the players were baseball veterans of the 1860s. Barker's participation gave him a second distinction: he took part in what is believed to be the game's first old-timers contest.

A noted singer and musician, Barker worked at various times as a clothing store salesman, decorative paperhanger, and dance instructor. He was also a substitute umpire in the National League during 1881.

BARMES, Bruce Raymond ("Squeaky")

Born: October 23, 1929, Vincennes. **Died:** January 25, 2014, Garner, North Carolina.
Height: 5'8". **Weight:** 165. **Batted:** left. **Threw:** right.
Debut: September 13, 1953. **Final Game:** September 27, 1953.
Positions, teams, years: outfield, Washington (AL) 1953.
Games: 5. **At-bats:** 5. **Home runs:** 0. **Average:** .200.

The son of a farmer, **Bruce Barmes** lettered in basketball, football and track at Lincoln High School in Vincennes, where there was no baseball team. During a three-year Air Force hitch, he spent twenty-eight months in the Azores as a control tower operator and played fast-pitch softball. After his discharge, Barmes (pronounced BAR-miss) attended a Washington tryout camp. The Senators signed him after he slammed the first pitch thrown to him over a fence.

In 1950, his first professional season, Barmes had a 31-game hitting streak and batted .372 for pennant-winning Orlando (Florida State). While playing for Charlotte, N.C. (Tri-State), in 1951 and 1952 he met and married a local girl and eventually made North Carolina his permanent home. His .311 average in 1951 helped Charlotte to a pennant. In 1952 he led the league with a .360 average and earned most valuable player honors.

A .320 season in 1953 at Chattanooga, Tenn. (Southern), earned Barmes a September call-up to the Senators. He was back in Chattanooga in 1954 and played there until 1957. He finished the '57 season with Omaha, Neb. (American Association), hitting .339 in 35 contests.

Even though he played through the 1960 campaign, the spray-hitting outfielder never again returned to the majors. In a dozen minor league seasons (including 1966, when he appeared in a single game for Charlotte as a 36-year-old), Barmes batted .318 in 1,439 contests. After leaving baseball he worked as a truck driver, welder and salesman.

In *Baseball Nicknames,* Barmes explained his nom de guerre. "A scout for the Washington Senators tagged me 'Squeaky' because I was always hollerin' at batters from my left field position," he told author James K. Skipper. "After a while, my voice would become hoarse."

BARMES, Clint Harold ("Barmie")

Born: March 6, 1979, Vincennes. **Lives:** Denver, Colorado.
Height: 6'1". **Weight:** 200. **Bats:** right. **Throws:** right.
Debut: September 5, 2003.
Positions, teams, years: shortstop (703), second base (306), third base (15), outfield (6), first base (1), Colorado (NL), 2003–2010, Houston (NL) 2011, Pittsburgh (NL) 2012–2014.
Games: 1,088. **At-bats:** 3,598. **Home runs:** 86. **Average:** .246.

Slick-fielding **Clint Barmes** is a distant relative of Bruce Barmes, who played for the 1953 Washington Senators.

In 1996 Barmes (pronounced BAR-miss) helped Vincennes Lincoln High School to a regional title. After two years at Olney (Ill.) Central College, he led Indiana State University in 2000 with a .375 average. That June the Colorado Rockies made him their tenth-round draft pick. His professional career began that summer with Portland, Ore. (Northwest).

Two seasons later, Barmes had a breakthrough year at Carolina and made the Southern League All-Star team. He batted .328 for Colorado Springs (Pacific Coast) in 2004 and in 2005 he took over as the Rockies' everyday shortstop and leadoff hitter. On Opening Day against the visiting San Diego Padres, he hit a game-winning, walk-off home run.

En route to an outstanding rookie season, Barmes suffered a broken left collarbone on June 5, 2005. At first, he said he'd fallen while lugging groceries up the stairs to his fourth-floor apartment. He later changed his story, explaining that he was actually carrying a package of deer meat provided by teammate Todd Helton. "I just didn't think it was right to bring Todd into something like this," Barmes told the *Denver Post.* He underwent surgery and was sidelined for nearly three months.

Barmes batted .220 in 2006, when rookie Troy Tulowitzki replaced him at shortstop. The Rockies won the NL pennant in 2007, but Barmes spent most of the year with Colorado Springs and wasn't on the Rockies' post-season roster. He began 2008 as a utility infielder, but took over as Colorado's everyday second baseman by the end of April and finished with a .290 average. In 2009 he clubbed 23 homers.

When Tulowitzki suffered a wrist injury in June 2010, Barmes switched back to shortstop. He served mainly as a defensive backup after Tulowitzki's return. The Rockies traded him to the Houston Astros prior to 2011, when he suffered a broken left hand during Spring Training and missed the first month of the season. After hitting .244 in 123 games as Houston's regular shortstop, he opted for free agency and signed with the Pirates.

Barmes was Pittsburgh's main shortstop in 2012, when he averaged .229. He batted .211 in 2013 and rookie Jordy Mercer replaced him. Barmes was a backup infielder for Pittsburgh in 2014, when the Pirates reached post-season for the first time since 1992. Sidelined by a strained left groin muscle from June 30 to August 25, he hit .245 in 48 contests. He became a free agent after the season and signed with the San Diego Padres for 2015.

BARNHART, Tucker Jackson ("Barnie")

Born: January 7, 1991, Indianapolis. **Lives:** Brownsburg.
Height: 5'11". **Weight:** 195. **Bats:** both. **Throws:** right.
Debut: April 3, 2014.
Positions, teams, years: catcher, Cincinnati (NL) 2014.
Games: 21. **At-bats:** 54. **Home runs:** 1. **Average:** .185.

Baseball scouts first noticed **Tucker Barnhart** during his sophomore year at Brownsburg High School, when he caught future Major League pitcher Drew Storen. Barnhart also played tennis at Brownsburg, where one of his teammates was future NBA star Gordon Hayward. Barnhart was Indiana's "Mr. Baseball" as a senior in 2009. He signed to play for Georgia Tech but decided on a professional career after the Cincinnati Reds took him in the tenth round of the draft.

Barnhart broke in with Cincinnati's rookie-level Gulf Coast League team in 2009 and played for Billings, Mont. (Pioneer), in 2010. In 2011 at Dayton, Ohio (Midwest), he was selected as the catcher on the Rawlings Minor League Baseball Gold Glove team. He was a Southern League all-star with Pensacola, Fla. (Southern) in 2013.

Projected to start the 2014 campaign at Louisville (International), Barnhart opened the year with Cincinnati when everyday Reds catcher Devin Mesoraco went on the disabled list. For Opening Day, the Reds hosted St. Louis. In the third game of the year Barnhart made his Major League debut against Cardinals right-hander Lance Lynn, another Brownsburg alumnus. "It was something I'll never forget," Tucker recalled. "It was special to see (Lynn) out there and give him a little wry smile."

When Mesoraco came off the disabled list on April 7, the Reds optioned Barnhart to Louisville. He spent the rest of the season shuttling between Louisville and Cincinnati, batting .185 in 21 appearances for the Reds.

BARRETT, Aaron James

Born: January 2, 1988, Evansville. **Lives:** Evansville.
Height: 6'4". **Weight:** 215. **Bats:** right. **Throws:** right.
Debut: March 31, 2014.
Positions, teams, years: pitcher, Washington (NL) 2014.
Games: 50. **Innings pitched:** 40.2. **Won/lost:** 3-0. **Earned run average:** 2.66.

Aaron Barrett was drafted four times before he finally signed a professional contract. Barrett helped Evansville Central High School to sectional and regional titles in 2006, when the Los Angeles Dodgers made him their 44th-round pick. He decided instead to attend Wabash Valley College in Mount Carmel, Ill. The Minnesota Twins took him in the 20th round of the 2008 draft after he helped Wabash Valley win the Great Rivers Athletic Conference title.

Opting to move on to a four-year school, Barrett opened the 2009 season with the University of Mississippi as a starting pitcher. That June the Texas Rangers drafted him in the 27th round. He returned to Ole Miss for his senior year and signed with Washington after the Nationals made him their ninth-round pick for 2012.

Switching to the bullpen, Barrett came into his own at Hagerstown, Md. (South Atlantic), in 2012 with 16 saves and a 2.60 ERA. In 2013 he was the named the Eastern League's top reliever with a 2.15 ERA and 26 saves for Harrisburg, Pa. He won a berth on the Washington roster during Spring Training in 2014. On Opening Day, he struck out two batters in the ninth inning at New York's Citi Field and got credit for the win in a 10-inning, 9–7 win over the Mets.

The Nationals optioned Barrett to Syracuse, N.Y. (International) on August 1 and recalled him a month later, when rosters expanded to 40. He finished the year with a 3–0 record and a 2.66 ERA in 50 big league appearances. He was with the Nationals when they clinched the NL East Division, giving Washington its first championship of any kind since 1933 when the Senators (who became the Minnesota Twins in 1961) won the 1933 AL pennant.

Barrett was the fifth Washington pitcher in the decisive fourth game of the NL Division Series with San Francisco. He relieved Matt Thornton in the seventh inning and surrendered the game-winning run, throwing a wild pitch with the bases loaded that gave the Giants a 3–2 lead. "It hurts now," Barrett announced on Twitter the following day, "but we will come back stronger than ever."

BARRETT, Timothy Wayne
Born: January 24, 1961, Huntingburg. **Lives:** Aurora.
Height: 6'1". **Weight:** 185. **Batted:** left. **Threw:** right.
Debut: July 18, 1988. **Final Game:** August 9, 1988.
Positions, teams, years: pitcher, Montreal (NL) 1988.
Games: 4. **Innings pitched:** 9.1. **Won/Lost:** 0–0.
Earned run average: 5.79.

A graduate of Pike Central High School in Petersburg, **Tim Barrett** spent a season at Wabash Valley Junior College in Mount Carmel, Ill., before starring at Indiana State University for three years. He signed with the Montreal Expos prior to the 1984 season as an undrafted free agent.

Barrett split the 1984 season between three clubs. He went 7–2 with a 1.94 ERA in 13 games at Gastonia, N.C. (South Atlantic), before compiling a 5–4, 2.30 record at West Palm Beach (Florida State). He finished the season at Jacksonville, Fla. (Southern), with a 1–1 mark and a 2.29 ERA in two appearances.

Relying on a changeup, slider and an above-average fastball, Barrett worked his way up to Indianapolis (American Association) by 1985. Working in relief, he went 10–1 for the Indians in 1987 to lead the American Association with a .909 winning percentage. He went 8–1 with a 1.99 ERA in 1988 to earn a promotion to Montreal. Back with Indianapolis in 1989, he was traded to Albuquerque (Pacific Coast) after just eight games and a 1–3 record. Barrett went 4–2 for the Dukes.

Bothered by arm trouble since 1986, Barrett retired prior to the 1990 season and accepted a coaching position at Lawrenceburg High School. He later worked as a supervisor for a Seagram's distillery.

BAUMANN, Charles John ("Paddy")
Born: December 20, 1885, Indianapolis. **Died:** November 20, 1969, Indianapolis.
Height: 5'9". **Weight:** 160. **Batted:** right. **Threw:** right.
Debut: August 10, 1911. **Final Game:** September 8, 1917.
Positions, teams, years: second base (150), third base (52), outfield (41), Detroit (AL) 1911–1914, New York (AL) 1915–1917.
Games: 299. **At-bats:** 904. **Home runs:** 4. **Average:** .274.

Paddy Baumann spent seven seasons as a Major League utilityman but had a long career in baseball as a player, manager and umpire. A lifelong Indianapolis resident, Baumann broke in with Richmond, Ind. (Indiana-Ohio), in 1908. "He had played much semi-pro ball around Indianapolis and vicinity, and his work attracted Clarence Jessup, the manager of the Quaker City club, who signed the local player up for the season," according to the *Indianapolis Sun*.

At New Bedford, Mass. (New England), in 1911 Baumann roomed with future Hall of Famer Rabbit Maranville. Detroit acquired him that June and he spent the next four years with the Tigers, playing second, third and the outfield. Baumann took Ty Cobb's place in center field for one game on May 16, 1912, the day after Cobb was suspended for going into the stands to pummel a heckler. Two days later

Baumann and his Tiger teammates protested Cobb's suspension by refusing to take the field for a game with the Athletics. It was the first players strike in big league history.

The New York Yankees obtained Baumann's contract from Providence, R.I. (International), prior to the 1915 season. He spent the next three seasons as a backup player, batting .292 in 1915 and .287 in 1916. After a .218 season in 1917 he returned to the minors and continued to play until 1928, when he finished his career with Dallas (Texas). He managed in the Texas League and later umpired in the Three-I League.

After leaving baseball, Baumann was a maintenance worker at the J.O. Holcomb Company in Indianapolis.

BEACHY, Brandon Alan

Born: September 3, 1986, Kokomo. **Lives:** Kokomo.
Height: 6'3". **Weight:** 215. **Bats:** right. **Throws:** right.
Debut: September 20, 2010.
Positions, teams, years: pitcher, Atlanta (NL) 2010–2013.
Games: 46. **Innings pitched:** 267.2. **Won/Lost:** 14–11. **Earned run average:** 3.23.

Brandon Beachy earned the Class 2A Mental Attitude Award in 2005, when his .430 batting average sparked Kokomo's Northwestern High School to the state championship game. Primarily a third baseman as a prep, he became Indiana Wesleyan University's closer as a sophomore in 2007.

Undrafted after his junior year in 2008, Beachy was pitching for a summer league team in Virginia when he caught the eye of an Atlanta Braves scout. Beachy signed and reported to Danville, Va. (Appalachian). He spent most of 2009 at Myrtle Beach, S.C. (Carolina).

Beachy enjoyed a breakout year at Mississippi in 2010, when he was named to the midseason Southern League all-star team. A 3–1 record with a 1.47 ERA in 27 games earned him a promotion to Gwinnett, Ga. (International). After going 2–0 with a 2.17 ERA for Gwinnett, he reported to the Arizona Fall League. Before the regular season ended, Atlanta summoned him for a start against the two-time defending NL champion Philadelphia Phillies.

In 2011 Beachy took over as Atlanta's fifth starter. After going on the disabled list in May with a strained side muscle, he returned in June with an 11-strikeout performance against Toronto. He finished the year with a 7–3 mark and a 3.68 ERA, fanning 169 batters in 141.2 innings. Beachy was 5–5 with a league-leading 2.00 ERA in mid–June 2012 when he suffered a partial elbow tear. He underwent reconstructive surgery and missed the remainder of the season.

Beachy rejoined Atlanta's rotation in July 2013 and went 2–1 in five starts. In the spring of 2014 the elbow problem resurfaced, and he underwent a second operation that sidelined him for the year. He became a free agent in December when the Braves didn't tender him a 2015 contract.

A pre-law and criminal justice student, Beachy is the first Indiana Wesleyan alumnus to reach the Major Leagues. His college roommate, Josh Worrell, is the son of former Major League pitcher Todd Worrell.

BECK, Ernest George Bernard ("Eaglebeak")

Born: February 21, 1890, South Bend. **Died:** October 29, 1973, South Bend.
Height: 5'11". **Weight:** 165. **Batted:** right. **Threw:** right.
Debut: May 15, 1914. **Final Game:** May 15, 1914.
Positions, teams, years: pitcher, Cleveland (AL) 1914.
Games: 1. **Innings pitched:** 1. **Won/Lost:** 0–0. **Earned run average:** 0.00.

A one-game big leaguer with the Cleveland Naps in 1914, spitball pitcher **George Beck** broke into organized ball with McLeansboro (Southern Illinois) in 1920 and pitched a 1–0 no-hitter against Vincennes on September 15. In 1913 he compiled a 17–12 record for Nashville, Tenn. (Southern).

The Philadelphia Phillies drafted Beck after the season and sold his contract to the Boston Braves in October 1913. "Manager George Stallings ... believes he's landed a first-class twirler," *The Sporting News* reported on January 15, 1914.

Cleveland obtained Beck in a waiver deal on May 5, 1914. Ten days later, in his only appearance for the Naps, he pitched the eighth inning of a 6–3 loss to the Athletics in Philadelphia. He returned to the minors soon after.

Beck was out of baseball from 1917–1918 due to World War I military service. In 1920 he returned to play for Moline, Ill. (Three-I), but never again pitched in the majors. Before retiring, he played for Des Moines, Iowa (Western), and Peoria. Ill. (Three-I), in 1921, for Rockford, Ill. (Three-I), in 1922 and 1923, and for Sioux Falls, S.D. (Tri-State), in 1924.

Returning to South Bend, Beck became a foundry worker for the Sibley Corporation.

BEJMA, Aloysius Frank ("Ollie," "The Polish Falcon")

Born: Alojzy Frank Bejma, September 12, 1907, South Bend. **Died:** January 3, 1995, South Bend.
Height: 5'10". **Weight:** 165. **Batted:** right. **Threw:** right.
Debut: April 24, 1934. **Final Game:** October 1, 1939.
Positions, teams, years: second base (174), shortstop (42), third base (23), outfield (9), St. Louis (AL) 1934–36, Chicago (AL) 1939.
Games: 316. **At-bats:** 906. **Home runs:** 14. **Average:** .245.

Lifelong South Bend resident **Ollie Bejma**, the son of Polish immigrants, was a boyhood favorite of Charles Schulz, the beloved cartoonist. Bejma (pronounced BAY-ma) quit school at age 16 to go to work, first for South Bend Toy and later with Studebaker. He spent five years playing for Studebaker's company baseball team, In 1929 he signed with Indianapolis (American Association) and batted .287 in 56 games.

Bejma spent most of the next two seasons with Quincy, Ill. (Three-I), hitting .344 in 1930 and .319 in 1931, when the St. Louis Browns acquired him after the season. He spent the next two years in the Texas League, averaging .287 for Longview (which moved there from Wichita Falls) in 1932 and .274 in 1933 at San Antonio.

Joining the Browns for 1934, Bejma batted .271 as a spare infielder. He slumped to .192 in 1935 and was temporarily demoted to San Antonio. He spent all of 1936 in St. Louis, hitting .259 as a backup at second and third. Back with San Antonio for 1937, he averaged .320.

Bejma joined St. Paul (American Association) for the 1938 season and led the Saints with 25 homers, 114 RBI and a .326 batting average. In the MVP ballot, he tied for top honors with Milwaukee pitcher Whit Wyatt. Third was 19-year-old Minneapolis outfielder Ted Williams, a future Hall of Famer.

In 1939 Bejma was back in the big leagues as a platoon second baseman for the Chicago White Sox. He returned to the minors for good in 1940 and left baseball after the 1943 season. Back in South Bend, he worked for Studebaker and played semi-pro ball for a team in Michigan City. He later worked as a security guard at Notre Dame. Bejma also became one of the area's top bowlers. He was part of five-man state championship team in 1954, and two years later he finished tenth in a national tournament.

In the "Peanuts" comic strip for February 21, 1974, Snoopy the beagle has a trivia question for his pal Woodstock, a little yellow bird: "Who played shortstop for St. Paul when they won the American Association pennant in nineteen thirty-eight?" In the last panel, Woodstock grins smugly while a dejected Snoopy ponders: "How'd he ever hear of Ollie Bejma?"

Growing up in St. Paul, "Peanuts" creator Charles Schulz was a great baseball fan. He was 15 years old in 1938, the year the Saints won the league pennant, and his favorite player was Ollie Bejma. "I have three children and 12 grandchildren," Bejma explained to Eugene Murdock, author of *Baseball Players and Their Times*, "and each one has an autographed copy of that cartoon and they wouldn't part with it for $1,000."

Ollie's nephew, Louis "Shorty" Bejma, played for Chanute, Kan. (Kansas-Oklahoma-Missouri), in 1947.

BENES, Alan Paul

Born: January 21, 1972, Evansville. Lives: Chesterfield, Missouri.
Height: 6'5". **Weight:** 215. **Batted:** right. **Threw:** right.
Debut: September 19, 1995. **Final Game:** May 28, 2003.
Positions, teams, years: pitcher, St. Louis (NL) 1995–1997, 1999–2001, Chicago (NL) 2002–2003, Texas (AL) 2003.
Games: 115. **Innings pitched:** 494. **Won/Lost:** 29–28. **Earned run average:** 4.59.

A first-round draft pick (16th overall) of the St. Louis Cardinals in 1993, former Creighton University standout **Alan Benes** (pronounced

BEN-ess) reached the Major Leagues after pitching Louisville to the 1995 American Association playoff title. In 1996 his 13–10 record helped the Cardinals to a first-place finish in the NL Central Division.

When Alan's older brother Andy signed with St. Louis for the 1997 season, they became the first Hoosier siblings to become Major League teammates since 1911, when Grover and Lou Lowdermilk pitched for the Cardinals.

On May 16, 1997, Benes pitched no-hit ball against Atlanta through eight and two-thirds innings before giving up a double to Michael Tucker. The Braves went on to score a run off reliever John Frascatore in the 13th for a 1–0 victory. "He's the type of guy who can go out and throw a no-hitter every five days because he throws the ball so hard and because of his breaking pitches," Andy Benes said of his kid brother.

Shoulder problems curtailed Alan's season in July 1997. He underwent arthroscopic surgery in early September and spent 1998 and most of 1999 on the disabled list. He rejoined St. Louis in September 1999 and appeared in 30 games as a reliever in 2000.

A graduate of Lake Forest (Ill.) High School in suburban Chicago, Benes joined the Cubs as a free agent prior to 2002. Chicago sent him to the Texas Rangers in May 2003, but reacquired him less than four weeks later. He pitched in the Cardinals' minor league system from 2004 through 2006 before retiring.

In its May/June 2014 edition, *Baseball Digest* identified Alan and Andy Benes as one of 14 players who batted against their brothers in Major League competition. Alan, in his lone at-bat against Andy, lined out to him. Andy faced Alan twice and had a pair of singles.

Alan is a member of Evansville's Sports Hall of Fame.

BENES, Andrew Charles ("Big Train," "Rainman")

Indiana Baseball Hall of Fame, 2009.
Born: August 20, 1967, Evansville. **Lives:** St. Louis, Missouri.
Height: 6'6". **Weight:** 235. **Batted:** right. **Threw:** right.
Debut: August 11, 1989. **Final Game:** September 29, 2002.
Positions, teams, years: San Diego (NL) 1989–1995, Seattle (AL) 1995, St. Louis (NL) 1996–1997, Arizona (NL) 1998–1999, St. Louis (NL) 2000–2002.
Games: 403. **Innings pitched:** 2,505.1. **Won/Lost:** 155–139. **Earned run average:** 3.97.

Andy Benes was one of baseball's premier pitchers in the 1990s. A product of Evansville Central High School, Benes spent two years playing baseball, football and basketball at the University of Evansville. He began to concentrate on baseball in 1988, his junior year. At one point he reeled off almost 40 consecutive scoreless innings.

Benes went 16–3 with a 1.42 ERA for the Purple Aces in 1988, and the San Diego Padres made him the No. 1 pick in the June draft. He spent that summer playing for the gold medal-winning U.S. team at the Seoul Olympics. Later he signed a $235,000 contract with the Padres and started the 1989 campaign at Wichita, Kan. (Texas). By August he was pitching for San Diego. A power pitcher with a sinking fastball and a deceptive curve, Benes won 15 games in 1991, 13 in 1992 and 15 again in 1993 for the Padres

Frustrated by his team's poor records in 1993 and 1994, Benes was frequently the subject of trade talks. When San Diego shipped him to Seattle in 1995 he went 7–2 in 12 starts to help the Mariners reach the AL Championship Series.

Benes became a free agent after the season and signed with St. Louis. In 1996 his 18–10 record led the Cardinals to the NLCS. He became a free agent again after 1997 and signed with the Arizona Diamondbacks, an expansion team. His 3–2 victory over San Francisco on April 5, 1998, was the first win in Diamondbacks history, and his 14 victories tied a record for the most wins by a pitcher for an expansion team.

Against Cincinnati on September 13, 1998, Benes came within two outs of becoming the first pitcher since 1969 to throw a no-hitter for a first-year club. He had to settle for a 5–0 one-hitter after giving up a one-out single in the ninth to Reds rookie first baseman Sean Casey.

Benes became a free agent once more after the 1999 season and rejoined the Cardinals. In 2000 he gave up four home runs in one inning, a Major League record. Despite an arthritic knee, his 12–9 record helped St. Louis to the 2000 NLCS.

Benes struggled through a 7–7 record in 2001 and nearly quit in 2002 due to chronic knee problems. During a three-month stretch on the disabled list, however, he developed a split-finger fastball. He came back and went 5–1 with a 1.56 ERA in his final 12 regular season starts, spurring the Cardinals to the NL Central Division title. He announced his retirement after the season.

Benes was the Opening Day pitcher for San Diego in 1993, 1994 and 1995, and for Arizona in 1998. In 1993 the Cardinals made his younger brother Alan their top selection in the June draft. Another brother, Adam, pitched in the St. Louis organization from 1995 to 2000. Drew Benes, Andy's son, was drafted by the Cardinals out of Arkansas State University in 2007 and pitched in the minors and independent leagues from 2010 to 2013.

Andy was inducted into the Indiana Baseball Hall of Fame in 2009. He's also a member of the University of Evansville Hall of Fame (Class of 1995) and the Evansville Sports Hall of Fame.

He inherited the nickname "Big Train" from Hall of Fame right-hander Walter Johnson. He was dubbed "Rainman" in 1990 when inclement weather forced the postponement of several games he was supposed to start.

BENZ, Joseph Louis ("Butcher Boy," "Blitzen Joe")

Born: January 21, 1886, New Alsace. **Died:** April 22, 1957, Chicago, Illinois.
Height: 6'1". **Weight:** 196. **Batted:** right. **Threw:** right.
Debut: August 16, 1911. **Final Game:** May 2, 1919.
Positions, teams, years: Chicago (AL) 1911–1919.
Games: 251. **Innings pitched:** 1,359.2. **Won/Lost:** 77–75. **Earned run average:** 2.43.

Pitcher **Joe Benz** earned his nicknames by working as an apprentice in his family's Batesville butcher shop and, according to legend, by accidentally tossing a baseball through the window of a Blitzen-Benz automobile. It's more likely "Blitzen" stemmed from the German word for lightning, since his grandfather emigrated from what is now Germany.

Benz started playing baseball for Batesville teams when he was about 14. He joined the Chicago White Sox following an exchange of letters between his father and team owner Charles Comiskey. Benz, who spent his entire nine-year career with the White Sox, relied on a spitter and a knuckleball. In 1913 he made a trip around the world with the Sox and reportedly spent $400 on evening clothes. "Only two other guys in my town even seen clothes this fine," he said.

In 1914 Benz had a 2.26 ERA and led the White Sox with 48 appearances and 283.1 innings pitched, despite a record of 15 wins and 19 defeats—the most in the AL. On May 31 at Chicago's Comiskey Park, he pitched a 6–1 no-hitter against a Cleveland lineup that included future Hall of Famers Joe Jackson and Nap Lajoie.

Benz's best year was 1915, when he was 15–11 with a 2.11 ERA. A spot starter by 1916, he went 7–3 in 1917 for the pennant-winning Sox but saw no action in their World Series triumph over the New York Giants. After an 8–8 record in 1918, he made one relief appearance for Chicago in 1919 before refusing assignment to a minor league team and retiring.

Making his home in Chicago, Benz continued to play for semi-pro clubs. He earned a living at various times as a tavern owner, stationery salesman, engineer and surveyor, as well as a custodian at St. Kilian's Catholic Church. Benz died at the age of 71, three days after suffering a stroke.

BERGMAN, Alfred Henry ("Dutch")

Born: September 27, 1889, Peru. **Died:** June 20, 1961, Fort Wayne.
Height: 5'7". **Weight:** 155. **Batted:** right. **Threw:** right.
Debut: August 29, 1916. **Final Game:** September 12, 1916.
Positions, teams, years: second base, Cleveland (AL) 1916.
Games: 8. **At-bats:** 14. **Home runs:** 0. **Average:** .214.

One of the University of Notre Dame's all-time great athletes, **Al Bergman** earned 11 letters between 1911 and 1915. He was the first Fighting Irish athlete to win varsity letters in four sports in one year, starring in baseball, basketball, football and track. A gridiron teammate of Knute Rockne and Gus Dorais, Bergman holds the Notre Dame record for the longest kickoff return: 105 yards against Loyola in 1911, a year when the playing field was 110 yards long.

Bergman joined Cleveland in August 1916 and played in eight games, three of them as a second baseman. He curtailed his baseball career to serve as a field artillery captain during World War I. Following the armistice, Bergman played for Greenville, S.C. (South Atlantic), batting .260 in 69 games in 1919.

Bergman left baseball to become a plant manager for the American Stationery Company in Peru. In 1923 he contracted tuberculosis. Although he lived to be 71 years old, he spent most of his remaining years in hospitals.

His brothers Art and Joe, also nicknamed Dutch, played football for Notre Dame. Art Bergman, known as "Dutch II," coached the Washington Redskins in 1943.

BERRY, Claude Elzy ("Admiral")

Born: February 14, 1880, Losantville. **Died:** February 1, 1974, Richmond.
Height: 5'7". **Weight:** 165. **Batted:** right. **Threw:** right.
Debut: April 22, 1904. **Final Game:** October 3, 1915.
Positions, teams, years: catcher, Chicago (AL) 1904, Philadelphia (AL) 1906–1907, Pittsburgh (Federal League) 1914–15.
Games: 245. **At-bats:** 753. **Home runs:** 3. **Average:** .219.

An excellent defensive catcher, **Claude Berry** played professional baseball from 1902 to 1917. His light hitting kept him in the minor leagues for all but five of those seasons. Berry reached the majors with Chicago in 1904, but after three games the White Sox sent him to Indianapolis (American Association). He played briefly for Connie Mack's Philadelphia Athletics at the end of 1906 and at the start of the 1907 season.

Berry spent 1908 through 1912 as the regular catcher for San Francisco (Pacific Coast). He hit .244 for the Seals in 1909. On June 8, 1909, he was behind the plate for all 24 innings of a 1–0 win over Oakland.

In 1913 Berry played for Portland, Ore., in the PCL, and then joined the Pittsburgh Stogies of the newly-formed Federal League in 1914. He hit .238 as Pittsburgh's regular backstop. In 1915 he caught Frank Allen's no-hitter over the St. Louis Terriers. Berry's batting average slipped to .192 that year, and when the FL collapsed he returned to the minors. He retired after spending 1916 and 1917 with Kansas City (American Association).

The son of a doctor, Berry moved to Richmond in 1919 and began a long and prosperous career as a realtor. He named one of his sons Tyrus in honor of Detroit Tigers outfielder Ty Cobb. Berry collected coins and always carried an Indian head cent minted in his birth year. When Berry died just three days short of his 94th birthday, he was one of the nation's oldest ex-big leaguers.

According to his family, Berry's nickname "Admiral" stemmed his from his flashy wardrobe. "Most of us think it was because of the way he dressed," said his son Tyrus. "He was a dapper dresser."

BEVILLE, Henry Monte

Born: February 24, 1875, Dublin. **Died:** January 24, 1955, Grand Rapids, Michigan.
Height: 5'11". **Weight:** 180. **Batted:** left. **Threw:** right.
Debut: April 24, 1903. **Final Game:** October 8, 1904.
Positions, teams, years: catcher (108), first base (31), New York (AL) 1903–1904, Detroit (AL) 1904.
Games: 145. **At-bats:** 454. **Home runs:** 0. **Average:** .203.

Long before Bill Dickey, Yogi Berra, Elston Howard, Thurman Munson and Jorge Posada, **Monte Beville** was the New York Yankees catcher. The son of a Civil War veteran, Beville was a longtime Indianapolis resident. One of his neighbors was John T. Brush, the clothing store magnate who later owned the New York Giants.

Beville played for the semi-pro Logansport Ottos in 1896 before making his organized baseball debut with Indianapolis (Western) in 1897. When New York first joined the AL in 1903 as the Highlanders, Beville and Jack O'Connor shared the catching duties. Neither hit well (Beville batted .194 while O'Connor averaged .203), and in July 1904 the Highlanders traded Beville to Detroit. He played his final Major League game with the Tigers in 1904. From 1905 to 1908 he played for Milwaukee (American Association).

In 1909 Beville wrapped up his career with Rochester, N.Y. (Eastern). He played before the refinement of protective gear for catchers, and the lower part of his right leg was permanently tinged a deep purple by hundreds of foul tips.

Settling in Grand Rapids, Mich., Beville was employed at a clothing store and continued to work well past retirement age.

BIGBIE, Larry Robert

Born: November 4, 1977, Hobart. **Lives:** Stevensville, Maryland.
Height: 6'4". **Weight:** 190. **Bats:** left. **Throws:** right.
Debut: June 23, 2001. **Final Game:** June 4, 2006.
Positions, teams, years: outfield, Baltimore (AL) 2001–2005, Colorado (NL) 2005, St. Louis (NL) 2006.
Games: 392. **At-bats:** 1,227. **Home runs:** 31. **Average:** .267.

Larry Bigbie is the first Hobart native to reach the Major Leagues. A star middle infielder/first baseman at Hobart High School, he was also an all-state quarterback for the Brickies football squad. At Ball State University in 1999 Bigbie hit .417 to earn Mid-America Conference player-of-the-year honors. He was the Baltimore Orioles' first-round pick (21st overall) in the 1999 draft.

Bigbie's professional career began that summer at Bluefield, W. Va. (Appalachian League). He was playing for Bowie, Md. (Eastern), in 2001 when Baltimore summoned him, and he batted .229 in 47 games for the Orioles. He opened the 2002 campaign with Rochester (International)., and on May 6 he went 6-for-6 at Indianapolis to become the first Rochester player with six hits in a single game since 1921.

In 2004 Bigbie took over as Baltimore's left fielder. The Orioles traded him to Colorado in July 2005 and the following December the Rockies dealt him to the St. Louis Cardinals. He played in the Los Angeles Dodgers chain in 2007.

According to the Mitchell Report on Steroid Abuse in Baseball, issued in December 2007, Bigbie admitted he had purchased and used performance-enhancing substances from 2001 to 2005. The report said he was "cooperating with federal authorities in connection with their investigations." Despite the notoriety, he signed to play for the Yokohama BayStars of Japan's Central League and hit .255 with eight homers in 72 games in 2008. He sat out the 2009 season, but returned in 2010 and batted .403 as the designated hitter for the Edmonton Capitals of the independent Golden Baseball League.

In 2010 Bigbie was inducted into Ball State's Athletics Hall of Fame.

BIGGS, Charles Orval

Born: September 15, 1906, French Lick. **Died:** May 24, 1954, French Lick.
Height: 6'1". **Weight:** 185. **Batted:** right. **Threw:** right.
Debut: September 3, 1932. **Final Game:** September 24, 1932.
Positions, teams, years: pitcher, Chicago (AL) 1932.
Games: 6. **Innings pitched:** 24.2. **Won/Lost:** 1–1. **Earned run average:** 6.93.

While **Charlie Biggs** appeared in just six big-league games, his pro baseball career lasted from 1929 to 1942. Biggs was pitching for a French Lick sandlot squad when a scout offered him a contract. He played for the Mission Reds (Pacific Coast) from 1929 to 1932, compiling a 12–21 record over three-plus seasons. He finished the 1932 season with Tyler (Texas), where he went 14–16 with a 2.94 ERA.

Biggs joined the White Sox in September 1932 and started against the Browns in St. Louis. "The youngster, who reported to the Sox from the Tyler Texas League club today, pitched well for five innings," the *Chicago Tribune* reported. Biggs gave up a home run to St. Louis leadoff man Debs Garms, the first batter he faced, but settled down and got the win in a 13–8 White Sox triumph. Biggs made three more starts and two relief appearances for Chicago, walking a dozen in 24.2 innings while striking out only one batter. He never again pitched in the Major Leagues.

Following a 10–16 record for El Dorado, Ark. (Dixie), in 1933, Biggs got into a salary dispute and left organized ball. After four semi-pro seasons, he spent 1938 in the South Atlantic League. Biggs divided the year between Spartanburg, N.C., and Augusta, Ga., compiling a 20–11 record.

After ending his playing days with Augusta,

Ga. (South Atlantic), in 1942, Biggs returned to French Lick to live on a farm. He was working at the French Lick Springs Hotel in 1954 when he suffered a stroke and died at the age of 47.

BILDILLI, Emil ("Hill Billy")

Born: September 16, 1912, Diamond. **Died:** September 16, 1946, Hartford City.
Height: 5'10". **Weight:** 170. **Batted:** right. **Threw:** left.
Debut: August 24, 1937. **Final Game:** May 1, 1941.
Positions, teams, years: pitcher, St. Louis (AL) 1937–1941.
Games: 41. **Innings pitched:** 148. **Won/Lost:** 4–8. **Earned run average:** 5.84.

Emil Bildilli died on his 34th birthday, less than 48 hours after throwing his last pitch. Born in the town of Diamond near Terre Haute, Bildilli attended Clinton High School and played sandlot ball throughout Indiana. He began the 1937 season with Terre Haute (Three-I), compiling a 7–7 record in 15 games before moving on to Johnstown, Pa. (Middle Atlantic), where he went 5–4 in 11 contests. He joined the St. Louis Browns in August 1937, appearing in four contests and losing his only decision.

In 1938 the left-handed curveball specialist went 18–4 for Springfield, Ill. (Three-I), and 1–0 for San Antonio (Texas). He had a 22–9 mark at San Antonio in 1939, and in two starts for the Browns that season he went 1–1.

Bildilli won a berth on the Browns' Opening Day roster in 1940. In his first start of the year on April 29, he beat the visiting New York Yankees 2–1. After giving up a leadoff triple followed by a single, he allowed no more hits and retired the last 19 batters he faced. St. Louis rejected a cash offer from the Detroit Tigers for Bildilli, who went on to post a 2–4 record in 28 games, including 11 starts. After two appearances in 1941, the Browns assigned him to Toledo (American Association). He quit baseball and joined the Muncie fire department.

Bildilli continued to play in the semi-pro ranks, and by 1946 he was pitching for the Fort Wayne Electricians club. During the morning hours of September 15 he was driving back to Muncie after a game in Fort Wayne when he was involved in a one-car accident about five miles north of Hartford City. He suffered severe head injuries and died the next day. Fire department officials praised him as "one of the best fireman Muncie ever had."

In 1981 Bildilli was posthumously inducted into the Delaware County Hall of Fame in Muncie.

BILLIARD, Harry Pree ("Pre," "Newt")

Born: November 11, 1883, Monroe. **Died:** June 3, 1923, Wooster, Ohio.
Height: 6'0". **Weight:** 190. **Batted:** right. **Threw:** right.
Debut: July 31, 1908. **Final Game:** October 3, 1915.
Positions, teams, years: pitcher, New York (AL) 1908, Indianapolis (Federal League) 1914, Newark (Federal League) 1915.
Games: 52. **Innings pitched:** 171. **Won/Lost:** 8–8. **Earned run average:** 3.95.

Contemporary newspaper accounts describe **Harry Billiard** as "a pitcher with terrific speed, ... bothered at times by lack of control." Raised in Wooster, Ohio, Billiard played for local teams before signing with Meridian, Miss. (Cotton States), in 1906. In 1908 he made the jump from Meridian to the New York Highlanders (later known as the Yankees).

In 1909 he was back in the minors with Lynchburg (Virginia). Pitching that year against Portsmouth, the *Washington Post* reported that Billiard walked the bases loaded and then struck out the side in the first, second and third innings. He played for Macon, Ga., and Augusta, Ga. (South Atlantic), in 1909 and pitched for San Antonio (Texas) in 1910 and for Terre Haute (Central) in 1911 before joining Indianapolis (Federal) in 1913.

Billiard was a big league player again in 1914 when the Federal League declared itself a major circuit. He was the fifth man in the Hoosiers' starting rotation, going 8–7 with a 3.71 ERA. Indianapolis finished first, but moved to Newark, N.J., for 1915 due to economic reasons. Plagued by control problems, he walked one batter for each of his 28 full innings and was soon gone from majors.

Back in Wooster, Billiard became a partner in an auto garage. He came down with typhoid fever in May 1923 and died five weeks later at the age of 39.

BLAEMIRE, Rae Bertrum

Born: February 8, 1911, Gary. **Died:** December 23, 1975, Champaign, Illinois.
Height: 6'0". **Weight:** 178. **Batted:** right. **Threw:** right.
Debut: September 13, 1941. **Final Game:** September 23, 1941.
Positions, teams, years: catcher, New York (NL) 1941.
Games: 2. **At-bats:** 5. **Home runs:** 0. **Average:** .400.

By September 1941, manager Bill Terry's New York Giants had been eliminated from pennant contention. The Giants began promoting farmhands from their minor league affiliates, including **Rae Blaemire**, a 30-year-old journeyman catcher from Jersey City (International).

In Cincinnati on September 13, Blaemire and pitcher Hugh East formed an all-rookie battery for New York. Blaemire went 2-for-5 in a 6–4 loss. Several of the September call-ups reportedly impressed Terry.

Whether Blaemire was one of them became academic when Mel Ott replaced Terry as manager of the Giants prior to the 1942 season. Blaemire returned to the minors, his big league career finished after just two games. He spent part of 1946—his final year—as player-manager for Grand Forks, N.D. (Northern).

After leaving the pro ranks, Blaemire settled in Champaign, Ill., and played in the semi-professional Eastern Illinois League. From 1962 to 1965 he served as league president. He suffered a fatal heart attack just ten months after retiring from an automobile agency.

BLEMKER, Raymond ("Buddy")

Indiana Baseball Hall of Fame, 2001.
Born: August 9, 1937, Huntingburg. **Died:** February 15, 1994, Evansville.
Height: 5'11". **Weight:** 190. **Batted:** right. **Threw:** left.
Debut: July 3, 1960. **Final Game:** July 3, 1960.
Positions, teams, years: pitcher, Kansas City (AL) 1960.
Games: 1. **Innings pitched:** 1.2. **Won/Lost:** 0–0. **Earned run average:** 27.00.

In 1960 **Ray Blemker** was the fourth and final Kansas City pitcher in a 13–2 loss at Boston. Blemker's slate in his only Major League outing included a wild pitch and a hit batsman. The statistics from his only big league contest belie a distinguished sports career.

Blemker starred in baseball, basketball and football at Huntingburg High School. At Georgia Tech he was a team captain in basketball, scoring 1,266 career points and receiving second-team All-America honors. Between 1957 and 1959 he won 18 games for the Yellowjackets baseball squad.

Blemker declined a $25,000 bonus in 1958 to complete his college degree and broke in with Sioux City, Iowa (Three-I), in 1959. A year later he was in the Major Leagues. Despite a good curve and favorable scouting reports, he quit baseball after 1962 to spend more time with his family.

Settling in Henderson, Ky., Blemker worked as an investigator for the U.S. Department of Labor. He was active in youth baseball until his death from leukemia at age 56. Few of the youngsters he coached ever learned of his athletic prowess.

In 2001 Blemker was inducted into the Indiana Baseball Hall of Fame.

BOEHLER, George Henry

Born: January 2, 1892, Lawrenceburg. **Died:** June 23, 1958, Lawrenceburg.
Height: 6'2". **Weight:** 180. **Batted:** right. **Threw:** right.
Debut: September 13, 1912. **Final Game:** September 7, 1926.
Positions, teams, years: pitcher, Detroit (AL) 1912–1916, St. Louis (AL) 1920–21, Pittsburgh (NL) 1923, Brooklyn (NL) 1926.
Games: 61. **Innings pitched:** 202.1. **Won/Lost:** 6–12. **Earned run average:** 4.71.

Nine nondescript Major League seasons mask the impressive career of lifelong Lawrenceburg resident **George Boehler**, a sidearm pitcher with a blazing fastball. Boehler (pronounced BAY-ler) won 20 or more games seven times in the minor leagues, including a 38-victory season in 1922. He led the PCL in strikeouts in 1924 (216) and 1925 (278).

Boehler's professional career began with Springfield (Ohio State) in 1911. On April 23 he pitched a 7–1 no-hitter against Lima. He won 27 games for Newark (Ohio State) in 1912, earning a late-season promotion to the Detroit Tigers. Dispatched to St. Joseph, Mo. (Western), early in 1913, he again notched 27 wins. He spent 1914 through 1916 with the Tigers before returning to the minors, and in

1920 he won 20 games for Joplin, Mo. (Western).

Following two brief stretches with the St. Louis Browns in 1920 and 1921, Boehler won 38 games for Tulsa, Okla. (Western), in 1922. No pitcher has had more victories in this century except in the PCL, where the schedule extended to around 200 contests in some seasons.

Boehler joined Pittsburgh for part of 1923, but prior to the 1924 campaign the Pirates traded him to Oakland (Pacific Coast). He won 26 games that year and 23 in 1925. On May 28, 1925, he held Sacramento hitless for nine and two-third innings, but lost 2–0 on two hits and an error in the tenth. He spent 1926 with the Brooklyn Dodgers and rejoined Oakland in 1927, helping the Oaks to the PCL title with 22 victories. It was his final 20-win season.

In 1929 Boehler appeared as a baseball extra in the comedy film *Fast Company*, along with Irish Meusel, Jigger Statz, Truck Hannah and several other players. After a 6–11 record for Nashville (Southern Association) in 1930, he retired with a career minor league record of 248 wins and 202 losses. He returned to Lawrenceburg, where he worked for the James Walsh & Co. distillery for nearly 25 years.

BOGAR, Timothy Paul

Born: October 28, 1966, Indianapolis. **Lives:** Bloomington, Illinois.
Height: 6'2". **Weight:** 198. **Batted:** right. **Threw:** right.
Debut: April 21, 1993. **Final Game:** July 1, 2001.
Positions, teams, years: shortstop (441), third base (118), first base (60), second base (36), pitcher (2), outfield (2), New York (NL), 1993–1996, Houston (NL) 1997–2000, Los Angeles (NL) 2001.
Games: 701. **At-bats:** 1,516. **Home runs:** 24. **Average:** .228.
Innings pitched: 2. **Won/Lost:** 0-0. **Earned run average:** 4.50.
Manager: Texas (AL) 2014 (14–8).

A hard-working, versatile utilityman, **Tim Bogar** once played every position in a minor league game. After attending Buffalo Grove (Ill.) High School and Eastern Illinois University, Bogar was the New York Mets' eighth-round pick in the 1987 free-agent draft. His first stop in professional ball was at Little Falls, N.Y. (New York-Penn). On the last day of the 1991 season Bogar played all nine positions for Tidewater (International).

He joined New York in 1993 as a backup infielder, but became the starting shortstop in June. Late in the season Bogar injured his left hand while sliding into the plate on an inside-the-park homer and had to undergo surgery. Healthy again in 1994, he was relegated to a backup role. Houston acquired Bogar prior to the 1997 season and he spent time as the Astros' regular shortstop. In 2000 he appeared in two games as a relief pitcher.

Bogar became a free agent prior to 2001 and signed with the Los Angeles Dodgers, but suffered recurrent hamstring injuries. He opened the 2002 season with Colorado Springs (Pacific Coast). He retired after just 13 games.

Returning to baseball in 2004, Bogar won manager of the year honors at Greeneville, Tenn. (Appalachian League). With Lexington, Ky., in 2005, he was voted the South Atlantic League's top managerial prospect. He managed Akron, Ohio (Eastern), in 2006 and 2007 and returned to the majors in 2008 with the Tampa Bay Rays, who created the post of quality assurance coach for him.

In 2009 Bogar joined the Red Sox as manager Terry Francona's first-base coach. In 2010 he became Boston's third-base coach, and in 2011 he took over as bench coach. Bobby Valentine replaced Francona in 2012, and friction developed between the manager and some of his coaches. Valentine was dismissed after the season and Bogar's contract wasn't renewed.

Bogar managed Arkansas (Texas) in 2013 and joined the Texas Rangers in 2014 as bench coach. He was named interim manager on September 5 after manager Ron Washington resigned due to an off-the-field personal matter. The Rangers went 14–8 under Bogar, including a 12–1 run from September 12–25.

After Texas named Jeff Banister as manager for 2015, Bogar joined the Los Angeles Angels as special assistant to the general manager.

BONIN, Ernest Luther ("Bonnie")

Born: January 13, 1889, Greenhill. **Died:** January 3, 1966, Sycamore, Ohio.
Height: 5'9". **Weight:** 178. **Batted:** left. **Threw:** right.

Debut: April 13, 1913. **Final Game:** May 16, 1914.
Positions, teams, years: outfield, St. Louis (AL) 1913, Buffalo (Federal League) 1914.
Games: 21. **At-bats:** 77. **Home runs:** 0. **Average:** .182.

After only one American League plate appearance, **Luther Bonin** jumped to the Federal League. Bonin entered the pro ranks with Canton, Ohio (Ohio-Pennsylvania), in 1910 and averaged .281 over 124 games. He was batting .386 in 18 contests for Columbus, Ohio (American Association), in 1911 when he left organized ball.

Bonin joined the St. Louis Browns for 1913 and batted for pitcher Mack Allison in the seventh inning of a 7–2 loss to the Chicago White Sox. Soon afterwards, the Browns shipped him to Columbus, where he appeared in 32 games and hit .287.

In 1914 Bonin signed with Buffalo of the newly-formed Federal League. He played right field and batted cleanup for the Blues in the FL's first contest in Baltimore on April 13, 1914. In Buffalo's next game on April 17, he hit a ball into the Terrapin Park bleachers for an apparent home run. As he passed the coach's box, manager Larry Schafly patted him on the back. The umpire, claiming Schafly's action violated the rules, called Bonin out. Instead of a homer, Bonin was credited with a triple in Buffalo's 4–3 win.

Bonin batted .184 in 20 games for Buffalo. Out of organized ball for 1915, he returned with Muskegon, Mich. (Central), in 1916 and hit .281 in 32 contests. He returned to Ohio after his baseball career and worked as a farmer. Bonin suffered from poor health for the last eight years of his life, dying at age 76 due to a heart ailment.

BOOTCHECK, Christopher Brandon

Born: October 24, 1978, La Porte. **Lives:** Atlanta, Georgia.
Height: 6'5". **Weight:** 210. **Bats:** right. **Throws:** right.
Debut: September 9, 2003.
Positions, teams, years: pitcher, Anaheim (AL) 2003, Los Angeles (AL) 2005–2008, Pittsburgh (NL) 2009, New York (AL) 2013.
Games: 91. **Innings pitched:** 148.1. **Won/Lost:** 3–7. **Earned run average:** 6.55.

Chris Bootcheck's father, Dan Bootcheck, compiled a 41–27 record as a left-handed pitcher in the Detroit Tigers system from 1966 to 1973.

After two years at Michigan City Rogers High School, Chris transferred to La Porte, where he starred in basketball and played baseball for the legendary Ken Schreiber. As a senior in 1997 he went 15–2 with a 1.14 earned run average and 198 strikeouts.

In three years at Auburn University, Bootcheck (pronounced BOO-check) compiled a 25–10 record. He toured Japan with Team USA in 1999 and in 2000 he was the Anaheim Angels' top draft pick (20th overall). His first stop in pro ball was with Rancho Cucamonga (California) in 2001. He joined the Angels in September 2003 and spent all of 2004 at Salt Lake City, Utah (Pacific Coast).

Converted from a starting pitcher to a reliever, Bootcheck shuttled between Salt Lake and Los Angeles in 2005 and 2006. He went on the disabled list in May 2006 when he pulled a hamstring while running onto the field during a brawl between the Angels and Oakland Athletics.

Bootcheck spent all of 2007 in Los Angeles as a long reliever. In July 2008 the Angels assigned his contract to Salt Lake. He compiled a 3–2 record with 20 saves at Indianapolis (International) in 2009, earning an August promotion to the Pittsburgh Pirates. He spent 2010 with the Yokohama BayStars of Japan's Central League.

Returning to the U.S. in 2011 to play in the Tampa Bay Rays organization, Bootcheck finished the year with the Lotte Giants of the Korean Baseball Organization. He pitched in the Detroit system in 2012 and signed a minor league contract with the Yankees for 2013. He went 10–7, 3.69 in 24 games (including 23 starts) for Scranton/Wilkes-Barre, Pa. (International) and during June he made one relief appearance for New York.

"No one wants to be that old guy hanging on in Triple-A," Bootcheck told *Baseball America* in 2013. "But when you love the game so much like I do, I'll let my performance dictate how long I play."

Bootcheck signed a minor league contract with the Phillies for 2014, dividing the year between Lehigh Valley (International) and

BOWEN, Sutherland McCoy ("Cy," "Sub," "Dad")

Born: February 17, 1871, Kingston. **Died:** January 25, 1925, Greensburg.
Height: 6'0". **Weight:** 175. **Batted:** right. **Threw:** right.
Debut: April 28, 1896. **Final game:** June 3, 1896.
Positions, teams, years: pitcher, New York (NL) 1896.
Games: 2. **Innings pitched:** 12. **Won/Lost:** 0–1. **Earned run average:** 6.00.

Pitcher **Cy Bowen** joined the Giants in 1896 when fellow Hoosier Amos Rusie refused to re-sign with New York. That season the Giants were in the second year of owner Andrew Freedman's ruinous eight-year reign. Freedman, a Tammany Hall politician, had gone through three managers in 1895. Before 1896 ended, he would fire one more as the once-proud New York franchise dropped to seventh place in a twelve-team league.

Bowen pitched impressively during Spring Training in Florida. When the season started, the Giants had won only once in eight tries when he started against the Boston Beaneaters. A New York newspaper reported that he "made a very creditable showing" in a 6–3 loss.

Soon after, the Giants sent Bowen to the New York Metropolitans (Atlantic). He rejoined the Giants in June for a relief appearance against Chicago. He was pitching for the Metropolitans when the team was expelled, and finished the year with Hartford, Conn., another Atlantic League club. He went 18–11 for Hartford in 1897.

Bowen spent a dozen years in organized baseball, finishing his career in 1910 with Grand Rapids, Mich. (Central). Nicknamed after Cy Young, Bowen was known as "Sub" in Greensburg, where he settled after retiring. Bowen owned and operated a grocery store at the time of his death.

BOYD, Raymond C. ("Nuts")

Born: February 11, 1887, Hortonville. **Died:** February 17, 1920, Hortonville.
Height: 5'10". **Weight:** 160. **Batted:** right. **Threw:** right.
Debut: September 24, 1910. **Final game:** October 12, 1911.
Positions, teams, years: pitcher, St. Louis (AL) 1910, Cincinnati (NL) 1911.
Games: 10. **Innings pitched:** 58.1. **Won/Lost:** 2–4. **Earned run average:** 3.09.

In 1920, Spanish influenza ravaged the central Indiana town of Hortonville so badly that the town's church services had to be cancelled. Two days later, the epidemic claimed one of Hortonville's most popular residents: 33-year-old ex–Major League pitcher **Ray Boyd**.

Boyd entered pro baseball in Iowa during 1908, playing for Keokuk and Burlington (Central Association). He married Flora Pierce of Westfield, Ind., prior to the 1909 season, when he had a 23–12 record for pennant-winning Burlington. One of his victories was a June 18 no-hitter against Jacksonville.

That October, Flora died of typhoid fever after Ray "had just recently returned from the season's play," according to the *Sheridan* (Ind.) *News*, "…and had just completed the erection of a new home to which the young couple would have moved in a few days."

Boyd pitched for Ottumwa, Iowa (Central Association), in 1910, compiling a 24–11 slate to earn a shot with the St. Louis Browns. He was 0–2 in three appearances for St. Louis and opened the 1911 campaign back in Ottumwa. His 30–7 record led the league as the Speedboys finished first, and before the end of the year he was back in the majors with Cincinnati. In seven appearances for the Reds he was 2–2 with a 2.66 ERA.

Before the start of the 1912 campaign, Cincinnati sent Boyd to Birmingham, Ala. (Southern Association), where he went 23–11 as the Barons won the league title. In February 1913, when Boyd married Evangeline Carey in Noblesville, newspaper reports indicated he would go to Spring Training with the Chicago Cubs. He pitched that year for Birmingham, where arm miseries limited him to just three games.

Boyd went 9–10 for Chattanooga, Tenn. (Southern Association), in 1914. He joined Oakland (Pacific Coast) in 1915 and had a 6–5, 2.62 record before suffering a broken right wrist in mid-June. After an 8–23 slate for Oakland in 1916, he joined Bloomington, Ill. (Three-I), for 1917. On May 19 he pitched a no-hit game against Peoria.

Following that season, Boyd retired to his Hamilton County farm. He served in the armed forces during World War I.

BRADLEY, Philip Poole

Born: March 11, 1959, Bloomington. **Lives:** Columbia, Missouri.
Height: 6'0". **Weight:** 185. **Batted:** right. **Threw:** right.
Debut: September 2, 1983. **Final game:** September 29, 1990.
Positions, teams, years: outfield, Seattle (AL) 1983–1987, Philadelphia (NL) 1988, Baltimore (AL) 1989–1990, Chicago (AL) 1990.
Games: 1,022. **At-bats:** 3,695. **Home runs:** 78. **Average:** .286.

A two-sport standout in college, **Phil Bradley** was the second Indiana-born former big leaguer to play in Japan.

When Bradley was nine years old, his father coached baseball at Virginia State University, where Phil's idol was the team's star player, future Major League outfielder Al Bumbry.

After graduation from Macomb (Ill.) High School in 1977, Bradley went to the University of Missouri on a football scholarship. A three-time All-Big Eight quarterback (1978–79–80), he led Mizzou to three post-season bowl games (Liberty, Hall of Fame, and Liberty again). He set a conference total offense record (6,459 yards) that lasted ten years.

Bradley was an outfielder for Missouri baseball teams that won the 1980 Big Eight title and went to the NCAA Tournament in 1980 and 1981. In his senior year, he batted .457. Considered too small for the National Football League, he rejected offers from a Canadian gridiron team to sign with the Seattle Mariners, who made him their third-round draft pick in 1981.

Breaking in with Bellingham, Wash. (Northwest) in 1981, Bradley batted .301. He hit .331 for Bakersfield (California) in 1982 and .323 in 1983 at Salt Lake City, Utah (Pacific Coast), before joining the Mariners. He hit over .300 in each of his first three full Major League seasons, slugging 26 homers with 88 RBI in 1985. "We call him 'Smoothie' because everything he does is silky smooth," Mariners skipper Chuck Cottier told the *Chicago Tribune's* Mike Kiley. "He's very intelligent. You always have to be thinking as a quarterback, and baseball's no different. Phil's mind is always on the game."

At Boston's Fenway Park On April 29, 1986, Bradley fanned against Red Sox right-hander Roger Clemens to set a record. Bradley was Clemens' twentieth strikeout victim, breaking the old mark of 19 shared by Steve Carlton (1969), Tom Seaver (1970) and Nolan Ryan (1974).

Unhappy in Seattle, Bradley was traded to the Philadelphia Phillies prior to the 1988 campaign. He homered in the first night contest at Chicago's Wrigley Field on August 8, but rain cancelled the game—along with Bradley's home run.

After three mediocre seasons with three different teams (Philadelphia in 1988, Baltimore in 1989–1990, White Sox in 1990), Bradley signed with the Yomiuri Giants of Japan's Central League for 1991. Following Jim Hicks as the second Hoosier-born ex-big leaguer to play in Japan, Bradley batted .282 with 21 homers for the Giants.

After returning to the U.S., Bradley became the baseball coach at Westminster (Mo.) College, where he also taught sports history classes. He later worked as special assistant to the executive director of the Major League Baseball Players Association. He also served as a volunteer assistant coach for the University of Missouri women's softball team.

BRANDT, William George

Born: March 21, 1915, Aurora. **Died:** May 16, 1968, Fort Wayne.
Height: 5'8". **Weight:** 170. **Batted:** right. **Threw:** right.
Debut: September 20, 1941. **Final game:** October 4, 1943.
Positions, teams, years: pitcher, Pittsburgh (NL) 1941–1943.
Games: 34. **Innings pitched:** 80.2. **Won/Lost:** 5–3. **Earned run average:** 3.57.

Bill Brandt spent his first two years in organized baseball with Hutchinson, Kan. (Western Association), winning 13 games in 1938 and again in 1939. In 1940 Brandt won 17 at Gadsden, Ala. (Southeastern), and in 1941 he had 15 wins for Harrisburg, Pa. (Inter-State). That September he joined the Pittsburgh Pirates, making two appearances and losing his only decision.

Back in the minors at the start of 1942, Brandt

won 15 for Toronto (International) to earn another trial with Pittsburgh. He spent all of 1943 with the Pirates, pitching mostly in relief, and posted a 4–1 record with a 3.16 ERA. He spent all of 1944 and 1945 in military service and, for a time, pitched for the U.S. Navy's Great Lakes team. He retired after splitting 1946 between Hollywood, Calif. (Pacific Coast), Columbus, Ohio (American Association), and Chattanooga, Tenn. (Southern).

Brandt settled in Fort Wayne, where he worked for General Electric and played for the company's semi-professional team. In 1947 the squad won the National Baseball Congress title, with Brandt pitching the championship game.

After helping the G-E's to another title in 1948, he attempted a comeback in 1949 with Sherbrooke, Quebec (independent Atlantic). In 1950 he was a member of the Fort Wayne Capeharts squad that went to Japan for the Inter-Hemispheric Semi-Pro World Championship Series. Fort Wayne beat Osaka's All-Kanebo Club for the title, four games to one.

In 1971 Brandt was inducted into the Northeast Indiana Baseball Association Hall of Fame.

BROWN, Charles Edward ("Farmer")

Born: August 17, 1871, Bluffton. **Died:** April 3, 1938, Monclova, Ohio.
Height: 6'0". **Weight:** 180. **Batted:** unknown. **Threw:** left.
Debut: August 4, 1897. **Final game:** August 14, 1897
Positions, teams, years: pitcher, Cleveland (NL) 1897.
Games: 4. **Innings pitched:** 24.1. **Won/Lost:** 1–2. **Earned run average:** 7.77.

Charlie Brown broke into professional baseball with Scranton, Pa. (Eastern), in 1895 and spent 1896 with Grand Rapids, Mich. (Western). In 1897 he played for two Interstate League teams, Dayton and Toledo, before joining the Cleveland Spiders.

On August 4, 1897, in Louisville, Brown started the second game of a doubleheader for Cleveland. The Spiders had lost the first game when Jesse Burkett was ejected and Cleveland manager Patsy Tebeau refused to send out a replacement. Still fuming when the second game started, Burkett and several teammates gave half-hearted efforts. Louisville won 7–4 and Brown was pinned with the loss. Seven days later in Cleveland, Brown pitched a complete-game 12–6 win over Pittsburgh.

In 1898 Brown returned to Dayton and had a 14–13 slate. He spent part of 1899 in Dayton before leaving organized ball. A good-hitting pitcher, he batted .300 in 1897 for Dayton.

Brown worked as a teamster after leaving baseball.

BROWN, Elmer Young ("Shook")

Born: August 25, 1883, Southport. **Died:** January 23, 1955, Indianapolis.
Height: 5'11". **Weight:** 172. **Batted:** left. **Threw:** right.
Debut: September 16, 1911. **Final game:** April 14, 1915.
Positions, teams, years: pitcher, St. Louis (AL) 1911–1912, Brooklyn (NL) 1913–1915.
Games: 43. **Innings pitched:** 188.2. **Won/Lost:** 7–11. **Earned run average:** 3.48.

Breaking in with Marion (Ohio State) at age 24 in 1908, **Elmer Brown** went 15–11. Out of organized ball in 1909, he returned in 1910 with Akron, Ohio (Ohio-Pennsylvania), and had a 21–7 record. A 22–5 record for Akron in 1911 earned him a shot with the St. Louis Browns, where he split two decisions in five September contests.

Brown made 23 appearances for St. Louis in 1912, going 5–8 with a 2.99 ERA. Back in the minors in 1913, he went 16–13 for Montgomery, Ala. (Southern Association), and led the league with 156 strikeouts. Brooklyn bought his contract for $7,000 that August and he saw action with the Dodgers in three games.

During Spring Training in 1914, Brown suffered a badly sprained ankle. When he recovered, a line drive struck him above the eye during batting practice, causing a wound that needed eight stitches. He spent part of the season with Newark, N.J. (International). He pitched sparingly for Brooklyn in 1914 and 1915, never living up to expectations.

Released by the Dodgers early in 1915, Brown divided the rest of the year between New Orleans (Southern Association) and Newark, which shifted to Harrisburg, Pa., in July. He was out of baseball in 1916 and 1917, then came back briefly in 1918 with Newport

News (Virginia). He had a 7–6 record when the league suspended operations in May due to World War I.

Brown's only NL complete-game victory came on June 17, 1914, at the expense of the Philadelphia Phillies and Pete Alexander, a future Hall of Famer.

After retiring from baseball, Brown returned to Indianapolis and managed a bowling alley for a time. He later worked as a millwright for the Evans Milling Company.

BROWN, Kevin Lee

Born: April 21, 1973, Valparaiso. **Lives:** Austin.
Height: 6'2". **Weight:** 200. **Batted:** right. **Threw:** right.
Debut: September 12, 1996. **Final game:** September 22, 2002.
Positions, teams, years: catcher, Texas (AL) 1996–1997, Toronto (AL) 1998–1999, Milwaukee (NL) 2000–2001, Boston (AL) 2002.
Games: 85. **At-bats:** 189. **Home runs:** 7. **Average:** .254.

Catcher **Kevin Brown** earned four letters in baseball and two in basketball at Pike High School in Petersburg. He was the 1994 Great Lakes Valley Player of the Year at the University of Southern Indiana and twice earned NCAA Division II All-America honors.

In the June 1994 draft the Texas Rangers, with no first-round selection, made Brown their top choice in the second round. His professional career began that summer with Hudson Valley (New York-Penn). At Tulsa, Okla. (Texas), in 1996 Brown belted 26 homers with 86 RBI to earn a September call-up to the Rangers. *USA Today* ranked him the top prospect in the Texas organization.

The Rangers sent Brown to Toronto in March 1998, and in July 2000 the Blue Jays traded him to the Milwaukee Brewers. He spent parts of 2000 and 2001 with Indianapolis (American Association). After becoming a free agent, he signed with Tampa Bay for 2002. The Devil Rays released him in mid-season and he joined the Boston organization, appearing in two games with the Red Sox before the season ended.

Brown retired after spending part of 2003 with Palm Beach (Florida State) in the St. Louis Cardinals system.

BROWN, Mordecai Peter Centennial ("Three-Finger," "Miner," "Brownie," "The Royal Rescuer")

National Baseball Hall of Fame, 1949. Indiana Baseball Hall of Fame, 1979.
Born: October 19, 1876, Nyesville. **Died:** February 14, 1948, Terre Haute.
Height: 5'10". **Weight:** 175. **Batted:** both. **Threw:** right.
Debut: April 19, 1903. **Final game:** September 4, 1916.
Positions, teams, years: pitcher (481), outfield (3), second base (1), St. Louis (NL) 1903, Chicago (NL) 1904–1912, Cincinnati (NL) 1913, St. Louis (Federal) 1914, Brooklyn (Federal) 1914, Chicago (Federal) 1915, Chicago (NL) 1916.
Games: 485. **Innings pitched:** 3,172.1. **Won/Lost:** 239–130. **Earned run average:** 2.06.
At bats: 1,143. **Home runs:** 2. **Average:** .206.
Manager: St. Louis (Federal) 1914 (50–63).

Ty Cobb once said the most devastating pitch he ever faced was **Three-Finger Brown's** curveball. Ironically, that pitch—a cross between a split-finger fastball and a knuckler—was the residue of a disfiguring childhood accident that also provided Brown with his unique nickname.

Brown grew up on a farm near Rosedale in west central Indiana. He was named Mordecai for an uncle, Peter after his father, and Centennial because of his birth in the United States' hundredth year.

Brown's right hand was mangled by a corn grinder when he was seven and the accident cost him his index finger. While the hand was still in a cast, he suffered further injuries in a fall that left his middle finger and pinky crooked and misshapen.

After attending Nyesville High School, Brown worked as a coal miner and played baseball for town teams in Clinton, Shelburn and Coxville. He started out as a catcher and third baseman, but soon discovered that the deformed digits gave his pitches an unhittable spin. "That old paw served me pretty well in its time," Brown said years later. "It gave me a firmer grip on the ball, so I could spin it over the hump. It gave me a greater dip."

In 1901 the 24-year-old Brown began his professional career with Terre Haute (Three-I). He reached the majors in 1903 with St. Louis. After one season the Cardinals traded him to Chicago, where he developed into one of baseball's premier pitchers. These were the Tinker-to-Evers-to-Chance Cubs, NL champions of 1906, 1907, 1908 and 1910.

Brown won 20 or more games from 1906 through 1911, including 29 in '08. From 1906 to 1910 his highest ERA was a stringent 1.86. His 1.04 ERA in 1906 remains the lowest by an NL hurler in the modern era (post–1900). Brown pitched in four World Series for Chicago, throwing a two-hitter against the White Sox in 1906. In 1907 and 1908, when the Cubs were world champions, he had a combined 3–0 record in Series play with an ERA of 0.00.

Brown slipped to 5–6 in 1912 at age 35 and was released. He joined the Cincinnati Reds in 1913 and went 11–12. When the Federal League began operations in 1914, Brown became player-manager of the St. Louis Terriers. He stepped down as manager in July with the Terriers in seventh place. In August he joined the Brooklyn Tip-Tops, another FL club. In 1915 he helped the Chicago Whales win the FL pennant with a 17–8 record.

After the FL folded, Brown rejoined the Cubs for 1916. He went 2–3 in his final year with Chicago and returned to the minors, where he continued to play and manage. He retired following the 1920 season with Terre Haute, where his professional career had begun two decades earlier.

During his halcyon years in Chicago, Brown's biggest rival was Christy Mathewson of the New York Giants. When Mathewson no-hit the Cubs 1–0 in 1905, Brown was the losing pitcher. Brown proceeded to win his next nine decisions against Mathewson, culminating with a triumph on the last day of the 1908 season that gave Chicago the NL pennant. The two squared off for a final time on Labor Day in 1916. Mathewson won, giving him a 13–12 edge. The game marked the last big league appearance for both men.

Brown's 57 career shutouts are tenth on the all-time list. His 2.06 lifetime ERA is third. He also pitched effectively in relief. From 1908 to 1911 his 32 saves were the most in the NL.

In 1911 he won 21 games and saved 13 more. No other 20-game winner has ever notched as many saves.

For a time Brown managed a semi-pro team in Lawrenceville, Ill. He later returned to Terre Haute, where he operated a filling station until 1945. He suffered a stroke in 1947. His death at the age of 71 was attributed to diabetes.

In 1949 Brown became the first Indiana native elected to the Hall of Fame. Thirty years later he was one of the original 16 members of Indiana's Baseball Hall of Fame. The western Indiana town of Nyesville, his birthplace, erected a granite monument in his honor in 1994. His biography, *Three-Finger: The Mordecai Brown Story*, was published in 2006 by Cindy Thomson and Scott Brown.

Brown's stellar relief work earned him the nickname "The Royal Rescuer." Although he often appears in contemporary newspaper reports as "Three-Finger," his teammates called him Mort, Brownie, or Miner.

BRUNTLETT, Eric Kevin

Born: March 29, 1978, Lafayette. **Lives**: Santa Rosa, California.
Height: 6'0". **Weight**: 200. **Bats**: right. **Throws**: right.
Debut: June 27, 2003. **Final game**: October 4, 2009.
Positions, teams, years: shortstop (181), outfield (101), second base (83), third base (48), first base (5), Houston (NL) 2003–2007, Philadelphia (NL) 2008–2009.
Games: 512. **At-bats**: 789. **Home runs**: 11. **Average**: .231.

Eric Bruntlett played in championship games at the high school and collegiate levels as well as in the World Series. At Lafayette Harrison High School, Bruntlett was a member of the National Honor Society and scored 1470 on his Scholastic Aptitude Test. He was also a football and baseball standout who contributed a pair of hits in Harrison's 3–1 win over Fort Wayne Concordia in the 1995 state championship game at Bush Stadium in Indianapolis.

The Los Angeles Dodgers drafted Bruntlett in 1996 (72nd round) but he opted to attend Stanford University. Primarily a shortstop, he took part in three College World Series and reached the championship game as a senior. He graduated in 2000 with a degree in economics. The Houston Astros drafted him that June and assigned him to Martinsville, Va. (Appalachian). In June 2004 he went from New Orleans (Pacific Coast) to the Astros.

Bruntlett was a utility infielder for Houston's first-ever pennant winner in 2005. The Astros dealt him to Philadelphia in November 2007. In 2008 the Phillies won the NL pennant, and in Game Two of the World Series Bruntlett slammed a pinch-hit homer against the Tampa Bay Rays. He scored what turned out to be the deciding run in Game Five, when the Phillies wrapped up the Series.

On August 23, 2009, in New York, Bruntlett had an unassisted triple play to preserve Philadelphia's 9–7 win over the Mets. Playing second base, he snared Jeff Francoeur's line drive, stepped on second to force Luis Castillo and tagged Daniel Murphy, who was running from first. It was the fifteenth one-man triple play in baseball history and only the second to end a game. Bruntlett needed a few moments before he realized the play had ended the game. "I didn't know how to react," he told reporters. "I didn't know what to do."

Bruntlett went to Spring Training in 2010 with Washington, but the Nationals released him in April. He finished his playing days that year with Scranton/Wilkes-Barre, Pa. (International), the top farm club of the New York Yankees.

BUENTE, Jay Phillip

Born: September 28, 1983, Evansville. **Lives**: Evansville.
Height: 6'2". **Weight**: 185. **Batted**: right. **Threw**: right.
Debut: May 27, 2010. **Final game**: July 26, 2011.
Positions, teams, years: pitcher, Florida (NL) 2010–2011, Tampa Bay (AL) 2011.
Games: 10. **Innings pitched**: 16. **Won/Lost**: 0–1.
Earned run average: 7.31.

After winning academic all-city honors at Evansville's Reitz High School, **Jay Buente** pitched for Purdue University from 2003 to 2006. The Florida Marlins took him in the 14th round of the 2006 draft and he pitched that summer for Jamestown, N.Y. (New York-Penn).

A 5–1, 3.39 record for New Orleans (Pacific Coast) in 2009 earmarked Buente (pronounced (BEN-tee) as a potential big league set-up man. He was 0–1 for New Orleans with a 2.70 earned run average in May 2010 when he joined the Marlins. Scheduled to pitch in the Arizona Fall League, he developed shoulder tendinitis and missed the final three weeks of the season. In October the Marlins sent him outright to New Orleans.

Florida briefly brought Buente back in May 2011 when pitcher Josh Johnson went on the disabled list. Claimed by Tampa Bay at the end of the month, Buente made one appearance for the Rays before he was optioned to Durham (International). He spent all of 2012 on the disabled list and became a free agent after the season.

In 2013 Buente retired after going 1–3 in six games for Lancaster of the independent Atlantic League.

BULLINGTON, Bryan Paul

Born: September 30, 1980, Indianapolis. **Lives:** Mokena, Illinois.
Height: 6'4". **Weight:** 210. **Bats:** right. **Throws:** right.
Debut: September 18, 2005.
Positions, teams, years: pitcher, Pittsburgh (NL) 2005, 2007, Cleveland (AL) 2008, Toronto (AL) 2009, Kansas City (AL) 2010.
Games: 26. **Innings pitched:** 81.2. **Won/Lost:** 1–9.
Earned run average: 5.62.

Pitcher **Bryan Bullington**, a two-sport star at Madison High School and Indiana's 1999 Mr. Baseball, was the No. 1 pick in the 2002 draft. Bullington averaged 25 points per game for his high school basketball team. He went 32–3 as a pitcher for the baseball club, and in 1999 his one-hit shutout over Fort Wayne Carroll gave Madison the State 3A title.

As a Ball State University sophomore in 2001, Bullington set a school record with 119 strikeouts and became the Mid-American Conference all-time strikeout leader. In June 2002 he became the third Hoosier native (along with Jeff King in 1986 and Andy Benes in 1988) to be picked first overall in the annual draft. When he signed that October, the Pittsburgh Pirates gave him a club-record $4 million bonus.

Bullington split the 2003 season between Hickory, N.C. (South Atlantic), and Lynchburg, Va. (Carolina). Shoulder problems delayed his Triple-A debut in 2005, but he compiled a 9–5 slate that year for Indianapolis (International) to earn a September call-up to Pittsburgh. Sidelined for all of 2006 after shoulder surgery, he went 11–9 for Indianapolis in 2007 to merit another promotion to the Pirates.

In August 2008 Bullington went to the Cleveland Indians in a waiver deal. Two months later the Toronto Blue Jays claimed him. He split 2009 between Toronto and Las Vegas (Pacific Coast). Prior to 2010 he signed a minor league contract with the Kansas City Royals and opened the year with Omaha, Neb. (Pacific Coast). Promoted in May, he earned a start against the Yankees on August 15 and pitched eight shutout innings for his first Major League win.

After the season, Bullington signed a contract with the Hiroshima Toyo Carp of Japan's Central League. He pitched in an exhibition game at Hiroshima hours before a powerful earthquake struck Japan's northeast coast on March 11, 2011. Opting to stay in Japan despite concerns about radiation leaks from a damaged nuclear power plant, he compiled a 13–11 record for Hiroshima with a 2.42 ERA. He was 7–14 for the Carp in 2012 and 11–9 in 2013. In both seasons, his ERA was 3.23. He went 9–8 in 2014 with a 4.58 ERA.

Bryan's high school basketball coach was his father, Larry, a former two-sport star at Marshall High School in Indianapolis. Larry Bullington played for the 1970 Indiana All-Star basketball team and earned baseball MVP honors at Ball State in 1972. In 2003 the elder Bullington coached Pike High School in Indianapolis to the state 4A basketball title.

BURNSIDE, Sheldon John ("Shelly")

Born: December 22, 1954, South Bend. **Lives:** Montgomery, Alabama.
Height: 6'5". **Weight:** 200. **Batted:** right. **Threw:** left.
Debut: September 4, 1978. **Final game:** September 16, 1980.
Positions, teams, years: pitcher, Detroit (AL) 1978–1979, Cincinnati (NL) 1980.
Games: 19. **Innings pitched:** 30. **Won/Lost:** 2–1. **Earned run average:** 6.00.

With Montgomery, Ala. (Southern), on June 24, 1976, **Sheldon Burnside** pitched a seven-inning no-hitter in an 8–0 win over Charlotte. Three years later, he was the third of four pitchers for Indianapolis (American Association) in a 5–0 no-hit victory over Evansville.

Burnside spent part of his boyhood in Cleveland. Due to his father's employment, his family moved to Canada when he was about 10. He was on the basketball team at Michael Power High School in Etobicoke, Ontario, and was also an excellent tennis player.

Burnside played first base for Toronto-area sandlot baseball teams and didn't start pitching until he was 15. He signed a contract with the Detroit Tigers in 1974 and entered pro ball in 1975 with Bristol, Va. (Appalachian).

After a 14–5 record for Evansville (American Association), Burnside joined Detroit in September 1978. He began the 1979 season with the Tigers but was loaned to Indianapolis (American Association), the top farm club of the Cincinnati Reds. After the year, Detroit traded him to Cincinnati. He pitched in seven games for the Reds in 1980, his final big league season.

Returning to Montgomery, Ala., where he'd pitched in the Southern League in 1976 and 1977, Burnside managed a United Parcel Service center.

BUSH, Owen Joseph ("Donie," "Ownie")

Indiana Baseball Hall of Fame, 1979.
Born: October 8, 1887, Indianapolis. **Died:** March 28, 1972, Indianapolis.
Height: 5'6". **Weight:** 140. **Batted:** both. **Threw:** right.
Debut: September 18, 1908. **Final game:** September 15, 1923
Positions, teams, years: shortstop (1,866), third base (43), second base (26), Detroit (AL) 1908–1921, Washington (AL) 1921–1923.
Games: 1,945. **At-bats:** 7,210. **Home runs:** 9. **Average:** .250.
Manager: Washington (AL) 1923, Pittsburgh (NL) 1927–1929, Chicago (AL) 1930–1931, Cincinnati (NL) 1933 (497–539).

Nearly seven decades in organized ball as a shortstop, manager, executive and scout earned **Donie Bush** the title of "Mr. Baseball" in Indianapolis. In 1967 Victory Field, the longtime home of the American Association's Indianapolis Indians, was renamed Bush Stadium in his honor.

Bush grew up on the Eastside of Indianapolis and played semi-pro ball for area teams. His professional career began in 1905 with Sault Sainte Marie, Mich. (Copper Country Soo). After a good year with South Bend (Central) in 1907, the Detroit Tigers acquired Bush's contract and assigned him to Indianapolis. He helped the Indians finish first in 1908 and by mid-September he was playing in Detroit. Known as "Ownie" around Indianapolis, he was tagged "Donie" (pronounced "DOE-nee") early in his career and the nickname stuck.

Bush became Detroit's starting shortstop the following year and held the job for 13 seasons helping the Tigers to a pennant in 1909. "There has never been a greater lead-off man than Donie," sportswriter Hugh Fullerton noted in 1921. Batting in front of Ty Cobb for much of his career, Bush led the league in bases on balls five times. He was also a fine base runner and a superb fielder with excellent range. Some consider him the finest shortstop in Tiger history.

The Tigers sent Bush to Washington in 1921. Two years later he became the Senators' player-manager. Released after a fourth-place finish, he returned to Indianapolis and managed the Indians from 1924–1926. In 1927 he took over as manager of the Pirates and led Pittsburgh to the NL pennant. The Pirates lost the World Series in four games to one of the greatest New York Yankee teams of all time.

Dismissed by the Pirates in 1929, Bush managed the Chicago White Sox in 1930–1931 and returned to the NL in 1933 as skipper of the Cincinnati Reds. He also managed Minneapolis in 1932 and again from 1934–1938. In 1939 he was manager and part owner of another American Association squad, the Louisville Colonels. After the 1940 season he and his partner, Indianapolis banker Frank McKinney, sold the franchise.

The following year Bush and McKinney purchased the Indianapolis Indians. Bush served as team president and general manager, and took over as field boss for 1943 and part of 1944. The Cleveland Indians purchased the Indianapolis franchise in 1951. Four years later the team was again on the market and in danger of being moved to another city. Bush, who'd been a scout for the Boston Red Sox from 1953–1955, helped arrange for the Indians to become a community-owned team. With the franchise remaining in Indianapolis, he served as president and general manager. At baseball's 1963 winter meetings, Major League executives named him "King of Baseball."

Bush retired from the Indians in 1969. During Spring Training in 1972 he was scouting in Florida for the White Sox when he took ill. He returned to Indianapolis and died there three weeks later at age 84.

In 1979 Bush was one of the original 16 members of the Indiana Baseball Hall of Fame. The Indianapolis Oldtimers' man-of-the-year award is named for him.

BUTERA, Andrew Edward

Born: August 9, 1983, Evansville. **Lives:** Lake Mary, Florida.
Height: 6'1". **Weight:** 200. **Bats:** right. **Throws:** right.
Debut: April 9, 2010.
Positions, teams, years: catcher (242), first base (3), pitcher (3), Minnesota (AL) 2010–2013, Los Angeles (NL) 2013–2014.
Games: 251. **At-bats:** 667. **Home runs:** 8. **Average:** .183.
Innings pitched: 1.2. **Won/Lost:** 0–0. **Earned run average:** 6.75.

A second-generation Major League catcher, **Drew Butera** lettered in golf and starred for the baseball team at Bishop Moore High School in Lake Mary, Fla. A 48th-round draft pick by the Toronto Blue Jays in 2002, he enrolled that fall at the University of Central Florida.

The Mets took Butera (pronounced "BYOO-tair-uh") in the fifth round of the 2005 draft. He signed with New York and broke in that summer with Brooklyn (New York-Penn). In 2007 he went to the Minnesota Twins organization as part of a three-player swap. He batted .219 for New Britain, Conn. (Eastern), in 2008 and hit .211 in 2009 for Rochester, N.Y. (International).

Butera joined the Twins in 2010 as the backup to Joe Mauer, the AL's reigning Most Valuable Player. When Mauer went on the disabled list in May 2011, Butera took over as Minnesota's everyday catcher. He batted .167 in 93 games and was behind the plate for Francisco Liriano's 1–0 no-hit win over the White Sox. Optioned to Rochester at the end of March 2012, he rejoined the club at the beginning of May. He batted .198 in 42 games and pitched a scoreless inning of relief in a 16–4 loss to Milwaukee on May 20.

In July 2013 the Twins dealt Butera to the

Dodgers. He joined Los Angeles in September, seeing action in four contests. He spent 2014 as a backup catcher for the Dodgers, who won the NL West Division title. He pitched a scoreless ninth inning in a 13–3 loss to Miami on May 14, when fastball was clocked in the mid-90s. Butera became the fifth catcher in history to catch no-hitters in both leagues on May 25, 2014, when he was behind the plate for Josh Beckett's 6–0 masterpiece against the Phillies.

When the Dodgers placed him on waivers after the season, the Los Angeles Angels claimed Butera.

Sal Butera, Drew's father, caught for the Twins, Tigers, Montreal Expos, Reds and Blue Jays from 1980 to 1988. Sal, a native of Richmond Hill, N.Y., was playing for Evansville (American Association) when Drew was born.

BUTLAND, Wilburn Rue ("Bill")

Born: March 22, 1918, Terre Haute. **Died:** September 19, 1997, Terre Haute.
Height: 6'5". **Weight:** 185. **Batted:** right. **Threw:** left.
Debut: May 29, 1940. **Final game:** May 10, 1947.
Positions, teams, years: pitcher, Boston (AL) 1940, 1942, 1946–1947.
Games: 32. **Innings pitched:** 150.2. **Won/Lost:** 9–3. **Earned run average:** 3.88.

Long, lean **Bill Butland** starred for Terre Haute's Gerstmeyer High School before entering professional baseball with St. Augustine (Florida State) in 1936. He had back-to-back 19 win seasons for Crookston, Minn. (Northern), in 1938 and in 1939 with Minneapolis (American Association).

In 1940 the sidearm specialist joined the Boston Red Sox, rooming with legendary outfielder Ted Williams. He was 1–2 with a 5.57 ERA in three starts by early July, when Boston shipped him to Scranton, Pa. (Eastern).

After a 12–11, 3.76 slate at Louisville (American Association) in 1941, Butland rejoined the Red Sox for 1942. He'd seen little action by August 6, when manager Joe Cronin gave him a start at Fenway Park. "Bill Butland, who spends most of his time sunning himself in the Boston Red Sox bullpen," reported the *Associated Press*, "came out of semiretirement today and shut out the Philadelphia Athletics 2–0 for his first victory of the season."

The four-hitter was the first of seven consecutive victories for Butland, one each over the other AL teams. On August 16 he beat the Senators 6–4 at Fenway. He pitched a 7–4 win over the visiting Yankees on August 20 and defeated the Indians 4–1 on August 26 in Boston, allowing three hits. On August 30 he made it five in a row with a 12–6 home win over the St. Louis Browns.

The streak continued into the next month, when Butland threw a two-hit, 2–0 victory over the Tigers at Fenway Park on September 3, followed by a 6–1 win on September 13 over the White Sox at Chicago's Comiskey Park. The streak finally ended at Yankee Stadium on September 19. Although the Red Sox won 9–6, Butland gave up 10 hits and six runs over seven innings and wasn't involved in the decision.

In December 1942 Butland entered the army. His best years were behind him when he returned in 1946. "When I did come back after three years the arm was bad," he told the *Terre Haute Tribune-Star*. "It was explained to me I tore a muscle in the shoulder and when it grew back it shortened up."

Butland won his only decision in five games for the Red Sox in 1946 and finished the year with Louisville. After one appearance for Boston in 1947 he was back in the minors for good. He pitched for Louisville in 1946, Roanoke, Va. (Piedmont), in 1947, Hollywood, Calif. (Pacific Coast), in 1948, Toledo (American Association) in 1949 and 1950, and ended his career in 1950 with Syracuse, N.Y. (International).

Making Terre Haute his home after baseball, Butland worked as a pipefitter for Commercial Solvents and later in the plastics industry as a machine operator for Ethyl Visqueen.

BYERS, James William ("Big Bill")

Born: October 3, 1877, Bridgeton. **Died:** September 8, 1948, Baltimore, Maryland.
Height: 5'7". **Weight:** 210. **Batted:** left. **Threw:** right.
Debut: April 15, 1904. **Final game:** June 4, 1904.
Positions, teams, years: catcher (16), first base (1), St. Louis (NL) 1904.
Games: 19. **At-bats:** 60. **Home runs:** 0. **Average:** .217.

As an 18-year-old in 1896, sturdy-looking **Bill Byers** played for the independent Logansport

Ottos. He broke into organized baseball two years later, and went on to play in 18 different cities in a dozen different states during a 15-year professional career.

Byers got his start with Dayton (Inter-State) in 1898, when *The Sporting News* described him as a "very fast thrower to the bases and a heavy left-handed batter." He finished the year with New Orleans (Southern), and from 1899 to 1903 he wore the uniforms of Paterson, N.J., Newark, N.J., Syracuse, N.Y., Bristol, Conn., Portsmouth, Va., Jersey City, Philadelphia (an Atlantic League franchise), Marion, Ind., Indianapolis, Harrisburg, Pa., Minneapolis, Tacoma, Wash., and Seattle.

In 1904 the St. Louis Cardinals used six different catchers. The first was Byers, who debuted with a 3-for-4 performance in a 5–4 loss to visiting Pittsburgh on Opening Day. He had only 10 more hits in his next 56 at-bats, however, and in June St. Louis released him to Baltimore (Eastern), where he batted .243 in 55 games.

Brooklyn acquired his contract in September 1904, but Byers never appeared in another Major League contest. He returned to Baltimore for 1905, hitting .325 in 91 games. He was part of Baltimore's pennant-winning team in 1908 and played for the team through 1911. He ended up his career with Trenton, N.J. (Tri-State), in 1912.

Byers returned to Baltimore after his playing days and died there at age 70 of a cerebral hemorrhage.

CALLAHAN, Wese LeRoy ("Cotton")

Born: July 3, 1888, Lyons. **Died:** September 13, 1953, Dayton, Ohio.
Height: 5'7". **Weight:** 155. **Batted:** right. **Threw:** right.
Debut: September 7, 1913. **Final game:** September 21, 1913.
Positions, teams, years: shortstop, St. Louis (NL) 1913.
Games: 7. **At-bats:** 14. **Home runs:** 0. **Average:** .286.

Fair-haired **Wes Callahan** started his career with Linton (Eastern Illinois) in 1908, batting .182 in nine contests. Primarily a shortstop, he spent 1910 and 1911 with Winchester, Ky. (Blue Grass). He batted .309 in 1910, when his 147 hits tied for the league lead.

Callahan joined Battle Creek (Southern Michigan) in 1912. In 1913 he was hitting .285 after 109 games when the St. Louis Cardinals shelled out $5,000 for him and pitcher Dick Niehaus. Callahan appeared in seven games for last-place St. Louis in his lone big-league season.

Moving to Jacksonville, Fla. (South Atlantic), for 1914, he played second base and hit .275 in 113 contests. Callahan spent 1915 with two teams—Jackson (Southern Michigan) and Grand Rapids, Mich. (Central). He played for Wheeling, W. Va. (Central), in 1916, batting .266 as the starting second baseman. In 1917 he hit .245 for South Bend (Central), which moved to Peoria, Ill., in July.

In 1918 Callahan signed with Portland, Ore. (Pacific Coast International), but wound up enlisting for World War I military duty. After his playing days, he was involved in newspaper work in Cincinnati. He died from liver cancer at a Veterans Administration hospital at 65.

CAMPBELL, David Alan ("Chopper")

Born: September 3, 1951, Princeton. **Lives:** Longwood, Florida.
Height: 6'3". **Weight:** 210. **Batted:** right. **Threw:** right.
Debut: May 6, 1977. **Final game:** October 1, 1978.
Positions, teams, years: pitcher, Atlanta (NL) 1977–1978.
Games: 118. **Innings pitched:** 158. **Won/Lost:** 4–10. **Earned run average:** 3.82.

Dave Campbell starred in four sports at Oakland City's Wood Memorial High School, turning down scholarship offers from Indiana University (as a pitcher) and Purdue (as a catcher) to attend East Tennessee State.

In 1974 Campbell signed with the Atlanta Braves as a non-drafted free agent after accompanying friends to a tryout. He joined Atlanta in 1977 following just two games at the Triple-A level with Richmond, Va. (International). Pitching in relief, he was a pleasant surprise for the last-place Braves, leading the team in appearances (65) and saves (13).

Campbell's ERA rose from 3.03 in his rookie year to 4.83 in 1978. Atlanta traded him to the Montreal Expos during Spring Training in 1979, but he developed arm problems and never again pitched in the majors.

After leaving baseball, Campbell became a teacher at Lyman High School in Longwood, Fla. His wife, the former Cindy Erb, was the 1974 Miss New Hampshire. They met when she threw out the first ball prior to a 1977 Braves game.

Campbell's nickname stems from the prodigious sideburns he wore during his college days.

CAREY, Max George ("Scoops")
National Baseball Hall of Fame, 1961. Indiana Baseball Hall of Fame, 1979.
Born: Max George Carnarius, January 11, 1890, Terre Haute. **Died:** May 30, 1976, Miami, Florida.
Height: 5'11". **Weight:** 170. **Batted:** both. **Threw:** right.
Debut: October 3, 1910. **Final game:** September 29, 1929.
Positions, teams, years: outfield, Pittsburgh (NL) 1910–1926, Brooklyn (NL) 1926–1929. **Games:** 2,476. **At-bats:** 9,363. **Home runs:** 70. **Average:** .285.
Manager: Brooklyn (NL) 1932–1933 (146–161).

One of the game's fastest runners, Hall of Famer **Max Carey** led the NL in stolen bases ten times between 1913 and 1925. His career total of 738 steals was a league record until Lou Brock broke it in 1974. Carey stole home 33 times in his career, second only to Ty Cobb's lifetime total of 54. He was also an excellent center fielder who set several defensive records. His total of 339 career assists is the modern NL mark and his league record 6,363 career putouts stood until it was eclipsed by Willie Mays. A consistent hitter and a fine bunter, he was one of baseball's first great switch hitters.

Carey became a professional baseball player almost by accident. He played for Concordia College in Fort Wayne, where he was studying for the Lutheran ministry. After graduating in 1909 Carey planned to enroll at Concordia Seminary in St. Louis. He tried out for the South Bend (Central) team, adopting the name "Carey" to protect his amateur status. After the 1909–1910 school year, he rejoined South Bend and his baseball career began to blossom. His plans for the ministry ended, but his alias stuck.

Late in 1910 Carey joined Pittsburgh and a year later he took over as the Pirates' leadoff hitter. In 1922 he stole 51 bases in 53 attempts. His record of 31 successful consecutive steals stood until 1975. Carey was considered one of the brainiest players of his era. "He was just as fast between the ears as he was with his feet," said sportswriter Joe Williams. "That's what made him harder to stop than a run in a silk stocking."

Carey batted over .300 seven times with a career high of .343 in 1925. He hit for the cycle against Brooklyn on June 20, 1925. That fall he batted .458 in the Pirates' World Series triumph over the Washington Senators.

In 1926 Carey teamed with two other future Hall of Fame outfielders, KiKi Cuyler and Paul Waner. That season Carey was involved in a squabble that led to his exile from Pittsburgh. Bill McKechnie managed the Pirates, but team stockholder Fred Clarke had appointed himself as a managerial assistant. Clarke, a former Pittsburgh field boss, kept second-guessing McKechnie's decisions. Carey and several other players asked the front office to remove Clarke from the bench. The move backfired and Carey and the others were dispatched. In mid–August he went to Brooklyn for the waiver price.

Carey remained with the Dodgers through 1929, but in 1930 he rejoined Pittsburgh as a coach. He became manager of the Dodgers in 1932. Brooklyn fired Carey after the 1933 season and offered the job to Carey's first base coach, Casey Stengel. At Carey's urging, Stengel accepted the job and launched his legendary managerial career.

Between 1944 and 1952 Carey was involved with several teams in the All-American Girls Professional Baseball League. He served as league president from 1945 to 1949. In 1955 he was a scout for the Baltimore Orioles. He briefly managed minor league teams in 1955 and 1956.

After leaving baseball in 1957, Carey worked as a dog-racing official in Miami Beach. In 1961 the Veterans Committee elected him to the Hall of Fame, and in 1962 he joined the Northeast Indiana Baseball Association Hall of Fame. In 1979 he was part of the original group inducted into the Indiana Baseball Hall of Fame. In 2001, a 6-foot-tall bronze and marble statue of Carey was dedicated at Terre Haute's Memorial Stadium.

Max inherited his nickname from George "Scoops" Carey, a big league first baseman at the turn of the century. The two Careys were not related.

CARMICHAEL, Chester Keller

Born: January 9, 1888, Muncie. **Died:** August 22, 1960, Rochester, New York.
Height: 5'11". **Weight:** 200. **Batted:** right. **Threw:** right.
Debut: September 5, 1909. **Final game:** September 23, 1909.
Positions, teams, years: pitcher, Cincinnati (NL) 1909.
Games: 2. **Innings pitched:** 7. **Won/Lost:** 0–0. **Earned run average:** 0.00.

Chet Carmichael broke into baseball with Vincennes, Ind. (Eastern Illinois) in 1908, when his .800 winning percentage (16-4) topped the Eastern Illinois League. He finished the year at Cedar Rapids, Iowa (Three-I), going 4-1 in five games.

After an 11-16 year for Cedar Rapids in 1909 Carmichael joined the Reds and made two relief appearances. He mishandled two of three chances for an inglorious .333 lifetime fielding average.

Less than a year later, Carmichael made history with Buffalo, N.Y., of the Eastern League. On Aug. 9, 1910, he threw a 1-0 perfect game against Jersey City, the first in the history of the Eastern League. Forty-two years would pass before the circuit (renamed the International League in 1912).saw another.

In 1910 Carmichael won 13 and lost 12 for Buffalo. He retired after a 3-7 record for Chattanooga, Tenn. (Southern), in 1911 and settled in Honeoye Falls, N.Y., south of Rochester, where he operated an electrical work and carpentry business.

CARROLL, Jamey Blake

Born: February 18, 1974, Evansville. **Lives:** Rockledge, Florida.
Height: 5'10". **Weight:** 170. **Batted:** right. **Threw:** right.
Debut: September 11, 2002. **Final game:** September 27, 2013.
Positions, teams, years: second base (638), third base (316), shortstop (264), outfield (21), pitcher (1), Montreal (NL) 2002–2004, Washington (NL) 2005, Colorado (NL) 2006–2007, Cleveland (AL) 2008–2009, Los Angeles (NL) 2010–2011, Minnesota (AL) 2012–2013, Kansas City (AL) 2013.
Games: 1,276. **At-bats:** 3,671. **Home runs:** 13. **Average:** .272.
Innings pitched: 1. **Won/Lost:** 0–0. **Earned run average:** 0.00.

Infielder **Jamey Carroll**, a 1992 graduate of Castle High School in Newburgh, batted .394 for the University of Evansville in 1996. A 14th-round draft pick by Montreal that June, he toiled in the Expos' farm system through 2001. He logged 1,156 minor league at-bats between 1996 through 1999 before hitting his first home run as a professional. He spent all or parts of the 2000–2002 campaigns with Ottawa, Ontario (International), Montreal's top farm club, where he became one of the most popular players of all time.

After seven seasons and 785 games in the minors, Carroll joined Montreal in 2002 as a 28-year-old rookie. His first hit was a single against another Evansville native, Alan Benes of the Chicago Cubs. Primarily a backup middle infielder for the Expos, Carroll scored the final run in Montreal history before the franchise moved to Washington after the 2004 season.

The Nationals sent him to Colorado prior to 2005, and in 2006 he batted .300 for the Rockies. In 2007 Carroll's 13th-inning sacrifice fly against San Diego on the final day of the season clinched the NL Wild Card berth for Colorado. The Rockies went on to win the pennant, and he made one appearance in a four-game World Series loss to the Boston Red Sox. The Rockies traded him to Cleveland after the Series and he spent 2008 and 2009 as a valuable utility player for the Indians.

A free agent after the season, Carroll signed with the Dodgers for 2010 and wore number 14 in honor of Dodgers great and fellow Hoosier Gil Hodges, one of Jamey's father's heroes. In 131 games he batted .291. "You always know he's ready to go every night," said Los Angeles manager Don Mattingly, another Indiana native. "He's the guy you don't truly appreciate until you see him play every day."

Penciled in as the Dodgers' utility infielder for 2011, Carroll wound up playing 146 games and batting .290 after injuries to third baseman Casey Blake and shortstop Rafael Furcal.

A free agent after the season, Carroll signed with Minnesota for 2012 and hit .268 in 138 contests. He opened the 2013 season with the Twins, who dealt him to Kansas City in August. In October he declined a minor league assignment and became a free agent. He went to Spring Training in 2014 with Washington, but was released at the end of March.

A member of Evansville's Sports Hall of Fame, Carroll grew up rooting for the Cincinnati Reds and Pete Rose. Jamey's brother Wes, a minor league infielder from 2003 to 2005, became the University of Evansville's baseball coach in 2009.

CARY, Scott Russell ("Red")

Born: April 11, 1923, Kendallville. **Died:** February 28, 2011, Coldwater, Michigan.
Height: 5'11". **Weight:** 168. **Batted:** left. **Threw:** left.
Debut: May 1, 1947. **Final game:** September 17, 1947.
Positions, teams, years: pitcher, Washington (AL) 1947.
Games: 23. **Innings pitched:** 54.2. **Won/Lost:** 3–1. **Earned run average:** 5.93.

One of ten children, **Scott Cary** began his baseball career in 1942 and spent the next three seasons in military service. After a 22–7 record in 1946 for Orlando (Florida State), he jumped from Class D ball to the majors in 1947 with the Washington Senators.

He saw action mostly as a mop-up man until late August when Senators owner Clark Griffith, impressed by Cary's six shutout innings in a charity exhibition game, asked Washington skipper Ossie Bluege to give the freckle-faced redhead a start. Cary got his chance on August 24 and posted a 7–4 win over the St. Louis Browns. In his next start he beat the Athletics to up his record to 3–0 (he'd also won a game as a reliever) before finally losing a game.

"He can't brush you back with his fastball and his curve isn't the sharpest in the league," Bluege told reporters. "But he can thread the needle with that ball and as soon as he learns a batter's blind spot he's got him."

Back in the minors in 1948, Cary went 14–10 with Charlotte, N.C. (Tri-State). Later that year Washington sent him to the Browns. Unhappy with the contract offer from St. Louis for 1949, he voluntarily retired before the season.

Cary returned to Michigan, his home since 1932, and became a farmer. He also operated the Cary Farms Trucking business and coached Little League and Babe Ruth League teams in Bronson, Mich. In 1976 he was inducted into the Northeast Indiana Baseball Association Hall of Fame.

A month before his death at age 87, Scott and his wife, the former Mary Hurley, celebrated their 65th wedding anniversary.

CASTLE, Donald Hardy

Born: February 1, 1950, Kokomo. **Lives:** Senatobia, Mississippi.
Height: 6'1". **Weight:** 205. **Batted:** left. **Threw:** left.
Debut: September 11, 1973. **Final game:** September 29, 1973.
Positions, teams, years: designated hitter, Texas (AL) 1973.
Games: 4. **At-bats:** 13. **Home runs:** 0. **Average:** .308.

At Coldwater (Miss.) High School in 1968, **Don Castle** struck out 20 of 21 batters in a game and threw back-to-back no-hitters. That summer Castle was named American Legion player of the year after pitching Memphis to victory in the Legion World Series. The Washington Senators made him the eighth pick in the June 1968 draft.

A potent hitter as an amateur, Castle played first base and the outfield in his first professional season with Burlington, N.C. (Carolina), in 1969. During Spring Training in 1972 he suffered a ruptured spleen.

Castle reached the majors in 1973 after batting .325 at Spokane, Wash. (Pacific Coast). By then the Senators had shifted to Texas. Rangers manager Billy Martin used him once as a pinch-hitter and three times as a designated hitter. Castle finished his playing career in the Yankee system, playing for Syracuse, N.Y. (International), in 1975 and from 1976 to 1978 at West Haven, Conn. (Eastern).

After retiring, Castle became the hitting coach for Northwest Mississippi Community College in Senatobia. Jim Miles, the school's coach and athletic director, had roomed with Castle at Denver (American Association).

Castle's cousin, Joe Gibbon, was a Major League pitcher from 1960 to 1972.

CATES, Eli Eldo

Born: January 26, 1877, Greens Fork. **Died:** May 29, 1964, Anderson.
Height: 5'9". **Weight:** 175. **Batted:** right. **Threw:** right.
Debut: April 20, 1908. **Final game:** September 29, 1908.
Positions, teams, years: pitcher (19), second base (3), Washington (AL) 1908.
Games: 40. **Innings pitched:** 113.2. **Won/Lost:** 4–8. **Earned run average:** 2.53.
At-bats: 59. **Home runs:** 0. Average: .186.

Pitching for Oakland in the Pacific Coast League, **Eli Cates** threw two no-hitters in less than a year. The first was a 7–0 win over Fresno on September 2, 1906. On June 25, 1907, he held Portland hitless in a 2–1 win.

A product of Greens Fork High School, Cates broke in with a 4–4 record at Toledo, Ohio (American Association), in 1898 and went 11–10 in 1899. Pitching for Oakland, he won 24 games in 1906 and 21 in 1907, when his 226 strikeouts led the PCL.

Cates spent 1908 with the Washington Senators as a 31-year-old rookie. On June 25 at Boston, he and Cy Young hooked up in a scoreless duel for 13 innings before the Red Sox won 2–1. When Washington shortstop Gorge McBride was injured on September 23, manager Joe Cantillon moved second baseman Jim Delahanty to short and replaced Delahanty with Cates.

Back in the minors in 1909, Cates spent his last season with Indianapolis of the Federal League in 1913, one year before the FL attained big league status. An excellent hitter, he batted .298 in his final campaign to go with a 12–8 won-loss record.

Born near Richmond, Cates lived most of his life in the Anderson area. He and his brother owned a tavern for many years. Cates later worked as a bartender at the Anderson Eagles Home, retiring in the mid-1940s.

CHANEY, Darrel Lee

Born: March 9, 1948, Hammond. **Lives:** Sautee Nacoochee, Georgia.
Height: 6'2". **Weight:** 188. **Batted:** both. **Threw:** right.
Debut: April 11, 1969. **Final game:** September 30, 1979.
Positions, teams, years: shortstop (621), second base (137), third base (133), catcher (1), Cincinnati (NL) 1969–1975, Atlanta (NL) 1976–1979.
Games: 915. **At-bats:** 2,113. **Home runs:** 14. **Average:** .217.

Darrel Chaney played in three World Series as part of Cincinnati's "Big Red Machine." A three-sport star at Morton High School in Hammond, Chaney passed up football scholarship offers from colleges like Notre Dame and Ohio State to sign with Ball State, where he would have been able to play baseball as well. He signed with the Reds in 1966 after Cincinnati picked him in the second round of the draft.

Chaney's first stop in professional baseball was Sioux Falls, S.D. (Northern), in 1966, where he led the league in putouts and assists. He enlisted in the U.S. Army Reserves during the Vietnam era, trained as an artillery specialist at Fort Sill, Okla., and missed parts of the 1967 and 1968 seasons.

Chaney joined the Reds in 1969 as a backup infielder, first to Woody Woodward and later to Dave Concepcion at shortstop, and to Joe Morgan at second base. He took part in three World Series with Cincinnati, winning a ring in 1975 when the Reds defeated the Boston Red Sox in seven games.

The Reds traded Chaney to the Atlanta Braves for 1976. He took over as the Braves' everyday shortstop and batted .252 in 153 contests. He remained in Atlanta through 1979, mostly in a backup role.

After retiring, Chaney worked as a radio and television announcer for the Braves along with Ernie Johnson, Skip Caray and Pete Van Wieren. He was also involved in real estate sales and charity work for the Hemophilia Society of Georgia. Chaney served on the board of directors for the Major League Baseball Alumni Association and as chairman of the board for Major League Alumni Marketing.

Chaney is a motivational speaker and devout Christian. He wrote an autobiography with Dan Hettinger called *Welcome to the Big Leagues ... Every Man's Journey to Significance: The Darrel Chaney Story*.

Keith Chaney, Darrel's son, played briefly in the Atlanta organization.

CHAPMAN, Glenn Justice ("Pete")

Born: January 21, 1906, Cambridge City. **Died:** November 5, 1988, Richmond.

Height: 5'11". **Weight:** 170. **Batted:** right. **Threw:** right.
Debut: April 18, 1934. **Final game:** September 30, 1934.
Positions, teams, years: outfield (40), second base (14), Brooklyn (NL) 1934.
Games: 67. **At-bats:** 93. **Home runs:** 1. **Average:** .280.

Pete Chapman played for the Brooklyn Dodgers in Casey Stengel's first year as a manager. Chapman spent the rest of his 16-year professional career in the minor leagues, including two separate hitches with the Indianapolis Indians (American Association).

Primarily an outfielder, Chapman split his first professional season between Richmond, Ind. (Central), and Topeka, Kan. (Western). He played for Indianapolis for part of 1932 and most of 1933.

In October 1933 the Dodgers obtained Chapman from Indianapolis via the Rule 5 draft. He spent part of the year in Brooklyn as a backup at second base and at the corner outfield posts, and in 53 contests for Albany, N.Y. (International), he batted .330.

Chapman was back in the minors for 1935 and rejoined Indianapolis in 1938, hitting .308 in 149 games. After spending 1940 and 1941 with Oakland (Pacific Coast), Chapman sat out the 1942 season. He returned during the war years and played for St. Paul (American Association) from 1943 to 1945. His final year was 1946, when he got into a dozen games for Grand Forks, N.D. (Northern), at age 40.

After retirement, Chapman was active in youth baseball. He managed an American Legion junior club from 1954–1962, and in 1958 his team won a state title.

Chapman served as Richmond's city clerk from 1959 to 1963. An active Mason, he was awarded the Indiana Masonic Grand Lodge Award of Gold.

CLOSSER, Jeffrey Darrin ("JD")

Born: January 15, 1980, Beech Grove. **Lives:** Garner, North Carolina.
Height: 5'10". **Weight:** 205. **Batted:** both. **Threw:** right.
Debut: June 30, 2004. **Final game:** October 1, 2006.
Positions, teams, years: catcher, Colorado (NL) 2004–2006.
Games: 160. **At-bats:** 447. **Home runs:** 10. **Average:** .239.

Playing for Alexandria's Monroe High School in 1998, **JD Closser** was Indiana's Mr. Baseball and the recipient of the Class 2A L.V. Phillips Mental Attitude Award. Arizona took him in the fifth round of that year's amateur draft and he reported to the Diamondbacks' Arizona League affiliate.

In 1999, when he batted .324 in 76 games, the switch-hitting Closser (pronounced "CLOSS-sir") was an all-star at Missoula, Mont. (Pioneer). He finished the year with South Bend (Midwest), hitting .241 in 52 contests. After a full season with South Bend in 2000, Arizona traded him to the Colorado Rockies. He batted .291 at Lancaster (California) in 2001 and .283 in 2002 and for Carolina (Southern).

Playing for Tulsa, Okla. (Texas) on his wedding day, June 4, 2003, Closser hit a game-winning home run in a 13-inning contest with El Paso. He joined the Rockies in June 2004 and replaced Charles Johnson as Colorado's everyday catcher, hitting .319 in 36 games. He struggled in 2005, batting .219 in 93 contests and wound up platooning with veteran Mark Greene.

Closser split the 2006 season between Colorado and Colorado Springs (Pacific Coast). The Milwaukee Brewers claimed him after the season and traded him to the Oakland Athletics in May 2007. He helped Oakland's top farm club, the Sacramento River Cats, to the 2007 Pacific Coast League championship.

From 2008 to 2011, Closser played for minor league clubs in the Cubs, Yankees, Padres and Dodgers systems. His playing days ended in 2011 with the Edmonton, Alb., Capitals of the independent North American League.

Closser is the owner of Going Pro Baseball Academy in Raleigh, N.C.

COGGINS, Richard Allen

Born: December 7, 1950, Indianapolis. **Lives:** Riverside, California.
Height: 5'8". **Weight:** 170. **Batted:** left. **Threw:** left.
Debut: August 29, 1972. **Final game:** July 7, 1976.
Positions, teams, years: outfield, Baltimore (AL) 1972–1974, Montreal (NL) 1975, New York (AL) 1975–1976, Chicago (AL) 1976.
Games: 342. **At-bats:** 1,083. **Home runs:** 12. **Average:** .265.

Rich Coggins was one of two rookies who helped Baltimore win the 1973 AL East Division title. With his regular outfielders slumping earlier in the year, Orioles manager Earl Weaver turned to Coggins and Al Bumbry. As a platoon player, Coggins hit close to .400 over the last six weeks of the season to finish at .319. When Baltimore met the Oakland Athletics in the 1973 AL Championship Series, he became the first Hoosier-born African American to play in a post-season game.

The Orioles drafted the speedy Coggins in the 21st round in 1968 out of Garey High School in Pomona, Calif. He entered pro ball that year with Aberdeen, S.D. (Northern), and in August 1972 he was batting .282 with 20 homers for Rochester, N.Y. (International), when he joined Baltimore.

After a .243 season in 1974, Coggins went to the Montreal Expos in a five-player trade. Early in 1975 the Expos peddled him to the New York Yankees. By then he had developed a thyroid condition that would curtail his career. The Yanks traded him to the White Sox in May 1976. Less than a month later Chicago shipped him to Philadelphia. He never played a game for the Phillies, and at age 25 his big league career was finished.

Rich's cousins, Don and Les Shy, played professional football.

COLEMAN, Robert Hunter ("Marse Bob," "Uncle Bob," "Old Carpet Slippers")

Indiana Baseball Hall of Fame, 1980.
Born: September 26, 1890, Huntingburg. **Died:** July 16, 1959, Boston, Massachusetts.
Height: 6'2". **Weight:** 190. **Batted:** right. **Threw:** right.
Debut: June 13, 1913. **Final game:** September 9, 1916.
Positions, teams, years: catcher, Pittsburgh (NL) 1913–1914, Cleveland (AL) 1916.
Games: 116. **At-bats:** 228. **Home runs:** 1. **Average:** .241.
Manager: Boston (NL) 1943–1945 (128–165).

Brief stints as a Major League catcher and manager only scratch the surface of **Bob Coleman's** half-century in professional baseball. Known as "Mr. Baseball" in Evansville, where he made his home, the long-jowled Coleman helped develop future Hall of Famers Hank Greenberg and Warren Spahn while managing in the minor leagues.

In 1910 Coleman joined Springfield, Ill. (Three-I), as a husky 19-year-old. He joined Pittsburgh in 1913 and spent all of 1914 with the Pirates before returning to the minors. He resurfaced in 1916 with the Cleveland Indians. Coleman's managerial career began in 1919. He would manage at either the minor- or major-league level every season through 1957—except for 1926, 1932 and 1943, when he coached for big league clubs.

For 24 of those 35 campaigns, Coleman managed in the Three-I League. He spent 20 seasons with Evansville teams, managing future big league stars like Greenberg, Tommy Bridges, Pete Fox, Whit Wyatt and Birdie Tebbetts when the Detroit Tigers owned the franchise. Spahn, Dick Donovan, Del Crandall, Johnny Logan, Wes Covington and Felix Mantilla played for Coleman when Evansville was a Braves farm club.

Coleman also managed at Mobile, Ala. (Southern Association), Terre Haute (Three-I), San Antonio, (Texas), Knoxville, Tenn. (Sally), Decatur, Ill. (Three-I), Beaumont (Texas), St. Paul (American Association), Springfield, Ill. (Three-I), Scranton, Pa. (New York-Penn) and Milwaukee (American Association). From 1957 through 1986 his 2,496 career wins were the most by any minor league manager.

Coleman coached for the Boston Red Sox in 1926 and for Detroit in 1932. He joined the coaching staff of the Boston Braves in 1943 after the Three-I League suspended operations due to World War II. The following year he took over for Casey Stengel as manager and guided Boston to a sixth-place finish. Del Bissonette replaced him in 1945 with the team in seventh place. After the Three-I League resumed operations in 1946, Coleman returned to Evansville.

When the Evansville franchise disbanded after the 1957 season, Coleman became a scout for the Braves, who by now were in Milwaukee. In the summer of 1959 Coleman was diagnosed with pancreatic cancer, and Braves owner Lou Perini flew him from Evansville to Boston for treatment. Coleman died there at age 68. Casey Stengel, by then one of baseball's most successful skippers with the New York Yankees, praised Coleman as "a man who could do almost anything in baseball. He was a great leader of youth. His knowledge of the game was great."

A member of the Evansville Sports Hall of Fame, Coleman was inducted into the Indiana Baseball Hall of Fame in 1980.

COLLINS, Orth Stein ("Buck")

Born: April 27, 1880, Lafayette. **Died:** December 13, 1949, Fort Lauderdale, Florida.
Height: 6'0". **Weight:** 150. **Batted:** left. **Threw:** right.
Debut: June 1, 1904. **Final game:** July 27, 1909.
Positions, teams, years: outfield (7), pitcher (1), New York (AL) 1904, Washington (AL) 1909.
Games: 13. **At-bats:** 24. **Home runs:** 0. **Average:** .250.
Innings pitched: 1. **Won/Lost:** 0–0. **Earned run average:** 0.00.

Over the years, legends like Earle Combs, Joe DiMaggio, Mickey Mantle and Bernie Williams have played center field for the New York Yankees. So have less famous men like **Orth Collins**.

Collins began his professional career in 1903 at Clarksville, Tenn. (Kitty). In May 1904 he went from Rochester, N.Y. (Eastern), to New York, then known as the Highlanders. A Washington, D.C., resident by now, he was "one of Washington's best bowlers last season," according to *The Sporting News*, "and he was known to every bowler in that city."

In his first game with the Highlanders, Collins played center field and batted sixth against Detroit at New York's Hilltop Park. After hitting .353 in five contests and 17 at-bats, he was back in Rochester.

From 1905 to 1908 Collins drifted around the minors. He opened the 1909 season with Terre Haute (Central) and, after 29 games and a .267 average, he moved on to Buffalo, N.Y. (Eastern). Collins was batting .294 through 31 contests on July 5 when he refused to play the second game of a doubleheader, claiming that his monthly salary was only $200 when Buffalo manager George Smith had promised him $250 a month if he made the team.

Turned down and suspended, Collins went home to Washington and signed with the Senators on July 13, 1909. He saw action in eight games with Washington, including one as a relief pitcher, before the Senators dispatched him to Buffalo (American Association). He continued to play minor league ball through 1912 and managed Cotton States League teams in Greenwood, Miss., and Meridian, Miss., for parts of 1911 and 1912.

COLLINS, William Shirley ("Cush")

Born: March 27, 1882, Chesterton. **Died:** June 26, 1961, San Bernardino, California.
Height: 6'0". **Weight:** 170. **Batted:** both. **Threw:** right.
Debut: April 14, 1910. **Final game:** October 5, 1914.
Positions, teams, years: outfield (210), third base (1), Boston (NL) 1910–1911, Chicago (NL) 1911, Brooklyn (NL) 1913, Buffalo (Federal) 1914.
Games: 228. **At-bats:** 773. **Home runs:** 3. **Average:** .224.

As a 28-year-old rookie in 1910, **Bill Collins** was part of an all-new outfield for the Boston Doves (today's Atlanta Braves). Collins stole 36 bases and his .977 fielding percentage was one of the NL's best. On October 6, 1912, he hit for the cycle in natural order (single, double, triple, homer) and finished the year with a .242 average. Despite his contributions, Boston finished last for a second consecutive year.

During Spring Training in 1911 Collins and several teammates shaved their heads in a show of determination, and newspaper reporters dubbed them "the Convicts." Collins was spared another last-place finish when Boston traded him to the Chicago Cubs that June. After spending all or parts of three seasons with Newark, N.J. (International), he returned to the majors with Brooklyn in 1913 and hit .189 on 32 contests.

Back with Newark at the outset of the 1914 season, Collins had a final, injury-plagued fling in the majors that year with Buffalo of the Federal League. "Ever since the season began he has been the object of all sorts of accidents, and has been out of the game for the greater part of the year," *The Sporting News* reported on August 13, 1914. "His first misfortune consisted of a broken finger on his left hand. Scarcely had this mended when he sprained his right ankle. Out of the game three weeks, he returned for one day and the next was taken seriously ill with ptomaine poisoning. This lasted a week and in his first game he broke the fore finger [sic] of his right hand. That is now practically well, but next he sprained his left ankle, sliding into third base, and is now hobbling around on crutches, not knowing what will happen next."

The injuries limited Collins to 21 games for Buffalo and a .149 average. He spent his last three years with Cedar Rapids, Iowa (Central Association), and batted .337 in 1915 to lead the league. He managed the team for parts of the 1916 and 1917 seasons before retiring. After baseball, he headed west and spent 14 years as head switchman for the Kaiser Steel Corporation in Fontana, Calif. He died at 79 from pneumonia complicated by diabetes.

CORHAN, George LeRoy ("Irish," "Cody," "Spider")

Born: October 21, 1887, Logansport. **Died:** November 24, 1958, San Francisco, California.
Height: 5'9". **Weight:** 165. **Batted:** right. **Threw:** right.
Debut: April 20, 1911. **Final game:** September 2, 1916.
Positions, teams, years: shortstop, Chicago (AL) 1911, St. Louis (NL) 1916.
Games: 135. **At-bats:** 426. **Home runs:** 0. **Average:** .211.

A fixture at shortstop for the Pacific Coast League's San Francisco Seals from 1912 to 1920, **Roy Corhan** turned down a big league contract in 1914 to remain in the PCL.

Corhan (pronounced core-han) spent most of his boyhood in Indianapolis. He went to Manual High School, worked in his father's grocery store, and played third base for the Tuxedos, a local sandlot club whose shortstop was Donie Bush, another future major leaguer.

In 1906 Corhan's family moved to Albuquerque, N.M., and he entered pro ball in 1907 with Pueblo, Colo. (Western). After a .262 season in 1910 for St. Joseph, Mo. (Western), the slick-fielding Corhan made his Major League debut in 1911 with the Chicago White Sox. A severe beaning that June limited him to just 43 games and a .214 average.

Corhan opened the 1912 season with San Francisco and quickly became a local favorite. In 1914, when he batted .293, he declined a Federal League offer to remain with the Seals. He helped San Francisco to PCL pennants in 1915 and 1917.

In 1916 Corhan left San Francisco to play for the St. Louis Cardinals. He was batting .210 after 82 games when rookie Rogers Hornsby replaced him at shortstop. Hornsby went on to a Hall of Fame career while Corhan was back with San Francisco by season's end, hitting .278 in 47 games. His final season was 1920, when he batted .280.

Corhan remained an avid Seals booster and joined several old-timers associations. "After his playing days Corhan became an insurance broker," noted the *San Francisco Chronicle*, "but in order to find him his clients often had to wait until a Seals game ended." In a 1937 fan ballot he was named to the all-time Seals team, along with notables like Lefty Gomez, Paul Waner, Earl Averill, Lefty O'Doul and Joe DiMaggio.

Corhan suffered a fatal heart attack a month after his 71st birthday.

CORIDAN, Philip F.

Born: August 19, 1858, Walpole (now Fortville). **Died:** July 1, 1915, Indianapolis.
Height: unknown. **Weight:** unknown. **Batted:** left. **Threw:** right.
Debut: July 16, 1884. **Final game:** July 17, 1884.
Positions, teams, years: second base (2), outfield (1), Chicago (Union Association) 1884.
Games: 2. **At-bats:** 7. **Home runs:** 0. **Average:** .143.

Phil Coridan briefly played for the Chicago Browns of the Union Association of Professional Base Ball Clubs, which challenged the NL and the American Association as the country's third big league in 1884. Chicago, Altoona, Baltimore, Boston, Cincinnati, Philadelphia, St. Louis and Washington were the league's charter members.

Prior to 1884 Coridan was a member of a Fort Wayne club called the Golden Eagles. On May 9, 1884, the *Indianapolis Times* reported that "Phil Corridan [sic] is playing second base with the St. Louis Reserves, and playing it well." Not long afterwards, he joined the Fort Wayne Hoosiers (Northwestern). "He is a number one fielder, and a hard hitter," noted the *Fort Wayne Daily News* on June 4.

Released in July by Fort Wayne, Coridan

signed with Chicago. He played in two games in two days for the Browns, who transferred to Pittsburgh in August and adopted the name Stogies. An outfielder-second baseman, he headed to Birmingham, Ala. (Southern), in 1885 and batted .131 in 40 games before disappearing from organized ball.

The son of Irish immigrants, Coridan worked as a bartender in Indianapolis after leaving baseball. He died of pulmonary tuberculosis at age 56. His birthplace, Walpole, is known today as Fortville.

CORRIDEN, John Michael, Jr. ("Jack")

Born: October 6, 1918, Logansport. **Died:** June 4, 2001, Indianapolis.
Height: 5'6". **Weight:** 160. **Batted:** both. **Threw:** right.
Debut: April 20, 1946. **Final game:** April 20, 1946.
Positions, teams, years: pinch runner (1), Brooklyn (NL) 1946.
Games: 1. **At-bats:** 0. **Home runs:** 0. **Average:** —.

Johnny Corriden's Major League career was one of the briefest in history. The son of Red Corriden, a big league player, coach and manager, Johnny attended Cathedral High Shool in Indianapolis before it had a baseball team. He later played center field for Indiana University, earning letters in 1939 and 1940.

Corriden worked out with the Cubs while his father was a coach for Chicago. "One day, while he was still going to Indiana University, he asked me what I thought he should do," Red told *The Associated Press* in 1946. "I told him to get his education first and then follow the same profession I did."

Instead, Johnny signed in 1941 with Olean, N.Y. (PONY). After a .313 season with Montreal (International) in 1945, he opened the 1946 campaign with Brooklyn. By now his father was a member of the Dodgers coaching staff.

Johnny pinch-ran for fellow Hoosier Billy Herman in the seventh inning of a 9–8 win over the New York Giants. He wasn't even on the field for a complete inning. He scored a run and, two days later, was optioned to Mobile, Ala. (Southern Association).

All told, Corriden spent eight seasons in organized baseball. He finished his career as a player-manager with Salisbury (North Carolina State) in 1949. He made Indianapolis his home after leaving baseball and retired from Wheaton Van Lines in 1981.

CORRIDEN, John Michael, Sr. ("Red," "Lollypop," "Buddy Boy")

Born: September 4, 1887, Logansport. **Died:** September 28, 1959, Indianapolis.
Height: 5'9". **Weight:** 165. **Batted:** right. **Threw:** right.
Debut: September 8, 1910. **Final game:** May 15, 1915.
Positions, teams, years: shortstop (145), third base (47), second base (12), outfield (1), St. Louis (AL) 1910, Detroit (AL) 1912, Chicago (NL), 1913–1915.
Games: 223. **At-bats:** 640. **Home runs:** 6. **Average:** .205.
Manager: Chicago (AL) 1950 (52–72).

One of the best-loved coaches in baseball history, **Red Corriden** was a pawn in a scheme to bilk Ty Cobb of the Detroit Tigers out of a batting title. His son, John Corriden, Jr., appeared in one game for Brooklyn while Red coached the Dodgers.

Corriden broke in with Charleston (Eastern Illinois) in 1907. After batting .308 for Omaha, Neb. (Western), in 1910, he joined the St. Louis Browns. At the time, the unpopular Cobb and Nap Lajoie were locked in a duel for the league batting crown. On the last day of the season, the Browns were playing a doubleheader with Lajoie's Cleveland team. Corriden started both games at third base, and St. Louis manager Jack O'Connor ordered the rookie to play on the edge of the outfield grass. Lajoie took advantage of the situation, bunting safely six times and going eight-for-eight. Lajoie almost edged Cobb for the title and the prize that went with it, a new Chalmers automobile. AL president Ban Johnson investigated the incident and tossed O'Connor out of the league, but cleared Corriden of any wrongdoing.

Corriden spent all of 1911 and part of 1912 with Kansas City (American Association) before joining the Tigers in 1912. Involved in a post-season three-team trade between Detroit, Cincinnati and the Cubs, Corriden wound up in Chicago for 1913. In 1914 he replaced Cubs shortstop Al Bridwell, who had jumped to the Federal League.

After just six games with Chicago in 1915 Corriden returned to the minors. As a third baseman for Louisville (American Association) in 1916-1917, Corriden was part of the team's "Iron Man Infield," playing every inning of 232 straight games along with first baseman Jay Kirke, second baseman Joe McCarthy and shortstop Roxy Roach.

Corriden left baseball in 1920, but returned to play in the Western League from 1921-1924. He coached and managed in the minors until 1930, when he became a scout for the Cubs. He coached for Chicago from 1931-1940, the Dodgers from 1941-1946, and the New York Yankees in 1947-1948. He spent 1949 at San Diego (Pacific Coast).

In 1950 Corriden joined the White Sox coaching staff. That May he took over for Jack Onslow as Chicago's manager. Under Corriden the Sox went 52-72 and finished sixth. Replaced by Paul Richards prior to 1951, Corriden rejoined the Dodger organization as a scout. He retired after the 1958 season due to illness.

Mostly a shortstop in the majors, Corriden also played third, second and the outfield. As a Brooklyn coach he often served as a buffer between players and manager Leo Durocher. "Everybody likes him," the prickly Durocher said of Corriden. "No man ever has had fewer enemies," wrote John C. Hoffman in the *Chicago Sun-Times*.

Corriden suffered a fatal heart attack while watching the telecast of a Dodgers-Braves playoff game in 1959.

COUNSELL, Craig John ("Counse")

Born: August 21, 1970, South Bend. **Lives:** Fort Myers, Florida.
Height: 6'0". **Weight:** 180. **Bats:** left. **Throws:** right.
Debut: September 17, 1995. **Final game:** September 28, 2011.
Positions, teams, years: second base (574), shortstop (478), third base (385), first base (4), outfield (1), Colorado (NL) 1995, 1997, Florida (NL) 1997-1999, Los Angeles (NL) 1999, Arizona (NL) 2000-2003, Milwaukee (NL) 2004, Arizona (NL) 2005-2006, Milwaukee (NL) 2007-2011.
Games: 1,624. **At-bats:** 4,741. **Home runs:** 42. **Average:** .255.

Craig Counsell played for two World Series winners and was an unlikely hero in the Florida Marlins' surprising triumph in the 1997 Fall Classic.

An 11th-round draft pick by the Colorado Rockies in 1992, Counsell attended Whitefish Bay (Wis.) High School and the University of Notre Dame prior to breaking in with Bend, Ore. (Northwest). A contact hitter and an excellent fielder, he joined the Rockies in 1995.

In 1997 the Rockies traded Counsell to Florida, where he batted .299 in a platoon role at second base. He hit .429 in the NLCS, and in the World Series with the Cleveland Indians his sacrifice fly in the bottom of the ninth sent Game Seven into extra innings. In the eleventh inning, he scored the run that made Florida the world champs.

Counsell's 1998 season ended in August when a pitched ball shattered his jaw. The Marlins traded him to Los Angeles in June 1999. Released by the Dodgers in March 2000, he signed with the Diamondbacks organization.

After batting .348 in 50 games with Tucson, Ariz. (Pacific Coast), Counsell joined Arizona. In 2001 and 2002 he started at shortstop and second base for the Diamondbacks. He starred in the 2001 NLCS, hitting .381 against the Atlanta Braves to earn MVP honors. He won a second championship ring when Arizona beat the New York Yankees in the World Series.

"You can apply any number of terms to him: overachiever, you know, one of those guys that makes the most out of his talent," Arizona skipper Bob Brenly told *USA Today*. "But outside of the two big guys in our rotation [Randy Johnson and Curt Schilling] and Gonzo [outfielder Luis Gonzalez], he's probably been our most valuable player this season with his versatility."

In December 2003 the Diamondbacks dealt Counsell to the Milwaukee Brewers as part of a nine-player trade. He became a free agent after the 2004 season and rejoined Arizona. After two more years with the Diamondbacks, he filed for free agent status and signed for a second hitch with the Brewers. Milwaukee reached the NL Division Series in 2008, and in 2009, at age 39, he batted .285 in 130 games. For the Brewers' final 2010 home game, he was in the starting lineup at shortstop as a tribute to his contributions to the team.

Counsell bowed out after the 2011 season,

when Milwaukee lost to the St. Louis Cardinals in the NLCS. In 2012 he took a job in the Brewers front office as a special assistant to the general manager.

One of the few Major Leaguers who didn't wear batting gloves, Counsell was famous for the unique batting stance he employed until 2008. With his back to the pitcher and his feet perpendicular to the mound, he held his bat high in the air, moving it erratically. A 2010 *Sporting News* article proclaimed him the 13th-smartest athlete in sports.

John Counsell, Craig's father, was an outfielder in the Minnesota Twins organization from 1964 to 1969. The elder Counsell served as the Milwaukee Brewers' director of community relations from 1978–1988 and Craig practically grew up in Milwaukee's County Stadium clubhouse. John was Notre Dame's captain in 1964. Twenty-eight years later, Craig followed in his father's footsteps as a co-captain for the Fighting Irish.

CRAMER, William Wendell
Born: May 22, 1891, Bedford. **Died:** September 11, 1966, Fort Wayne.
Height: 6'0". **Weight:** 175. **Batted:** right. **Threw:** right.
Debut: June 25, 1912. **Final game:** June 25, 1912.
Positions, teams, years: pitcher, Cincinnati (NL) 1912.
Games: 1. **Innings pitched:** 2.1. **Won/Lost:** 0–0. **Earned run average:** 0.00.

After three seasons in the Blue Grass League, **Bill Cramer** joined the Cincinnati Reds in 1912. In his lone appearance he pitched two and one-third innings of relief in an 11–0 loss to the Chicago Cubs. "He wasn't in action in Cincinnati often enough to get a real line on him," reported *Sporting Life*, "and on the one occasion he found himself under championship fire he tossed the ball around as if it were a hot potato just off the skillett [sic]."

Relying on a spitter and an emery ball, Cramer came to the Reds from Frankfort, Ky. (Bluegrass), where he'd compiled an 8–2 record. Returning to Frankfort after his short stint with the Reds, he finished the year with a 14–6 mark.

Cramer's best season was 1914, when he had a 19–13 slate for Fort Wayne (Central). Out of organized ball in 1915, he returned in 1916 with Terre Haute (Central) and went 11–15 before leaving for good.

Cramer moved to Florida and later to West Virginia before settling in Fort Wayne for the last 24 years of his life. He played for and managed industrial league teams in Fort Wayne until he was in his mid-forties.

CRANDALL, James Otis ("Otie," "Doc")
Born: October 8, 1887, Wadena. **Died:** August 17, 1951, Bell, California.
Height: 5'10". **Weight:** 180. **Batted:** right. **Threw:** right.
Debut: April 24, 1908. **Final game:** August 31, 1918.
Positions, teams, years: pitcher (302), second base (71), shortstop (8), outfield (4), first base (1), New York (NL) 1908–1913, St. Louis (Federal League) 1914–1915, St. Louis (AL) 1916, Boston (NL) 1918.
Games: 500. **Innings pitched:** 1,546.2. **Won/Lost:** 102–62. **Earned run average:** 2.92. **At-bats:** 887. **Home runs:** 9. **Average:** .285.

Dubbed the "Physician of the Pitching Emergency" by Damon Runyon, **Doc Crandall** was one of Major League baseball's first relief specialists.

During the early years of the 20th Century, the northwestern Indiana hamlet of Wadena barely had more than 50 residents. The town's baseball team, the Plowboys, included two men who would reach the big leagues: Doc and slugging outfielder Cy Williams, both Wadena High School alums. Also on the club were Doc's brothers Karl and Arnold, who went on to play in the minor leagues.

Crandall's professional career began in 1906 with Cedar Rapids, Iowa (Three-I), and two years later he joined the New York Giants. Future Hall of Famer Christy Mathewson, the Giants' ace pitcher, described him as "a raw country boy" who was at his best "when things looked darkest." Crandall was also a good hitter and fielder, and Giants' manager John McGraw often used him as a pinch-hitter. Doc occasionally filled in at second base and shortstop.

Crandall's best year was 1910, when he had 17 wins and four losses, including a 7–1 record as a reliever. From 1910 to 1912 he led the league in relief victories. In six years with the Giants he went 67–36 and played in three World Series. In the fifth game of the 1911 Series against the Philadelphia Athletics, Crandall knocked in the tying run with a two-out, pinch-hit double in the bottom of the ninth. He stayed in the game as a pitcher, earning the victory when the Giants scored in their half of the tenth.

The Giants traded Crandall to the St. Louis Cardinals in August 1913, but reacquired him a week later. He jumped to the Federal League in 1914, alternating between the mound and second base for the St. Louis Terriers. In two FL seasons, he went 13–9 and 21–15. When the league folded after 1915, he was awarded to the St. Louis Browns.

Early in 1916 the Browns released Crandall to Oakland (Pacific Coast). Later that season the Oaks sent him to Los Angeles and he began a long association with the Angels. Except for a brief stint with the Boston Braves in 1918, he spent 1917 through 1926 with Los Angeles. He won 20 games or more five times, and in 1925 he batted .356. In 1924 his 2.71 ERA led the PCL. On April 7, 1918, he was one strike away from pitching a no-hitter against Salt Lake City when his brother Karl stroked a single.

In 1927 and for part of 1928, Crandall owned, managed and pitched for Wichita, Kan. (Western). He retired as a player after the 1929 season. His minor league slate included 249 wins and a 2.96 earned run average. Two years later Crandall returned to the majors as a coach with the Pirates and stayed in Pittsburgh until 1934. He managed and coached in the minors through 1938. When he was manager of Des Moines, Iowa (Western), in 1935, the team's catcher was his son, Jim.

A member of the Pacific Coast League Hall of Fame, Crandall settled in Southern California after leaving baseball. He was a bit player in *The Babe Comes Home*, a 1927 film comedy starring Babe Ruth. Toward the end of his life, Crandall suffered a series of strokes that left him paralyzed.

CRAWFORD, Kenneth Daniel
Born: October 31, 1894, South Bend. **Died:** November 11, 1976, Pittsburgh, Pennsylvania.
Height: 5'9". **Weight:** 145. **Batted:** left. **Threw:** right.
Debut: September 6, 1915. **Final game:** October 3, 1915.
Positions, teams, years: first base (14), outfield (4), Baltimore (Federal League) 1915.
Games: 23. **At-bats:** 82. **Home runs:** 0. **Average:** .244.

Outfielder-first baseman **Ken Crawford** is one of a handful of Twentieth Century players who played in neither the AL nor the NL but still qualify as big leaguers. In 1914–1915, the Federal League challenged the two existing major circuits. With teams in eight cities, the Feds induced stars like Three-Finger Brown and Joe Tinker to leave their AL and NL clubs.

Both older circuits filed lawsuits in an attempt to bankrupt the FL. In January 1915 the Feds countered with an antitrust suit against the other two leagues. While U.S. District Court Judge Kenesaw Mountain Landis withheld his decision, the Feds finished their second season mired in debt.

That winter the warring factions reached a settlement. FL owners withdrew their lawsuit after gaining partial compensation from the AL and NL. Two FL magnates purchased Major League clubs: Phil Ball bought the St. Louis Browns and Charles Weeghman purchased the Chicago Cubs. In 1916 Weeghman moved the Cubs to his Federal League ballpark, which in 1927 was renamed Wrigley Field. In 1920 Judge Landis became baseball's first commissioner. Crawford had been playing for an independent team called the Pittsburgh Collegians before joining the Baltimore Terrapins in September 1915. The *Baltimore Sun* reported that the 20-year-old rookie "goes to first pretty fast and from all reports has quite a lot of nerve on the basepaths."

When the FL folded, so did Crawford's pro baseball career. He returned to Pittsburgh, where he worked as a gasoline salesman, and later for the Taylor-Wharton Iron and Steel Company.

CRIGER, Louis
Indiana Baseball Hall of Fame, 2004.
Born: February 3, 1872, Elkhart. **Died:** May 14, 1934, Tucson, Arizona.
Height: 5'10". **Weight:** 165. **Batted:** right. **Threw:** right.
Debut: September 21, 1896. **Final game:** June 3, 1912.
Positions, teams, years: catcher (984), first base (10), outfield (1), third base (1), Cleveland (NL)

1896–1898, St. Louis (NL) 1899–1900, Boston (AL) 1901–1908, St. Louis (AL) 1909, New York (AL) 1910, St. Louis (AL) 1912.
Games: 1,012. **At-bats:** 3,202. **Home runs:** 11. **Average:** .221.

All but forgotten today, **Lou Criger** was one of the greatest defensive catchers in baseball history. He was Cy Young's favorite batterymate. Criger (rhymes with "trigger") and Boston teammate Chick Stahl became the first Hoosiers to play in the modern World Series in 1903. Criger's 156 assists that year is still a record for Red Sox catchers.

In 1896 Criger joined the Cleveland Spiders, whose star pitcher was Cy Young. The small and agile Criger soon became Young's personal catcher. Wherever Young went, Criger followed: from Cleveland to the St. Louis Cardinals in 1899, and to the Boston Pilgrims when the AL began operations in 1901. Pitcher Bill Dinneen, a Boston teammate, once said that Young "couldn't have made that record [511 career wins] without Criger in there."

Criger was behind the plate for Boston's first AL game in 1901. He caught every inning for Boston in the 1903 Fall Classic. Later, he revealed that he'd been offered a $12,000 bribe to throw the Series from gamblers who wanted the Pittsburgh Pirates to win.

Criger caught Cy Young's perfect game against the Philadelphia Athletics on May 5, 1904, as well as no-hitters by Young in 1908 and New York's Tom Hughes in 1910. The no-hit game by Hughes was the first in Yankees history. Prior to the 1907 season, Criger helped train the University of Notre Dame baseball team. The Fighting Irish responded with a 20–3 record.

Lou and Young parted company prior to 1909 when Boston sent Criger to the St. Louis Browns. "In Criger, St. Louis will get one of the greatest catchers that ever donned a glove," said Young. "I've pitched to him so long that he seems a part of me."

Criger's defensive skills were so formidable that he was still considered one of the best catchers in baseball when the Browns traded him to the New York Highlanders in 1910, even though he was 38 years old and hadn't hit over .200 since 1902.

Despite a slight build and frail appearance, Criger was a rugged competitor who frequently covered spike wounds with gauze pads to keep on playing. Around 1906 he was stricken with spinal neuralgia and missed all but seven games. In 1907 he reclaimed his job as Boston's top catcher.

Criger retired after 1910. He joined the Browns as a coach and played in one game in 1912. Soon afterwards he retired to a farm near Jones, Mich. In 1914 he developed tuberculosis of the knee joint and doctors amputated his left leg. He returned to Elkhart, nearly destitute and broken in health. In 1922 a pension from the AL, one of the first in baseball history, enabled him to relocate to Arizona's salubrious climate. When he died, Criger was 62 years old and working in a Tucson bakery managed by his twin sons.

The northern Indiana chapter of the Society for American Baseball Research was named for Criger in 1998. In 2004 he was elected to the Indiana Baseball Hall of Fame. A monument to Criger was dedicated in Elkhart's Riverview Park in 2012.

Elmer Criger, Lou's brother, played minor league ball and won 22 games for Jackson (Southern Michigan) in 1909.

CROUSE, Clyde Ellsworth ("Buck")
Indiana Baseball Hall of Fame, 1981.
Born: January 6, 1897, Anderson. **Died:** October 23, 1983, Muncie.
Height: 5'8". **Weight:** 158. **Batted:** left. **Threw:** right.
Debut: August 1, 1923. **Final game:** September 28, 1930.
Positions, teams, years: catcher, Chicago (AL) 1923–1930.
Games: 470. **At-bats:** 1,306. **Home runs:** 8. **Average:** .262.

Buck Crouse, who spent much of his big league career as a backup to Hall of Fame catcher Ray Schalk, won the International League's most valuable player award at the age of 40. Crouse spent most of his life in Muncie and was one of the area's best-liked, most respected athletes.

Crouse entered professional baseball in 1921 with Jackson, Mich. (Central). He joined the Chicago White Sox in 1923 and served as

Schalk's understudy through 1926. In 1925 Crouse batted .351 in 54 games. For the next two seasons he was part of a catching tandem, first with Harry McCurdy and later with Moe Berg. Against Washington on May 12, 1929, Crouse managed an unassisted double play—extremely rare for a catcher. He had an excellent throwing arm, averaging nearly one assist per game.

After the 1930 campaign Crouse returned to the minors. He helped Alexandria, Va., to the Cotton States League pennant in 1929, earning MVP honors. He joined Buffalo, N.Y., in 1931, and in 1936 he helped the Bisons win the International League championship. In May 1937 he became player-manager for Baltimore (International). The 40-year-old Crouse led the Orioles to the playoffs, winning league MVP honors. In 1940 he spent his final year in baseball as a coach for Indianapolis (American Association).

Returning to Muncie, Crouse worked for the Hemingway Glass Company and later for the Acme-Lees Company, an automobile moldings manufacturer. He occasionally played for the Muncie Citizens, a semi-professional team.

Crouse, who died at 86 years, is in the Indiana Baseball Hall of Fame (Class of 1981), the Buffalo Bison Hall of Fame and the Delaware County Athletic Hall of Fame.

CROWE, George Daniel ("Big Daddy")

Indiana Baseball Hall of Fame, 2004.
Born: March 22, 1921, Whiteland. **Died:** January 18, 2011, Rancho Cordova, California.
Height: 6'2". **Weight:** 210. **Batted:** left. **Threw:** left.
Debut: April 16, 1952. **Final game:** April 30, 1961.
Positions, teams, years: first base (407), second base (1), Boston (NL) 1952, Milwaukee (NL) 1953, 1955, Cincinnati (NL), 1956–1958, St. Louis (NL) 1959–1961.
Games: 702. **At-bats:** 1,727. **Home runs:** 81. **Average:** .270.

George Crowe, Indiana's first black Major League baseball player, was also the state's first Mr. Basketball. Crowe's athletic career began at Franklin High School, where he starred in both sports. The Grizzlies lost to Frankfort in the 1939 state basketball tournament championship game, but in a statewide poll Crowe was the top vote-getter and became the first official Mr. Basketball.

The bespectacled Crowe played baseball and basketball and competed in track and field at Indiana Central College (known today as the University of Indianapolis). He earned a baccalaureate degree in 1943 and immediately entered the army. He served as a first lieutenant in the China-Burma-India Theatre.

After the war Crowe played baseball for the New York Black Yankees of the Negro National League and also for professional basketball teams like the Los Angeles Red Devils and the New York Renaissance.

A first baseman, Crowe signed with the Boston Braves in 1949, two years after the integration of the Major Leagues. With pennant-winning Pawtucket, R.I., in '49, his 106 RBI topped the New England League. At Hartford, Conn., in 1950 he won Eastern League MVP honors, leading the league in runs (122), hits (185) and batting (.353). In 1951 his 189 hits and 119 RBI led the American Association as he helped Milwaukee win the pennant.

Crowe became the first African American player in Braves history in 1952, serving as a backup to Earl Torgeson and later to Joe Adcock. Prior to 1956 the Braves traded Crowe to the Cincinnati Reds, where Ted Kluszewski was the everyday first baseman. When Kluszewski was injured in 1957, Crowe began playing regularly. He responded with 31 home runs and a .271 batting average in 133 games.

By now Crowe was recognized as a leader among African American players and a mentor to younger blacks around the league. In 1960, Reds outfielder Vada Pinson told *Sports Illustrated* that Crowe "took me right under his wing. He came up to me and said, 'If there are any problems, you come to me. I'm your father, your big daddy up here.'"

Cincinnati sent Crowe to the St. Louis Cardinals for 1959. That year he led the NL with 17 pinch hits. By the time he left the majors in 1961, his 14 career pinch-hit home runs were a Major League record.

For two years after retiring, Crowe was a Cardinals scout and served as a coach during Spring Training. He later worked for Pan American Airways in San Francisco. He eventually moved to New York's Long Island, working as a physical education teacher. He retired in 1971 and moved to Long Eddy, N.Y., a rustic hamlet in the Catskills.

For 11 years Crowe lived in a one-room log cabin with no electricity, running water or central heating. "In these hills I'm free, I don't have to punch anyone else's time clock," he told *Inside Sports* magazine in 1981. He later moved into a more conventional abode and spent winters with a daughter in California.

Crowe is a member of the Indiana Baseball, Indiana Basketball and University of Indianapolis halls of fame. Franklin High School's baseball field is named for him.

During the 1950s, Crowe's older brother Ray (also an Indiana Central graduate) coached Crispus Attucks High School of Indianapolis to a 179–20 record and a pair of state basketball titles. In 2012 a University of Indianapolis residence building was renamed Ray & George Crowe Hall.

CUPPY, George Joseph ("Nig," "Snail," "Maceo")

Born: George Joseph Koppe, July 3, 1869, Logansport. **Died:** July 27, 1922, Elkhart.
Height: 5'7". **Weight:** 160. **Batted:** right. **Threw:** right.
Debut: April 16, 1892. **Final game:** August 7, 1901.
Positions, teams, years: pitcher (302), outfield (11), Cleveland (NL) 1892–1898, St. Louis (NL) 1899, Boston (NL) 1900, Boston (AL) 1901.
Games: 313. **Innings pitched:** 2,283.2. **Won/Lost:** 162–98. **Earned run average:** 3.48.
At bats: 1,066. **Home runs:** 1. **Average:** .233.

In the last decade of the Nineteenth Century, Cy Young and **Nig Cuppy** formed an outstanding pitching tandem for the NL's Cleveland Spiders. Cuppy, whose best pitch was a rising fastball, exasperated batters with a deliberate windup. He was one of the first pitchers to wear a fielder's glove.

A Logansport High School alumnus, Cuppy's sandlot baseball success in his hometown led to a professional contract in 1890 with Dayton, Ohio (Tri-State). His work at Meadville, Pa. (New York-Penn) attracted Spiders player-manager Patsy Tebeau, who brought Cuppy to Cleveland for the 1892 season. The rookie responded with a 28–13 record. In the fourth game of the 1892 post-season NL championship, he took the defeat in a 4–0 loss to the Boston Beaneaters.

From 1893 to 1896 Cuppy produced records of 17–10, 24–15, 26–14 and 25–14. His three shutouts in 1894 topped the NL. In 1895 he and Young combined for six. Cleveland played the Baltimore Orioles that year in the Temple Cup Series, and Cuppy split a pair of decisions. In the 1896 Temple Cup, he started the third game despite a sore arm as the Spiders lost to Baltimore in four straight games.

Cuppy's arm problems continued to plague him, and after 1896 he won just 42 games against 32 defeats. In July 1898 Cleveland teammates told *The Sporting News* he "will never be able to pitch ball again." But he got temporary relief from John "Bonesetter" Reese, whose self-taught methods of "bloodless surgery" resembled modern-day chiropractic technique.

After the season, Cuppy was one of several players transferred from Cleveland to St. Louis by Frank DeHaas Robison, who owned both teams. Cuppy played for the Boston Beaneaters in 1900 and in 1901 he joined the Boston Puritans of the newly-formed AL.

Cuppy returned to Elkhart prior to 1902 and opened a billiard hall and tobacco store. He suffered from Bright's disease, a kidney ailment, and died at the age of 53 following a bout with pneumonia.

In less enlightened times, the name "Nig" was often bestowed upon dark-complected players. Antonio Maceo, a contemporary Cuban revolutionary hero, was the source of another Cuppy nickname. "Snail" refers to Cuppy's slow pitching pace. A contemporary newspaper account mentions his "plodding, deliberate tactics." Another describes Cuppy as "delaying the delivery of the ball to the utmost possible limit," until the opposing hitter was "in a nervous frenzy and generally an easy victim."

CURTIS, Chad David

Born: November 6, 1968, Marion. **Lives:** Ada, Michigan.
Height: 5'10". **Weight:** 175. **Batted:** right. **Threw:** right.
Debut: April 8, 1992. **Final game:** September 30, 2001.
Positions, teams, years: outfield (1,141), second base (3), California (AL) 1992–1994, Detroit (AL)

1995–1996, Los Angeles (NL) 1996, Cleveland (AL) 1997, New York (AL) 1997–1999, Texas (AL) 2000–2001.
Games: 1,204. **At-bats:** 4,017. **Home runs:** 101. **Average:** .264.

Chad Curtis, who was married in a baseball uniform, grew up in Michigan after his family left Indiana when he was a year old. His parents later moved to Arizona, where Curtis graduated from Benson (Ariz.) Union High School. He played at a pair of junior colleges, Yavapai and Cochise County, and an NAIA school, Grand Canyon, where he won All-America honors.

The California Angels selected Curtis in the 45th round of the 1989 free agent draft. On May 2, 1990, during his second professional season at Quad City (Midwest), he married Candace Reynolds. The wedding, scheduled for 10:30 a.m., was delayed until 1 p.m. With a game scheduled for 2 p.m., Curtis changed into his baseball uniform prior to the ceremony. As soon as the nuptials were completed he left for the ballpark.

An excellent base stealer, Curtis was a spray hitter ideally suited for the number-two slot in the batting order. An infielder during his college days, he switched to the outfield while in the minors. In April 1995 the Angels traded him to the Detroit Tigers. "It was home. I was always a Tigers fan," he told the *Arizona Daily Star*. In Tiger Stadium he displayed unprecedented power with a 21-homer season.

In 1996 the Los Angeles Dodgers acquired Curtis after throat cancer sidelined their regular center fielder, Brett Butler. A free agent after the season, Curtis signed with the Cleveland Indians, who traded him to the New York Yankees in early June. He was a valuable role player for the Yanks, seeing action in center and left and batting .284. During the 1998 season he played all three outfield positions as New York won 114 games, an American League record.

Curtis was a surprise star for the Yanks in the 1999 World Series against the Atlanta Braves. He hit two home runs in Game Three, including a walk-off blast in the bottom of the tenth. Traded to the Texas Rangers in December 1999, he retired after the 2001 season.

After leaving baseball, Curtis earned a degree from Cornerstone University in Grand Rapids, Mich. In 2012 he was working as a high school weight training instructor in western Michigan when several female students accused him of sexual misconduct. Tried and found guilty in 2013, Curtis was sentenced to seven to ten years at a correctional facility in Adrian, Mich.

DALE, James Carl
Born: December 7, 1972, Indianapolis. **Lives:** Cookeville, Tennessee.
Height: 6'2". **Weight:** 215. **Batted:** right. **Threw:** right.
Debut: September 7, 1999. **Final game:** September 26, 1999.
Positions, teams, years: pitcher, Milwaukee (NL) 1999.
Games: 4. **Innings pitched:** 4. **Won/Lost:** 0–1. **Earned run average:** 20.25.

Reliever **Carl Dale** went to high school in Cookeville, Tenn., and starred at Winthrop University in Rock Hill, S.C. An 11–4 record and 2.82 ERA in 1994 earned him Big South Conference pitcher-of-the-year honors. *Baseball America* projected him as a possible mid-first-round draft pick, praising his "above-average fastball and curveball to go with a bulldog mentality."

St. Louis selected Dale in the second round of the 1994 draft. He launched his pro career that summer with New Jersey (New York-Penn). In January 1996 the Cardinals traded him to Oakland. He underwent elbow surgery in August 1997 and in August 1998 the Athletics sent him to Milwaukee. Less than three weeks later he reached the Major Leagues, making four relief appearances for the Brewers

Dale became a free agent after the 1999 season and signed with Kansas City, but the Royals released him in Spring Training. He joined the Cleveland organization and split 2000 between Akron, Ohio (Eastern), and Buffalo, N.Y. (International). Released by the Indians that August, he signed with the Boston Red Sox and finished the year at Trenton, N.J. (Eastern).

After the 2000 season Dale left baseball, returning to Cookeville and taking a job with Tennessee Tech University's maintenance department. He also taught baseball lessons and coached a Babe Ruth League team.

DARINGER, Clifford Clarence ("Shanty," "Rabbit")

Born: April 10, 1885, Hayden. **Died:** December 26, 1971, Sacramento, California.
Height: 5'7". **Weight:** 155. **Batted:** left. **Threw:** right.
Debut: April 20, 1914. **Final game:** September 29, 1914.
Positions, teams, years: shortstop (24), third base (19), second base (14), Kansas City (Federal League) 1914.
Games: 64. **At-bats:** 160. **Home runs:** 0. **Average:** .263.

One of three brothers who played professional baseball, **Cliff Daringer** was in the starting lineup for the first game at what would become Wrigley Field.

Lorenzo Daringer (pronounced DAH-ring-er), Cliff's father, had played baseball while serving in the Union Army during the Civil War. Lorenzo raised five sons and a daughter on the family farm in Hayden.

After two seasons with the amateur North Vernon (Ind.) Reds, Cliff signed with Lynchburg (Virginia State) for 1906. The following year his brother Howard, older by two years, joined Peoria, Ill. (Three-I). In 1909 Rollie Daringer, who was three years younger than Cliff, signed with Saginaw (Southern Michigan).

Cliff began the 1913 season with Covington, Ky., in the outlaw Federal League. In June the franchise moved to Kansas City, and he finished the year with a .316 average and a league-leading 86 runs.

In 1914 the FL challenged the AL and NL as a third major circuit. Daringer served as Kansas City's backup infielder, playing shortstop, second and third base. During the first game at Chicago's Weeghman Park on April 23, 1914, he played shortstop and batted seventh in the Packers' 1–0 win over the host Chifeds. After the FL folded, the Chicago Cubs acquired the ballpark and began playing home games there in 1916. In 1927 the facility was renamed Wrigley Field.

Daringer retired from baseball after spending 1915 and 1916 in the Three-I League. Starting in 1910 he made his home in Sacramento, Calif., where he'd spent the 1909 and 1910 seasons in the Pacific Coast League. He worked as a department store salesman in and around the Sacramento area.

Cliff was the first of the three Daringer brothers to pass on when he died at age 86.

DARINGER, Rolla Harrison

Born: November 15, 1888, Hayden. **Died:** May 23, 1974, Seymour.
Height: 5'10". **Weight:** 155. **Batted:** left. **Threw:** right.
Debut: September 19, 1914. **Final game:** April 23, 1915.
Positions, teams, years: shortstop, St. Louis (NL) 1914–1915.
Games: 12. **At-bats:** 27. **Home runs:** 0. **Average:** .148.

Rollie Daringer was the only member of his family who played in either the American or National Leagues. Cliff Daringer played in the upstart Federal League in 1914, while another brother, Howard, spent 1907 through 1920 in the minors.

Rollie broke in with Saginaw (Southern Michigan) in 1909. He spent his next four seasons with Dubuque, Iowa (Three-I), batting .240 in 1910, .217 in 1911, .266 in 1912 and .299 in 1913.

Late in 1914 the St. Louis Cardinals acquired Daringer from Peoria, Ill. (Three-I). where he was hitting .256 in 37 contests. "Daringer is reported to be a great fielder," the *St. Louis Post-Dispatch* reported, "but a little shy in the hitting."

Rollie began the 1915 season with St. Louis but was back in Peoria after 10 appearances and an .087 average. He spent 1916 and 1917 with Bloomington, Ill. (Three-I). Following World War I army service in 1918, he played for Milwaukee (American Association), Oklahoma City (Western) and Houston (Texas) from 1919 to 1921. A speedy shortstop, he stole 53 bases for Dubuque in 1912.

After his baseball career ended, Rollie managed the Daringer farm in Hayden. For many years, the farm was the site of family reunions. One of Rollie's closest friends was Indiana governor Edgar Whitcomb, who was from nearby Seymour. Governor Whitcomb's visits to the Daringer farm in a chauffeur-driven limousine always caused excitement in Hayden.

DAUSS, George August ("Hookie")
Indiana Baseball Hall of Fame, 2006.
Born: George August Daus, September 22, 1889, Indianapolis. **Died:** July 27, 1963, St. Louis, Missouri.
Height: 5'10". **Weight:** 168. **Batted:** right. **Threw:** right.
Debut: September 28, 1912. **Final game:** September 19, 1926.
Positions, teams, years: pitcher (538), outfield (1), Detroit (AL) 1912–1926.
Games: 538. **Innings pitched:** 3,390.2. **Won/Lost:** 223–182. **Earned run average:** 3.30.
At-bats: 1,124. **Home runs:** 6. **Average:** .238.

George Dauss, who was elected to the Indiana Baseball Hall of Fame in 2006, spent his entire 15-year career in Detroit. His 223 victories is the highest career total by a Tigers pitcher.

Dauss, who at some point added as extra "S" to his last name, grew up in Indianapolis. He played baseball for Manual High School and for a semi-pro club called the Atlee Sawmakers. Professional teams were reluctant to sign him because of his size. He grew a few inches taller and added some weight and joined South Bend (Central) in 1909, but drew his release before he could pitch in an official contest. After a brilliant performance in an exhibition game, he joined Duluth, Minn. (Minnesota-Wisconsin). He won 19 and lost 10 that year, and in 1911 he went 21–11 for Winona, Minn. (Minnesota-Wisconsin).

The Tigers obtained Dauss late in 1912 from St. Paul (American Association). He joined a veteran Detroit team that included Ty Cobb, Sam Crawford and fellow Hoosier Donie Bush, a friend since elementary school. Dauss (whose effective curveball earned him the nickname "Hookie") remained in the Tigers rotation for the next 14 years.

While Detroit failed to win a pennant during that period, Dauss won 15 or more games seven times and had ten winning seasons. In 1914 he won 24 games. He had 21 victories in both 1918 and 1923.

Dauss was Detroit's Opening Day starter in 1914, 1920 and 1924. He led AL pitchers in hit batsmen in 1914 (19), 1916 (16) and 1915 (21). An excellent fielder, he is the winningest pitcher born in Indianapolis. He was also the last pitcher Shoeless Joe Jackson faced. Jackson singled off Dauss in a game at Detroit on Sept. 27, 1920. After the season, Jackson was banned for his part in the 1919 World Series scandal.

Friendly and good-natured, Dauss teamed with the fiery Cobb throughout his Major League career. After the 1926 season, an irregular heartbeat forced Dauss's retirement. "I wasn't a great pitcher and never pitched any remarkably good games," he said. "But I managed to win a lot of games where I held the opposing club to four of five hits."

The only other pitchers with 223 or more career wins who never made it to the World Series are Ferguson Jenkins (284), Ted Lyons (260), Jim Bunning (224) and Mel Harder (223).

Dauss operated a farm in the St. Louis area after leaving baseball and worked as a detective for the Pinkerton Agency. He spent the final 18 years of his life in Fenton, Mo. Ray "Bud" Dauss, George's brother, was an Indianapolis auto dealer who served as a city councilman.

DAVIDSON, William Simpson
Born: May 10, 1887, Lafayette. **Died:** May 23, 1954, Lincoln, Nebraska.
Height: 5'10". **Weight:** 170. **Batted:** right. **Threw:** right.
Debut: September 29, 1909. **Final game:** September 18, 1911.
Positions, teams, years: outfield, Chicago (NL) 1909, Brooklyn (NL) 1910–1911.
Games: 225. **At-bats:** 808. **Home runs:** 1. **Average:** .235.

Former University of Arizona football player **Bill Davidson** entered professional baseball with Fort Dodge (Iowa State) in 1905, hitting .238. In 1906 he led the league with a .344 average. Later that season he joined Lincoln, Neb. (Western), and hit .339 in 16 games. He remained in Lincoln through September 1909, when the Cubs obtained him. He appeared in two contests for Chicago with one hit in seven at-bats.

On April 13, 1910, the Cubs traded Davidson and two other players to the Brooklyn Superbas for right-hander Harry McIntyre. "Brooklyn received three youngsters who have their careers before them in infielder 'Tony' Smith and Outfielder 'Happy' Smith and W.S. Davidson," *The Sporting News* reported, "while [Chicago manager Frank] Chance obtains one of the greatest pitchers in the two big leagues."

The deal sent Davidson from the powerhouse Cubs to the Superbas, a perennial NL doormat during the early Twentieth Century. Along with Zack Wheat and Jack Dalton, Davidson was part of an all-rookie Brooklyn outfield in 1910. In his lone year as a big league regular, Davidson played centerfield and hit .238 with a team-high 27 stolen bases.

After a .233 season for Brooklyn in 1911, Davidson returned to the Western League, this time with Omaha, Neb. He spent 1913 to 1915 at Sioux City, Iowa (Western), helping the club to a first-place finish in 1914 with a .286 average.

That was Davidson's final season. He returned to Nebraska, where he worked for the Department of Roads and Irrigation. He spent the last twelve years of his life in Lincoln.

DEXTER, Charles Dana

Born: June 15, 1876, Evansville. **Died:** June 9, 1934, Cedar Rapids, Iowa.
Height: 5'7". **Weight:** 155. **Batted:** right. **Threw:** right.
Debut: April 17, 1896. **Final game:** September 27, 1903.
Positions, teams, years: outfield (403), catcher (116), third base (81), first base (76), second base (41), shortstop (39), Louisville (NL) 1896–1899, Chicago (NL) 1900–1902, Boston (NL) 1902–1903.
Games: 774. **At-bats:** 2,876. **Home runs:** 16. **Average:** .261.

A member of the Evansville Sports Hall of Fame, **Charlie Dexter** played all over the diamond. His personal life was even more erratic.

The son of an Evansville waterworks engineer, Dexter starred for a local semi-pro team known as the Cooks. He enrolled at the University of the South in Sewanee, Tenn., in 1894 and returned to Evansville in 1895 to play for the city's Southern Association team. "Dexter belongs to a good family," noted the *Columbus* (Ohio) *Dispatch*. He plays ball for a living simply because of his infatuation for the game."

The following year, Dexter joined the Louisville Colonels of the NL. He batted .279 in 1896, .280 in 1897, and .314 in 1898, when he stole 44 bases. He slumped to .258 in 1899. After the league expelled the Louisville franchise, he joined the Chicago Cubs for 1900. In July 1902 the Cubs traded him to the Boston Beaneaters (later the Braves). The 1903 campaign was his last in the majors.

On December 30, 1903, Dexter was one of 1,600 on hand for a performance at Chicago's Iroquois Theater. A fire broke out that would claim around 600 lives. Dexter and Frank Houseman, another ballplayer, burst open a locked exit door and enabled hundreds of people to escape the holocaust. "While the frightened beasts around you fought and struck at women and children and trampled on them, you—in the face of death—tried to save my life," wrote a boy who survived the holocaust. "You are a hero."

Dexter arranged his own release from Boston before the 1904 season and returned to Louisville (by now a member of the minor league American Association), where he played third base and served as team captain. Midway through the 1905 season he moved from Louisville to Des Moines, Iowa (Western).

On October 1, 1905, Dexter was out carousing in Des Moines when he got into an argument with Harry Bateman, an old friend who played for Milwaukee (American Association). Dexter, known for his hot temper, stabbed Bateman in the chest and seriously wounded him. Dexter was arrested, but Bateman recovered and refused to press charges.

During his eight-year big league tenure Dexter caught, played the outfield and all four infield positions. For a time he worked for an Evansville newspaper during the off-season. A very popular player, he managed five different minor league clubs before leaving baseball after 1908.

At various times, Dexter managed a music store, worked in the restaurant business and sold clothing. In June 1934 he traveled from his home in Des Moines to visit relatives in St. Louis. On the return trip he stopped in Cedar Rapids, Iowa. Using a false name, Dexter checked into a hotel room where he shot and killed himself.

DIETZ, Richard Allen ("Mule")

Born: September 18, 1941, Crawfordsville. **Died:** June 28, 2005, Clayton, Georgia.
Height: 6'1". **Weight:** 195. **Batted:** right. **Threw:** right.
Debut: June 18, 1966. **Final game:** September 30, 1973.
Positions, teams, years: catcher (532), first base (36), San Francisco (NL) 1966–1971, Los Angeles (NL) 1972, Atlanta (NL) 1973.
Games: 646. **At-bats:** 1,829. **Home runs:** 66. **Average:** .261.

A high school baseball and football star in Greenville, S.C., **Dick Dietz** signed with the Giants in 1960. He played the outfield for El Paso in 1963 and led the Texas League with a .354 average and 128 runs, as well as 26 errors. He was a catcher-first baseman for Phoenix (Pacific Coast) in 1966 when he joined San Francisco.

In 1968 Dietz (pronounced "deets") was involved in two memorable events. At Los Angeles on May 31, Dodgers pitcher Don Drysdale was working on a record-tying fifth straight shutout with a 3–0 lead in the ninth. The Giants had the bases loaded with no outs when a 2–2 pitch clipped Dietz's left arm, apparently forcing in a run to end Drysdale's streak. But home plate umpire Harry Wendelstedt ruled it a ball, claiming that Dietz had moved into the pitch. "The pitch was hard and I just couldn't move," Dietz told the *Los Angeles Times*. "All I could do was flinch before it hit me." After Dietz flew out, Drysdale retired the next two batters for the win. Drysdale pitched another shutout in his next start, eventually setting a Major League record with 58 scoreless innings.

Later that summer, on September 17, Dietz caught Gaylord Perry's 1–0 no-hit victory over St. Louis at San Francisco's Candlestick Park. In 1970 he became San Francisco's full-time catcher and was named to the NL All-Star team. In his first at-bat as an All-Star, he led off the bottom of the ninth inning with a pinch-hit home run. The homer sparked a game-tying rally and the NL went on to win in the bottom of the 12th.

Dietz finished the 1970 season with 22 home runs, a .300 average and 107 RBI, the most by a Giants catcher since the franchise left New York for San Francisco.

After a 19-homer, .252 campaign in 1971 the Giants wanted to trade him to an AL team. The Dodgers claimed Dietz on waivers, however, and he wound up playing for Los Angeles in 1972. A broken bone in his right wrist shelved him for most of the season. The Dodgers sent him to Atlanta in March 1973 and he finished his big league career with the Braves.

After serving as president of a sports clinics business, Dietz returned to baseball in 1990 as a minor league coach in the Giants organization. He later managed minor league and independent league teams.

Stubborn determination earned Dietz his nickname. After a severe beaning in 1971 he refused to come out of the lineup and continued to play with his head swathed in bandages.

Dietz, who spent his last years in Pawley's Island, S.C., died from a heart attack at age 63. "He was fun to be around," pitcher Bob Bolin, a Giants teammate, told the *Greenville* (S.C.) *News*. "He had a wonderful sense of humor and loved to play the game. I would say if anybody enjoyed life any better than Dick, I don't know who it was."

DISTEL, George Adam ("Dutch")

Born: April 15, 1896, Madison. **Died:** February 12, 1967, Madison.
Height: 5'9". **Weight:** 165. **Batted:** right. **Threw:** right.
Debut: June 21, 1918. **Final game:** June 27, 1918.
Positions, teams, years: second base (5), shortstop (2), outfield (1), St. Louis (NL) 1918.
Games: 8. **At-bats:** 17. **Home runs:** 0. **Average:** .176.

A veteran of 17 professional campaigns, infielder **Dutch Distel** played eight games for the St. Louis Cardinals in 1918.

Distel entered organized ball with Middlesboro, Ky. (Appalachian), in 1914. He began the 1918 season with Little Rock, Ark. (Southern), and was hitting .317 when he joined the Cardinals. He played second, short and the outfield before St. Louis sent him to Milwaukee (American Association).

When Little Rock won the Southern Association pennant in 1920, Distel batted .252 as the Travelers' everyday second baseman. Back in Madison after the season, he attended a local amateur game where he spotted a 17-

year-old shortstop named Tommy Thevenow. Impressed, Distel convinced him to sign a professional contract. Thevenow wound up spending 15 years in the big leagues.

Distel's best year was 1925, when he batted .323 for Wichita Falls (Texas). He left baseball after spending 1930 at Quincy, Ill. (Three-I). In 1932 he purchased a tavern in Madison, which he operated until 1951.

DORSETT, Brian Richard
Indiana Baseball Hall of Fame, 2008.
Born: April 9, 1961, Terre Haute. **Lives:** Terre Haute.
Height: 6'3". **Weight:** 215. **Batted:** right. **Threw:** right.
Debut: September 8, 1987. **Final game:** June 4, 1996.
Positions, teams, years: catcher (134), first base (6), Cleveland (AL) 1987, California (AL) 1988, New York (AL) 1989–1990, San Diego (NL) 1991, Cincinnati (NL) 1993–1994, Chicago (NL) 1996.
Games: 163. **At-bats:** 411. **Home runs:** 9. **Average:** .224.

Brian Dorsett caught for seven different organizations in 11 seasons before becoming an everyday Major League player in 1994.

Dorsett (pronounced DORSE-ett) was a football, basketball and baseball star at Terre Haute North High School and a first-team All-Missouri Valley Conference pick in baseball at Indiana State University. A tenth-round draft pick by Oakland in 1983, he broke in that year with Medford, Ore. (Northwest).

Oakland traded Dorsett to Cleveland in 1987 and he reached the Major Leagues that year with the Indians. From 1988 to 1992 he played for minor league affiliates of the California Angels, New York Yankees, San Diego Padres and Pittsburgh Pirates before signing with the Cincinnati Reds as a free agent in 1993. He was batting .299 with 18 homers for Indianapolis (American Association) in July 1993 when he was summoned to Cincinnati after Reds catcher Joe Oliver slashed his arm on a knife while trying to empty a dishwasher.

In 1994 Dorsett spent his first Opening Day in a big league uniform. He batted .245 that year, compiling 216 at-bats—more than he had in his six previous big league campaigns. He was back in Indianapolis in the spring of 1995 after the Reds signed catchers Damon Berryhill and Benito Santiago. He joined the Chicago Cubs as a free agent during Spring Training in 1996, appearing in 17 games before he was optioned to Iowa (American Association). Limited to nine games by an ankle injury, he retired after the season.

Dorsett owns and operates a pair of Terre Haute car dealerships and was involved with the Terre Haute Acton Track from 2008 through 2010. He did color commentary for Indianapolis Indians telecasts in 2003. He managed the Terre Haute Rex, a collegiate summer baseball team in the Prospect League, from 2010 to 2012 and won 2012 manager of the year honors. He was a member of the Indiana Baseball Hall of Fame's Class of 2008.

Dorsett married his high school sweetheart, Gina Mascari. Brandon Dorsett, their son, pitched for Indiana State University and signed with the Toronto Blue Jays organization in 2012.

DOSTER, David Eric
Born: October 8, 1970, Fort Wayne. **Lives:** New Haven.
Height: 5'10". **Weight:** 185. **Batted:** right. **Threw:** right.
Debut: June 16, 1996. **Final game:** October 3, 1999.
Positions, teams, years: second base (101), third base (7), shortstop (5), Philadelphia (NL) 1996, 1999.
Games: 138. **At-bats:** 202. **Home runs:** 4. **Average:** .233.

David Doster starred for New Haven High School from 1986 to 1989, hitting .445 with 37 homers and setting a state record with 137 runs. A first-team All-Missouri Conference selection at Indiana State University in 1993, he was a 27th-round draft pick by the Philadelphia Phillies.

Doster (pronounced "DAH-stir") made his pro debut with Spartanburg, S.C. (South Atlantic), in 1993 and hit .274. In 1994 at Clearwater he was the Florida State League's best defensive second baseman, and his 42 doubles set a club record. During the FSL playoffs he clubbed six homers in eight games.

Promoted to the Eastern League for 1995, Doster helped Reading, Pa., to its first title since 1973. His 39 two-base hits broke a 61-year-old franchise record. He opened the 1996 campaign with Scranton/Wilkes-Barre, Pa.

(International), and joined the Phillies after former Indiana University star Mickey Morandini went on the disabled list. Doster batted .267 in 39 contests with the Phillies.

After spending 1997 and 1998 with Scranton/Wilkes-Barre, Doster returned to Philadelphia in 1999 and hit .196 in 99 games. He was back with Scranton/Wilkes-Barre again in 2000 and moved on to the Yokohama BayStars of Japan's Central League, where he averaged .272 in 2001.

Doster returned to the U.S. in 2002 for another tour of duty with Scranton/Wilkes-Barre. He spent 2003 with Nashville, Tenn. (Pacific Coast). His 32-game hitting streak in 2004 at Fresno, Calif. (Pacific Coast), set a franchise record. It was the longest in the PCL since 1933, when Joe DiMaggio hit safely in 61 consecutive games for the San Francisco Seals.

Doster opened the 2005 season with the Mexican League's Tuneros de San Luis and hit .280 in 34 games. He finished the year with Tucson, Ariz. (Pacific Coast), batting .338 before calling it a career.

In 2007 Doster was inducted into the Northeast Indiana Baseball Association Hall of Fame. He went into the Reading Phillies Hall of Fame in 2012. For a time, he had an off-season job in Fort Wayne as a substitute teacher.

DOWNEY, Alexander Cummings ("Alex," "Red")

Born: February 6, 1889, Aurora. **Died:** July 10, 1949, Detroit, Michigan.
Height: 5'11". **Weight:** 174. **Batted:** left. **Threw:** left.
Debut: September 14, 1909. **Final Game:** October 7, 1909.
Positions, teams, years: outfield, Brooklyn (NL) 1909.
Games: 19. **At-bats:** 78. **Home runs:** 0. **Average:** .256.

In September 1909 a pair of outfielders debuted with the Brooklyn Superbas, as the Dodgers were then known. **Red Downey** had led the Texas League with a .346 average at Oklahoma City while the other rookie, Zack Wheat, had batted .246 for Mobile, Ala. (Southern). In his first game, a 1–0 Brooklyn win at Philadelphia, Downey batted third and played center field while Wheat was in left, hitting second.

Wheat went on to a Hall of Fame career while Downey never again played in the Major Leagues after that season. Downey would go on to become a major player in corporate America.

The son of a U.S. court of claims judge in Washington, D.C., Downey was named for his grandfather, Indiana's 23rd Supreme Court Justice. His professional baseball career began in 1908 and ended in 1914. In 1911 his 48 stolen bases for Austin topped the Texas League.

After leaving baseball, Downey returned to college and graduated from Georgetown Law School in 1917. Downey entered the army after earning his degree. In June 1918 he was commissioned a lieutenant colonel in the U.S. Army Air Corps.

Following World War I, Downey became a close business associate of auto magnate Walter Chrysler. After the formation of the Chrysler Corporation in 1925, he served as the organization's purchasing agent. He became vice president of the Dodge truck division in 1928 and later served as head of Chrysler's Fargo Motor Company. In 1937 he was named president of Chrysler's Airtemp division in Dayton, Ohio, which manufactured air-conditioning equipment.

Downey retired in 1940, but when the U.S. entered World War II he returned to supervise Dodge's production of bomber engines. He died of heart disease at age 60.

DUGGAN, James Elmer ("Jim," "Mer")

Born: June 1, 1885, Whiteland. **Died:** December 5, 1951, Indianapolis.
Height: 5'10". **Weight:** 165. **Batted:** left. **Threw:** left.
Debut: June 29, 1911. **Final Game:** June 29, 1911.
Positions, teams, years: first base, St. Louis (AL) 1911.
Games: 1. **At-bats:** 4. **Home runs:** 0. **Average:** .000.

Except for one game with the St. Louis Browns, first baseman **Elmer Duggan** spent his entire 11-year professional career in the minor leagues.

Duggan graduated from Whiteland High School and attended Franklin College before entering pro ball with Atlanta (Southern Association) in 1906. He was playing for Holyoke, Mass. (Connecticut), in 1911 when the franchise folded on June 20. A few days later, the

Browns summoned him to Detroit for a game with the Tigers. Batting seventh, Duggan went hitless in four at-bats, drew a walk, drove in a run and scored once in a 6–5 St. Louis victory. It would be his only Major League appearance.

Duggan's last six seasons were in the Three-I League. Starting in 1912, he spent four years with Decatur, Ill., and in 1915 he was the Commodores' playing manager. He split the 1916 season between Rock Island, Ill., and Davenport, Iowa. He finished his career in 1917 as a player-manager with Alton, Ill.

In 1918 Duggan entered the army. He was on board a ship bound for Europe when World War I ended.

Johnny Duggan, Elmer's brother, was a minor league outfielder.

DUMOULIN, Daniel Lynn ("Low Down," "Dummy")

Born: August 20, 1953, in Kokomo. **Lives:** Kokomo.
Height: 6'0". **Weight:** 175. **Batted:** right. **Threw:** right.
Debut: September 5, 1977. **Final game:** October 1, 1978.
Positions, teams, years: pitcher, Cincinnati (NL) 1977–1978.
Games: 8. **Innings pitched:** 10.1. **Won/Lost:** 1–0. **Earned run average:** 7.84

Elbow problems finished **Dan Dumoulin's** promising pitching career. As a Little League player, Dumoulin (pronounced duh-MOO-lin) helped the Kokomo Northside All-Star team to a state title. He later starred at Kokomo High School, where his teammates included another future Major League pitcher, Tom Underwood.

Dumoulin left high school after his junior year to work for Chrysler. Selected by the Reds in the 21st round of the 1972 draft, he didn't sign until 1974 and spent his first professional season with Billings, Mont. (Pioneer).

By 1977 Dumoulin was pitching for Indianapolis (American Association), where his fastball was clocked at about 95 miles per hour. Promoted to Cincinnati in September, he made five relief appearances for the Reds. Back with Indianapolis in 1978, he was 12–6 in 32 games (16 as a starter, 16 as a reliever) before rejoining Cincinnati, where he went 1–0 with a 1.80 ERA in three games as a reliever.

Dumoulin's elbow problems began that year. He had a 2–2 record and 5.79 ERA for Indianapolis in 1979 when he underwent surgery. The operation didn't help. "The elbow just didn't look right," he told the *Kokomo Perspective*. "It was crooked. I couldn't straighten it out."

Dumoulin never pitched another inning. His baseball career ended when he was 27 years old. Returning to his hometown, he took a job as a plant operator with Kokomo Glass and Fuel. He and his wife Joan, a police officer, raised four children.

DUNNE, Michael Dennis ("Ice")

Born: October 27, 1962, South Bend. **Lives:** Peoria, Illinois.
Height: 6'4". **Weight:** 190. **Batted:** right. **Threw:** right.
Debut: June 5, 1987. **Final Game:** October 3, 1992.
Positions, teams, years: pitcher, Pittsburgh (NL) 1987–1989, Seattle (AL) 1989, San Diego (NL) 1990, Chicago (AL) 1992.
Games: 85. **Innings pitched:** 474.1. **Won/Lost:** 25–30. **Earned run average:** 4.08.

In 1987, his first Major League season with the Pittsburgh Pirates, **Mike Dunne** won 13 games and was named the year's top rookie pitcher. He went on to win just 12 more big league contests.

Dunne lettered in baseball, basketball and golf at Limestone Community High School in Bartonville, Ill. At Bradley University, where one of his teammates was future big league third baseman Jim Lindeman, Dunne was 8–2 with a 2.44 ERA as a junior in 1984. That June, the St. Louis Cardinals made him their top selection (seventh overall) in the draft. Named to the U.S. Team for the 1984 Olympics in Los Angeles, he pitched two scoreless innings of relief versus Italy.

Dunne's pro career began in 1985 with Arkansas (Texas). On April 1, 1987, St. Louis sent him to Pittsburgh along with catcher Mike LaValliere and third baseman Andy Van Slyke for catcher Tony Pena. "That was a bad day for me," Dunne told the *Peoria Journal Star*. "I took it pretty hard. It happened on April Fool's Day and I thought it was a joke."

Dunne began the 1987 season with Vancouver, B.C. (Pacific Coast) and joined the Pirates in June. He went 13–6 with an NL-best .684 winning percentage and was second to San Diego's Benito Santiago in the rookie-of-the-year ballot. In 1988 Dunne was Pittsburgh's Opening Day starter. He slipped to 7–11 that year, and in 1989 the Pirates traded him to the Seattle Mariners, where he dipped to 2–9 with a 5.27 ERA.

Pitching for the San Diego Padres in 1990, Dunne had an 0–3, 5.65 record. In 1992 he went 2–0 for the Chicago White Sox with a 4.26 ERA, but spent most of the year with Colorado Springs, where his 10–6, 2.78 record helped the SkySox win the Pacific Coast League championship.

Arm injuries sidelined Dunne for most of 1993, when he was 1–1 with a 5.47 ERA for Sarasota (Florida State). In an unsuccessful 1994 comeback attempt with Scranton/Wilkes-Barre, Pa., (International), a Philadelphia Phillies farm team, he went 2–2 with a 5.22 ERA.

Dunne settled in Peoria. Ill., after retiring. He taught at the Midwest Baseball Academy and co-directed the Future Stars Biddy basketball League. From 2000 to 2009 he was Bradley University's pitching coach.

DUNWOODY, Todd Franklin

Born: April 11, 1975, Lafayette. **Lives:** West Lafayette.
Height: 6'1". **Weight:** 190. **Batted:** left. **Threw:** left.
Debut: May 10, 1997. **Final Game:** June 21, 2002.
Positions, teams, years: outfield, Florida (NL) 1997–1999, Kansas City (AL) 2000, Chicago (NL) 2001, Cleveland (AL) 2002.
Games: 295. **At-bats:** 915. **Home runs:** 11. **Average:** .233.

In 1992 **Todd Dunwoody** helped West Lafayette's Harrison High School to a Class 3A football title. He also starred for the Raiders baseball team, which reached the IHSAA semifinals in 1993. Dunwoody's high school baseball teammates included future Major Leaguers Erik Sabel and Eric Bruntlett, as well as Josh Loggins, who played in the minors from 1998 to 2005. As a member of the Indiana Bulls travel squad, Dunwoody teamed with Scott Rolen, who also made it to the big leagues.

A center fielder, Dunwoody was Florida's seventh-round draft choice in 1993. In 1996 he was the Marlins' top minor league player after a 24-homer, 93 RBI, .277 season at Portland, Maine (Eastern). From 1997 to 1999 he split time between the Marlins and Charlotte, N.C. (International). He was voted the best hitter and most exciting player in the International League for 1997.

Florida traded Dunwoody to Kansas City for the 2000 campaign. After the season he joined the Chicago Cubs as a free agent. A free agent again after 2001, He signed with the Cleveland organization and spent part of 2002 with the Indians. Between 2003 and 2005 he played for Triple-A clubs in the St. Louis, Cleveland and Minnesota organizations.

Dunwoody retired after 2005 and served as hitting coach for South Bend (Midwest) in 2006. He later worked as sales manager for the Mike Raisor Ford dealership in Lafayette.

Dunwoody comes from an athletic family. His older brother, Chad Dunwoody, coached Lafayette Central Catholic to IHSAA Class A boys basketball titles in 1998, 2000 and 2003. Steve Dietrich, Todd's cousin, coached West Lafayette to the 1998 3A girls basketball state title. Todd's aunt, Jan Conner, was a coach for girls' hoops squads at Warren Central, Benton Central and Martinsville. In 1997–1998 Conner's Benton Central teams won back-to-back state crowns.

EARL, William Scott ("Scotty")

Born: September 18, 1960, Seymour. **Lives:** Indianapolis.
Height: 5'11". **Weight:** 165. **Batted:** right. **Threw:** right.
Debut: September 10, 1984. **Final Game:** September 30, 1984.
Positions, teams, years: second base, Detroit (AL) 1984.
Games: 14. **At-bats:** 35. **Home runs:** 0. **Average:** .114.

A smart base runner with fair power, second baseman **Scott Earl** was stuck behind Lou Whitaker in the Detroit Tigers organization and played just 14 Major League games.

After graduation from Jennings County High School, Earl attended Glen Oaks Community College in Centerville, Mich., and Eastern Kentucky University. Detroit selected him in the 14th round of the 1981 free-agent draft. In 1984 at Evansville (American Association) he hit .251 with 11 homers and joined the Tigers that September.

Baseball America projected Earl as the Tigers' second baseman of the future, but Whitaker's reign in Detroit continued through the decade. Earl returned to the minors in 1985 and spent two seasons with Nashville (American Association). In 1987 a broken bone in his left leg limited him to 89 games at Toledo (American Association).

Prior to 1988 Earl left Detroit as a six-year minor league free agent and signed with the Cincinnati Reds organization. In 1989 he played for Toledo, Ohio (Detroit's top minor league club), and Columbus, Ohio (the top affiliate of the New York Yankees), before retiring.

Earl eventually became a sales representative for Edgcomb Metals in Indianapolis. His wife, Stacia Jordan, was a star volleyball player at Ball State University.

EDGERTON, William Albert

Born: August 16, 1941, South Bend. **Lives:** Foley, Alabama.
Height: 6'2". **Weight:** 185. **Batted:** left. **Threw:** left.
Debut: September 3, 1966. **Final Game:** April 25, 1969.
Positions, teams, years: pitcher, Kansas City (AL) 1966–1967, Seattle (AL) 1969.
Games: 17. **Innings pitched:** 20.2. **Won/Lost:** 1–2. **Earned run average:** 4.79.

Bill Edgerton starred in baseball and basketball for Mishawaka's Penn High School before signing with the New York Mets in 1963. Released that summer, he joined the Kansas City Athletics organization.

In 1966 Edgerton went 17–4, including 12 straight triumphs, to help Mobile, Ala., to the Southern League title. Promoted to the Athletics in September, he lost his only decision. He pitched briefly for the A's again in 1967. He spent all of 1968 in the Pacific Coast League, dividing the year between Seattle (the top farm club of the California Angels) and San Diego (the Philadelphia Phillies' Triple-A affiliate).

In September 1968 the Seattle Pilots (an expansion team scheduled to join the AL the following year) purchased Edgerton's contract. Soon after, he became the first player to sign with the new club. His stay with the Pilots lasted less than a month. By the end of April he was back in the PCL.

From 1969 until 1971 Edgerton drifted from one minor league system to another, pitching for farm clubs of the Baltimore Orioles, Los Angeles Dodgers and Milwaukee Brewers. His final stop was at Evansville (American Association).

Following his baseball career Edgerton worked in law enforcement in West Palm Beach, Fla. He eventually returned to northern Indiana, where he worked for AM General, the company that manufactures HumVee military vehicles.

Edgerton was among the big league players from 1947 to 1979 who fought Major League Baseball's vesting requirements for pensions and medical benefits. "To me, it all boils down to the fact that you can't just buck big business," Edgerton told Doug Gladstone, the author of the 2010 book *A Bitter Cup of Coffee: How MLB and the Players Association Threw 874 Retirees a Curve*. "Baseball is a steamroller, and it's rolled right over guys like me."

EDINGTON, Jacob Frank ("Stumpy," "Frank")

Born: July 4, 1891, Koleen. **Died:** November 11, 1969, Bastrop, Louisiana.
Height: 5'8". **Weight:** 170. **Batted:** left. **Threw:** left.
Debut: June 20, 1912. **Final Game:** July 13, 1912.
Positions, teams, years: outfield, Pittsburgh (NL) 1912.
Games: 15. **At-bats:** 53. **Home runs:** 0. **Average:** .302.

Like Hall of Fame manager Casey Stengel, **Stump Edington's** pro baseball career started in the Blue Grass League in 1910. Originally a pitcher, Edington switched to the outfield and in his second season batted .333 for Lexington, Ky. (Blue Grass).

In June 1912 Edington was hitting .372 when Lexington sold his contract to Pittsburgh. He batted .302 in just 15 games for the Pirates. "I came from a small town in Indiana—Lyons. Population 800," he said years later. "And I made one trip to New York with the Pirates. Honus Wagner [Pittsburgh's great shortstop] knew I was scared and he took me by the hand

and led me across Broadway. I never forgot that."

After his short stay with the Pirates, Edington was back in the minors for good. He developed into one of the top leadoff hitters in Texas League history, beginning in 1922 with Beaumont. Sent to Fort Worth during the 1923 campaign, he teamed with fellow Indiana native Clarence "Big Boy" Kraft to help the Panthers win pennants in 1923, 1924 and 1925. In six Texas League seasons Edington batted .319.

Edington's baseball career spanned 18 years and also included stops in the Central, Western, Pacific Coast, South Atlantic and Piedmont leagues, as well as the American Association. He spent 1918 in military service and left baseball after the 1928 season.

Built like a fireplug, Edington was a native of the southwestern Indiana town of Koleen in Greene County and a graduate of Lyons High School. He worked as a deputy sheriff in Beaumont, Texas, and later moved to Bastrop, La., where he became an optometrist.

ELLER, Horace Owen ("Hod")

Born: July 5, 1894, Muncie. **Died:** July 18, 1961, Indianapolis.
Height: 5'11". **Weight:** 185. **Batted:** right. **Threw:** right.
Debut: April 16, 1917. **Final Game:** September 15, 1921.
Positions, teams, years: pitcher (160), first base (2), second base (1), Cincinnati (NL) 1917–1921.
Games: 163. **Innings pitched:** 863. **Won/Lost:** 60–40. **Earned run average:** 2.62.
At-bats: 308. **Home runs:** 1. **Average:** .221.

Hod Eller, who spent his entire five-year big league career with the Cincinnati Reds, was the winning pitcher in the final game of the tainted 1919 World Series. Eller's specialty was the shine ball, a pitch that owed its sharp hop and dip to substances like talcum powder or paraffin.

Eller's family moved to Danville, Ill., when he was about seven years old. He started his professional career in 1913 with Champaign, Ill. (Illinois-Missouri). In 1915 his 19 wins for Moline, Ill. (Three-I), tied for the league lead. The Chicago White Sox gave him a tryout in the spring of 1916 but returned him to the minor leagues before the season began. At the end of the year he started for an independent team in an exhibition game against Cincinnati. Although the Reds won, he pitched effectively. Cincinnati drafted him that fall.

Eller went 10–5 in 1917 and 16–12 in 1918, his first two Major League seasons. On May 11, 1919, he pitched a 6–0 no-hitter against the St. Louis Cardinals. His 20–9 record that year helped the Reds to their first NL pennant. Cincinnati faced the White Sox in the best-of-nine World Series, and Eller started and won the fifth and eighth games. In his first win, a 5–0 shutout, he set a Series record by striking out six consecutive batters.

The Reds beat the White Sox in eight contests, and in 1920 several Chicago players admitted to conspiring with gamblers to fix the outcome. Eller maintained that the White Sox were playing to win in the two games he started. Reds outfielder Edd Roush claimed in Lawrence Ritter's *The Glory of Their Times* that Eller had been approached by a gambler prior to his first start. "He showed me five thousand-dollar bills, and said they were mine if I'd lose the game," Roush quoted Eller, who told the man "if he didn't get damn far away from me real quick he wouldn't know what hit him."

In 1920 baseball outlawed trick pitches, including Eller's shine ball. He went 13–12 with a 2.95 ERA that year and in 1921 slipped to 2–2, 4.98 in 13 appearances after reporting late for Spring Training. At the end of that year the Reds traded him to Oakland (Pacific Coast). He retired after a 3–6 record and 3.33 ERA at Indianapolis (American Association) in 1924.

Eller settled in Indianapolis and spent 22 years with the police department, retiring in 1947. He later worked as a driver for a liquor distributorship and as a security guard for Indiana Gear Works. In 1954 he made an unsuccessful run for nomination as Marion County sheriff.

ELLIOTT, Harold Bell ("Rowdy")

Born: July 8, 1890, Kokomo. **Died:** February 12, 1934, San Francisco, California.
Height: 5'9". **Weight:** 160. **Batted:** right. **Threw:** right.
Debut: September 24, 1910. **Final game:** October 2, 1920.

Positions, teams, years: catcher, Boston (NL) 1910, Chicago (NL) 1916–1918, Brooklyn (NL) 1920.
Games: 157. **At-bats:** 402. **Home runs:** 1. **Average:** .241.

The 21-year baseball career of talented but troubled **Rowdy Elliott** began in 1907 with Charleston, Ill. (Eastern Illinois). He played for Kewanee, Ill. (Central Association), in 1908–1909 and Birmingham. Ala. (Southern) in 1910 before the Boston Doves (today's Atlanta Braves) gave him a three-game trial.

In 1911 Elliott returned to Birmingham, where he developed into an outstanding catcher despite a reputation as a hard man to handle. Following a dispute with his manager in 1912, he was traded to Nashville, Tenn. (Southern), where team officials accused him of "not doing his best, dissipating, playing off sick, leading younger players astray and doing nearly everything not intended to promote the best interests of a club," according to the *San Francisco Examiner*.

Elliott spent the next four years in the Pacific Coast League, playing for Venice, Calif., in 1913 and 1914 and for Oakland in 1915 and 1916. He batted .301 for Oakland in 1915 and managed the club from June 20 to August 1. In 1916 the Oaks dealt him to the Chicago Cubs, where he shared catching duties with Art Wilson in 1917. He spent most of 1918 in the U.S. Navy.

In 1919 Elliott was back in the PCL, batting .293 for Oakland in 96 games. He returned to the majors with Brooklyn in 1920 and caught part of a 26-inning, 1–1 contest at Boston on May 1. It was the longest game in Major League history.

Back in the minors in 1921, Elliott continued to play through 1927, when he batted .20 for Shreveport, La. (Texas). He settled in San Francisco, and for a time was married to Helen Kearns, whose brother Doc managed boxing great Jack Dempsey.

In 1934, penniless and drunk, Elliott fell through the light well of an apartment and died from his injuries. He was 43 years old.

EPPARD, James Gerhard

Born: April 27, 1960, South Bend. **Lives:** Rapid City, South Dakota.
Height: 6'2". **Weight:** 180. **Batted:** left. **Threw:** left.
Debut: September 8, 1987. **Final Game:** October 1, 1990.
Positions, teams, years: outfield (18), first base (10), California (AL) 1987–1989, Toronto (AL) 1990.
Games: 82. **At-bats:** 139. **Home runs:** 0. **Average:** .281.

During a 12-year professional career, **Jim Eppard** won four minor league batting titles. Eppard played for Citrus College in Azusa, Calif., and the University of California before the Oakland Athletics took him in the 11th round of the 1982 draft. In his first year as a professional he hit .376 for Medford, Ore., to lead the Northwest League. Three years later at Modesto, his .345 average led the California League.

Throughout Eppard's years in the Oakland chain, there were always other players ahead of him, including Danny Goodwin and Rob Nelson at first base and Jose Canseco, Luis Polonia and Stan Javier in the outfield.

Prior to the 1987 season Oakland traded Eppard to the California Angels. He batted .341 for Edmonton, Alb., that summer to lead the Pacific Coast League. He earned a September promotion to the Angels and batted .333 in eight contests. He split 1988 between Edmonton and California, averaging .283 in 56 games with the Angels.

Released after the 1989 season, Eppard signed a minor league contract with the Toronto Blue Jays for 1990. Playing for Syracuse, N.Y., he led the International League in hitting with a .310 mark. He bowed out of the majors after six pinch-hitting appearances with Toronto. He spent 1992 with Indianapolis (American Association), hitting .267 in 97 games, and ended his playing days in 1993 with St. Paul (independent Northwest), where he hit .296 in 65 contests.

In 1994 Eppard began managing and coaching in Colorado's farm system. After eight years with the Rockies he moved to the Angels organization in 2003. In May 2012 he returned to the Major Leagues as hitting instructor for the Los Angeles Angels. He spent 2013 as hitting coach for the Angels, who released him after the season.

ERSKINE, Carl Daniel ("Oisk," "The Gentleman from Indiana")

Indiana Baseball Hall of Fame, 1979.

Born: December 13, 1926, Anderson. **Lives:** Anderson.
Height: 5'10". **Weight:** 165. **Batted:** right. **Threw:** right.
Debut: July 25, 1948. **Final Game:** June 14, 1959.
Positions, teams, years: pitcher, Brooklyn (NL) 1948–1957, Los Angeles (NL) 1958–1959.
Games: 335. **Innings pitched:** 1,718.2. **Won/Lost:** 122–78. **Earned run average:** 4.00.

Carl Erskine, one of the Brooklyn Dodgers' legendary "Boys of Summer," pitched in five World Series and threw a pair of no-hitters. He was Brooklyn's Opening Day pitcher in 1951 and 1953, 1954 and 1955.

Erskine starred in baseball and basketball at Anderson High School and joined the navy after graduation. He signed with Brooklyn in 1946 for $3,500 and began his professional career with Danville, Ill. (Three-I). Since Erskine had signed with the Dodgers while still in military service, baseball commissioner A.B. Chandler nullified the contract and declared him a free agent. The Dodgers signed Erskine for a second time, outbidding the Boston Braves with a $5,000 offer.

Erskine possessed an extraordinary fastball and had the ability to change speeds on his curve and changeup. He also had a deceptive delivery and good control. By 1948 he was pitching in Brooklyn. In his first big league start he injured his shoulder and for the rest of his career he frequently pitched in pain.

In 1949 Erskine compiled an 8–1 record, mostly as a reliever, to help Brooklyn win the NL pennant. He went 14–6 in 1952 after moving into the starting rotation. On June 19 that year he no-hit the Cubs. Chicago's only baserunner was pitcher Willard Ramsdell, who walked in the third inning.

The Dodgers won another pennant in 1952, and Erskine split two decisions in the World Series against the New York Yankees. Erskine's .769 winning percentage in 1953 led the NL and his 20–6 record helped Brooklyn to another flag. The Dodgers again faced the Yankees in the World Series, and in Game Three his 14 strikeouts set a record that stood until 1963. In 1954 he compiled an 18–15 record for the second-place Dodgers. Brooklyn won the 1955 pennant and Erskine, who went 11–8 during the season, drew one Series start against the Yanks. He failed to earn a decision, but Brooklyn won its first and only World Series title.

Erskine, who lived in the borough's Bay Ridge section, was by then one of the team's most popular players. The nickname "Oisk" stems from the Brooklynese pronunciation of his last name.

Bothered by a sore elbow in 1956, Erskine went 13–11. On May 12 he pitched a second no-hitter, this time against the arch-rival New York Giants. The Dodgers won another pennant, and lost to the Yankees once more in the Series. Erskine was the starting and losing pitcher in the fourth game.

In 1957 arm miseries limited Erskine to seven starts and a 5–3 record. He moved with the team to Los Angeles for the 1958 season and started the first game ever played at the Los Angeles Coliseum. His record for '58 was 4–4. He was 0–3 in June 1959 when he retired, just 28 days short of qualifying as a ten-year man for his pension. "When your time comes," he told *The Associated Press*, "the decision is not too hard to make. You know what's right."

From 1961 to 1973 Erskine coached the Anderson College baseball team, earning collegiate coach-of-the-year honors for 1965. He enrolled at Anderson as a 32-year-old freshman, and in 1984 the school awarded him an honorary degree. He sold insurance for several years, and in 1963 he began working for First National Bank. In 1972 Erskine became First National's executive vice president. He became its president in 1983. For a time he served as vice president of the Major League Baseball Players Alumni Association. He serves on the advisory board of the Baseball Assistance Team, a non-profit organization dedicated to helping former players through financial and medical difficulties.

The articulate Erskine did some broadcast work for ABC's Wide World of Sports as well as the Game of the Week telecast. He occasionally serves as a color commentator for Indianapolis Indians telecasts.

In 1969 the Dodgers drafted Gary Erskine, Carl's son, out of Anderson High School. After another son, Jimmy, was born with Down syndrome, Carl became involved with the Special Olympics.

In 1979 Erskine was inducted into the Indiana Baseball Hall of Fame, and in 2010 he was elected to the Northeast Indiana Baseball Association Hall of Fame. A six-foot tall bronze statue was erected in front of Anderson's Carl D. Erskine Rehabilitation and Sports Medicine Center to honor Erskine's baseball and civic achievements. Anderson's Erskine Elementary School, built on land donated by Erskine, is named for him. In Brooklyn, Erskine Street was created and named for him. Anderson High School retired the No. 17 baseball jersey Erskine wore as a prep. The Indiana Historical Society selected him as one of the state's Living Legends in 1999.

Erskine's *Tales From the Dodger Dugout* came out 2000. In 2005 he published a second book, *What I Learned From Jackie Robinson*, with Burton Rocks as co-author.

EUBANK, John Franklin ("Honest John," "The Slinger from Servia")

Born: September 9, 1872, Servia. **Died**: November 3, 1958, Bellevue, Michigan.
Height: 6'2". **Weight:** 215. **Batted:** right. **Threw:** right.
Debut: September 19, 1905. **Final game:** August 2, 1907.
Positions, teams, years: pitcher (42), outfield (2), first base (1), second base (1), Detroit (AL) 1905–1907.
Games: 47. **Innings pitched:** 233.1. **Won/Lost:** 8–13. **Earned run average:** 3.12.
At-bats: 108. **Home runs:** 0. **Average:** .204.

John Eubank began his professional baseball career in 1903 with Greenville, Miss. (Cotton States), as a 30-year-old pitcher-outfielder. A good-hitting pitcher, he spent the next two seasons at Fort Dodge (Iowa State). He went 23–9 in 1905 before joining the Detroit Tigers in September as a 33-year-old rookie.

Relying exclusively on his fastball, Eubank went 4–10 with the sixth-place Tigers in 1906. "His effectiveness was always impaired by the lack of a curve ball," reported *Sporting Life* in January 1907, "…the result being that he would mystify his opponents as a rule for five or six innings, after which a bombardment usually began."

Eubank began tinkering with a spitball, and he was 3–3 with a 2.67 ERA in 1907 when the Tigers dispatched him to Indianapolis (American Association). With Houston in 1910 the 37-year-old Eubank's .714 won-loss percentage led the Texas League. From 1911 to 1916 he played semi-pro ball, and in 1917 he was a member of the independent Goshen (Ind.) Grays.

A native of the northeastern Indiana hamlet of Servia, Eubank eventually settled in Bellevue, Mich., where he worked as a farmer and as a carpenter. He continued to pitch in Michigan semi-pro leagues until he was well past 50 years of age.

EVERITT, William Lee ("Big Bill," "Wild Bill," "Bad Bill")

Born: December 13, 1868, Fort Wayne. **Died:** January 19, 1938, Denver, Colorado.
Height: 6'0". **Weight:** 185. **Batted:** left. **Threw:** right.
Debut: April 18, 1895. **Final game:** June 24, 1901.
Positions, teams, years: first base (341), third base (310), outfield (43), second base (3), Chicago (NL) 1895–1900, Washington (AL) 1901.
Games: 698. **At-bats:** 2,842. **Home runs:** 11. **Average:** .317.

Bill Everitt starred for Chicago's National League franchise for six years. During that stretch, the team's nickname changed from the White Stockings to the Colts to the Orphans, and finally to the Cubs.

Everitt's family moved to Colorado when he was a boy and he developed his skills on Denver's sandlots. He joined San Francisco (California) in 1890 and batted .283. After stints with San Jose (California) in 1891 and 1892, Augusta, Ga. (Southern), in 1893 and Detroit (Western) in 1894, he joined Chicago in 1895 and hit .358 as a rookie.

Originally a shortstop, Everitt spent most of his first three seasons in Chicago playing third base and frequently batting in the leadoff spot. He averaged over .300 for his first five seasons.

A less-than-adequate fielder, Everitt was a fine base runner and a master of the bunt. One contemporary claimed that until he joined Chicago, big league catchers positioned themselves well behind the batter. His carefully-placed bunts forced receivers to move closer to home plate.

Everitt switched to first base in 1898, replacing the legendary Cap Anson. He was appointed team captain in 1899. He had appeared in just 23 games by May 1900, when the Cubs traded him to Kansas City (Western). He remained in Chicago, refusing to report to the minor league club.

The following year, the Western League—renamed the American League—gained Major League status and the Kansas City franchise shifted to Washington. Everitt reported for duty but was cut loose in June after batting .191 in 33 games. He finished the year with Denver, hitting .295 in 67 contests. He played for Colorado Springs (Western) in 1902 and 1903 and was out of organized ball for 1904 before returning to Denver for a final fling in 1905. In 1906 he was Denver's non-playing manager.

Everitt served as president of the Colorado Wrecking Company after leaving baseball. When he died at 69, the *Denver Post* hailed him as the "foremost player in Denver's history."

FARMER, Howard Earl ("Farm Club")

Born: January 18, 1966, Gary. **Lives:** Gary.
Height: 6'3". **Weight:** 185. **Batted:** right. **Threw:** right.
Debut: July 2, 1990. **Final Game:** October 1, 1990.
Positions, teams, years: pitcher, Montreal (NL) 1990.
Games: 6. **Innings pitched:** 23. **Won/Lost:** 0–3. **Earned run average:** 7.04.

When **Howard Farmer** started for the Montreal Expos against the Atlanta Braves in 1990, he became the first black Indiana native to pitch in the Major Leagues.

An outstanding player at Gary's Horace Mann High School, Farmer was the Toronto Blue Jays' first-round draft pick (25th overall) in 1985. He opted to attend Jackson State University instead, and in 1987 he compiled a 7–4 record with a 3.51 ERA.

Selected by the Montreal Expos in the seventh round of the 1987 draft, Farmer broke in with Jamestown, N.Y. (New York-Penn). A 12–9 record and 2.20 ERA at Jacksonville, Fla., in 1989 earned him recognition as one of the Southern League's top prospects. He pitched for Indianapolis (American Association) for all or part of four seasons, 1989 to 1992. He started the 1993 campaign with Montreal's new farm club at Ottawa, Ont. (International), before the Expos traded him to the Milwaukee Brewers organization.

Arm trouble sidelined Farmer for all of 1994. He retired in 1995 after pitching one game for Chattanooga, Tenn. (Southern). His repertoire included a fastball, slider and changeup.

Mike Farmer, Howard's younger brother, reached the majors in 1996 with the Colorado Rockies.

FARMER, Michael Anthony

Born: July 3, 1968, Gary. **Lives:** Hammond.
Height: 6'1". **Weight:** 193. **Batted:** both. **Threw:** left.
Debut: May 4, 1996. **Final game:** June 8, 1996.
Positions, teams, years: pitcher, Colorado (NL) 1996.
Games: 7. **Innings pitched:** 28. **Won/Lost:** 0–1. **Earned run average:** 7.71.

Like his older brother Howard, **Mike Farmer** reached the Major Leagues as a pitcher—but not until after switching from the outfield. A product of Roosevelt High School in Gary, Mike attended Jackson State University, compiling an 8–2 mark with a 3.43 ERA in 1988 and a 6–4, 2.63 slate in 1989, when he was the Southwestern Athletic Conference pitcher of the year.

In 1989 Farmer signed with the Philadelphia Phillies as a non-drafted free agent. He batted .268, .238 and .241 in his first three professional seasons. He made the South Atlantic League All-Star team in 1991 when his 77 RBI at Spartanburg, S.C., led all Phillies minor leaguers.

Farmer started pitching in 1992 at Clearwater (Florida State). In December 1993 the Colorado Rockies took him in the minor league draft. The following year, he underwent surgery for elbow problems. He bounced back in 1995 with a 10–5 record at New Haven, Conn. (Eastern).

During the players strike in the spring of 1995 Farmer crossed picket lines, in need of cash to pay for surgery to correct his son's clubfoot. In May 1996 he was the first replacement player to make Colorado's 25-man roster when the Rockies promoted him from Colorado Springs (Pacific Coast). Farmer spent 1997 through 1999 with Colorado Springs before leaving the U.S. to pitch for the Doosan

Bears of Korea's Dream League. In Korea he went 10–9 in 2000 and 1–2 in 2001 before retiring.

In 1996 Farmer discussed his brother Howard with *USA Today*. "I was his little brother who followed in his shadow," Mike said. "When I became a pitcher, I thought one day we would face each other. I don't know how I ended up left-handed and he was right-handed because I tried to do everything he did. But I couldn't throw right-handed for nothing."

FEHRING, William Paul ("Dutch")

Indiana Baseball Hall of Fame, 1999.
Born: May 31, 1912, Columbus. **Died:** April 13, 2006, Palo Alto, California.
Height: 6'0". **Weight:** 195. **Batted:** both. **Threw:** right.
Debut: June 25, 1934. **Final game:** June 25, 1934.
Positions, teams, years: catcher, Chicago (AL) 1934.
Games: 1. **At-bats:** 1. **Home runs:** 0. **Average:** .000.

Dutch Fehring earned his nickname when he played football at Central High School in Columbus, Ind. After he ran back a blocked punt for a 70-yard touchdown, a local sportswriter dubbed Fehring "The Flying Dutchman."

At Purdue, Fehring won a total of nine letters in baseball, basketball and football. A switch-hitting catcher, Dutch had a career .297 average. He started at left tackle for the Boilermakers from 1931 to 1933 and played on two Big Ten title teams. He roomed with John Wooden during basketball road trips, and the two remained friends for life.

After graduation in 1934 Fehring turned down several pro football offers to sign with the Chicago White Sox. He appeared in one big league game as a catcher and struck out in his only at-bat. The White Sox sent him to Dallas (Texas) and he finished the season at Longview, Texas (West Dixie).

Fehring left baseball after that season and returned to Purdue, where he coached freshman teams in three sports. From 1936 to 1942 he served as the Boilermakers' head baseball coach while working with the football squad as an assistant coach.

During World War II, Fehring served in the navy as a senior grade lieutenant. Afterwards he worked as an assistant football coach to Bud Wilkinson, first at Oklahoma and later at UCLA. It was Fehring who recommended Wooden for the Bruins coaching post.

In 1949 Stanford athletic director Everett Dean (a native Hoosier who had coached basketball and baseball at Indiana University) hired Fehring as an assistant coach in both football and baseball. He served as a football assistant for 17 years and became Stanford's head baseball coach in 1956. He helped develop future Major Leaguers Bob Boone, Frank Duffy and Don Rose. He retired in 1967 after leading Stanford to third place in the College World Series.

Fehring was Stanford's intramurals director until 1977. From 1963 to 1977 he served as president of the U.S. Baseball Federation. A member of the Stanford Athletic and American Baseball Coaches halls of fame, he was elected to the Indiana High School Basketball Hall of Fame in 1979. Twenty years later, he was inducted into the Indiana Baseball Hall of Fame. He was one of the first members of Purdue's Athletic Hall of Fame.

A longtime resident of Menlo Park, Calif., Fehring died at age 93.

FERGUSON, Cecil Benoni

Born: August 27, 1883, Ellsworth. **Died:** September 5, 1943, Montverde, Florida.
Height: 5'10". **Weight:** 165. **Batted:** right. **Threw:** right.
Debut: April 19, 1906. **Final game:** July 21, 1911.
Positions, teams, years: pitcher, New York (NL) 1906–1907, Boston (NL) 1908–1911.
Games: 142. **Innings pitched:** 698. **Won/Lost:** 29–46. **Earned run average:** 3.34.

A promising member of a New York Giants pitching staff that boasted Christy Mathewson and Joe McGinnity, **Cecil Ferguson** became a doctor after his baseball career ended prematurely.

Ferguson broke into organized ball in 1903 when Terre Haute (Central), strapped for pitchers, gave him a start. Two years later he was pitching for Louisville (American Association). Late in 1906 the Giants acquired him and he went 2–1 in 22 appearances for New York, all but one in relief.

Along with teammate and fellow Indiana

native Doc Crandall, Ferguson was an early bullpen specialist. In 1907 he went 3–1, and that December the Giants sent him to the Boston Doves in an eight-player trade. He went 12–11 for Boston in 1908, but suffered an arm injury. In 1909 he compiled a 5–23 record for a last-place team, leading the league in defeats. During the next two seasons he pitched sparingly for the Doves.

Memphis, Tenn. (Southern), purchased Ferguson's contract in July 1911, but he refused to join the club until 1912, when he posted a 9–18 record. He retired from baseball after going 1–6, 3.21 for Venice, Calif. (Pacific Coast), in 1913.

Ferguson entered the American School of Osteopathy in Kirksville, Mo., and became a physician. A sports medicine pioneer, he worked with the Brooklyn Dodgers, the University of Notre Dame and the University of Illinois. For a time, he coached the osteopathic school's baseball team.

Sporting Life described Ferguson as ambidextrous and a "clever" basketball player. In the winter of 1906–1907 he and Three-Finger Brown were teammates in a Terre Haute YMCA basketball league.

Ferguson eventually settled in Miami, Fla. He suffered a heart attack and died at age 60 while on a fishing trip near Orlando, Fla.

FINCH, Joel D.

Born: August 20, 1956, South Bend. **Lives:** Granger.
Height: 6'2". **Weight:** 175. **Batted:** right. **Threw:** right.
Debut: June 12, 1979. **Final game:** September 27, 1979.
Positions, teams, years: pitcher, Boston (AL) 1979.
Games: 15. **Innings pitched:** 57.1. **Won/Lost:** 0–3. **Earned run average:** 4.87.

Joel Finch lettered in baseball, basketball and cross country at South Bend's Washington High School and pitched his American Legion team to a 1973 state title. The following year he signed with the Boston Red Sox and went 6–3 for Elmira, N.Y. (New York-Penn). He developed into a big league prospect in 1977 with a 15–7, 3.22 season at Bristol, Conn. (Eastern).

In June 1979 Finch joined the Red Sox from Pawtucket, R.I. (International). He debuted with a five-inning, two-hit relief stint against the Kansas City Royals. Boston sent him back to the minors in August. He finished the year with a 9–1 record and a 2.63 ERA for Pawtucket and an 0–3 record with the Red Sox.

Finch suffered an arm injury and spent 1980 at Pawtucket, where he went 1–5 with a 3.54 ERA in 16 games. He retired after going 6–7, 3.74 for Pawtucket in 1981. He eventually became a sales representative for Yellow Freight. According to David Finch, his father, the "D" in Joel's name is only an initial and nothing more.

FISHER, Chauncey Burr ("Peach," "Whoa Bill," "Fish")

Born: January 8, 1872, Anderson. **Died:** April 27, 1939, Los Angeles, California.
Height: 5'11". **Weight:** 175. **Batted:** right. **Threw:** right.
Debut: September 20, 1893. **Final game:** July 6, 1901.
Positions, teams, years: pitcher, Cleveland (NL) 1893–1894, Cincinnati (NL) 1894, 1896, Brooklyn (NL) 1897, New York (NL) 1901, St. Louis (NL) 1901.
Games: 66. **Innings pitched:** 444.2. **Won/Lost:** 21–26. **Earned run average:** 5.44.

Pitcher **Chauncey Fisher** was part of Indiana's first Major League brother combination. His baseball career began in 1890 in his native Anderson (Indiana State). Late in 1893 he joined the Cleveland Spiders after compiling a 17–17 record with a 2.36 earned run average for Buffalo, N.Y. (Eastern). During the 1894 season Cleveland dealt him to Cincinnati, but before the year was out he was back in Buffalo.

Pitching for Indianapolis in 1895, Fisher topped the Western League in wins (38) and winning percentage (.818). According to *The Sporting News*, he was "undoubtedly the best pitcher in the Western League ... and had Cincinnati not had a prior claim on his services nearly every club in the National League would have gone after him."

Fisher split 1896 between Cincinnati (where he had a 10–7 record in 27 contests) and Indianapolis (going 6–3 in nine games). He joined Brooklyn for 1897 and went 9–7 in 20 contests before heading back to the minors. He spent the next two years in the Western League. He helped the Chicago White Sox win the AL pennant in 1900, one year before the league became a major circuit. He began the 1901 season with the New York Giants, who traded him to the St. Louis Cardinals in May. He left baseball after the season.

Fisher also played roller polo, serving as team captain for an Indianapolis club. He met his future wife, Essie Paine, at a Fort Wayne ballpark. Fisher operated a wrecking company in Anderson for many years. Two years before his death, he relocated to southern California.

Tom Fisher, Chauncey's younger brother, pitched for the NL's Boston Beaneaters in 1904.

FISHER, Maurice Wayne

Born: February 16, 1931, Uniondale. **Lives:** Fredericktown, Ohio.
Height: 6'5". **Weight:** 210. **Batted:** right. **Threw:** right.
Debut: April 16, 1955. **Final game:** April 16, 1955.
Positions, teams, years: pitcher, Cincinnati (NL) 1955.
Games: 1. **Innings pitched:** 2.2. **Won/Lost:** 0–0. **Earned run average:** 6.75.

Born in northeastern Indiana, **Maury Fisher** grew up near Cincinnati. As a 13-year-old sandlot player, he threw a no-hitter in the first game he pitched. Fisher lettered in baseball, basketball and football at Greenhills (Ohio) High School. During his prep career he pitched seven no-hit games and won all-state honors in football.

When Fisher graduated in 1949, ten different teams offered him contracts. He signed with the Cincinnati Reds and reported to Muncie (Ohio-Indiana). One of his wins that year was a 6–0 no-hitter against Richmond.

A freak accident prior to the 1950 season damaged Fisher's vision. "My brother and I were just fooling around with a rubber band, and he snapped it and it went into my eye," Fisher explained to Richard Tellis in *Once Around the Bases*, "It started hemorrhaging behind the eye, and they took me in and operated on it, but I lost my sight in that eye."

Fisher had a combined 2–13 record that summer for Lockport, N.Y. (PONY), and Ogden, Utah (Pioneer). In 1951 he went 7–6 at Ogden and 0–1 for Columbia, S.C. (South Atlantic). He bounced back in 1952 with a 14–10 season at Salisbury, N.C. (Inter-State) and followed with a 16–7 record for Columbia in 1953.

Fisher appeared in one game with the Reds in 1955 at Cincinnati's Crosley Field. He was the second of five pitchers in a 9–5 loss to the Milwaukee Braves. Shortly afterward, the Reds dispatched him to San Francisco (Pacific Coast). He left baseball after pitching for Sacramento, Calif. (Pacific Coast) and Amarillo, Texas (Western), in 1956.

Fisher eventually joined General Motors and worked as a senior tool designer for GM's Fisher Body Division, retiring in 1988.

FISHER, Thomas Chalmers ("Red")

Born: November 1, 1880, Anderson. **Died:** September 3, 1972, Anderson.
Height: 5'10". **Weight:** 185. **Batted:** right. **Threw:** right.
Debut: April 17, 1904. **Final game:** October 3, 1904.
Positions, teams, years: pitcher (31), outfielder (6), Boston (NL) 1904.
Games: 39. **Innings pitched:** 214. **Won/Lost:** 6–16. **Earned run average:** 4.25.
At-bats: 99. **Home runs:** 2. **Average:** .212.

Tom Fisher followed his brother Chauncey into professional baseball, breaking in with Bloomington, Ill. (Central), in 1900. Tom spent the next three seasons at Shreveport, La. (Southern Association).

A good-hitting pitcher, Fisher batted .368 in 1903 and occasionally played the outfield. His 24 victories that season earned him a promotion to the Boston Beaneaters (currently the Atlanta Braves). The chunky redhead spent 1904 in the NL and was back in the minors with Shreveport in 1905.

Fisher went 24–12 for Shreveport in 1906. On September 1 he pitched a perfect game against Montgomery, striking out 15 batters in a 4–0 win. He played for two other Southern Association teams—Mobile, Ala., in 1908 and Atlanta from 1909 to 1911—before joining Anniston, Ala. (Southeastern), in 1911. He was a player-manager at Shreveport, Mobile and Anniston.

Fisher retired after the 1911 season and returned to Anderson, where he opened a feed and coal business. He later worked for the Union Grain Company, and also served for a time as director of the Anderson Chamber of Commerce.

FITZSIMMONS, Fred Landis ("Fitz," "Fat Freddie")

Indiana Baseball Hall of Fame, 1992.
Born: July 28, 1901, Mishawaka. **Died:** November 18, 1979, Yucca Valley, California.
Height: 5'11". **Weight:** 185. **Batted:** right. **Threw:** right.
Debut: August 12, 1925. **Final game:** July 16, 1943.
Positions, teams, years: pitcher, New York (NL) 1925-1937, Brooklyn (NL) 1937-1943.
Games: 513. **Innings pitched:** 3,223.2. **Won/Lost:** 217-146. **Earned run average:** 3.51.
Manager: Philadelphia (NL) 1943-1945 (104-180).

Fred Fitzsimmons's interest in baseball was encouraged by his father, a Mishawaka police chief and a former sandlot player. During Fred's 19-year career, he won more games than several notable Hall of Fame pitchers. His Fitzsimmons began working on a knuckleball at age 15. Developing complete confidence in the pitch, he threw it with great accuracy. "The knuckleball is Freddy's chief stock in trade, along with a veiled delivery that makes him look like a whirling dervish before he sends the ball platewards," wrote Edgar Brands in a 1940 *Sporting News* article.

In 1920 Fitzsimmons made his professional debut with a 3-9 record for Muskegon, Mich. (Central). In 1922 he moved from Muskegon to Indianapolis (American Association), where he compiled a 40-31 record in all or part of four seasons.

In the summer of 1925 Fitzsimmons joined John McGraw's New York Giants. He went 6-3 that year, and in 1926 his 14 wins led the team. He never had a losing season between 1925 and 1934, and from 1928 to 1937 he and Carl Hubbell gave New York a potent righty-lefty combination. Fitzsimmons compiled a 20-9 record in 1928, and in 1930 his .731 winning percentage led the NL. He was New York's Opening Day starter in 1931. A fine fielder and fair hitter, he hit a grand slam home run in '31.

Appearing in two World Series for the Giants, Fitzsimmons was the losing pitcher in Game 3 versus the Washington Senators in 1933. He underwent arm surgery in July 1935, but by September he was pitching again. In the 1936 Series he dropped a pair of decisions—one a two-hitter—to the New York Yankees.

In June 1937 the Giants traded Fitzsimmons to the Brooklyn Dodgers. He went 16-2 for the Dodgers in 1940, topping the NL with an .889 percentage. He pitched in only 13 games for Brooklyn in 1941, when the Dodgers won their first pennant since 1920. The 40-year-old Fitzsimmons started the third game of the World Series against the New York Yankees. He pitched seven scoreless innings, but had to leave after a line drive struck his left leg.

Fitzsimmons, who also coached for the Dodgers, made one appearance in 1942. In 1943 he was 3-4 after nine appearances when he left Brooklyn in July to manage the Phillies. Philadelphia finished seventh that year and came in last in 1944. The Phils were in the basement when he resigned in late June 1945. Far from finished in baseball, he coached for the Boston Braves, Giants, Chicago Cubs and Kansas City Athletics from 1948 to 1966. In 1956 he managed Binghamton, N.Y. (Eastern).

Fitzsimmons earned his nickname by gaining 50 or more pounds over the years. He spent two years as general manager of the Brooklyn Dodgers of the All-America Football League.

Early in his career, Fitzsimmons purchased a ranch in California. He and his wife eventually moved to Yucca Valley, Calif., where he helped coach a local high school team. He died of a heart attack at age 78.

Fitzsimmons' 217 wins for the Giants and Dodgers surpass the career totals of Hall of Famers Stan Coveleski, Jesse Haines, Don Drysdale, Bob Lemon, Hal Newhouser, Dazzy Vance, Lefty Gomez, Sandy Koufax and Dizzy Dean. In Hall of Fame balloting between 1948 and 1962, however, Fitzsimmons received only 38 total votes.

The Mishawaka High School alum entered the Indiana Baseball Hall of Fame in 1992. In 2009 the baseball field at Mishawaka's Baker Park was named for him. Pete DeKever's biography, *Freddie Fitzsimmons: A Baseball Life*, was published in 2014.

FODGE, Gene Arlan ("Suds")

Born: July 9, 1931, South Bend. **Died:** October 27, 2010, Mishawaka.
Height: 6'0". **Weight:** 175. **Batted:** right. **Threw:** right.
Debut: April 20, 1958. **Final game:** July 21, 1958.

Positions, teams, years: pitcher, Chicago (NL) 1958.
Games: 16. **Innings pitched:** 39.2. **Won/Lost:** 1–1.
Earned run average: 4.76.

At South Bend Central High School, **Gene Fodge** starred in basketball and tennis and captained the baseball team. He signed with the Chicago Cubs in 1950 after graduation and entered pro baseball in 1951 with Janesville (Wisconsin State). In his debut he struck out 16 batters.

Fodge spent 1952–1953 in the U.S. Marine Corps. Stationed at California's El Toro air base, he played baseball, basketball and football. He returned to baseball in 1954 and spent two seasons pitching for Des Moines, Iowa (Western). On July 26, 1955, he tied a league record when his shutout streak reached 32 innings. He finished the year with a 16–10 record and a 2.28 ERA.

In 1956 Fodge moved up to Los Angeles of the Pacific Coast League. Bolstered by his 19 wins, the Angels gave Los Angeles its last minor league pennant. He split 1957 between three teams, Fort Worth (Texas), Portland, Ore. (Pacific Coast), and Memphis, Tenn. (Southern).

Fodge began the 1958 season with the Cubs. His lone big league victory was a complete-game 15–2 win over the Dodgers at the Coliseum. Twice that year Chicago optioned him to Fort Worth, where he went 8–3 with a 2.23 ERA.

Bothered by elbow problems in 1957, Fodge retired after the 1958 campaign. He became a salesman in South Bend and later worked at the Morris Inn, the University of Notre Dame's on-campus hotel.

A minor league teammate gave Fodge the nickname "Suds," but its origins are unclear. Some sources maintain it was due to a fondness for beer. Others claim Fodge earned it because he was frequently driven from the mound to an early shower.

FOX, Ervin ("Pete")

Indiana Baseball Hall of Fame, 1980.
Born: March 8, 1909, Evansville. **Died:** July 5, 1966, Detroit, Michigan.
Height: 5'11". **Weight:** 165. **Batted:** right. **Threw:** right.
Debut: April 12, 1933. **Final game:** September 23, 1945.
Positions, teams, years: outfield, Detroit (AL) 1933–1940, Boston (AL) 1941–1945.
Games: 1,461. **At-bats:** 5,636. **Home runs:** 65. **Average:** .298.

The Detroit Tigers' right fielder during most of the Depression years, strong-armed **Pete Fox** was a capable hitter and base runner.

The son of an Evansville fire captain, Fox attended Central High School and pitched in sandlot leagues before signing with the local Three-I League club in 1929. At Beaumont in 1932 Fox led the Texas League with a .357 average. Called "Rabbit" by Beaumont fans because of his speed, Fox's nickname evolved into "Peter Rabbit" and, eventually, "Pete."

Fox joined the Tigers in 1933 and played for pennant-winning teams in 1934, 1935 and 1940. In 1934 he set a record for the most doubles (six) in a seven-game World Series. When Detroit bested the Chicago Cubs in 1935, he batted a Series-high .385. Although Fox compiled a 29-game hitting streak in '35, his best season was 1937 when he batted .331. In 1938 his .994 fielding percentage topped AL outfielders. "He was always quiet, not a colorful personality to the fans," said Rick Ferrell, a contemporary who pitched for rival teams. "But you noticed that he always made the right play."

By 1941 Fox was a part-time player for the Red Sox, but he reclaimed a starting role in 1943 after Boston regulars like Ted Williams and Dom DiMaggio entered military service. At age 35 in 1944, Fox made the AL All-Star team for the first time. He also made a run at the batting title, finishing at .315.

The 1945 season was his last in the majors, but Fox remained in baseball. After playing in the Pacific Coast League in 1946 he managed at Pawtucket, R.I. (New England), Waterloo, Iowa (Three-I), and Hot Springs, Ark. (Cotton States). He later scouted for the Chicago White Sox.

When cataracts impaired Fox's vision in the early Fifties, he took a job with a Detroit firm owned by a boyhood friend from Evansville. He died at 57, a victim of cancer. A member of Evansville's Sports Hall of Fame, he was inducted into the Indiana Baseball Hall of Fame in 1980. His son Don pitched in the Red Sox chain in 1966. Another son, James, was an all-city football player at Evansville's Bosse High School.

FOX, Jacob Quirin

Born: July 20, 1982, Greenfield. **Lives:** Greenfield.
Height: 6'0". **Weight:** 220. **Bats:** right. **Throws:** right.
Debut: July 19, 2007.
Positions, teams, years: outfield (47), catcher (32), third base (31), first base (24), Chicago (NL) 2007, 2009, Oakland (AL) 2010, Baltimore (AL) 2010–2011.
Games: 193. **At-bats:** 489. **Home runs:** 20. **Average:** .237.

Jake Fox, who played his first big league game the day before his 25th birthday, starred in baseball, basketball and football at Cathedral High School in Indianapolis. He was the Chicago Cubs' third-round pick out of the University of Michigan in 2003, and his professional career began that summer with the Cubs' Arizona Rookie League affiliate.

Developing into a power hitter in 2006, Fox combined for 21 homers at Daytona (Florida State) and West Tenn (Southern). Promoted to the Cubs in July 2007, he debuted as a pinch-hitter at Wrigley Field against the San Francisco Giants the day Barry Bonds hit his 752nd and 753rd home runs to pull within two of Hank Aaron's career record.

Fox spent 2008 in the minors. He returned to Chicago in late May 2009 after hitting .409 with 17 homers in 45 games at Iowa (Pacific Coast). As a part-time outfielder-third baseman, he hit .269 for the Cubs with 11 home runs in 82 contests.

Chicago traded Fox to Oakland in December 2009. In June 2010 the Athletics shipped him to the Orioles. After shuttling between Baltimore and Norfolk, Va. (International) in 2011, he became a free agent and signed a minor league contract with Pittsburgh. He played for Indianapolis (International) until he was released in late June 2012. He finished the year with Scranton/Wilkes-Barre, Pa. (International), the top farm club of the Philadelphia Phillies.

Fox opened the 2013 season with the Somerset (N.J.) Patriots of the independent Atlantic League. He hit .310 with 25 homers in 96 contests and the Arizona Diamondbacks signed him to a minor league contract. A free agent again after the season, he played for Somerset and the Mexican League's Vaqueros Laguna in 2014 before returning to organized ball with Reading, Pa. (Eastern), the Phillies' Double-A farm club, where he had 22 homers and a .308 average in 78 contests. Released by Philadelphia after the season, he inked a minor league pact with the Toronto Blue Jays for 2015.

A catcher in high school, college and through his first four pro seasons, Fox began playing first base and the outfield in 2007. His wife Allison was a cross country runner at Michigan. Terry Fox, Jake's father, played baseball for Indiana State and served as Cathedral's athletic director.

FRENCH, Charles Calvin ("Frenchie")

Born: October 12, 1883, Indianapolis. **Died:** March 30, 1962, Indianapolis.
Height: 5'6". **Weight:** 140. **Batted:** left. **Threw:** right.
Debut: May 23, 1909. **Final game:** September 13, 1910.
Positions, teams, years: second base (64), shortstop (23), outfield (16), Boston (AL) 1909–1910, Chicago (AL) 1910.
Games: 105. **At-bats:** 377. **Home runs:** 0. **Average:** .207.

Infielder **Charlie French** was the leadoff hitter for the Chicago White Sox in the first game ever played at Comiskey Park.

The lifelong Indianapolis resident began his professional career in 1905 with Henderson, Ky. (Kitty). When the franchise folded in mid-July he joined the Vincennes club, but one month later the league shut down due to a Yellow Fever epidemic. As Evansville's second baseman in 1908, French helped the Evas to the Central League title. He led the league in hits (170) and batting average (.339).

French's speed and hustling play drew comparisons to another Indianapolis native, Detroit shortstop Donie Bush. A 1908 newspaper account noted that Charlie "covers a wonderful amount of ground, hits the ball well, and does many other things that a good ball player should do."

The Boston Red Sox drafted French for the 1909 campaign. He briefly held the second base job, but was sidelined by a mid-season injury. He was a utility player for Boston in 1910, and that May the Red Sox sent him to Chicago.

When the White Sox opened their new park on July 1, 1910, French was the starting second baseman and batted at the top of the order. Chicago dispatched him to Montreal (Eastern) in 1911, and he continued to play in the minor leagues until 1920. He also managed in the minors.

During his playing days, French was one of the smallest big league players. After leaving baseball, he spent over three decades working as a coffee roaster for the Kothe-Wells-Bauer Company in Indianapolis.

FREUND, Lawrence Joseph ("Lentz")

Born: July 5, 1875, Jeffersonville. **Died:** November 5, 1933, Jeffersonville.
Height: 5'10". **Weight:** 180. **Batted:** unknown. **Threw:** right.
Debut: August 2, 1896. **Final game:** August 3, 1896.
Positions, teams, years: catcher, Louisville (NL) 1896.
Games: 2. **At-bats:** 5. **Home runs:** 0. **Average:** .200.

Lentz Freund, who was from just across the Ohio River in Jeffersonville, Ind., joined Louisville in August 1896 when the Colonels needed an extra catcher.

Freund (pronounced "friend") played organized baseball for two seasons. In 1896 he caught for Hopkinsville, Ky. (independent Pennyrile), before the league disbanded and reorganized as the Kentucky-Indiana League. He played for Henderson, Ky. (Kentucky-Indiana) before heading to Louisville.

After catching two games for the Colonels, Freund was involved in an on-field controversy. During an August 9 game at Cincinnati, a row started between Louisville outfielder Fred Clarke and umpire Bud Lally. Reds management had a policy against ruffianism, and over a dozen policemen poured onto the field to get between the combatants. Freund, who wasn't in uniform, crossed the field with a bat in his hands to watch the action. Clarke and Lally were taken into custody and Freund was later arrested when the police learned his identity. All charges were eventually dropped.

Freund, who never signed a contract with Louisville, split the 1897 season between Asheville, N.C. (Southeastern), and Springfield, Ohio (Interstate). He never again played organized ball. His career ended prematurely due to what a contemporary newspaper account described as "a fondness for the pace that kills."

Freund occasionally worked as a butcher. He died of a heart attack at age 58.

FRIEND, Robert Bartmess ("Warrior," "Nervous")

Indiana Baseball Hall of Fame, 1979.
Born: November 24, 1930, Lafayette. **Lives:** Blawnox, Pennsylvania.
Height: 6'0". **Weight:** 190. **Batted:** right. **Threw:** right.
Debut: April 28, 1951. **Final game:** September 24, 1966.
Positions, teams, years: pitcher, Pittsburgh (NL) 1951–1965, New York (AL) 1966, New York (NL) 1966.
Games: 602. **Innings pitched:** 3,611. **Won/Lost:** 197–230. **Earned run average:** 3.58.

The only pitcher to win two All-Star games, **Bob Friend** spent 15 of his 16 big league seasons with Pittsburgh. He was the Pirates Opening Day starter seven times, in 1954, 1956–57–58 and 1960–61–62.

Friend holds several other unique distinctions. In 1955 he became the first to lead the league in earned run average while pitching for a last-place team. He was the winning pitcher in the last game the New York Giants played at the Polo Grounds in 1957. When the Mets played their first game there in 1962, he was Pittsburgh's starter. During an April 1963 game with Cincinnati, he surrendered the first of Pete Rose's career record 4,256 hits.

Friend came from an athletic family. His older brother, Paul, played outfield for Purdue University and was the Boilermakers' MVP in 1942. A great high school baseball and football player at West Lafayette High School, Bob also played basketball and golf.

In the fall of 1949 Friend enrolled at Purdue. He signed with the Pirates in 1950 and compiled a 12–9 record that year at Waco, Texas (Big State). One of his wins was a no-hitter against Wichita Falls. He finished the year at Indianapolis (American Association), winning two of six decisions.

The Pirates were the NL's worst team in the years following World War II, finishing higher than seventh only twice between 1946 and 1957. In 1950 Branch Rickey took over as general manager and began rushing talented young players to the Major Leagues.

Friend joined the Pirates pitching staff in 1951 with only one year of professional experience. In his first four years he won 28 games against 50 losses. Pitching for a last-place team in 1955, he went 14–9 and his 2.84 ERA led the league. "I really learned how to pitch in the Major Leagues because I only had one year in the minor leagues," he told *Sports Collectors Digest's* Paul Green.

Friend had a 2–1 record in All-Star competition. He started and won the 1956 contest and took a loss in relief in 1958. He started the first of two All-Star games in 1960 and earned the victory.

Relying on a fastball and a sinker, Friend led the NL with 22 wins in 1958. He slipped to 8–19 the following season, but his 18–12 record in 1960 helped Pittsburgh win the pennant. Although he lost his only two decisions against the New York Yankees, the Pirates won the World Series. "My first start in the second game, I pitched pretty well for four innings," he told Bill Schulman of *Yankees Magazine*, "but I was lifted for a pinch-hitter when we were behind 3-0. We went on to lose that game about 16-3. My second start, in Game 6, I just didn't pitch very well."

In 1961 Friend struggled through a 14–19 season, but in 1962 he rebounded with an 18–14 slate. His five shutouts tied for the NL lead. Prior to 1966 the Pirates traded Friend to the Yankees, and that June the Yanks sent him to the Mets. Friend had a combined 6–12 record with the two New York clubs and retired after the season.

Friend, who earned an economics degree from Purdue in 1957, was active in the fledgling players association. He was the Pirates' player representative for ten years and served as the NL player representative for five years. From 1967 to 1975 he served as controller of Pennsylvania's Allegheny County. In 1976 he joined an insurance brokerage, eventually becoming a vice president.

While the origin of his nickname "Warrior" is unclear, teammates dubbed him "Nervous" because he paced through the clubhouse prior to each start, massaging his pitching arm.

In 1979 Friend was inducted into the Indiana Baseball Hall of Fame. His son Bobby toured with the Professional Golfers Association.

FRITZ, Laurence Joseph ("Moose," "Zeb")

Born: February 14, 1949, East Chicago. **Died:** July 22, 2010, Munster.
Height: 6'2". **Weight:** 225. **Batted:** left. **Threw:** left.
Debut: May 30, 1975. **Final game:** May 30, 1975.
Positions, teams, years: pinch hitter, Philadelphia (NL) 1975.
Games: 1. **At-bats:** 1. **Home runs:** 0. **Average:** .000.

Larry Fritz's Major League career consisted of two pitches. In a 1975 game at Philadelphia against the Houston Astros, he batted for Larry Christenson, the Phillies starting pitcher. Swinging at the second pitch he saw, Fritz lined out to left field. "I knew it was an out when I hit it," he told the *Pittsburgh Post's* Gene Collier, "but I ran past first base and back to the dugout and my feet felt like they never touched the ground."

Fritz starred in baseball, football and basketball at Whiting High School. He was a member of the Whiting American Legion team that won the 1965 state title. The Detroit Tigers made him their ninth-round draft pick in 1967, but he entered Arizona State University. He played just one season for the Sun Devils.

Picked by the New York Mets in the second round of the 1969 draft, Fritz broke into pro baseball that summer as a first baseman-outfielder. In his first three seasons, he led three different leagues in homers. He had 13 home runs with a league-leading 66 RBI in 1969 at Marion, Va. (Appalachian), followed by 24 homers at Visalia (California) in 1970 and 20 for Memphis, Tenn. (Texas), in 1971. He missed the last seven weeks of the 1970 season when he went on active duty with the Indiana National Guard.

Traded to the Philadelphia organization prior to 1974, Fritz split 1975 between three teams, Reading, Pa. (Eastern), Toledo, Ohio

(International), and the Phillies. He joined Philadelphia in May, but was back in the minors by June. He spent the next two seasons with the Rieleros de Aguascalientes (Mexican). He won the league batting title in 1976 with a .355 average and hit .341 in 1977.

Forced to quit baseball by knee problems, Fritz returned to Whiting and worked as a truck driver. He retired from Metro Intermodal Trucking of Lansing, Ill., in 2004.

GAFF, Brent Allen ("Willy")

Born: October 5, 1958, Fort Wayne. **Lives:** Albion.
Height: 6'2". **Weight:** 200. **Batted:** right. **Threw:** right.
Debut: July 7, 1982. **Final game:** September 30, 1984.
Positions, teams, years: pitcher, New York (NL) 1982–1984.
Games: 58. **Innings pitched:** 126.1. **Won/Lost:** 4–5. **Earned run average:** 4.06.

As a pitcher in the New York Mets organization during the late Seventies and early Eighties, **Brent Gaff's** contemporaries included Dwight Gooden, Ron Darling, Sid Fernandez, Rick Aguilera, Walt Terrell, Roger McDowell and Randy Myers.

At Churubusco High School, Gaff played baseball, basketball, football and volleyball. After pitching the Wayne Komets to the finals of the Connie Mack Senior Division National Tournament in 1976, he enrolled at Central Arizona College.

The Mets took Gaff in the sixth round of the 1977 draft. His baseball career began a year later with Wausau, Wis. (Midwest), where he went 1–13 with a 5.77 ERA. The following year, he turned things around with a 10–5, 2.98 slate at Wausau. In 1980 he helped Jackson, Miss., win a Texas League division title.

After a brief stint at Shea Stadium in 1982, where he made five starts in seven appearances, New York converted Gaff into a reliever. Pitching for Tidewater (International) in the 1983 Triple-A World Series, he earned a save in the deciding game against Portland (Pacific Coast).

Gaff spent most of 1984 in New York and went 3–2 with one save. Near the end of the season he suffered a shoulder injury that never completely healed. He spent almost all of 1985 on the disabled list, and the Mets released him that November.

After leaving baseball, Gaff worked at a home improvement company. He was elected to the Northeast Indiana Baseball Association Hall of Fame in 2003.

GATES, Joseph Daniel ("Moose")

Born: October 3, 1954, Gary. **Died:** March 28, 2010, Gary.
Height: 5'7". **Weight:** 175. **Batted:** left. **Threw:** right.
Debut: September 12, 1978. **Final game:** June 24, 1979.
Positions, teams, years: second base (16), third base (1), Chicago (AL) 1978–1979.
Games: 24. **At-bats:** 40. **Home runs:** 0. **Average:** .175.

Stocky **Joe Gates** bore a strong resemblance to another second baseman, Hall of Famer Joe Morgan.

At Gary Roosevelt High School, Gates played baseball, basketball and ran track. After graduation in 1973 he attended Manatee Junior College in Bradenton, Fla. In 1974 he signed with Kansas City as an undrafted free agent and attended the Royals' Baseball Academy near Sarasota, Fla. He spent that summer with Kansas City's Gulf Coast League team and won the batting title with a .379 average.

In 1975 Gates stole 55 bases and scored 115 runs for Waterloo, Iowa (Midwest). With Jacksonville, Fla., in 1976 he was the Southern League player of the year. The Royals traded him to the Chicago White Sox in April 1978. That season he batted .332 for Knoxville, Tenn. (Southern), to capture another hitting crown. His 85 runs and 161 hits also topped the league. Gates played eight games with the White Sox at the end of the 1978 season and 16 more in 1979. Back in the minors in 1980, he played for Pittsburgh and Texas affiliates before retiring after 1982.

Returning to Gary, Gates coached baseball and volleyball at Wirt High School. He was back in pro baseball from 2003 to 2009 as a bench coach for the Gary SouthShore RailCats of the independent Northern League. When he died at age 55, team president and general manager Roger Wexelberg praised Gates as "the ultimate ambassador of the RailCats and of baseball in Gary."

GIBSON, Kyle Benjamin

Born: October 23, 1987, Greenfield. **Lives:** Fort Myers, Florida.
Height: 6'6". **Weight:** 220. **Bats:** right. **Throws:** right.
Debut: June 29, 2013.
Positions, teams, years: pitcher, Minnesota (AL) 2013–2014.
Games: 41. **Innings pitched:** 230.1. **Won/Lost:** 15–16. **Earned run average:** 4.92.

Kyle Gibson sat out his sophomore high school season when the IHSAA ruled him ineligible after he transferred from Indianapolis Cathedral to Greenfield-Central. He went 7–2 in his junior year and 8–6 with an 0.98 ERA as a senior. "I was really skinny and didn't really throw that hard," he told the *Minneapolis Star Tribune*. "I think senior year, I was throwing 86–91 [miles per hour], so it wasn't like I was a super prospect."

The Philadelphia Phillies selected Gibson in the 36th round of the 2006 draft. That fall he enrolled at the University of Missouri, where he developed into one of the nation's top prospects. In 2009 he went 10–3 with 123 strikeouts in 99 innings, but his stock dipped when his fastball dropped to the mid-80s in his final college start. Diagnosed with a stress fracture in his right forearm, Gibson went to the Minnesota Twins in the first round of the draft (22nd overall).

Gibson sat out the rest of the 2009 season and began his pro career in 2010 with Fort Myers (Florida State). After going 4–1, 1.87 in seven games he jumped to New Britain (Eastern) and went 7–5, 3.68 in 16 starts. By year's end he was pitching for Rochester, N.Y. (International), posting a 1.72 ERA in three starts.

Back in Rochester for 2011, Gibson was 3–8 with a 4.81 ERA at the end of July when an elbow injury ended his season. That September he underwent reconstructive surgery. He returned late in 2012, making a combined 13 appearances for the Twins' rookie team (Gulf Coast), Fort Myers and Rochester and going 0–2 with a 4.13 ERA.

After a successful showing in the Arizona Fall League, Gibson opened 2013 at Rochester. By late June he was 7–5 with a 2.92 ERA when he joined the Twins' starting rotation. In 10 starts he went 2–4 with a 6.53 ERA. He opened 2014 as Minnesota's fifth starter. In an up-and-down season, Gibson had a 22-inning scoreless streak but finished the year with a 13–12 record and a 4.47 ERA.

GICK, George Edward ("Gickie")

Born: October 18, 1915, Dunnington. **Died:** August 12, 2008, Lafayette.
Height: 6'0". **Weight:** 190. **Batted:** both. **Threw:** right.
Debut: October 3, 1937. **Final game:** April 21, 1938.
Positions, teams, years: pitcher, Chicago (AL) 1937–1938.
Games: 2. **Innings pitched:** 3. **Won/Lost:** 0–0. **Earned run average:** 0.00.

George Gick's big league career consisted of two games spread over two seasons. "He was a flamethrower," one of his contemporaries told the *Lafayette Journal and Courier*. "All the guys wanted to be George Gick. He was a big, strong, good-looking fellow, and all the girls were crazy about him."

Gick, who grew up on a farm, was a graduate of Pine Township High School in Benton County. He played high school, American Legion and semi-pro ball, and after a tryout he signed with the Chicago White Sox. Pitching for Rayne, La. (Evangeline), he went 15–10 with a league-leading 2.41 ERA. Before the season was over he made two more stops, first at Longview (East Texas), and finally at Comiskey Park in Chicago.

In his big league debut against the St. Louis Browns on October 3, 1937, Gick pitched the last two frames of a game that was called after five innings due to darkness. He picked up a save for Monty Stratton's 15th win. Stratton, the legendary White Sox ace, spent one more year with the Sox before losing a leg in an off-season hunting accident. Stratton came back to pitch in the minors, compiling a 35–21 record over five seasons. James Stewart portrayed him in the 1949 film *The Stratton Story*.

The 1938 season was also Gick's last in the majors. He pitched in one more game for Chicago before the White Sox sent him to Shreveport, La. (Texas), where he compiled a 5–8 record. Gick, who relied mostly on a fastball, developed arm trouble from overuse. He went to Spring Training with the Sox in 1939 but retired before the season started.

Gick spent time as a farmer in Tippecanoe and Benton counties, and later worked at a Lafayette aluminum plant and the State Highway Department. He retired from the animal disease diagnostic laboratories at Purdue University's Veterinary Clinic. Gick was 92 when he passed on.

GILL, Warren Darst ("Doc")

Born: December 21, 1878, Ladoga. **Died:** November 26, 1952, Laguna Beach, California.
Height: 6'1". **Weight:** 175. **Batted:** right. **Threw:** right.
Debut: August 26, 1908. **Final game:** September 29, 1908.
Positions, teams, years: first base, Pittsburgh (NL) 1908.
Games: 27. **At-bats:** 76. **Home runs:** 0. **Average:** .224.

As a 29-year-old rookie in 1908, **Doc Gill** indirectly affected the outcome of the NL pennant race.

Before starting his baseball career with Fort Scott, Kan. (Missouri Valley), in 1902, Gill earned a degree from Washington University in St. Louis. He pitched and played the outfield until 1906, when he switched to first base.

Gill opened the 1908 season with Grand Rapids, Mich. (Central). "He is big and husky and fields his position in clever style," noted the *Fort Wayne Journal Gazette*. He was batting .267 through 96 games when the Pittsburgh Pirates acquired him in late August.

Pittsburgh was in a three-team pennant scramble with the New York Giants and Chicago Cubs. In the bottom of the ninth inning in a scoreless game with the Cubs on September 4, 1908, the Pirates loaded the bases. The next batter singled and the runner from third scored. Gill, who was on first, slowed down when he saw the runner cross the plate and didn't touch second base. The Cubs tagged second, claiming Gill should be out on a force play. But the lone umpire, Hank O'Day, ruled that the run counted, giving Pittsburgh a 1–0 triumph. The ump later admitted he hadn't been watching Gill, and promised to call the play correctly the next time he saw it.

O'Day got that chance on September 23 during a Cubs-Giants contest in New York. In the bottom of the ninth, New York scored what looked like the winning run. But Giants rookie Fred Merkle failed to run to second from first on the play, and O'Day called Merkle out when Chicago's Johnny Evers tagged second base. With darkness gathering, the game ended in a tie. The contest was rescheduled for October 8 at the Polo Grounds. This time the Cubs won, taking a third consecutive pennant. "Merkle's Boner" became part of baseball lore, thanks in part to Doc Gill.

Gill opened the 1909 season with Minneapolis (American Association) and helped the Millers to pennants in 1910, 1911 and 1912. In 1911 his 55 stolen bases led the league. He went to Spring Training with the Chicago White Sox in 1910 and the Washington Senators claimed him in August 1910, but he never returned to the Major Leagues.

By 1913 Gill, a Kansas City Dental College graduate, had a practice in Los Angeles and wanted to play for a West Coast team. He opened the year with Los Angeles (Pacific Coast), but was released at the end of June after batting .183 in 20 games.

Gill later practiced in Long Beach and taught dentistry at the University of Southern California. A veteran of both the Spanish-American War and World War I, he spent the last four years of his life in Laguna Beach.

Roy Gill, Doc's younger brother, pitched in the minor leagues from 1905–1907 and 1909–1910.

GILLENWATER, Claral Lewis ("Gilly")

Born: May 20, 1900, Sims. **Died:** February 27, 1978, Bradenton, Florida.
Height: 6'0". **Weight:** 187. **Batted:** right. **Threw:** right.
Debut: August 20, 1923. **Final game:** September 8, 1923.
Positions, teams, years: pitcher, Chicago (AL) 1923.
Games: 5. **Innings pitched:** 21.1. **Won/Lost:** 1–3. **Earned run average:** 5.48.

Born in northern Indiana, pitcher **Claral Gillenwater** grew up in southern Ohio. His lone big league victory was a shutout.

In 1920 Gillenwater joined Peoria, Ill. (Three-I), and in 1921 he became the property of the San Francisco Seals (Pacific Coast). In 1922 San Francisco assigned him to Saginaw, Mich. (Michigan-Ontario), where Gillenwater pitched ineffectively, and the Seals reassigned him to Evansville (Three-I). "Failing to make good there," says a contemporary newspaper article, "the Seals sent him to Des Moines, where he again flivvered. Then Nashville, Tenn., decided to take a chance with him, but scratched him after a few ineffective attempts to win. Columbia, S.C., in the South Atlantic League, then took Gillenwater, but released him after a short trial."

Released by San Francisco in 1923, Gillenwater signed with Muskegon, Mich. (Michigan-Ontario), and promptly won 10 of 11 decisions. The Chicago White Sox acquired him in August. After one disastrous relief appearance (seven hits and five runs in two innings), he started against the Boston Red Sox on August 25th at Comiskey Park. He won 3–0, giving up four singles. It would be Gillenwater's only big league victory. He lost his next three decisions and the White Sox returned him to Muskegon.

Gillenwater continued to pitch in the minors through 1928. Over the years, various newspapers around the country reported his first name as Claude, Clyde, Claren, or some other misnomer.

After leaving baseball, Gillenwater returned to Saginaw and played for area semi-pro teams. The son of a barber who learned the trade as a youth, he opened and operated Frederick's Barber Shop in Saginaw for many years before retiring to Ruskin, Fla.

GILMORE, Leonard Preston ("Meow")

Born: November 3, 1917, Fairview Park. **Died:** February 18, 2011, Oklahoma City, Oklahoma.
Height: 6'3". **Weight:** 175. **Batted:** right. **Threw:** right.
Debut: October 1, 1944. **Final game:** October 1, 1944.
Positions, teams, years: pitcher, Pittsburgh (NL) 1944.
Games: 1. **Innings pitched:** 8. **Won/Lost:** 0–1. **Earned run average:** 7.88.

After leading the Eastern League with 21 victories in 1944, **Len Gilmore** pitched the final game of the season for the Pittsburgh Pirates.

A graduate of Clinton High School, Gilmore played for Indiana State University's freshman baseball team before signing with Refugio (Texas Valley) in 1938. He was in and out of organized baseball until 1943, when he requested a tryout at Pittsburgh's wartime Spring Training camp in Muncie. Impressed, the Pirates signed Gilmore and sent him to Albany, N.Y. (Eastern), where he compiled a 13–5 record.

Gilmore went 21–5 for Albany in 1944. The Pirates promoted him at the close of the Eastern League campaign along with teammates Al Gionfriddo, Bill Rodgers and Vic Barnhart. On the last day of the season, Pittsburgh clinched second place in the first game of a doubleheader with the Phillies. Gilmore started the nightcap and pitched seven solid innings. Rusty due to inactivity, he gave up four runs in the eighth inning of a 7–1 loss.

In 1945 the Pirates shipped Gilmore to Oakland (Pacific Coast), in 1945, where he went 14–13. Casey Stengel took over as Oakland's manager in 1946 and, said Gilmore, "If there's one man in this life I hated, it'd be Casey Stengel." The two men didn't get along, and after Gilmore lost his only start, Stengel dispatched him to Milwaukee (American Association).

From 1947 to 1949 Gilmore pitched for Oklahoma City, Okla. (Texas), compiling records of 12–10, 5–7 and 13–11. He left baseball after the 1952 season with a 128–94 record over 11 minor league seasons.

Gilmore, who made his home in Jones, Okla., spent 26 years with the Oklahoma City Fire Department. He retired in 1974 as a captain. His nickname stemmed from a California gasoline brand called Gilmore, which had a lion as its trademark.

GLENALVIN, Robert Joseph ("Glen")

Born: Edward W. Dowling, January 17, 1867, Indianapolis. **Died:** March 24, 1944, Detroit, Michigan.
Height: 5'9". **Weight:** 160. **Batted:** both. **Threw:** right.
Debut: July 12, 1890. **Final game:** September 16, 1893.
Positions, teams, years: second base, Chicago (NL) 1890, 1893.
Games: 82. **At-bats:** 311. **Home runs:** 4. **Average:** .283.

Bob Glenalvin changed his name before entering pro baseball because his minister father, Rev. William Worth Dowling, objected to his career choice. Bob reached the big leagues in the wake of a players' revolt.

Glenalvin's family moved to St. Louis when he was about 10 years old. In 1887 he broke into pro ball with Lincoln, Neb. (Western). "Always fond of baseball and athletic sports," *The Sporting Life* reported, "…Dowling began playing semi-professional, and on account of the objection of his parents he adopted the name of R.J. Glenalvin."

In 1890 the members of the Brotherhood of Baseball Players, unhappy with the reserve clause and salary limits of the two big leagues (NL and American Association) jumped their teams to create the Players' League. Chicago Colts manager Cap Anson lost several key players, including Fred Pfeffer, his regular second baseman since 1883. Glenalvin, who started the year at Wheeling, W.Va. (Tri-State), took over Pfeffer's post in mid-season and batted .268 in 66 games. When the Players' League folded prior to the 1891 season, Pfeffer came back to Chicago and reclaimed the second base post.

Glenalvin returned to the minors and spent 1891 as playing manager for Portland, Ore. (Pacific Northwestern). Portland finished first and squared off against San Jose, the California League pennant winner, for the championship of the West Coast. In the final game, Glenalvin kicked an opposing player, argued with the umpire and ordered his team off the field, resulting in a 9–0 forfeit. *The Sporting News* insisted he "can not control his temper, and it is not expected that a man this handicapped can handle a baseball team."

Yet Glenalvin continued as a player-manager with Los Angeles (California) in 1892 and 1893. He rejoined Chicago in 1894 and hit .344 in 16 games before a severe spiking ended his season, as well as his days as a Major League player. He was back in the minors in 1894, batting .305 as playing manager for Detroit (Western). He managed and played for six more minor league clubs before ending his career with St. Paul (Western) in 1899.

Glenalvin returned to St. Louis, where he worked for his father as an assistant editor for the Christian Publishing Company. He umpired in the minor leagues from 1912 to 1914 and again in 1921. Eventually he settled in Detroit, where he worked as a machine operator for the Kelsey Wheel Company.

GLENN, Harry Melville ("Husky")

Born: June 9, 1890, Shelburn. **Died:** October 12, 1918, St. Paul, Minnesota.
Height: 6'1". **Weight:** 200. **Batted:** left. **Threw:** right.
Debut: April 14, 1915. **Final game:** May 12, 1915.
Positions, teams, years: catcher, St. Louis (NL) 1915.
Games: 6. **At-bats:** 16. **Home runs:** 0. **Average:** .313.

One of the most versatile athletes to come out of western Indiana, catcher **Harry Glenn** was a victim of the 1918 Spanish influenza pandemic.

Glenn was a baseball, basketball and football star in high school and had a reputation as a good amateur boxer. He played for Shelburn's town team and spent his first pro season with Vincennes (Kitty) in 1910.

In 1911 Glenn was hitting .320 for Vincennes after 79 games when he moved on to Nashville, Tenn. (Southern Association), for three contests. He spent 1912 with Nashville, hitting .234, and rebounded in 1913 with a .330 average for Akron, Ohio (Inter-State).

Glenn joined St. Paul (American Association) in 1914. He started the 1915 season with the St. Louis Cardinals, but returned to St. Paul and batted .296 in 63 games. He quickly became one of the Saints' most popular players. He was batting .282 for St. Paul in 1917 when an injury knocked him out of the lineup. "His spirit and pep helped make the Saints a machine that threatened to run off with the pennant," noted the *St. Paul Pioneer Press*, "but in the closing weeks of the race he suffered a split finger and was forced to retire." Without Glenn, St. Paul dropped to second place behind Indianapolis.

Glenn enlisted in the army in June 1918, as World War I raged in Europe, and trained at an aviation mechanics school in St. Paul. He managed and played for the unit's baseball team, and occasionally received permission to rejoin the Saints. He averaged .283 in 50 games in what would be his final season.

That autumn Glenn came down with an apparent cold. His condition worsened, and within a few days he was dead at age 28. "He had a world of friends who mourn his death," the *Terre Haute Tribune* reported.

Glenn was engaged to a lady from Terre Haute. They had planned to marry after the war.

GOAR, Joshua Mercer ("Jot")

Born: January 31, 1870, New Lisbon. **Died:** April 4, 1947, New Castle.
Height: 5'9". **Weight:** 160. **Batted:** right. **Threw:** right.
Debut: April 18, 1896. **Final game:** May 1, 1898.
Positions, teams, years: pitcher, Pittsburgh (NL) 1896, Cincinnati (NL) 1898.
Games: 4. **Innings pitched:** 15.1. **Won/Lost:** 0–1. **Earned run average:** 15.85.

Jot Goar had two brief Major League stints. The lifelong New Lisbon resident became a local celebrity while pitching for a Cambridge City sandlot team. In an era when the curveball was still a novelty, Goar frequently staged exhibitions for curious townsfolk. He started his professional career with Muncie (Indiana State) in 1890. From 1891 to 1894 he played for independent teams, including the Carthage (Ind.) Stars.

Goar re-entered the pro ranks in 1895 with Toledo, Ohio (Western), but became disenchanted when his manager wanted him to play the outfield when he wasn't pitching. Toledo traded him to Terre Haute and he finished the year with a combined 13–19 record.

After the season, Goar signed with Connie Mack's Pittsburgh Alleghenies for 1896. He made three relief appearances for Pittsburgh and lost his only decision. He returned to the Western League, this time with Grand Rapids, Mich., and went 5–6 with a 3.06 ERA.

The Cincinnati Reds signed Goar for 1897 and assigned him to Indianapolis, his fourth Western League team. He responded with his best season, winning 25 games and posting a 1.39 ERA for the pennant-winning Hoosiers. "Jot Goar is by long odds the greatest pitcher in the Western League," Connie Mack told *The Sporting News*.

Goar joined the Reds for 1898, but illness and a wrist injury limited him to one game over the next two years. He resurfaced in 1900 with Indianapolis in the AL, a year before the league became a major circuit.

After leaving baseball, Goar's career consisted of business, farming, and employment as New Lisbon's postmaster.

GRAMAN, Alex Joseph

Born: November 17, 1977, Huntingburg. **Lives:** Carmel.
Height: 6'4". **Weight:** 210. **Batted:** left. **Threw:** left.
Debut: April 20, 2004. **Final game:** July 17, 2005.
Positions, teams, years: pitcher, New York (AL) 2004–2005.
Games: 5. **Innings pitched:** 6.1. **Won/Lost:** 0–0. **Earned run average:** 18.47.

Alex Graman had a seven-run lead before he threw his first Major League pitch. Graman (pronounced GRA-mun) attended Huntingburg's Southridge High School and Indiana State University before joining the New York Yankee organization as a third-round draft pick in 1999. That year at Staten Island, N.Y., he was the New York-Pennsylvania League's top prospect with a 6–3 record and 2.99 ERA.

Summoned from Columbus (International) by the Yankees early in the 2004 season, Graman started against the White Sox at Comiskey Park. New York scored seven runs in the top of the first inning. It was the biggest cushion afforded a pitcher making his big league debut since 1895. He lasted two and two-thirds innings in a game that was interrupted twice by rain. He pitched in one more contest before returning to the minors.

Graman spent time with Columbus and New York in 2005 before the Yankees released him in July. In August he signed with the Cincinnati Reds and went 2–1 for Louisville (International). The Reds cut him loose after the season.

In 2006 Graman signed with the Seibu Lions of Japan's Pacific League and took over as the team's closer in 2007. His 31 saves and 1.42 ERA helped Seibu to a first-place finish in 2008. The Lions bested the Yomiuri Giants in the Japan Series, with Graman earning a pair of saves. Pitching sparingly in 2009 and 2010 due to injuries, he went 2–1 with a 4.26 ERA in 29 games for the Lions in 2011.

Over six seasons in Japan, Graman went 13–18 with 52 saves and a 3.82 ERA. He signed with the Kia Tigers (Korea Baseball Organization) for 2012, but failed a physical and returned to the U.S.

GRAY, Charles A.

Born: June 1864 (exact date unknown), Indianapolis. **Died:** June 1, 1900, Indianapolis.
Height: unknown. **Weight:** unknown. **Batted:** unknown. **Threw:** unknown.
Debut: April 23, 1890. **Final game:** June 23, 1890.
Positions, teams, years: pitcher, Pittsburgh (NL) 1890.
Games: 5. **Innings pitched:** 31. **Won/Lost:** 1–4. **Earned run average:** 7.55.

Charlie Gray broke into organized baseball in 1889 as a member of the Danville, Ill., club of the short-lived Illinois-Indiana League. A year later, when a players' revolt decimated big league rosters, he pitched for one of the worst teams in history.

In 1890 members of a newly-formed union called the Brotherhood of Baseball Players jumped their NL and American Association teams to form the Players' League. The top two pitchers for the NL's Pittsburgh Alleghenies, Pud Galvin and Harry Staley, jumped to the Pittsburgh Burghers of the Players' League.

Neither club prospered. On the day of Gray's big league debut with the Alleghenies, both Pittsburgh teams played home games. Only 150 fans turned out to see the Alleghenies play, while around 500 showed up for the Burghers contest.

Gray started four games for the Alleghenies and walked 24 batters in 31 innings. In a May 24 loss at Philadelphia he issued 11 walks and threw four wild pitches. The *Chicago Tribune* reported on July 2 that Pittsburgh "has turned Pitcher Gray out on the cold world." After an unsuccessful tryout with the New York Giants he finished the year with Ottawa, Iowa (Illinois-Iowa). After that, he disappeared from organized baseball.

Gray's old team, the Alleghenies, went on to finish last with a 23–113 record. The Players' League collapsed after the 1890 season.

GROSSMAN, Harley Joseph

Born: May 5, 1930, Evansville. **Died:** September 5, 2003, Evansville.
Height: 6'0". **Weight:** 170. **Batted:** right. **Threw:** right.
Debut: April 22, 1952. **Final game:** April 22, 1952.
Positions, teams, years: pitcher, Washington (AL), 1952.
Games: 1. **Innings pitched:** 0.1. **Won/Lost:** 0–0. **Earned run average:** 54.00.

Harley Grossman, a member of Evansville's Sports Hall of Fame, pitched one-third of an inning for the Washington Senators at Fenway Park in his lone big league appearance.

Fellow Evansville resident Ivan Keuster, who managed Washington's Kitty League affiliate in Fulton, Ky., signed Grossman to a Senators' contract after his graduation from Reitz High School in 1948. "At the time Ivan signed me I had a chance to sign with a team in the Boston Braves' organization," Grossman told the *Chattanooga* (Tenn.) *Times*, "but I preferred going with Keuster to Fulton, Ky., in 1949."

Pitching for Keuster's Fulton Railroaders that year, Grossman led the Kitty League with 19 wins against 10 defeats. Back with Fulton in 1950 he went 13–8 with a 2.72 earned run average. In 1951 his 10–2 record, mostly in relief, helped Charlotte, N.C., win the Tri-State pennant.

Grossman opened the 1952 season with the Senators. On April 22 he came on in relief against the Boston Red Sox with two out in the sixth inning. He gave up a single and a home run before recording the final out. Soon afterward the Senators assigned him to Chattanooga (Southern). Bothered by elbow trouble, he quit baseball after a 4–9 record at Scranton, Pa. (Eastern) in 1953.

Grossman eventually enrolled at the University of Evansville and worked as a stockbroker and as a manager for Thompson-McKinnon Securities. Keith Grossman, one of Harley's five children, played baseball at Indiana State. Harley's daughter Kim, who once worked as Nolan Ryan's secretary, married former Major League utilityman Harry Spilman.

GROTT, Matthew Allen

Born: December 5, 1967, La Porte. **Lives:** Sun City, Arizona.
Height: 6'1". **Weight:** 210. **Batted:** left. **Threw:** left.
Debut: May 4, 1995. **Final game:** May 6, 1995.
Positions, teams, years: pitcher, Cincinnati (NL) 1995.
Games: 2. **Innings pitched:** 1.2. **Won/Lost:** 0–0. **Earned run average:** 21.60.

Matt Grott, who pitched in three different farm systems before reaching the Major Leagues, grew up in Arizona. He went to Apollo High

School in Glendale and attended Phoenix College. In 1989 he signed with Oakland as a free agent. The Athletics traded him to the Montreal Expos in 1991, and after the season the Cincinnati Reds selected him in the Triple-A Rule 5 draft.

Grott, who relied mainly on his control and a breaking pitch, worked mostly in relief during his first five professional campaigns. "I've really had to perfect the way I pitch, as opposed to a guy who had a 95-mph fastball and can throw it by people," he told *Baseball America*, "I can't do that. I have to trick people every now and then."

Grott became a starter in 1994, when his 10-3 record and league-leading 2.55 ERA helped Indianapolis win the American Association flag. He joined the Reds in May 1995 and was back in Indianapolis after two relief appearances.

After the season Grott became a minor league free agent. In 1996 he went to Spring Training with the Philadelphia Phillies and pitched for three different minor league clubs—Scranton-Wilkes Barre, Pa., (International) in the Phillies' chain, and two Baltimore Orioles affiliates, Rochester, N.Y. (International), and Bowie, Md. (Eastern).

When the year ended, Grott again became a free agent and joined with the Milwaukee Brewers. He retired after a 3-1 record with four saves in 55 games for Tucson, Ariz. (Pacific Coast) in 1997.

GRUBE, Jarrett George
Born: November 5, 1981, Fort Wayne. **Lives:** Fort Wayne.
Height: 6-4. **Weight:** 220. **Bats:** right. **Throws:** right.
Debut: May 31, 2014.
Positions, teams, years: pitcher, Los Angeles (AL) 2014.
Games: 1. **Innings pitched:** 0.2. **Won/lost:** 0-0. **Earned run average:** 13.50.

Jarrett Grube made his big league debut at the age of 32 after toiling in the minors for more than a decade.

Grube (pronounced "groob") grew up in the northeast Indiana town of Corunna and played baseball and basketball at DeKalb High School in Waterloo. He helped the Barons to conference titles in 1999 and 2000 and went 8-2 with a 1.30 ERA as a senior. His 172 career strikeouts at Vincennes University broke a school record. In two years at the University of Memphis, he had a 14-9 record with a 3.18 ERA.

The Colorado Rockies took Grube in the tenth round of the 2004 draft, and that year he joined Tri-City (Northwest). Released in 2009, he pitched for Southern Maryland (independent Atlantic) before signing with Seattle in 2010. The Mariners cut him in July 2012, and two weeks later he joined the Los Angeles Angels organization.

Grube was pitching for Salt Lake City (Pacific Coast) in 2014 when the Angels called him up at the end of May. "You try to keep that glimmer of hope alive," said Grube, who was in his eleventh professional campaign. "It's the reason you play, to get to the majors. I can't say I had given up, but there are definitely small thoughts like that. You try to ignore them."

Grube's parents, wife and mother-in-law flew from Fort Wayne to the Bay Area for his debut against the Oakland Athletics. He recorded the last two outs of an 11-3 loss, giving up a homer to Yoenis Cespedes. On June 2 the Angels optioned him to Fort Wayne, where he finished the year. He became a free agent after the season.

HANKINS, Donald Wayne
Born: February 9, 1902, Pendleton. **Died:** May 16, 1963, Winston-Salem, North Carolina.
Height: 6'3". **Weight:** 183. **Batted:** right. **Threw:** right.
Debut: April 23, 1927. **Final game:** September 3, 1927.
Positions, teams, years: pitcher, Detroit (AL) 1927.
Games: 20. **Innings pitched:** 42.2. **Won/Lost:** 2-1. **Earned run average:** 6.33.

He pitched in the majors for just one season, but **Don Hankins** was on hand for three memorable moments in big league history.

Hankins's family moved from Indiana to Brooksville, Fla.. when he was a toddler. As a boy, he suffered a broken right elbow. The injury never healed properly, and he was bothered by pain throughout his baseball career.

Joining Tampa (Florida State) in 1921, Hankins saw action in three games and split two decisions. After a 7–14 slate for Tampa in 1922, he moved to Lakeland (Florida State) in 1923 and improved to 11–5. After undistinguished seasons with Chattanooga, Tenn. (Southern), in 1924 and Reading, Pa. (International), in 1925, he joined Newark, N.J. (International), in 1926. His 16–7, 3.73 record attracted interest from the Detroit Tigers.

Hankins opened the 1927 campaign in Detroit and appeared in 20 games, all but one as a reliever. On May 31, teammate Johnny Neun executed an unassisted triple play against the visiting Cleveland Indians. In Detroit on July 8, Hankins surrendered the 27th of Babe Ruth's 60 home runs. On July 18, Hankins saw Ty Cobb, in Detroit with the Philadelphia Athletics, stroke the 4,000th hit of his career off Tigers pitcher Sam Gibson.

The Tigers sent Hankins to Toronto (International) for 1928, where he went 12–16 with a 4.02 ERA. He continued to pitch in the minors through 1931.

Hankins worked for Willson Products in Reading, Pa., and later for Allied Safety Equipment in Houston. In 1949 he moved to Winston-Salem, N.C. Eventually he became vice president of the West Hankins Realty Company in Fayetteville, N.C.

HANSKI, Donald Thomas

Born: Donald Thomas Hanyzewski, February 27, 1916, La Porte. **Died:** September 2, 1957, Worth, Illinois.
Height: 5'11". **Weight:** 180. **Batted:** left. **Threw:** left.
Debut: May 6, 1943. **Final game:** May 13, 1944.
Positions, teams, years: first base (5), pitcher (3), Chicago (AL) 1943–1944.
Games: 11. **At-Bats:** 22. **Home runs:** 0. **Average:** .227.
Innings pitched: 4. **Won/Lost:** 0–0. **Earned run average:** 9.00.

While his cousin, Ed Hanyzewski, pitched for the Cubs, **Don Hanski** was on Chicago's Southside playing for the White Sox. Hanski's and Hanyzewski's fathers were brothers. Hanski legally changed his last name, prompting *Los Angeles Times* columnist Al Wolf to write that Don "came to the rescue of headline writers by amputating a few letters."

A graduate of South Bend's Washington High School, Hanski signed with Neosho, Mo. (Arkansas-Missouri) in 1938. He never played a game for Neosho, however, and didn't return to organized ball until 1943 when he joined the White Sox.

Primarily a pitcher, Hanski also filled in at first base for Chicago. He appeared in nine games in '43 and two more in 1944 before the White Sox assigned him to Hollywood, Calif. (Pacific Coast). He finished the year with San Diego, another PCL team, compiling a 2–7 record.

Hanski entered the army in February 1945 and remained on the White Sox roster until his discharge in 1946. Chicago optioned him to Memphis, Tenn. (Southern), in April 1947, where he went 3–2 with a 4.56 ERA.

That season was Hanski's last in organized ball, but he continued to play for semi-pro teams in the Chicago area like the Cole Lenzis, Orland Park Athletic Club and the Worth (Ill.) A.C. In 1950 he managed the South squad in the Greater Chicago Semi-Pro League All-Star game. A heart condition forced him to quit in 1951. The Worth and Lenzis teams proclaimed July 19, 1951, Don Hanski Day, with the gate receipts from the game turned over to the former hurler.

Hanski, who settled in the Chicago suburb of Worth, eventually became the town's postmaster. He also headed the local volunteer fire department and served as president of local youth baseball leagues. He suffered a fatal heart attack and died in 1957 at age 41.

HANYZEWSKI, Edward Michael

Born: September 18, 1920, Union Mills. **Died:** October 8, 1991, Fargo, North Dakota.
Height: 6'1". **Weight:** 200. **Batted:** right. **Threw:** right.
Debut: May 12, 1942. **Final game:** September 26, 1946.
Positions, teams, years: pitcher, Chicago (NL) 1942–1946.
Games: 58. **Innings pitched:** 218. **Won/Lost:** 12–13. **Earned run average:** 3.30.

Ed Hanyzewski joined the Cubs pitching staff ten months after an impressive exhibition game performance against Chicago.

Hanyzewski (pronounced "Hanna-ZESS-key") lost only one game in three years at South Bend's Washington High School, where he also starred in football and basketball. In

1937 he pitched South Bend's Post 357 team to the semifinals of the American Legion national tournament.

In 1940 Hanyzewski entered the University of Notre Dame. The following summer he joined a South Bend semi-pro team called the Studebaker Athletics. On June 26, 1941, he started for the Athletics against the Cubs in an exhibition game at South Bend's Lippincott Park and struck out 14 in a 2–0 loss. The Cubs scored both runs when a Studebaker outfielder misjudged a fly ball. "I was never any better than I was that night," he told a reporter years later.

Hanyzewski returned to Notre Dame in the fall of 1941, but turned pro after getting married that November. He signed with the Cubs and started the 1942 season as the property of Chicago's Tulsa, Okla. (Texas), farm club. His work in spring training, however, earned him a berth on the Cubs Opening Day roster. The Cubs optioned him to Milwaukee (American Association) after six appearances.

Hanyzewski divided the 1943 season between Chicago and Milwaukee, posting an 8–7 record with a 2.56 earned run average for the Cubs. He saw limited action in 1944 and 1945 due to an arm injury. On May 11, 1944, while wearing a four-leaf clover under his cap, he beat the Phillies 5–3 to end a 13-game losing streak.

After three appearances in 1946, the Cubs dispatched Hanyzewski to Nashville, Tenn. (Southern). He went 1–3 there and finished the season in Tulsa, where he went 8–2. Released by the Cubs during Spring Training, he had an unsuccessful tryout with the Cleveland Indians before retiring.

Hanyzewski returned to South Bend and became a member of the police department. He rejoined the Studebaker Athletics and pitched a no-hitter against a team from Battle Creek, Mich., on August 16, 1948. After retiring from the police department in 1967, he worked as head of security for South Bend's Clay High School until 1980.

A college football referee during the fall, Hanyzewski spent his summers in Minnesota. He moved to the Pelican Rapids, Minn., after retirement.

Ed's cousin, Don Hanski, played for the White Sox in 1943–1944.

HARGAN, Steven Lowell ("Harg")
Indiana Baseball Hall of Fame, 2011.
Born: September 8, 1942, Fort Wayne. **Lives:** Palm Springs, California.
Height: 6'3". **Weight:** 170. **Batted:** right. **Threw:** right.
Debut: August 3, 1965. **Final game:** September 15, 1977.
Positions, teams, years: pitcher, Cleveland (AL) 1965–1972, Texas (AL) 1974–1976, Toronto (AL) 1977, Texas 1977, Atlanta (NL) 1977.
Games: 354. **Innings pitched:** 1,632. **Won/Lost:** 87–107. **Earned run average:** 3.92.

Elbow problems hampered **Steve Hargan** for much of his 12-year career. After lettering in baseball, basketball, football, track and cross country at Fort Wayne's South Side High School, Hargan had offers from five Major League teams. After one semester at Ball State, he signed with the Cleveland Indians for 1961 and spent his first year at Selma, Ala. (Alabama-Florida).

Hargan joined the Indians for the last two months of the 1965 season after a 13–5 record at Portland, Ore. (Pacific Coast). He developed into one of Cleveland's top starters in 1966, winning 13 games with a 2.48 ERA—third best in the AL. In 1967 he posted a 14–13 record and a 2.62 ERA, and his six shutouts tied for the AL lead. He was named to the All-Star team but didn't get to play.

Hargan's arm trouble began in 1968. Taking regular cortisone shots for pain, he slumped to 8–15 and finished the year in the bullpen. After the season he underwent surgery. His fastball had lost its zip, however, and he slipped to 5–14 in 1969. Following a brief stay in Wichita, Kan. (American Association), in 1970, Hargan rebounded with an 11–3 slate for the Indians while mixing a curve, slider and changeup in with his fastball. "I guess I learned to pitch," he told *The Sporting News.*

In 1971 Hargan was Cleveland's Opening Day starter. He was mostly ineffective, due in part to a right ankle hairline fracture. He compiled a 1–13 record with a 6.21 ERA. After disappointing seasons with Cleveland and Portland in 1972 and at Oklahoma City (American

Association) in 1973, the Indians dealt him to Texas.

Hargan rebounded in 1974 with a 12-9, 3.95 slate for the Rangers. Following two more seasons in Texas, the fledgling Toronto Blue Jays selected Hargan in the expansion draft. He opened the 1977 campaign with Toronto, but returned to Texas in a May trade. A few weeks later the Rangers shipped him to the Atlanta Braves.

Cut loose after the season, Hargan went back to the minors and worked on developing a forkball in an unsuccessful comeback attempt. A lifelong bachelor, he left baseball and made his home in Palm Springs, Calif., where he owned the Sanco pumping service.

In 2003 Hargan was voted into the Northeast Indiana Baseball Association Hall of Fame.

He was a member of the Indiana Baseball Hall of Fame's Class of 2011.

HARGRAVE, Eugene Franklin ("Bubbles")

Indiana Baseball Hall of Fame, 2005.
Born: July 15, 1892, New Haven. **Died:** February 23, 1969, Cincinnati, Ohio.
Height: 5'10". **Weight:** 174. **Batted:** right. **Threw:** right.
Debut: September 18, 1913. **Final game:** September 6, 1930.
Positions, teams, years: catcher, Chicago (NL) 1913–1915, Cincinnati (NL) 1921–1928, New York (AL) 1930.
Games: 852. **At-Bats:** 2,533. **Home runs:** 29. **Average:** .310.

Bubbles Hargrave was one of two Twentieth Century catchers who won NL batting titles. His nickname came about in part due to an ebullient personality, and also because of a tendency to stutter when he pronounced the letter "B."

A New Haven High School alum, Hargrave worked in the upholstery business as a youth. He spent his first three pro campaigns with Terre Haute (Central), batting .285 in 1911, .292 in 1912 and .309 in 1913.

At the end of the 1913 season Hargrave joined the Chicago Cubs. He played sparingly in Chicago, appearing in a total of 41 contests through 1915. The Cubs shipped him to Kansas City (American Association) for 1916, and he toiled in the minors for the next five seasons. The Cincinnati Reds acquired him after a .335 season in 1920 with St. Paul (American Association).

Hargrave batted over .300 six times in his eight seasons with Cincinnati, including six straight .300-plus seasons from 1922 to 1927. In 1926 he averaged .353, ending Rogers Hornsby's six-year reign as NL batting champ. Although he had only 326 at-bats, Hargrave appeared in 105 games, five more than the required minimum. He remained the only catcher to win the league batting title until 1938, when Cincinnati's Ernie Lombardi hit .342. Underrated defensively, Hargrave tied for the league lead in double plays in 1923.

Released by the Reds after the 1928 season, Hargrave was back in St. Paul as a player-manager for the 1929 season. At age 37, his .369 average helped the Saints to a second-place finish. In 1930, his final big league season, he joined the New York Yankees as a backup to future Hall of Famer Bill Dickey. Hargrave sat out the 1933 season and retired after spending part of 1934 as a playing manager at Cedar Rapids, Iowa (Western).

Hargrave operated restaurants in St. Paul and Cincinnati after leaving baseball. In 1940 he made Cincinnati his permanent home. He retired in 1966 as a supervisor for the William Powell Valve Company. Elected to the Reds Hall of Fame and the Northeast Indiana Baseball Association Hall of Fame in 1962, he was inducted into the Indiana Baseball Hall of Fame in 2005.

Pinky Hargrave, his younger brother, was a big league catcher from 1923 to 1933.

HARGRAVE, William McKinley ("Pinky")

Born: January 31, 1896, New Haven. **Died:** October 3, 1942, Fort Wayne.
Height: 5'8". **Weight:** 180. **Batted:** both. **Threw:** right.
Debut: May 18, 1923. **Final game:** September 23, 1933.
Positions, teams, years: catcher (442), third base (8), outfield (1), Washington (AL) 1923–1925, St. Louis (AL) 1925–1926, Detroit (AL) 1928–1930, Washington (AL) 1930–1931, Boston (NL) 1932–1933.
Games: 650. **At-Bats:** 1,601. **Home runs:** 39. **Average:** .278.

A catcher like his older brother Bubbles, **Pinky Hargrave** spent 22 years in baseball. Pinky, whose red hair led to his nickname, was named for the 25th U.S. president.

Hargrave attended New Haven High School and lived primarily in Fort Wayne, where he played sandlot ball until signing with Waterbury, Conn. (Eastern), in 1919. In 1922 he averaged .321 for New Haven, Conn. (Eastern). The Washington Senators drafted him after the season.

In 1923, his rookie year, Hargrave batted .288 in 33 games for Washington. He got into 24 contests in 1924, hitting .152 for the pennant-winning Senators. With teammate Muddy Ruel handling all the catching duties, Hargrave didn't see action during Washington's seven-game World Series triumph over the New York Giants.

In June 1925 Hargrave was part of a three-player trade between Washington and the St. Louis Browns. He platooned with Leo Dixon for the Browns in '25, batting .290. In 1926 he hit .281 while sharing catching chores with Wally Schang. St. Louis sent Hargrave to the Detroit Tigers in January 1926 as part of a seven-player deal.

Demoted to Toronto (International) for all of 1927, Hargrave returned to Detroit in 1928 as the Tigers' regular catcher and batted .274. A part-timer again in 1929, he hit .330. Washington purchased his contract in September 1930. His second tour of duty with the Senators ended in 1931 after he batted .325 in 40 games.

The Boston Braves picked up Hargrave for the waiver price in December 1931. A broken ankle sidelined him for much of 1932. He was batting .178 in 1933 when the Braves dispatched him to Albany, N.Y. (International). Hargrave's Major League career was over, but he continued to play in the minors until 1938. He was the 1934 American Association MVP when he batted .356 and helped Minneapolis to the pennant.

When his playing days ended, Hargrave returned to Fort Wayne. Working for City Utilities, he was involved in recreation programs and directed Fort Wayne's youth baseball programs. He was working at a baseball field at Dwenger Park when he suffered a heart attack and died at age 46.

Hargrave was a member of the Northeast Indiana Baseball Association Hall of Fame's Class of 1964. A right-handed batter in his first four big league seasons, he was a switch hitter from 1928 to 1932. In 1933 he was strictly a left-handed batter.

HARMON, Charles Byron ("The Glove")

Indiana Baseball Hall of Fame, 1995.
Born: April 23, 1924, Washington. **Lives:** Cincinnati, Ohio.
Height: 6'2". **Weight:** 175. **Batted:** right. **Threw:** right.
Debut: April 17, 1954. **Final game:** September 15, 1957.
Positions, teams, years: third base (112), outfield (82), first base (13), Cincinnati (NL) 1954–1956, St. Louis (NL) 1956–1957, Philadelphia (NL) 1957.
Games: 289. **At-Bats:** 592. **Home runs:** 7. **Average:** .238.

While he wasn't Cincinnati's first black player, versatile **Chuck Harmon** was the first African American to play for the Reds.

An outstanding baseball and football player at Washington High School, Harmon helped the Hatchets win state basketball titles in 1941 and 1942. As a University of Toledo freshman he sparked the Rockets to the championship game of the 1943 National Invitational Tournament. Later that year he left school to enter the navy. For a time he played on the Great Lakes Naval Station's black baseball squad. His roommate, Larry Doby, went on to integrate the AL in 1947 with the Cleveland Indians.

Discharged in 1946, Harmon returned to Toledo and earned three more letters in basketball. In the 1947–1948 and 1948–1949 seasons he was the team's second-leading scorer. He also played two more years of college baseball in 1947 and 1948. In 1947 he briefly played for the Indianapolis Clowns of the Negro American League, going by the name "Charlie Fine" to maintain his amateur status.

In 1947 Harmon signed with the St. Louis Browns and batted .270 in 54 games for Gloversville-Johnstown, N.Y. (Canadian-American). Out of organized ball in 1948, he played for the independent Fort Wayne General Electric team. In 1949 he rejoined Gloversville-Johnstown and later that season shifted to Olean, N.Y. (PONY), where he hit .351 in 31 contests.

Harmon continued to pursue a two-sport career. In 1950 he had an unsuccessful tryout with the Boston Celtics of the National Basketball Association. During the 1951–1952 season, he became one of the first black coaches for an integrated pro hoops team when he coached and played for the Utica (N.Y.) Pros of the American Basketball League.

From 1950 to 1953 Harmon put together four consecutive .300-plus seasons in the minors. He batted .375 in 1951 for pennant-winning Olean with a league-leading 143 RBI. The Cincinnati Reds acquired him in 1953, and he batted .311 for Tulsa, Okla. (Texas), where he was the first black player in franchise history.

In 1954 Harmon joined the Reds as a corner infielder. When he pinch-hit on Opening Day, he became the first African American to play for the Reds. The previous batter, pinch-hitter Nino Escalera, was Cincinnati's first black player, but Escalera was a native of Puerto Rico. Harmon downplayed his role as a pioneer. "I was just interested in making the team," he said years later.

Harmon remained with the Reds as a backup at first, third and the outfield until 1956, when he was traded to St. Louis. In 1957 the Cardinals dealt him to the Philadelphia Phillies. A year later he returned to the minor leagues, and his .310 average in 1959 helped Salt Lake City to its first Pacific Coast League title. He finished his career with Hawaii (Pacific Coast) in 1961.

Making his home in Indianapolis, Harmon operated a service station until 1969. In 1970 he moved to Cincinnati, where worked as director of recreation for a Job Corps center. He joined MacGregor Athletic Products in 1972 as national baseball promotions manager. "My job was to go around and scout the minor leagues and find out who were the good young ballplayers in each organization," he told *Sports Collectors Digest*. He later served as deputy clerk and administrative assistant for the Ohio First District Court of Appeals. He also worked as a part-time scout for the Indiana Pacers of the American Basketball Association in the early 1970s.

Harmon was elected to the Indiana Basketball Hall of Fame in 1989 and in 1995 he entered the Indiana Baseball Hall of Fame. He is also a member of the University of Toledo Athletic Hall of Fame. Harmon Field, a Little League diamond in his native Washington, is named for him. His biography, *First Black Red* by Marty Ford Pieratt, came out in 2011.

As a big leaguer, Harmon had three different gloves—one each for the outfield, first base and third base—which led to his nickname.

HARTLEY, Grover Allen ("Slick")

Born: July 2, 1888, Osgood. **Died:** October 19, 1964, Daytona Beach, Florida.
Height: 5'11". **Weight:** 175. **Batted:** right. **Threw:** right.
Debut: May 13, 1911. **Final game:** September 30, 1934.
Positions, teams, years: catcher (435), first base (19), second base (13), third base (4), outfield (2), shortstop (1), New York (NL) 1911–1913, St. Louis (Federal League) 1914–1915, St. Louis (AL) 1916–1917, New York (NL) 1924–1926, Boston (AL) 1927, Cleveland (AL), 1929–1930, St. Louis (AL) 1934.
Games: 569. **At-Bats:** 1,319. **Home runs:** 3. **Average:** .268.

Grover Hartley was named for U.S. President Grover Cleveland and Allen G. Thurman, Cleveland's running mate in his unsuccessful bid for reelection in 1888. He caught for five teams in three Major Leagues during a 14-year big-league career.

Hartley played shortstop at Osgood High School as well as for sandlot and semi-pro teams. After reading a newspaper article that said catching was the quickest route to the bigs leagues, he switched positions. He made his pro debut in 1909 with Battle Creek (Southern Michigan Association), but was released after breaking a finger in his second game.

In 1910 Hartley joined Decatur, Ill. (Northern Association), and a year later he was a member of the New York Giants. After backing up Chief Meyers and Art Wilson for three seasons, he was traded to Cincinnati for 1914.

Before the season began, Hartley got into a contract dispute with Reds owner Garry Herrmann and jumped to the St. Louis Terriers of the upstart Federal League. In his two years with the Terriers he batted .288 and .274. He caught in 113 games in 1915, the only time in his career that he was behind the plate in a hundred or more contests.

When the Federal League failed after the 1915 season, Hartley remained in St. Louis as a member of the Browns. On September 7, 1915, he was behind the plate for Dave Davenport's no-hitter against the Cubs. In a game with the Yankees on September 19, 1916, he managed an unassisted double play.

Hartley returned to the minors in 1918 as a player-manager for Columbus, Ohio (American Association). He spent seven years with Columbus and had a career-high .351 average in 1920.

In 1924 Giants manager John McGraw brought Hartley back to the Polo Grounds. He remained with New York until 1926, when he moved on to Indianapolis (American Association). In 1927 he was back in the majors, this time with the Boston Red Sox. He batted .275 at the age of 39, and after the season he went to Cleveland in a waiver deal. The Indians wanted him as a coach, and he saw no action in 1928. In 1929 he played in 24 games.

Hartley appeared in his last big league contest in 1930, going 3-for-4. At 46, he was the oldest position player to start a Major League contest—a record that stood until 2004, when Julio Franco started a game at first base for the Atlanta Braves. Hartley was also the last active player from the Federal League.

Returning to Columbus after retiring, Hartley became a salesman. He was soon back in baseball, coaching for the Pittsburgh Pirates (1931–1933), Browns (1934–1936) and later the Giants (1946). He managed in the minors for years and settled in Daytona Beach, Fla., in 1947 after serving as skipper of the local Florida State League club.

Despite playing for four pennant-winning Giants teams (1911–1912–1913, 1924), Hartley never appeared in a World Series game. A music lover, he played the mandolin, guitar and violin. His nickname stemmed from his shrewd selection of pitches while behind the plate.

HAWKINS, LaTroy ("Satch")

Born: December 21, 1972, Gary. **Lives:** Prosper, Texas.
Height: 6'5". **Weight:** 220. **Bats:** right. **Throws:** right.
Debut: April 29, 1995.
Positions, teams, years: pitcher, Minnesota (AL) 1995–2003, Chicago (NL) 2004–2005, San Francisco (NL) 2005, Baltimore (AL) 2006, Colorado (NL) 2007, New York (AL) 2008, Houston (NL) 2008–2009, Milwaukee (NL) 2010–2011, Los Angeles (AL) 2012, New York (NL) 2013, Colorado (NL) 2014.
Games: 1,000. **Innings pitched:** 1,428.2. **Won/Lost:** 72-93. **Earned run average:** 4.33.

A baseball and basketball standout at Gary West High School, **LaTroy Hawkins'** chief rival was Gary Roosevelt's Glenn Robinson, a future NBA star. "I loved basketball," Hawkins told *Elkhart Truth* sportswriter Steve Krah. "I wasn't working toward being a Major League ballplayer at all."

Nevertheless, Hawkins turned down a basketball scholarship offer from Indiana State University to play professional baseball. A seventh-round draft pick of the Minnesota Twins in 1991, he was the Midwest League's pitcher-of-the-year in 1993, going 15–5 for Fort Wayne with a 2.06 ERA and 179 strikeouts. In 1994 he vaulted from the Class-A ranks to the Triple-A level with a combined 18–6 record for three teams.

Hawkins debuted with the Twins in 1995 as a starter. Some 35 family members made the trip from Gary to Minneapolis when he pitched his first game at the Metrodome. On May 17, 1998, he was the starting pitcher when David Wells of the Yankees threw a perfect game against the Twins.

After going 10–14 with a 6.66 ERA in 1999, Hawkins switched to the bullpen. He had 14 saves in 2000 and 28 in 2001. Moving to a setup role, he helped Minnesota to division titles in 2002 and 2003. He became a free agent prior to 2004 and signed with the Chicago Cubs. He struggled as a closer in Chicago, and in May 2005 the Cubs traded him to the San Francisco Giants. Dealt to Baltimore prior to

2006, he joined Colorado for 2007 and made two appearances for the Rockies in that year's World Series.

The Yankees signed Hawkins as a free agent for 2008, and on July 31 New York swapped him to Houston. In 2009 he pitched for Team USA in the World Baseball Classic. A free agent again after the season, he signed a two-year pact with Milwaukee and pitched for the Brewers in 2010 and 2011. A free agent once more after the season, he joined the Los Angeles Angels for 2012.

Hawkins signed with the New York Mets for 2013, and at age 40 he was considering retirement. But after going 3–2, 2.93, and earning his 100th career save, he came back in 2014 for a second tour of duty with Colorado. "This will be my 20th season; I've played for 10 teams in 44 ballparks," he told *Sports Illustrated*. As the Rockies's closer, he had 23 saves with a 4–3 mark and a 3.31 ERA and made his 1,000th career appearance.

A loose, live arm, reminiscent of Satchel Paige's, earned Hawkins his nickname. He has a pit bull tattoo on his left arm with the inscription "Top Dog." To help Little League baseball in Gary, he paid for uniforms, insurance and a riding lawnmower. For Friday home games at US Steelyard, home of the Gary Southshore RailCats (independent American Association), he provides 500 free tickets to youth groups. The right field bleacher area at the ballpark is called the "Hawk's Nest" in his honor. "People talk all the time about wanting to give back, but this guy does it," RailCats assistant general manager Kevin Spudic told *USA Today Sports Weekly*.

HEILMAN, Aaron Michael

Born: November 12, 1978, Logansport. **Lives:** Chicago, Illinois.
Height: 6'5". **Weight:** 230. **Batted:** right. **Threw:** right.
Debut: June 26, 2003. **Final game:** July 15, 2011.
Positions, teams, years: pitcher, New York (NL) 2003–2008, Chicago (NL) 2009, Arizona (NL) 2010–2011.
Games: 477. **Innings pitched:** 630. **Won/Lost:** 35–46. **Earned run average:** 4.40.

Aaron Heilman pitched Logansport High School to the semifinal round of the 1996 IHSAA tournament as a junior. In his senior year he was Indiana's top prep player. The Yankees selected him in the 55th round of the 1997 draft, but he decided to attend the University of Notre Dame.

In 1999 Heilman pitched for Team USA, competing in 14 cities in ten states as well as Japan. He was a first-round draft pick of the Minnesota Twins in 2000, but returned to Notre Dame for his senior year. After a 15–0 season with the Fighting Irish, the New York Mets made him the 18th overall selection in the 2001 draft. His pro career began that year with St. Lucie (Florida State).

Heilman joined the Mets in 2003 and went 3–10 in his first two seasons. Despite a one-hit shutout against the Florida Marlins in April 2005, the Mets switched him to the bullpen. "Starting has always been my first love," he told MLB.com. "You know when you're going to pitch, so you can prepare and have a weekly routine. Relieving is great because you don't have to wait five days if you have a bad outing, but at the same time, you never know, so you're on call pretty much every day."

In 2005 Heilman compiled a 5–3 record with a 3.17 ERA, mostly in middle relief. He took the loss in Game 7 of the 2006 NLCS against St. Louis. He continued as a setup man for New York in 2007 and 2008.

The Mets sent Heilman to Seattle in December 2008 as part of a three-team, 11-player trade that also involved the Cleveland Indians. In January 2009 the Mariners shipped him to the Chicago Cubs, where he went 4–4 with a 4.11 ERA. The Cubs dealt him to Arizona for 2010, where he went 5–8, 4.50 and finished the season as the Diamondbacks' closer.

Released by Arizona in July 2011, Heilman pitched in the International League for Lehigh Valley (a Philadelphia Phillies affiliate) and Indianapolis (a Pittsburgh Pirates farm club). After spending 2012 at Round Rock, Texas (Pacific Coast), in the Texas Rangers' organization, he retired from baseball.

In his book *Notre Dame Baseball Greats*, Cappy Gagnon wrote that Heilman would be "the consensus choice as the starting pitcher" on the all-time Fighting Irish team.

Heilman has a degree in management information systems. His father, Joe Heilman, ran track at Indiana State. A sister, Michelle, played softball for St. Joseph's College.

HEINZMAN, John Peter

Born: September 27, 1863, New Albany. **Died:** November 10, 1914, Louisville, Kentucky.
Height: unknown. **Weight:** unknown. **Batted:** right. **Threw:** right.
Debut: October 2, 1886. **Final game:** October 2, 1886.
Positions, teams, years: first base, Louisville (American Association) 1886.
Games: 1. **At-Bats:** 5. **Home runs:** 0. **Average:** .000.

Jack Heinzman, who pitched, played first base and the outfield in the minor leagues, was the son of a Kentucky baseball pioneer. His father, John Heinzman, organized a top amateur club in Louisville and was once a teammate of the legendary Pete Browning.

In his first pro season, 1884, Heinzman batted .288 in 19 games at Harrisburg, Pa. (Eastern). He hit .244 in 1885 for Macon, Ga. (Southern). He was playing for Macon in 1886 when the Southern League ceased operations on September 4 due to an earthquake near Charleston, S.C.

Heinzman returned to Louisville and joined the semi-pro J.A. Etheridge club, which defeated the big-league Louisville Colonels of the American Association in an exhibition game on October 1, 1886. The following day, with four players sidelined by injury, the Colonels borrowed Heinzman for a regular-season contest with the Baltimore Orioles. With only 500 fans on hand due to chilly weather, he played first base and went 0-for-5 in Louisville's 7–3 triumph. It was his only big league appearance.

After the 1889 season Heinzman left organized baseball and returned to Louisville. He managed and played for semi-pro teams while working as a stationkeeper at Louisville's Central Police Station. For two years he served as treasurer of Louisville's police union. He continued to play for local teams until he was past 40 years of age.

In February 1914 Heinzman suffered several broken ribs in a fall. He died from complications at the age of 51.

HENDRICKSON, Donald William ("Rubber-Arm Don," "Blackman," "The Van Dyke Spinach Man")

Born: July 14, 1913, Kewanna. **Died:** January 19, 1977, Norfolk, Virginia.
Height: 6'2". **Weight:** 204. **Batted:** right. **Threw:** right.
Debut: July 4, 1945. **Final game:** April 24, 1946.
Positions, teams, years: pitcher, Boston (NL) 1945–1946.
Games: 39. **Innings pitched:** 75.1. **Won/Lost:** 4–9. **Earned run average:** 4.90.

Before signing to play in the New York Yankees organization, **Don Hendrickson** pitched for an offshoot of the House of David baseball team.

After graduation from South Bend Central High School, Hendrickson entered Ball State University. He left after one semester to play for the City of David, a barnstorming team whose players wore full beards.

In the winter of 1935–1936, Hendrickson and his teammates went on a 21-week tour of the Philippines. He once estimated that during a single season he played 250 games and traveled 80,000 miles by bus. "If you want to see the country," he said, "spend a season playing with the House of David."

The Yanks signed Hendrickson for 1937, and that year he went 11–10 with a 3.53 ERA for Akron, Ohio (New York-Pennsylvania). In 1938 he won 21 games for Norfolk, Va. (Piedmont). Sidelined for much of 1939 by a broken leg, he joined Kansas City (American Association) in 1940 and went 16–7. Midway through 1944 the Blues traded him to the Milwaukee Brewers, another American Association club.

The Boston Braves acquired Hendrickson in July 1945. He went 4–8 for the Braves with a 4.93 ERA in 37 outings, all but one as a reliever. After appearing in two games for the Braves in 1946, he returned to Kansas City. He retired after the 1947 season and returned to South Bend, where he operated a restaurant and saloon until 1970.

Hendrickson's various nicknames refer to his durability, his dark complexion and a resemblance to a bearded character in a vegetable advertisement. He spent the last year of his life living with a daughter in Norfolk.

HENLINE, Walter John ("Butch")

Born: December 20, 1894, Fort Wayne. **Died:** October 9, 1957, Sarasota, Florida.
Height: 5'10". **Weight:** 175. **Batted:** right. **Threw:** right.
Debut: April 13, 1921. **Final game:** July 18, 1931.
Positions, teams, years: catcher (608), outfield (6), first base (4), New York (NL) 1921, Philadelphia (NL) 1921–1926, Brooklyn (NL) 1927–1929, Chicago (AL) 1930–1931.
Games: 740. **At-Bats:** 2,101. **Home runs:** 40. **Average:** .291.

Butch Henline, who caught and umpired in the Major Leagues, was the first Twentieth Century NL player to hit three home runs in one game.

A weaver in his youth, Henline was a sandlot baseball star in the Fort Wayne area. His work with a Cleveland semi-pro squad earned him a contract with Indianapolis (American Association) in 1918. He entered the army before ever playing a game. Discharged in 1919, he split the season between Indianapolis and Bloomington, Ill. (Three-I).

In 1921 Henline went from Indianapolis to the New York Giants. After one at-bat, the Giants traded him to the Phillies. Philadelphia fans criticized the deal, which sent popular outfielder Irish Meusel to New York for Henline and two other players. Henline proved to be a fine acquisition for the Phils, however, averaging .304 from 1921 to 1926. As a rookie in 1921, his .983 fielding percentage topped NL catchers.

Henline's three-homer game took place September 15, 1922, against the St. Louis Cardinals. He became the first NL batter to accomplish the feat since 1896, when Ed Delahanty of the Phillies belted four homers in a single game. In 1923 Henline batted a career-high .324. Philadelphia sent him to Brooklyn prior to 1927, and he spent three years with the Dodgers as a part-timer.

Henline began the 1930 campaign at Toledo, Ohio (American Association), but joined the Chicago White Sox later that summer. Early in 1931 the Sox returned him to Toledo. He played in the minors until 1936, and then went into the motel business in Sarasota, Fla.

While Henline was playing for Brooklyn, Bill Klem (an umpire who would enter the Hall of Fame in 1953) suggested he would be a good ump. "I went home to Sarasota Fla., that season and worked a couple of softball games," Henline told the *Pittsburgh Press* in 1946. "Then I took on a few baseball games."

With help from Klem, Henline landed an umpiring job in the Southeastern League in 1939. He worked in the International League from 1940 through 1944 and joined the NL staff in 1945. In 1947 he was part of the umpiring crew for the All-Star game at Chicago's Wrigley Field. He left the NL after 1948 and spent six years as supervisor of umpires for the Florida International League.

Henline died at 62 after a seven-month battle with cancer. He is a member of the Northeast Indiana Baseball Association Hall of Fame's Class of 1964.

HENNING, Ernest Herman ("Pete")

Born: December 28, 1887, Crown Point. **Died:** November 4, 1939, Dyer.
Height: 5'11". **Weight:** 185. **Batted:** right. **Threw:** right.
Debut: April 17, 1914. **Final game:** October 3, 1915.
Positions, teams, years: pitcher, Kansas City (Federal League) 1914–1915.
Games: 68. **Innings pitched:** 345. **Won/Lost:** 14–25. **Earned run average:** 3.83.

The son of German immigrants, **Pete Henning** spent most of his professional career pitching for major and minor league teams in Kansas City.

Henning progressed from Crown Point sandlot teams to semi-pro clubs in Indiana, Michigan and Wisconsin. In 1913 he joined Covington, Ky., of the Federal League, which moved to Kansas City in mid-June. His 18 wins topped the circuit.

When the FL became a major circuit in 1914, Henning posted a 5–10 record. In 1915 he went 9–15 with a 3.17 ERA. The FL folded after that season, and in 1916 he spent time with Kansas City (American Association) and Topeka, Kan. (Western).

Henning served in the army during World War I and was discharged in 1919 as a corporal. He pitched for Kansas City before and after the war, and then left baseball permanently.

Eventually he went to work for the Crown Point Telephone Company.

Returning home from a trip to the Calumet district one early morning, he stopped to push a stalled car on the Lincoln Highway east of Dyer in northwestern Indiana. Another vehicle came up from behind and struck Henning, who died shortly afterwards. He was 51 years old.

HERMAN, William Jennings Bryan ("Owl Eyes," "Banjo Eyes," "Old Popeyes")

National Baseball Hall of Fame, 1975. **Indiana Baseball Hall of Fame, 1979.**
Born: July 7, 1909, New Albany. **Died:** September 5, 1992, West Palm Beach, Florida.
Height: 5'11". **Weight:** 180. **Batted:** right. **Threw:** right.
Debut: August 29, 1931. **Final game:** August 1, 1947.
Positions, teams, years: second base (1,813), third base (71), first base (27), Chicago (NL) 1931–1941, Brooklyn (NL) 1941–1943, 1946, Boston (NL) 1946, Pittsburgh (NL) 1947.
Games: 1,922. **At-Bats:** 7,707. **Home runs:** 47. **Average:** .304.
Manager: Pittsburgh (NL) 1947, Boston (AL) 1964–1966 (189–274).

An adroit defensive player and an excellent hit-and-run man, **Billy Herman** was the NL's premier second baseman during the Thirties and early Forties. He spent 50 years in baseball as a player, manager, coach and scout. The legendary Casey Stengel, a shrewd judge of baseball talent, called Herman "one of the two or three smartest players ever to come into the National League."

Born on a farm, Herman was named for three-time Democratic presidential candidate William Jennings Bryan. At New Albany High School, Billy was a steady, if unspectacular, pitcher-infielder. He developed into a prospect while playing sandlot ball in the Louisville area.

The Louisville Colonels (American Association) signed Herman in 1928 and assigned him to Vicksburg, Miss. (Cotton States), where he batted .332. He hit over .300 at each minor league stop. Despite a .350 season at Louisville in 1931, New York Giants manager John McGraw rejected Herman as "too frail." In late August '31 the Chicago Cubs acquired Billy as the heir apparent to second baseman Rogers Hornsby, another future Hall of Famer.

An ideal number-two hitter, Herman batted over .300 eight times in a 15-year career and helped the Cubs to pennants in 1932, 1935 and 1938. In 1935 his 227 hits and 57 doubles led the NL. Contemporary accounts said he covered second base "like a blanket." He would eventually tie a record by leading the NL in putouts for seven years. In ten All-Star games he batted .433.

Traded to Brooklyn in May 1941, Herman helped the Dodgers to their first pennant in 21 years. After batting .256 in 1942, he rebounded with a .330 season in 1943. He spent the next two seasons in the navy. In 1945 he managed the NL team in the Navy World Series on Oahu Island.

When Herman returned to baseball in 1946 the Dodgers traded him to the Boston Braves. In 1947 the Braves dealt him to Pittsburgh, where he became the Pirates' player-manager. Pittsburgh finished in a tie for seventh place, and he was fired before the final game of the season.

Back in the minors for 1948, Herman was a player-coach for Minneapolis (American Association) and batted .452 in ten games. He took over as manager before the season ended. His last year as a player was in 1950, when he batted .307 in 71 games for Oakland (Pacific Coast) at age 41.

Herman managed Richmond, Va. (Piedmont), in 1951 before returning to the majors as a coach with Brooklyn (1952–1957) and the Milwaukee Braves (1958–1959). During that eight-year stretch, he went to five World Series (1952, '53, '55, '57 and '58).

From 1960 to 1964 Herman was a coach for the Red Sox, and in October '64 he took over as manager. Boston finished ninth in 1965 and 1966, and late in the '66 campaign he was fired. "Nothing against Billy Herman," Sox pitcher Dennis Bennett told Peter Golenbock, author of *Fenway: An Unexpurgated History of the Boston Red Sox*. "I thought he was a fine manager, but he was just a nice guy in the wrong situation, and most of the players took advantage of the fact."

After a year as coach for the California Angels in 1967, Herman managed Bradenton, Fla. (Gulf Coast Rookie), in 1968, and in 1969 he moved on to Tri-City (Northwest). He worked in player development for the Oakland Athletics before returning to the big leagues as a San Diego Padres coach from 1978 to 1979.

Prominent brown eyes led to Herman's nicknames. He was a member of the Baseball Hall of Fame's Class of 1975. In 1979 he was inducted into the Indiana Baseball Hall of Fame.

An excellent golfer, Herman moved to Florida in 1968. His son, Billy Jr., played briefly in the minors. Herman's granddaughter Cheri is the wife of Mitch Daniels, Indiana's governor from 2005 to 2013.

HERRMANN, Martin John ("Lefty")

Born: January 10, 1893, Oldenburg. **Died:** September 11, 1956, Cincinnati, Ohio.
Height: 5'10". **Weight:** 150. **Batted:** left. **Threw:** left.
Debut: July 10, 1918. **Final game:** July 10, 1918.
Positions, teams, years: pitcher, Brooklyn (NL) 1918.
Games: 1. **Inning Pitched:** 1. **Won/Lost:** 0–0. **Earned run average:** 0.00.

As more and more of his players—15 by season's end—left in 1918 to serve in the armed forces, Brooklyn Robins manager Wilbert Robinson began casting about for pitching help. Perhaps it was Robinson's desperation that made **Marty Herrmann** a big leaguer for one game.

The U.S. had been at war with Germany since April 1917, but it wasn't until June of the following year that Provost Marshal General Enoch Crowder issued a "work or fight" order. Crowder's decree drove many players into military service or defense-related work. Before the season was over, nine Brooklyn pitchers would be in uniform.

With a doubleheader scheduled in Cincinnati for July 10, Robinson recruited Herrmann, a local sandlot hurler. With the Reds on top by 7–0 in the eighth inning of the first game, Herrmann replaced Brooklyn starter Jack Coombs and pitched a hitless frame, allowing one walk.

By the end of the second game (a 5–0 Cincinnati triumph) Herrmann was an ex–Major Leaguer. He never pitched in another professional contest and spent the rest of his life in Cincinnati, working as a plumber.

Marty's grandson, Ed Herrmann, caught for five Major League teams from 1967 to 1978.

HICKS, James Edward

Born: May 18, 1940, East Chicago. **Lives:** Houston, Texas.
Height: 6'3". **Weight:** 205. **Batted:** right. **Threw:** right.
Debut: September 19, 1964. **Final game:** April 20, 1970.
Positions, teams, years: outfield (40), first base (10), Chicago (AL) 1964–1966, St. Louis (NL) 1969, California (AL) 1969–1970.
Games: 93. **At-Bats:** 141. **Home runs:** 5. **Average:** .163.

The son of a steel mill foreman, outfielder-first baseman **Jim Hicks** was the first Indiana native to play professional baseball in Japan.

Hicks starred in baseball, basketball and football at Gary Roosevelt High School. He earned a football scholarship to the University of Illinois, but left in 1959 to sign with the Chicago White Sox. He broke into pro ball with a .318 average for Holdrege (Nebraska State) in '59. He progressed through the Chicago farm system and spent most of the 1964 season at Indianapolis (American Association) before joining the White Sox at the tail end of the year.

For the next three seasons, Hicks shuttled between Indianapolis and Chicago. In 1967 he won team MVP honors at Indianapolis. That October, the White Sox peddled him to the St. Louis Cardinals. Despite spending part of 1968 on active duty with the Army Reserves, Hicks turned in an outstanding year at Tulsa, Okla. (Pacific Coast). He slugged 23 home runs with a league-leading .366 average, and Tulsa finished the season with the PCL's best record. In the playoffs, Tulsa defeated Spokane four games to one, and Hicks was named league MVP.

The Cardinals traded Hicks to the California Angels in May 1969. Except for four games with the Angels in 1970, he spent three consecutive seasons with the PCL's Hawaii Islanders where he batted .309, .330 and .326. Due to a knee injury in 1970, he appeared in just 86 games for Hawaii. In 1973 he signed with the Hiroshima Carp of Japan's Central

League. He spent two years in Japan, averaging .250 in 1973 and .242 in 1974.

While still playing baseball, Hicks earned a business degree from Indiana University's Gary branch. After returning from Japan he settled in Houston, where he worked as a supervisor for Continental Airlines.

HILDEBRAND, Oral Clyde ("Hildy")

Born: April 7, 1907, Indianapolis. **Died:** September 8, 1977, Southport.
Height: 6'3". **Weight:** 175. **Batted:** right. **Threw:** right.
Debut: September 8, 1931. **Final game:** July 28, 1940.
Positions, teams, years: pitcher, Cleveland (AL) 1931–1936, St. Louis (AL) 1937–1938, New York (AL) 1939–1940.
Games: 258. **Innings pitched:** 1,430.2. **Won/Lost:** 83–78. **Earned run average:** 4.35.

The first Indiana-born pitcher selected to a Major League All-Star team, **Oral Hildebrand** was a two-sport standout in high school and college.

Hildebrand started playing baseball when he entered Southport High School. Originally an outfielder, he became a pitcher after the graduation of Southport's top hurler, Chuck Klein, who went on to star in the big leagues as a slugging outfielder.

A star center for the Southport basketball squad, Hildebrand entered Butler University in 1928. At Butler's newly-opened Butler Field House on December 13, 1928, he scored 18 points as the Bulldogs snapped the University of Pittsburgh's 27-game win streak. Butler finished the season with a 17–2 record and won the Amateur Athletic Union's national collegiate title.

Hildebrand also pitched for the Bulldog baseball team. During the summer, he played for the powerful Indianapolis Power and Light Company club, which won the 1928 national industrial tournament in Detroit.

For the 1929–1930 season, Hildebrand was named captain of Butler's basketball team. In February 1930 he was declared ineligible, based on charges he'd received payment the previous summer while playing for a baseball team from Brazil, Ind. Soon afterwards, he signed with Indianapolis (American Association) and compiled a 3–10 record with a 4.34 ERA in his first pro campaign. "I was wild and didn't amount to much that first year," he told *The Sporting News*.

Hildebrand had an 11–8 mark for Indianapolis in 1931 when Cleveland acquired him. He developed into a reliable starter for the Indians, winning 56 games against 46 losses from 1931 to 1936. He was Cleveland's Opening Day pitcher in 1934.

Contemporaries credited Hildebrand with a fair fastball, a good curve and an excellent change of pace. His best season was 1933, when he won 16 games and topped the league with six shutouts. That summer he was a member of the AL team for the inaugural All-Star Game in Chicago (Chuck Klein, who Hildebrand had replaced at Southport, was a starting outfielder for the NL). Of the four AL pitchers selected, Hildebrand was the only one who didn't get to play.

In January 1937 the Indians traded Hildebrand to the St. Louis Browns. After two seasons with a second-division club, he joined the Yankees for 1939. His 10–4 record helped New York to a fourth consecutive pennant. He started the fourth and final game of the World Series, pitching four scoreless innings as the Yanks swept the Cincinnati Reds.

The Yanks released Hildebrand in August 1940. He pitched for St. Paul (American Association) in 1941 and briefly for Indianapolis in 1942 before quitting baseball. Returning to Southport, he worked as a tool and die maker for the Link-Belt Division of the Ford Motor Company.

During the 1935–1936 season Hildebrand played professionally for the Indianapolis Kautskys of the Midwest Basketball Conference. After leaving baseball, he frequently worked out with the Butler basketball team. He was elected to the Indiana Basketball Hall of Fame in 1995.

HILLMAN, John Eric

Born: April 27, 1966, Gary. **Lives:** Denver, Colorado.
Height: 6'10". **Weight:** 235. **Batted:** left. **Threw:** left.
Debut: May 18, 1992. **Final game:** May 30, 1994.
Positions, teams, years: pitcher, New York (NL) 1992–1994.

Games: 49. **Innings pitched:** 232. **Won/Lost:** 4–14. **Earned run average:** 4.85.

Eric Hillman, at one time one of the tallest players in Major League history, is the tallest man ever to play pro baseball in Japan.

Hillman grew up in suburban Chicago and attended Homewood-Flossmoor High School before entering Eastern Illinois University. Picked by the New York Mets in the 16th round of the 1987 draft, he began his career that season with Little Falls, N.Y. (New York-Penn).

Hillman debuted with the Mets in 1992, joining Seattle Mariners pitcher Randy Johnson as the only other 6-foot, 10-inch player in big league history (6-foot, 11-inch Jon Rauch became the tallest player in baseball history when he debuted with the White Sox in 2004).

Poised to move into the Mets starting rotation in 1994, Hillman struggled and was soon back in the minors. He compiled a 10–1 record at Norfolk, Va. (International), and became a free agent after the season.

At the urging of Bobby Valentine, his manager at Norfolk, Hillman signed with the Chiba Lotte Marines of Japan's Pacific League for 1995. He had a 12–9 mark with a 2.87 ERA in his first year in Japan. "Nineteen ninety-five was the first year that I had ever started and finished with the same team," he told Robert Fitts, author of *Remembering Japanese Baseball*.

In 1996 Hillman went 14–9, 2.40. A free agent again after his second year with Chiba, he received offers from the Anaheim Angels, the Toronto Blue Jays and a handful of other teams. He decided to remain in Japan, however, and signed a two-year pact with Tokyo's Yomiuri Giants. Rotator cuff problems in 1997 confined Hillman to six innings. The Yomiuri club released him in 1998 and he returned to the U.S.

In 2000 Hillman made an unsuccessful comeback attempt with the Houston Astros organization. From 2005–2008 he worked as an analyst for FSN Rocky Mountain's Colorado Rockies telecasts. He and his wife Heather own Pure Puppy Inc., a company that develops and sells dog care products, including natural-ingredient shampoos and conditioners.

HISNER, Harley Parnell ("Jim")
Born: November 6, 1926, Maples. **Lives:** Monroeville.
Height: 6'1". **Weight:** 185. **Batted:** right. **Threw:** right.
Debut: September 30, 1951. **Final game:** September 30, 1951.
Positions, teams, years: pitcher, Boston (AL) 1951.
Games: 1. **Innings pitched:** 6. **Won/Lost:** 0–1. **Earned run average:** 4.50.

Jim Hisner was the last pitcher to face Joe DiMaggio in a regular-season contest.

Although Hisner (pronounced (HICE-ner) signed his first contract in 1945, his professional career didn't begin until two years later. He spent two years in the army after graduating from Hoagland High School in northeastern Indiana. Discharged in 1947, he joined Scranton, Pa. (Eastern). His 11–3, 2.48 record helped Scranton win the 1948 league title.

In 1949 Hisner was pitching for Louisville, and when the 1951 American Association season ended he joined the Red Sox. He started the last game of the year for Boston at Yankee Stadium. New York had already clinched the AL pennant, and the game had no bearing on the standings. The Yankees clipped Hisner for a run in the second and two more in the third en route to a 3–0 victory.

DiMaggio, New York's legendary center fielder, had an infield single off Hisner in one official trip to the plate—his last hit in a regular-season game—and came out of the lineup. "It was the one and only time I saw him play," said Jim, "and I pitched against him."

The game at Yankee Stadium was Hisner's lone big league appearance. He played in the minors until 1953, dividing his final season between Syracuse, N.Y. (International), Dallas (Texas) and Wichita Falls, Tex. His 14–5 record spurred Wichita Falls to the 1953 Big State League pennant.

Shoulder trouble, which began in 1948, curtailed Hisner's career. After leaving baseball he spent 33 years as a machinist at Rea Magnet Wire in Fort Wayne, retiring in 1987. He also played for semi-pro teams around the Midwest, tying a National Baseball Congress tournament record in 1957 with four wins for a Fort Wayne team. Pitching for the Anderson

(Ind.) Fallstaffs in the 1958 tourney, he threw a no-hitter against Grand Rapids, Mich.

In 1976 Hisner was inducted into the Northeast Indiana Baseball Association Hall of Fame.

HOCKETT, Oris Leon ("Brown")

Born: September 29, 1909, Amboy. **Died:** March 23, 1969, Torrance, California.
Height: 5'9". **Weight:** 182. **Batted:** left. **Threw:** right.
Debut: September 4, 1938. **Final game:** September 7, 1945.
Positions, teams, years: outfield, Brooklyn (NL) 1938–1939, Cleveland (AL) 1941–1944, Chicago (AL) 1945.
Games: 551. **At-Bats:** 2,165. **Home runs:** 13. **Average:** .276.

Oris Hockett, a line-drive hitting outfielder, became an everyday player during World War II.

When Hockett was a youngster his family moved to Dayton, Ohio, where he starred in football at Roosevelt High School. He attended college at Denison and Michigan State, eventually leaving to work as a logger in Alabama. Alabama Poly (now Auburn University) offered him a football scholarship, and he enrolled there as a pre-medical student.

Hockett left school after a year and returned to Dayton. In 1931 he set off for California in a Model-T Ford, but ran out of money in Nebraska. He signed a contract with a minor league team in Norfolk (Nebraska State), where he played under the name Jim Brown, possibly to retain his amateur status. Records indicate that he also enrolled at Nebraska State Teachers College.

Hockett was out of organized ball in 1934 and again in 1937. After batting .341 for Dayton (Middle-Atlantic) in 1938, he joined the Brooklyn Dodgers. He played sparingly in 1938–1939 before the Dodgers sent him to Milwaukee (American Association). With Nashville, Tenn. (Southern), he batted .363 in 1940 and .359 in 1941 and returned to the majors with Cleveland.

In 1942, after many other big leaguers had entered military service, Hockett became the Indians' starting right fielder. An off-season job as a toolmaker at Goodyear Aircraft in Dayton exempted him from the draft. His best year was 1944, when he batted .289 and made the AL All-Star team. The *Cleveland Plain Dealer* described him as "a strong, well-knit, hustling, battling fellow who seems to have muscles even in his eyebrows."

Cleveland sent Hockett to the White Sox in December 1944. He spent 1945 as Chicago's primary center fielder, batting .293 at age 35—although he maintained he was five years younger. His career ended in 1946, when the regulars began returning from the service.

Hockett eventually settled in southern California. He died of a heart attack at age 59.

HODGES, Gilbert Ray ("Bud," "The Quiet Man")

Indiana Baseball Hall of Fame, 1979.
Born: April 4, 1924, Princeton. **Died:** April 2, 1972, West Palm Beach, Florida.
Height: 6'1". **Weight:** 200. **Batted:** right. **Threw:** right.
Debut: October 3, 1943. **Final game:** May 5, 1963.
Positions, teams, years: first base (1,908), outfield (79), catcher (64), third base (32), second base (1), outfield (1), Brooklyn (NL), 1943, 1947–1957, Los Angeles (NL) 1958–1961, New York (NL) 1962–1963.
Games: 2,071. **At-Bats:** 7,030. **Home runs:** 370. **Average:** .273.
Manager: Washington (AL) 1963–1967, New York (NL) 1968–1971 (660–753).

A baseball legend in Indiana and New York, **Gil Hodges** was a power-hitting first baseman for the Brooklyn Dodgers. He later guided the Mets to their first pennant and a stunning upset in the World Series.

The son of a coal miner, Hodges lettered in four sports at Petersburg High School. At St. Joseph's College in Rensselaer, he continued to star in athletics. While playing shortstop in 1943 for an Indianapolis industrial league team, Hodges signed a contract with the Dodgers. He joined Brooklyn without playing in the minor leagues and appeared in the final game of the year as a third baseman.

When the season ended Hodges entered the Marine Corps and saw combat in the Pacific. Discharged with the rank of sergeant, he resumed his baseball career in 1946 with Macon, Ga. (South Atlantic), where Dodgers management planned to convert him into a catcher. He rejoined Brooklyn in 1948, but by then future Hall of Famer Roy Campanella was the Dodgers' regular backstop. Hodges changed positions again, this time switching to first base.

Almost overnight, he developed into one of the league's best. Hodges was named to seven NL All-Star teams (1949–51, '53–55 and '57) and helped Brooklyn to six pennants (1947, '49, '52–53, '55–56). In his finest year, 1954, Hodges hit .304 with 42 home runs and 130 RBI. From 1949 to 1955 he drove in over a hundred runs each season. He averaged around 32 homers a year from 1950 to 1957.

Hodges' most awesome display of power came against the Boston Braves on August 31, 1950, when he belted four homers in a single game. He had 14 grand slams during his career, an all-time league high. His lifetime total of 370 homers was an NL record for right-handed batters.

Hodges also excelled on defense, leading NL first basemen in fielding three times. Brooklyn shortstop Pee Wee Reese once said that Hodges—one of the most physically powerful players of all time—wore a first baseman's glove "only because it's fashionable."

On Brooklyn's "Boys of Summer" teams, Hodges was an acknowledged leader. He was a favorite of Ebbets Field fans, who cheered for him throughout his dreadful 0-for-21 slump during the 1952 World Series. "Poor performance was not appreciated in Brooklyn. And the fans let you know it," noted Larry Moffi in *This Side of Cooperstown*. "With one exception: Gil Hodges. They never booed Hodges."

After marrying Brooklyn resident Joan Lombardi in 1948, Hodges made his year-round home there. He went to Los Angeles in 1958 when the Dodgers relocated to the West Coast. In 1959 he appeared in his seventh World Series as Los Angeles beat the Chicago White Sox in six games. His .391 average topped all Dodgers batters.

Prior to the 1962 season, the fledgling New York Mets took Hodges in the expansion draft. At age 38 he opened the year as the Mets' first baseman. Injuries limited him to 54 contests. In May 1963 New York traded Hodges to the Washington Senators, who named him manager. The Senators' victory total increased in each of his five years at the helm.

After guiding Washington to a sixth-place finish in 1967 he returned to New York, this time as skipper of the Mets. The club had been the NL doormat since its inaugural season, but its farm system was beginning to deliver talented young players. He almost didn't get through his first year, suffering a heart attack in September 1968.

Hodges recovered, and a year later to the date the Mets won the NL Eastern Division title. New York won the 1969 pennant with a three-game sweep of the West Division champion Atlanta Braves. The Mets went up against the heavily-favored Baltimore Orioles in the World Series. After a Game One loss, the Mets rocked the sports world with four consecutive victories. Tom Seaver, the Mets' star pitcher, said that during the final six weeks of the '69 season, Hodges was "an infallible genius."

The Mets finished third in both 1970 and 1971. During spring training in 1972, just two days before his 48th birthday, Hodges suffered a coronary and died instantly. He was mourned in Indiana, in New York and throughout baseball.

The recipient of the Lou Gehrig Memorial Award for 1959, Hodges is still remembered in his native state and his adopted city. A Little League Field in Brooklyn is named for him, and the Gil Hodges Memorial Bridge spans the inlet between Brooklyn and Rockaway. The bridge over the east fork of White River in Indiana's Pike County bears his name.

With Frank Slocum, Hodges authored *The Game of Baseball* in 1969. Books written about Hodges include *The Gil Hodges Story*, by Milton Shapiro (1960); *Gil Hodges: Baseball's Miracle Man*, by John Devaney (1973); *Gil Hodges: The Quiet Man*, by Marino Amoruso (1991); *Praying for Gil Hodges: A Memoir of the 1955 World Series and One Family's Love of the Brooklyn Dodgers*, by Thomas Oliphant (2005); and *Gil Hodges: The Brooklyn Bums, The Miracle Mets, and the Extraordinary Life of a Baseball Legend* (2012), by Tom Clavin and Danny Peary.

Gil's brother Bob pitched in the minor leagues in 1947. His son, Gil Jr., played college ball at C.W. Post. Gil Jr. was drafted by the Mets and spent the 1971 and 1972 seasons with New York farm clubs.

Hodges was nicknamed "Bud" by his boyhood friends. The "Quiet Man" sobriquet came from the classic 1952 John Ford film, with John Wayne in the title role.

During his 14 years on the Hall of Fame ballot, Hodges received 3,010 votes—the most of any player who has yet to be elected. In 1979 he was inducted into the Indiana Baseball Hall of Fame.

HOFFERTH, Stewart Edward

Born: January 27, 1913, Logansport. **Died:** March 7, 1994, Valparaiso.
Height: 6'2". **Weight:** 195. **Batted:** right. **Threw:** right.
Debut: April 19, 1944. **Final game:** June 15, 1946.
Positions, teams, years: catcher, Boston (NL) 1944–1946.
Games: 136. **At-Bats:** 408. **Home runs:** 4. **Average:** .216.

A rifle-armed catcher, **Stew Hofferth** was the 1943 American Association MVP.

Hofferth (pronounced HOE-fert) graduated from Kouts High School in northwestern Indiana and worked at Inland Steel, where he played for the company baseball team. His first professional season was 1936, with Tallahassee, Fla. (Georgia-Florida). He spent 1937 and 1938 at Nashville, Tenn. (Southern), and in 1939 the Brooklyn Dodgers acquired his contract. He served as player-manager for Brooklyn farm teams at Americus, Ga., in 1940 and Valdosta, Ga. in 1941, both in the Georgia-Florida League.

Hofferth spent 1942 with Toronto (International), and baseball commissioner Kenesaw Mountain Landis declared him a free agent after the season. Stew joined Indianapolis (American Association) in 1943 and batted .301 to earn MVP honors. "That the Indians finished in second place was due in large part to Hofferth's magnificent backstopping and timely swatting," wrote the *Boston Post*'s Howell Stevens.

The Boston Braves obtained Hofferth for 1944 and he spent the next two seasons as a backup catcher. In 1946 the Braves traded him to Brooklyn for New Albany, Ind., native Billy Herman. Dodger management wanted Hofferth to manage in the minors, but he refused and was out of baseball in 1947. He returned in 1948, spending time at St. Paul (American Association) and Cambridge, Md. (Eastern Shore), where he was once again a playing manager. Cambridge won 21 of 32 games under Stew, who batted .335 in his final season.

Hofferth returned to Indiana and resumed his work at Inland Steel, eventually becoming a foreman and retiring after 37 years. Despite a series of strokes in his later years, he remained a baseball enthusiast and an avid golfer.

Hofferth's son Ted played baseball for Valparaiso University.

HOLT, Tyler Andrew

Born: March 10, 1989, Marion. **Lives:** Gainesville, Florida.
Height: 5-10. **Weight:** 190. **Bats:** right. **Throws:** right.
Debut: July 6, 2014.
Positions, teams, years: outfield, Cleveland (AL) 2014.
Games: 36. **At-bats:** 71. **Home runs:** 0. **Average:** .268.

Born in Indiana and raised in Florida, **Tyler Holt** hit .608 in 2007 as a Gainesville High School senior. Prior to his junior year at Florida State University, he spent the summer playing center field for Team USA. He batted .371 in 22 games for the U.S. squad, which defeated Germany in the title game of the 2009 World Baseball Challenge in Prince George, British Colombia.

The Cleveland Indians made Holt their tenth pick in the 2010 draft. He broke in that year with a .286 average for Lake County (Midwest). In 2011 he hit .254 with 34 stolen bases at Kinston, N.C. (Carolina), and played solid defense.

Holt came into his own in 2014, batting .298 for Akron, Ohio (Eastern), before earning a promotion to Columbus, Ohio (International). He was hitting .302 when Cleveland brought him up to replace injured center fielder Michael Bourn. "It's a dream come true," Tyler told reporters.

During August, Holt bounced back and forth between Cleveland and Columbus. He finished the year with a combined .305 average and 31 stolen bases for Akron and Columbus. With the Indians he batted .268, playing errorless ball in 28 games in right field, nine in center and one in left.

HOUTZ, Fred Fritz ("Lefty")

Born: September 4, 1875, Connersville. **Died:** February 15, 1959, St. Marys, Ohio.
Height: 5'10". **Weight:** 170. **Batted:** left. **Threw:** left.
Debut: July 23, 1899. **Final game:** July 26, 1899.
Positions, teams, years: outfield, Cincinnati (NL) 1899.
Games: 5. **At-Bats:** 17. **Home runs:** 0. **Average:** .235.

Fred Houtz was a fleet-footed outfielder for 15 professional seasons, all but one of them in the minor leagues. In 1909 he played in one of the earliest night games in history.

Houtz started out in pro baseball with Galveston in 1899, when he topped the Texas Association with 16 homers and a .395 average in 78 contests. He spent part of the season with the Cincinnati Reds. It would be his only stint in the Major Leagues. By August he was back in the minors with St. Paul (Western).

Houtz played for minor league squads for the remainder of his career, including pennant-winning teams at Galveston (Texas Association) in 1899, Butte, Mont. (Pacific Northwest), in 1902, Boise, Idaho (Pacific National), in 1904, and Chillicothe (Ohio State) in 1913.

With Boise in 1904 Houtz's 33 doubles, 18 triples, 49 stolen bases and .343 average were career bests. At Montgomery, Ala., in 1906, he led the Southern Association with 86 runs scored. With Zanesville, Ohio (Central), on July 7, 1909, he homered in a game played after dark under electric lights at Grand Rapids, Mich.

From 1910 to 1914 Houtz played in the Ohio State League, first at Lima in 1910–1911 and then with Chillicothe in 1913–1914. He was out of baseball in 1912.

Houtz lived in Wapakoneta, Ohio, for most of his life. A lifelong bachelor, he died from chronic heart problems at age 83.

HUHN, Emil Hugo ("Hap," "Hunnie")

Born: March 10, 1892, North Vernon. **Died:** September 5, 1925, Camden, South Carolina.
Height: 6'0". **Weight:** 180. **Batted:** right. **Threw:** right.
Debut: April 10, 1915. **Final game:** June 30, 1917.
Positions, teams, years: first base (116), catcher (49), outfield (1), Newark (Federal League) 1915, Cincinnati (NL) 1916–1917.
Games: 184. **At-Bats:** 560. **Home runs:** 1. **Average:** .229.

Hap Huhn was the Cincinnati Reds catcher in a game that saw pitchers for both teams throw no-hitters for nine innings.

Known for his sunny disposition, Huhn (pronounced "hoon") broke into professional baseball in 1910 with Maysville, Ky. (Blue Grass). He reached the majors after hitting .295 for Seattle (Northwestern) in 1914. Playing for the Newark (N.J.) Peppers of the upstart Federal League in 1915, he appeared in 124 games, mostly as a first baseman.

The Federal League folded after the season and Huhn joined Cincinnati. He spent the next two seasons with the Reds, mostly as a backup. At Chicago on May 2, 1917, Huhn caught Reds right-hander Fred Toney. Through the first nine innings, neither Toney nor Cubs pitcher Jim Vaughn allowed a base hit. Cincinnati finally managed a single in the top of the tenth and went on to score a run. Toney threw one more hitless frame in the bottom of the tenth for a 1–0 no-hit victory.

Huhn played for Milwaukee (American Association) from 1918 to 1920. By 1918, when he made his off-season home in Adrian, Mich., he spent part of the year working at a defense-related job with Nordyke & Marmon Company of Indianapolis.

As the everyday first baseman for Augusta, Ga. (South Atlantic), in 1921 Huhn batted 359. For the next three seasons he played first base for Mobile, Ala. (Southern), averaging .311 in 1922, .345 in 1923 and .292 in 1924.

In 1925 Huhn returned to Augusta as the Tygers' player-manager. "Emil Huhn is a competent leader," wrote Bob Parks, the Augusta correspondent for *The Sporting News*. "Taciturn he is, but quick to act. He is a smart baseball player and a leader who is quick to discern the weaknesses of his machine, and equally as quick to provide remedial measures for those weaknesses."

Coming home from a game in Charlotte, N.C., the car Huhn was driving overturned near Camden, S.C. Although five other players in the vehicle suffered relatively minor injuries, Huhn and outfielder Frank Reiger were killed. He was 33 years old and left a wife and three children.

HUNTER, Raymond Thomas III

Born: July 3, 1986, Indianapolis. **Lives:** Indianapolis.
Height: 6'3". **Weight:** 260. **Bats:** right. **Throws:** right.
Debut: August 1, 2008.
Positions, teams, years: pitcher, Texas (AL) 2008–2011, Baltimore (AL) 2011–2014.
Games: 226. **Innings pitched:** 616.1. **Won/lost:** 42–31. **Earned run average:** 4.32.

After a meteoric rise through the Texas Rangers system, right-hander **Tommy Hunter** recorded his first Major League win on his birthday.

In 2005 Hunter's 9–4 record, 110 strikeouts and 1.28 ERA led Cathedral High School of Indianapolis to Indiana's Class 4A semistate championship. Selected by the Tampa Bay Devil Rays in the 18th round of the draft, he instead opted to attend the University of Alabama. After his freshman year in 2006, he played for the gold medal-winning U.S. team at the World University Games in Havana. In 2007 he went 7–5 with a 3.87 ERA for the Crimson Tide and the Texas Rangers drafted him in the compensation round with the 54th pick overall.

Hunter broke in that season with Spokane, Wash. (Northwest). He started the 2008 campaign with Bakersfield (California) and moved on to Frisco (Texas) and Oklahoma (Pacific Coast) before joining the Rangers in August. He moved into the Rangers' starting rotation in 2009 and notched his first big league victory in a 3–1 win over Tampa Bay on July 3, his 23rd birthday.

A ribcage injury sidelined Hunter for the start of the 2010 season. Rejoining the Rangers rotation in June, he went 13–4 with a 3.73 ERA as Texas won its first AL pennant. In Game Four of the World Series with San Francisco, he started and took the loss in the Giants' 4–0 triumph. San Francisco won the Series in five games.

In July 2011 Hunter had a 1–1 record when the Rangers dealt him to Baltimore, where he went 3–3. In 2012 he shuttled between the Orioles and the minors, finishing the year in the bullpen as Baltimore lost to the Yankees in the AL Division Series.

Hunter became a full-time reliever in 2013. Appearing in 68 games, he went 6–5 with four saves and a 2.81 ERA. After trading Jim Johnson to Oakland, the Orioles named Hunter their closer for 2014. He lost the job after going 1–1 with 11 saves and a 6.06 in 19 appearances and went on the disabled list in late May with a strained left groin muscle. Demoted to middle relief when he returned, Hunter pitched effectively the rest of the year. He finished the year with a 3–2 mark and a 2.97 ERA as the Orioles finished first in the AL East.

According to Rich Andriole, his high school coach, Hunter assists with Cathedral's yearly Christmas baseball camp. "I think one of the greatest things about Tommy Hunter," Andriole told the *Indianapolis Star*, "…is that he's never forgotten where he's come from."

Despite his bulky size, Hunter is an excellent all-around athlete who was a linebacker on Cathedral's football team. As a pre-teen, he won a pair of Junior Olympic national judo titles.

INKS, Albert John

Born: January 27, 1871, Ligonier. **Died:** October 3, 1941, Ligonier.
Height: 6'3". **Weight:** 175. **Batted:** left. **Threw:** left.
Debut: September 2, 1891. **Final game:** June 23, 1896.
Positions, teams, years: pitcher, Brooklyn (NL) 1891–1892, Washington (NL) 1892, Baltimore (NL) 1894, Louisville (NL) 1894–1895, Philadelphia (NL) 1896, Cincinnati (NL) 1896.
Games: 89. **Innings pitched:** 603.2. **Won/Lost:** 27–46. **Earned run average:** 5.52.

A slender southpaw with a penchant for fancy clothes, **Bert Inks** graduated from Ligonier High School and pitched for the University of Notre Dame before signing a pro contract in 1890. In 1891 he went 14–5 at Fort Wayne (Northwestern) before moving to Duluth, Minn. (Western Association), where he had a 9–5 record. That September he reached the big leagues with the Brooklyn Bridegrooms, going 3–10 with a 4.03 ERA in 13 games.

In 1892 Inks pitched briefly for two big league clubs, Brooklyn and the Washington Senators. He spent most of the year at Binghamton, N.Y. (Eastern), compiling a 21–10 record. He had 23 wins and 15 losses in 1893, when he pitched for a pair of Eastern League teams, Binghamton and Springfield, Mass.

Inks joined Baltimore for 1894, the year the Orioles won the NL pennant. He wasn't around for the celebration. During the season, Baltimore skipper Ned Hanlon replaced every pitcher from the Orioles' Opening Day staff. Inks was 9–4 with a 5.55 ERA when Hanlon dispatched him to the lowly Louisville Colonels, who finished the 1894 campaign in the NL basement.

In 1895 Inks started for the Colonels on Opening Day. He lost 20 of 27 decisions as Louisville again came in last. The Colonels dealt him to Philadelphia for 1896. He was 0–1 in three appearances when the Phillies sent him to Cincinnati. In three games with the Reds, Inks went 1–1. He finished the year in St. Paul (Western).

Inks was back in the Eastern League in 1897, first with Springfield and later with Buffalo, N.Y. In late July, *The Sporting News* reported that he was "stricken with rheumatism, and on the advice of his physicians will retire from the diamond." He never again pitched in organized baseball.

A good hitter, Inks batted .371 in 1892 and .357 in 1893 and averaged .300 over his five big league campaigns. Contemporary accounts indicate he was popular with the ladies. *The Sporting News* called him a "dandy of the diamond," claiming Inks brought a trunk of clothes on road trips while his teammates customarily brought only a single clean change.

Inks came from a pioneer family in Ligonier and for the last 34 years of his life operated the town's only movie theater and playhouse, the Crystal Theater. Will Inks, Bert's brother, was a minor league outfielder.

One of Bert's biggest fans was future baseball commissioner Ford Frick, who grew up in Brimfield, Ind., just east of Ligonier. "Believe me, Burt [sic] Inks was 'big stuff,'" Frick recalled in his memoir, *Games, Asterisks and People*. "He rated first rung on the ladder with Levi Crume, the local Civil War Hero, who fought at Shiloh and Chickamauga."

IRELAN, Harold ("Grump")

Born: August 5, 1890, Burnettsville. **Died:** July 16, 1944, Carmel.
Height: 5'7". **Weight:** 165. **Batted:** both. **Threw:** right.
Debut: April 23, 1914. **Final game:** October 6, 1914.
Positions, teams, years: second base (44), shortstop (3), third base (2), first base (2), Philadelphia (NL) 1914.
Games: 67. **At-bats:** 165. **Home runs:** 1. **Average:** .236.

Although his big league career lasted only one season, **Hal Irelan** spent most of his life in baseball as a player, manager, club owner and scout.

Irelan started out as an infielder with Marion (Northern State of Indiana) in 1909. The Philadelphia Phillies bought his contract after the 1911 season. After stops at Sacramento, Calif. (Pacific Coast), Rochester, N.Y. (International), and New London, Conn. (Eastern), he reached the majors in 1914. Primarily a second baseman, he played all four infield positions with the sixth-place Phillies and had six hits in a dozen pinch-hitting appearances.

When Philadelphia optioned him to Montreal (International) for 1915, Irelan's days as a Major Leaguer were over. He played in the minors until 1926, except for 1918–1919, when he was voluntarily retired, and 1925, when he was sidelined by illness.

Between 1921 and 1936 Irelan managed at Kingsport, Tenn. (Appalachian), Greenville, S.C. (Cotton States), Decatur, Ill. (Three-I), Quincy, Ill. (Three-I), Des Moines, Iowa (Western), and Fargo-Moorhead, N.D. (Northern). From 1928–1932 he owned and operated the Quincy club, and for part of 1934 at Des Moines he did double duty as general manager.

In 1937 Irelan became a scout for the Cleveland Indians. One year later he discovered Lou Boudreau while the future Hall of Famer was playing for the University of Illinois.

While playing for the Phillies, Irelan lived in the town of Burnettsville, a dozen miles west of Logansport. Toward the end of his life he made Indianapolis his home. He died of a heart attack at age 53 while visiting his daughter in Carmel.

Irelan's nickname stemmed from his serious demeanor.

JACKSON, Henry Everett

Born: June 23, 1861, Union City. **Died:** September 14, 1932, Chicago, Illinois.
Height: 6'2". **Weight:** 185. **Batted:** right. **Threw:** right.

Debut: September 13, 1887. **Final game:** September 28, 1887.
Positions, teams, years: first base, Indianapolis (NL) 1887.
Games: 10. **At-bats:** 38. **Home runs:** 0. **Average:** .263.

In September 1887 the Indianapolis Hoosiers of the NL were mired in last place. Horace Fogel, the third Indianapolis manager that season, was unsatisfied with first baseman Otto Schomberg, whose wild throws had contributed to several losses during a recent road trip. Fogel recruited **Henry Jackson**, the star first baseman for an amateur club in Union City, a town east of Muncie that straddles the Ohio border.

When the rangy Jackson debuted against the New York Giants in a game at Athletic Park in Indianapolis, about twenty friends from his hometown were on hand. The *Indianapolis Sentinel* praised Jackson's batting and fielding in a 7–4 Hoosiers win, describing him as "the Union City giant." During his brief career, Jackson was one of the tallest big league players.

Indianapolis finished the 1887 season with a 37–89 record and in 1888 Harry Spence replaced Fogel. Gone, too, was Jackson, who never again played in the majors. After splitting 1888 between Allentown, Pa. (Central), and Jackson, Mich. (Tri-State), he disappeared from organized ball.

JAMES, Jeffrey Lynn ("Jesse")

Born: September 29, 1941, Indianapolis. **Died:** May 7, 2006, Indianapolis.
Height: 6'3". **Weight:** 195. **Batted:** right. **Threw:** right.
Debut: April 13, 1968. **Final game:** October 1, 1969.
Positions, teams, years: pitcher, Philadelphia (NL) 1968–1969.
Games: 35. **Innings pitched:** 147.1. **Won/Lost:** 6–6. **Earned run average:** 4.52.

A baseball, football and basketball player as a prep, **Jeff James** pitched the first no-hitter in the history of Washington High School in Indianapolis. He once set a city record with 18 strikeouts in a seven-inning game.

James attended Indiana State University for two years before signing with the Philadelphia Phillies, spending his first pro season at Elmira, N.Y. (New York-Pennsylvania), in 1961.

Except for 1963 at Magic Valley (Twin Falls, Idaho), when his 16 wins led the Pioneer League, James didn't post a winning record until 1967. He developed into a top prospect that summer, winning 11 straight games for San Diego (Pacific Coast) en route to a 13–5 season. "He has a good live fastball, has gained good control and is a fierce competitor," said San Diego manager Bob Skinner.

James spent 1968 with the Phillies as a reliever and spot starter and pitched a shutout against the Chicago Cubs in July. By 1969 he was back in the minors with Eugene, Ore. (Pacific Coast). He rejoined Philadelphia in September after leading the PCL with 155 strikeouts.

In 1970 the Phillies returned James to Eugene, where he went 6–14. He split the following season between Eugene and Hawaii (Pacific Coast), going 6–10 before retiring from baseball.

James, who was nicknamed for the legendary western outlaw, spent six years in the U.S. Army Reserves. After leaving baseball he settled in Oregon, where he worked for a lumber company.

JOHN, Thomas Edward ("T.J.")

Indiana Baseball Hall of Fame, 1996.
Born: May 22, 1943, Terre Haute. **Lives:** Long Lake, Minnesota.
Height: 6'3". **Weight:** 180. **Batted:** right. **Threw:** left.
Debut: September 6, 1963. **Final game:** May 25, 1989.
Positions, teams, years: pitcher, Cleveland (AL) 1963–1964, Chicago (AL) 1965–1971, Los Angeles (NL) 1972–1974, 1976–1978, New York (AL) 1979–1982, California (AL) 1982–1985, Oakland (AL) 1985, New York (AL), 1986–1989.
Games: 760. **Innings pitched:** 4710.1. **Won/Lost:** 288–231. **Earned run average:** 3.34.

Tommy John's 288 career victories is the highest total for an Indiana-born pitcher. He also spent more seasons in the Major Leagues (26) than any other Hoosier. John made history after undergoing a revolutionary medical procedure, now commonly referred to as "Tommy John surgery."

A two-sport star at Terre Haute's Gerstmeyer High School, he was a straight-A student and class valedictorian. In 1961 John declined numerous college basketball scholarship offers to sign with the Cleveland Indians.

John's first pro team was Dubuque, Iowa (Midwest), in 1961, and by 1963 he was pitching for Cleveland. In January 1965 he went to the Chicago White Sox in a three-way trade involving the Indians and Kansas City Athletics. He developed into an excellent starting pitcher in Chicago, relying on a sinker and pinpoint control. He twice led the AL in shutouts (1966–1967), and in 1968 he compiled a 10–5 record and made the AL All-Star squad. From 1966 through 1968 he was among the league ERA leaders.

In December 1971 the White Sox traded John to the Los Angeles Dodgers for slugger Dick Allen. In 1973 John had the NL's best winning percentage (.696). He was en route to an even better season in 1974, with a 13–3 record in mid-July when the medial collateral ligament in his left elbow ruptured.

Dodgers team physician Frank Jobe performed experimental surgery in September 1973. Dr. Jobe laced John's tendons back and forth across the joint, and then repositioned the tendons. In December, John underwent a second, even riskier, procedure when Dr. Jobe re-channeled the ulnar nerve, or funny bone, from its normal position to the front of John's elbow.

After the operations, John's left arm was crippled. "I couldn't use it at all," he said. "I couldn't open a car door.... My wife had to cut my food and feed me." By July 1975 John regained feeling in his fingers, and that autumn he pitched in an instructional league.

In 1976 the pitcher with the "bionic arm" returned to the majors. John had a 10–10 record, earning NL Comeback of the Year honors. In 1977 he won 20 games for the first time in his career and led the Dodgers to a pennant. His 17 wins in 1978 helped Los Angeles to a second consecutive World Series. Both years, Los Angeles lost to the New York Yankees.

When the Dodgers refused him a three-year contract, John became a free agent and signed with the Yanks for 1979. During his first year in pinstripes, John went 21–9. His 22 wins helped New York to a division title in 1980, and in 1981 he made his final World Series appearance against the Dodgers.

In August 1982 New York sent John to the Angels, and in July 1985 he joined the Oakland Athletics. A free agent again prior to 1986, he signed with the Yankees for a second time. He retired after the 1986 season to become an assistant coach at the University of North Carolina. After just four weeks, however, he resigned and returned to the Yankees. He had one last big year for New York in '87, going 13–6. He had a 2–7 record and was a dozen games short of 300 career wins when the Yanks released him in May 1989. "Winning 300 games was a goal to shoot for, and nothing more," he claimed. "...I just enjoyed playing baseball."

John became the baseball coach at Westminster Academy in Miami, winning honors as Florida's high school coach of the year in 1992. After working as a television commentator for the Minnesota Twins and Yankees, John returned to the field as a coach in the Montreal Expos organization and as a manager in the Yankees system. From 2007 to 2009 he managed the Bridgeport, Conn., Bluefish of the independent Atlantic League.

A four-time All-Star (1968, 1978–79–80), John is the fifth-winningest left-handed pitcher in Major League history. He compiled a 2–1 record in World Series play and had a 4–1 slate in five league championship series—two with the Dodgers, two more with the Yankees and one with the Angels.

During his professional career John attended Indiana State University, served in the Indiana Air National Guard and was active in the Fellowship of Christian Athletes. He received the 1976 Fred Hutchinson Award (for overcoming a major physical disability), as well as the 1981 Lou Gehrig Memorial Award (for outstanding character).

John was elected to the Indiana Baseball Hall of Fame in 1996. He is the subject of three books: *The Tommy John Story*, written with Joe Musser, *The Sally and Tommy John Story: Our Life in Baseball*, and *My Twenty-Six Years in Baseball*, co-authored with Dan Valenti.

John's son, Tommy John III, spent two seasons playing for independent league teams.

Pat Mannelly, John's son-in-law, was the long snapper for the Chicago Bears football team in the 2007 Super Bowl.

JOHNS, Douglas Alan

Born: December 19, 1967, South Bend. **Lives:** Plantation, Florida.
Height: 6'2". **Weight:** 185. **Batted:** right. **Threw:** left.
Debut: July 8, 1995. **Final game:** October 2, 1999.
Positions, teams, years: pitcher, Oakland (AL) 1995–1996, Baltimore (AL) 1998–1999.
Games: 114. **Innings pitched:** 386. **Won/Lost:** 20–22. **Earned run average:** 5.13.

Indiana native **Doug Johns**, who graduated from Nova High School in Fort Lauderdale, Fla., and earned a psychology degree from the University of Virginia in 1990, also played professional baseball in Italy.

A 16th-round draft pick by Oakland in 1990, he entered pro ball that year with the Athletics' rookie club in the Arizona League. In 1991 at Madison, Wis. (Midwest), he pitched mostly in relief but threw a no-hitter against Burlington. He progressed to the Triple-A level in 1994, working mainly as a starter for Tacoma, Wash. (Pacific Coast).

Johns led the PCL with a 2.89 ERA in 1994. In 1995 he became one of eight rookie pitchers to debut with Oakland. His first outing was a memorable one. He started the first game of a July doubleheader against the Toronto Blue Jays. After Oakland's Mark McGwire was hit by a pitch in the bottom of the third, Johns was ejected in the top of the fourth when his first throw sailed behind Toronto batter John Olerud.

Johns was 5–3 as a rookie, but struggled through a 6–12 record in 1996 and finished the year in Oakland's bullpen. Released by the Athletics in March 1997, he briefly pitched for Omaha, Neb. (American Association), and then moved on to a pro league in Italy. Pitching for the Angels of Parma, Johns was the winning pitcher in the 1997 European championship game.

Later that year Johns returned to the U.S. and signed with the Baltimore organization. He split the next two seasons between the Orioles and Rochester, N.Y. (International). He signed with Oakland prior to the 2000 season, but quit baseball after the Athletics sold his contract to the Orix BlueWave of Japan's Pacific League.

JOHNSON, Elmer Ellsworth ("Hickory")

Born: June 12, 1884, Beard. **Died:** October 31, 1966, Hollywood, Florida.
Height: 5'9". **Weight:** 185. **Batted:** right. **Threw:** right.
Debut: April 24, 1914. **Final game:** October 6, 1914.
Positions, teams, years: catcher, New York (NL) 1914.
Games: 11. **At-bats:** 12. **Home runs:** 0. **Average:** .167.

When the New York Giants traded catcher Grover Hartley, an Indiana native, to the Cincinnati Reds in December 1913, they replaced him with another Hoosier, **Elmer Johnson**.

Johnson, who spent most of his life in Frankfort, Ind., entered professional baseball in 1908 with Springfield, Ill. (Three-I). Dispatched to Taylorville (Eastern Illinois) for more seasoning, he returned to Springfield after hitting .297 in 30 games. He continued to play for Springfield through 1910, and in 1909 his 10 homers topped the league.

Johnson turned in two solid years at Omaha, Neb. (Western), averaging .289 in 1912 and .327 in 1913. A good baserunner, he stole 19 bases in 1913. In 1914 he joined the Giants as a 30-year-old rookie. "The Hoosier athlete is broad of beam and has an immense pair of shoulders. His demeanor is calm and his temperament all that a catcher's should be," Sid Mercer wrote in *The Sporting News*.

As a backup to Chief Meyers and Larry McLean, Johnson appeared in just 11 contests. He returned to the minors in 1915 and left organized ball after hitting .338 in 1916 for Lincoln, Neb. (Western).

Returning to Frankfort, Johnson played for a local industrial league team until 1922. He worked for the Indiana Brass Company, and moved to Florida in 1960 after the death of his wife.

Johnson's resiliency at a tough, demanding position earned him his nickname.

JOHNSON, Otis L. ("Ote," "Otey," "Home Run")

Born: November 5, 1883, Fowler. **Died:** November 9, 1915, Johnson City, New York.

Height: 5'9". **Weight:** 185. **Batted:** both. **Threw:** right.
Debut: April 12, 1911. **Final game:** September 21, 1911.
Positions, teams, years: shortstop (47), second base (15), third base (3), New York (NL) 1911.
Games: 71. **At-bats:** 209. **Home runs:** 3. **Average:** .234.

Infielder **Otis Johnson**, who once worked as a glass-blower in Muncie during the off-season, spent part of 1911 with the New York Highlanders.

Signed by Dallas (Texas) in 1903 at the recommendation of fellow Hoosier Claude Berry, Johnson learned the game on Muncie's sandlots. Late in 1904 he moved on to Little Rock, Ark. (Southern Association). He joined Charleston, S.C. (South Atlantic), in 1907, when his 10 home runs led the league.

Portland, Ore. (Pacific Coast), acquired Johnson's contract that September and for the next three seasons he starred at shortstop and third base for the Beavers. In 1909 at Chutes Park in Los Angeles, he hit one of the longest homers in PCL history.

After spending the 1910 campaign at Jersey City, N.J. (Eastern), Johnson joined the Highlanders (who became known as the Yankees in 1913). "He is a glassblower and makes from $6 to $7 a day in the wintertime blowing fruit jars at Muncie, Ind.," wrote New York sports reporter Mark Roth. Johnson suffered an arm injury and committed 31 errors in 71 games—21 at short, nine at second and one as a third baseman.

Johnson spent the rest of his career in the minor leagues. A fan favorite wherever he played, the good-natured switch-hitter averaged .323 as the shortstop for the pennant-winning Binghamton Bingos (New York State) in 1913. In 1914 he joined Elmira (New York State) and led the league with 13 homers.

By 1915 Johnson made his home in Johnson City, N.Y. That November, four days after his 32nd birthday, he and three companions went hunting about four miles west of Oswego, N.Y. While chasing a fox, Johnson fell and his shotgun discharged. The blast struck him in the stomach and he died from his wounds.

JOHNSON, Wallace Darnell

Born: December 25, 1956, Gary. **Lives:** Gary.
Height: 6'0". **Weight:** 173. **Batted:** both. **Threw:** right.
Debut: September 8, 1981. **Final game:** August 3, 1990.
Positions, teams, years: first base (78), second base (16), Montreal (NL) 1981–1983, San Francisco (NL) 1983, Montreal 1984, 1986–1990.
Games: 428. **At-bats:** 569. **Home runs:** 5. **Average:** .255.

Gary Roosevelt High School and Indiana State University graduate **Wallace Johnson** was one of the Major Leagues' top pinch hitters toward the latter part of his career. In 1979 Johnson and Larry Bird were teammates when the future Boston Celtics great briefly played for Indiana State's baseball squad.

The Montreal Expos took Johnson in the sixth round of the 1979 draft after he led Indiana State to a Missouri Valley Conference title. He entered pro ball that year with Jamestown, N.Y. (New York-Pennsylvania), and batted .338. At West Palm Beach (Florida State) in 1980 he was the league leader in stolen bases (58) and batting average (.334).

Johnson joined Montreal in September 1981. His pinch-hit double against the Mets on the next-to-last day of the season clinched the NL East title for the Expos, who reached the post-season for the first (and only) time in franchise history. In 1982 he was Montreal's Opening Day second baseman. He batted .193 in 36 contests and finished the year in Wichita, Kan. (American Association), where he hit .352.

The Expos traded Johnson to the San Francisco Giants in 1983. Released after the season, he rejoined the Expos for 1984. He spent all of 1985 at Indianapolis, where he batted .309 and made the American Association all-star team as an outfielder.

Johnson, who played mostly first base in the majors, returned to Montreal in 1986. He topped the NL in pinch hits with 17 in 1987 and 22 in 1988. He batted .309 in 86 games in 1988, averaging .344 as a pinch hitter. On May 2, 1988, his two-out single in the ninth broke up a perfect game bid by Cincinnati's Ron Robinson.

Johnson's big league career ended in 1990 with the Expos. He returned to Gary and opened an accounting firm. "I left Indiana State with a degree," he told Phil Rogers of the *Chicago Tribune*. "I never felt baseball would be there forever. I tried to stay abreast of what was happening in my field during the offeason."

From 1995 to 1997 Johnson was back in baseball as a coach in the Atlanta Braves organization. He was the Chicago White Sox's third base coach from 1998 to 2002.

In 1996 Johnson was inducted into the Indiana State University Hall of Fame.

JONES, Barry Louis
Indiana Baseball Hall of Fame, 2010
Born: February 15, 1963, Centerville. **Lives:** Murrysville, Pennsylvania.
Height: 6'4". **Weight:** 225. **Batted:** right. **Threw:** right.
Debut: July 18, 1986. **Final game:** May 22, 1993.
Positions, teams, years: pitcher, Pittsburgh (NL) 1986–1988, Chicago (AL) 1988–1990, Montreal (NL) 1991, Philadelphia (NL) 1992, New York (NL) 1992, Chicago (AL) 1993.
Games: 348. **Innings pitched:** 433. **Won/Lost:** 33–33. **Earned run average:** 3.66.

A three-sport athlete at Centerville High School in eastern Indiana, relief pitcher **Barry Jones** spurned a contract offer from the Texas Rangers in 1981 in favor of an Indiana University baseball scholarship.

The third-round draft pick by Pittsburgh in 1984, Jones signed with the Pirates and joined Watertown, N.Y. (New York-Pennsylvania). He converted from a starter to short relief in 1985 at Prince William (Carolina) with excellent results.

Jones joined the Pirates in mid–July 1986. In 1988, his first full season in the majors, Pittsburgh traded Jones to the Chicago White Sox. In 1989 he spent three months on the disabled list with an elbow injury. Healthy again in 1990, he became a set-up man for Sox closer Bobby Thigpen and posted an 11–4 record with a 2.31 ERA.

After the season, Chicago sent Jones to the Montreal Expos in a five-player deal. In 1991 he led the NL with 77 appearances and had 13 saves. The Expos traded him prior to 1992, this time to Philadelphia. The Phillies released him in August 1992 and he signed with the New York Mets. He became a free agent after the season and signed once more with the White Sox, who released him in June 1993. He finished his career in 1994 with New Orleans (American Association).

In 2010 Jones was inducted into the Indiana Baseball Hall of Fame.

JUSTIS, Walter Newton ("Smoke," "Choo-Choo")
Born: August 17, 1883, Moores Hill. **Died:** October 4, 1941, Greendale.
Height: 5'11". **Weight:** 195. **Batted:** right. **Threw:** right.
Debut: July 12, 1905. **Final game:** August 1, 1905.
Positions, teams, years: pitcher, Detroit (AL), 1905.
Games: 2. **Innings pitched:** 3.1. **Won/Lost:** 0–0. **Earned run average:** 8.10.

Walt Justis, who pitched four no-hitters for Lancaster (Ohio State) during the 1908 season, won 20 or more games three times during his eight years as a professional.

Justis's career began in 1905. Later that year he and Eddie Cicotte, another 21-year-old first-year pro, found themselves pitching for the Detroit Tigers. While Justis's Major League career would end after two games, Cicotte went on to star for the Chicago White Sox and was implicated in the 1919 World Series scandal.

Justis spent the next four years pitching for Lancaster, Ohio, an Ohio-Pennsylvania League team in 1906–1907 and part of the Ohio State League for 1908–1909. He went 22–19 in 1907, 25–17 in 1908 and 19–17 in 1909. He pitched an 18-inning 1–0 shutout in 1907. In 1908 he threw four no-hit games for the pennant-winning Lanks, and his 298 strikeouts led the league. The no-hitters came on July 19 vs. Mansfield, August 2 vs. Portsmouth, September 8 vs. Lima and September 13 vs. Marion. He pitched another no-hitter in 1909 against Marion. In 1910 he joined Dayton, Ohio (Central), and went 24–16.

After three more minor league seasons, Justis left organized ball. Settling in the southeastern Indiana town of Greendale, he worked for the Old Quaker Distillery in Lawrenceburg and played for a local semi-pro team. At Christmas he would dress as Santa Claus, soliciting funds to clothe and feed the poor. Justis, whose nicknames stemmed from his blazing fastball, died of a heart attack at 58 years of age.

KAHLE, Robert Wayne
Born: November 23, 1915, New Castle. **Died:** December 16, 1988, Inglewood, California.

Height: 6'0". Weight: 170. Batted: right. Threw: right.
Debut: April 21, 1938. Final game: June 22, 1938.
Positions, teams, years: pinch-hitter, pinch-runner, Boston (NL) 1938.
Games: 8. At-bats: 3. Home runs: 0. Average: .333.

Bob Kahle pinch-hit and pinch-ran in just eight big league games with the Boston Bees in 1938, but he played in the minors from 1934 to 1947.

A basketball star at Richmond's Morton High School, Kahle (pronounced "collie") signed with the Indianapolis Indians (American Association) in 1934. The Indians assigned him to Fort Wayne (Central), where he played shortstop. After the league disbanded in late May, he joined Danville, Va. (Bi-State).

In 1937 Kahle batted .306 for Indianapolis, and Boston drafted him for 1938. "I guess I must have been too anxious at the Boston training camp in 1938," he later told the *Philadelphia Record*, "for I tried to do everything and in the end came up with a sore arm." The injury limited him to eight appearances and he finished the year with Hartford, Conn. (Eastern), batting .184 in 10 games.

Boston sent Kahle to the New York Yankees' farm team at Newark, N.J. (International), at the end of March 1939. After 24 contests, the Yanks returned him to Boston, which sold him to Hollywood, Calif. (Pacific Coast). An excellent fielder with an accurate throwing arm, he became one of the PCL's top third basemen and batted .312 in 1940 and .320 in 1941.

The Philadelphia Athletics conditionally acquired Kahle in September 1940. Due to a contract dispute, he never played for the A's and returned to Hollywood for two more seasons. He spent 1943 through 1945 in the U.S. Navy and was back in the PCL for 1946. He split that year between Hollywood and Sacramento, Calif., batting .287. In 1947, his final season, he hit .300 for Little Rock, Ark. (Southern Association). He batted .293 over ten minor league seasons.

After leaving baseball, Kahle worked in Hollywood as a film studio painter. He was a founder of the Little League organization in Westchester, Calif., as well as St. Jerome Roman Catholic Church in Los Angeles. He died of lung cancer in 1988.

KELLER, Ronald Lee

Born: June 3, 1943, Indianapolis. Lives: Johns Island, South Carolina.
Height: 6'2". Weight: 200. Batted: right. Threw: right.
Debut: July 9, 1966. Final game: September 27, 1968.
Positions, teams, years: pitcher, Minnesota (AL) 1966, 1968.
Games: 9. Innings pitched: 21.1. Won/Lost: 0-1. Earned run average: 3.38.

The first Indiana native to reach the Major Leagues through baseball's annual draft, **Ron Keller** pitched for the Minnesota Twins for parts of two seasons.

From 1957 to 1961 Keller earned six letters in baseball and basketball at Cathedral High School in Indianapolis. "He was a very intelligent player," said Cathedral teammate Garry Donna. "He always threw strikes and kept the ball down."

Keller majored in accounting at Indiana University, where he pitched for ex-big leaguer Ernie Andres. Between his junior and senior years, he played in the Central Illinois Collegiate League.

In June 1965 baseball held its first amateur draft in New York City. The Kansas City Athletics, picking first, chose Arizona State outfielder Rick Monday. The Twins made Keller their eighth pick, two rounds before the New York Mets selected Nolan Ryan, a future member of the Hall of Fame. Keller joined St. Cloud, Minn. (Northern), and led the league with nine wins while striking out 132 batters in 111 innings.

The following year Keller progressed from Wilson, N.C. (Carolina), to Charlotte, N.C. (Southern), to Denver (American Association). He joined the defending AL champion Twins after an injury to veteran pitcher Camilo Pascual.

Keller spent all of 1967 in the minors and rejoined the Twins in 1968. When Minnesota tried to return him to Denver in 1969, Keller retired from baseball. "I felt I had nothing more to prove in the minors," he said. "(Twins owner Calvin) Griffith refused to trade me, and wouldn't believe my threats to quit baseball."

Keller entered the securities field and eventually became a registered investment advisor. His son, Jason Keller, is a Hollywood screenwriter.

KERINS, John Nelson

Born: July 15, 1858, Indianapolis. **Died:** September 8, 1919, Louisville, Kentucky.
Height: 5'10". **Weight:** 177. **Batted:** right. **Threw:** right.
Debut: May 1, 1884. **Final game:** June 15, 1890.
Positions, teams, years: first base (334), catcher (163), outfield (71), third base (4), shortstop (2), second base (1), Indianapolis (American Association) 1884, Louisville (American Association) 1885–1889, Baltimore (American Association) 1889, St. Louis (American Association) 1890.
Games: 557. **At-bats:** 2,227. **Home runs:** 20. **Average:** .252.
Manager: Louisville (American Association) 1888, St. Louis (American Association) 1890 (12–12).

A first baseman and catcher for most of his career, **Jack Kerins** also managed in the big leagues.

Kerins started playing semi-pro ball for the Indianapolis Capitals in 1878. He became the first Indianapolis native to reach the Major Leagues when he joined the Indianapolis Hoosiers of the American Association in 1884. He batted only .216 that year, but his .972 fielding percentage led all first basemen.

When the Association dropped the Indianapolis franchise prior to 1885, Kerins joined the Louisville Colonels. His batting average improved to .243. Primarily a catcher in 1886, his average jumped to .269. While watching a sandlot game in downtown Indianapolis, he discovered pitcher Toad Ramsey. With Kerins as his personal catcher, Ramsey won 75 games for Louisville in 1886 and 1887. "Ramsey's unusual success was to a considerable degree due to the able catching of Kerins," *The Sporting News* reported.

Playing first base and serving as Louisville's team captain in 1887, Kerins had his best season, batting .294 with a league-leading 19 triples. In a July game with the Philadelphia Athletics, he was involved in a collision at home plate that left him with a broken right hand and two dislocated fingers. He returned to action three weeks later, but his injuries may not have healed completely and he was never again the same player.

In 1888, when he batted .235 in 83 contests, Kerins was the third of four managers for seventh-place Louisville. Released by the Colonels after two games in 1889, he caught on with the Baltimore Orioles and saw action in 16 contests. He finished the year with a .290 average.

Kerins moved on to his third American Association club, the St. Louis Browns, in 1890. He was the second of five Browns skippers that season, replacing Tommy McCarthy before giving way to Chief Roseman. St. Louis won nine of 17 games with Kerins at the helm. He made 18 appearances, mostly as a first baseman, and his average dwindled to .127.

The 1890 campaign was Kerins' last. Settling in Louisville, he worked at a variety of jobs. He umpired in the American Association in 1891, and for a time he was a barkeeper at a saloon. He was employed as a houseman at the Tyler Hotel at the time of his death at the age of 71. Kerins was buried in a potter's field, but his old fans were determined to provide him with a more dignified resting place and a headstone. Eventually, he was reinterred in Louisville's Cave Hill Cemetery.

KIERMAIER, Kevin James

Born: April 22, 1990, Fort Wayne. **Lives:** Fort Wayne.
Height: 6-1. **Weight:** 195. **Bats:** left. **Throws:** right.
Debut: September 30, 2013.
Positions, teams, years: outfield, Tampa Bay (AL) 2013–2014.
Games: 109. **At-bats:** 331. **Home runs:** 10. **Average:** .263.

As a senior, Kevin Kiermaier helped Fort Wayne's Bishop Luers High School to Class 2A state titles in football (2007) and baseball (2008). Switching to the outfield, Kiermaier (pronounced "KEER-my-er") batted .426 with 13 triples as a freshman at Parkland College (Champaign, Ill.). He earned MVP honors when Parkland won the 2009 Division II Junior College World Series in Enid, Okla.

The Tampa Bay Rays took Kiermaier in the 31st round of the 2010 draft. He broke in that summer with a .303 average in 57 games for Princeton, W. Va. (Appalachian). Playing for Montgomery, Ala. (Southern), and Durham, N.C. (International), in 2013, he ranked as the top defensive outfielder in the Rays organization.

Kiermaier joined Tampa Bay in late September 2013 after Rays center fielder Desmond Jennings suffered a strained hamstring. In the 163rd game of the year, an AL wild-card tiebreaker that saw Tampa Bay beat Texas to reach the playoffs, Kiermaier saw action as a defensive replacement. He became the first player in Major League history to make his debut in a single-game tiebreaker, and the second to do it in his team's 163rd (or later) game of a season (in 1964, Elvio Jimenez of the Yankees debuted in New York's 164th and final game).

In 2014 Kiermaier shuttled between Durham and Tampa Bay until a wrist injury shelved Wil Myers, the Rays right fielder. Playing all three outfield positions, the lightning-fast Kiermaier showed surprising power with 10 homers in 108 contests. He finished the year with a .263 average.

His rise from late-round draft pick to big league outfielder impressed baseball pundits. "You can call it a Cinderella story," Kiermaier told the *Tampa Bay Times*, "but there was a lot of hard work and I'm just thankful for the opportunity."

KING, Jeffrey Wayne ("Kinger")

Born: December 26, 1964, Marion. **Lives:** Wexford, Pennsylvania.
Height: 6'1". **Weight:** 175. **Batted:** right. **Threw:** right.
Debut: June 2, 1989. **Final game:** May 21, 1999.
Positions, teams, years: third base (586), first base (488), second base (121), shortstop (11), outfield (1), Pittsburgh (NL), 1989–1996, Kansas City (AL) 1997–1999.
Games: 1,201. **At-bats:** 4,262. **Home runs:** 154. **Average:** .256.

Versatile **Jeff King**, the top pick in the 1986 draft, didn't achieve stardom until his eighth professional season.

King's family moved from Indiana to California before he started school. From there they relocated to Colorado, where he starred at shortstop for Rampart High School in Colorado Springs. The Chicago Cubs drafted him in 1983, but King didn't sign and took a scholarship offer from the University of Arkansas.

In three years with the Razorbacks, he batted .372 with 42 home runs.

The Sporting News named him college player of the year for 1986, and the Pittsburgh Pirates—hoping King could provide immediate help at third base—made him their number one draft pick. He batted just .235 in his first professional season at Prince William (Carolina), and didn't reach the Major Leagues until 1989.

King spent all of 1990 with Pittsburgh, which optioned him to Buffalo (American Association) in 1991 and again in 1992. After hitting .345 in seven games for the Bisons in '92, he returned to the majors to stay. That September 20 at Pittsburgh he hit a line drive to Phillies second baseman (and Indiana University alum) Mickey Morandini, who executed the ninth unassisted triple play in big league history.

The following year King began to live up to expectations, batting .295 with 98 runs batted in. Back and wrist injuries slowed him in 1994 and again in 1995. In 1996 he developed into one of baseball's top power hitters with a career-high 30 homers, 111 RBI and a .271 average. "He's fundamentally and mechanically the best player I've ever seen. He just doesn't know it," Pittsburgh shortstop Jay Bell told *Baseball America*. "He's doing things now that he was capable of doing his entire career."

Against the Cincinnati Reds on April 30, 1996, King blasted a solo homer and a grand slam to become only the third player in history to hit two home runs in the same inning twice. His previous two-homer inning came on August 8, 1995, versus San Francisco.

After the season the Pirates sent King to Kansas City in a six-player transaction. In his first two seasons with the Royals, he had 112 RBI in 1997 and 93 in 1998. An excellent fielder at third base and a capable second baseman, King moved to first base in 1996 due to chronic shoulder problems. Recurrent back injuries forced his retirement in May 1999 at age 34.

Jack King, Jeff's father, played in the minor leagues from 1954 to 1955 and later directed Athletes in Action's baseball ministry. Jeff's brother Jim was drafted twice but never signed a professional contract.

KINZER, Matthew Roy

Born: June 17, 1963, Indianapolis. **Lives:** Fort Wayne.
Height: 6'2". **Weight:** 210. **Batted:** right. **Threw:** right.
Debut: May 18, 1989. **Final game:** May 26, 1990.
Positions, teams, years: pitcher, St. Louis (NL) 1989, Detroit (AL) 1990.
Games: 9. **Innings pitched:** 15. **Won/Lost:** 0–2. **Earned run average:** 13.20.

Matt Kinzer, a two-sport standout at Purdue University, had brief careers in pro football and Major League baseball. Kinzer grew up in Markle and earned all-state honors in baseball and football at Norwell High School in Ossian, where he also played basketball.

The Cleveland Indians drafted Kinzer in 1981, but instead he accepted a football scholarship from Purdue University. He was the Boilermakers' punter from 1981 to 1983. He won three letters in baseball at Purdue, and in the summer of 1983 he led the amateur Atlantic Collegiate League with a 1.26 ERA while compiling a 7–0 record.

In June 1984 the St. Louis Cardinals drafted Kinzer in the second round. He spent his first professional season with Arkansas (Texas). In 1987 he threw a no-hitter for the Travelers against Tulsa. He became a full-time reliever in 1988 and joined the Cardinals the following year. Detroit acquired him in a five-player trade in December 1989, and in 1990 he pitched in one game for the Tigers. Released that July, he pitched briefly in the Baltimore Orioles organization.

During the 1987 National Football League players' strike, Kinzer signed with the Detroit Lions as a replacement player. In his lone professional appearance, he punted seven times for a 34-yard average.

Kinzer served as Columbia City High School's athletic director when his athletic career ended and also scouted for the Tampa Bay Devil Rays. He later became an adviser for Reynolds Sports Management. In 2004 he was elected to the Northeast Indiana Baseball Association Hall of Fame.

Lee Kinzer, Matt's father, signed with a St. Louis Cardinals' farm team in 1950 but never played. Matt's son Taylor, a pitcher/designated hitter for Homestead High School and Taylor University, spent three seasons in the Los Angeles Angels chain.

KITTLE, Ronald Dale ("Kitty")

Indiana Baseball Hall of Fame, 2010
Born: January 5, 1958, Gary. **Lives:** Chesterton.
Height: 6'4". **Weight:** 200. **Batted:** right. **Threw:** right.
Debut: September 2, 1982. **Final game:** August 13, 1991.
Positions, teams, years: outfield (353), first base (72), Chicago (AL) 1982–1986, New York (AL) 1986–1987, Cleveland (AL) 1988, Chicago (AL) 1989–1990, Baltimore (AL) 1990, Chicago (AL) 1991.
Games: 843. **At-bats:** 2,708. **Home runs:** 176. **Average:** .239.

The AL Rookie of the Year for 1983, **Ron Kittle's** baseball career almost ended before he reached the majors.

The bespectacled Kittle was a three-sport letterman at Wirt High School in Gary and signed with the Los Angeles Dodgers as a free agent in 1977. After unproductive, injury-plagued stops at Clinton (Midwest) and Lethbridge, Alb. (Pioneer), the Dodgers released him in July 1978. He returned to Gary as an iron worker. Later that summer, he underwent surgery for a pinched nerve caused by two crushed neck vertebrae.

In 1979 Kittle got a second chance when the Chicago White Sox signed him after a special tryout arranged by former Sox pitcher Billy Pierce. Kittle developed into a prospect in 1981 with a 40-homer year at Glens Falls, N.Y. (Eastern). In 1982 his 50 home runs and 144 RBI for Edmonton, Alb. (Pacific Coast), earned him Minor League Player of the Year honors.

Playing left field for the division-champion White Sox in 1983, Kittle won Rookie of the Year honors. His 35 homers eclipsed the club's freshman record of 27 by Zeke Bonura in 1934. "I swing at everything," Kittle quipped. "That way they don't know how to pitch to me." In 1984 his 32 home runs topped Chicago for a second consecutive year, but his average plummeted from .254 to .215. He clubbed 26 homers in 1985 despite losing three weeks due to a shoulder injury.

In July 1986 the White Sox traded Kittle to the New York Yankees. Neck problems limited him to 59 games for the Yanks in 1987. Released by New York after the season, he signed with Cleveland for 1988. Strictly a designated hitter by now, Kittle batted .258 for the Indians with 18 homers in 75 games. In 1989 he returned to the White Sox as a free agent. By mid–June, Kittle was batting .302 with 11 homers in 51 games when he underwent season-ending surgery for a herniated disc. He split the 1990 campaign between Chicago and the Baltimore Orioles and closed out his career with the White Sox in 1991.

A lifelong Indiana resident, Kittle founded Indiana Sports Charities in 1989 and has been involved in a variety of charitable causes since his retirement. In 1996 he was selected to carry the Olympic flame through Crown Point during the torch run for the Atlanta Games.

Kittle managed independent league teams in Merrillville and Schaumberg, Ill. In 2005 he published *Tales from the White Sox Dugout*, co-authored with former Chicago sportswriter Bob Logan.

Kittle is a member of the Indiana Baseball Hall of Fame's Class of 2010.

KLEIN, Charles Herbert ("Tiger," "The Hoosier Hercules," "The Hoosier Hammerer")
National Baseball Hall of Fame, 1980. **Indiana Baseball Hall of Fame, 1981.**
Born: October 7, 1904, Indianapolis. **Died:** March 28, 1958, Indianapolis.
Height: 6'0". **Weight:** 185. **Batted:** left. **Threw:** right.
Debut: July 30, 1928. **Final game:** June 11, 1944.
Positions, teams, years: outfield (1600), first base (1), Philadelphia (NL) 1928–1933, Chicago (NL) 1934–1936, Philadelphia (NL) 1936–1939, Pittsburgh (NL) 1939, Philadelphia (NL) 1940–1944.
Games: 1,753. **At-bats:** 6,486. **Home runs:** 300. **Average:** .320.

Chuck Klein, a slugging outfielder for the Philadelphia Phillies during the Depression years, was the first Indiana native to play in the All-Star Game.

At Southport High School, Klein was a member of the varsity baseball, football, basketball and track teams. He later played for Indianapolis semi-pro clubs and worked in steel mills before signing with Evansville (Three-I) in 1927. After the season, Fort Wayne (Central) purchased his contract. Klein was batting .331 with 26 home runs through 88 games in 1928 when he joined the Phillies. He took over in right field and batted .360 with 11 homers in 64 contests.

Playing in Philadelphia's Baker Bowl during the live-ball era of the late Twenties and early Thirties, Klein compiled amazing statistics in his first five-and-a-half big league seasons. In 1929, his first full year, he batted .365 and his league-leading 43 home runs set an NL record. Klein had a pair of 26-game hitting streaks in 1930, finishing with 40 homers and a .386 average. He led the NL with 59 doubles and 158 runs and his 44 assists set a record for outfielders that has never been broken. In 1931 he hit .337 and led the league in homers (31), runs (121) and RBI (121).

In 1932, when he was the NL MVP, Klein batted .348 with 137 RBI. His 38 homers tied for the league lead. He led the NL in hits (226), runs (152) and stolen bases (20) to become the first live-ball era player to win both the home run and base-stealing titles. When he set a record with 200 or more hits for a fifth consecutive season in 1933, he was the NL's starting right fielder in the Major League's first All-Star Game (Cleveland pitcher Oral Hildebrand, another Indianapolis native, was selected to the AL team but didn't play).

Writing for the *Indianapolis Times* in 1957, Harold Baker described Klein in his heyday: "He got the biggest love out of going to the ball park every day; studying the pitchers until he got his chance to swing; trotting out to right field and chess-playing the opposing hitters; rough-housing with the boys in the shower room; poker and bridge and bull sessions with his player buddies in hotel rooms and on the easy-going train circuit. A wonderful guy was having a wonderful time."

Klein won the Triple Crown in '33, leading the league with 28 homers, 120 RBI and a .368 average. Although he led the league in five other offensive categories, Klein finished second in the MVP ballot behind pitcher Carl Hubbell of the pennant-winning New York Giants. With Philadelphia, Klein averaged 36 homers a year, 139 RBI, 229 hits and a .359 batting average. He belted six grand slams and hit for the cycle twice. But during his first six campaigns, the Phillies had only one winning season.

In November 1933, Klein became the first player to be traded after winning the Triple

Crown when Philadelphia dealt him to the Chicago Cubs. Playing for a perennial pennant contender, he got off to a fine start in 1934 and once again made the NL All-Star team. He suffered a leg injury in July and missed 37 games, finishing with 20 homers and a .301 average as Chicago came in third. The Cubs won the pennant in 1935, but Klein had another sub-par season with 21 homers and a .293 average in 119 games. It was the first time he failed to hit .300 or better. Benched for much of the pennant drive, Klein's home run in Game Five of the World Series led to a 3–0 Cubs victory over Detroit. The Tigers went on to win the Series in six games.

Chicago traded Klein back to the Phillies in May 1936. On July 10, he hit four home runs in a game with the Pittsburgh Pirates. Bothered by injuries in 1937, Klein hit 15 homers and averaged .325. In 1938 he averaged .247 with eight home runs. Cut loose by Philadelphia in June 1939, he signed with Pittsburgh. Klein rejoined the Phillies for a third hitch in 1940. He got into 116 games, hitting .218 with seven homers. From 1941 to 1944 he served mostly as a pinch-hitter. He was a player-coach for his last three seasons.

After retiring, Klein operated a Philadelphia tavern. He returned to Indianapolis in 1948, suffering from a debilitating illness aggravated by malnutrition and excessive drinking. He died at age 53 from a cerebral hemorrhage.

Klein was on the Hall of Fame ballot for 15 years but was passed over each time. The Veterans Committee finally selected him for Cooperstown in 1980. In 1981 he was elected to the Indiana Baseball Hall of Fame.

An Indianapolis sports complex was named for Klein in 1985. In 2000 *The Sporting News* ranked him No. 92 on its all-time greatest players, while *Baseball America* listed him as No. 65 that same year. In 2004 the Society for American Baseball Research's Centennial Celebrity voted Klein the most prominent baseball figure born a hundred years earlier.

KNEPPER, Charles

Born: February 18, 1871, Anderson. **Died:** February 6, 1946, Muncie.
Height: 6'4". **Weight:** 190. **Batted:** right. **Threw:** right.
Debut: May 26, 1899. **Final game:** September 26, 1899.
Positions, teams, years: pitcher, Cleveland (NL) 1899.
Games: 27. **Innings pitched:** 219.2. **Won/Lost:** 4–22. **Earned run average:** 5.78.

Charlie Knepper's four victories for the Cleveland Spiders in 1899 were the highest total for the worst team in Major League history.

Reportedly an excellent boxer as a young man, Knepper was a star pitcher for independent teams around Indiana. In 1896 and 1898 he had trials with Indianapolis (Western), which sent him to Youngstown, Ohio (Interstate), for the 1898 season. He developed into a prospect at Youngstown with a 20–16 record for a last-place team that won just 53 contests.

In May 1899 Knepper joined Cleveland, a team that was part of a syndicate that also owned the St. Louis Perfectos. After his debut, the *Cleveland Plain Dealer* noted: "He evidently thinks he is Samson, with his strength in his hair, for he is in great need of a hair cut. Knepper has a good drop ball that should be troublesome, but he could not control it."

After the syndicate shifted its best players to St. Louis, Cleveland won only 20 games against 134 losses. Knepper, who completed all 26 of his starts for the hapless Spiders, finished with a 4–22 record. The only other pitcher with as many wins, right-hander Jim Hughey, went 4–30.

Cleveland disbanded after the season. Knepper, who was on the St. Louis reserve list for 1900 but didn't play, resurfaced in 1901. After a combined record of 2–6 for St. Paul and Des Moines, Iowa, of the Western League, he was gone from organized ball. He settled in Muncie, where he worked for the Warner Gear Company and later at the Eagles Club.

KNOLL, Charles Elmer ("Punch")

Born: October 7, 1881, Evansville. **Died:** February 8, 1960, Evansville.
Height: 5'7". **Weight:** 170. **Batted:** right. **Threw:** right.
Debut: April 27, 1905. **Final game:** October 4, 1905.
Positions, teams, years: outfield (63), catcher (5), first base (2), Washington (AL) 1905.
Games: 79. **At-bats:** 244. **Home runs:** 0. **Average:** .213.

Punch Knoll, whose pro career began in his hometown, spent thirty years in baseball and managed six minor league pennant winners.

Knoll was Evansville's first batter when the River Rats played their inaugural contest in 1901. Before the summer ended, he moved to Nashville, Tenn. (Southern Association). He played there until 1904, when Washington drafted him. The Senators released him after the 1905 season, and in 1906 he was back in the minors with New Orleans (Southern Association).

For the next eleven years, Knoll was a player-manager in the Central League—first at Evansville from 1907 to 1909, and then Dayton, Ohio, from 1910 through 1912. He led the league in homers with 12 in 1908, and with 11 in both 1909 and 1911.

Knoll guided Dayton to a first-place finish in 1911. He returned to Evansville in 1913 and remained there through 1917. He led the River Rats to pennants in 1908 and 1915, the year Evansville's historic Bosse Field opened.

Out of baseball in 1918, Knoll operated a tavern in Evansville. In 1919 he joined Evansville's team in the rejuvenated Three-I League. He was a playing manager at Ludington, Mich. (Central), in 1920. From 1921 to 1924 he was player-manager at Bay City, Mich. (Michigan-Ontario), which finished first in 1923 and 1924. He was back in the Three-I League with Danville, Ill., from 1925 to 1926 and with Quincy, Ill., in 1927. Returning to the Central League, he managed Fort Wayne in 1928. In 1929 he was a non-playing manager at Wilkes-Barre, Pa. (New York-Pennsylvania). He finished his managing career with Fort Wayne in 1930, logging three at-bats at the age of 48.

Knoll had 2,500 lifetime hits, all but 52 in the minors. He prepared many players for the Major Leagues, including outfielder Chuck Klein. Klein, also an Indiana native, went on to a Hall of Fame career after playing for Knoll at Fort Wayne in 1928. Klein credited Punch for developing his fielding skills.

After leaving baseball, Knoll retired to his orchard farm. When the Three-I League celebrated its fiftieth anniversary in 1951 he was honored as "Mr. Baseball." Knoll is a member of the Evansville Sports Hall of Fame. His daughter Thelma married Syl Simon, who played for the St. Louis Browns in 1923–24.

KNOLLS, Oscar Edward ("Hub")

Born: December 18, 1883, Valparaiso. **Died:** July 1, 1946, Chicago, Illinois.
Height: 6'2". **Weight:** 190. **Batted:** unknown. **Threw:** right.
Debut: May 1, 1906. **Final game:** May 6, 1906.
Positions, teams, years: pitcher, Brooklyn (NL) 1906.
Games: 2. **Innings pitched:** 6.2. **Won/Lost:** 0–0. **Earned run average:** 4.05.

The son of German immigrants, **Hub Knolls** split a pair of decisions at Evansville (Central) in 1905. As a 22-year-old rookie with just one year's professional experience, he went to spring-training in 1906 with the Chicago Cubs of Tinker-to-Evers-to-Chance fame. Although Knolls pitched effectively in exhibition games, the Cubs shipped him to the Brooklyn Superbas at the end of April.

Knolls made two relief appearances for Brooklyn. In his lone at-bat, he hit a double, and he muffed his lone chance in the field for an error. Describing him as a "big prairie pitcher," *The Sporting Life* reported that Knolls jumped Brooklyn and returned to Chicago to pitch for the semi-pro Marquettes team.

Knolls later sought reinstatement from baseball's National Commission and returned to organized ball in 1908. He spent that year in the Tri-State League, splitting time between Johnstown, Pa., and Trenton, N.J. He played for Denver (Western) in 1909 and 1910.

After leaving baseball, Knolls returned to Chicago and worked as a commercial agent for the Railway Express Agency. For many years he was a member of Chicago's Old Timers Baseball Association. He died from heart disease at age 62.

KONOPKA, Bruno Bruce

Born: September 16, 1919, Hammond. **Died:** September 27, 1996, Denver, Colorado.
Height: 6'2". **Weight:** 190. **Batted:** left. **Threw:** left.
Debut: June 7, 1942. **Final game:** September 29, 1946.
Positions, teams, years: first base (23), outfield (1), Philadelphia (AL) 1942–1943, 1946.
Games: 45. **At-bats:** 105. **Home runs:** 0. **Average:** .238.

A fine all-around athlete, **Bruno Konopka's** football skills earned him a mention in *Ripley's Believe It or Not*.

Konopka, whose family moved to Colorado soon after his birth, was a three-sport standout at Denver's Manual High School. During a football contest on October 23, 1937, Konopka punted from deep in his own end zone. The ball traveled 77 yards in the air and landed on the opposing team's 25-yeard line. Then it kept on bouncing and rolling until it came to rest 30 yards behind the opposition's goal line. The punt was measured at 132 yards, six inches, and was listed as a "world record" in *Ripley's*.

After rejecting a contract offer from the St. Louis Browns, Konopka accepted a baseball and basketball scholarship from the University of Southern California. In 1942 he served as captain for the first Trojan baseball team coached by the legendary Rod Dedeaux. The pull-hitting first baseman briefly played for Connie Mack's Philadelphia Athletics in 1942 and 1943 before spending two years in the navy. He rejoined the A's in 1946, but lost the first base post to Ferris Fain. Bruno returned to the minors and ended his pro career in 1947 after stints with Atlanta and Little Rock, Ark., in the Southern Association.

Konopka, who earned a degree in business administration from USC, went to work for the Coors Brewing Company and played for the company's semi-pro baseball squad. In 1947 he was the MVP at the National Baseball Congress Tournament in Wichita, Kan., batting .514 for the runnerup Golden (Colo.) Coors squad. Later, he worked as a realtor and as a stockbroker. In 1993 he retired from Denver's parks and recreation department. In 1996 Konopka was one of several old-time players from the Denver area who were honored prior to a Colorado Rockies game at Mile High Stadium.

KRAFT, Clarence Otto ("Big Boy")

Born: June 9, 1887, Evansville. **Died:** March 25, 1958, Fort Worth, Texas.
Height: 6'0". **Weight:** 190. **Batted:** right. **Threw:** right.
Debut: May 1, 1914. **Final game:** May 15, 1914.
Positions, teams, years: first base, Boston (NL) 1914.
Games: 3. **At-bats:** 3. **Home runs:** 0. **Average:** .333.

Playing for one of the best teams in Texas League history, **Big Boy Kraft** was one of the greatest minor league sluggers of all time.

Kraft earned his nickname when he grew to six feet at an early age. He played for an Evansville YMCA championship team in basketball and was also a sandlot baseball star. Originally a pitcher and outfielder, he broke in with Evansville (Central) in 1910 and went to McLeansboro (Southern Illinois) after one at-bat. McLeansboro shifted to the Kitty League at mid-season.

Drafted by the Cleveland Naps for 1911, Kraft played in three different leagues before the Brooklyn Superbas acquired him for 1914. Brooklyn sold his contract to the Boston Braves. Back with Brooklyn after three games, he became the center of controversy when the Superbas tried to assign him to Newark, N.J. (International). Before the conflict was resolved, the Player's Fraternity threatened to shut down all of baseball by striking on Kraft's behalf.

From 1915 through 1917, Kraft played in four different minor league cities. He joined Fort Worth (Texas) in 1918 and spent part of the year in France with the U.S. Army. Back with Fort Worth in 1919, he helped the Panthers to six consecutive pennants. His .352 batting average topped the league in 1921, and he won three consecutive home run titles with 32 in both 1922 and 1923 and an eye-popping 55 in 1924. His 196 runs batted in during the '24 season is a league record that still stands.

When he retired after the 1924 season at age 37, one sportswriter credited Kraft with twenty-seven Texas League records. He opened a Ford dealership in Fort Worth which "became crowded with visitors," former big leaguer Bobby Bragan told Jeff Guinn, author of *When Panthers Roared: The Fort Worth Cats and Minor League Baseball*, "but no one wanted to buy a car. Instead, they all wanted to talk baseball with Kraft. Finally, he felt forced to post a notice that no one could come in and discuss baseball without purchasing a car first."

During the Depression, Kraft returned to baseball as Fort Worth's team president. He was elected county judge in 1942, a post he held until retirement in 1948.

KRALY, Steve Charles ("Lefty")
Born: April 18, 1929, Whiting. **Lives:** Johnson City, New York.
Height: 5'10". **Weight:** 152. **Batted:** left. **Threw:** left.
Debut: August 9, 1953. **Final game:** September 15, 1953.
Positions, teams, years: pitcher, New York (AL) 1953.
Games: 5. **Innings pitched:** 25. **Won/Lost:** 0–2. **Earned run average:** 3.24.

Pint-sized **Steve Kraly** threw two no-hitters for Whiting High School, where he also lettered in basketball and track.

Most scouts ignored him because of his small stature, but the New York Yankees offered Kraly (pronounced KRAH-lee) a contract after a brief stint at Indiana University. In 1949, his first professional season, he compiled a 15–10 record for Independence, Mo. (Kansas-Oklahoma-Missouri), followed by an 18–6 slate in 1950 for Joplin, Mo. (Western Association). One of his teammates at Independence and Joplin was future Yankee center fielder Mickey Mantle.

Returning from a two-year army hitch in 1953, Kraly had a 19–2 record and a league-leading 2.08 ERA for Binghamton, N.Y. (Eastern). That August, with the Yankees battling for the pennant, Mantle urged manager Casey Stengel to promote Kraly. "I don't care how small he is, he can win up here," Mantle insisted.

Kraly appeared in five games for New York. Although he didn't play in the World Series, he earned a championship ring when the Yanks beat the Brooklyn Dodgers in seven games. He spent the next three seasons in the Yankee chain and developed arm trouble in 1955.

Released by New York prior to the 1958 season, Kraly continued to pitch until 1960. He ended his career with Indianapolis (American Association).

Kraly worked for IBM after leaving baseball. He also served as an official scorer for the Binghamton Mets of the Eastern League.

LaMASTER, Noble Wayne
Indiana Baseball Hall of Fame, 1988.
Born: February 13, 1907, Speed. **Died:** August 4, 1989, New Albany.
Height: 5'8". **Weight:** 170. **Batted:** left. **Threw:** left.
Debut: April 19, 1937. **Final game:** August 29, 1938.
Positions, teams, years: pitcher, Philadelphia (NL) 1937–1938, Brooklyn (NL) 1938.
Games: 71. **Innings pitched:** 295.1. **Won/Lost:** 19–27. **Earned run average:** 5.82.

Stocky southpaw **Wayne LaMaster** pitched in the minor leagues for ten seasons before reaching the majors. He once lost a big league game in which he didn't allow a batter to reach base.

Born in the unincorporated community of Speed, just north of Sellersburg in southeastern, Indiana, LaMaster was a graduate of Jeffersonville High School. He played for Indiana semi-pro teams in Austin and Seymour before signing with Jackson, Miss. (Cotton States), in 1927. In 1932 he led Charleston, W.Va., to the Middle Atlantic League pennant with a 17–6 record. His 177 strikeouts and 2.27 ERA led the league.

Drafted by the Phillies for 1937, LaMaster joined Philadelphia's starting rotation as a 30-year-old rookie. His 19 losses that year were a league high, but he had a team-high 15 victories.

LaMaster was the Phillies' Opening Day hurler in 1938, the year he developed arm problems. In a May 5 start against the Cubs at Wrigley Field, a strained arm forced him out of the game with a 3-and-1 count on leadoff hitter Stan Hack. Relief pitcher Tom Reis finished the walk, which was charged to LaMaster. Hack scored the first of four Chicago runs in a 21–2 victory, and LaMaster was charged with the loss.

That August, Philadelphia dealt LaMaster to Brooklyn. He underwent surgery in the spring of 1939, but later that year came back to pitch for Montreal (International). He remained with Montreal through 1940 and appeared in four games for Durham, N.C. (Piedmont), in 1941 before retiring.

LaMaster lived in Sellersburg during most of his baseball career. He later moved to Jeffersonville, where he worked for the Marhoefer Packing Company. In 1988 he was inducted into the Indiana Baseball Hall of Fame.

Wayne and his wife Dorothy shared a birthdate, February 13, which was also their wedding date. "The idea was mine, and about the smartest idea I ever had," LaMaster told Bruce Dudley of the *Louisville Courier-Journal*. "I don't have to buy but one present!"

LARMORE, Robert McKahan ("Red")

Born: December 6, 1896, Anderson. **Died:** January 15, 1964, St. Louis, Missouri.
Height: 5'10". **Weight:** 185. **Batted:** right. **Threw:** right.
Debut: May 14, 1918. **Final game:** June 22, 1918.
Positions, teams, years: shortstop, St. Louis (NL) 1918.
Games: 4. **At-bats:** 7. **Home runs:** 0. **Average:** .286.

Even though he played in the Major Leagues, baseball may not have been **Bob Larmore's** best sport.

Larmore moved to St. Louis at an early age. He starred in football, basketball and baseball at Central High School, where he batted .485 as a junior in 1917. Before graduating in 1918 at the advanced age of 21, he signed with the Cardinals. "The contract signed by Larmore yesterday permits him to finish his high school course," the *St. Louis Post-Dispatch* reported on February 9.

The red-haired Larmore appeared in four games for the Cardinals that year and also spent time with Houston (Texas) and Sioux City, Iowa (Western). In July he enlisted in the U.S. Navy.

Dividing the 1919 campaign between Houston and Dallas in the Texas League, Larmore batted .240. He opened the 1920 season at Joplin. Mo. (Western). He batted .194 in 22 games and moved on to Cedar Rapids, Iowa (Three-I), where he hit .266 in 111 contests. That was his last season in organized ball.

Larmore, whose family founded an ice cream factory in Anderson, Ind., in 1901, briefly attended the University of Missouri in the Twenties. In time he became an officer of the Sealtest Foods Company.

The winner of several city handball titles in St. Louis, Larmore was runnerup at the 1929 national championships. He maintained an active interest in sports until his death at age 67 following a long illness.

LARSEN, Don James ("Gooney Bird," "Night Rider," "The Ghoul")

Indiana Baseball Hall of Fame, 2005.
Born: August 7, 1929, Michigan City. **Lives:** Hayden Lake, Idaho.
Height: 6'4". **Weight:** 215. **Batted:** right. **Threw:** right.
Debut: April 18, 1953. **Final game:** July 7, 1967.
Positions, teams, years: pitcher (412), outfield (2), St. Louis (AL) 1953, Baltimore (AL) 1954, New York (AL) 1955–1959, Kansas City 1960–1961, Chicago (AL) 1961, San Francisco (NL) 1962–1964, Houston (NL) 1964–1965, Baltimore (AL) 1965, Chicago (NL) 1967.
Games: 412. **Innings pitched:** 1,548. **Won/Lost:** 81–91. **Earned run average:** 3.78.
At-bats: 596. **Home runs:** 14. **Average:** .242.

Don Larsen turned in baseball's most dramatic performance in the 1956 World Series.

Larsen played basketball at Michigan City High School before his family moved to California in 1944. At San Diego's Point Loma High, he played basketball and baseball, and in the summer of 1946 he starred in American Legion tournament play.

In 1947 Larsen signed with the St. Louis Browns and debuted with Aberdeen, S.D. (Northern). After a 17–11 slate at Aberdeen in 1948, the gangly right-hander suffered from arm trouble and control problems. He spent the next two seasons with four different clubs.

Following a two-year army hitch, Larsen joined the Browns in 1953 and went 7–12. After the season the Browns moved to Baltimore. Larsen, the Orioles' Opening Day starter in 1954, won three games versus a league-leading 21 defeats. In November 1954, Baltimore sent him to the Yankees as part of a 17-player deal.

Larsen went 9–1 for Denver (American Association) in 1955 to earn a promotion to New York, where he went 9–2 to help the Yanks win the AL flag. He took the loss in the fourth game of the World Series against the Brooklyn Dodgers, who went on to win in seven games for their first and only Series title.

Larsen went 11–5 for New York in 1956. In a World Series rematch with Brooklyn, Larsen started Game Two at Ebbets Field but didn't get past the second inning. In Game Five at Yankee Stadium three days later, he started again. This time Larsen beat the Dodgers 2–

0, allowing no hits and no walks for the first perfect game since 1922. It was the first no-hit performance in Series history. "Even though I pitched a no-hitter and retired 27 men in a row I hardly can believe it," Larsen told reporters. "Of coure I've dreamed of it—the no-hitter, but, Oh, Lord, never the perfect game."

Larsen's 10–4 slate in 1957 helped the Yanks to another pennant. In Game Three of the World Series against the Milwaukee Braves, he earned the win with seven and one-third innings of relief work. Larsen was the starter and losing pitcher in Game Seven.

The Yankees won a fourth consecutive AL title in 1958, as Larsen went 9–6 despite elbow problems. In another New York-Milwaukee Series, he threw seven shutout innings in the Yanks' Game Three win. Larsen started the seventh game, coming out in the third inning as New York went on to win 6–2.

Larsen slipped to 6–7 in 1959 and that December the Yanks sent him to Kansas City as part of a six-player deal that brought Roger Maris to New York. Larsen won just one of 11 decisions for the Athletics in 1960 and spent part of the year in the minors. By 1961, when Kansas City shipped him to the Chicago White Sox, he was primarily a relief pitcher.

When the White Sox dealt him to the San Francisco Giants in 1962, Larsen wound up with another pennant winner. In the World Series against the Yankees, he pitched in relief in Game Four and got the win.

After a 7–7 record in 1963, the Giants dealt Larsen to Houston. He went 4–8, 2.26 for the Colt .45s in 1964. In 1965 he made one appearance for Houston before he went to Baltimore. Released by the Orioles in the spring of 1966, he spent the year with Phoenix (Pacific Coast). Larsen closed out his big league career in 1967 with three relief appearances for the Chicago Cubs. He spent time with Tacoma, Wash. (Pacific Coast), and San Antonio (Texas) in 1968 before retiring.

Larsen was last active player from the old St. Louis Browns. A good hitter, he established a Major League batting record for pitchers in 1953 with seven consecutive hits. In 1958 he batted .306. He had 42 career homers.

After leaving baseball, Larsen worked as a paper company salesman in San Jose, Calif. On July 18, 1999, he returned to Yankee Stadium to throw out the first pitch. Incredibly, New York's David Cone threw a perfect game that day against the Montreal Expos.

With Mark Shaw, Larsen wrote a 1996 autobiography entitled *The Perfect Yankee*. Larsen's cousin, Phillip Hoose, published *Perfect, Once Removed* in 2006.

A fondness for breaking curfew earned Larsen the nickname "Night Rider." Teammates called him "The Ghoul" because of his predilection for morbid comic books.

In 2004 Larsen was elected to the Indiana Baseball Hall of Fame.

LAZAR, John Daniel ("Lazer Beam")

Born: November 14, 1943, in East Chicago. **Lives:** Munster.
Height: 6'1". **Weight:** 190. **Batted:** left. **Threw:** left.
Debut: June 21, 1968. **Final game:** October 2, 1969.
Positions, teams, years: pitcher, Chicago (AL) 1968–1969.
Games: 17. **Innings pitched:** 34. **Won/Lost:** 0–1.
Earned run average: 5.56.

Danny Lazar graduated in 1961 from Griffith High School, where he played baseball, basketball and football. At Indiana State University he set school records with 16 strikeouts in a single game and an 0.84 ERA for the 1965 season.

A 31st-round draft pick by the Chicago White Sox In 1965, Lazar (pronounced "lay-zer") rapidly progressed from rookie league Sarasota, Fla., to Class A Clinton, Iowa (Midwest), to Triple-A Indianapolis (Pacific Coast).

Back in Class A ball for 1966, Lazar went 14–9, 2.42 for Lynchburg, Va. (Carolina). In 1967 at Evansville (Southern) he compiled a 2.30 ERA, losing the league lead by a fraction of a percentage point.

Promoted to Chicago in 1968, Lazar missed the final month of season due to arm problems. "There was inflammation of the tendon and, though I tried relieving a few times, I was through for the year," he told White Sox beat writer Edgar Munzel.

Lazar split the 1969 campaign between the White Sox and Tucson, Ariz. (Pacific Coast). His career ended after six games with Tucson in 1970.

A woodworking enthusiast, the bespectacled Lazar earned a bachelor of science degree in education and taught industrial education at Indiana high schools in East Chicago, Griffith and Highland. Eventually he became president of Slugger Corporation of America, which produced hydraulic bar and billet shears.

Lazar was inducted into Indiana State University's Hall of Fame in 2009.

LEIBOLD, Harry Loran ("Nemo," "Socks")

Born: February 17, 1892, Butler. **Died:** February 4, 1977, Detroit, Michigan.
Height: 5'6". **Weight:** 157. **Batted:** left. **Threw:** right.
Debut: April 12, 1913. **Final game:** October 2, 1925.
Positions, teams, years: outfield (1,120), third base (1), Cleveland (AL) 1913–1915, Chicago (AL) 1915–1920, Boston (AL) 1921–1923, Washington (AL) 1923–1925.
Games: 1,268. **At-bats:** 4,167. **Home runs:** 3. **Average:** .266.

A singles hitter and excellent baserunner with a strong throwing arm, **Nemo Leibold** spent two years with Milwaukee (American Association) before joining the Cleveland Naps in 1913. In Cleveland, Leibold (pronounced "lie-bold") played in the same outfield with the legendary Shoeless Joe Jackson. During 1915, Leibold and Jackson were traded to the Chicago White Sox in separate deals.

Platooning in right field for Chicago from 1915 to 1920, Leibold helped the White Sox to pennants in 1917 and 1919. In 1920 eight Chicago players, including Jackson, were implicated in throwing games in the 1919 World Series. Leibold, one of the honest players, had managed just one hit in 18 Series at-bats after hitting .302 during the 1919 season.

In 1920 Leibold slipped to .220 and Chicago sent him to the Red Sox. Playing center field for Boston in 1921, he had his best season with a .306 average. In 1923 the Red Sox traded him to Washington, where he played for pennant winners in 1924 and 1925. Leading off the eighth inning of the seventh game of the 1924 World Series, Leibold stroked a pinch-hit double that sparked a game-tying rally. The Senators went on to win in the twelfth inning for their only Series triumph.

Leibold returned to the minor leagues in 1926, and in 1928 he become player-manager for Columbus, Ohio (American Association). "Leibold has always been a smart player, smart at bat, smart playing the batters and smart on the bases. If he can impart this knowledge to his men he is sure to be a successful manager," wrote Manning Vaughan of the *Milwaukee Sentinel*.

Leibold went on to manage minor league clubs in Reading, Pa. (New York-Pennsylvania), Syracuse, N.Y. (International), Rocky Mount, N.C. (Piedmont), Clarksdale, Miss. (Cotton States), Scranton Pa. (Eastern), and Louisville (American Association). His teams won four minor league pennants (Scranton in 1939–1940–1943 and Louisville in 1946). His Louisville club lost the 1946 Junior World Series in seven games to Montreal (International).

The 1948 season was his last as a skipper. Over 21 minor league seasons, he compiled a career record 1,527 wins and 1,422 losses. The pint-sized Leibold had a gargantuan temper. In 1946 he was suspended for 45 days for bumping, shoving and verbally assaulting an umpire.

Nicknamed for a newspaper comic strip called "Little Nemo in Slumberland," he lived most of his life in Detroit and scouted for the Tigers in 1950–1951. He suffered a fatal heart attack at age 85.

LEPPERT, Donald George ("Moose")

Indiana Baseball Hall of Fame, 2003.
Born: October 19, 1931, Indianapolis. **Lives:** Naples, Florida.
Height: 6'2". **Weight:** 220. **Batted:** right. **Threw:** right.
Debut: June 18, 1961. **Final game:** September 16, 1964.
Positions, teams, years: catcher, Pittsburgh (NL) 1961–1962, Washington (AL) 1963–1964.
Games: 190. **At-bats:** 532. **Home runs:** 15. **Average:** .229.

Don Leppert, a member of the Indiana Baseball Hall of Fame's Class of 2003, spent 31 years in pro ball as a player, coach and manager.

The burly catcher played baseball at Washington High School in Indianapolis and later at Wabash College, where he was also a member of the football and track squads. After a four-year hitch with the U.S. Air Force, he signed with the Milwaukee Braves and began his career in 1955 at Corpus Christi, Texas (Big State).

In 1961 Leppert joined the Pittsburgh Pirates as a 29-year-old rookie. On June 18 he became the first Indiana native to hit a home run in his first big league at-bat. Traded to the Washington Senators after the 1962 season, he hit three homers in one game against the Boston Red Sox on April 11, 1963. He was selected to the AL All-Star team that year, but didn't play.

The 1964 season was Leppert's last in the majors. He spent spent the next two years in the minors. In 1967 he managed Gastonia, N.C. (Western Carolina).

Over a 19-year-span, Leppert coached for three Major League teams: Pittsburgh (1968–1976), the Toronto Blue Jays (1977–1979) and the Houston Astros (1980–1985).

Returning to the minors, Leppert earned Midwest League manager-of-the-year honors in 1987 when he led Kenosha, Wis., a Minnesota Twins affiliate, to a championship. He earned three World Series rings (Pirates in 1971; Twins in 1987 and 1991).

Two of Leppert's sons, both catchers, were drafted by Major League teams. Toronto selected Steve Leppert (Avon Worth High School, Pittsburgh) in 1977 and he spent three years in the minors. Tim Leppert (Brown County High School, Nashville, Ind.) was drafted by the Twins in 1989, but didn't sign.

LEWIS, Richie Todd ("Hellcat," "Bulldog," "Rooster")

Born: January 25, 1966, Muncie. **Lives:** Melbourne, Florida.
Height: 5'6". **Weight:** 175. **Batted:** right. **Threw:** right.
Debut: July 31, 1992. **Final game:** June 4, 1998.
Positions, teams, years: pitcher, Baltimore (AL) 1992, Florida (NL)1993–1995, Detroit (AL) 1996, Oakland (AL) 1997, Cincinnati (NL) 1997, Baltimore (AL) 1998.
Games: 217. **Innings pitched:** 293.1. **Won/Lost:** 14–15. **Earned run average:** 4.88.

During his 17 years in professional baseball, **Richie Lewis** pitched for 19 different teams in the United States, Canada and Mexico.

Lewis was a three-sport star at Muncie Southside High School, where his father, Larry Lewis, coached the baseball squad. At Florida State University between 1985 and 1987, the stocky right-hander threw 392 innings for a school record. Relying on an excellent curve ball, he struck out 520 batters and helped the Seminoles to the title game of the 1986 College World Series.

After he led the nation with 15 wins and 196 strikeouts in 1987, the Montreal Expos took Lewis in the second round of the draft. He broke in that summer with Indianapolis (American Association), but the heavy college workload began to take a toll. Lewis's next three seasons were cut short by elbow problems, and he underwent surgery in 1991. The Expos traded him to Baltimore that August, and in 1992 he made it to the majors with the Orioles as a starter.

Despite his chronic arm problems, the fledgling Florida Marlins took Lewis in the expansion draft prior to 1993. He spent the next three seasons with Florida as a middle reliever and enjoyed his best season in '93 with a 6–3 record and 3.26 ERA.

Between 1996 and 2003, Lewis was a baseball nomad. At various times he signed contracts with San Diego, Detroit, Oakland, Cincinnati, Philadelphia, the New York Mets, Cleveland, and the Chicago Cubs. He also made stops at Edmonton, Alb. (Pacific Coast), in Canada as well as two Mexican League outposts, Reynosa and Campeche.

Lewis served as pitching coach for the Los Angeles Dodgers Class-A affiliate in Columbus, Ga. (South Atlantic), in 2006 and 2007.

Throughout his career, Lewis was listed as 5-foot–10. In a 2000 interview, he admitted he was actually four inches shorter. "I kept my spikes on when I got measured," he told Phillip B. Wilson of the *Indianapolis Star*.

LIEBHARDT, Glenn John

Born: March 10, 1883, Milton. **Died:** July 13, 1956, Cleveland, Ohio.
Height: 5'10". **Weight:** 175. **Batted:** right. **Threw:** right.
Debut: October 2, 1906. **Final game:** August 5, 1909.
Positions, teams, years: pitcher, Cleveland (AL) 1906–1909.
Games: 90. **Innings pitched:** 612.2. **Won/Lost:** 36–35. **Earned run average:** 2.17.

Born five miles west of Richmond in the town of Milton, **Glenn Liebhardt** spent part of his youth in Indianapolis.

After pitching for an independent team in

Greenfield, Ind., he moved to Arizona in 1903 seeking work as a cowboy. "Before he learned the uses of the branding iron and how to rope cattle," Henry P. Edwards wrote in the *Cleveland Plain Dealer*, "he heard the Los Angeles club needed pitchers. He could not resist the call of the game and left Arizona flat to go to the Pacific Coast."

Playing for Los Angeles (Pacific National) in 1903, Liebhardt learned how to throw a spitball. After the franchise folded he signed with Spokane, Wash. (Pacific National), and finished with an 8–10 record. Pitching for Rock Island, Ill. (Three-I), in 1904, he hurled a 2–0 no-hitter against Bloomington, Ill.

In 1906 Liebhardt had a breakout year at Memphis, Tenn., leading the Southern Association with a league-record 35 wins. Late that year he joined the Cleveland Naps and went 2–0. In 1907 he had an excellent rookie season, going 18–14 with a 2.05 ERA. He lost his first six decisions in 1908, but wound up with a 15–16 slate as the Naps made an unsuccessful run at first place. He took the loss in the contest that decided the pennant as Detroit finished first by half a game.

After a 1–5 record in 1909, Liebhardt returned to the minors and played for another five years. Pitching for Columbus, Ohio (American Association), he won 23 games in 1910 and 19 in 1911. In 1912 he went from Columbus to Minneapolis (American Association), posting a combined 10–11 record. He was back in Memphis for the 1913 and 1914 seasons, going 15–14 in his final campaign.

After leaving baseball, Liebhardt returned to Cleveland, where he worked for a department store and played semi-pro ball. He later managed a paint store.

His son, Glenn Ignatius Liebhardt, who was born in Cleveland, pitched for the Philadelphia Athletics in 1930 and the St. Louis Browns in 1936 and 1938. Another son, Terry Liebhardt, played in the minors in 1937.

LIND, Adam Alan
Born: July 17, 1983, Muncie. **Lives:** Anderson.
Height: 6'2". **Weight:** 195. **Bats:** left. **Throws:** left.
Debut: September 2, 2006.
Positions, teams, years: first base (304), outfield (224), Toronto (AL) 2006–2014.
Games: 953. **At-bats:** 3,407. **Home runs:** 146. **Average:** .273.

Adam Lind was Indiana's Mr. Baseball in 2002 when he set a state record with a .675 batting average for Anderson Highland High School. That fall he entered the University of South Alabama, and as a draft-eligible sophomore in 2004 he led the Sun Belt Conference with a .392 average. The Toronto Blue Jays made him their third-round pick that June.

A first baseman in college, Lind reported to Auburn, N.Y. (New York-Penn), in the summer of 2004 and hit .312 in his pro debut. In 2005 he made the Florida State League all-star team, batting .313 at Dunedin. After winning MVP honors with a .310 average at New Hampshire (Eastern) in 2006, he hit .400 in 33 games for Syracuse, N.Y. (International). Later that season he earned a promotion to the Blue Jays. In the last game of the year, his two-run homer at Yankee Stadium lifted the Jays to a 7–5 win over New York.

Lind shuttled between Toronto and Syracuse in 2007 and 2008, playing mostly in left field. He came up for good in late June 2008, hitting .282 in 88 contests. As the Blue Jays' primary designated hitter in 2009, he slammed 35 homers, drove in 114 runs and batted .305. On September 29 he belted three homers in an 8–7 win over Boston, and at season's end he was cited as the year's top DH.

After signing a four-year, $18 million contract with the Blue Jays prior to 2010, Lind regressed to 23 homers, 72 RBI and a .237 average. Hampered by back trouble in 2011, he batted .251 in 125 games with 26 homers and 87 RBI. He opened the 2012 season as Toronto's cleanup hitter and first baseman. He hit .186 in 34 games and was back in the minors by mid–May. In 32 games for Las Vegas (Pacific Coast), he batted at a .392 clip and returned to Toronto, where he finished the year with 11 homers and a .255 average in 93 contests.

In 2013 Lind rebounded with a .288 average and 23 homers. Back and foot injuries limited him to 96 games in 2014. He batted .321, but his home run total dropped to six and after the season Toronto traded him to the Milwaukee Brewers.

LINDBLOM, Joshua William

Born: June 15, 1987, Lafayette. **Lives:** Lafayette.
Height: 6'4". **Weight:** 240. **Bats:** right. **Throws:** right.
Debut: June 1, 2011.
Positions, teams, years: pitcher, Los Angeles (NL) 2011–2012, Philadelphia (NL) 2012, Texas (AL) 2013, Oakland 2014.
Games: 110. **Innings pitched:** 136.2. **Won/Lost:** 5–8. **Earned run average:** 3.82.

A standout for Harrison High School in West Lafayette, **Josh Lindblom** was 8–2 as a senior in 2005 with a 2.30 ERA and 117 strikeouts in 76 innings. The Astros made him their third-round pick in the June draft, but he turned down a $500,000 offer from the Astros to attend the University of Tennessee. "I was only 17," Lindblom (pronounced LIN-bloom) told the *Orange County Register*. "I knew I wasn't ready to play in the minor leagues. I needed to grow up in a lot of ways."

In 2007 Lindblom transferred to Purdue, where a 96-mph fastball made him one of the nation's top college relievers. The Los Angeles Dodgers took him in the second round of the 2008 draft and assigned him to Great Lakes (Midwest), hoping to convert him into a starter. Midway through 2009 the Dodgers switched him back to the bullpen. He responded with a 3–0 record and 2.54 ERA, mostly in relief, at Albuquerque, N.M. (Pacific Coast).

Lindblom made 40 appearances for Albuquerque in 2010, all but 10 as a reliever, and slipped to 3–2, 6.54. In 2011 the Dodgers demoted him to Double-A Chattanooga, Tenn. (Southern), where he worked as a closer. He joined Los Angeles at the end of May and went 1–0, 2.73 in 27 games as a setup man. He began the 2012 campaign with the Dodgers, who sent him to the Philadelphia Phillies at the trade deadline. His season totals included a 3–5 slate with a 3.55 ERA in 74 contests, all in relief.

Traded to Texas before the 2013 season, Lindblom became a starter. He went 1–3, 5.46 in eight games for the Rangers and 8–4, 3.08, in 20 contests with Round Rock, Texas (Pacific Coast). That December he was on the move again, this time to Oakland in a four-player deal. He spent most of 2014 with Sacramento, Calif. (Pacific Coast), starting 16 of 17 contests and compiling a 4–3, 5.79 record.

Designated for assignment by the Athletics on November 28, Lindblom was claimed by Pittsburgh on December 8. Released by the Pirates on December 12, he signed to play for the Lotte Giants of the Korea Baseball Organization in 2015.

LOFTON, Kenneth ("K-Lo")

Indiana Baseball Hall of Fame, 2013.
Born: May 31, 1967, East Chicago. **Lives:** Phoenix, Arizona.
Height: 6'0". **Weight:** 180. **Batted:** left. **Threw:** left.
Debut: September 14, 1991. **Final game:** September 29, 2007.
Positions, teams, years: outfield, Houston (NL) 1991, Cleveland (AL) 1992–1996, Atlanta (NL) 1997, Cleveland (AL) 1998–2001, Chicago (AL) 2002, San Francisco (NL) 2002, Pittsburgh (NL) 2003, Chicago (NL) 2003, New York (AL) 2004, Philadelphia (NL) 2005, Los Angeles (NL) 2006, Texas (AL) 2007, Cleveland (AL) 2007.
Games: 2,103. **At-bats:** 8,120. **Home runs:** 130. **Average:** .299.

During his 17-year big league career, **Kenny Lofton** played for eleven teams and reached the post-season eleven times. A basketball star in high school and college, Lofton began concentrating on baseball only after signing a professional contract. He quickly became one of the game's finest center fielders and leadoff hitters, as well as an excellent bunter, baserunner, and base stealer.

Lofton was a four-year starter for the baseball squad at Washington High School in East Chicago. He also led the basketball team to the semifinals of the 1985 state tournament. Recruited by Lute Olsen, Lofton accepted a basketball scholarship from the University of Arizona. He was the Wildcats' sixth man as a sophomore point guard in 1988 when Arizona reached the NCAA Final Four. In 1989 he set Wildcat single-season and career records for steals.

In the spring of 1988 Lofton joined Arizona's baseball team. Although he played sparingly, the Houston Astros made him their 17th-round pick in the June draft. Continuing to play basketball for Arizona, he signed with Houston and batted .214 that summer for Auburn, N.Y. (New York-Penn). Two years later at Osceola, he led the Florida State League with a .331 average. He joined Houston in September 1991, and that December the Astros traded him to Cleveland. He batted .285 in his first full season and his 66 stolen bases were an AL rookie record.

Lofton developed into an outstanding player with the Indians, leading the AL in steals each year from 1992 to 1996. He topped the league in assists (1994–95, 1998), hits (1994) and triples (1995). He helped Cleveland to AL East division titles in 1995 and 1996. After helping the Indians to the 1995 AL pennant with a .458 average in the Division Series with Seattle, he became the first black Indiana native to play in the World Series. Cleveland lost in six games to the Atlanta Braves, but Lofton tied a Series record with two stolen bases in one inning.

In 1996 Lofton became the Indians' all-time leading base stealer. Cleveland sent him to Atlanta as part of a four-player deal for 1997. Despite missing 40 games due to injuries, he batted .333 as the Braves won the NL East title. A free agent after the season, he rejoined the Indians. After four years in Cleveland he signed as a free agent with the Chicago White Sox, who traded him in July 2002 to the pennant-bound San Francisco Giants. In the World Series against the Anaheim Angels, he hit .290 in a losing effort.

The Pittsburgh Pirates signed Lofton for 2003 and traded him to the Chicago Cubs that July. A free agent again in 2004, he joined the New York Yankees, who dealt him to Philadelphia after the season. No longer an everyday player at age 38, he batted .335 in 110 games for the Phillies in 2005. After hitting .301 for the Dodgers in 2006, he split the 2007 season—his last—between Texas and the Indians. At year's end he became a free agent, but didn't sign for 2008.

Lofton's best single-season average, .349, came in 1994. In 42 post-season games with six different teams, he batted .225. He hit .269 in 40 Championship Series contests, and in two World Series he averaged .250. He batted .357 in six All-Star Games, and won Gold Glove awards each year from 1993–1996. In 2011 he served as a guest instructor at Cleveland's Spring Training camp.

Lofton, who owns a degree in television and radio, is active in charitable causes for disadvantaged children in East Chicago. In 1995 he was named East Chicagoan of the year, and the street where he grew up was renamed Kenny Lofton Lane. In 2013 he became the Indiana Baseball Hall of Fame's 164th inductee.

LOWDERMILK, Grover Cleveland ("Slim")

Born: January 15, 1885, Sandborn. **Died:** March 31, 1968, Odin, Illinois.
Height: 6'4". **Weight:** 190. **Batted:** right. **Threw:** right.
Debut: July 3, 1909. **Final game:** May 12, 1920.
Positions, teams, years: pitcher, St. Louis (NL) 1909, 1911, Chicago (NL) 1912, St. Louis (AL) 1915, Detroit (AL), 1915–1916, Cleveland (AL) 1916, St. Louis (AL) 1917–1919, Chicago (AL) 1919–1920.
Games: 122. **Innings pitched:** 590.1. **Won/Lost:** 23–39. **Earned run average:** 3.58.

The single-season minor league strikeout king, **Grover Lowdermilk** spent 16 seasons in baseball, including nine with six different Major League clubs. He won 20 or more games four times in the minors. Although his fastball drew comparisons to the great Walter Johnson's, control problems plagued Lowdermilk throughout his career.

In 1907 Lowdermilk broke in with Decatur, Ill. (Three-I), and struck out seven batters in his lone appearance before moving to Mattoon (Eastern Illinois). He helped Mattoon win the pennant with an 0.93 ERA, 33 wins and 458 strikeouts, all league-leading numbers. His combined strikeout total of 465 is a minor league record that has never been broken.

Back with Decatur in 1908, Lowdermilk threw a no-hitter on August 14 to beat Peoria 6–2. He reached the big leagues with the St. Louis Cardinals in 1909 and went 0–2, 6.21 in seven games.

After a 25–9 record for Springfield, Ill. (Three-I), in 1910, Lowdermilk went to the Cardinals' Spring Training camp in 1911. "Roger Bresnahan was the manager and catcher for the Cards and he asked me why I couldn't win for him like I did at Springfield," Lowdermilk recalled. "Well, I told him it was because I had a good, smart catcher, Bob Coleman."

Lowdermilk saw action in 11 games for St. Louis that year, going 0–1 with a 7.36 ERA. He spent the rest of his career shuttling between the majors and minors. His highest victory total came in 1915, when he split the year between the St. Louis Browns and Detroit Tigers and had 13 victories against 18 losses.

Lowdermilk landed with the Chicago White Sox in 1919 and pitched one inning against the Cincinnati Reds in that year's World Series, in which several Chicago players conspired to fix the games. "I don't think we could have beaten Cincinnati anyway," he said in a 1960 interview. "They had a great ballclub."

Lowdermilk ended his baseball career at Columbus, Ohio (American Association), in 1922 and settled in Odin, Ill., where he worked as a miner.

Lou Lowdermilk, Grover's younger brother, also pitched in the majors.

LOWDERMILK, Louis Bailey

Born: February 23, 1887, Sandborn. **Died:** December 27, 1975, Centralia, Illinois.
Height: 6'1". **Weight:** 180. **Batted:** right. **Threw:** left.
Debut: April 20, 1911. **Final game:** May 16, 1912.
Positions, teams, years: pitcher, St. Louis (NL) 1911–1912.
Games: 20. **Innings pitched:** 80. **Won/Lost:** 4–5. **Earned run average:** 3.38.

Lou Lowdermilk and his brother Grover were St. Louis Cardinals teammates during the 1911 season.

Lou entered professional baseball in 1907 and pitched for five minor league teams in four different leagues before joining the Cardinals in 1911. He and Grover became the first brother combination to pitch for St. Louis.

By July 11, 1911, the Cardinals were contending for the NL pennant with a 43–32 record. Early that morning, the train taking them to Boston left the tracks. While the St. Louis players were unhurt, 56 passengers were injured, 12 of them fatally.

The Lowdermilks and their teammates joined in the rescue efforts. "I saw enough horrors to last me all through my life," St. Louis outfielder Steve Evans told newsmen.

After the accident, the Cardinals dropped out of contention. "The sights and surroundings of the wreck," offered *Spalding's*, "...unnerved the players, and their downfall began from that week." St. Louis wound up in fifth place with a 75–74 record.

Lou Lowdermilk finished his rookie season with a 3–4 record in 16 games. He was 1–1 in four games in 1912 before returning to the minors. In 1913 he had a 20–19 record for Fort Wayne (Central). He was 4–7 at Grand Rapids, Mich. (Central), in June 1914 when South Bend, Ind. (Southern Michigan), acquired him. He threatened to jump to the Federal League, but reconsidered and posted a 15–6 record for his new club.

Lowdermilk's career ended in 1916 after a combined 14 wins and 17 losses for three teams in two different leagues. After serving in the army during World War I, he settled in southern Illinois and worked as a coal miner and artist.

LYNN, Michael Lance

Born: May 12, 1987, Indianapolis. **Lives:** Wilsonville, Oregon.
Height: 6'5". **Weight:** 240. **Bats:** right. **Throws:** right.
Debut: June 2, 2011.
Positions, teams, years: pitcher, St. Louis (NL) 2011–2014.
Games: 119. **Innings pitched:** 616. **Won/Lost:** 49–28. **Earned run average:** 3.46.

A star player for Brownsburg High School's undefeated state championship team, **Lance Lynn** went on to pitch for the University of Mississippi and Team USA before signing with the St. Louis Cardinals.

In 1999 Lynn played for the Brownsburg team that reached the Little League World Series. He helped Brownsburg High School to three consecutive IHSAA title games. Going 16–0 as a senior in 2005, Lynn got the win as Brownsburg defeated Evansville North for the state 4A title.

Drafted by the Seattle Mariners that year, Lynn instead went to Ole Miss and helped the Rebels to an NCAA regional title in 2007. That summer he earned a silver medal at the Pan American Games in Rio de Janeiro, Brazil, where the American squad finished second to Cuba.

The Cardinals drafted Lynn in 2008 with a supplemental first-round pick (39th overall), and he divided the year between Batavia, N.Y. (New York-Penn), and Quad Cities (Midwest). He had an 11–4 record at Springfield, Mo. (Texas), in 2009 and in 2010 he went 13–10 at

Memphis, Tenn. (Pacific Coast). He set a franchise record by fanning 16 batters in a PCL playoff game.

A starter in the minors, Lynn shifted to the bullpen in June 2011 when the Cardinals recalled him from Memphis. Sidelined in early August with a strained oblique muscle, he returned for post-season play. He scored relief wins in the NLCS and in the World Series, where St. Louis beat the Texas Rangers in seven games.

Moving into the Cardinals rotation in 2012, Lynn went 18–7, 3.78 in 35 games (including 29 starts). He picked up a relief win in Game 2 of the NLDS against Washington. In Game 4 he relieved again, giving up a walk-off homer and losing to Nationals closer Drew Storen, another Brownsburg alumnus. The Cardinals went on to win the NLDS and met San Francisco in the NLCS. Lynn started and took the loss in Game 5.

Lynn shed about 40 pounds prior to the 2013 campaign, when he helped St. Louis to another pennant with a 15–10, 3.97 season. He won two games against the Dodgers in the NLCS. In the World Series with the Red Sox, he started and took the loss in Game Four.

In 2014 Lynn again posted a 15–10 record, but his ERA tumbled to 2.74. The Cardinals advanced to the NLCS, where they lost to the Giants. "He won a lot of games earlier in his career without earning much respect. That changed this year," wrote Jeff Gordon in the *St. Louis Post-Dispatch*. "His maturation was evident in the playoff, too, as he posted a 3.08 ERA in his two starts. He is now 'top of the rotation' material."

Lynn's wife, the former Lauren Grill, played shortstop for the Ole Miss softball team and set school records in slugging and on-base percentage.

LYONS, Curt Russell

Born: October 17, 1974, Greencastle. **Lives:** Lexington, Kentucky.
Height: 6'5". **Weight:** 230. **Batted:** right. **Threw:** right.
Debut: September 19, 1996. **Final game:** September 29, 1996.
Positions, teams, years: pitcher, Cincinnati (NL) 1996.
Games: 3. **Innings pitched:** 16. **Won/Lost:** 2–0. **Earned run average:** 4.50.

Once a top pitching prospect for the Cincinnati Reds, **Curt Lyons** threw his last pitch at age 25.

A product of Madison Central High School in Richmond, Ky., Lyons was the sixth pick by the Reds in the 1992 draft. He developed an excellent changeup in 1993 following arm surgery.

Despite more arm problems in 1996, Lyons showed promise with a 13–4 record at Chattanooga, Tenn. He was the Southern League's pitcher of the year, and his 176 strikeouts topped all Double-A hurlers He joined the Reds that September and went 2–0 in three starts.

After more arm trouble in the spring of 1997, Cincinnati traded him to the Chicago Cubs. On Opening Day that year, he was the starting pitcher for Iowa (American Association) at Indianapolis. Unable to overcome his arm ailments, he finished the year with an 0–2 mark. The Cubs released him after the season.

Lyons rejoined the Cincinnati organization for 1998, appearing in three games for Chattanooga. He played in the New York Yankees chain in 1999, and in 2000 he hooked up with independent teams in Atlantic City, N.J. (Atlantic) and Yuma, Ariz. (Western). Before the year ended, he also pitched for a Cleveland Indians farm club.

After leaving baseball, Lyons became proprietor of Commonwealth Technology, a printing and copying service in Lexington, Ky.

MAGGERT, Harl Vestin ("Vee")

Born: February 13, 1883, Cromwell. **Died:** January 7, 1963, Fresno, California.
Height: 5-8. **Weight:** 155. **Batted:** left. **Threw:** right.
Debut: September 4, 1907. **Final game:** October 3, 1912.
Positions, teams, years: outfield, Pittsburgh (NL) 1907, Philadelphia (AL) 1912.
Games: 77. **At-bats:** 248. **Home runs:** 1. **Average:** .250.

Longtime Pacific Coast League standout **Harl Maggert** was barred from organized baseball after a betting scandal.

Born in the northeastern Indiana town of Cromwell, Maggert got his start in 1906 with Fort Wayne (Interstate Association). When the league folded in July he caught on with Sharon, Pa. (Ohio-Pennsylvania). Toward the end of the 1907 season he joined Pittsburgh and appeared in six games for the second-place Pirates.

Maggert spent two seasons with Springfield, Mass. (Connecticut State), and then joined the Oakland Oaks, where he became one of the PCL's top base stealers. After playing for Connie Mack's Philadelphia Athletics in 1912, Maggert returned to the PCL, this time with the Los Angeles Angels. He led the league in runs scored from 1913 to 1915 and helped the Angels to a pennant in 1916. He played for San Francisco in 1918 and shifted to Salt Lake City for the 1919–1920 campaigns

During an 11-year PCL career, Maggert engaged in disputes and altercations with opposing players, teammates, umpires and, on one occasion, his own manager. *The Sporting News* described him as "a foxy, wide-awake player, and but for his ill-temper would easily be held as an idol by the public."

In November 1920 Maggert was one of several players indicted for criminal conspiracy and collusion, the result of fixing contests between the Salt Lake City and Vernon, Calif., clubs during the 1919 season—the same year as the World Series scandal involving the Chicago White Sox. Since throwing ballgames violated no California laws, all charges were dropped. Nevertheless, PCL officials expelled Maggert along with three other players.

Finished with baseball, Maggert eventually settled in Berkeley, Calif., where he worked in the feed and fuel business. About two years before his death, he moved to Fresno to live with his son, Harl Warren Maggert. The younger Maggert, who was born in Citrus Heights, Calif., in 1914, was an outfielder-third basemen for the Boston Braves in 1938.

MANN, John Leo

Born: February 4, 1898, Fontanet. **Died:** March 31, 1977, Terre Haute.
Height: 5'11". **Weight:** 160. **Batted:** right. **Threw:** right.
Debut: April 18, 1928. **Final game:** May 23, 1928.
Positions, teams, years: third base, Chicago (AL) 1928.
Games: 6. **At-bats:** 6. **Home runs:** 0. **Average:** .333.

His big league career consisted of just six contests, but **Johnny Mann** was involved in baseball from 1919 to 1932.

Mann broke in with Terre Haute (Three-I) in 1919 and spent his next two seasons playing shortstop for Evansville (Three-I). In 1922 he went to Spring Training with the Detroit Tigers.

At Macon, Ga. (South Atlantic), in 1926, Johnny teamed up with his younger brother, infielder Raymond "Pete" Mann. In 1927 Johnny moved on to Wichita Falls (Texas) while Pete remained in Macon. On July 13 that year, Pete died at home plate when a pitched ball struck him in the chest.

Despite injuries and his brother's death, Johnny made the Chicago White Sox roster for Opening Day in 1928. But Bill Cissell beat him out for the second base job, and Johnny returned to the minor leagues for good. At Macon in 1930, he suffered a broken arm in a collision at third base with a runner. His last stop was at Hartford, Conn. (Eastern), for the 1931–1932 campaigns.

Born in Fontanet, just northeast of Terre Haute, Mann grew up there and returned after leaving baseball. In the fall of 1933 he was returning from a hunting trip when a hit-and-run driver struck him. Although the accident eventually cost him a leg, Mann recovered and lived to be 79 years old.

MATTINGLY, Donald Arthur ("Donnie Baseball")

Indiana Baseball Hall of Fame, 2001.
Born: April 20, 1961, Evansville. **Lives:** Evansville and Hermosa Beach, California.
Height: 6'0". **Weight:** 175. **Batted:** left. **Threw:** left.
Debut: September 8, 1982. **Final game:** October 1, 1995.
Positions, teams, years: first base (1,634), outfield (76), third base (3), second base (1), New York (AL), 1982–1995.
Games: 1,785. **At-bats:** 7,003. **Home runs:** 222. **Average:** .307.
Manager: Los Angeles (NL), 2011–2014 (354–293).

The finest New York Yankee first baseman since Lou Gehrig and the greatest Yankee never to play in the World Series, **Don Mat-**

tingly was a six-time AL All-Star. His six grand slam home runs in one season set a Major League record.

At Reitz Memorial High School in Evansville, Mattingly was an Indiana all-star defensive back in football and an all-city and all-conference performer in basketball. In 1978 he led the undefeated Tigers baseball squad to a state title. Reitz Memorial lost to Blackford High School in 1979, Mattingly's senior year, when his two triples tied a 66-year-old championship game record. The IHSAA presented him with the L.V. Phillips Mental Attitude Award.

Most big league teams expected Mattingly to enroll at Indiana State University. But when the Yankees took him in the 19th round of the 1979 draft, Mattingly signed for a $22,500 bonus. That summer he played for Oneonta, N.Y. (New York-Penn), and in 1980 at Greensboro, N.C., he led the South Atlantic League with a .358 average.

Mattingly appeared in seven games for New York in September 1982. In June 1983 he took over as the Yanks' everyday first baseman. He batted .343 in 1984 to become the first Yankee batting champion since Mickey Mantle in 1956. In 1985 Mattingly was the AL MVP when he topped the league in six offensive categories. He drove in 145 runs to become New York's first RBI league-leader since Roger Maris in 1961.

In a 1986 poll of Major Leaguers, Mattingly was selected as the best player in baseball. A .352 average that season made him the eighth Yankee to hit .350 or better. His 53 doubles broke Gehrig's team record, while his 238 hits eclipsed the club record set by Earle Combs.

In 1987 a disc problem in his back ended Mattingly's 335-game playing streak. Despite the injury, he set a big league record with six grand slam home runs, including two in a single contest on June 29. Between July 8–18 he tied a big league mark with home runs in eight consecutive contests. He batted .311 in 1988 and .303 in 1989, becoming the first Yankee to bat .300 or better in six consecutive seasons since Joe DiMaggio.

Mattingly's average dipped to .256 in 1990, when he was disabled by back trouble from late July to mid–September 1990. Named team captain in 1991, he rebounded with a .288 average, although chronic back problems limited him to nine home runs. He was New York's most effective hitter in 1992 with a .287 average and 86 RBI.

In 1993 the Yankees were in a pennant race for the first time in Mattingly's career. He responded with a .291 average, 17 homers and 86 RBI as the Yanks finished second in the AL East. At Anaheim on July 23, 1994, he joined Babe Ruth, Gehrig, DiMaggio, Yogi Berra and Mantle as a member of New York's 2,000-hit club. With the Yankees atop their division, a players' strike ended Mattingly's chances for post-season play. Despite the back ailments and persistent tendinitis in his right wrist, he managed to bat .304. In November 1994 he earned his ninth career Gold Glove, a record for AL first basemen.

Hampered by an eye infection in 1995 and missing playing time due to the degenerative disc and a pulled hamstring, Mattingly was still a superb fielder and a welcome clubhouse presence. He batted .288 with seven homers and 49 RBI in 128 games. He finally made it to post-season play when the Yankees earned the Wild Card spot. Despite Mattingly's .417 average (10-for-24), New York lost to Seattle in a best-of-five division series.

After the season Mattingly became a free agent and was reportedly considering a move to a team closer to his Evansville home. Despite his diminished skills, he was still a fan favorite in New York. "I never heard him get booed at home or on the road," said Yankees infielder Randy Velarde. That November, Mattingly announced plans to take a sabbatical in 1996—the year new manager Joe Torre led the Yankees to a World Series triumph over the Atlanta Braves.

Mattingly officially retired in January 1997, leaving with a .307 career average and 1,099 RBI for his 14-year career. The Yankees retired his uniform number, 23, that August. In 2004 Mattingly returned to New York as a hitting coach. Along with Joe Torre, he shifted to the Los Angeles Dodgers for the 2008 season and served as Torre's bench coach.

When Torre stepped down after the 2010

campaign, Mattingly replaced him as the Dodgers' field boss. After finishing third in 2011 and second in 2012, the Dodgers won NL West Division titles in 2013 and 2014.

A member of the Evansville Sports Hall of Fame, Mattingly was a three-time recipient of the Sid Mercer Memorial Award (1984–85–86) and the winner of the 1993 Lou Gehrig Award as the player who best exemplified Gehrig's character. He was inducted into the Indiana Baseball Hall of Fame in 2001.

Mattingly, whose brother Randy was a quarterback in the National Football and Canadian Football leagues, had two sons who played professional baseball. The Yankees made first baseman Taylor Mattingly their 42nd-round pick in 2003 while the Dodgers took second baseman Preston Mattingly with a supplemental first-round pick in 2006.

MAUCK, Alfred Maris ("Hal")

Born: March 6, 1869, Princeton. **Died:** April 27, 1921, Princeton.
Height: 5'11". **Weight:** 185. **Batted:** right. **Threw:** right.
Debut: April 29, 1893. **Final game:** August 10, 1893.
Positions, teams, years: pitcher, Chicago (NL) 1893.
Games: 23. **Innings pitched:** 143. **Won/Lost:** 8–10. **Earned run average:** 4.41.

At age 19, **Al Mauck** began his career with Lafayette, Ind. (Central Inter-State). After leading Birmingham, Ala. (Southern), to a pennant in 1892, he joined Cap Anson's Chicago Colts (today's Cubs). Anson, a Hall of Fame member, called his 1893 club "a team of great promise and poor performances." Chicago finished ninth in the 12-team NL, the franchise's worst-ever showing to that point.

Mauck started 18 games for Chicago in 1893, the third-highest total behind Wild Bill Hutchinson (40) and Willie McGill (34). Mauck's most memorable outing was a 4–0 win over Cincinnati on June 22. On July 1 he lost 1–0 to the New York Giants and Indiana native Amos Rusie, a future Hall of Fame member.

It would be Mauck's only big league season. He returned to the minors in 1894, spending part of the year at Indianapolis (Western). At Des Moines, Iowa (Western Association), in 1897 he won 24 of the team's 67 victories.

Mauck retired after 1900 and umpired for a time in the Southern and Three-I leagues. He later worked for the Southern Railroad and served as Princeton's town marshal. He spent nine years as deputy fish and game commissioner for the State of Indiana, retiring due to illness in December 1920. He died about five months later at age 52.

MAURER, Robert John

Born: January 7, 1967, Evansville. **Lives:** Evansville.
Height: 6'3". **Weight:** 200. **Batted:** left. **Threw:** left.
Debut: September 8, 1991. **Final game:** October 4, 1992.
Positions, teams, years: first base, Texas (AL) 1991–1992.
Games: 21. **At-bats:** 25. **Home runs:** 0. **Average:** .120.

Rob Maurer starred in baseball, football and wrestling at Evansville's Mater Dei High School and attended the University of Evansville. His college teammate Andy Benes was the St. Louis Cardinals' first-round pick in the 1988 draft, while the Texas Rangers took Maurer in the sixth round.

Maurer (pronounced "mah-wer") started out at Butte, Mont. (Pioneer), in 1988 and led the league with a .391 average. In 1991 at Oklahoma City (American Association) he made a run at a triple crown, finishing with a .301 average, 20 homers, 77 RBI batted in, and a league-leading 41 doubles. "He just kept hitting and driving in runs," Oklahoma City manager Tommy Thompson told *Baseball America*. "He was our most consistent player."

At the end of the 1991 season Maurer played in 13 games for the Rangers. He batted .288 in 1992 for Oklahoma City and returned to Texas for eight more games. During Spring Training in 1993 he injured his right knee, underwent surgery, and missed the entire year. He came back for one more season in 1994 and batted .258 with 11 homers in 61 games for Oklahoma City.

MAY, Merrill Glend ("Pinky")

Indiana Baseball Hall of Fame, 2003.
Born: January 18, 1911, Laconia. **Died:** September 4, 2000, Corydon.
Height: 5–11. **Weight:** 165. **Batted:** right. **Threw:** right.
Debut: April 21, 1939. **Final game:** October 3, 1943.

Positions, teams, years: third base (646), shortstop (1), Philadelphia (NL) 1939–1943.
Games: 655. **At-bats:** 2,215. **Home runs:** 4. **Average:** .275.

Before Scott Rolen, **Pinky May** was considered the finest Hoosier-born third baseman.

A native of the southeastern Indiana town of Laconia, May lettered in baseball, basketball and track at Boone Township High School and also played for the local baseball team. At Indiana University, he was the baseball squad's center fielder. He signed with the New York Yankees after the Hoosiers won the 1932 Big Ten Conference title.

May's professional career started that year with Cumberland, Md. (Middle Atlantic). At Durham, N.C. (Piedmont), in 1933 he shifted from the outfield to third base. He developed a reputation as an excellent fielder and a solid hitter, but the Yanks had perennial All-Star Red Rolfe at third base. Pinky languished in the minors until the Philadelphia Phillies drafted him after the 1938 season.

May batted .287 for the Phils in 1939 and was named to the 1940 NL All-Star team. He led NL third basemen in fielding in 1939, 1941 and 1943 and eventually became the Phillies' team captain. He entered the navy after the '43 season and missed the next two campaigns.

Released by Philadelphia in 1946, May became a minor league manager in 1947. He continued to manage minor league clubs through 1971, winning pennants with Albany, N.Y. (Eastern), in 1949, Sherbrooke, Quebec (Provincial), in 1953, Keokuk, Iowa (Three-I), in 1955 and Peninsula (Carolina) in 1965.

During twenty-five years, May's teams won 1,624 games—one of the highest totals in minor league history. Roger Maris, Russ Nixon, Mudcat Grant, Hal McRae and future Hall of Famer Johnny Bench all played for him on their way to the majors.

Pinky, who picked up his nickname during his college years, retired to Corydon. When he died in 2000 at age 89, May was Indiana's oldest former big leaguer. He was elected to the Indiana Baseball Hall of Fame in 2003.

Milt May, Pinky's son, was a Major League catcher from 1970 to 1984.

MAY, Milton Scott

Born: August 1, 1950, Gary. **Lives:** Bradenton, Florida.
Height: 6–0. **Weight:** 190. **Batted:** left. **Threw:** right.
Debut: September 8, 1970. **Final game:** September 30, 1984.
Positions, teams, years: catcher, Pittsburgh (NL) 1970–1973, Houston (NL) 1974–1975, Detroit (AL) 1976–1979, Chicago (AL) 1979, San Francisco (NL) 1980–1983, Pittsburgh (NL) 1983–1984.
Games: 1,192. **At-bats:** 3,693. **Home runs:** 77. **Average:** .263.

The son of former big league third baseman and longtime minor league manager Pinky May, **Milt May** grew up around baseball. Milt lived in Indiana until his family moved to St. Petersburg, Fla., before his tenth birthday. As soon as school was out, Milt would join his father and serve as a batboy for whichever team Pinky was managing.

A shortstop and third baseman in high school, Milt switched to catching in 1968 when the Pittsburgh Pirates took him in the 11th round of the draft. That summer he played for Bradenton, Fla. (Gulf Coast). A minor league all-star his first three professional seasons, he made the jump to Triple-A Columbus, Ohio (International), in 1970 and joined the Pirates toward the end of the year.

May backed up Pittsburgh catcher Manny Sanguillen when the Pirates won the 1971 pennant. In Game Four of the '71 World Series with the Baltimore Orioles—the first night game in Series history—May drove in the winning run with a pinch-hit single.

As Sanguillen's understudy again in 1972, May batted .281 in 57 games. He took over as the everyday catcher in 1973 when Sanguillen moved to right field after the death of Roberto Clemente in a plane crash. The Pirates eventually abandoned the experiment, and May was traded to Houston when Sanguillen went back behind the plate.

In 1974, his first year with the Astros, May batted .289 and led NL catchers in fielding with a .993 percentage. His three-run homer at San Francisco on May 4, 1975, made headlines. Bob Watson, who was on second base when May homered, crossed home plate with what was ballyhooed as the millionth run in

Major League baseball history. Subsequent research, however, concluded that those calculations were inaccurate, and it's not certain who actually scored baseball's millionth run.

Houston dealt May to the Detroit Tigers for 1976, but he suffered a fractured ankle after six games and missed the rest of the year. He served as Detroit's primary catcher for the next two campaigns and in 1979 the Tigers shipped him to the Chicago White Sox. A free agent after the season, May signed with San Francisco for 1980. In 1981 he batted .310 in 97 games for the Giants. He returned to Pittsburgh in a 1983 trade, and closed out his playing days in 1984 with the Pirates.

May served as a bank vice president in Bradenton, Fla., before rejoining Pittsburgh as an advance scout in 1986. In 1987 he became a roving instructor in the Pirates organization. A year later he became Pittsburgh's batting coach, a post he held for ten years.

Before leaving baseball in 2002, he also coached for the Florida Marlins, Colorado Rockies and Tampa Bay Devil Rays. He returned in 2010 as a hitting coach for Baltimore's rookie-level affiliate in the Gulf Coast League. He continued in that post through 2014.

A veteran of the U.S. Army Reserves, May owns Catchers Marina on Anna Maria Island in Florida. The marina's services include boat rentals, boat repairs, sightseeing tours and charter fishing.

May's wife, the former Brenda Boyd, is the daughter of a former Florida state senator. Their son, Milt Jr., was a catcher-third baseman at Manatee Community College in Florida. Pat Osburn, Milt Sr.'s brother-in-law, pitched for the Reds and Brewers from 1974 to 1975.

McCABE, Joseph Robert ("Joe Bob")

Born: August 27, 1938, Indianapolis. **Lives:** Naples, Florida.
Height: 6-0. **Weight:** 190. **Batted:** right. **Threw:** right.
Debut: April 18, 1964. **Final game:** May 22, 1965.
Positions, teams, years: catcher, Minnesota (AL) 1964, Washington (AL) 1965.
Games: 28. **At-bats:** 46. **Home runs:** 1. **Average:** .174.

A three-sport athlete at Lebanon High School, **Joe McCabe** played for prominent amateur baseball teams like the Lebanon Merchants and the Southside Saints of Indianapolis before enrolling at Purdue University. He hit .432 for the Boilermakers in 1960 to win Big Ten MVP honors. After graduation that year, McCabe signed with the Washington Senators and reported to Erie, Pa. (New York-Pennsylvania).

The Senators became the Minnesota Twins in 1961 and McCabe split the year between Nashville, Tenn. (Southern Association), and Wilson, N.C. (Carolina). After a six-month stint in the U.S. Army Reserves, he batted .290 for Vancouver, B.C. (Pacific Coast), in 1962. *The Sporting News* proclaimed him "the Twins' catcher of the future."

In 1961 McCabe was playing for Dallas-Fort Worth (Pacific Coast) when he suffered a shoulder separation. He continued to play despite the injury, but was never the same and finished the year with a .216 average in 107 contests.

McCabe opened the 1964 season in Minnesota, where he was reunited with former Purdue teammate Bernie Allen, the Twins' second baseman. McCabe saw action in 14 games before Minnesota sent him to Charlotte, N.C. (Southern), where he hit .274 in 27 games. In October 1964 the Twins traded him to the expansion Washington Senators.

After 14 games in 1965, the Senators dispatched McCabe to Honolulu (Pacific Coast). That August, prior to a game at Victory Field in Indianapolis, McCabe received a key to the city from Lebanon mayor Herb Ransdell. During the contest—which took place on Friday the 13th—McCabe suffered a fractured right index finger. He finished the year with a .226 average in 72 games and retired.

McCabe worked as an instructor at a baseball school in Bradenton, Fla. Later, he earned a pilot's license and flew for United Airlines.

McCARTHY, Thomas Patrick

Born: May 22, 1884, Fort Wayne. **Died:** March 28, 1933, Mishawaka.
Height: 5'7". **Weight:** 170. **Batted:** unknown. **Threw:** right.
Debut: May 10, 1908. **Final game:** July 7, 1909.

Positions, teams, years: pitcher, Cincinnati (NL), 1908, Pittsburgh (NL) 1908, Boston (NL) 1908–1909.
Games: 25. **Innings pitched:** 150. **Won/Lost:** 7–9. **Earned run average:** 2.34.

During the first 39 days of his rookie season, **Tom McCarthy** was traded twice and pitched for three different teams.

In 1906, his first year in pro ball, McCarthy helped Mount Clemens (Southern Michigan) to a first-place finish. After an 18–12 season at Newark, N.J. (Eastern), in 1907, he joined the Cincinnati Reds. His big league debut came on May 10, 1908, in St. Louis, when he started against the Cardinals in the second game of a doubleheader. McCarthy took the loss, and before the month was out the Reds shipped him to the Pittsburgh Pirates.

Pittsburgh won the 1908 pennant, but without McCarthy's help. He pitched twice for the Pirates, including one start, before a June 18 trade sent him to the Boston Doves. He was 7–3 with a pair of shutouts and a 1.63 ERA for Boston by August 5, when he suffered a slight arm fracture, the result of an awkward slide into home plate.

Returning to the Doves in 1909, McCarthy was 0–5 when Boston demoted him to Hartford (Connecticut State) in July. He helped Hartford to a pennant, and in 1910 he moved up to Indianapolis (American Association). Before the year was out, he was back with Hartford. He went 15–9 there in 1911 and retired due to a back injury.

In 1915 McCarthy moved from Fort Wayne to Mishawaka. He died at age 47 after an extended illness.

McCAULEY, Allen A. ("Mac," "Pop")

Born: March 4, 1863, Indianapolis. **Died:** August 24, 1917, Indianapolis.
Height: 6–0. **Weight:** 180. **Batted:** left. **Threw:** left.
Debut: June 21, 1884. **Final game:** October 6, 1891.
Positions, teams, years: first base (180), pitcher (10), outfield (3), Indianapolis (American Association) 1884, Philadelphia (NL) 1890, Washington (American Association) 1891.
Games: 192. **At-bats:** 677. **Home runs:** 2. **Average:** .251.
Innings pitched: 76. **Won/Lost:** 2–7. **Earned run average:** 5.09.

Fastball specialist **Al McCauley** pitched for a Danville, Ind., town team in 1883, where one of his teammates was future Hall of Famer Sam Thompson. With the independent Evansville club in 1884, McCauley and catcher Len Sowders formed a rare left-handed battery.

By June, McCauley was a big league pitcher-outfielder-first baseman for the Indianapolis Hoosiers (American Association). Released in early August by Indianapolis, the versatile McCauley became a baseball nomad, changing teams seventeen times over a 14-year professional career. At Peoria, Ill., in 1889, McCauley's .317 average led the Central Interstate League.

In 1890 McCauley returned to the majors as the everyday first baseman for the Philadelphia Phillies. He batted .244 in 112 games and was back in the minors for 1891. That summer the Washington Senators of the American Association gave McCauley his third big league trial, and he hit .282 in 59 contests. On August 6, 1891, he played an entire game at first base without a putout.

McCauley returned to the minors in 1892 and continued to bounce around. He spent the 1893 season with Los Angeles of the independent California League, managed by Indianapolis native Bob Glenalvin. He bowed out after playing for Rockford, Ill. (Western Association), in 1897.

A widower, McCauley died at age 54 in the Marion County Poor Asylum.

McCLENDON, Lloyd Glenn ("Legendary Lloyd")

Indiana Baseball Hall of Fame, 2010
Born: January 11, 1959, Gary. **Lives:** Chesterton.
Height: 5–10. **Weight:** 190. **Batted:** right. **Threw:** right.
Debut: April 6, 1987. **Final game:** August 11, 1994.
Positions, teams, years: outfield (260), first base (101), catcher (50), third base (9) Cincinnati (NL) 1987–1988, Chicago (NL) 1989–1990, Pittsburgh (NL) 1990–1994.
Games: 570. **At-bats:** 1,204. **Home runs:** 35. **Average:** .244.
Manager: Pittsburgh (NL) 2001–2005 (336–446), Seattle (AL) 2014 (87–75).

He had an eight-year big league career and coached and managed in the majors, but **Lloyd McClendon's** most spectacular performance took place in Williamsport, Pa., when he was 12 years old.

Growing up in Gary, McClendon was a standout player who pitched and batted his team to the 1971 Little League World Series. In tournament play, he drew five walks and hit five home runs—each on the first pitch. His team lost the championship game to Taiwan in extra innings.

An all-state pick at Gary's Roosevelt High School, McClendon played college ball at Valparaiso University. The New York Mets drafted him as a catcher in 1980 and he reported to Kingsport, Tenn. (Appalachian), that summer. After the 1982 season the Mets dealt McClendon to the Cincinnati Reds in a trade that brought pitcher Tom Seaver back to New York. At Denver in 1986, McClendon's 24 homers topped the American Association.

Breaking in with the Reds in 1987, McClendon spent two years with Cincinnati as a utility player. The Cubs picked him up in 1989 and traded him to Pittsburgh the following season. He batted .291 in a backup role in 1991, helping the Pirates to the NL Championship Series. He remained with Pittsburgh through 1994.

Always a tough out in post-season play, McClendon went 10-for-16 (a .625 average) in 11 games for the Cubs (1989) and Pirates (1991-92). On October 13, 1992, his two hits in one inning tied a Championship Series record.

McClendon became a coach in the Pirates organization in 1996 and took over as Pittsburgh's hitting instructor a year later. He managed instructional league teams in the off-season. Prior to the 2001 season he took over as skipper of the Pirates. "Managing is something I wanted to do since my playing days," said McClendon, who became the first Indiana-born African American to manage a big league team.

The Pirates hadn't finished at .500 or above since 1992 and continued to struggle during McClendon's first season as skipper. During the seventh inning of a home game with Milwaukee on June 26, 2001, Pittsburgh's Jason Kendall was called out on a close play at first base. McClendon argued the call and was ejected. He dislodged the first base bag, tucked it under his arm and stormed off into the dugout. The Pirates went on to win 7-6 in 12 innings, and Major League Baseball slapped McClendon with a $1,000 fine. "If it guarantees us a win, I'll steal second base tonight," he quipped.

After five losing seasons, McClendon was fired in September 2005. He joined Detroit's coaching staff in 2006, and the Tigers won AL pennants in '06 and 2012. During his seven years in Detroit, Tiger hitters won four batting titles (Magglio Ordonez in 2007; Miguel Cabrera in 2011-12-13). Hired to manage Seattle for 2014, McClendon led the Mariners to a third-place finish in the AL West with an 87-75 record.

Staying involved with baseball in his hometown, McClendon became a minority owner of the Gary SouthShore Railcats of the independent Northern League. In 2010 he was inducted into the Indiana Baseball Hall of Fame.

In the 2010 draft the Tigers selected Valparaiso outfielder Bo McClendon, Lloyd's son, in the 39th round.

McCOOL, William John ("Cool Billy")
Indiana Baseball Hall of Fame, 2013.
Born: July 14, 1944, Batesville. **Died:** June 8, 2014, Summerfield, Florida.
Height: 6'2". **Weight:** 195. **Batted:** right. **Threw:** left.
Debut: April 24, 1964. **Final game:** July 8, 1970.
Positions, teams, years: pitcher, Cincinnati (NL) 1964-1968, San Diego (NL) 1969, St. Louis (NL) 1970.
Games: 292. **Innings pitched:** 528.1. **Won/Lost:** 32-42. **Earned run average:** 3.59.

Left-hander **Billy McCool** reached the majors at 19 and pitched his last big league game before his 27th birthday.

At Lawrenceburg High School, McCool played basketball, football and baseball, and also starred in American Legion ball. He signed with the Cincinnati Reds in 1963 and joined Tampa (Florida State), where he went 5-13 with a 2.01 ERA for a last-place team. Before the season was over he was pitching for San Diego (Pacific Coast), one step away from the Major Leagues.

In 1964 McCool took over as Cincinnati's top left-handed reliever. He posted a 6-5 record with 17 saves and a 2.43 ERA as the Reds finished one game out of first place. He had 21 saves and a 4.29 ERA in 1965, followed by a 2.48 ERA in 1966 with 18 saves. In 1966 he was named to the NL All-Star team.

By now McCool had developed a slider to go with his fastball, which ranked among the best in the majors. For part of 1967 he was in the Reds starting rotation, going 3–7 with a 3.43 ERA. A mid-season wrist injury in 1968 put him on the disabled list.

San Diego took McCool in the post-season expansion draft, but a knee injury had curtailed his effectiveness. He went 3–5 for the Padres in 1969 with a team-high seven saves in 54 relief appearances. San Diego shipped him to St. Louis in 1970. His big league career ended that July when the Cardinals sent him to Tulsa, Okla. (American Association). He retired after spending the 1972 season with Kansas City Royals and Minnesota Twins farm teams.

For a time during his playing days, McCool was co-owner of a Lawrenceburg drug store. After moving to Ohio he became a sportscaster for a Dayton television station. He spent 30 years as a salesman for a steel distributing company and authored a 1977 book called *The Billy McCool Pitching Digest: A Guide to Effective Baseball Pitching.*

McCool, who moved to Florida in 2004, entered the Indiana Baseball Hall of Fame in 2013.

McDONALD, David Bruce ("Mac," "Cheeseburger")

Born: May 20, 1943, New Albany. **Lives:** Pompano Beach, Florida.
Height: 6-3. **Weight:** 215. **Batted:** left. **Threw:** right.
Debut: September 15, 1969. **Final game:** September 26, 1971.
Positions, teams, years: first base (15), outfield (1), New York (AL) 1969, Montreal (NL) 1971.
Games: 33. **At-bats:** 62. **Home runs:** 1. **Average:** .145.

The son of a former National Football League player, **Dave McDonald** spurned college gridiron offers to pursue a baseball career. Les McDonald, Dave's father, was a University of Nebraska football standout who went on to play for the Chicago Bears, Philadelphia Eagles and Detroit Lions from 1937 to 1940. Dave was born in New Albany while his father worked at a munitions plant during World War II.

At Grand Island (Neb.) High School, McDonald was an all-state end in football and an all-conference basketball guard. Nebraska and several other Big Eight colleges offered him football scholarships, but his father advised him to play baseball. "He told me: 'Baseball is easier on you physically,'" Dave explained in a 1969 *Sporting News* interview. "'You're not as likely to get hurt, so you can play it longer, and if you want to stay with it all your life, baseball has plenty of jobs for a good man.'"

Since his high school had no baseball team, McDonald played for Grand Island's American Legion squad. After hitting .365 in 1961 he signed with the New York Yankees and launched his pro career in 1962. In 1963 he led the Western Carolinas League with 21 home runs, splitting the year between Shelby, N.C., and Statesville, N.C.

Originally a catcher, McDonald switched to first base in 1965 at Greensboro, N.C. (Carolina). At Syracuse, N.Y. (International), in 1969 his 24 homers and .281 average earned him a September promotion to New York.

The Yankees traded McDonald to Montreal in May 1970. That December the Expos sent him to the San Francisco Giants, who shipped him back to Montreal for 1971. After 24 games the Expos sent him to Winnipeg, Manitoba, where his 17 homers and .309 average earned him a berth on the International League All-Star team. He played for the New York Mets' top farm club at Tidewater (International) from 1972 through 1974 before leaving baseball.

McDonald attended Nebraska in the off-season, eventually earning a degree. He worked as a freight company supervisor in North Carolina, and for a time served as an assistant baseball coach at Gardner-Webb University in Boiling Springs, N.C.

MEEKIN, George Jouett

Born: February 21, 1867, New Albany. **Died:** December 14, 1944, New Albany.
Height: 6'1". **Weight:** 180. **Batted:** right. **Threw:** right.
Debut: June 13, 1891. **Final game:** July 8, 1900.
Positions, teams, years: pitcher (324), outfield (7), first base (1), Louisville (American Association) 1891–1892, Washington (NL) 1892–1893, New

York (NL) 1894–1899, Boston (NL) 1899, Pittsburgh (NL) 1900.
Games: 339. **Innings pitched:** 2,605.1. **Won/Lost:** 152–133. **Earned run average:** 4.07.
At-bats: 1,099. **Home runs:** 15. **Average:** .243.

Jouett Meekin, one of early baseball's most feared flamethrowers, may have ruined his pitching arm while enjoying a spectacular season in 1894.

The son of James Meekin, who once ran for mayor of New Albany, Jouett caught for a local squad called the Browns before entering professional baseball in 1887 with St. Paul (Western Association). In 1891 he reached the big leagues with the Louisville Colonels of the American Association.

After switching to the NL in 1892, Louisville released Meekin, and league president Nick Young awarded him to Washington. Years later, Meekin said his career took off after catcher Duke Farrell joined the Senators in 1893. "Farrell really taught me how to pitch," Meekin told *The Sporting News*. "He spent hours studying the weaknesses of the batters and then he'd go over them with me until we had those weak points down pat."

Meekin went 10–15 for Washington in 1893, and that winter the Senators traded him to the Giants. In New York's rotation he joined another Indiana native, Amos Rusie. Nicknamed "The Iron Twins," Rusie won 36 games in 1894 while Meekin compiled 33 victories against 9 losses. Meekin's .786 winning percentage led the NL.

The Giants finished second, but defeated the pennant-winning Baltimore Orioles in four straight games to take the 1894 Temple Cup Series—a forerunner of the modern Fall Classic. Afterwards, Young Sport's Library of New York published a dime novel based on his life called *The Mighty Meekin*. "The book is interesting owing to its wide variance from the truth," noted the *New Albany Evening Tribune*.

After pitching 418 innings in 1894, Meekin developed chronic arm problems. From 1895 to 1897 he posted records of 16–12, 26–13, and 20–11. The soreness persisted and in 1898 he dipped to 16–18. In August 1899 the Giants sold his contract to the Boston Beaneaters. His Major League career ended after an 0–2 slate with the Pittsburgh Pirates in 1900.

A fastball pitcher, Meekin was an excellent fielder. He was also a capable batsman who hit three triples in a game against the Cleveland Spiders on July 4, 1894.

After leaving baseball, Meekin spent over 25 years with the New Albany Fire Department. He died at age 77 of complications resulting from injuries sustained in a fall.

METZGER, Clarence Edward ("Butch")

Born: May 23, 1952, Lafayette. **Lives:** Sacramento, California.
Height: 6'1". **Weight:** 185. **Batted:** right. **Threw:** right.
Debut: September 8, 1974. **Final game:** June 28, 1978.
Positions, teams, years: pitcher, San Francisco (NL) 1974, San Diego (NL) 1975–1977, St. Louis (NL) 1977, New York (NL) 1978.
Games: 191. **Innings pitched:** 293.1. **Won/Lost:** 18–9. **Earned run average:** 3.74.

Before **Butch Metzger** started school, his family moved to California. He developed into a baseball star at Sacramento's John F. Kennedy High School, and in 1970 the San Francisco Giants took him with their second pick in the draft. His nine losses that year at Great Falls, Mont., were the most in the Pioneer League.

In 1974 Metzger went 12–10 at Phoenix (Pacific Coast), earning a September promotion to San Francisco. He won his only decision, and the Giants sent him to the San Diego Padres that December in a three-player deal. In 1975 he went 15–7 as a starter for Honolulu (Pacific Coast). He joined the Padres at the end of the season and won his only decision.

Metzger began the 1976 season in San Diego's bullpen, winning his first ten decisions to tie the NL record by Hooks Wiltse of the New York Giants in 1904. "I felt like I could do a good job if they gave me a chance," he told Phil Collier of the *San Diego Tribune*. "But I never really expected anything like this." Metzger finished with an 11–4 record and 16 saves, and shared NL Rookie of the Year honors with Cincinnati pitcher Pat Zachry.

When Metzger got off to a slow start in 1977, the Padres shipped him to St. Louis. He bounced back with the Cardinals, notching seven saves and a 4–2 slate. St. Louis put him on waivers during Spring Training in 1978 after a personality conflict developed between Metzger and manager Vern Rapp.

Claimed by the New York Mets, Metzger developed shoulder problems. After going 1–3 with a 6.57 ERA for New York in 1978, his big league career was over. The Mets sent him to the Philadelphia Phillies and Metzger spent the rest of the year at Oklahoma City (American Association). Cut by the Phillies before the 1979 season opened, he pitched briefly for Caracas, Venezuela (Inter-American), before the league folded at the end of June.

Metzger retired after spending all of 1980 with the Atlanta Braves' top farm club at Richmond, Va. (International). He returned to Sacramento, where he became a fireman and also a part-time scout for the California Angels. Seventeen years after his last big league game, he attempted a comeback. With the Major League players on strike in 1995, he crossed the picket lines as a replacement player with the Giants. San Francisco released him when the strike ended.

MIDDLETON, James Blaine ("Rifle Jim")

Born: May 28, 1889, Argos. **Died:** January 12, 1974, Argos.
Height: 5'11". **Weight:** 165. **Batted:** right. **Threw:** right.
Debut: April 18, 1917. **Final game:** September 18, 1921.
Positions, teams, years: pitcher, New York (NL) 1917, Detroit (AL) 1921.
Games: 51. **Innings pitched:** 157.2. **Won/Lost:** 7–12. **Earned run average:** 4.51.

During a professional baseball career that lasted from 1910 to 1929, pitcher **Jimmy Middleton** was a seven-time 20-game winner in the minor leagues.

Middleton's career began in 1910, when he won a combined 21 games for Decatur, Ill. (Northern Association), and Springfield, Ill. (Three-I). He won 20 in 1912 and 21 in 1913 for Springfield. He went 26–10 for Davenport, Iowa, in 1914, when his 1.24 ERA for the pennant-winning Blue Sox topped the Three-I League.

Middleton joined Louisville (American Association) in 1915, posting a 21–9 record in 1916 when the Colonels finished first and defeated Omaha (Western) in the Minor League Championship Series.

The New York Giants obtained Middleton for 1917. After a 1–1 record with a 2.75 ERA in 13 games, he was back with Louisville. Dealt to Kansas City (American Association) for 1918, Middleton left baseball to work on a livestock farm in La Porte. He returned in 1920 with Toledo (American Association), going 26–14. He spent 1921 with the Detroit Tigers and, after a 6–11 season, his big league career was over.

Middleton continued to pitch for Portland, Ore. (Pacific Coast), in 1922–1923; for pennant-winning Fort Worth (Texas), winner of the 1924 Dixie Series; for Minneapolis (American Association) from 1925–1927; for Seattle (Pacific Coast) in 1928; and for Minneapolis again in 1929. With Fort Worth in 1924, he pitched a seven-inning, 3–0 no-hitter against Beaumont. In 1926 he went 20–15 for Minneapolis.

Middleton, who compiled a 259–182 record in the minors, also managed Portland in 1922–1923 and Seattle in 1928. When his baseball career ended, he returned to the northern Indiana town of Argos and worked for the Marshall County Highway Department.

MILES, Donald Ray

Born: March 13, 1936, Indianapolis. **Died:** April 26, 2011, Houston, Texas.
Height: 6-1. **Weight:** 210. **Batted:** left. **Threw:** left.
Debut: September 9, 1958. **Final game:** September 20, 1958.
Positions, teams, years: outfield, Los Angeles (NL) 1958.
Games: 8. **At-bats:** 22. **Home runs:** 0. **Average:** .182.

The first Indianapolis native to play in the Major Leagues since Chuck Klein in 1944, outfielder **Don Miles** was an outstanding athlete who lettered in baseball, football, wrestling and track at Ben Davis High School. He also played a year of football at Indiana Central College (presently the University of Indianapolis).

According to *Los Angeles Examiner* sports reporter Bob Hunter, Miles was playing for a semi-pro team in Indianapolis in 1956 when he spotted Brooklyn Dodgers scout Stan Feezle in the stands. Feezle, who had discovered Gil Hodges and Carl Erskine, departed without talking to Miles. "As the scout left the ball park, Miles suddenly missed him," wrote Hunter. "He chased Feezil [sic] three blocks down the street to prevent him from leaving town before presenting a contract."

Miles signed for $200 and broke in with Kokomo (Midwest), hitting .312 with 23 homers. In 1957 he was the Big State League's Most Valuable Player after a 28-homer, .316 season for pennant-winning Victoria, Texas.

In Victoria, Miles met and eventually married Louise O'Connor, the daughter of team owner Tom O'Connor, a multi-millionaire businessman. Don spent time with Victoria and St. Paul (American Association) in 1958 before a September promotion to the Dodgers, by now relocated to Los Angeles.

Miles opened the 1959 season with Spokane, Wash. (Pacific Coast), but returned to Victoria in time to help the Rosebuds win the Texas League pennant. Before the 1960 season began, the Dodgers sold his contract to Victoria.

Tom O'Connor suffered a heart attack after the season, and Miles left baseball to help run family affairs. O'Connor eventually recovered, and in 1965 Miles shed 82 pounds for a comeback attempt with Dallas-Forth Worth (Texas), a Chicago Cubs farm club. He retired again after hitting .224 in 43 games.

Miles returned once more in 1968 with the Dodgers' Bakersfield (California) affiliate. He averaged .254 in 22 contests and left baseball for good.

MILLER, Charles Bruce

Indiana Baseball Hall of Fame, 2012.
Born: March 4, 1947, Fort Wayne. **Lives:** Fort Wayne.
Height: 6-1. **Weight:** 185. **Batted:** right. **Threw:** right.
Debut: August 4, 1973. **Final game:** August 28, 1976.
Positions, teams, years: third base (115), second base (41), shortstop (20), San Francisco (NL) 1973–1976.
Games: 196. **At-bats:** 553. **Home runs:** 1. **Average:** .246.

While playing Major League baseball, **Bruce Miller**—a college graduate with a degree in education and a minor in mathematics—spent his off-seasons as a substitute math teacher.

Miller grew up on a farm and played baseball and basketball for Columbia City High School. As a junior in 1969 he batted .354 for Indiana University's baseball squad, earning All-Big Ten Conference shortstop honors.

Selected by the Chicago White Sox in the 20th round of the 1970 draft, Miller batted .276 that summer for Duluth-Superior, Minn. (Northern). The White Sox shipped him to the California Angels in August 1972. In April 1973 the Angels traded him to San Francisco. Miller batted .313 that year for Salt Lake City (Pacific Coast) and joined the Giants in August.

Miller began 1974 with Phoenix (Pacific Coast) and finished the year as a backup infielder for the Giants. With San Francisco in 1975, Miller split third base duties with Steve Ontiveros and batted .239. He appeared in 12 games for the Giants in 1976, but spent most of the year with Phoenix.

After sitting out the 1977 campaign, Miller became a free agent. But his baseball career was over, and he returned to Fort Wayne to accept a full-time teaching post at North Side High School. He coached the school's baseball team from 1985 to 2005.

In 1984 Miller was named to the Northeast Indiana Baseball Association Hall of Fame. He entered the Indiana Baseball Hall of Fame in 2012.

MILLER, Dyar K ("Big D")

Indiana Baseball Hall of Fame, 2007.
Born: May 29, 1946, Batesville. **Lives:** Indianapolis.
Height: 6'1". **Weight:** 195. **Batted:** right. **Threw:** right.
Debut: June 9, 1975. **Final game:** September 2, 1981.
Positions, teams, years: pitcher, Baltimore (AL) 1975–1977, California (AL) 1977–1979, Toronto (AL) 1979, New York (NL) 1980–1981.
Games: 251. **Innings pitched:** 465.1. **Won/Lost:** 23–17. **Earned run average:** 3.23.

One of the 16 members of New Point High School's Class of 1964, **Dyar Miller** grew up on a Decatur County farm. He played for New Point's baseball and basketball teams and pitched and caught for an American Legion club in southern Indiana's Tri-County League. At Utah State University he played baseball and basketball, but he returned to Indiana when the school dropped baseball in 1968.

Miller was playing for an amateur team in Batesville in 1968 when the Phillies offered him a contract as a catcher. Released after four games with Huron, S.D. (Northern), he signed with the Baltimore Orioles for 1969—this time as a pitcher. At Stockton (California) that year he was 4–4 with a 2.33 ERA. He gradually developed into one of Baltimore's top prospects, and in June 1975, after a 5–0 record and 2.20 ERA with Rochester, N.Y. (International), he joined the Orioles as a 29-year-old rookie.

Miller registered 16 saves for the Orioles before going to the California Angels in June 1977 as part of a two-player swap. As a setup man for the Angels in 1978 he went 6–2 with a 2.65 ERA. Toronto bought his contract on June 6, 1979, and on July 30 shipped him to Denver (American Association), the top farm club of the Montreal Expos. The Expos released Miller during Spring Training in 1980 and he signed a minor league contract with the Mets. Promoted to New York that June, he compiled a 1.93 ERA in 31 games.

After closing out his big league career with the Mets, Miller signed on as a player-coach in 1981 with Louisville (American Association), a St. Louis Cardinals affiliate. In December 1983 he underwent surgery for colon cancer. He appeared in six games for Louisville in 1984 before retiring as an active player.

Miller continued to coach in the Cardinals system until 1987, when he joined the Chicago White Sox for a two-year stint as a bullpen coach. He also coached minor league teams for the Detroit Tigers and Cleveland Indians before returning to the St. Louis organization in 1995. In 2012 he served as the Cardinals bullpen coach, and after the season the Houston Astros hired him as their minor league pitching coordinator.

Miller's family lived in Missouri when he was a boy and he grew up rooting for St. Louis. A member of an air force reserve unit during his playing days, he holds a degree in history. His full name is Dyar K Miller—the K is only an initial.

In 2007 Miller was inducted into the Indiana Baseball Hall of Fame. His son, Matthew Miller, pitched for the University of Evansville.

MILLER, Frederick Holman ("Speedy")

Born: June 28, 1886, Fairfield. **Died:** May 2, 1953, Brookville.
Height: 6'2". **Weight:** 190. **Batted:** left. **Threw:** left.
Debut: July 8, 1910. **Final game:** August 15, 1910.
Positions, teams, years: pitcher, Brooklyn (NL) 1910.
Games: 6. **Innings pitched:** 21. **Won/Lost:** 1–1. **Earned run average:** 4.71.

Except for a six-game stint with the Brooklyn Superbas, **Speedy Miller** spent his professional baseball career in the South. Miller's nickname referred to his fastball, not his foot speed.

Miller broke in with Jackson, Miss. (Cotton States), in 1907. In 1908 his 18–6 record helped Jackson win the pennant. The Cleveland Naps acquired him at the end of the season but shipped him to Columbia, S.C. (South Atlantic), for 1909. He went 12–17 with 196 strikeouts for a last-place team.

In July 1910 Miller joined Brooklyn. His first appearance for the Superbas was a start in Pittsburgh against the defending World Series champion Pirates. He threw six and one-third innings to get the win. He lost his only other decision, and in six games he allowed 13 walks while notching just two strikeouts. A fractured ankle curtailed his stay in the majors.

After sitting out the 1911 season, Miller returned to organized ball in 1912 with Montgomery, Ala. (Southern). He went 2–1 in nine games before moving on to Charlotte, N.C. (Carolina Association), where he was 6–6 before calling it quits.

Returning to Indiana, Miller lived on a farm near the town of Brookville in the eastern part of the state. He continued to play for local baseball teams as late as the 1940s. He died from a cerebral hemorrhage at age 66.

MILLER, Ralph Joseph ("Hack")

Born: February 29, 1896, Fort Wayne. **Died:** March 18, 1939, Fort Wayne.
Height: 6-0. **Weight:** 190. **Batted:** right. **Threw:** right.
Debut: April 14, 1920. **Final game:** September 30, 1924.
Positions, teams, years: third base (101), shortstop

(48), second base (3), first base (3), outfield (1), Philadelphia (NL) 1920–1921, Washington (AL) 1924.
Games: 163. **At-bats:** 557. **Home runs:** 3. **Average:** .248.

A two-sport standout, **Ralph Miller** was considered one of Fort Wayne's finest all-around athletes. In three Major League seasons, he played for a pair of tail-end clubs and one pennant winner.

Miller spent his first professional campaign as a shortstop for Waterloo, Iowa (Central Association), in 1916. He appeared in 90 games for the Loons in 1917 before shifting to Fort Wayne (Central) late that season. He was in the army for the 1918–1919 seasons, spending 18 months with an aerial squadron in France and Germany.

Mustered out of service as a sergeant, Miller opened the 1920 season with the Philadelphia Phillies and split third base duties with left-handed hitting Russ Wrightstone. The Phillies finished in the basement that year and last again in 1921, when Miller batted .304 as a backup. In a game with the Boston Braves on April 28, Miller hit a grand slam home run. Teammate Lee Meadows also connected for a bases-loaded homer. Seventy-six seasons passed before the Phillies would have two grand slams in the same contest.

Miller spent part of the 1921 season with Louisville (American Association). Sold to San Francisco (Pacific Coast) prior to 1922, he joined Reading, Pa. (International), in 1923.

In July 1924 Washington acquired Miller. He appeared in nine games for the pennant-winning Senators, who beat the Giants four games to three in the World Series. Miller got into four contests after regular third sacker Ossie Bluege switched to shortstop to replace the injured Roger Peckinpaugh.

Washington cut Miller after the season and he spent the next four years in the American Association, including a hitch with Indianapolis (American Association) in 1927–1928. Out of organized ball in 1930–1931, he came back with Fort Wayne (Central) in 1932. He played nine games for Keokuk, Iowa (Mississippi Valley), in 1933 before retiring.

An all-around athlete who attended Fort Wayne's St. Paul's High School, Miller was a member of the Fort Wayne Hoosiers of the American Basketball League and also played semi-pro football. After leaving organized baseball, he played for independent teams.

Miller contracted peritonitis following an appendectomy and died at age 43. He is a member of the Northeast Indiana Baseball Association Hall of Fame, Class of 1963.

MILLER, Roscoe Clyde ("Ross," "Roxy," Rubberlegs")

Born: December 2, 1876, Greenville. **Died:** April 18, 1913, Corydon.
Height: 6'2". **Weight:** 190. **Batted:** right. **Threw:** right.
Debut: April 25, 1901. **Final game:** July 30, 1904.
Positions, teams, years: pitcher, Detroit (AL) 1901–1902, New York (NL) 1902–1903, Pittsburgh (NL) 1904.
Games: 102. **Innings pitched:** 772.2. **Won/Lost:** 39–45. **Earned run average:** 3.45.

Fastball pitcher **Roscoe Miller** broke into the majors with a 23-win season. He pitched his last big league game just three years later.

Miller's first stop in pro baseball was at Mansfield, Ohio (Inter-State), in 1897. After a league-leading 28 wins for the Haymakers in 1899, he moved on to the Detroit Tigers of the American League for 1900. The newly-formed AL was a minor league circuit, but attained big league status in 1901. Miller started and won Detroit's first-ever AL contest and finished the year with a 23–13 slate. His 35 complete games and 332 innings pitched that season are AL rookie records.

Detroit's Opening Day starter again in 1902, Miller had a 6–12 record in July 1902 when he jumped the team over a salary dispute. He signed with John McGraw's New York Giants, losing nine of 10 decisions to finish with a 7–20 slate. Miller appeared in 15 games for New York in 1903, going 2–5. The Giants released him at the end of the season and he joined Pittsburgh. He had a 7–8 record when the Pirates cut him loose in September 1904.

Miller split the 1905 season between Seattle and San Francisco in the Pacific Coast League, winning 19 against 26 losses. He joined Des Moines, Iowa (Western), for 1906 and led the Champions to a first-place finish with a 28–15 slate. After a 15–19 record in 1907, he was gone from baseball.

In 1912, Miller moved to Corydon to work in his father's grocery store. He developed tuberculosis and died at age 36, leaving a wife and three children.

Known as Ross Miller in southern Indiana, he apparently picked up the nickname "Rubberlegs" after bouncing from one team to another between 1902 and 1904. "Roxy" was a play on his first name.

MILLER, Walter W.

Born: October 19, 1884, Spiceland. **Died:** March 1, 1956, Marion.
Height: 5'11". **Weight:** 180. **Batted:** right. **Threw:** right.
Debut: September 20, 1911. **Final game:** October 6, 1911.
Positions, teams, years: pitcher, Brooklyn (NL) 1911.
Games: 3. **Innings pitched:** 11. **Won/Lost:** 0–1. **Earned run average:** 6.55.

Walt Miller lived in Gas City as a young man, playing for a town team called the Marion Owls and working as a glassblower during the winter months. Miller spent five seasons with Grand Rapids, Mich., from 1903 to 1907, leading the Central League with 24 victories in 1905. He went 13–12 for the Wolverines in 1906 when they won the league title.

Miller spent the next three seasons at Fort Wayne (Central), compiling a 21–14 slate in 1909 despite a brief suspension for assaulting an umpire during a July contest in Zanesville, Ohio. "Miller engaged in an argument over balls and strikes," according to the *South Bend Times*, "and during the latter part of the game, Miller was so angered that he could not restrain himself from overstepping the boundary and soon he was in a fistic encounter with the indicator man."

With Fort Wayne in 1910 Miller went 25–9. He was 15–13 for Atlanta (Southern Association) in September 1911 when Brooklyn obtained him. He lost his only decision in two starts and one relief appearance for the Dodgers, giving up 16 hits and six walks without striking out a batter. Back with Atlanta for 1912, he was 1–3 in nine games before returning to Grand Rapids.

Out of organized baseball in 1913, Miller came back in 1914 and pitched for Grand Rapids and Terre Haute. After three games with Evansville (Central) in 1915, his professional career was over. Miller, who made his home in the town of Red Bridge near Marion, owned and operated a gasoline station and grocery store. He died of kidney disease at age 71.

MOORE, Charles Wesley

Born: December 1, 1884, Jackson County. **Died:** July 29, 1970, Portland, Oregon.
Height: 5–10. **Weight:** 160. **Batted:** right. **Threw:** right.
Debut: April 16, 1912. **Final game:** May 13, 1912.
Positions, teams, years: shortstop (2), second base (1), third base (1), Chicago (NL) 1912.
Games: 5. **At-bats:** 9. **Home runs:** 0. **Average:** .222.

As a 27-year-old rookie in 1912, **Charley Moore** played in the Chicago Cubs infield alongside Hall of Fame legends Joe Tinker and Johnny Evers.

Moore's family left Indiana for Oregon when he was a toddler. He spent most of his youth in Gardner, Ore., before moving to Portland. He played baseball for Oregon's Columbia University, a preparatory school.

In 1906 Moore joined Portland. Ore. (Pacific Coast), and finished the year with Los Angeles. A holdout in 1907, he played for an independent team in Portland before returning to organized ball with Aberdeen, Wash. (Northwest), in 1908. At Peoria, Ill., in 1910, his 82 runs topped the Three-I League.

Primarily a shortstop, Moore suffered from recurrent vision problems since his prep school days, when a pitched ball struck him in the head. "He was able to gauge the ball effectively while at bat and kept up his reputation as a strong batsman," the *Chicago Tribune* reported. "But in the field, ground balls that came to him below his knee or for which he had to run hard proved deceptive and marred his fielding record."

The Cincinnati Reds drafted Moore after 1910 and assigned him to Los Angeles for 1911. In his second stint in the PCL, he batted .298 and stole 54 bases. His vision cleared up after a surgical procedure—his fourth—late that summer.

The Cubs obtained Moore for 1912 and he

made his debut in a 20–5 loss at St. Louis. Replacing Ed Lennox at third base, he took the field with Tinker at shortstop and Evers at second base. Chicago's manager was Frank Chance, another Hall of Famer who was in his final year at the Cubs' helm.

Chicago returned Moore to Los Angeles after four more appearances. He spent the rest of his baseball career in the minors, and managed Atlanta (Southern Association) for part of the 1933 season.

After leaving baseball, Moore worked as a mechanic for the Port of Portland.

MORAN, Roy Ellis ("Deedle," "Morrie," "Nig")

Born: September 17, 1884, Vincennes. **Died:** July 18, 1966, Atlanta, Georgia.
Height: 5-8. **Weight:** 155. **Batted:** right. **Threw:** right.
Debut: September 3, 1912. **Final game:** September 15, 1912.
Positions, teams, years: outfield, Washington (AL) 1912.
Games: 7. **At-bats:** 13. **Home runs:** 0. **Average:** .154.

Roy Moran, who played briefly for the second-place Washington Senators in 1912, spent much of his career as a wide-ranging left fielder and prolific base stealer for the Atlanta Crackers of the Southern League.

Moran's first stop in professional baseball was with pennant-winning Vincennes (Kitty) in 1906. He split the 1907 season between Peoria, Ill. (Three-I), and Jacksonville, Ill. (Iowa State), before joining Atlanta in 1908. He helped the Crackers to a first-place finish in 1909 and became a year-round Atlanta resident after the season.

In 1911 Atlanta sent Moran to Chattanooga, Tenn., and his 11 home runs led the league. He was batting .259 for Chattanooga in 1912 when the Senators acquired him. He had just two hits in 13 at-bats, but drew eight walks for a .476 on-base percentage.

Moran spent the next two seasons in the Pacific Coast League with Sacramento. He was with the club in September 1914 when it moved to San Francisco and became the Mission Wolves. A trade in February 1915 brought him back to Atlanta, where a newspaper proclaimed him "one of the most popular ball players that has ever worn an Atlanta uniform." When a fire destroyed his home in 1917, Atlanta fans staged a day in Moran's honor on June 24. He topped the league that year with 177 hits as the Crackers won the pennant.

Moran retired in June 1918 after balking at a trade that would have sent him to Memphis. He took a job in the automobile industry and later worked as a building contractor. He died from heart disease at age 71.

MORE, Forrest Thedore

Born: September 30, 1881, Hayden. **Died:** August 17, 1968, Columbus.
Height: 6'0". **Weight:** 180. **Batted:** right. **Threw:** right.
Debut: April 15, 1909. **Final game:** September 8, 1909.
Positions, teams, years: pitcher, St. Louis (NL) 1909, Boston (NL) 1909.
Games: 25. **Innings pitched:** 98.2. **Won/Lost:** 2–10. **Earned run average:** 4.74.

In his lone big league season, **Forrest More** went from bad to awful when he was traded from a seventh-place team to a tail-end club.

Starting in 1906, More spent three seasons with Springfield, Ill. (Three-I). In 1908 his 20–7 record and league-leading .741 winning percentage for the first-place Senators caught the attention of the St. Louis Cardinals.

More joined St. Louis in 1909, but after 15 games and a 1–5 record, the Cards dealt him to the Boston Rustlers. More appeared in 15 games for Boston and posted an identical 1–5 mark. St. Louis came in seventh that year while Boston finished in the basement.

His days as a big leaguer ended after the 1909 season, but More continued to pitch in the minors. He went 18–12 for Chattanooga, Tenn. (Southern Association), in 1910 and remained with the club until 1913, when the Lookouts sent him to Nashville, Tenn.

The Vols released More after a 12–15 season in 1914. He returned to Indiana, where he continued to play for independent teams. In 1922 he helped the North Vernon Reds to a first-place finish in the Southern Indiana Semi-Pro League.

More made his home in Vernon, working in the timber business until his retirement.

MORRISON, Philip Melvin

Born: October 18, 1894, Rockport. **Died:** January 18, 1955, Lexington, Kentucky.
Height: 6'2". **Weight**: 190. **Batted**: both. **Threw**: right.
Debut: September 30, 1921. **Final game**: September 30, 1921.
Positions, teams, years: pitcher, Pittsburgh (NL) 1921.
Games: 1. **Innings pitched**: 0.2. **Won/Lost**: 0-0. **Earned run average**: 0.00.

Phil Morrison, who appeared in one big league contest, briefly teamed with his younger brother Johnny as a member of the Pittsburgh Pirates' pitching staff.

Phil was a native of the southwestern Indiana town of Rockport, while Johnny was born a year later in Pellville, Ky., less than 20 miles to the southeast. Phil played for teams in Owensboro, Ky., before serving in the U.S. Army during World War I.

Late in the summer of 1920 Phil signed with Birmingham, Ala. (Southern Association), where his brother was en route to a 26-13 season. In 1921 Johnny moved on to the Pirates, while Phil replaced him in Birmingham's starting rotation and went 21-13. On July 20 Phil threw a seven-inning no-hitter against Mobile.

Phil joined Pittsburgh in mid-September and appeared in one game at St. Louis, pitching two-thirds of an inning in a 12-4 loss to the Cardinals. Johnny continued to pitch for the Pirates, winning 25 games in 1923, but Phil's Major League career was over. He returned to Birmingham in 1922 and went 22-15. He split the 1923 season between Birmingham and Atlanta, going 6-20.

Severe rheumatism kept Morrison out of baseball in 1924 and 1925. He went to spring training with Pittsburgh in 1926, and the Pirates dealt him to Indianapolis (American Association). After six games with the Indians he retired for good and returned to Owensboro.

Phil died at a Veterans Administration hospital in Lexington, Ky., at age 60. Johnny, who won 103 games against 80 losses in a 10-year career with Pittsburgh and the Brooklyn Dodgers, died in Louisville in 1966.

MOSS, Charles Malcolm

Born: April 18, 1905, Sullivan. **Died:** February 5, 1983, Savannah, Georgia.
Height: 6'0". **Weight:** 175. **Batted:** right. **Threw:** left.
Debut: April 24, 1930. **Final game:** August 13, 1930.
Positions, teams, years: pitcher, Chicago (NL) 1930.
Games: 12. **Innings pitched:** 18.2. **Won/Lost:** 0-0. **Earned run average:** 6.27.

A picaresque figure in Hoosier baseball history, **Mal Moss** was a two-sport college star who became an attorney, served as a wartime naval officer and worked for a major corporation.

Mal's family moved to Winchester, Ky., shortly after his birth. After graduation from Bingham Military School in Asheville, N.C., he entered Vanderbilt University. A member of the Commodores' baseball team, he also served as captain of the basketball squad and helped the school to its first Southeast Conference hoops title in 1927.

After graduating cum laude that year, Moss signed with Louisville (American Association and enrolled in Vanderbilt's law school. He continued to pitch for the Colonels in 1928, recording a 10-22 mark. Despite a 9-18 record in 1929, the Cubs bought his contract and he opened the 1930 season in Chicago. That same year Moss, who had switched to the University of Chicago, earned his law degree.

In August 1930 the Cubs traded Moss to Minneapolis (American Association), where he compiled a 5-3 mark in a dozen games. He pitched for Los Angeles (Pacific Coast) the next two seasons, going 15-14 in 1931. On June 12 he threw a no-hit victory against Sacramento. He had an 11-8 record for Los Angeles in 1932.

Moss began working at a Chicago law firm after the 1931 season. He left baseball in 1932 to become a full-time attorney, and he joined a Chicago mortgage company in 1934.

In 1942 Moss took a leave of absence to enlist in the U.S. Navy. Accepting a commission, he served as a beachmaster during operations at Iwo Jima and Okinawa and earned two battle stars. He left the service in 1945 with the rank of lieutenant commander.

Relocating to Los Angeles after the war, Moss resumed his career in the mortgage business. In 1954 he returned to Chicago as counsel for the Mid-America Office of the Prudential Insurance Company. For many years he made his home in Evanston, Ill. He moved to Savannah, Ga., after retiring.

Moss died at age 77 after a brief illness.

MOWE, Raymond Benjamin

Born: July 12, 1889, Rochester. **Died:** August 14, 1968, Sarasota, Florida.
Height: 5-7. **Weight:** 160. **Batted:** left. **Threw:** right.
Debut: September 25, 1913. **Final game:** October 3, 1913.
Positions, teams, years: shortstop, Brooklyn (NL) 1913.
Games: 5. **At-bats:** 9. **Home runs:** 0. **Average:** .111.

Ray Mowe's eight years in organized baseball included a brief stint with the Brooklyn Dodgers.

After spending the 1909 season with an amateur team in La Porte, Ind., Mowe (rhymes with 'how') signed with Elgin, Ill. (Northern Association), for 1908. When the league disbanded in July he joined Newark (Ohio State), and by year's end he was playing for Indianapolis (American Association).

Describing Mowe as "a modest, gentlemanly lad," a 1910 article in the *Fort Wayne Journal-Gazette* reported he was "in the baseball game professionally in order that he may obtain money with which to put himself through a college course."

In 1911 Mowe batted .199 as the Indians' everyday shortstop. He wound up in Springfield, Ohio (Central), for 1912, where he improved to .266. He opened the 1913 campaign with Troy (New York State), where he batted .286 with 40 stolen bases.

Acquired by Brooklyn in September 1913, Mowe saw limited action in his short big-league stay. The Dodgers assigned him to Newark, N.J. (International), for 1914, and he was with the franchise in 1915 when it shifted to Harrisburg, Pa. The club returned to Newark in 1916, where Mowe took part in 26 games. He split the 1917 season between Newark and Springfield, Mass. (Eastern), before leaving baseball.

Mowe taught school in Rochester, Ind., during his playing days. From 1918 to 1923 he served as director of athletics and football coach at Earlham College. A respected basketball referee, he officiated state championship games in 1922, 1924 and 1925. He later worked as a sporting goods merchant and as a sales manager for the Westinghouse Corporation.

Mowe was in his late seventies when he moved to Sarasota, Fla., where he died at age 79.

MUFFETT, Billy Arnold ("Muff")

Born: September 21, 1930, Hammond. **Died:** June 15, 2008, Monroe, Louisiana.
Height: 6'1". **Weight:** 198. **Batted:** right. **Threw:** right.
Debut: August 3, 1957. **Final game:** April 28, 1962.
Positions, teams, years: pitcher, St. Louis (NL) 1957–1958, San Francisco (NL) 1959, Boston (AL) 1960–1962.
Games: 125. **Innings pitched:** 376.1. **Won/Lost:** 16–23. **Earned run average:** 4.33.

Named for 1930 Indianapolis 500 winner Billy Arnold, **Billy Muffett** grew up in Texas and lettered in baseball, football and basketball at Fort Worth's North Side High School. During more than four decades in baseball, Muffett teamed with Stan Musial, Willie Mays and Ted Williams, and coached Bob Gibson, Steve Carlton, Nolan Ryan and Jack Morris.

Muffett broke in with Helena, Ark. (Cotton States), in 1949. In 1951 he helped Monroe, La. (Cotton States), to a pennant, leading the league with 22 wins and a 2.25 ERA. He spent 1952 and 1953 with a U.S. Army artillery unit.

In 1954 Muffett returned to baseball. During the 1955 Texas League playoffs he pitched a 10–0 no-hitter for Shreveport, La., against San Antonio. In November 1955 the St. Louis Cardinals acquired him in the Rule 5 draft, and in 1956 and 1957 he posted back-to-back 14-win seasons at Houston (Texas).

Muffett joined St. Louis in August 1957, going 3–2 with a 2.25 ERA and eight saves. On September 23 in Milwaukee he gave up a game-winning home run to Henry Aaron that gave the Braves the NL pennant. The Cardinals finished second, eight games back.

St. Louis traded Muffett to the San Francisco Giants after a disappointing 1958 campaign. In July 1959 the Giants sent him to Minneapolis (American Association), Boston's top farm club. He resurfaced with the Red Sox in 1960, going 6–4 in 23 games, including 14 starts. He went 3–11 in 1961 and, after one start for Boston in 1962, his days as a Major League pitcher were over.

Muffett continued to play in the minors and was part of the Atlanta squad that won the 1962 International League Governors' Cup. The Crackers went on to beat Louisville (American Association) in the Junior World Series.

At Richmond, Va. (International), in 1963 and 1964 he helped develop future New York Yankees pitching star Mel Stottlemyre. "He was a tremendous help to me, pushing me to be more aggressive in the strike zone, and talking to me about the mental part of pitching," Stottlemyre wrote in his autobiography, *Pride and Pinstripes.*

Muffett ended his playing days in 1965 at Tulsa, Okla. (Texas), where he doubled as a coach. In 1966 he caught on as a full-time pitching coach in the St. Louis organization. He joined St. Louis in 1967, the year the Cardinals defeated the Red Sox in the World Series.

In 1971 Muffett switched to the California organization and served as the Angels' pitching coach from 1975 to 1977. In 1979 he moved to the Tigers' minor league system. In 1985, his first year as Detroit's pitching coach, the Tigers beat the Padres in the World Series. He remained with Detroit through 1994, when he retired from baseball at the age of 64.

Muffett's weight ballooned to around 250 while he coached in Detroit. He shed more than 80 pounds after he was diagnosed with throat cancer in 1987. He spent his retirement years in Monroe, La., where he'd met and married the former Janet Lusk in 1950. Their marriage lasted nearly 58 years.

MURPHY, Leo Joseph ("Red," "Murph")

Born: January 7, 1889, Terre Haute. **Died:** August 12, 1960, Racine, Wisconsin.
Height: 6-1. **Weight:** 179. **Batted:** right. **Threw:** right.
Debut: May 2, 1915. **Final game:** September 25, 1915.
Positions, teams, years: catcher, Pittsburgh (NL) 1915.
Games: 31. **At-bats:** 41. **Home runs:** 0. **Average:** .098.

Leo Murphy, who spent a season as a backup catcher for the Pittsburgh Pirates, was involved in baseball for most of his 71 years.

Murphy's first year in organized ball was 1911, when he batted .323 for Champaign-Urbana, Ill. (Illinois-Missouri). After two years as a second-string backstop with Columbus, Ohio (American Association), he helped Sioux City, Iowa (Western), to a first-place finish in 1914 with a .323 average. The Pirates drafted him after the season. He spent all of 1915 in Pittsburgh, where his teammates included three other Hoosiers, Max Carey, Babe Adams and Fritz Scheeren.

In 1916 Murphy returned to Columbus, and he spent 1917–1918 with Milwaukee (American Association). In 1919 he joined the Fairbanks-Morse club (Beloit, Wis.) of the Midwest League, an outlaw circuit made up of industrial teams.

Murphy, who lived in Chicago for part of his career in organized ball, spent 1924 through 1926 with a Midwest League team in Racine, Wis., which became his permanent home. After a brief return to organized ball with Waco (Texas) in 1927 and Winston-Salem, N.C. (Piedmont), in 1928, he returned to the industrial leagues as a player and manager. He retired after 1933.

A factory worker after his baseball days, Murphy returned to the game as an investor in the Racine Belles of the All-American Girls Professional Baseball League. He served on the Belles strategy board and in 1945 took over as manager. In 1946 he guided the Belles to a pennant and a playoff victory. Racine was still one of the league's elite teams through 1949, Murphy's final season as manager.

MUSGRAVES, Dennis Eugene ("Denny")

Born: December 25, 1943, Indianapolis. **Lives:** Centralia, Missouri.
Height: 6'4". **Weight:** 188. **Batted:** right. **Threw:** right.
Debut: July 9, 1965. **Final game:** July 29, 1965.
Positions, teams, years: pitcher, New York (NL) 1965.
Games: 5. **Innings pitched:** 16. **Won/Lost:** 0–0. **Earned run average:** 0.56.

Before signing with the New York Mets, **Dennis Musgraves** pitched the University of

Missouri to a Big Eight Conference title and to the championship game of the College World Series.

Musgraves, who grew up in Missouri, was captain of the baseball and basketball teams at Hazelwood High School in St. Louis. He continued as a two-sport athlete at Mizzou, posting a 7–2 record for the baseball team as a sophomore in 1964. His 2–1, two-hit victory over Maine in the semifinals propelled Missouri to the title game against Minnesota, the eventual NCAA champion.

Shortly afterward the Mets signed Musgraves for a reported $100,000 bonus, the largest in club history at the time. By the time he was promoted from Buffalo, N.Y. (International), to the Mets in July 1965, he had already developed elbow problems. "I think I got it pitching in cold weather," Musgraves told the *St. Louis Post-Dispatch*. "I had been used to the hot weather here and when I got to Buffalo I didn't adjust very well."

Injured again in a July 29 game with the Chicago Cubs, Musgraves went on the disabled list and underwent surgery in October 1965. He appeared in four games for Greenville, S.C. (Western Carolinas), in 1966 before more arm problems ended his season.

Converted into a reliever in 1968, Musgraves continued to pitch for the Mets farm clubs through 1970. His career ended in 1971 with Omaha, Neb. (American Association), the top farm club of the Kansas City Royals.

After baseball, Musgraves worked as an analyst for an insurance company in Columbia, Mo. Wilson Musgraves, Denny's father, was a pitcher-outfielder-first baseman in the Boston Braves organization in 1946–1947.

MUSSER, Neal Gordon

Born: August 25, 1980, Lafayette. **Lives:** Port St. Lucie, Florida.
Height: 6'1". **Weight:** 235. **Batted:** left. **Threw:** left.
Debut: April 21, 2007. **Final game:** May 29, 2008.
Positions, teams, years: pitcher, Kansas City (AL) 2007–2008.
Games: 18. **Innings pitched:** 25.2. **Won/Lost:** 0–1. **Earned run average:** 4.21.

A star pitcher for Benton Central High School in Oxford, Ind., **Neal Musser** went 8–2 as a senior. Selected by the Mets in the second round of the 1999 draft, he passed up a scholarship offer from Texas A&M to sign with New York.

Musser launched his pro career that summer with the Mets' rookie Gulf Coast League affiliate. He compiled a 2.06 ERA during his first two pro seasons, and his fastball, changeup and curve showed potential. The Mets questioned his durability—he pitched in just eight games in 1999 and seven in 2000—and released him after the 2005 season.

Arizona signed Musser for 2006. After seven starts for their Tucson, Ariz. (Pacific Coast), farm club, the Diamondbacks cut him. Kansas City gave him a contract and moved him to the bullpen. "I think it fits my personality well," he told *Baseball America*'s Alan Eskew. "I don't have to hold anything back on the hitters. I can just go right after them."

Musser opened the 2007 season with Omaha, Neb. (Pacific Coast), and was recalled three times by the Royals. A broken finger ended his season, but he recovered in time to help Team USA win the World Cup in Taiwan. He pitched ten shutout innings in the tournament, and got the win in a 5–1 triumph over South Africa.

Musser spent most of 2008 at Omaha and made one relief appearance for Kansas City. Released at season's end, he signed with Houston for 2009 and saw action in four games at Round Rock, Texas (Pacific Coast). After the Astros cut him, he went 2–2 in 22 games for an independent team at Lancaster, Pa. (Atlantic).

In 2010 Musser signed a minor league contract with the Mets, but New York released him during Spring Training.

NEHF, Arthur Neukom ("Little Arthur," "The Terre Haute Terror")

Indiana Baseball Hall of Fame, 1989.
Born: July 31, 1892, Terre Haute. **Died:** December 18, 1960, Phoenix, Arizona.
Height: 5'9". **Weight:** 176. **Batted:** left. **Threw:** left.
Debut: August 13, 1915. **Final game:** October 3, 1929.
Positions, teams, years: pitcher (451), outfield (4), Boston (NL) 1915–1919, New York (NL) 1919–1926, Cincinnati (NL) 1926–1927, Chicago (NL) 1927–1929.
Games: 451. **Innings pitched:** 2,707.2. **Won/Lost:** 184–120. **Earned run average:** 3.20.
At-bats: 915. **Home runs:** 8. **Average:** .210.

Pitching for the New York Giants, left-hander **Art Nehf** twice defeated the crosstown rival Yankees in games that decided the World Series. "Never gifted with the size or stuff of a Rube Waddell or Bob Grove," columnist Red Smith wrote in 1960, "he was nevertheless one of the finest of all left-handers, with control and curves and courage and intelligence and complete mastery of his trade."

After graduation from Terre Haute's Wiley High School, Nehf entered Rose Polytechnic Institute. In 1911 he batted .468 for Rose Poly's baseball team and pitched a no-hitter against Indiana State. In 1914 he earned an electrical engineering degree.

Nehf played for Negaunee, Mich., of the independent Copper League in 1912. In 1913, while still a Rose Poly undergrad, he signed with Kansas City (American Association). He finished the year at Sioux City, Iowa (Western). In 1914 he moved on to Terre Haute (Central), where he won 19 games and led the league with 218 strikeouts and a 1.39 ERA. Pitching for Terre Haute on July 24, 1915, he hurled a 1-0 no-hitter against Erie.

The Boston Braves bought Nehf's contract on August 15, 1915. A control artist and curveball specialist, he pitched in a dozen games as a rookie and went 5-4 with a 2.54 ERA. In 1917 he compiled a 17-8 record, throwing 41 consecutive scoreless innings from September 13 through October 4. He went 15-15 in 1918, pitching all 21 innings of a 2-0 loss to visiting Pittsburgh on August 1.

In August 1919 the Braves traded Nehf to the Giants. He was an immediate success in New York, winning 21 games in 1920. In 1921 his 20-10 record helped the Giants to the pennant, and he pitched a complete-game 1-0 win over the Yankees in Game Eight of the best-of-nine World Series.

Nehf's 19 victories led the Giants to another pennant in 1922. The Giants again beat the Yanks in the Series, this time in five games, with Nehf winning the final contest. In 1923 he had 13 wins for the first-place Giants, and took the loss in Game Six of the Fall Classic as the Yankees scored their first World Series triumph.

In 1924 Nehf went 14-4 as the Giants won a fourth consecutive pennant and lost to the Washington Senators in a seven-game Series. In the opening game, he outdueled Walter Johnson 4-3 in 12 innings. He lost to Tom Zachary 2-1 in Game 6.

When the Giants slipped to second place in 1929, Nehf's 11 wins were his fewest in ten full seasons. After a 107-60 record in 226 games with New York, the Giants dealt him to Cincinnati in 1926. Bothered by neuritis, he appeared in just nine games that season and lost his only decision. Cut loose by the Reds in August 1927, he joined the Chicago Cubs and finished the year with a 4-6 record.

Nehf rebounded with 13 wins for Chicago in 1928. In 1929 he went 8-5 as a reliever and spot starter for the first-place Cubs, who lost to the Philadelphia Athletics in the World Series. He made his final post-season appearance that fall, relieving in a pair of games without a decision. In five different World Series, he appeared in a dozen games and went 4-4 with a 2.16 ERA.

The 1929 season was Nehf's last. He finished his career with 182 complete games and 28 shutouts. He was also a good fielder, participating in a dozen double plays in 1920 to tie an NL record. A career .210 hitter, he hit five home runs in 1924, including two in one game on July 29. He was the Giants' Opening Day starter in 1922 and 1923.

Making Phoenix his home after baseball, Nehf became a successful insurance executive. A heart attack in 1932 forced him into early retirement. He remained active in sandlot baseball and arranged Major League tryouts for several local players. One of them, outfielder Hank Leiber, played for the Giants and Cubs from 1933 to 1942.

Nehf succumbed to cancer at age 68. In 1959, the year before his death, he was named to the Arizona Sports Hall of Fame. In 1965 the baseball facility on the campus of his alma mater (now known as Rose-Hulman Institute of Technology) was named Nehf Field. He was elected to the Indiana Baseball Hall of Fame in 1989.

NELSON, William F.

Born: September 28, 1863, Terre Haute. **Died:** June 23, 1941, Terre Haute.

Height: unknown. Weight: unknown. Batted: unknown. Threw: right.
Debut: September 3, 1884. Final game: September 10, 1884.
Positions, teams, years: pitcher, Pittsburgh (American Association) 1884.
Games: 3. Innings pitched: 26. Won/Lost: 1-2. Earned run average: 4.50.

Before entering organized ball, **Billy Nelson** earned fame as a member of a prominent semi-pro team called the Terre Haute Blues. He joined Muskegon, Mich. (Northwestern), in 1884, compiling a 9-18 record with a 1.72 ERA before the league disbanded in August.

Nelson finished the 1884 season with the Pittsburgh Alleghenies of the American Association, one of three big leagues operating that year. During an eight-day span he pitched in three games, defeating the Toledo Blue Stockings on September 6 for his lone big league victory.

From 1885 through 1889 Nelson played every position except catcher for Toledo, Ohio (Western), Lincoln, Neb. (Western), Dubuque, Iowa (Central Inter-State), and Terre Haute (Illinois-Indiana). The 1889 Terre Haute club ("considered for many years as the city's best team ever," wrote *Terre Haute Tribune-Star* contributor Mike McCormick) finished first and swept runnerup Danville in the best-of-seven playoffs.

Nelson spent his entire life in Terre Haute. He was a minor league umpire until 1897, when a thrown ball struck him in the head. He also worked as a blacksmith and as a hotel clerk.

NEWKIRK, Joel Inez ("Sailor")

Born: May 1, 1896, Kyana. Died: January 22, 1966, Eldorado, Illinois.
Height: 6'0". Weight: 180. Batted: right. Threw: right.
Debut: August 20, 1919. Final game: April 23, 1920.
Positions, teams, years: pitcher, Chicago (NL) 1919-1920.
Games: 3. Innings pitched: 8.2. Won/Lost: 0-1. Earned run average: 7.27.

A World War I veteran, **Joel Newkirk** pitched in just five professional games. Newkirk honed his baseball skills during a five-year hitch in the U.S. Navy. In 1919 the spitball specialist reportedly hurled 72 consecutive shutout innings for a sandlot team in his hometown of Norris City, Ill.

That July, Newkirk signed with the Chicago Cubs and appeared in one Major League contest. He opened the 1920 season with Chicago but, after two appearances and an 0-1 slate, the Cubs sold his contract to the Columbus, Ohio, Senators (American Association). He split a pair of decisions in two games with Columbus, and finished the year back in Chicago with a semi-pro club called the Winton Six.

Newkirk, who served as commander of an American Legion post in Eldorado, Ill., worked in a steel mill and eventually became a general foreman.

Joel's younger brother, right-hander Floyd Newkirk, also played Major League baseball. Floyd, an Illinois native, threw a no-hitter for St. Paul (American Association) in 1933 and pitched in one game for the New York Yankees in 1934.

NEWLIN, Maurice Milton ("Newt," "Newly")

Born: June 22, 1914, Bloomingdale. Died: August 14, 1978, Houston, Texas.
Height: 6'0". Weight: 176. Batted: right. Threw: right.
Debut: September 20, 1940. Final game: September 17, 1941.
Positions, teams, years: pitcher, St. Louis (AL) 1940-1941.
Games: 15. Innings pitched: 33.2. Won/Lost: 1-2. Earned run average: 6.42.

Maurice Newlin graduated from high school in Wichita and played semi-pro baseball in Kansas before breaking in with Fairbury (Nebraska State) in 1936. He toiled for six different independent clubs until 1939, when he hooked up with Topeka, Kan. (Western Association), a St. Louis Browns farm team.

Newlin got credit for 26 of Topeka's 72 wins that season for a share of the league lead. Promoted to San Antonio (Texas) for 1940, he went 23-8 with a 1.98 ERA and topped the league in wins, winning percentage and innings pitched (287). The Browns purchased Newlin's contract that September. In his lone appearance, he started against the Chicago White Sox and threw no-hit ball until the fifth inning. He got credit for the win in a 7–6 Browns triumph.

Newlin opened the 1941 season with the Browns, but returned to San Antonio in mid–May. He was back in St. Louis at the end of June and pitched in 14 games, losing his only two decisions. He spent 1942 through 1945 as a U.S. Navy seabee. He never returned to the big leagues after World War II, although he pitched for five different minor league teams from 1946 to 1948.

After quitting baseball, Newlin worked as a salesman. He died of a malignant brain tumor at age 64.

NEWMAN, Raymond Francis

Born: June 20, 1945, Evansville. **Lives:** Myrtle Beach, South Carolina.
Height: 6'5". **Weight:** 205. **Batted:** left. **Threw:** left.
Debut: May 16, 1971. **Final game:** May 24, 1973.
Positions, teams, years: pitcher, Chicago (NL) 1971, Milwaukee (AL) 1972–1973.
Games: 45. **Innings pitched:** 63.2. **Won/Lost:** 3–3. **Earned run average:** 2.97.

Ray Newman played for Muskegon (Mich.) High School and Muskegon Community College before signing with the Detroit Tigers in 1964. Drafted by the Cubs that November, he spent 1967 and 1968 in the U.S. Navy.

Returning to baseball in 1969, Newman became a full-time relief pitcher. After posting a 1.80 ERA in 11 games at Tacoma, Wash. (Pacific Coast), he earned a promotion to the Cubs in mid–May 1971.

Newman hurled five perfect innings in relief in a July 18 win over Montreal, but gained notoriety for riding a bicycle from his Chicago apartment to Wrigley Field. "It's cheap transportation," he told *Chicago Sun-Times* reporter Edgar Munzel. Bushy-haired and high-strung, Newman compiled a 3.55 ERA for Chicago while striking out 35 batters in 38 innings.

Toward the end of Spring Training in 1972 the Cubs sent Newman to the Milwaukee Brewers in a three-player deal. After the trade, Chicago manager Leo Durocher described him as "this nut who used to ride a bicycle to the ballpark."

In 1972 and 1973 Newman shuttled between the Brewers and their top farm team, helping Evansville win the '72 American Association title with a 6–2 record, 13 saves and a 2.05 ERA.

Traded to the Detroit Tigers in 1973, Newman spent two more seasons with Evansville before leaving baseball.

NEWTON, Eustace James ("Doc")

Born: October 26, 1877, Mount Carmel. **Died:** May 14, 1931, Memphis, Tennessee.
Height: 6'0". **Weight:** 185. **Batted:** left. **Threw:** left.
Debut: April 27, 1900. **Final game:** May 7, 1909.
Positions, teams, years: pitcher (178), first base (2), Cincinnati (NL) 1900–1901, Brooklyn (NL) 1901–1902, New York (AL) 1905–1909.
Games: 180. **Innings pitched:** 1,201.2. **Won/Lost:** 54–72. **Earned run average:** 3.22.
At-bats: 436. **Home runs:** 0. **Average:** .172.

Doc Newton threw the first no-hitter in Pacific Coast League history and set a Major League record for the most errors by a pitcher in one season.

The son of a prominent doctor and Indiana state legislator, Newton played baseball for a local team in the Bartholomew County town of Hope. From 1899 to 1901 he attended the Central College of Physicians and Surgeons in Indianapolis, where his father was an instructor.

Newton made his professional debut in 1897 with Norfolk, Va. (Atlantic), posting a 15–12 mark with a 1.90 ERA. By 1899 he was pitching for the Western League franchise in Indianapolis, where he had made his home. He pitched a 5–0 no-hitter versus Milwaukee on June 9, and his 15–11 slate helped Indianapolis to a first-place finish.

Joining Cincinnati for 1900, Newton went 9–15. The Reds dealt him to the Brooklyn Superbas in July 1901, and he finished the season with 17 errors—a modern-era record for big league pitchers. After a 15–14 showing with Brooklyn in 1902, he jumped to Los Angeles (Pacific Coast) for 1903. Newton led the PCL—where the seasons continued through autumn—with 35 wins in 1903 and 39 in 1904. On November 8, 1903, he won a 2–0 no-hitter against Oakland. In 1904 his 28 errors in 33 games set a PCL record.

After recovering from diphtheria, Newton joined the AL's New York Highlanders in 1905. On August 4, he and catcher Mike Powers formed what is believed to be the only all-medical school graduate battery in big league history. Through 1909 Newton managed 19 wins for the Highlanders against 25 losses. Hampered by his erratic fielding and a lack of control, he issued 11 walks in a single game with the St. Louis Browns on September 8, 1905. He was repeatedly disciplined for insubordination or dissipation, and in 1906 *Sporting Life* reported that he "wore out too many shoes leaning on bar-rests."

Newton was New York's Opening Day starter in 1909, but after three more appearances the Highlanders dispatched him to Toronto (Eastern). He pitched in the minors through 1915 for Louisville (American Association), Memphis, Tenn. (Southern Association), Galveston (Texas) and Chattanooga, Tenn. (Southern Association).

Despite his degree, Newton never practiced medicine. He was working as a warehouse superintendent for the Memphis Terminal Corporation when he died from food poisoning at age 53, not long after suffering a nervous breakdown.

NICHOLSON, Ovid Edward

Born: December 30, 1888, Salem. **Died:** March 24, 1968, Salem.
Height: 5-9. **Weight:** 155. **Batted:** left. **Threw:** right.
Debut: September 17, 1912. **Final game:** September 26, 1912.
Positions, teams, years: outfield, Pittsburgh (NL) 1912.
Games: 6. **At-bats:** 11. **Home runs:** 0. **Average:** .455.

Fleet-footed outfielder **Ovid Nicholson** once stole 111 bases in a single season.

After moving from Indiana to Kansas for health reasons in 1910, Nicholson spotted a newspaper ad regarding tryouts for the Great Bend club of the Kansas State League. "Although his experience was virtually nil, he made the club because of fine natural ability," according to the *Evansville Courier-Journal*.

In 92 games for Great Bend that summer, Nicholson hit .254. In 1911 he moved on to Frankfort, Ky. (Blue Grass), and batted .313. Frankfort finished first in 1912, sparked by Nicholson's .352 average and 111 steals.

In a six-game trial with the Pittsburgh Pirates that September, Nicholson had five hits in 11 at-bats. Back in the minors for 1913, he batted .315 for Wichita, Kan. (Western), and hit .305 in 1914 with 60 steals. In 1916 he swiped 50 bases in 102 games for Hannibal, Mo. (Three-I).

After the 1917 season, Nicholson entered military service and retired from baseball. In 1918 he married Nellie Donica, whose brother Harry was Ovid's teammate in Frankfort.

In 1926 Nicholson resurfaced as player-manager of the Ludington, Mich., squad, which began the year in the Central League. In June the circuit merged with the Michigan-Ontario League to form the Michigan State League.

Nicholson then left baseball for good and moved to Kenosha, Wis., where he operated a clothing store for women. He retired in 1953 and returned to Indiana, where he and Nellie spent the rest of their lives.

NILL, George Charles ("Rabbit")

Born: July 14, 1881, Fort Wayne. **Died:** May 24, 1962, Fort Wayne.
Height: 5-7. **Weight:** 160. **Batted:** right. **Threw:** right.
Debut: September 27, 1904. **Final game:** June 22, 1908.
Positions, teams, years: second base (113), third base (75), shortstop (47), outfield (36), Washington (AL) 1904–1907, Cleveland (AL) 1907–1908.
Games: 296. **At-bats:** 963. **Home runs:** 3. **Average:** .212.

During five Major League seasons, **Rabbit Nill** played second base, third base, shortstop, and all three outfield positions. Foot speed and a small frame earned him his nickname.

"I started my career as a baseball player with the famous Shamrocks of Fort Wayne," Nill told the *Fort Wayne News* in 1908. "We played Sunday games chiefly, visiting a number of small towns in Indiana and Illinois.... All of the members of the team were Irish except yours truly [Nill's ancestry was German]. The boys adjusted to my deficiency in this respect by placing a letter 'O' in front of my name and I was known all over the section as O'Nill."

Danville, Ill. (Three-I), signed Nill to his professional contract in 1901. He batted .298 that year and topped the league with 125 runs. After a .253 season in 1902, he moved to Colorado Springs (Western) where he hit .301 in 1903 and .285 in 1904.

The Senators purchased Nill's contract in August 1904. Though never an everyday player, he became a fan favorite in Washington. "Nill is a sawed-off little chap, but gets around fast and covers ground well," reported *Sporting Life* in 1905.

In August 1907 the Senators traded Nill to the Cleveland Naps, where his big league career ended in 1908. He played for eight different minor league clubs through 1914. After his professional career ended, he joined a Fort Wayne semi-pro team called the Blackbirds.

Nill operated a garage for a time and worked for the Fort Wayne Tool and Die Company until his retirement in 1954. He was elected to the Northeast Indiana Baseball Association Hall of Fame in 1963.

Dr. John Nill, Rabbit's son, was president of the Allen County Board of Health and served as team physician for Bishop Luers High School for over a quarter century. Both Nills are members of Fort Wayne's Baseball Hall of Fame.

O'NEILL, Philip Bernard ("Peaches")

Born: August 30, 1879, Anderson. **Died:** August 2, 1955, Anderson.
Height: 5'11". **Weight:** 165. **Batted:** right. **Threw:** right.
Debut: April 16, 1904. **Final game:** August 4, 1904.
Positions, teams, years: catcher (5), first base (1), Cincinnati (NL) 1904.
Games: 8. **At-bats:** 15. **Home runs:** 0. **Average:** .267.

In 1900 the premier sport at the University of Notre Dame wasn't football, but baseball, and that year's Fighting Irish squad included four future Major Leaguers: pitchers Norwood Gibson and Burt Keeley, third baseman James "Red" Morgan and catcher **Peaches O'Neill**.

An Anderson High School alumnus, O'Neill studied law while playing for Notre Dame from 1899 to 1902. *Notre Dame Scholastic*, the school's weekly newspaper, reported in March 1901 that "O'Neill will be behind the bat again with his big yellow glove and his big mellow smile, to cheer up the rooters with his jolly 'Peaches! Old hoss!' O'Neill is playing the same steady game, and his arm has lost none of its force and accuracy."

After graduation in 1902, O'Neill signed with Le Mars, Iowa (Iowa-South Dakota). He opened the 1903 campaign in his hometown of Anderson (Central). During the season the team shifted to Grand Rapids, Mich.

In 1904 O'Neill joined the Cincinnati Reds as a backup to Heinie Peitz and George Schlei, who shared the catching duties. In August the Reds tried to send O'Neill to Louisville (American Association), but he refused to report. "Phil O'Neill, the Cincinnati catcher, rebels on [sic] the idea of going to Louisville," reported *Sporting Life* in August 1904. In September, the weekly indicated that Peaches squeezed five days additional pay out of the Reds by threatening to sue.

Practicing law in Anderson, O'Neill played for independent teams in Guthrie, Indian Territory (present-day Oklahoma), in 1904, and Youngstown, Ohio, in 1905. In 1906 he was planning a return to organized ball with Sioux City, Iowa (Western), when an arm injury ended his baseball career.

Settling in Anderson, O'Neill became a full-time attorney. He was a member of the firm of O'Neill, Scott and Schrenker and served as president of the Madison County Bar Association. He helped college baseball teams prepare for their seasons at Indiana University (1903), Purdue (1905) and DePauw (1907).

ORME, George William

Born: September 16, 1891, Lebanon. **Died:** March 16, 1962, Indianapolis.
Height: 5–10. **Weight:** 160. **Batted:** right. **Threw:** right.
Debut: September 14, 1920. **Final game:** September 17, 1920.
Positions, teams, years: outfield, Boston (AL) 1920.
Games: 4. **At-bats:** 6. **Home runs:** 0. **Average:** .333.

The son of an Irish-born butcher, **George Orme** attended Manual High School in Indianapolis, where he spent most of his life.

Orme (pronounced (OR-mee) entered professional baseball in 1912 with Galesburg, Ill. (Central). He was out of organized ball in 1917 and 1918 before resurfacing in the Michigan-Ontario League in 1919. He spent most of the year with Flint, Mich., before joining pennant-winning Saginaw, Mich., late in the season.

In 1920 Orme batted .327 for Brantford, Ontario. (Michigan-Ontario). The Boston Red Sox acquired him at the end of August. Orme drew three bases on balls during his brief big league career, including two in the same inning. Hitting in the leadoff slot in a game at Detroit's Navin Field on September 17, he batted twice in the seventh inning and walked both times.

Orme was back with Brantford as a player-manager in 1921 and led the team to a second-place finish. He continued to play in the minors through 1925, managing Michigan-Ontario League clubs in Flint (1922), and Kitchener, Ontario (1925).

After leaving baseball, Orme took a job as a structural ironworker in Indianapolis. He continued to play for semi-pro teams while serving as a part-time scout. Orme retired in 1957. While playing cards at the Iron Workers Union Hall in 1962, he suffered a heart attack and died at age 70.

OYLER, Raymond Francis ("Oil Can Harry")

Born: August 4, 1938, Indianapolis. **Died:** January 26, 1981, Redmond, Washington.
Height: 5-11. **Weight:** 165. **Batted:** right. **Threw:** right.
Debut: April 18, 1965. **Final game:** October 1, 1970.
Positions, teams, years: shortstop (502), second base (11), third base (3), first base (1), Detroit (AL) 1965-1968, Seattle (AL) 1969, California (AL) 1970.
Games: 542. **At bats:** 1,265. **Home runs:** 15. **Average:** .175.

A batboy for his hometown minor league team as a youth, **Ray Oyler** grew up to be a slick-fielding, light-hitting shortstop for a World Series winner.

In 1952 Oyler won a contest to become the first official batboy for the Indianapolis Indians (American Association). At Cathedral High School in Indianapolis, he won letters in baseball and basketball and quarterbacked the football squad to a city title. In 1956 he played for the semi-pro Marion, Ind., Blue Sox.

After a four-year Marine Corps hitch, Oyler signed with the Detroit Tigers in 1960. With Knoxville, Tenn., in 1962 his .961 fielding average topped the South Atlantic League. He joined the Tigers in 1965, and for the next three years served mainly as a backup to All-Star shortstop Dick McAuliffe.

Detroit manager Mayo Smith switched McAuliffe to second base in 1967 to make room for Oyler, who batted .207 in 148 games and 367 at-bats. In an effort to see the ball better, Oyler began wearing yellow-tinted eyeglasses during Spring Training in 1968. "He looks like a German tank commander," quipped teammate Norm Cash.

The Tigers won the 1968 AL pennant, with Oyler batting .135 after going hitless over his last 37 at-bats. For the World Series, Smith benched Oyler and moved center fielder Mickey Stanley to shortstop. Detroit beat the St. Louis Cardinals in seven games, with Oyler seeing action in four contests as a late-inning defensive replacement for Stanley.

The Seattle Pilots, an expansion club, drafted Oyler prior to the 1969 season. He batted .165 in 106 games as Seattle's primary shortstop. A local disc jockey **facetiously** organized a Ray Oyler Fan Club, which grew to as many as 50,000 fans. The Pilots left Seattle after one season to become the Milwaukee Brewers.

In December 1969 Oyler went to the Oakland Athletics in a four-player trade. In April 1970 Oakland dealt him to the California Angels, his final big league stop. He played for Salt Lake City and Hawaii in the Pacific Coast League before quitting baseball.

Settling in Redmond, Wash., Oyler worked for the Boeing Corporation and later for a bowling center. He suffered a fatal heart attack at age 42.

PACTWA, Joseph Martin ("Packy")

Born: June 2, 1948, Hammond. **Died:** March 10, 2009, Hutchins, Texas.
Height: 5'11". **Weight:** 185. **Batted:** left. **Threw:** left.
Debut: September 15, 1975. **Final game:** September 28, 1975.
Positions, teams, years: pitcher, California (AL) 1975.
Games: 4. **Innings pitched:** 16.1. **Won/Lost:** 1-0. **Earned run average:** 3.86.

After nine years in the minors as an outfielder-first baseman, **Joe Pactwa** reached the big leagues as a pitcher.

A graduate of North Thornton High School

in Calumet, Ill., Pactwa signed with the New York Yankees out of Chicago's Loop Junior College in 1966. In 1970 he batted .285 with 25 homers for Manchester, N.H. (Eastern). After spending part of the 1971 season in the Minnesota Twins organization, he returned to the Yankee chain. He switched to pitching in 1972, and in 1973 at West Haven, Conn. (Eastern), he went 12-6 with a 3.18 ERA.

Before the 1975 season the Yankees sold Pactwa's contract to the Tampico Alijadores of the Mexican League. As a pitcher and part-time designated hitter, he had a 17-6 record and batted .299. Pactwa added four more wins in post-season play as Tampico defeated the Union Laguna Algodoneros and the Monterrey Sultanas in the playoffs before besting the Cordoba Cafeteros in the finals.

That September, Pactwa joined the Angels. He beat the Minnesota Twins and Bert Blyleven 1-0 for his lone Major League decision. "With a screwball, slider and fastball, he is hoping to be the kind of pitcher the Angels can use," opined Ron Rapoport in the *Los Angeles Times*. "And if the American League ever repeals the designated-hitter rule, he's all set."

Back with Tampico for 1976, Pactwa finished his career in the Mexican League. He went from Tampico to the Saltillo Saraperos in 1977 and retired after playing first base for the Coahuila Mineros in 1978. Attempting a comeback with the Reynosa Broncos in 1982 at age 33, he went 0-1 in two starts before finally calling it quits.

Pactwa died in Hutchins, Texas, a southern suburb of Dallas, when he was 60 years old.

PARKER, Jarrod Brent

Born: November 24, 1988, Fort Wayne. **Lives:** Bluffton.
Height: 6'1". **Weight:** 195. **Bats:** right. **Throws:** right.
Debut: September 27, 2011.
Positions, teams, years: pitcher, Arizona (NL) 2011, Oakland (AL) 2012-2013.
Games: 62. **Innings pitched:** 384. **Won/Lost:** 25-16. **Earned run average:** 3.68.

Jarrod Parker, the Arizona Diamondback's first-round draft pick in 2007 (and the ninth selection overall), spent two years at Wayne High School in Fort Wayne before switching to Ossian's Norwell High. As a junior, his 8-1, 1.19 record helped Norwell to a berth in the 2006 IHSAA 3A championship game at Victory Field in Indianapolis. He started against Jasper High School and left with a 7-6 lead, but Jasper went on to win 13-12. Parker spent the summer playing for Team USA in the World Junior Championships in Cuba. He had a 1-0 record with an 0.77 ERA as the Americans took the silver medal behind Korea.

With a fastball that reached 98 miles per hour, Parker was ranked among the nation's top prep prospects in 2007. That April he signed a letter of intent with Georgia Tech, and in May he won honors as Indiana's Gatorade Player of the Year.

In the June 2007 draft, Parker was the first high school pitcher selected. Nine days later, he threw a shutout and hit a home run as undefeated Norwell beat Evansville Memorial to win the state 3A title. Parker finished the season with a 12-0 slate and an 0.10 ERA, earning Indiana's Mr. Baseball honors from *Hoosier Diamond* magazine. In August he signed with the Diamondbacks for an estimated $2.1 million.

Parker began his pro career in 2008 with a 12-5, 3.44 record at South Bend (Midwest). He divided 2009 between Visalia (California) and Mobile, Ala. (Southern), but his season ended abruptly at the end of July when he experienced elbow tightness. That October, he underwent Tommy John surgery and sat out all of 2010. Healthy again in 2011, he helped Mobile to the Southern League title with an 11-8, 3.79 slate.

Parker joined Arizona in September 2011 and started the Diamondbacks' next-to-last game of the season against Los Angeles. He pitched shutout ball into the sixth inning before leaving without a decision. Traded to Oakland in December 2011, he developed into a solid starting pitcher for the Athletics in 2012. Along with Tommy Milone, Travis Blackley, A.J. Griffin and Dan Straily, Parker led an all-rookie rotation down the stretch. He finished with a 13-8. 3.47 record as the A's overtook the Rangers to win the AL West.

In 2013 Parker helped Oakland to another division title with a 12-8, 3.97 slate. In 18 starts from May 28 to September 4, he went 9–0 with a 2.59 ERA, the longest unbeaten streak by an A's pitcher since Lefty Grove in 1931. Parker beat Detroit in the third game of the ALDS. He was set to be Oakland's 2014 Opening Day starter, but a second Tommy John surgery shelved him for the year.

For two seasons at Wayne High School, Jarrod teamed with his older brother, Justin Parker. An infielder, Justin went on to play for Wright State University and spent three years with minor league clubs in the Arizona and Milwaukee systems.

PARRETT, Jeffrey Dale

Born: August 26, 1961, Indianapolis. **Lives:** Versailles, Kentucky.
Height: 6'4". **Weight:** 185. **Batted:** right. **Threw:** right.
Debut: April 11, 1986. **Final game:** September 28, 1996.
Positions, teams, years: pitcher, Montreal (NL) 1986–1988, Philadelphia (NL) 1989–1990, Atlanta (NL) 1990–1991, Oakland (AL) 1992, Colorado (NL) 1993, St. Louis (NL) 1995–1996, Philadelphia (NL) 1996.
Games: 491. **Innings pitched:** 724.2. **Won/Lost:** 56–43. **Earned run average:** 3.80.

Jeff Parrett's family left Indiana for West Virginia when he was six months old and eventually settled in Kentucky. Parrett went from Lafayette High School in Lexington to the University of Kentucky, and in 1983 the Milwaukee Brewers took him in the ninth round of the draft.

Originally a starter, Parrett switched to the bullpen in 1984. Pitching for Stockton in 1985, he led the California League with a 2.75 ERA. Montreal acquired him after the 1985 season and he opened the 1986 season with the Expos. When Montreal optioned him to Indianapolis (American Association) that June, he became the second Indianapolis-born Major Leaguer to play pro ball in his native city (the first was shortstop Donie Bush in 1908).

In 1988, his first full season with Montreal, Parrett went 12–4 with a 2.65 ERA. Traded to Philadelphia in December, his dozen wins in 1989 topped NL relievers. The Phillies sent him to Atlanta in August 1990. Released by the Braves before the 1992 season, he signed with Oakland as a setup man. He contributed a 9–1 record and a 3.02 ERA as the Athletics won the AL West title.

A free agent after the season, Parrett joined the Colorado Rockies, an expansion team, in 1993. An elbow injury at the end of July shelved him for the rest of the season. After spending 1994 with Omaha, Neb. (American Association), he resurfaced with St. Louis in 1995. In 1996 the Cardinals traded Parrett to Philadelphia, where the ten-year veteran finished his big league career.

Parrett retired to Versailles, Ky., where he coaches baseball at Woodford County High School. He led the team to its first state title in 2012.

PENNER, Kenneth William

Born: April 24, 1896, Boonville. **Died:** May 28, 1959, Sacramento, California.
Height: 5'11". **Weight:** 170. **Batted:** left. **Threw:** right.
Debut: September 11, 1916. **Final game:** September 4, 1929.
Positions, teams, years: pitcher, Cleveland (AL) 1916, Chicago (NL) 1929.
Games: 9. **Innings pitched:** 25.1. **Won/Lost:** 1–2. **Earned run average:** 3.55.

Ken Penner won 331 games, all but one in the minor leagues. During 45 years as a player, coach, manager and scout, he pitched in portions of two Major League campaigns, 13 years apart.

Born in the southwestern Indiana town of Boonville, Penner attended Dale High School. In 1913, when he was 17 years old, he broke in with Columbus, Miss. (Cotton States). He went 22–11 in 1916 for pennant-winning Marshalltown, Iowa, leading the Central Association with a 1.41 ERA. That September he joined the Cleveland Indians, appearing in four games with a 1–1 record.

Cleveland sent Penner to Portland, Ore., for 1917, and he spent the next nine seasons in the Pacific Coast League. After a 21–18 record in 1917, he shifted to Salt Lake City for 1918. In 1919 he returned to Portland. The Beavers dealt Penner to Sacramento, where he pitched from 1920 to 1923. At Vernon, Calif., in 1924 he went 24–13. He split the 1925 season between Vernon and Wichita, Kan. (Western), combining for a 21–12 mark.

Penner joined Houston in 1926, and in 1927

his 2.52 ERA led the Texas League. In 1928 he reached the 20-victory plateau for a fifth time with a 20–8 record for the pennant-winning Buffaloes. He joined Indianapolis (American Association) in 1929, and a wire service story described his "splendid control, a slow ball that shows the seam and a fast one that is fast."

On August 1 the Chicago Cubs bought Penner's contract. In five relief appearances for the first-place Cubs, Penner lost his only decision but posted a 2.84 ERA. He earned part of a World Series share, but made no post-season appearances against the Philadelphia Athletics. The Cubs dispatched him to Louisville (American Association) that December in return for another Indiana-born pitcher, Malcolm Moss.

In 1930 Penner played on a pennant-winning team for a third time in as many years, going 10–8 for Louisville. He was 17–8 in 1931, and in 1932 he earned his 300th career victory.

From 1934 to 1938 Penner was a player-manager for four different clubs, including Louisville in 1934–1935, Crookston, Minn. (Northern), in 1936, Montgomery, Ala. (Southeastern), in 1937, and Bellingham, Wash. (Western International), in 1938. He served as a non-playing skipper at Bellingham in 1939 and at Pocatello, Idaho (Pioneer), in 1940.

Back in the Pacific Coast League in 1941, Penner spent three more seasons with Sacramento as a coach and occasional player before finally hanging up his spikes at age 47. He spent one more year in uniform as the non-playing manager at Rochester, N.Y. (International), in 1944.

Penner was a capable batter who saw occasional duty as a pinch-hitter. A popular figure in West Coast baseball, he made his home in Sacramento for many years. In 1945 he became a scout for the Cardinals, and St. Louis named him supervisor of its West Coast scouts in 1957.

Soon afterward, Penner was diagnosed with amyotrophic lateral sclerosis (Lou Gehrig's disease). In October 1958 in Sacramento, more than 30 players from Major-League and minor-league teams staged a benefit game to help raise money for Penner's medical bills. He died at age 63.

PENNINGTON, Brad Lee

Born: April 14, 1969, Salem. **Lives:** Salem.
Height: 6'5". **Weight:** 205. **Batted:** left. **Threw:** left.
Debut: April 17, 1993. **Final game:** September 22, 1998.
Positions, teams, years: pitcher, Baltimore (AL) 1993–1995, Cincinnati (NL) 1995, Boston (AL) 1996, California (AL) 1996, Tampa Bay (AL) 1998.
Games: 79. **Innings pitched:** 75.2. **Won/Lost:** 3–6. **Earned run average:** 7.02.

A rangy left-hander with a heater that topped out in the high 90s, **Brad Pennington** drew comparisons to Mitch "Wild Thing" Williams, another erratic flame-throwing reliever who pitched from 1986 to 1997.

Big league clubs passed over Pennington when he graduated from Eastern High School in Pekin, Ind. He attended Bellarmine University before transferring to Vincennes University. The Baltimore Orioles took him in the twelfth round of the 1989 draft.

During his first three minor league seasons Pennington struck out 324 batters in 237 innings, but he also issued 264 bases on balls while compiling an 8–28 record. He developed into a top prospect in 1992 when he cut down on his walks. In 1993 he joined the Orioles, who envisioned him as their future closer. He shuttled between Baltimore and Rochester N.Y. (International), in 1993 and 1994.

In June 1995 the Orioles traded Pennington to the Cincinnati Reds, his favorite team as a youngster. A free agent after the season, he signed with Boston for 1996. That May, the Red Sox put Pennington on waivers and California claimed him. He made eight appearances for the Angels before they dispatched him to Vancouver, B.C. (Pacific Coast). After a Spring Training trial with the New York Yankees, he spent the 1997 season in the Kansas City Royals organization. He relieved in one contest for the Tampa Bay Devil Rays during their first year in 1998.

After pitching for Syracuse, N.Y. (International), in 1999, Pennington was out of baseball in 2000. He came back in 2001 with the independent Allentown, Pa., Ambassadors (Northern) before retiring.

PERZANOWSKI, Stanley ("Perz")

Born: August 25, 1950, East Chicago. **Lives:** Syracuse.

Height: 6'2". **Weight:** 170. **Batted:** both. **Threw:** right.
Debut: June 20, 1971. **Final game:** September 27, 1978.
Positions, teams, years: pitcher, Chicago (AL) 1971, 1974, Texas (AL) 1975–1976, Minnesota (AL) 1978.
Games: 37. **Innings pitched:** 142.2. **Won/Lost:** 5–11. **Earned run average:** 5.11.

After an injury ended his career as a hurdler at Hammond's Morton High School, **Stan Perzanowski** quit the track team and joined the baseball squad. As a senior in 1968, he was the team's MVP. He was pitching for Anderson (Ind.) College when the Chicago White Sox picked him in the 16th round of the 1971 draft.

Between 1968 and 1970 Perzanowski made stops at Sarasota, Fla. (Gulf Coast), Duluth-Superior, Minn. (Northern), Appleton, Wis. (Midwest), and Tucson, Ariz. (Pacific Coast). In 1971 he went 11–0 in 13 starts for Asheville, N.C. (Southern), to earn a promotion to the White Sox. In five games with Chicago he lost his only decision. He finished the year at Tucson, where he went 7–4.

In 1972 Perzanowski led the PCL in losses with a 5–17 mark. He spent the next two years at Iowa (American Association). He went 14–8 in 1973 and 13–8 in 1974, when he appeared in two more games for the White Sox.

After the '74 season, Perzanowski joined Zulia of Venezuela's winter league. His 4–3 record and 1.82 ERA attracted interest from the Senators, who acquired him in February 1975. He went 3–3 in a dozen games that year for Washington.

In June 1976 the Senators traded Perzanowski to Cleveland. Released after a 7–7, 6.10 year at Salt Lake City (Pacific Coast), he signed with the Minnesota Twins. Pitching mostly in relief for Toledo, Ohio (International), in 1978, he earned a return trip to the majors with a 5–1, 2.46 performance. He had a 2–7 record in 13 games for the Twins, who returned him to Toledo for 1979. He appeared in four games with the Mud Hens before ending his career.

Perzanowski, who attended Anderson College in the off-season, was inducted into the Hammond Sports Hall of Fame in 1997. His cousin Ron Perranoski pitched for the Dodgers, Twins, Tigers and Angels from 1961 to 1973.

PETEREK, Jeffrey Allen

Born: September 22, 1963, Michigan City. **Lives:** Niles, Michigan.
Height: 6'2". **Weight:** 195. **Batted:** right. **Threw:** right.
Debut: August 14, 1989. **Final game:** September 22, 1989.
Positions, teams, years: pitcher, Milwaukee (AL) 1989.
Games: 7. **Innings pitched:** 31.1. **Won/Lost:** 0–2. **Earned run average:** 4.02.

After throwing a pair of no-hitters for Three Oaks (Mich.) River Valley High School in 1980, **Jeff Peterek** played for Lake Michigan College (Benton Harbor, Mich.), the University of Mary Hardin-Baylor (Belton, Texas), and Western Kentucky. In 1985 he signed with the Milwaukee Brewers as an undrafted free agent.

Peterek (pronounced "peter-reck") debuted that summer with Beloit, Wis. (Midwest). His 15 wins and three shutouts for Stockton in 1986 led the California League. Pitching for Stockton and El Paso (Texas) in 1987 he combined for a 13–6 slate. He opened the 1988 season at El Paso, going 7–1, and finished at Denver (American Association), where he went 7–6.

In August 1989 Peterek had a 9–9 record and a 3.61 ERA at Denver when the injury-depleted Brewers promoted him. "I'm the type of pitcher who has to change speeds, mix things up and try to keep the hitters off balance to take the sting out of their bats and get the groundball outs," he told the Madison, Wis., *Capital Times*. "I'm not the kind of guy who's going to blow the ball past hitters and get a lot of strikeouts."

Peterek debuted with seven innings of two-hit ball in Milwaukee's 5–4 come-from-behind win over the Yankees, with Tony Fossas getting the win in relief. His final big league appearance came on his 26th birthday.

Back in Denver for 1990, Peterek bowed out of baseball after spending 1991 in the Atlanta Braves' system. He eventually founded the Field of Dreams Real Estate company in Three Oaks, Mich.

PHEGLEY, Joshua Aaron

Born: February 12, 1988, Terre Haute. **Lives:** Indianapolis.

Height: 5-10. **Weight:** 225. **Bats:** right. **Throws:** right.
Debut: July 5, 2013.
Positions, teams, years: catcher, Chicago (AL) 2013-2014.
Games: 76. **At-bats:** 241. **Home runs:** 7. **Average:** .207.

A baseball and football star at Terre Haute North High School, **Josh Phegley** hit .592 as a senior in 2006 to win *Hoosier Diamond* magazine's Mr. Baseball award. Later that summer, he helped Terre Haute's Wayne Newton Post #346 to a second-place finish at the American Legion World Series in Cedar Rapids, Iowa.

As a junior at Indiana University, Phegley batted .344 with 17 homers and 66 RBI to help the Hoosiers win the Big Ten Tournament. That June, the Chicago White Sox made him a supplemental first round pick (38th overall). He debuted that summer with Kannapolis, N.C. (South Atlantic).

Assigned to Winston-Salem, N.C. (Carolina), for 2010, Phegley was diagnosed with idiopathic thrombocytopenic purpura—ITP, a platelet disorder resulting in blood clotting issues. "The normal blood platelet count is between 150,000 and 350,000," he said. "I had the lowest reading you could have, without it being zero. You feel like you're in top physical condition, and you hear that you could be dying.... It was kind of scary."

After six weeks of treatments with no baseball activity, Phegley returned to action and batted a combined .284 in 48 games with Winston-Salem, Bristol, Va. (Appalachian), and Birmingham, Ala. (Southern). He was scheduled to play in the Arizona Fall League when the condition returned. Since doctors believed Phegley's platelets were being destroyed in his spleen (a non-vital organ that acts primarily as a blood filter), Josh opted for a splenectomy. "I thought if I wanted to be ready for next season, I needed to get home, have the operation, and have plenty of time to recover," he said.

The surgery took place in November 2010, and on Opening Day 2011, Phegley was back on duty. He hit .242 in 116 contests. splitting the year between Birmingham and Charlotte, N.C. (International). He batted .266 for Charlotte in 2012, when his .996 fielding percentage earned him a Rawlings minor league Golden Glove. He was hitting .316 for Charlotte in July 2013 when he was called up by the White Sox. He batted .206 in 65 games with Chicago.

Phegley started the 2014 campaign with Charlotte and made the International League team for the Triple-A All-Star Game for a third consecutive year. He rejoined the White Sox in September and hit .216 in 11 contests. After the season, Chicago sent him to the Oakland Athletics in a six-player trade that brought pitcher Jeff Samardzija (a native of Merrillville, Ind.) to the White Sox.

PHILLIPS, Heath Michael ("Philly")

Born: March 24, 1982, Evansville. **Lives:** Lake City, Florida.
Height: 6'3". **Weight:** 275. **Batted:** left. **Threw:** left.
Debut: September 5, 2007. **Last game:** September 30, 2007.
Positions, teams, years: pitcher, Chicago (AL) 2007.
Games: 6. **Innings pitched:** 7.1. **Won/Lost:** 1-1. **Earned run average:** 3.68.

Well-traveled **Heath Phillips** played a major role in getting Team USA to the 2008 Olympics.

A graduate of Central High School in Evansville, Phillips was the tenth pick of the Chicago White Sox in the 2000 draft. He enrolled at Lake City (Fla.) Community College, where he compiled a 7-6 record with a 3.09 ERA before signing with Chicago in 2001.

Over his first three minor league seasons, Phillips compiled a 12-31 record. But his 3.57 ERA during that stretch, along with an impressive strikeout/walk ratio, earned him a berth with Birmingham, Ala. (Southern), for 2004. That year he went 12-10, 4.02 with 107 whiffs versus 36 walks. He split the 2005 season between Charlotte, N.C. (International), and Birmingham.

Phillips broke through in 2006 with a 13-5, 2.96 record and was named to the mid- and post-season all-star teams. That August, he joined Team USA for the Americas Olympic qualifying tournament in Havana. He was the winning pitcher in the opening game with Canada, and in his next start he beat the Dominican Republic. In the title contest, Team USA defeated Cuba to qualify for the 2008 Games in Beijing, China.

After a 13-7 record with Charlotte in 2007,

Phillips joined the White Sox in September. He became a free agent after the season, pitching for farm teams of the New York Yankees, Tampa Bay Rays and Kansas City Royals between 2008 and 2009.

Phillips spent 2010 with Tampa Bay's top farm club at Durham, N.C. (International). He pitched for independent Atlantic League teams in Long Island in 2011 and Sugar Land, Texas, in 2012 before retiring.

PIGNATIELLO, Carmen Peter ("Piggy")
Born: September 12, 1982, Hammond. **Lives:** Aurora, Illinois.
Height: 6'0". **Weight:** 205. **Batted:** right. **Threw:** left.
Debut: August 16, 2007. **Final game:** April 7, 2008.
Positions, teams, years: pitcher, Chicago (NL) 2007–2008.
Games: 6. **Innings pitched:** 2.2. **Won/Lost:** 0–0. **Earned run average:** 6.75.

A Cubs fan as a youngster, **Carmen Pignatiello** grew up in Chicago's south suburbs. In 1999 he pitched for the gold medal-winning U.S. team at the World Junior Championship in Taiwan. He earned Chicago Catholic League co–MVP honors in 2000 with a 14–0 record and an 0.79 ERA for Providence Catholic High School in New Lenox, Ill. Gatorade named him the 2000 Illinois High School Player of the Year.

In 1999 Pignatiello signed a letter of intent with Mississippi State, but he opted for a professional career when the Cubs took him in the 20th round of the 2000 draft. Primarily a starter from 2000 through 2004, he switched to the bullpen at Iowa (Pacific Coast) in 2005.

Pignatiello became a six-year free agent after the 2006 season, but re-signed with the Cubs for 2007. With Chicago battling for the Central Division title, he joined the Cubs that August. He made his Major League debut at Wrigley Field before a crowd that included his wife, parents, sister, and his 76-year-old grandfather, for whom he was named.

"Pitching for the team you grew up rooting for in your hometown," Carmen told MLB.com's Carrie Muskat, "and having your family here to watch you and having the people who have supported me throughout the years here—to go out and pitch a solid inning, it doesn't get any better than that."

Pignatiello opened 2008 with the Cubs but spent most of the year at Iowa. He joined the Minnesota Twins organization for 2009, but was released after four games. He finished the year as a starter for the Schaumburg (Ill.) Flyers of the independent Northern League and left baseball after the season.

In 2012 Pignatiello resurfaced as a pitching coach for the independent Joliet (Ill.) Slammers (Frontier). After leaving baseball, he worked as a Nationwide insurance agent in Palos Heights, Ill.

PILARCIK, Alfred James
Indiana Baseball Hall of Fame, 1987.
Born: July 3, 1930, Whiting. **Died:** September 20, 2010, Schererville.
Height: 5'10". **Weight:** 180. **Batted:** left. **Threw:** left.
Debut: July 13, 1956. **Final game:** September 24, 1961.
Positions, teams, years: outfield, Kansas City (AL) 1956, Baltimore (AL) 1957–1960, Kansas City (AL) 1961, Chicago (AL) 1961.
Games: 668. **At-bats:** 1,614. **Home runs:** 22. **Average:** .256.

Al Pilarcik, a hustling outfielder with good speed and a strong arm, grew up in Whiting, Ind., rooting for the Chicago Cubs. The son of a Slovakian immigrant, Pilarcik (pronounced "pill-ARE-sick") won seven letters in three sports at Whiting High School and captained the football team. In 1948 he signed with the New York Yankees and played for Independence, Kan. (K-O-M).

Except for an army hitch that cost him the 1953 and 1954 seasons, Pilarcik toiled in the Yankee chain until the Kansas City Athletics bought his contract prior to 1956. He was batting .325 with 18 homers and 75 RBI that year for Columbus, Ohio (International), when he joined the A's in July.

In 1957 Pilarcik's 15 assists were second in the AL. That December, Kansas City sent him to Baltimore in a four-man deal. He batted .243 for the Orioles in 1958 and .282 in 1959.

A part-timer in 1960, Pilarcik was in right field on September 28 at Boston's Fenway Park when Ted Williams belted his 521st career home run. The ball rolled off the façade, and Pilarcik caught it when it came down. After Williams circled the bases, he returned to the dugout and announced his immediate retirement. Pilarcik pocketed the ball but, he said, "John Rice, the umpire, made me give it up."

The Orioles sent Pilarcik back to Kansas City in January 1961. In June the Athletics traded him to the Chicago White Sox. He retired after the season. A tough out, he struck out just 150 times in 1,859 plate appearances.

Pilarcik earned a degree from Valparaiso University during his playing days. He taught physical education and coached baseball at Dyer Central High School and later at Lake Central High. He retired in 1987 and was elected to the Indiana Baseball Hall of Fame that same year. In 2009 he was inducted into Whiting's Wall of Fame.

PLESAC, Daniel Thomas
Indiana Baseball Hall of Fame, 2011.
Born: February 4, 1962, Gary. **Lives:** Crown Point.
Height: 6'5". **Weight:** 205. **Batted:** left. **Threw:** left.
Debut: April 11, 1986. **Final game:** September 28, 2003.
Positions, teams, years: pitcher, Milwaukee (AL) 1986–1992, Chicago (NL) 1993–1994, Pittsburgh (NL) 1995–1996, Toronto (AL) 1997–1999, Arizona (NL) 1999–2000, Toronto (AL) 2001–2002, Philadelphia (NL) 2002–2003.
Games: 1,064. **Innings pitched:** 1,072. **Won/Lost:** 65–71. **Earned run average:** 3.64.

A three-time All-Star, reliever **Dan Plesac** pitched for six teams during his 18 Major League seasons.

Plesac (pronounced "PLEE-sack") grew up in Gary. When he was a sophomore his family moved to Crown Point, where he starred in baseball and basketball at Crown Point High School. The St. Louis Cardinals made him their second-round pick in the 1980 draft. Instead he went to North Carolina State University, joining his older brother Joe on the Wolfpack baseball squad. Joe Plesac, a right-hander, was drafted by the San Diego Padres in 1982 and spent six years in the minors.

Milwaukee took Dan in the first round (26th overall) of the 1983 draft. He spent that summer at Paintsville, Ky., where his nine wins led the Appalachian League. In 1986 he joined the Brewers and over the next five years he picked up 124 saves. His 33 saves in 1989 were a team record, and Plesac was selected to AL All-Star teams in 1987, 1988 and 1989. Bothered by bursitis and tendinitis, he lost the closer's job in 1991. "To put it bluntly," he told Chuck Greenwood of *Sports Collectors Digest*, "I guess I saw the penthouse, and then I saw the outhouse soon after that."

In an attempt to strengthen his weakened shoulder, Plesac made ten starts that year and four more in 1992. After the '92 season, Plesac signed with the Cubs as a free agent. He appeared in 111 games for Chicago in 1993 and 1994, mostly as a set-up man. Granted free agency, he joined Pittsburgh for 1995. In November 1996 the Pirates dealt him to Toronto. He was 0–3 with an 8.34 ERA in June 1999 when the Blue Jays traded him to Arizona. Plesac's 2–1 record and 3.32 ERA helped the Diamondbacks win the NL West Division.

By now the 38-year-old Plesac was contemplating retirement. "I can walk away with my head held high," he told *USA Today*. "There aren't many who can say they've played 15 years." But after a 5–1, 3.15 season for Arizona in 2000, he filed for free agency and rejoined the Blue Jays. In May 2001 he became the 12th Major Leaguer to pitch in 900 games. A year later Toronto sent him to the Philadelphia, where he appeared in his 1,000th game and recorded his 1,000th strikeout. Plesac returned for one more campaign, posting a 2–1 record with a 2.70 ERA for the Phillies. His 1,064 appearances as a hurler placed him fourth behind Jesse Orosco (1,243), Dennis Eckersley (1,071) and Hoyt Wilhelm (1,070).

After working on-air for Comcast SportsNet Chicago from 2005 to 2008, Plesac became an analyst for MLB Network in 2009. An avid harness racing fan, he also served as president of a family business called DTP Standardbreds, Inc. Business holdings include the 40-acre Three-Up-Three-Down Farm in northern Indiana, as well as racehorses in Illinois, New Jersey and Ontario.

Plesac is a member of the North Carolina State University athletic hall of fame. In 2011 he joined his brother-in-law, legendary Andrean High School coach Dave Pishkur, as a member of the Indiana Baseball Hall of Fame.

PORTER, Odie Oscar
Born: May 24, 1877, Borden. **Died:** May 2, 1903, Borden.

Height: unknown. **Weight:** unknown. **Batted:** unknown. **Threw:** left.
Debut: June 16, 1902. **Final game:** June 16, 1902.
Positions, teams, years: pitcher, Philadelphia (AL) 1902.
Games: 1. **Innings pitched:** 8. **Won/Lost:** 0–1. **Earned run average:** 3.38.

Odie Porter achieved two firsts in his one and only Major League appearance. He became the first Indiana University alumnus to reach the big leagues and the first Hoosier native to play for a pennant winner in baseball's modern era (1901 to present).

Porter started as an outfielder and took up pitching in high school at Borden Institute. He enrolled at Indiana in 1899 and quickly earned a reputation as one of the Midwest's top college players. "He is a south paw," reported Indiana University's *Daily Student* newspaper, "and he has all the speed, curves and steadiness in the box necessary to make his name dreaded by the opposing batsmen."

Porter played for the Hoosiers again in 1900 but didn't return to school for the fall semester. He apparently played for an independent team in the Bloomington area, and may have spent part of 1901 playing for Dayton, Ohio (Western Association).

Two months into the 1902 season, the Philadelphia Athletics' pitching staff was depleted by injuries. On June 16 the Athletics were in Chicago for a series with the White Sox. Porter started for Philadelphia, giving up seven runs in the first inning and two more in the second. The Sox added another run in the fifth and went on to win 10–5 with Porter going the distance.

That was Porter's lone big league appearance. The Athletics went on to win the American League pennant, but Porter never again pitched professionally at any level. For years, baseball history books listed Philadelphia's one-game starter from 1902 as "J. James Porter"—a name Odie may have adopted to protect his collegiate eligibility.

Soon afterward Porter came down with lung disease and relocated to Colorado for his health. Terminally ill, he returned to Indiana in the spring of 1903. He died just 320 days after his one day in the Major Leagues.

PROUGH, Herschel Clinton ("Bill")

Born: November 28, 1888, Markle. **Died:** December 29, 1936, Richmond.
Height: 6'3". **Weight:** 185. **Batted:** right. **Threw:** right.
Debut: April 27, 1912. **Final game:** April 27, 1912.
Positions, teams, years: pitcher, Cincinnati (NL) 1912.
Games: 1. **Innings pitched:** 3. **Won/Lost:** 0–0. **Earned run average:** 6.00.

Clint Prough won 20 games or more seven times during 18 years in professional baseball, even though he pitched for nine teams that finished last or in next-to-last place.

Prough (as in "how") began his career with Keokuk, Iowa (Central Association), in 1908. In 1909 he won 20 games and pitched a 1–0 no-hitter against Waterloo. The St. Louis Browns bought Prough's contract toward the end of the season, but he was back with Keokuk for 1910.

At Birmingham, Ala. (Southern) in 1911, Prough went 21–13. He joined Cincinnati for 1912 and became the third of four Reds pitchers in a 23–4 loss at Pittsburgh on April 27. After that lone appearance Cincinnati returned him to Birmingham, and Prough's 14–10 record helped the Barons to a first-place finish. After a 23–6 mark in 1913 the Chicago White Sox acquired him. He saw no action with the Sox, who dealt him to Oakland (Pacific Coast) for 1914.

That was the start of an 11-year PCL stint for Prough, who remained with the Oaks though 1918. During his five years with Oakland, the team finished fifth or sixth each year in a six-team league. He lost 20 games or more from 1914 to 1917. On June 4, 1916, he pitched no-hit ball through ten innings against San Francisco, surrendering a hit in the eleventh. He came out after 14 frames as Oakland went on to win 1–0 in 18 innings. In 1917 he managed 22 wins against 22 defeats.

During Spring Training in 1919, Oakland traded Prough to Sacramento. He won 93 games for the Senators, posting 20-win seasons in 1920, 1921 and 1923. Prior to 1925, Sacramento shipped him to Shreveport, La. (Texas), where he finished his career. His stats in the minors include 269 wins, 252 losses, 2,003 strikeouts and a 3.08 ERA. His seven 20–

win seasons tie him for fourth on the all-time minor league list behind Spider Baum and Tony Freitas, with nine each, and Kewpie Barrett, who had eight.

Prough returned to Indiana after leaving baseball and made his home near Fort Wayne. He died at age 49 after a two-week illness.

PRUIETT, Charles Leroy ("Tex," "Bird-shot")

Born: April 10, 1883, Osgood. **Died:** February 6, 1953, Ventura, California.
Height: 5'8". **Weight:** 176. **Batted:** left. **Threw:** right.
Debut: April 26, 1907. **Final game:** July 18, 1908.
Positions, teams, years: pitcher, Boston (AL) 1907–1908.
Games: 48. **Innings pitched:** 232.1. **Won/Lost:** 4–18. **Earned run average:** 2.83.

Tex Pruiett, whose name belies his Hoosier roots, threw shutouts in three of his four big league victories.

Pruiett's nickname stemmed from his days in the Texas League. He broke in with Waco, (Texas) in 1905, and in 1906 he compiled a 22–15 season with an 11–7 mark at Dallas (Texas) to go with an 11–8 record at St. Paul (American Association). That August, St. Paul peddled the fastball specialist to the Boston Red Sox.

In 1907 Pruiett had a 3–11 record for the seventh-place Red Sox, along with a 3.11 ERA. His 18 relief appearances topped the AL, and two of his wins were shutouts. In July 1908 he was 1–7 with a 1.99 ERA in 13 games—his lone win was another shutout—when Boston traded him to the Cleveland Naps. He made no appearances for Cleveland, which released him to Toledo, Ohio (American Association), where he didn't pitch.

New Orleans (Southern) picked up Pruiett for 1909, and he went 14–13 for the Pelicans. He returned to Massachusetts in 1910 for a three-year hitch with New Bedford (New England), and on May 30 he threw a 1–0 no-hitter against Fall River. He compiled a 46–35 record for the Whalers, including an 18-win season in 1912.

Pruiett joined Oakland (Pacific Coast) in 1913. West Coast newspapers dubbed him "Bird-shot" in 1914 after his arrest at a Portland, Ore., theater, where he'd been placing birdshot between his teeth and propelling the pellets with a toothpick at chorus girls. He remained with the Oaks through 1917, amassing a 34–44 mark. His highest win total came in 1915, when he went 16–20.

After leaving baseball, Pruiett lived in Ojai, Calif., for many years and retired from the Tide Water Associated Oil Company of California.

PUCKETT, Troy Levi ("Puck," "Trojan," "Andy," "Rufus," "Ringtail")

Born: December 10, 1889, Winchester. **Died:** April 13, 1971, Winchester.
Height: 6'2". **Weight:** 186. **Batted:** left. **Threw:** right.
Debut: October 4, 1911. **Final game:** October 4, 1911.
Positions, teams, years: pitcher, Philadelphia (NL) 1911.
Games: 1. **Innings pitched:** 2. **Won/Lost:** 0–0. **Earned run average:** 13.50.

Troy Puckett's Major League career consisted of one relief appearance for the Philadelphia Phillies.

A 1908 graduate of Winchester High School, Puckett was a student at Wabash College when he played for Paducah, Ky. (Kitty), in 1911 under the name "Roy Brown."

Puckett joined the Phillies toward the end of the season. He took over for Earl Moore in the eighth inning of a 7–3 loss in the first game of a doubleheader with the Boston Rustlers at Philadelphia's Baker Bowl. "Earl Moore got his [lumps] in seven innings as a starter," reported the *Philadelphia Inquirer*, "after which a Mr. Puckett, one of next year's hopes from Paducah, Ky., debuted, and they finished the first end of the show by whaling Mr. Puckett."

Reserved for the next season by the Phillies, Puckett divided 1912 between Wilkes-Barre, Pa. (New York State), and Cairo, Ill. (Kitty). He started the 1913 season with Cairo and finished with Columbus, Ga. (South Atlantic), where he played through 1915.

Puckett, who earned a degree from Wabash in 1913, was a lifelong Winchester resident. After leaving baseball he operated his family's Puckett Dairy.

RADER, Donald Russell

Born: September 5, 1893, Wolcott. **Died:** June 26, 1983, Walla Walla, Washington.

Height: 5'10". **Weight:** 164. **Batted:** left. **Threw:** right.
Debut: July 25, 1913. **Final game:** October 1, 1921.
Positions, teams, years: shortstop (9), third base (1), outfield (1), Chicago (AL) 1913, Philadelphia (NL) 1921.
Games: 13. **At-bats:** 35. **Home runs:** 0. **Average:** .286.

Don Rader, who spent 13 years in organized ball, played for a pennant winner in his next-to-last season.

Born in Wolcott, 26 miles west of Logansport, Rader was about seven years old when his family moved to Oregon. In 1909 he helped Pendleton (Ore.) High School to a state title. In 1911 he turned down an offer from the Boston Red Sox to attend the University of Oregon, where he was the lone freshman on the basketball squad for the 1911–1912 season.

Before the season ended, "times got tough," Rader told the *Walla Walla* (Wash.) *Union-Bulletin*, and he left school. In 1913 he signed with Pendleton, Ore. (Western Tri-State). He joined the Chicago White Sox that July as a 19-year-old rookie and finished the year with Lincoln, Neb. (Western).

Rader began the 1914 season with Helena, Mont. (Union Association). When the league disbanded in August, he signed with Venice, Calif. (Pacific Coast). Except for 1918, when he served in the navy, Rader toiled for minor league clubs in the West, South and Midwest, mostly as a shortstop.

In January 1921 Rader joined a team of American professionals for a tour of Japan. The Detroit Tigers purchased his contract in April, but returned him to New Orleans (Southern Association) before he saw action in a Tigers uniform. The Philadelphia Phillies gave him a nine-game trial that summer.

Rader's best season was 1922, when he batted .318 while splitting the year between Dallas and Beaumont in the Texas League. In 1925 his .283 average helped Des Moines, Iowa (Western), to a first-place finish. After sitting out all of 1926, he returned to Lincoln (Western) for one more campaign in 1927. For part of 1937 he managed Lewiston, Idaho (Western International).

For a time, Rader worked as a car salesman in California. Eventually he moved to Walla Walla, where he worked in his father's sporting goods store. He died there just 10 weeks short of his 90th birthday.

RAMSEY, Thomas H. ("Toad")
Born: August 8, 1864, Indianapolis. **Died:** March 27, 1906, Indianapolis.
Height: 5'9". **Weight:** 180. **Batted:** right. **Threw:** left.
Debut: September 5, 1885. **Final game:** September 17, 1890.
Positions, teams, years: pitcher (248), outfield (4), Louisville (American Association) 1885–1889, St. Louis (American Association) 1889–1890.
Games: 250. **Innings pitched:** 2,100.2. **Won/lost:** 113–124. **Earned run average:** 3.29.
At-bats: 858. **Home runs:** 0. **Average:** .204.

For a brief period in the 1880s, left-hander **Tom Ramsey** was the greatest strikeout pitcher in big league baseball.

As a teenager, Ramsey played sandlot ball in Indianapolis while working primarily as an apprentice bricklayer. He accidentally sliced a tendon in the index finger of his pitching hand with a trowel and, when the injury failed to heal properly, he couldn't straighten his finger. The crooked digit enabled him to throw a ball so that it veered downward as it reached the plate. Known as the "drop curve," the pitch was almost unhittable.

Ramsey was allegedly discovered at age 16 by fellow Indianapolis resident John Kerins, another future big leaguer. At Kerins' recommendation, Ramsey joined a semi-pro club sponsored by the When Clothing Store. He quickly became the best pitcher in the Indianapolis Municipal League.

In 1885 Ramsey signed a professional contract with Chattanooga, Tenn. (Southern). Relying on his drop curve, he struck out 16 batters in one game and on May 30 he pitched a no-hit game against Nashville. At the end of August he reached the Major Leagues with the Louisville Colonels of the American Association.

With Kerins as his primary catcher, Ramsey established himself in 1886 as one of the top big league hurlers. He went 38–27, leading the league in complete games (66) and innings pitched (588.2) while striking out 499 batters (second only to the 513 by Baltimore Orioles left-hander Matt Kilroy). On August 9 he fanned 17 batters in a 6–0 win over the visiting New York Metropolitans.

Ramsey almost duplicated his win-loss figures in 1887 with a 37–27 slate. Despite a rule change that allowed batters four strikes, he had a league-leading 355 strikeouts. His career began to unravel in 1888, with heavy alcohol consumption contributing to an 8–30 record. He was 1–16 on July 17, 1889, when Louisville shipped him to the St. Louis Browns of the American Association. He won three of four decisions for the Browns.

Bobby Lowe, a Major League infielder from 1890 to 1907, claimed "there has never been a better left-hander" than Ramsey. "I played against him in some exhibition games along '89, when he was with Louisville and I was in the Western League," Lowe told *The Sporting News* in 1906. "I saw his drop ball then. He didn't have to start it high. He sent it in about waist high and it broke so quickly and so low that a batter couldn't get under it to hit it."

In 1890 Ramsey went 24–17, but the Browns released him in September after he engaged in a shouting match with volatile St. Louis owner Chris Von Der Ahe. Between 1891 and 1895 Ramsey played for minor league clubs in Denver (Western Association), Jacksonville, Ill. (Illinois-Iowa), Savannah, Ga. (Southern Association), and St. Joseph, Mo. (Western Association).

Returning to Indianapolis, Ramsey resumed his bricklaying career and played semi-pro ball for a team in Shelbyville. He later worked as a bartender in an establishment owned by his brother. Ramsey died of pneumonia at age 41. He is buried in an unmarked grave at Crown Hill Cemetery in Indianapolis.

A terrible fielder, Ramsey made 107 errors in 434 career chances. Although some maintain that his best pitch was a knuckleball, it's more likely he threw a variation of the forkball or knuckle-curve. The nickname "Toad" apparently stemmed from a peculiar squatting motion Ramsey frequently assumed before delivering a pitch.

RARIDEN, William Angle ("Bedford Bill")

Born: February 5, 1888, Bedford. **Died:** August 28, 1942, Bedford.
Height: 5'10". **Weight:** 168. **Batted:** right. **Threw:** right.
Debut: August 12, 1909. **Final game:** October 2, 1920.
Positions, teams, years: catcher (948), third base (3), second base (1), Boston (NL) 1909–1913, Indianapolis (Federal) 1914, Newark (Federal) 1915, New York (NL) 1916–1918, Cincinnati (NL) 1919–1920.
Games: 982. **At-bats:** 2,877. **Home runs:** 7. **Average:** .237.

In 1917 **Bill Rariden** was involved in one of the most controversial plays in World Series history. Two years later, he played in the most infamous Fall Classic of all time.

The son of a doctor, Rariden played baseball and football for Bedford High School. He worked as a fireman before joining Canton, Ohio (Central), in 1907. In August 1909, Canton sold his contract to the Boston Rustlers (today's Atlanta Braves), where he established himself as one the NL's top defensive catchers.

In 1914 Rariden defected to Indianapolis of the upstart Federal League. "He still spends the frigid months in Hoosierdom," the *Atlanta Constitution* reported, "and it was in part his love for his native state" that led to the decision. With Rariden handling most of the backstop duties, the Hoosiers finished first. In 1915 the team relocated to Newark, N.J., where he remained the top catcher for the Peppers.

When the FL folded, Rariden signed with the New York Giants for 1916. In 1917 he led NL catchers with a .984 fielding percentage and batted .271 to help New York win the pennant. In the best-of-seven World Series, the Chicago White Sox took a three games-to-two lead over the Giants.

Game Six at New York's Polo Grounds was scoreless after three innings when the White Sox put runners at first and third with no outs. The next Chicago batter grounded to Giants pitcher Rube Benton, who spotted the runner at third, Eddie Collins, hung up between home plate and the bag. Benton threw to third baseman Heinie Zimmerman, who relayed to Rariden as Collins headed home. Rariden chased Collins back toward third and fired the ball to Zimmerman. The lightning-quick Collins saw the plate unguarded and sprinted home, with Zimmerman in vain pursuit. The Sox scored twice more in the inning en route to a 4–2 triumph and the World Series title.

Zimmerman was branded as a goat, even though Rube Benton and first baseman Walter Holke failed to cover home plate with Rariden so far up the third base line.

During the winter months, Rariden worked as a farmer and electrician in Bedford. He wound up closer to home when the Giants traded him to Cincinnati after the 1918 season. In 1919 Rariden shared catching duties with Ivy Wingo for the pennant-winning Reds, who beat the White Sox in the World Series. Several Chicago players—the notorious "Black Sox"—were subsequently suspended for conspiring with gamblers to fix the contests.

In his two Series appearances, Rariden batted a combined .281 (9-for-32). In 1921 Cincinnati sent him to Atlanta (Southern Association), where he served as team captain. He managed the Crackers from May through July of 1922, when he resigned and returned to Bedford to harvest his peach crop.

Rariden farmed and operated a service station until the mid 1930s, when his health began to fail. He and his wife, the former Ruby Sellers, divided their time between Bedford and Florida until Bill's death at age 54.

RAY, Larry Dale
Born: March 11, 1958, Madison. **Lives:** Maumelle, Arkansas.
Height: 6'1". **Weight:** 195. **Batted:** left. **Threw:** right.
Debut: September 10, 1982. **Final game:** October 2, 1982.
Positions, teams, years: outfield, Houston (NL) 1982.
Games: 5. **At-bats:** 6. **Home runs:** 0. **Average:** .167.

Larry Ray won MVP honors in the Ohio River Valley Conference in 1976 while playing for Switzerland County High School in Vevay. A three-year letterman at Kentucky Wesleyan College, Ray was drafted in the fourth round by the Houston Astros in 1979.

Ray spent his first two professional campaigns with Daytona Beach (Florida State). At Columbus, Ga., in 1981, he led the Southern League with 107 RBI. In 1982 he hit .294 with 15 homers for Tucson, Ariz. (Pacific Coast).

That September Ray joined the Astros and pinch-hit for future Hall of Famer Nolan Ryan in his first big league at-bat. "To have made it this far and be from a small place like Vevay is amazing," Ray told the *Madison Courier's* Tim Hillman, "considering most professional players are from California, Texas, New York and all areas where they play baseball all year around."

Ray spent the next two seasons in the Pacific Coast League. In 1985 he joined Mexico City and helped the Diablos Rojos to the Mexican League title. He returned to Columbus for the 1986 season.

On June 30, 1986, Ray was in the Columbus lineup when Bo Jackson, the 1985 Heisman Trophy winner, made his pro baseball debut with Memphis. Ray overshadowed the former Auburn University two-sport standout, leading Columbus to a 9–5 road win with a pair of homers and a single.

Before leaving baseball, Ray played for the Pittsburgh Pirates' Vancouver, British Columbia (Pacific Coast), affiliate in 1987. Seven years after his baseball career ended, he moved to Arkansas and took a job in the automotive equipment field.

REED, Ronald Lee
Indiana Baseball Hall of Fame, 1990.
Born: November 2, 1942, La Porte. **Lives:** Lilburn, Georgia.
Height: 6'6". **Weight:** 215. **Batted:** right. **Threw:** right.
Debut: September 26, 1966. **Final game:** September 29, 1984.
Positions, teams, years: pitcher, Atlanta (NL) 1966–1975, St. Louis (NL) 1975, Philadelphia (NL) 1976–1983, Chicago (AL) 1984.
Games: 751. **Innings pitched:** 2,477.2. **Won/lost:** 146–140. **Earned run average:** 3.46.

Ron Reed, who gave up a pro basketball career to concentrate on baseball, reached postseason play seven times during a 19-year big league career.

A star performer at La Porte High School in baseball, basketball and football, Reed averaged 18.9 points per game for the University of Notre Dame basketball team between 1962 and 1965. Grade problems prevented him from playing for the Fighting Irish baseball squad until his senior year. Selected by the National Basketball Association's Detroit Pistons in 1965, he went unnoticed in that year's baseball draft. The Milwaukee Braves signed him in July 1965. He spent the rest of the summer pitching for West Palm Beach (Florida State).

During the winter of 1965–1966 Reed was the sixth man for the Pistons under coach Dave DeBusschere, who had given up Major League baseball in favor of basketball. From 1966 to 1967, Reed was the only man playing in both the NBA and the big leagues.

In 1966 the Braves relocated to Atlanta. Reed rose from Class A to the majors that year, and made two late-September starts for the Braves. After the season he returned to the Pistons, but he quit basketball in March 1967 to concentrate on his diamond career. "I had to make a decision sooner or later," he told Jerry Green of the *Detroit News*. "I'd been playing terrible basketball this year. I don't think I've been helping the team. I want to play a sport where I can help the team. I hope it's baseball."

Reed quickly developed into one of Atlanta's top starters, winning 13 of his last 17 decisions for an 18–10 record. The Braves won the NL West title, but were swept in the League Championship Series by New York's "Miracle Mets." Reed took the loss in Game Two.

Reed suffered a broken collarbone in March 1970 and never again posted a winning season in Atlanta. He still managed to tie a Major League record in 1975 by allowing only five home runs in 250.1 innings. Reed was Atlanta's starting and winning pitcher when teammate Henry Aaron hit his 500th and 600th career home runs, as well as his record-breaking 715th.

During a nine-month span in 1975 Reed was traded twice, first to the St. Louis Cardinals in March and again in December to Philadelphia. Phillies manager Danny Ozark moved him to the bullpen with excellent results. Reed teamed with southpaw Tug McGraw to give Philadelphia an effective relief tandem. "It worked out great for both of us," Reed told Bill Ballew of *Sports Collectors Digest*. "Every time we were brought in, we were fresh. When one of us got tired, the other one was there."

Between 1976 and 1983 Reed produced 57 wins and 91 saves, leading NL relievers with 13 wins in 1979. During that stretch the Phillies reached post-season play six times. In 1980 the Phils beat the Kansas City Royals for their first-ever World Series title, with Reed getting a save in the second contest.

At age 40 in 1983, he went 9–1 with eight saves to help Philadelphia win another pennant. Reed made four appearances in the World Series as the Phillies lost to the Baltimore Orioles. That December, Philadelphia traded him to the White Sox. He closed out his career in 1984 with a dozen saves and a 3.08 ERA for Chicago.

A 1968 NL All-Star, Reed is one of a handful of pitchers with 100 career wins, 100 saves and 50 complete games. Making his home in suburban Atlanta after baseball, he became a vice president for development for Marketing Event Partners Inc., a business consulting service.

Reed played for two Indiana Baseball Hall of Fame coaches—Ken Schreiber of La Porte (Class of 1979) and Notre Dame's Jake Kline (Class of 1980). In 1990 he joined them in the state shrine at Jasper. He was inducted into the National Polish-American Sports Hall of Fame in 2005.

REISING, Charles ("Pop")

Born: August 28, 1861, Lanesville. **Died:** July 26, 1915, Louisville, Kentucky.
Height: unknown. **Weight:** unknown. **Batted:** unknown. **Threw:** unknown.
Debut: July 19, 1884. **Final game:** July 20, 1884.
Positions, teams, years: outfield, Indianapolis (American Association) 1884.
Games: 2. **At-bats:** 8. **Home runs:** 0. **Average:** .000.

The son of German immigrants, **Charlie Reising** played for amateur teams like the Star Base Ball Club and the Kentons in Covington, Ky., before signing with the Indianapolis Hoosiers in July 1884. The Hoosiers were part of the American Association, one of three big leagues operating that year.

Leading off and playing right field in a 4–0 loss to the Toledo Blue Stockings on July 19, Reising went 0-for-4. "He failed to cover himself in glory at the bat," reported the next day's *Indianapolis State Sentinel*, "and did not play a brilliant game in his position."

Reising's big-league career ended after three days and one more game. He pitched that summer for Springfield (Ohio Association).

After hitting .147 in 38 games for Birmingham, Ala. (Southern Association), in 1885, Reising was out of organized ball in 1886. He played for Hastings, Neb. (Western), in 1887 and for Davenport, Iowa (Central Inter-State), in 1888. The Davenport squad was in first place when the league disbanded at the end of July. When the Inter-State League returned in 1889, he played for Burlington, Iowa.

Reising disappeared from baseball after the season and eventually settled in Louisville, where he operated a saloon at Twelfth and Market streets. A widower, Reising was a month short of his 54th birthday when he died of tuberculosis at his mother's home.

REITH, Brian Eric
Born: February 28, 1978, Fort Wayne. **Lives:** Parrish, Florida.
Height: 6'5". **Weight:** 220. **Batted:** right. **Threw:** right.
Debut: May 16, 2001. **Final game:** June 14, 2004.
Positions, teams, years: pitcher, Cincinnati (NL) 2001, 2003–2004.
Games: 73. **Innings pitched:** 127.2. **Won/lost:** 4–12. **Earned run average:** 5.92.

As a high school junior, **Brian Reith's** 90-mile-an-hour fastball helped Fort Wayne Concordia to the 1995 state championship game. Reith (pronounced "reeth") came down with mononucleosis as a senior and won just four of nine decisions. He scrapped plans to attend Purdue and signed with the Yankees when New York selected him in the sixth round of the 1996 draft.

In 2000 at Tampa, Reith was leading the Florida State League with a 2.18 ERA when the Yanks sent him to Cincinnati in a six-player deal. After one game at Triple-A Louisville (International) in 2001, the Reds pressed him into their starting rotation. Following an 0–7 slate that summer he spent all of 2002 in the minors. The Philadelphia Phillies claimed him that July, but in August the Reds reacquired him on waivers.

Reith shuttled back and forth between Cincinnati and Louisville in 2003 and 2004, pitching almost exclusively in relief. A free agent after the season, he signed with the Pittsburgh organization and spent 2005 with Indianapolis (International).

In 2007 and 2008 Reith played for the independent Somerset Patriots (Atlantic) before leaving for Taiwan to pitch for the Uni-President 7-Eleven Lions. He signed with Milwaukee for 2009. After the Brewers released him, he pitched that summer for independent teams in Joliet, Ill. (Northern), and Camden, N.J. (Atlantic), and for the Tigres de Quintana Roo of the Mexican League.

Reith is a member of the Northeast Indiana Baseball Association Hall of Fame's Class of 2010. He currently serves as a head coach and pitching coordinator for SCORE International Baseball's travel teams in Tampa, Fla.

REPKO, Jason Edward
Born: December 27, 1980, East Chicago. **Lives:** Kennewick, Washington.
Height: 5'11". **Weight:** 200. **Bats:** right. **Throws:** right.
Debut: April 6, 2005.
Positions, teams, years: outfield, Los Angeles (NL) 2005–2006, 2008–2009, Minnesota (AL) 2010–2011, Boston (AL) 2012.
Games: 360. **At-bats:** 700. **Home runs:** 16. **Average:** .224.

Jason Repko, who can play all three outfield positions, spent his first three professional seasons as a shortstop.

Repko's family moved from northwestern Indiana to the state of Washington when he was nine years old. The Los Angeles Dodgers made him their first-round pick (37th overall) in 1999 after he batted .581 for Hanford High School in Richland, Wash.

From 1999 to 2001 Repko played shortstop at Great Falls, Mont. (Pioneer), Yakima, Wash. (Northwest), and Wilmington, Del. (South Atlantic). He switched to the outfield in 2002 at Vero Beach (Florida State). "For me, shortstop was always a tough position," he told the *Las Vegas Review-Journal's* Matt Youmans. "My footwork wasn't that great and I didn't have great hands. I tried my hardest to improve and things just didn't work out."

Repko blossomed into a big league prospect in 2004, batting .291 at Jacksonville, Fla. (Southern), and .311 for Las Vegas, Nev. (Pacific Coast). In 2005 he shuttled between the Dodgers and Las Vegas.

A sprained ankle in 2006 shelved Repko for

more than two months, and after the season he underwent surgery. He sat out all of 2007 after suffering a torn hamstring in Spring Training. Bouncing back with a .283 season at Las Vegas in 2008, he rejoined the Dodgers for 22 games. After a .277 average for Las Vegas in 2009 he appeared in ten September contests for Los Angeles.

Cut loose by the Dodgers in March 2010, Repko signed with the Twins. In 2010 and 2011 he commuted between Minnesota and its top affiliate in Rochester, N.Y. (International). Boston signed him to a minor league contract for 2012, and he joined the Red Sox on April 15 when center fielder Jacoby Ellsbury went on the disabled list.

A week later, Repko injured his shoulder while making a catch and wound up on the 60-day DL. When he returned, Boston outrighted him to Pawtucket, R.I. (International). He became a free agent and joined the York, Pa., Revolution (independent Atlantic) for 2013. He retired after 24 games, but came back in 2014. After 30 games he suffered another hamstring injury that sidelined him for the rest of the year.

REPLOGLE, Andrew David

Born: October 7, 1953, South Bend. **Died:** April 10, 2012, Fort Myers Florida.
Height: 6'5". **Weight:** 205. **Batted:** right. **Threw:** right.
Debut: April 11, 1978. **Final game:** September 30, 1979.
Positions, teams, years: pitcher, Milwaukee (AL) 1978–1979.
Games: 35. **Innings pitched:** 157.1. **Won/lost:** 9–5. **Earned run average:** 4.00.

Andy Replogle, a member of an Indiana state high school championship team, pitched briefly but effectively in the Major Leagues.

A pitcher and third baseman at South Bend Clay High School, Replogle (pronounced REP-low-gull) had a 13–1 record as a sophomore in 1970, when the Colonials defeated Evansville Memorial in the IHSAA title game.

After one more year at South Bend Clay, Replogle's family moved to Fort Wayne. As a senior in 1972 he batted .412 and compiled a 15–1 record at Fort Wayne Snider. The New York Mets made him their fourth-round draft pick that June, but he passed on a contract to attend Kansas State University. Pitching for the Wildcats from 1973 to 1975, he set a school record with 25 career wins.

Signed by the St. Louis Cardinals after they took him in the ninth round of the 1975 draft, Replogle split his first pro season between Johnson City, Tenn. (Appalachian), and St. Petersburg (Florida State). The Baltimore Orioles acquired him in December 1977 and dealt him to Milwaukee in April 1978. Alternating between the Brewers' starting rotation and the bullpen that year, he went 9–5 with a 3.93 ERA.

After a lackluster Spring Training performance in 1979 the Brewers shipped Replogle to Vancouver, B.C. (Pacific Coast). That summer he made three relief appearances for Milwaukee. After two seasons in the minors, the Cincinnati Reds invited him to Spring Training in 1982. He tore a rotator cuff and retired from baseball.

Replogle, who took basketball MVP honors as a high school senior, earned a degree in radio, television and public relations from Kansas State in 1975. He installed telephone systems in Indianapolis before relocating to Florida in 1994, where he worked for the Estero Country Club at the Vines in Naples, Fla.

REYNOLDS, Charles Lawrence ("The Professor")

Born: May 1, 1865, Williamsburg. **Died:** July 3, 1944, Denver, Colorado.
Height: 5'9". **Weight:** 175. **Batted:** right. **Threw:** right.
Debut: May 8, 1889. **Final game:** August 19, 1889.
Positions, teams, years: catcher, Kansas City (American Association) 1889, Brooklyn (American Association) 1889.
Games: 13. **At-bats:** 46. **Home runs:** 0. **Average:** .217.

Mustachioed **Charlie Reynolds** played for a pennant winner in his lone big league season.

Reynolds' professional career began in 1886 with Leavenworth, Kan. (Western). When the club disbanded in 1887, he moved to Hastings, Neb. (Western), and was managing the club by season's end. He joined the Kansas City Blues (Western Association) for 1888.

By 1889 Reynolds was playing for the Kansas City Cowboys of the major-league American

Association. The *Denver Daily News* described the DePauw alumnus as "extremely popular with all patrons of the game and with his acquaintances. He is modest and unassuming and a well educated and intelligent gentleman. He neither drinks nor uses tobacco and is free from any habits or irregularities that impair the usefulness of ball players."

After one game with Kansas City, the Brooklyn Bridegrooms acquired Reynolds on May 22, 1889, for a reported $2,000. He and Joe Visner shared the catching duties while Bob Clark, Brooklyn's main backstop, recuperated from injuries.

The Bridegrooms finished first and met the NL champion New York Giants in the 1889 Dauvray Cup Championship Series, a forerunner of the modern Fall Classic. Reynolds saw no action in the series, won by the Giants six games to three.

In 1890 and 1891 Reynolds played for minor league clubs in Denver (Western Association) and Sacramento (California). He continued playing for amateur teams in Denver after leaving organized ball.

Reynolds spent the rest of his life in Denver, where he worked as a railroad conductor. He died of a heart attack at age 79.

RICE, Edgar Charles ("Sam," "Man o' War," "Rango")

National Baseball Hall of Fame, 1963. Indiana Baseball Hall of Fame, 1979.
Born: February 20, 1890, Morocco. **Died:** October 13, 1974, Rossmoor, Maryland.
Height: 5'9". **Weight:** 150. **Batted:** left. **Threw:** right.
Debut: August 7, 1915. **Final game:** September 18, 1934.
Positions, teams, years: outfield (2,270), pitcher (9), Washington (AL) 1915–1933, Cleveland (AL) 1934.
Games: 2,404. **At-bats:** 9,269. **Home runs:** 34. **Average:** .322.
Innings pitched: 39.1. **Won/Lost:** 1–1. **Earned run average:** 2.52.

A converted pitcher, Hall of Fame outfielder **Sam Rice** holds the career record for hits by an Indiana-born Major Leaguer.

Rice grew up in rural Illinois, just across the Indiana state line. In 1912, while he was trying out for a team in Galesburg, Ill. (Central Association), a tornado killed his wife, two children and four other family members. Rice failed to make the Galesburg club and worked at odd jobs around the Midwest until joining the U.S. Navy in January 1913. While serving aboard the *U.S.S. New Hampshire*, he took part in the occupation of Veracruz, Mexico, in April 1914.

In the summer of 1914, while the *New Hampshire* was docked in Norfolk, Va., Rice was pitching for the ship's baseball club. The nearby minor league team in Petersburg, Va., offered him a contract and bought his way out of the service. He finished the year as the Virginia League's top pitcher with a 9–2 record.

Rice joined the Washington Senators in August 1915. In 1916 he moved from the mound to right field, and in 1917 he led the team with a .302 average. He missed all but seven games in 1918 due to World War I army service and spent several months in France with an artillery unit.

In 1919 Rice rejoined Washington. He was 29 years old, with only one full Major League season under his belt. He quickly established himself as a solid hitter and a base stealer second only to Ty Cobb. In 1920 he led the AL with 63 stolen bases, and in 1923 he topped the league with 18 triples.

Rice's .334 average helped the Senators to a pennant in 1924, and he batted .207 in Washington's World Series triumph over the New York Giants. In 1925 he had the highest hit total (227) and the best batting average (.350) of his career as the Senators again finished first. Although Washington lost the Series in seven games to the Pittsburgh Pirates, Rice batted .364.

In the eighth inning of Game 3, after switching from right field to center, he was involved in one of the most controversial plays in baseball history. In pursuit of a long fly ball, Rice sailed over the right-center field barricade, tumbled into the stands and disappeared. When he resurfaced with the ball in his glove, the umpire called it a fair catch, touching off a heated protest by the Pirates. Asked if he'd actually made the catch, for years Rice would only reply: "The umpire said I did."

At age 40 in 1930, Rice batted .349. After hitting .310 in 1931 and .323 in 1932, he was relegated to part-time status in 1933 during Washington's run to another pennant. In his lone appearance against the Giants, he had a pinch-hit single. At 43, he became the oldest non-pitcher to play in the World Series.

Released in January 1934, Rice signed with the Cleveland Indians and batted .293 in a part-time role. He retired after the season with 2,987 career hits, the most for a Hoosier native. Asked why he retired just 13 hits short of the magic 3,000, Rice answered: "You must remember, there wasn't much emphasis on 3,000 hits when I quit. And to tell the truth, I didn't know how many hits I had."

Rice purchased a poultry farm in Maryland where he raised chickens and racing pigeons. A skilled golfer since his playing days, he continued to play well past his 80th year.

In 1963 he entered baseball's Hall of Fame and began attending the annual induction ceremonies. Prior to the 1965 event he wrote a letter about his 1925 World Series catch, leaving instructions that it was to be sealed until after his death. Eleven years later, after Rice died at age 84, the letter was opened. It read, in part: "I turned slightly to my right and had the ball in view all the way, going at top speed and about 15 feet from the bleachers jumped as high as I could and back handed and the ball hit the center of pocket in glove (I had a death grip on it).... At no time did I lose possession of the ball."

In 1979 Rice was elected to the Indiana Baseball Hall of Fame. The Little League Field in Morocco is named in his honor, and each year the town stages the Sam Rice Summer Festival. In 2008 McFarland & Company published Jeff Carroll's *Sam Rice: A Biography of the Washington Senators Hall of Famer*.

Known as "Eddie" in his youth, Rice appears to have picked up the nickname "Sam" when he played for Petersburg. The nickname "Rango" was a corruption of Rheingold, Rice's favorite beer brand as a young man in Illinois. Newspaper reporters dubbed him "Man o' War" (after the famous racehorse) because of his speed and his service at Veracruz.

RICHARD, Clayton Colby
Born: September 12, 1983, Lafayette. **Lives**: Lafayette.
Height: 6'5". **Weight**: 245. **Bats**: left. **Throws**: left.
Debut: July 23, 2008.
Positions, teams, years: pitcher, Chicago (AL) 2008–2009, San Diego (NL) 2009–2013.
Games: 147. **Innings pitched**: 773.1. **Won/Lost**: 46–47. **Earned run average**: 4.33.

At McCutcheon High School, **Clayton Richard** was the *Indianapolis Star's* Mr. Football for 2002. In 2003, when he won the Class 4A L.V. Phillips Mental Attitude Award, he was Indiana's Mr. Baseball. He was a four-year All-State selection in football and a *Parade Magazine* All-American.

At the University of Michigan, Richard doubled as a football quarterback and a relief pitcher on the baseball squad. His pro baseball career began in 2005 with Great Falls, Mont. (Pioneer), after the Chicago White Sox took him in the eighth round of the draft.

Heading into the 2008 season, Richard's career won-loss record in the minors was 17–23. He caught fire after a promotion to Charlotte, N.C. (International), winning his first six decisions. He started for the U.S. team at the Futures Game in July and was named to the Olympic squad, but he was promoted to the White Sox before the team left for Beijing.

In May 2009 Richard pitched his way into Chicago's starting rotation. On July 31 he went to San Diego in a five-player trade. In a dozen starts for the Padres he went 5–2. In 2010 his 14–9 slate helped San Diego contend for the NL West title. Bothered by shoulder problems in 2011, he went 5–9 and underwent season-ending surgery in July. He rebounded in 2012 with a 14–14, 3.99 season.

Richard entered 2013 as San Diego's No. 2 starter. On May 5 he went on the disabled list with an intestinal virus. He returned on May 27, but injured his shoulder in a game on June 21. "I went out and there was nothing," he told the *Lafayette Courier-Journal*. "The more I tried, the more it hurt, and it wasn't loosening up."

On July 15 Richard underwent season-ending surgery. Refusing an outright assignment after the season, he became a free agent. In February 2014 he underwent thoracic outlet syndrome surgery. After extensive rehabilitation, he signed a minor league contract with the Arizona Diamondbacks.

Richard returned to action on August 10, 2014, with Mobile, Ala. (Southern). He went 0–2 in three starts for the BayBears and finished the season in Reno, Nev. (Pacific Coast), where he was the winning pitcher in his lone appearance. A free agent again after the season, he signed a minor league pact with the Pittsburgh Pirates for 2015.

Richard's wife, the former Ashley Buckingham, was a standout volleyball player at Center Grove High School in Greenwood, Ind.

RICHARDS, Duane Lee

Born: December 16, 1936, Spartanburg. **Lives:** Palestine, Ohio.
Height: 6'3". **Weight:** 200. **Batted:** right. **Threw:** right.
Debut: September 25, 1960. **Final game:** October 1, 1960.
Positions, teams, years: pitcher, Cincinnati (NL) 1960.
Games: 2. **Innings pitched:** 3. **Won/Lost:** 0–0. **Earned run average:** 9.00.

Duane Richards lettered in baseball, basketball and track at Westmont High School in Hollansburg, Ohio, a few miles northeast of Richmond, Ind. After pitching in four consecutive games during the 1955 Ohio state high school tournament, he developed arm trouble that would plague his first four professional seasons. "I tore the ligaments from the elbow to the shoulder," he told the *Buffalo Evening News*.

Pitching for Cincinnati Reds farm teams in Fort Walton Beach, Fla. (Alabama-Florida), West Palm Beach (Florida), Palatka (Florida) and Wenatchee, Wash (Northwest), between 1955 and 1958, Richards compiled an unimpressive 23–30 slate. He bounced back in 1959 with a 16–10 record for Savannah, Ga. (South Atlantic).

A 1960 scouting report described Richards as "Aggressive with desire and might go all the way." That summer he went 12–17 for Nashville, Tenn. (Southern Association), to earn a September promotion to the Reds. In a six-day span he made two relief appearances against the Phillies—the first at Cincinnati's Crosley Field, the other at Shibe Park in Philadelphia.

Pitching for Macon, Ga. (South Atlantic), on July 3, 1962, Richards threw a 4–0 no-hitter against Norfolk-Portsmouth. In July 1963 the Reds swapped him to the New York Mets organization as part of a four-player trade. He left baseball after dividing the 1964 season between Williamsport, Pa. (Eastern), and Buffalo, N.Y. (International).

Richards worked as a lathe operator and eventually became a supervisor for Carlton Natco, a machine tools manufacturing company in Richmond.

RICHARDSON, Kenneth Franklin ("Pork Chops," "Rub")

Born: May 2, 1915, Orleans. **Died:** December 7, 1987, Woodland Hills, California.
Height: 5'10". **Weight:** 187. **Batted:** right. **Threw:** right.
Debut: April 14, 1942. **Final game:** May 2, 1946.
Positions, teams, years: second base (6), outfield (3), third base (1), first base (1), Philadelphia (AL) 1942, Philadelphia (NL) 1946.
Games: 12. **At-bats:** 35. **Home runs:** 0. **Average:** .114.

During 21 seasons, **Ken Richardson** played for 20 different teams in 14 leagues in a dozen states and two countries. All but four of his 2,172 career hits came in the minor leagues.

The son of a Santa Fe Railroad employee, Richardson played high school baseball and basketball in San Bernardino, Calif., before signing with Los Angeles (Pacific Coast) in 1934.

A jack-of-all-trades who played the infield and outfield, Richardson bounced around from Los Angeles to Ponca City, Okla. (Western Association), Moline, Ill. (Three-I), Chattanooga, Tenn. (Southern Association), Jersey City, N.J. (International), Minneapolis (American Association) and Williamsport, Pa. (Eastern), before joining Connie Mack's Philadelphia Athletics in 1942. Back with Williamsport after six games, he played for Hollywood, Calif. (Pacific Coast), from 1943 to 1945.

Richardson opened the 1946 season with the Philadelphia Phillies but went back to Hollywood in June. He sat out the 1947 season and returned in 1948 with Seattle (Pacific Coast). His best year came in 1949 at Spokane, Wash. (Western International), when he batted .324. His .322 average in 1951 helped Spokane to a first-place finish. He played for Western International League pennant-winners in Lewiston, Idaho, in 1953 and Vancouver, B.C., in 1954. He ended his playing days in 1955 with El Paso, Texas (West Texas-New Mexico), at the age of 40.

Richardson batted .282 in 2,336 minor league contests. A selective hitter whose 154 walks in 1950 led the Sunset League, he was also a good baserunner who topped the Western Association with 47 stolen bases in 1936.

Originally employed by Pacific Electric during off-seasons, he wound up spending 27 years in the motion picture industry. He worked as a grip on the television series *Gunsmoke* as well as films like *Give My Regards to Broadway*. He was an extra in the 1949 baseball movie *The Stratton Story*.

After a 21-year-hiatus, Richardson returned to the game in 1976 as manager of independent Victoria, Texas (Gulf States). He also managed a pair of Milwaukee Brewers affiliates, Newark, N.Y. (New York-Penn), in 1978 and Butte, Mont. (Pioneer), from 1979 to 1981.

Richardson, who spent most of his adult years in San Bernardino, succumbed to cancer at age 72. According to his daughter, Susan Gray, Richardson seemed to hit a home run whenever his wife served pork chops for dinner—hence his nickname. "I remember a fan at a ballgame yelling 'Come on, Pork Chops, hit one over the wall!'" Susan recalled. "I turned to see who was up at bat and it was my dad. I started crying and told the fan that was my daddy, and not to call him 'Pork Chops.'"

RICHARDSON, William Henry ("Jumbo," "Billy")

Born: January 24, 1878, Salem. **Died:** November 6, 1949, Sullivan.
Height: 5'11". **Weight:** 200. **Batted:** right. **Threw:** right.
Debut: September 20, 1901. **Final game:** October 6, 1901.
Positions, teams, years: first base, St. Louis (NL), 1901.
Games: 15. **At-bats:** 52. **Home runs:** 2. **Average:** .212.

At various times in his 71 years, **Will Richardson** worked as a printer, carpenter, saloonkeeper, miner and as a professional athlete. He played for amateur teams in Salem, Ind., before entering organized ball in 1898 with Galveston (Texas).

Richardson was a catcher-first baseman for Terre Haute (Three-I) in 1901 when the St. Louis Cardinals came to town in mid-September for an exhibition game. Terre Haute beat the big leaguers 10–8, and the Cardinals signed Richardson to replace their regular first baseman, Dan McGann. McGann had recently left the club after an argument with manager Patsy Donovan.

Richardson spent the rest of the year with the Cardinals. On September 25 his 11th-inning walk-off homer gave St. Louis a 2–1 win over Boston. According to the *St. Louis Globe Democrat*, Cardinals fans "swarmed upon the playing field after the youngster had crossed the pan, and, lifting him on their shoulders, carried him into the clubhouse."

After conditionally signing him for 1902, St. Louis opted not to purchase Richardson's contract. He returned to Terre Haute (by now in the Central League) and remained in the minors through 1908. His seven homers for Dayton in 1907 tied for the Central League lead.

After baseball, Richardson worked as a coal miner in Sullivan County. A robust physique earned him the nickname "Jumbo."

ROBBINS, Bruce Duane

Born: September 10, 1959, Portland. **Lives:** Noblesville.
Height: 6'1". **Weight:** 190. **Batted:** left. **Threw:** left.
Debut: July 28, 1979. **Final game:** September 23, 1980.
Positions, teams, years: pitcher, Detroit (AL) 1979–1980.
Games: 25. **Innings pitched:** 97.2. **Won/Lost:** 7–5.
Earned run average: 5.34.

Following a brilliant high school career, **Bruce Robbins** had a rapid rise to the Major Leagues.

Robbins grew up in Dunkirk, 15 miles northeast of Muncie. At Blackford High School in Hartford City, he was a standout pitcher-first baseman. In 1977 his 13-strikeout performance in the IHSAA semifinals led the Bruins to the title game at Bush Stadium in Indianapolis, where they lost to Logansport. Robbins fanned 202 batters in high school, the second-highest total in state history.

Turning down college scholarship offers from Purdue, Ohio State and Western Michigan, Robbins signed with Detroit in 1977 after the Tigers took him in the 14th round of the draft.

Robbins spent the 1977 season with Bristol, Va. (Appalachian). In July 1979, after a 7–1 record for Montgomery, Ala. (Southern), the Tigers summoned him. "I thought he [Detroit's assistant farm director] was going to tell me I had been called up to Triple-A, but when he told me I was going to the big leagues it really surprised me," Robbins told Doug Driscoll of the *Hartford News*.

Three months short of his 20th birthday, Robbins became the second-youngest Hoosier (behind left-hander Billy McCool, a Batesville native) to play big league ball in the post–World War II era.

Robbins split 1980 between Detroit and Evansville (American Association). He spent most of 1981 on the disabled list. After a 4–6 record at Birmingham, Ala. (Southern) in 1983, his career ended at 23.

Returning to Indiana, Robbins launched a successful business career. He eventually owned five companies, including an Internet recruiting firm. One of his businesses had $25 million in yearly sales.

Robbins, who became a born-again Christian at 21 while pitching in Venezuela's winter league, created Family Fest in 2009. Presented by A New Concept, Robbins' faith-based nonprofit organization, the festival at Westfield High School offered music concerts and motivational speakers.

Robbins' older brother Leroy was a star outfielder at Blackford High and the University of Kentucky. Drafted by the Athletics one day before Detroit selected Bruce, Leroy played in the Oakland organization from 1977–1980.

ROESLER, Michael Joseph

Born: September 12, 1963, Fort Wayne. **Lives:** Fort Wayne.
Height: 6'5". **Weight:** 195. **Batted:** right. **Threw:** right.
Debut: August 9, 1989. **Final game:** April 23, 1990.
Positions, teams, years: pitcher, Cincinnati (NL) 1989, Pittsburgh (NL) 1990.
Games: 22. **Innings pitched:** 31. **Won/Lost:** 1–1. **Earned run average:** 3.77.

After lettering in baseball, basketball and tennis at Fort Wayne's Bishop Luers High School, **Mike Roesler** was a starting pitcher for Ball State University's baseball squad from 1982 through 1985. Known for his laid-back demeanor, he once went missing from baseball practice at Ball State to play an intramural rugby game.

Selected by the Cincinnat Reds in the 17th round of the 1985 draft, Roesler (pronounced "ress-ler") broke in that year with Billings, Mont. (Pioneer). He went 8–2 with a 2.33 ERA as a starter. After a 9–13 mark for Cedar Rapids, Iowa (Midwest), in 1986 he switched to relief in 1987 at Tampa (Florida State).

A 6–4 record and a 3.25 ERA for Nashville, Tenn. (American Association), earned Roesler a promotion to Cincinnati in August 1989. In 17 relief appearances for the Reds, he went 0–1 with a 3.96 ERA. Traded to the Pittsburgh Pirates on April 3, 1990, he recorded his lone big league win on April 20 against the Chicago Cubs at Wrigley Field. Ten days later he was back in the minors for good.

On July 25, 1992, Roesler had a 3–5 slate with a 5.50 ERA for Buffalo, N.Y. (International), when he was removed from a game with visiting Oklahoma City. Heckled by fans behind the Buffalo dugout, Roesler cursed them and gestured rudely. The Pirates organization cut him loose after the incident. He finished his career in the Kansas City Royals system in 1993.

Roesler, who returned to Ball State in 1986 to earn a degree, worked for the Guardian Financial Group in Fort Wayne. He also pitched for the Indianapolis Giants, an amateur club for over–30-year-olds in the Indianapolis Men's Senior Baseball League. The Giants won the title in their age division at the 1999 MSBL World Series.

In 2006 Roesler was inducted into the Northeast Indiana Baseball Association Hall of Fame.

ROLEN, Scott Bruce

Born: April 4, 1975, Evansville. **Lives:** Carmel and Holmes Beach, Florida.
Height: 6'4". **Weight:** 245. **Batted:** right. **Threw:** right.
Debut: August 1, 1996. **Final game:** October 3, 2012

Positions, teams, years: third base, Philadelphia (NL) 1996–2002, St. Louis (NL) 2002–2007, Toronto (AL), 2008–2009, Cincinnati (NL) 2009–2012.
Games: 2,038. **At-bats:** 7,398. **Home runs:** 316. **Average:** .281.

Scott Rolen, the finest big league third baseman to come out of Indiana, was a three-sport star at Jasper High School. As a senior he went undefeated in singles tennis, made the Indiana All-Star basketball team with a 26.9 points-per-game average, and received the state's Mr. Baseball award. After signing a letter of intent to play baseball and basketball with the University of Georgia in 1993, he was the second-round draft pick of the Philadelphia Phillies. Opting for a baseball career, he joined Martinsville, Va. (Appalachian), that summer and quickly became one of Philadelphia's top prospects.

In August 1996 Rolen joined the Phillies. He was one at-bat away from losing his rookie status when he suffered a broken forearm on September 7. In 1997 he batted .283 with 21 homers and was the unanimous pick for NL Rookie of the Year.

In March 1998 Rolen signed a four-year, $10 million contract with the Phillies. With 31 home runs and a .290 average that season, he began rating comparisons to Mike Schmidt, Philadelphia's Hall of Fame third baseman. "Scott Rolen is a different sort of ballplayer," wrote Paul Hagen in *Baseball Digest*. "He's not only a cornerstone for the Phillies but also is a walking, talking advertisement for what is good about the sport."

Rolen missed a total of 84 games over the 1999 and 2000 campaigns due to back problems, aggravated by playing on the artificial turf at Philadelphia's Veterans Stadium. By 2001, critical of the home field playing surface and what he called the Phillies' lack of commitment to long-term success, he balked at signing a long-term pact. Although his 25 homers and .289 average helped the Phils to their first winning season in seven years, by June he was the target of Philadelphia fans' wrath.

Traded to St. Louis in June 2002, Rolen helped the Cardinals to the NL Central Division title. He batted .429 in the Cards' win over Arizona in the NLDS, but suffered a shoulder injury that sidelined him for the NLCS loss to San Francisco. Considered the best St. Louis third baseman since Ken Boyer, Rolen hit .286 with 28 home runs in 2003. A 34-homer, .314 season in 2004 helped the Cardinals to the NL pennant. He went 0–15 in the World Series as Boston swept St. Louis.

A shoulder injury in May 2005 ruined Rolen's season. He missed a month after surgery, and appeared in just 56 games before undergoing a season-ending second operation in July. Despite shoulder problems that hampered him for the second half of 2006, he bounced back with 22 homers and a .296 average. A feud erupted when St. Louis manager Tony LaRussa benched Rolen for Game Two of the NLCS. The Cardinals beat the Mets for the pennant and then bested Detroit in the World Series, aided by Rolen's .421 average.

Rolen slumped in early 2007 but was finally coming around when a recurrence of shoulder woes finished him in August. He batted .265 with eight home runs in 112 games. There was more friction in December with LaRussa. "If he plays hard and plays as well as he can, he plays," LaRussa told *USA Today Sports Weekly*. "If he doesn't, he can sit. If he doesn't like it, he can quit." Through his agent, Rolen replied: "I will not dignify Tony's comments with any response at this time." In January 2008 the Cards swapped Rolen to the Toronto Blue Jays. He missed the first five weeks of the season due to a hand injury that required surgery.

By the end of July 2009, Rolen was batting .320 when Toronto dealt him to Cincinnati. Rolen, who was hoping to be traded to a club closer to his home, quickly developed into a team leader for a youthful Reds squad. In 2010 his .285 average, 20 homers and 83 RBI helped Cincinnati to first place in the NL Central Division. In the All-Star Game at Anaheim on July 13, his seventh-inning single and daring first-to-third base running ignited a rally that led to a 3–1 win for the NL squad—its first triumph since 1996. Chronic shoulder problems limited him to a .242 average in 65 games in 2011 and .245 in 92 contests in 2012. He became a free agent after the season and never played again.

A seven-time All-Star (1998, 2000–04, 2006, 2010–11), Rolen won seven Gold Glove awards (1998, 2000–04, 2006). In 2001 he formed the Enis Furley Foundation (named for one of his dogs), as well as a Kentucky retreat called Camp Emma Lou (also named for one of Rolen's dogs), to assist critically ill children and their families.

ROUSH, Edd J
National Baseball Hall of Fame, 1962. Indiana Baseball Hall of Fame, 1979.
Born: May 8, 1893, Oakland City. **Died:** March 21, 1988, Bradenton, Florida.
Height: 5'11". **Weight:** 170. **Batted:** left. **Threw:** left.
Debut: August 20, 1913. **Final game:** September 27, 1931.
Positions, teams, years: outfield (1,848), first base (14), second base (1), Chicago (AL) 1913, Indianapolis (Federal) 1914, Newark (Federal) 1915, New York (NL) 1916, Cincinnati (NL) 1916–1926, New York (NL) 1927–1929, Cincinnati (NL) 1931.
Games: 1,967. **At-bats:** 7,363. **Home runs:** 68. **Average:** .323.

During an illustrious 18-year career, two-time bat champ **Edd Roush** was the NL's best defensive center fielder. The fiercely independent Roush (pronounced "rowsh") was a frequent holdout who loathed Spring Training and once sat out an entire season in a contract dispute.

The son of a dairy farmer and former semi-professional ballplayer, Roush attended Oakland City High School and played for town teams in southwestern Indiana before signing with Evansville (Kitty) in 1912. A natural southpaw, Roush frequently played the field as a right-hander. "I was born left-handed," he told Dave Koerner of the *Louisville Courier-Journal*, "but I learned to throw right-handed because back in my day you didn't have any gloves to fit the right hand, not around Oakland City, anyway." He continued to throw with both hands through his first big league season.

The Chicago White Sox acquired Roush from Evansville in August 1913 and sent him to Lincoln, Neb. (Western), after nine games. He was batting .171 in 35 at-bats when he quit the team and returned to Oakland City. In 1914 he signed to play for the Indianapolis Hoosiers of the upstart Federal League. The Hoosiers won the pennant, with Roush batting .325 in 74 games. The franchise shifted to Newark, N.J., for 1915, when Roush batted .298 as an everyday player.

The FL disbanded prior to 1916 and Roush joined the New York Giants, who swapped him to Cincinnati in July. Taking over center field for the Reds, he earned the 1917 NL batting title with a .341 average. Roush hit .333 in 1918, when Zach Wheat of Brooklyn topped the league with a .335 mark.

A .321 average in 1919 gave Roush another batting crown. Cincinnati won the pennant that year and beat the White Sox in the World Series, with Roush batting .214. One year later came the news that several Chicago players had conspired with gamblers to fix the Series outcome. For the rest of his life, Roush maintained that the Reds were the better team. "I don't know whether the whole truth of what went on there will ever come out," he told Lawrence Ritter in the baseball classic *The Glory of Their Times*. "Whatever it was, though, it was a dirty rotten shame. One thing that's always overlooked in the whole mess is that we could have beat them no matter what the circumstances!"

Roush, who wielded a 48-ounce bat (the heaviest in big league history), hit .338 in 1920. On June 8 he was ejected from a game at New York under unusual circumstances. During a lengthy on-field argument, Roush took a nap in center field. When play resumed, umpire Barry McCormack tossed him for delaying the contest. Roush hit .352 in 1921. He refused to sign his 1922 contract until late July and played just 49 games, again batting .352. His 41 doubles led the league in 1923, when he averaged .351. In 1924 he batted .348, topping the NL with 21 triples.

After two more stellar seasons (.339 in 1925, .323 in 1926), the Reds traded Roush back to the Giants for 1927. Stomach surgery limited him to 46 games in 1928, when he had a career-low .252 average. Roush hated playing in New York and didn't like John McGraw, the Giants' volcanic manager, who tried to cut Edd's salary after a .324 season in 1929. When Roush sat out the entire 1930 campaign, McGraw shipped him back to Cincinnati for 1931. Edd finished his playing days that year with the Reds. He returned as a Reds coach in 1938, but left after one season.

Roush saved money during his baseball career and made solid investments. He was elected president of the board of directors for Oakland City's First Bank and Trust Company, served on school and town boards, and ran the Montgomery County Cemetery. Baseball fields were named for him in Oakland City and in Bradenton, Fla, where he owned a winter home.

Edd and his wife, the former Essie Swallow, were married for 64 years—from 1914 until Essie's death in 1978. While there's never been an explanation for the spelling of his unusual first name, Edd's middle initial J was an homage to a pair of uncles named Jim and Joe. Roush died just prior to a 1988 Spring Training game in Bradenton at the age of 94.

In 1962 Roush was elected to the National Baseball Hall of Fame. A member of the Reds and Ohio Baseball halls of fame, he was part of the Indiana Baseball Hall of Fame's original induction class in 1979.

In 2006 his granddaughter, Dr. Susan Dellinger, published a book called *Red Legs and Black Sox: Edd Roush and the Untold Story of the 1919 World Series*. Mitchell Stinson followed in 2010 with *Edd Roush: A Biography of the Cincinnati Reds Star*.

RUSIE, Amos Wilson ("The Hoosier Thunderbolt")

National Baseball Hall of Fame, 1977. **Indiana Baseball Hall of Fame, 1979.**
Born: May 30, 1871, Mooresville. **Died:** December 6, 1942, Seattle, Washington.
Height: 6'1". **Weight:** 200. **Batted:** right. **Threw:** right.
Debut: May 9, 1889. **Final game:** June 9, 1901.
Positions, teams, years: pitcher (463), outfield (21), first base (1), Indianapolis (NL) 1889, New York (NL) 1890–1895, 1897–1898, Cincinnati (NL) 1901.
Games: 487. **Innings pitched:** 3,778.2. **Won/Lost:** 246–174. **Earned run average:** 3.07.
At-bats: 1,730. **Home runs:** 8. **Average:** .248.

Flame-throwing **Amos Rusie** was New York City's first sports hero.

Rusie grew up in Indianapolis and played for scrub teams on the city's Eastside as a youth. He switched from the outfield to pitching in his mid-teens and joined the Indianapolis Hoosiers of the NL in 1889. He was three weeks away from his 18th birthday when he made his big league debut. Reassigned to Burlington, Iowa (Central Interstate), due to control problems, he returned to Indianapolis in August and finished the year with a 12–10 record.

The Hoosiers folded after the season and Rusie wound up with the New York Giants for 1890. Starring for a sixth-place Giants squad, he went 29–34 with a league-leading 341 strikeouts over 548 innings. New York newspapers dubbed him "The Hoosier Thunderbolt." Pitching every other day, he went 33–20 in 1891 and struck out 337 batters. One of his wins was a 6–0 no-hitter against Brooklyn on July 31.

In 1892 Rusie went 32–31 with 304 strikeouts for a club that went 71–80. In 1893 the distance from the pitcher's box to home plate changed from 50 feet to 60 feet, six inches. Some historians cite Rusie's blinding speed as the reason for the change, but it was actually an attempt to restore balance between offense and defense.

Unaffected by the new rules, Rusie went 33–21 in 1893. He led the league with 208 strikeouts. His 218 walks were a modern Major League record that still stands. In 1894 Rusie topped all pitchers with 36 wins, 195 strikeouts and a 2.78 ERA. Right-hander Jouett Meekin, a native of New Albany, Ind., joined the Giants and fashioned a 33–9 record. Sportswriters dubbed the Hoosier tandem "the Iron Twins."

The Giants finished second to Baltimore that year and met the Orioles in the inaugural Temple Cup, a precursor of the modern World Series. Rusie won the first and third games while Meekin added a pair of wins as New York swept the Orioles.

Rusie was the toast of New York during the Gay Nineties. Fashionable Manhattan establishments began offering drinks like the Hoosier Cyclone and the Rusie Cocktail. Rusie was the city's first sports idol, the prototype for Christy Mathewson, Babe Ruth, Willie Mays, Mickey Mantle, Tom Seaver and Derek Jeter.

Teammate Buck Ewing explained to the *New York Telegram* what it was like to catch

Rusie's fastball: "I've caught some fast pitchers in my time, but I can't remember any one who holds the record for speed that Rusie did. I was behind the bat one day in Brooklyn when he was at his best, and every time he let that fast one come through it was as if the palm of my hand had been burned with a big sun glass."

Since 1892 however, Rusie had been unhappy with the New York club's tight-fisted ownership. Matters worsened after real estate attorney Andrew Freedman took control of the Giants in 1895. Rusie went 23–23 with 201 strikeouts that year, the most in the league. Freedman levied a series of fines against Rusie, claiming "indifference" on the pitcher's part. Calling the owner's actions unjust, Rusie sat out the entire 1896 season and sued the league. In the *New York Herald*, O.P. Caylor wrote that "the Giants without Rusie would be like *Hamlet* without the melancholy Dane."

In April 1897 the other owners, fearful of an attack on baseball's reserve clause, took over negotiations. Rusie rejoined the Giants that year, going 28–10 with a league-best 2.54 ERA. Bothered by arm trouble for the first few months of the 1898 campaign, Rusie finished with a 20–11 record.

More problems with Freedman led to a one-man strike by Rusie in 1899. He re-signed with the Giants for 1900 but remained in Indianapolis, sitting out another season due to domestic problems. New York traded him to the Cincinnati Reds for the 1901 season. After pitching in three games and losing his only decision, his Major League career ended at age 30.

Rusie worked at a variety of menial jobs around Indiana. In 1903 he played right field for Vincennes (Kitty). After moving to Washington State, he took a job as a ticket taker for Seattle (Northwestern). In 1921 he returned to New York, working at the Polo Grounds. Back in Washington in 1929, he was part of the grounds crew for home games at Seattle (Pacific Coast).

Rusie died at 71. He was all but forgotten until 1977, when he was elected to the Hall of Fame. In 1979 he was one of the charter members of the Indiana Baseball Hall of Fame.

RUSS, John

Born: April 1, 1860, Cannelton. **Died:** January 18, 1912, Louisville, Kentucky.
Height: unknown. **Weight:** unknown. **Batted:** unknown. **Threw:** unknown.
Debut: July 4, 1882. **Final game:** July 4, 1882.
Positions, teams, years: outfield (1), pitcher (1), Baltimore (American Association) 1882.
Games: 1. **At-bats:** 3. **Home runs:** 0. **Average:** .333.
Innings pitched: 3. **Won/Lost:** 0–0. **Earned run average:** 3.00.

John Russ, born on April Fool's Day, made his lone Major League appearance on the Fourth of July.

With a record of 3–25 on July 4, 1882, the Baltimore Orioles were last in the American Association. For that day's game with the host Louisville Eclipse, Baltimore manager Henry Myers recruited a pair of local amateurs, Monk Cline and John Russ.

The son of a German immigrant, Russ was 24 years old and a native of the Perry County port city of Cannelton on the Ohio River. He started the game in center field, batting ninth. In the seventh, he relieved starter Doc Landis and pitched the final three innings of the Orioles' 7–1 loss to the Eclipse.

That one game was the extent of Russ's professional baseball career. He appears to have spent most of his life in Louisville, where he worked as a painter and played for an amateur team called the Red Stockings. He died from cirrhosis of the liver at age 51.

SABEL, Erik Douglas

Born: October 14, 1974, Lafayette. **Lives:** Tucson, Arizona.
Height: 6'3". **Weight:** 193. **Batted:** right. **Threw:** right.
Debut: July 9, 1999. **Final game:** July 28, 2002.
Positions, teams, years: pitcher, Arizona (NL) 1999, 2001, Detroit (AL) 2002.
Games: 50. **Innings pitched:** 61. **Won/Lost:** 3–2. **Earned run average:** 5.02.

Erik Sabel's teammates at Lafayette Harrison High School included four other future pro ballplayers: infielder Eric Bruntlett (Astros, Phillies), outfielder Todd Dunwoody (Marlins, Royals, Cubs, Indians), plus catcher Josh Loggins and outfielder Brian Kennedy, who played in the minors. Sabel and Dunwoody gave Lafayette Harrison a formidable pitching tandem, leading the school to the 1993 IHSAA semifinals.

From 1994 to 1996 Sabel pitched for Tennessee Tech. In 1996 the Arizona Diamondbacks—taking part in the baseball draft for the first time—selected him in the 42nd round.

Sabel advanced through Arizona's minor league system through 1999, when he joined the Diamondbacks in mid-summer. "Randy Johnson's locker is just across the clubhouse from mine," he told the *Lafayette Journal & Courier*. "I watched him pitch when I was in high school. Now I'm on the same team."

After spending all of 2000 at Tucson, Ariz. (Pacific Coast), Sabel was back with the Diamondbacks as a middle reliever in 2001. He posted a 3–2 mark with a 4.38 ERA. Detroit acquired him in a waiver deal in July 2002, and after one appearance for the Tigers he returned to the minors. In 2003 he was back at Tucson, where his playing days ended.

Sabel worked as a pitching coach in the Diamondbacks system at Yakima, Wash. (Northwest), from 2005–2007, South Bend (Midwest) from 2008–2009, and Visalia (California) in 2010. In 2011 he became the baseball coach at Mountain View High School in Tucson.

SAMARDZIJA, Jeffrey Alan ("Shark")

Born: January 23, 1985, Merrillville. **Lives:** Valparaiso.
Height: 6'5". **Weight:** 225. **Bats:** right. **Throws:** right.
Debut: July 25, 2008.
Positions, teams, years: pitcher, Chicago (NL) 2008–2014, Oakland (AL) 2014.
Games: 222. **Innings pitched:** 777.2. **Won/Lost:** 36–48. **Earned run average:** 3.85.

After breaking nearly every receiving record at the University of Notre Dame, **Jeff Samardzija** (pronounced "suh-MAR-jah") gave up football to sign with the Chicago Cubs.

Samardzija was a three-sport letterman (football, basketball, baseball) at Valparaiso High School. He played center field for the baseball squad, batting .467 as a senior with seven home runs and 55 RBI. At Notre Dame he developed into an All-America wideout. He caught 77 passes for 1,249 yards and 15 touchdowns as a junior, helping the Fighting Irish to a berth in the 2006 Fiesta Bowl. He also developed into an All-Big East pitcher, compiling a 21–6 record in three seasons with Notre Dame's baseball squad.

The Cubs took Samardzija in the fifth round of the 2006 draft and signed him to a $7.25 million contract. He began his baseball career that summer with Boise, Idaho (Northwest), and finished the year with Peoria, Ill. (Midwest).

That autumn Samardzija returned to Notre Dame for his senior year. He had 78 receptions for 1,017 yards and caught a touchdown pass in the Sugar Bowl. He finished his college football career as the most accomplished wide receiver in Irish history, with single-season records for receiving yards (1,249) and touchdown catches (15).

Projected as a 2007 first-round NFL draft pick, Samardzija instead signed a five-year, $10 million contract that January with the Cubs. "Baseball is my first love," he explained. He pitched for Daytona (Florida State) and Tennessee (Southern) that year with mixed results.

Samardzija opened the 2008 season with Tennessee. A 4–1 record and 3.13 ERA for Iowa (Pacific Coast) earned him a July promotion to the Cubs. He continued to shuttle between Chicago and Iowa in 2009 and 2010, and he spent all of 2011 in the Cubs bullpen. Showing improved command during Spring Training in 2012, he won a spot in Chicago's starting rotation. Before the season ended, he was the staff ace with a 9–13 mark and a 3.81 ERA.

In 2013, Samardzija went 8–13 and his ERA rose to 4.34. Heading into 2014, during negotiations to extend his contract, rumors began to circulate that the rebuilding Cubs were willing to deal Samardzija for prospects. He started for Chicago on Opening Day, and after ten starts he was winless despite a league-leading 1.46 ERA.

On the Fourth of July the Cubs sent Samardzija to the Oakland Athletics in a blockbuster six-player trade. Named to the NL All-Star squad a few days later, Major League Baseball declared him ineligible for the game due to the league switch. "I'm just happy to be a part of it all, getting the chance to take part in the festivities," Samardzija told *USA Today's* John Perrotto. "I'd love to pitch but I can't, so I'll just sit back and enjoy the game."

Samardzija, 2–7 with a 2.83 ERA in Chicago, went 5–6 with a 3.14 ERA for the A's. Oakland finished second in the AL West to win a Wild Card berth, but lost to Kansas City as the Royals advanced to the ALDS. On December 9 Oakland traded Samardzija to the Chicago White Sox in a six-player deal. One of the players who went from the Sox to the A's was catcher Josh Phegley, a native of Terre Haute.

College baseball teammates gave Samardzija the nickname "Shark" because of the size and shape of his nose. Sam Samardzija, Jeff's father, was a semi-pro hockey player, and Jeff's older brother Sam Jr. played football and baseball at Indiana University.

SCHAFER, Jordan James

Born: September 4, 1986, Hammond. **Lives:** Tampa, Florida.
Height: 6'1". **Weight:** 205. **Bats:** left. **Throws:** left.
Debut: April 5, 2009.
Positions, teams, years: outfield, Atlanta (NL) 2009, 2011, Houston (NL) 2011–2012, Atlanta (NL) 2013–2014, Minnesota (AL) 2014.
Games: 436. **At-bats:** 1,223. **Home runs:** 12. **Average:** .229.

Jordan Schafer jumped from Double-A ball to the Atlanta Braves in 2009 and hit a home run in his first Major League at-bat.

David Schafer, Jordan's father, coached the junior varsity baseball team at Hobart High School before moving his family to Florida when Jordan was six years old. Jordan starred for the Winter Haven (Fla.) High School team and signed with Atlanta in 2005 as a third-round draft pick.

Schafer sputtered through his first two professional seasons but came into his own in 2007 with a .372 average in 30 games at Rome, Ga. (South Atlantic). Promoted to Myrtle Beach, S.C. (Carolina), he batted .294 in 106 contests and led all minor leaguers with a total of 176 hits. After that breakout season, he was rated Atlanta's top prospect.

In April 2008 Schafer was suspended for fifty games because of evidence he possessed, obtained or used human growth hormone, a banned substance. He struggled after joining Mississippi (Southern) in early June, but had a strong second half to finish the year with a .269 average.

Schafer went to Spring Training with Atlanta in 2009 and made the jump from Double-A to win the center field job. Against the Phillies on Opening Day, he went 2-for-3 and homered in his first trip to the plate. Shortly afterward, he suffered a wrist injury and was hitting .204 in early June when the Braves optioned him to Gwinnett (International). He underwent surgery that September and spent all of 2010 in the minors.

Schafer opened the 2011 campaign with Gwinnett and rejoined the Braves at the end of May. On July 31 Atlanta sent him to Houston as part of a five-player trade. In 2012 he batted .211 with 27 stolen bases for the Astros in 106 games.

Atlanta reacquired Schafer on waivers prior to 2013, and in 94 games he batted .247 with 22 steals. He was hitting .163 after 63 contests in 2014 when Minnesota claimed him on waivers. In 41 games with the Twins, he batted .285 and stole 15 bases.

An excellent gloveman with a strong throwing arm, Schafer's primary position is center field. "I feel I can play defense with everybody," he said. "I don't think there's a ball I can't get to when I'm out in the field."

SCHEEREN, Frederick ("Fritz," "Dutch")

Born: July 1, 1891, Kokomo. **Died:** June 17, 1973, Kittanning, Pennsylvania.
Height: 5'9". **Weight:** 159. **Batted:** right. **Threw:** right.
Debut: September 14, 1914. **Final game:** May 11, 1915.
Positions, teams, years: outfield, Pittsburgh (NL) 1914–1915.
Games: 15. **At-bats:** 34. **Home runs:** 1. **Average:** .265.

Fritz Scheeren's father, Tillman Scheeren, moved from Germany to Pennsylvania in the 1880s and spent six years in Kokomo, Ind., where Fritz was born. Tillman returned to Pennsylvania and settled in Ford City, where he became a successful businessman.

At Ford City High School, Fritz starred in baseball and football and attended Kiski, a college preparatory school in Saltsburg, Pa., before entering Lafayette College (Easton, Pa.) in the fall of 1912. He was a two-sport star at

Lafayette, playing fullback for the football team and manning center field for the baseball squad.

Prior to his junior year, Scheeren was playing for an amateur baseball squad in Bethlehem, Pa., when the Pittsburgh Pirates signed him to a Major League contract. He batted .290 in 11 games for the Bucs that September, playing in the outfield alongside Max Carey, a fellow Hoosier and future Hall of Fame member.

Scheeren appeared in four games with Pittsburgh in 1915, spending most of the year with Youngstown, Ohio (Central), where he hit .232.

After batting .282 in 118 games for Wheeling, W.Va. (Central), in 1916, Scheeren returned to Ford City and eventually took over his father's insurance company. The firm is still operated by his descendants. Scheeren was inducted into Pennsylvania's Armstrong County Sports Hall of Fame in 1973.

SCHELLHASE, Albert Herman ("Schelley")

Born: September 13, 1864, Evansville. **Died:** January 3, 1919, Evansville.
Height: 5'8". **Weight:** 148. **Batted:** right. **Threw:** right.
Debut: May 7, 1890. **Final game:** October 4, 1891.
Positions, teams, years: catcher (8), outfield (5), third base (1), shortstop (1), Boston (NL) 1890, Louisville (American Association) 1891.
Games: 15. **At-bats:** 45. **Home runs:** 0. **Average:** .133.

Al Schellhase's baseball career ended after he suffered an eye injury during a Major League game.

Schellhase (pronounced "shell-house") played for semi-professional clubs in Evansville and Mount Vernon before signing with Macon, Ga. (Southern), in 1885. He began the 1886 season with an independent team in Mobile, Ala., before joining Nashville, Tenn. (Southern), in April.

Primarily a catcher, the wiry Schellhase spent 1887 and 1888 with Syracuse, N.Y. (International), where he teamed with pitcher Bob Higgins, one of a handful of black players in organized ball during the 19th Century. Schellhase caught Higgins' first win for Syracuse against Oswego on May 31, 1887. In 1888, when Schellhase batted .273, Syracuse finished first with an impressive 81–30 record.

After a .246 average in 1889 for St. Joseph, Mo. (Western Association), he joined the Boston Beaneaters (today's Atlanta Braves) in 1890. Boston released him at the end of June and he spent the rest of the year with Sioux City, Iowa (Western Association).

Schellhase opened the 1891 campaign with Evansville (Northwestern) and returned to the majors with the Louisville Colonels. He was batting against the visiting Washington Nationals on September 15 when he fouled off a pitch that struck his left eye. "A doctor examined the wound," noted the next day's *Louisville Courier*, "and stated that while it was severe, it was not dangerous." He returned to action before the season ended.

In 1892 Schellhase signed with Evansville (Illinois-Iowa) as a player-manager. Vision problems made it impossible for him to continue, however, and he resigned on May 6. He opened a saloon in Evansville in 1893, which remained in operation until the advent of Prohibition in 1919. A popular figure in the Pocket City, he also bred racehorses.

"Schelley" is a member of Evansville's Sports Hall of Fame. He is related to Dave Schellhase, a Purdue University basketball standout who played for the Chicago Bulls from 1966 to 1968, and to Greg Schellhase, the hoops coach at Carmel's University High School who became athletic director at Zionsville High School in 2008.

SCHNEIDER, Daniel Louis

Born: August 29, 1942, Evansville. **Lives:** Tucson, Arizona.
Height: 6'3". **Weight:** 170. **Batted:** left. **Threw:** left.
Debut: May 12, 1963. **Final game:** April 27, 1969.
Positions, teams, years: pitcher, Milwaukee (NL) 1963–1964, Atlanta (NL) 1966, Houston (NL) 1967, 1969.
Games: 117. **Innings pitched:** 166.1. **Won/Lost:** 2–5. **Earned run average:** 4.71.

Dan Schneider played Little League and Babe Ruth League baseball in Evansville before his family moved to Tucson in 1958, where his father taught biochemistry at the University of Arizona.

Dan played basketball at Tucson's Rincon High School and earned all-state baseball honors. As a U. of Arizona freshman in 1962 he went 13-1, striking out 20 batters in a game against Utah. He compiled 186 strikeouts and a 1.30 ERA for the Wildcats, leading all college pitchers in victories. His lone setback was a 1-0 loss to Texas in the NCAA district championships.

Schneider considered a career as a Methodist minister before signing with the Milwaukee Braves in June 1962 for an estimated $100,000 bonus. He spent that summer with Louisville (American Association). In 1963 he went from Denver (Pacific Coast) to the Braves and had a 1-0 record in 30 games, mostly in relief. Schneider worked in 13 contests for Milwaukee in 1963, spending two months on the disabled list with a back injury.

In the minors for all of 1965, Schneider moved with the Braves to Atlanta in 1966 and went 4-6 in 18 games. After the season the Braves sent him to Houston. He spent his only full year as a Major Leaguer with the Astros in 1967. Back in the minors for all of 1968, he made six more appearances for Houston in 1969. He left baseball after playing for Tulsa, Okla. (American Association), a St. Louis Cardinals affiliate, in 1970.

Returning to Tucson, Schneider became the chief financial officer for Schneider, Bulua, Talerco, Inc., an insurance and financial services company. He stayed involved in baseball as a Little League coach and league president. After the Cleveland Indians abandoned their Spring Training base in Tucson, he headed a community group that brought in the Colorado Rockies.

Schneider is a member of Arizona's Pima County Sports Hall of Fame.

SCHULZ, Jeffrey Alan

Born: June 2, 1961, Evansville. **Lives:** Evansville.
Height: 6'1". **Weight:** 190. **Batted:** left. **Threw:** right.
Debut: September 2, 1989. **Final game:** May 15, 1991.
Positions, teams, years: outfield, Kansas City (AL) 1989-1990, Pittsburgh (NL) 1991.
Games: 40. **At-bats:** 78. **Home runs:** 0. **Average:** .244.

A teammate of Don Mattingly at Evansville Reitz Memorial High School, **Jeff Schulz** played in back-to-back IHSAA championship games. He was Evansville Memorial's designated hitter in 1978 when the Tigers defeated Blackford 7-1 at Bush Stadium in Indianapolis.

In the 1979 state title game, when Logansport dethroned Evansville Memorial 6-5 in ten innings, Schulz played center field and set a championship record with four hits. He attended Western Kentucky for a year before switching to Southern Indiana, where his .734 career slugging percentage set a school record.

The Kansas City Royals picked Schulz in the 23rd round of the 1983 draft, and in 1986 he returned to Bush Stadium with Omaha, Neb. (American Association). He remained in Omaha for most of the next four seasons. Playing briefly for Kansas City in 1989, Schulz had a pinch-hit single in his first big-league at-bat off future Hall of Famer Nolan Ryan. When the Royals released him prior to 1991, Schulz signed with Pittsburgh. He made three appearances with the Pirates before joining Buffalo, N.Y. (International), where he batted .300 in 122 contests.

Schulz spent 1992 in the American Association, splitting time between the Cubs' farm club at Iowa and Nashville, Tenn., the Reds' top affiliate. In 1993 he went to Italy to play for a professional team in Bologna. He retired after the season, but continued to play sporadically for a semi-pro team called the Indiana Outlaws. He served as hitting coach for the Evansville Otters (independent Frontier) in 2003.

In 2008 Schulz signed on as Evansville Mater Dei High School's baseball coach. "I feel that God blessed me with the knowledge of baseball and has given me patience with kids and the love of the game," he told Gordon Englehardt of the *Evansville Courier & Press*. "Playing professionally, it's such a business. It wasn't much fun. There's not a better feeling than seeing kids succeed."

Schulz's Wildcats overcame a 3-9 start in 2012 to finish with an 18-14-1 record and a berth in the Class 2A championship game at

Victory Field in Indianapolis, where they lost to No. 1-ranked Northfield. He resigned after the season with a career record of 98–50–1.

Schulz, who worked in real estate, continued to coach a local American Legion team.

SCHURR, Wayne Allen
Born: August 6, 1937, Garrett. **Lives:** Hudson.
Height: 6'4". **Weight:** 185. **Batted:** right. **Threw:** right.
Debut: April 15, 1964. **Final game:** July 11, 1964.
Positions, teams, years: pitcher, Chicago (NL) 1964.
Games: 26. **Innings pitched:** 48.1. **Won/Lost:** 0–0. **Earned run average:** 3.72.

Born about 20 miles north of Fort Wayne in the DeKalb County town of Garrett, **Wayne Schurr** played baseball and basketball at Salem Center High School. He attended Griffin Junior College in Van Wert, Ohio, before earning a degree in education from Michigan's Hillsdale College.

A two-sport star at Hillsdale, Schurr signed with the San Francisco Giants in 1959. That summer he went 6–2 with a 2.22 ERA for Michigan City, Ind. (Midwest). The lanky right-hander had a 13–11 record with a 3.18 ERA for Eugene, Ore. (Northwest), in 1960, and at Victoria (Texas) in 1961 he pitched a 1–0 no-hit game against San Antonio.

Schurr's Army Reserve unit was called up in October 1961 during the Berlin Crisis. After deactivation in 1962 he joined El Paso (Texas) and went 3–3 with a 3.38 ERA in a dozen games for the pennant-winning Sun Kings.

At Tacoma, Wash. (Pacific Coast), in 1963 Schurr became a full-time relief pitcher. That winter the Chicago Cubs took him in the Rule 5 draft. He made 26 relief appearances for the Cubs in 1964 before Chicago shipped him to Salt Lake City (Pacific Coast) in July. He spent all of 1965 as a starter for Salt Lake and pitched for Tacoma in 1966.

After the season the Cubs traded him to the California Angels, but Schurr, who had developed elbow problems, decided to call it a career. He settled in Hudson, a Steuben County hamlet, where he worked as a packaging engineer for Magnavox.

Schurr is a member of the Northeast Indiana Baseball Hall of Fame's Class of 1982.

SCHWIND, Arthur Edwin
Born: November 4, 1889, Fort Wayne. **Died:** January 13, 1968, Sullivan, Illinois.
Height: 5'8". **Weight:** 150. **Batted:** both. **Threw:** right.
Debut: October 3, 1912. **Final game:** October 3, 1912.
Positions, teams, years: third base, Boston (NL) 1912.
Games: 1. **At-bats:** 2. **Home runs:** 0. **Average:** .500.

Art Schwind leapfrogged from Chicago's sandlots to the big leagues in one season.

Schwind played shortstop for a Windy City semi-pro team called the Roseland Eclipse in 1911, and in the spring of 1912 he tried out for Evansville of the Class B Central League. Evansville manager Frank Shaughnessy liked what he saw and arranged for the speedy Schwind to play with Ottawa, Ontario, of the Class C Canadian League.

Schwind appeared in 96 of 98 contests for the pennant-winning Senators in 1912 and batted .274. That September the Boston Braves acquired him, and in the next-to-last game of the season he replaced Art Devlin at third base in a 13–4 loss to visiting Philadelphia. He went 1-for-2 in his only big league appearance.

Schwind spent the next four years in the Texas League, playing football and basketball in Chicago between seasons. He was with San Antonio in 1913, and in 1914 he played for Dallas. Schwind, according to a contemporary newspaper account, "is fast, covers a world of ground, and from first impressions is one of the neatest little infielders that has ever stepped up to the plate."

Schwind suffered a broken leg in the spring of 1915, when he divided the year between Dallas and Beaumont. Released in 1916 after 70 games with Beaumont, he enlisted in the Army in May 1917. While serving with an engineer unit in Washington, he went 6-for-15 in a handful of games for Tacoma (Northwest). When the U.S. entered the First World War, Schwind went to France. After the armistice he captained an undefeated Eighteenth Engineers baseball team, which beat a navy squad for the American Expeditionary Forces championship.

After the war Schwind made his home in Chicago, working as a fire department alarm operator. He played baseball for semi-pro clubs into the 1920s, including a stint with a team from Hammond, Ind. He also became a well-known dog breeder who raised prize-winning German shepherds.

Schwind lived in California and Washington State before returning to the Midwest. At the time of his death, he was a resident of the Masonic Home in Sullivan, Ill.

SCOTT, Lewis Everett ("Deacon, "Scotty")

Indiana Baseball Hall of Fame, 1986.
Born: November 19, 1892, Bluffton. **Died:** November 2, 1960, Fort Wayne.
Height: 5–8. **Weight:** 148. **Batted:** right. **Threw:** right.
Debut: April 14, 1914. **Final game:** July 27, 1926.
Positions, teams, years: shortstop (1,643), third base (3), second base (1), Boston (AL) 1914–1921, New York (AL) 1922–1925, Washington 1925, Chicago (AL) 1926, Cincinnati (NL) 1926.
Games: 1,654. **At-bats:** 5,837. **Home runs:** 20. **Average:** .249.

A star defensive shortstop, **Everett Scott** once held the Major League record for most consecutive games played.

Scott entered organized ball in 1909 and joined the Boston Red Sox in 1914. His fielding ability and bunting skills made him an immediate asset, and his quiet manner earned him the nickname "Deacon." He played for Boston's pennant-winning teams in 1915, 1916 and 1918.

When the Red Sox began to fade after World War I, owner Harry Frazee began peddling his star players. In December 1921, eleven months after selling Babe Ruth to New York, Frazee sent Scott to the Yankees in a six-player deal. "My transfer to New York was, of course, a very acceptable move," Scott told *Baseball Magazine's* F.C. Lane. "To get with a winning team is a natural ambition for any ball player and adds a little pep and encouragement to his work."

Scott helped the Yanks to first-place finishes in 1922 and 1923. He was New York's starting shortstop for the first game at Yankee Stadium on April 18, 1923. That year he led AL shortstops in fielding for the eighth straight season.

Scott's playing streak began on June 20, 1916, while he was with Boston. When the skein approached 900, statisticians discovered that he had long since passed the old standard by George Pinckney, a Brooklyn Bridegrooms third baseman who had appeared in 577 consecutive games between 1885 and 1890.

A general team slump ended Scott's streak in 1925, a year when the Yankees finished seventh. In an effort to shake up the team, manager Miller Huggins benched Scott after a game on May 5. "I never even thought about a record until after the string had reached 700 or 800 games," Scott told *The Sporting News*. "No one else paid any attention to the streak until it had reached about 900 games. I started game after game because my manager thought I was helping the team, not because I had a consecutive streak going."

Scott's record of 1,307 straight games lasted until 1933, when it was surpassed by Lou Gehrig. Invited to St. Louis for the record-breaking occasion, Scott declined. "Gehrig can probably stay in there for a good many more games, barring injury, if he cares to," Scott told the *Fort Wayne Journal-Gazette*, "but I believe he would be wise to take a rest when he feels that he needs it. It's the old legs that begin to feel the strain, sooner or later."

In June 1925 the Yankees released Scott to Washington. The Senators won the pennant, but he saw no action in the World Series. Scott, who batted .156 in 27 World Series contests, split the 1926 season between the Chicago White Sox and the Cincinnati Reds. From 1927 to 1929 he played for minor league teams in Baltimore (International), Toledo, Ohio (American Association), and Reading, Pa. (International).

After retiring as a player, Scott returned to Fort Wayne and operated several bowling alleys. An avid kegler himself, he won numerous city and state titles and bowled 300 over 50 times.

The Bluffton High School alum was inducted into Northeast Indiana Baseball Association Hall of Fame in 1962, and in 1986 he was elected to the Indiana Baseball Hall of Fame.

SCOTT, Rodney Darrell ("Cool Breeze")

Indiana Basebal Hall of Fame, 2014
Born: October 16, 1953, Indianapolis. **Lives:** Indianapolis.

Height: 6-0. **Weight:** 160. **Batted:** both (batted right, 1975). **Threw:** right.
Debut: April 11, 1975. **Final game:** August 21, 1982.
Positions, teams, years: second base (443), shortstop (153), third base (64), outfield (11), Kansas City (AL) 1975, Montreal (NL) 1976, Oakland (NL) 1977, Chicago (NL) 1978, Montreal (NL) 1979–1982, New York (AL) 1982.
Games: 690. **At-bats:** 2,132. **Home runs:** 3. **Average:** .236.

Versatile, volatile **Rodney Scott** played five different positions and changed uniforms six times during an eight-year stint in the Major Leagues.

A three-sport star for Indianapolis Arlington High School, Scott helped the Golden Knights to a City title in basketball and to a baseball sectional title in baseball. He tried out for the football team as a senior and won All-City honors. He was Arlington's top basketball scorer as a senior and made the Indiana All-Star squad. He also won All-State honors in baseball.

"I really want to play some form of pro sports," Scott told Harrison Howard of the *Indianapolis Star*. "I don't know which it will be. I like basketball very much. Baseball, too. I was All-City in football last year ... but a year of that has convinced me I'm too small for the sport. I do hope I can make it in pro basketball or baseball."

Scott signed a letter of intent to play basketball for Vincennes University, but he decided on a baseball career after the Kansas City Royals picked him in the 11th round in the 1972 draft. He spent four years in the minors, stealing a total of 85 bases for Waterloo, Iowa (Midwest), and San Jose (California) in 1974. He opened the 1975 season with Kansas City, and spent time that season with Omaha, Neb. (American Association), and Jacksonville, Fla. (Southern).

The Royals dealt Scott to Montreal in December 1975. In 1976 he batted .307 for Denver (American Association), the Expos' top farm club. He appeared in seven contests with Montreal that year, and in March 1977 the Expos traded him to Texas. Eleven days later the Rangers swapped him to Oakland. He batted .261 for the Athletics in his first full big league campaign and finished sixth in the AL with 33 stolen bases.

Oakland traded Scott to the Cubs prior to 1978. He divided the year between Chicago and Wichita, Kan. (American Association), averaging .282 in 78 games for the Cubs. He was on the move again that December when Chicago sent him to Montreal. For the next two years he was the Expos' everyday second baseman. He batted .238 in 1979 and .224 in 1980, when his 13 triples tied for the NL lead. In 1980 Scott stole 63 bases, while Montreal left fielder Ron LeFlore swiped 97 for a combined total of 160—a big league record for teammates.

During the strike-shortened 1981 campaign, when Montreal lost to the Dodgers in the NLCS, Scott stole 30 bases in 95 games. He batted just .205, however, and in 1982 the Expos released him after 14 games. That June he signed a minor league deal with the Yankees and hit .192 in 10 contests for New York before the Yanks dropped him in August.

In 1983 Scott was back in the Montreal system, playing for the Expos' top farm club in Wichita. He spent the next three seasons in the Mexican League, batting .309 for the Truchas de Toluca in 1984. He hit .280 for the Angeles de Puebla in 1985 and .276 for the Ganaderos de Tabasco in 1986. From 1990 to 1992 he was one of the many ex-big leaguers who played in the Florida-based Senior Professional Baseball Association.

Scott, who stole 205 bases in 690 Major League contests, believed shortstop was his best position. John Mayberry, a Kansas City teammate, nicknamed him "Cool Breeze" for his unflappable outlook.

Scott managed to get crossways with managers like Whitey Herzog (Royals), Bobby Winkles (Athletics), Herman Franks (Cubs) and Clyde King (Yankees), but was a personal favorite of Dick Williams, a Hall of Fame member who managed Scott in Oakland and Montreal. "Somebody's always going to dislike you or not like your ways," Scott told Dan Turner, author of *The Expos Inside Out*. "Everybody's going to like a guy who just does what they tell him to do."

In 2014 Scott was inducted into the Indiana Baseball Hall of Fame.

SEMBER, Michael David

Born: February 24, 1953, Hammond. **Lives:** Boca Raton, Florida.
Height: 6-0. **Weight:** 185. **Batted:** right. **Threw:** right.
Debut: August 18, 1977. **Final game:** October 1, 1978.
Positions, teams, years: third base (7), second base (1), shortstop (2), Chicago (NL) 1977–1978.
Games: 12. **At-bats:** 7. **Home runs:** 0. **Average:** .286.

Mike Sember played football and basketball for Hammond's Bishop Noll High School and didn't go out for baseball until his senior year in 1970.

At Tulsa University, Sember quarterbacked the freshman football team before deciding to concentrate on baseball. "During the spring of my freshman year, I was going to spring football and baseball," he told Springfield, Ill., *State Journal-Register* reporter Jim Ruppert, "and the football coach and I got into a hassle about playing football, so I quit and went to baseball."

From 1971 to 1974 Sember helped Tulsa to four consecutive Missouri Valley Conference titles and set a school record with 22 career homers. Tulsa reached the College World Series in 1971, losing to Arizona State in the final game of the double-elimination tournament.

A collegiate and academic All-America, Sember earned a communications degree in 1974. The Cubs made him their second-round draft pick that June, and he spent his first pro season with Midland (Texas). Chicago's front office envisioned him as a possible successor to longtime Cubs shortstop Don Kessinger.

In 1977 Sember was batting .245 for Wichita, Kan. (American Association), when he earned his first promotion to Chicago. The Cubs brought him up again in 1978 after a .239 season at Wichita.

Released by Chicago during Spring Training in 1979, Sember signed with the Toronto Blue Jays. He played 49 games for Toronto's top farm club at Syracuse, N.Y. (International), before leaving baseball at age 26.

Sember launched a marketing career, making his home in Florida and commuting to New York City. In 2011 he was inducted into Tulsa University's Sports Hall of Fame.

SENTENEY, Stephen Leonard

Born: August 7, 1955, Indianapolis. **Died:** June 18, 1989, Colusa, California.
Height: 6'2". **Weight:** 205. **Batted:** right. **Threw:** right.
Debut: June 6, 1982. **Final game:** September 30, 1982.
Positions, teams, years: pitcher, Toronto (AL) 1982.
Games: 11. **Innings pitched:** 22. **Won/Lost:** 0–0. **Earned run average:** 4.91.

Indianapolis native **Steve Senteney** was a 1973 graduate of Casa Robles High School in Citrus Heights, Calif. He attended St. Mary's College in Moraga, Calif.

After a Marine Corps hitch, Senteney signed with the Toronto Blue Jays as a free agent. He broke in with Medicine Hat, Alb. (Pioneer), in 1979 and in 1981 he went 10–5 with a 3.14 ERA for Knoxville, Tenn. (Southern).

Senteney jumped from Syracuse, N.Y. (International), to Toronto in 1982, making 11 relief appearances for the Blue Jays. Toronto traded him to the Mets in February 1983 and he opened the year with Tidewater (International). New York sent him to the Pittsburgh Pirates that June, and he spent the rest of the year with Hawaii (Pacific Coast).

After dividing the 1984 season between Hawaii and Nashua, N.H. (Eastern), Senteney joined the Seattle Mariners organization. He was 2–2 with a 4.50 ERA for Calgary, Alberta (Pacific Coast), before retiring.

Returning to Citrus Heights, Senteney remained active in baseball as a coach and as a semi-pro player for the Sacramento Smokies and the Tahoe Suns.

At about 9:50 p.m. on June 18, 1989, he was driving east on California's Highway 10 near Colusa when he was involved in a head-on collision with a westbound vehicle. The 33-year-old Senteney died instantly. Survivors included his wife, Monica, and their daughter, Karina.

SHANNER, Wilfred William

Born: November 4, 1894, Oakland City. **Died:** December 18, 1986, Evansville.
Height: 6'1". **Weight:** 195. **Batted:** left. **Threw:** right.
Debut: October 1, 1920. **Final game:** October 1, 1920.

Positions, teams, years: pitcher, Philadelphia (AL) 1920.
Games: 1. **Innings pitched:** 4. **Won/Lost:** 0–0. **Earned run average:** 6.75.

Near the end of the 1920 season, the Philadelphia Athletics were anchored in the AL cellar. A's manager Connie Mack, who frequently auditioned recruits in Major League contests, added **Bill Shanner** to his pitching staff. Shanner was a World War I Army veteran who lived in New Castle, Del., and worked as an accountant. He also pitched for the Pennsylvania Railroad's semi-pro baseball team.

On October 1, 1920, with three games left in the season, Mack started another rookie, Fred Heimach, against Washington at Philadelphia's Shibe Park. The Nationals lit up Heimach, a 19-year-old left-hander, for nine runs in five innings before Mack removed him for a pinch-hitter. The 25-year-old Shanner came on for the last four frames, giving up four more runs (three earned) in a 13–3 loss. "Shanner looked easier to hit than did Heimach," reported the *Washington Post*, "his high-hand toss coming up with about schoolboy speed."

It would be the lone big league appearance for the two rookie hurlers. Shanner started the 1921 season with Winston-Salem, N.C. (Piedmont), going 1–4 in eight games before Daytona Beach (Florida State) purchased his contract. He went 1–3 in seven appearances for the Florida squad before leaving organized ball.

Making Evansville his home, Shanner played semi-pro ball while working in the accounting department at Standard Oil of Indiana. He also umpired for many years. Before retiring, he worked in accounting at Hahn, Inc., an Evansville-based rotary tiller manufacturer.

Shanner and his wife, the former Florence Gullette, had been married for 69 years when he passed away at age 92.

SHELDON, Scott Patrick ("Shel")

Born: November 28, 1968, Hammond. **Lives:** League City, Texas.
Height: 6-3. **Weight:** 185. **Batted:** right. **Threw:** right.
Debut: May 18, 1997. **Final game:** October 5, 2001.
Positions, teams, years: third base (59), shortstop (52), second base (13), first base (11), outfield (5), catcher (4), pitcher (1), Oakland (AL) 1997, Texas (AL) 1998–2001.
Games: 141. **At-bats:** 285. **Home runs:** 8. **Average:** .235.

Scott Sheldon was the first American-born big leaguer to play all nine positions in a single contest.

The son of a peripatetic Amoco Oil Company executive, Sheldon was born in Hammond. He was less than a year old when his family moved to Texas. The Sheldons lived in Kansas City and Salt Lake City and made two stops in Chicago before settling in Houston when Scott was in middle school.

Sheldon was a star baseball player at Houston's Clear Lake High School and at the University of Houston. Oakland made him its eighth-round choice in 1991.

Working his way through the Athletics' chain, Sheldon reached the Major Leagues in 1997 as a 28-year-old rookie. After the season he became a free agent and signed with Texas. In 1998 he appeared in seven games with the Rangers, spending most of the year with Oklahoma (Pacific Coast). At Oklahoma in 1999 he made the PCL All-Star squad and rejoined the Rangers for a couple of games at season's end.

Sheldon opened the 2000 season with Texas as a utility player. On September 6, at Chicago's Comiskey Park, Sheldon played every position. Only two other players had played all nine positions in a single game: Bert Campaneris, a native of Cuba, with the Kansas City Athletics in 1975, and Minnesota's Cesar Tovar, a Venezuelan, in 1968.

"We were playing the White Sox, so it was close to where I was born in Hammond," Sheldon recalled. "My mom and dad were in town, and the wife and kids were there, so it was awesome. It'll be something I'll always remember."

After spending all of 2001 with the Rangers, Sheldon spent the next two years playing for the Orix BlueWave of Osaka in Japan's Pacific League. He returned to the U.S. for a final season in 2004, playing for Indianapolis (International), Altoona, Pa. (Eastern), and Nashville, Tenn. (Pacific Coast).

SHEPARD, Bert Robert ("Shep")

Born: June 28, 1920, Dana. **Died:** June 16, 2008, Highland, California.

Height: 5'11". **Weight:** 185. **Batted:** left. **Threw:** left.
Debut: August 4, 1945. **Final game:** August 4, 1945.
Positions, teams, years: pitcher, Washington (AL) 1945.
Games: 1. **Innings pitched:** 5.1. **Won/Lost:** 0–0. **Earned run average:** 1.69.

The only Major Leaguer with an artificial leg, **Bert Shepard** attended Clinton High School in western Indiana and played sandlot ball around the Terre Haute area before signing a professional contract. He bounced around with Jeanerette, La. (Evangeline), and Tiffin (Ohio State) in 1939; for Wisconsin Rapids (Wisconsin State) and Mount Airy, N.C. (Bi-State), in 1940; and with Anaheim (California) and Bisbee, Ariz. (Arizona-Texas), in 1941 before entering the army in 1942.

Commissioned an air corps second lieutenant, Shepard became a fighter pilot and went to England, where he flew combat missions for the Eighth Air Force. He also served as player-manager for the 55th Fighter Group's baseball squad. He was returning from a raid on Berlin on May 21, 1944, when his P-38 Thunderbolt was shot down behind enemy lines. When Shepard awoke in a German hospital, he learned that doctors had amputated his right leg below the knee.

Shepard returned to the United States in March 1945 as part of a prisoner of war exchange. While recuperating in Washington, D.C., he met Robert Patterson, the U.S. Undersecretary of War. When Shepard said he wanted to resume his baseball career, Patterson arranged for a tryout with the Washington Senators, hoping to encourage other badly wounded veterans. "I could pitch," he said, "so you couldn't tell I had a leg gone."

The Senators signed Shepard as a batting practice pitcher and used him in several fund-raising exhibition games against service teams. Battling the Detroit Tigers for the AL pennant, Washington added him to its roster after he beat the Brooklyn Dodgers in a July exhibition contest.

Shepard got a chance to pitch in a regular-season game against Boston in the nightcap of a doubleheader on August 4, 1945. With the Red Sox leading 14–1 in the fourth inning, he entered the game with the bases loaded and two out. He fanned the first batter he faced to end the inning, and pitched five more frames while giving up one run on three hits.

Prior to a Senators home game a few weeks later, Shepard received the Distinguished Flying Cross. "Now I know why nothing can stop the Army Air Corps," teammate Clyde Milan told the *Washington Times-Herald*. "If he can do what he does with one leg, what would he do with two good props under him?"

Shepard opened the 1946 season with Washington. When he hadn't pitched in a game by mid-season, he asked to be sent to the minors. The Senators shipped him to Chattanooga, Tenn. (Southern), where he went 2–2 in seven games. He also logged time with Duluth, Minn. (Northern), and Decatur, Ill. (Three-I). In the off-season, he barnstormed with an all-star team made up of Major League players.

In 1947 Shepard's career was interrupted again, this time by more surgery. But complications set in, and he had to undergo four additional operations. Out of baseball for two years, he joined Waterbury, Conn. (Colonial), as a player-manager in 1949. He appeared in 69 games that year as a pitcher-first baseman, compiling a 5–6 slate with a .229 average. He resurfaced in 1952 with St. Augustine (Florida) as a playing manager, and finished the season with Hot Springs, Ark. (Cotton States). He also played for Tampa (Florida International) in 1953 and for Modesto (California) in 1955.

During the off-season, Shepard was a typewriter salesman for IBM. After leaving baseball, he worked as a safety engineer for Hughes Aircraft; for several Southern California insurance agencies; and for Fluor Construction. His employment took him to the Middle East and South America before his retirement in 1983. "The reputation I got in baseball," he said, "and the confidence that I developed being able to play enabled me to get jobs."

Making his home in Hesperia, Calif., Shepard won national amputee golf titles in 1968 and 1971. He frequently returned to his native state to compete in an Indianapolis golf tournament for amputees.

Shepard died 12 days short of his 88th birthday.

SHEPHERD, Keith Wayne

Born: January 21, 1968, Wabash. **Lives:** Granger.
Height: 6'2". **Weight:** 205. **Batted:** right. **Threw:** right.
Debut: September 6, 1992. **Final game:** August 4, 1996.
Positions, teams, years: pitcher, Philadelphia (NL) 1992, Colorado (NL) 1993, Boston (AL) 1995, Baltimore (AL) 1996.
Games: 41. **Innings pitched:** 63. **Won/Lost:** 2–5. **Earned run average:** 6.71.

Injuries from a motorcycle accident in the summer of 1985 kept **Keith Shepherd** from playing football as a senior at Wabash High School, and sidelined him for much of the basketball season. He was still recovering at the start of the 1986 baseball season, when he went 11–3 with a 1.23 ERA and 143 strikeouts in 89⅔ innings. He was the starting and winning pitcher in a semistate game against La Porte. With Shepherd as its designated hitter, Wabash beat Marion 2–1 in the championship game. That same month, Pittsburgh took him in the eleventh round of the draft.

Shepherd spent the summer of 1986 with the Pirates' rookie team in the Gulf Coast League. In December 1988 Kansas City claimed him in the Rule 5 minor league draft. Released by the Royals in July 1989, he joined the Cleveland organization. The Indians cut him loose after the 1990 campaign, and in March 1991 he signed with the White Sox organization. He was a Southern League All-Star with Birmingham, Ala., in 1992 with a 2.14 ERA in 40 games. Chicago traded him to the Phillies organization that August and he debuted with Philadelphia in September.

The fledgling Rockies selected Shepherd in the second round of the expansion draft in November 1992, and he divided the 1993 season between Colorado and Colorado Springs (Pacific Coast). The Rockies dealt him to Boston in June 1994, but he developed shoulder problems and drew his release in July 1995. He pitched in the Florida Marlins system before resurfacing with the Baltimore Orioles in 1996. He played in the Mets system before closing out his career with a second tour in the Pirates organization in 1997.

In 1998 Shepherd pitched for the Brother Elephants of Taiwan's professional baseball league. He returned to Wabash High School as an assistant coach and continued to play for independent teams in northern Indiana like the Shady Nook Jackers.

Shepherd was elected to the Northeast Indiana Baseball Association Hall of Fame in 2009.

SIMON, Michael Edward

Born: April 13, 1883, Hayden. **Died:** June 10, 1963, Los Angeles, California.
Height: 5–11. **Weight:** 188. **Batted:** right. **Threw:** right.
Debut: June 27, 1909. **Final game:** September 30, 1915.
Positions, teams, years: catcher, Pittsburgh (NL) 1909–1913, St. Louis (Federal) 1914, Brooklyn (Federal) 1915.
Games: 379. **At-bats:** 1,069. **Home runs:** 1. **Average:** .225.

Mike Simon was the second Indiana University alumnus to play big league ball (behind pitcher Odie Porter) and IU's first position player to reach the majors. He was a teammate of Honus Wagner, the legendary Hall of Fame shortstop, and spent much of his career as a backup to George Gibson, one of the era's most durable catchers.

Simon grew up in Jennings County and was a member of the IU baseball squad in 1901. From 1903 to 1904 he played for independent teams in Parkersburg, W.Va.; Piqua, Ohio; and Muncie, Ind. In 1904 he broke into organized ball with Columbus, Ohio (American Association), and from 1905 to 1908 he played in the Three-I League. He managed Peoria, Ill., for part of the '05 season and split 1907 between Peoria and Cedar Rapids, Iowa.

After batting .217 for Cedar Rapids in '08, Simon joined Pittsburgh in 1909. Led by Wagner's .339 average, the Pirates finished first that season. With Gibson playing almost every day for Pittsburgh, Simon appeared in just 11 games and saw no action in the Pirates' seven-game World Series triumph over Detroit.

Simon appeared in 22 games in 1910, but got into 71 games in 1911, when Gibson slumped badly. That August, Simon left the team briefly due to the death of his nine-month-old son. "Simon will take the remains to North Vernon, Ind., his home, for burial, but his wife will be unable to accompany him," reported the *Washington Post*. "She has not fully recovered from an operation which she underwent recently for appendicitis, and the shock of the baby's death has rendered her condition such that it will likely be some time before her husband is able to leave her and resume his position on the catching corps of Manager [Fred] Clarke's outfit."

In 1912 Simon hit .301 in 42 contests. When Gibson went down with a broken ankle in 1913, Simon got into 92 games and batted .247. In 1914 he jumped to St. Louis of the outlaw Federal League, and appeared in 93 games for the last-place Terriers. He closed out his big league career with Brooklyn (Federal) in 1915.

Simon spent the next two years in the minors. His manager at Bloomington, Ill. (Three-I), in 1916 was Howard Daringer, another Jennings County native. Simon played for Vernon, Calif. (Pacific Coast), in 1917 and spent much of his later years in the West. He managed Tucson, Ariz. (Arizona-Texas), for part of 1939 and eventually worked as a truck driver for a dry cleaning establishment in Anaheim, Calif., where he spent his final years.

SIMON, Sylvester Adam ("Sammy")

Born: December 14, 1897, Evansville. **Died:** February 28, 1973, Chandler.
Height: 5–10. **Weight:** 170. **Batted:** right. **Threw:** right.
Debut: October 1, 1923. **Final game:** September 27, 1924.
Positions, teams, years: third base (6), shortstop (5), St. Louis (AL) 1923–1924
Games: 24. At-bats: 33. Home runs: 0. Average: .242.

A member of the Evansville Sports Hall of Fame, **Syl Simon** enjoyed a lengthy, productive professional baseball career despite a disfiguring hand injury.

Simon entered organized ball with Ludington, Mich. (Central), in 1920, where he played for former Major Leaguer and fellow Evansville native Punch Knoll. Out of organized baseball in 1921, Simon returned in 1922 to play for Knoll in Bay City, Mich. (Michigan-Ontario), where he batted .312.

After a .322 season for San Antonio (Texas) in 1923, Simon joined the St. Louis Browns and made his big league debut as a pinch-hitter. He spent all of 1924 with St. Louis as a backup infielder. The Browns assigned Simon to Tulsa, Okla. (Western), for 1925, and Milwaukee (American Association) purchased his contract in 1926. Prior to the season he married Thelma Knoll, the daughter of his former manager.

Simon batted .308 for the Brewers, and after the season he resumed his off-season work in Evansville as an upholsterer at a furniture manufacturing company. Late that October, according to the *St. Louis Post-Dispatch*, Simon "wanted a couple of pieces of wood sawed in two. The operator of the saw was gone. Syl decided to do it himself. Hardly had he commenced when the mishap occurred. His hand got caught in the machine and before he could extricate it, three fingers and part of the palm were ripped off."

In 2001 Simon's granddaughter, Sylvia Watters, told Dave Johnson of the *Evansville Courier-Journal*: "The little finger was the only one left intact. And all that was left of his thumb was a nub."

Milwaukee's front office sent Simon a letter of condolence, along with a check for $100 and a notice that he had been released. While his hand healed, Simon fashioned a bat with a padded steel grip along with a specially designed glove to compensate for his handicap.

Working out with Punch Knoll at Evansville's Bosse Field, Simon eventually joined a semi-pro team in nearby Mount Vernon, Ind., in 1927. About halfway through the season he signed with Evansville (Three-I), where he managed to bat .279 in 55 games.

Simon continued to put up impressive numbers for the next five years, batting .360 for Fort Wayne (Central) in 1928, .338 for Erie, Pa. (Central), in 1929, .364 in a second stint with Fort Wayne in 1930 and .319 for Bloomington, Ill. (Three-I), in 1931. He ended his career as a playing manager in 1931, batting .294 while guiding Quincy, Ill. (Three-I), to a third-place finish.

After retiring, Simon worked at the Servel refrigerator plant in Evansville and managed the company baseball team. He was later employed by Wessleman's grocery and was involved in an orchard business in Chandler, Ind., with Punch Knoll.

In 1973 Simon committed suicide by hanging himself from a rafter at a barn near his home in Chandler.

SINER, Hosea John

Born: March 20, 1885, Shelburn. **Died:** June 10, 1948, Sullivan.
Height: 5-10. **Weight:** 185. **Batted:** right. **Threw:** right.
Debut: July 28, 1909. **Final game:** August 23, 1909.
Positions, teams, years: third base (5), second base (1), shortstop (1), Boston (NL) 1909.
Games: 10. **At-bats:** 23. **Home runs:** 0. **Average:** .130.

In 1909 **Hosea Siner** was one of five Indiana-born members of Boston's NL team.

A native of the western Indiana mining town of Shelburn, the slick-fielding Siner broke in as a shortstop with Albany (Georgia State) in 1906. After stops at Calumet, Mich. (Northern Copper Country), South Bend (Central) and Monmouth, Ill. (Illinois-Missouri), he joined the Boston Rustlers (now the Atlanta Braves) in the summer of 1909.

Pitchers Cecil Ferguson, Forrest More and Tom McCarthy, and catcher Bill Rariden—all native Hoosiers—also played for Boston that year. "Siner has the natural ability to play ball," observed the *South Bend Tribune*, "but he does not hit the ball hard enough."

Siner went to Spring Training with Boston in 1910, but the Rustlers sold his contract to Monmouth, which was now in the Central League. In 1911 he enjoyed his finest year at Danville, Ill. (Three-I), where he batted .276 and made the all-star team as a second baseman.

A miner in his younger days, the strong and solidly built Siner liked to wrestle during the off-season. After the 1911 season he suffered a wrestling injury that limited him to just 52 games in 1912. He retired after helping Great Falls, Mont. (Union Association), to a first-place finish is 1913.

Returning to Indiana, Siner organized an independent team called the Shelburn Maroons. He owned a farm near Sullivan and operated a service station there for several years before his death at the age of 63.

SLAGLE, John A.

Born: John A. Schlagle, October 1869, Lawrence. **Died:** February 23, 1915, Indianapolis.
Height: 5'10". **Weight:** 175. **Batted:** left. **Threw:** right.
Debut: April 30, 1891. **Final game:** April 30, 1891.
Positions, teams, years: pitcher, Cincinnati (American Association) 1891.
Games: 1. **Innings pitched:** 1.1. **Won/Lost:** 0-0. **Earned run average:** 0.00.

John Slagle was pitching for an independent team in Muncie when the Galesburg, Ill., club of the Central Interstate League shifted to Indianapolis in late May of 1890. He went 0-4 in four games and, reported the *Indianapolis Sun* on June 16, "Slagle has not proved fast enough for Inter-State league company, and will be allowed to go."

In 1891 the major league American Association added a new team, Kelly's Killers of Cincinnati. When Cincinnati beat Columbus 15-6 on April 30, Slagle relieved starter Cannonball Crane.

It was the one and only big league game for Slagle, who split the rest of the year between Fort Wayne (Northwestern) and Oconto (Wisconsin State). Between 1892 and 1897 he pitched for ten different teams, taking turns at third base, shortstop and the outfield. In 1893 he went 16-5 for Easton, topping the Pennsylvania State League with a .762 winning percentage.

For the final game of the 1896 season Slagle was on the mound for Grand Rapids, Mich. (Western Association). With Kansas City's Charles "Count" Campau batting, *The Sporting News* reported that Slagle "pitched a large juicy potato instead of the ball, and he tossed a slow one over the plate." Campau swung, made contact, and started for first base before he realized the joke. "It was not exactly according to Hoyle," *TSN* noted, "but it was the last game of the season and everything went."

A native of the Marion County town of Lawrence, Slagle lived in St. Joseph, Mo., after leaving baseball. He eventually settled in Indianapolis, where he worked as a bartender. He died at age 45 of pulmonary tuberculosis.

SLUSARSKI, Joseph Andrew ("Slu")

Born: December 19, 1966, Indianapolis. **Lives:** Springfield, Illinois.
Height: 6'4". **Weight:** 195. **Batted:** right. **Threw:** right.
Debut: April 11, 1991. **Final game:** June 21, 2001.

Positions, teams, years: pitcher, Oakland (AL) 1991–1993, Milwaukee (AL) 1995, Houston (NL) 1999–2000, Atlanta (NL) 2001, Houston (NL) 2001.
Games: 118. **Innings pitched:** 305.2. **Won/Lost:** 13–21. **Earned run average:** 5.18.

Joe Slusarski was born in Indianapolis while his father, a native of Poland, was working on a master's degree. Slusarski's family later moved to Springfield, Ill., where he went to Sacred Heart-Griffin High School. He played college baseball for Lincoln Land Community College in Springfield and later for the University of New Orleans.

In 1987 Slusarski returned to Indianapolis with Team USA for the Pan American Games. He went 3–0 as the Americans took second behind Cuba. The Seattle Mariners picked him in the second round of the June 1987 draft, but he returned to New Orleans for his senior year. He went 13–6 for the Privateers in 1988.

Slusarski again pitched for Team USA that summer in the USA-Japan collegiate baseball series in Mito, Japan; at the Baseball World Cup in Parma, Italy; and in the Olympics in Seoul, Korea. With Cuba boycotting the Games, the Americans easily won the gold medal.

In June 1988, the Oakland Athletics took Slusarski in the second round of the draft. His professional career began in 1989 at Modesto, where his 13 wins led the California League. Set to open the 1991 season with Tacoma, Wash. (Pacific Coast), he found himself in Oakland's starting rotation due to an injury to Eric Show.

Slusarski wound up shuttling between the A's and Tacoma through 1994. During Spring Training in 1992 he stumbled against a cactus and damaged tendons in the middle finger of his pitching hand. "I couldn't grip the ball," he told *USA Today Baseball Weekly*. "The hand injury hung around all year, and it turned into a shoulder problem."

Unable to throw breaking pitches, Slusarski started overthrowing his fastball and injured his shoulder. Oakland released him in 1994, and he pitched for six different organizations until his retirement in 2001.

Slusarski pitched for minor league teams in New Orleans in 1995 and 1996, and from 1998 to 2001. In 1998 he helped the Zephyrs beat Buffalo in the Triple-A World Series between the pennant winners of the Pacific Coast League and the American Association. His alma mater, the University of New Orleans, hired him as its pitching coach in 2002.

The following year Slusarski was back in pro ball as a pitching coach in Houston's farm system. He remained in the Astros organization through 2006. He spent part of the 2009 season as the pitching coach for the Texas Rangers' Double-A affiliate in Frisco (Texas).

SMITH, Harry W.

Born: February 2, 1856, North Vernon. **Died:** June 4, 1898, North Vernon.
Height: 6'0". **Weight:** 175. **Batted:** right. **Threw:** right.
Debut: May 8, 1877. **Final game:** August 19, 1889.
Positions, teams, years: second base (17), outfield (14), catcher (9), Chicago (NL) 1877, Cincinnati (NL) 1877, Louisville (American Association) 1889.
Games: 35. **At-bats:** 132. **Home runs:** 0. **Average:** .220.

Harry Smith, the NL's first Indiana-born player, also was the first Hoosier native to play for the Cincinnati Reds and for the Chicago Cubs. Over the years, details of his career and his life after baseball often have been confused and clouded.

The NL began operations in 1876, and in 1877 Smith joined the Chicago White Stockings (who later became the Cubs). He played alongside future Hall of Famers Cap Anson and Al Spalding, seeing occasional action at second base and in the outfield.

On August 10 Chicago granted Smith his release so he could sign with Cincinnati. Contemporary newspaper accounts described him as a "hard-working player" who "can play second base or catch better than any man Cincinnati now has." He got into 10 games with the Reds as a catcher, outfielder and second baseman.

Smith disappeared from organized ball from 1878 to 1882, resurfacing in 1883 with Grand Rapids, Mich. (Northwestern). In 1884 he played two games for Stillwater, Okla. (Northwestern), and he joined an independent team in Fort Wayne in 1885. He also made seven appearances that season for Birmingham, Ala. (Southern).

Smith opened the 1886 season with Topeka, Kan. (Western), where he was the personal catcher for Jim McElroy, another former big leaguer. Smith and McElroy finished the year with an independent club in Nickerson, Kan. In 1887 Smith and McElroy moved to independent Wellington (Kansas State), where Smith served as field captain. The pair played for another independent outfit in Albuquerque, N.M., in 1888 and 1889.

Although Smith is listed as a one-game big league catcher for the Louisville (American Association) in 1889, there is speculation this may have been another player. In 1890 he joined Indianapolis (Central Inter-State) as a catcher and team captain. He took over as manager before the team disbanded in July.

After leaving baseball, Smith returned to his home in Queensville, about four miles northwest of Mount Vernon. Joseph Smith, Harry's father, owned some 800 acres of land in Jennings County. Harry's younger brother, Clifford Smith, served as a federal judge in Iowa from 1900 to 1908 before resigning to leave for Boston, where he became a central figure in the burgeoning Christian Science faith.

For many years, it was erroneously believed that Harry Smith had been hanged for murder in 1895 in Decatur, Ill. Newspaper coverage of the execution incorrectly described the condemned man, Charles N. "Pacer" Smith of Pendleton, Ind., as a former big leaguer with Chicago and Cincinnati.

While investigating Smith's career in 1968, National Baseball Hall of Fame historian Lee Allen heard from Howard Daringer, a former minor league player from Jennings County. Daringer, whose brothers Cliff and Rolla had been Major Leaguers, informed Allen that Smith had died in North Vernon at age 42.

In the summer of 1898, Smith was afflicted by a throat disease that lead to "severe paroxysms of coughing," according to a contemporary newspaper account. Medical treatment provided temporary relief, but edema of the throat resulted in strangulation. "The details of his death are too horrifying to contemplate," noted the newspaper, and we can not write them." The newspaper described Smith as "a universally respected young man" whose friends "were legion and numbered in every State in the Union."

SMITH, Rhesa Edward

Born: February 21, 1879, Mentone. **Died:** March 20, 1956, Tarpon Springs, Florida.
Height: 5'11". **Weight:** 170. **Batted:** right. **Threw:** right.
Debut: April 27, 1906. **Final game:** October 7, 1906.
Positions, teams, years: pitcher, St. Louis (AL) 1906.
Games: 19. **Innings pitched:** 154.2. **Won/Lost:** 8-11. **Earned run average:** 3.72.

After one season in the Major Leagues, **Ed Smith** went on to become a major figure in South Bend baseball as a player, college coach, manager and owner.

Born on a farm near the northern Indiana town of Mentone, Smith attended schools in Kosciusko County. He played for a town team in Kokomo before launching his professional career in 1901 with Colorado Springs (Western).

After Smith went 17-17 for Dayton, Ohio (Central), in 1905, the St. Louis Browns bought his contract for 1906. The *St. Louis Post-Dispatch* described him as "well clad, well set up, well educated, and in all a most confident and proper looking party." He went 8-11 that season, despite a midsummer illness that confined him to his home in South Bend for a time.

Smith spent the rest of his playing days in the minors. He pitched for Central League pennant-winners at South Bend in 1910 (where he went 22-13) and in 1913 at Grand Rapids, Mich. (compiling a 20-11 slate).

When Smith wasn't playing baseball he worked as a steamfitter in South Bend, and in 1910 and 1912 he was the pre-season coach for the University of Notre Dame baseball squad. From 1911 to 1914 he was a player-manager for teams in South Bend and Grand Rapids.

After retiring as a player, Smith managed South Bend to the 1915 Southern Michigan League title. In 1916 he became the owner of South Bend's Central League franchise, also serving as team president. From 1918 to 1949 he served as superintendent of buildings and grounds for South Bend's city schools.

An avid sportsman, Smith was playing golf

during a Florida vacation when he suffered a fatal heart attack at age 77. His body was returned to South Bend for burial.

SMITH, Willard Jehu ("Zeke," "Red")

Born: April 11, 1892, Logansport. **Died:** August 23, 1970, Bradenton, Florida.
Height: 5'8". **Weight:** 165. **Batted:** right. **Threw:** right.
Debut: September 17, 1917. **Final game:** September 1, 1918.
Positions, teams, years: catcher, Pittsburgh (NL) 1917–1918.
Games: 26. **At-bats:** 45. **Home runs:** 0. **Average:** .156.

Zeke Smith, once one of the most popular sports figures in Logansport, played baseball professionally for 17 seasons.

As a teenager, Smith established a reputation as one of Logansport's top bowlers. "Willard 'Zeke' Smith broke the record at the Elks' bowling alleys last night when he rolled three games with an average of 221⅔ pins, or 665 pins for the three games," the *Logansport Journal* reported on January 4, 1910. He also starred for the town baseball squad, and later that year he signed a contract with Hopkinsville, Ky. (Kitty).

In 1913 Smith moved from Cairo, Ill. (Kitty), to Nashville, Tenn. (Southern). In August 1917 he was playing for Birmingham, Ala. (Southern), when the Pittsburgh Pirates acquired him and four other players. Smith spent 1918 with Pittsburgh, serving as a third-string catcher. When the season ended in early September due to World War I, he took a job at a Pittsburgh ammunition plant.

After playing for Memphis, Tenn. (Southern), in 1919, Smith returned to Logansport and played for a semi-pro team called the Ottos in 1920. He joined Joplin, Mo. (Western), for 1921, but in 1922 he was back in Indiana, playing for local semi-pro squads.

Smith re-entered organized ball in 1923 with Toledo, Ohio (American Association), where he batted .335 in 115 games. During a two-month span in 1924, he belonged to Galveston (Texas), Denver (Western), Baltimore (International) and Wichita Falls (Texas). He played for Denver in 1925 and 1926 and for Quincy, Ill. (Three-I), in 1927 and 1928.

When Smith left the game for good, he owned and operated sporting goods stores in Logansport and Kokomo. He moved to Florida after retiring.

Known as "Red" when he played for the Pirates, Smith was referred to as "Zeke" in Logansport newspaper accounts throughout his lengthy career.

SOMERLOTT, John Wesley ("Jock," "Long John")

Born: October 26, 1882, Flint. **Died:** April 21, 1965, Butler.
Height: 6-0. **Weight:** 160. **Batted:** right. **Threw:** right.
Debut: September 19, 1910. **Final game:** May 25, 1911.
Positions, teams, years: first base, Washington (AL) 1910–1911.
Games: 29. **At-bats:** 103. **Home runs:** 0. **Average:** .204.

A popular figure in Indiana's Steuben County, **Jack Somerlott** once bought out his own contract for two cents.

Somerlott attended elementary school in Angola. In 1904 he joined an amateur team in Ligonier called the Meyers Earth Sellers. He was playing for a semi-pro Fort Wayne outfit in 1905 when friction developed between him and player-manager Jack Hardy, the team's catcher. "Tell you what I'll do, Jack," Somerlott told Hardy. "I'll give you every cent I've got for my release." Hardy agreed and, according to a 1910 *Washington Post* article, Somerlott "frisked his clothing, and allowed the manager to do the same, and the total output was two pennies. He handed the cash to Hardy and got his release."

In 1906 Somerlott's professional career began as a shortstop-third baseman at Winnipeg, Manitoba (Northern-Copper Country). In 1907 he played for pennant-winning Tecumseh (Southern Michigan), where he switched to first base in 1908. He spent the next two seasons with Terre Haute (Central) and in July 1910 Washington purchased his contract. He batted .222 in 16 games for the Senators.

Due to a severe eye infection, Somerlott reported late to Washington's 1911 spring camp. He wound up batting .175 in 13 games before the Senators returned him to Terre Haute in

June. By the end of the year he was Terre Haute's acting manager. He spent three more seasons in organized ball with teams in Evansville (Kitty), Troy (New York State), and Pittsfield, Mass. (Eastern).

Returning to Indiana after the 1914 season, Somerlott began farming in Steuben County, where he was known as "Mr. Baseball." Starting in 1922, he spent four years as player-manager for Angola's town team. He managed Fort Wayne's Lincoln Life ballclub in 1927.

Somerlott sold his farm in 1937 and purchased a business in Bronson, Mich., which he operated until retirement in 1947. In 1968 he was inducted into the Northeast Indiana Baseball Association Hall of Fame.

SPEECE, Byron Franklin ("Lord Byron")

Born: January 6, 1897, West Baden Springs. **Died:** September 29, 1974, Elgin, Oregon.
Height: 5'11". **Weight:** 170. **Batted:** right. **Threw:** right.
Debut: April 21, 1924. **Final game:** July 10, 1930.
Positions, teams, years: pitcher, Washington (AL) 1924, Cleveland (AL) 1925–1926, Philadelphia (NL) 1930.
Games: 62. **Innings pitched:** 167.1. **Won/Lost:** 5–6. **Earned run average:** 4.73.

By Speece's 23-year professional career includes 246 victories, all but five of them in the minor leagues. Using an accentuated underhand delivery, he pitched for a World Series winner, two Junior World Series champions, and the first-place team in a national semi-pro tournament.

The son of a farmer, Speece played high school baseball and football in West Baden Springs, and spent part of his youth and early manhood in Norfolk, Neb. His baseball career was delayed twice, first by World War I, when he served in the army and played for a regimental baseball team. Pitching for a Nebraska semi-pro team in 1920, he suffered an elbow ligament injury and sat out the 1921 season.

Speece broke into organized ball in 1922, leading Norfolk (Nebraska State) to a pennant with a 14–9 record. The Washington Senators obtained him after a 26–14 year at Omaha, Neb. (Western), in 1923. As a 27-year-old rookie in 1924 he went 2–1 with a 2.67 ERA in 21 games for Washington, all but one in relief. The Senators bested the New York Giants in a seven-game World Series, with Speece making a relief appearance in Game Three, a 6–4 loss at the Polo Grounds.

Prior to 1925, Washington sent Speece and rookie outfielder Carr Smith to Cleveland for 35-year-old right-hander Stan Coveleski, a four-time 20-game winner who had slipped to 15–16 for the Indians in 1924. Coveleski rebounded in 1925 with 20 wins for Washington and a league-leading 2.84 ERA.

Speece went 3–5 for the Indians in 1925, and Cleveland dispatched him to Indianapolis (American Association) in early May 1926. He went 17–10 for Indianapolis that summer, and Toledo acquired him in 1927. The Mud Hens finished first in the American Association, giving Casey Stengel the first pennant of his lengthy managerial career. Toledo went on to beat Buffalo (International) in the Junior World Series, five games to one. In Game Four, Speece got the win with four and two-thirds innings of scoreless relief work.

In 1928 Speece played for another Junior World Series winner. He went to Spring Training that year with the Pittsburgh Pirates, who sent him to Indianapolis before the season began. He went 12–10 in a second tour of duty for Indianapolis, which won the pennant and defeated Rochester in post-season play.

Speece had a 9–2 record for Indianapolis in 1929, and the Philadelphia Phillies drafted him for 1930. He compiled a 13.05 ERA with no decisions for the last-place Phillies, finishing the year with Newark, N.J. (International).

Although he never returned to the majors, Speece's career was far from over. Newark sent him to Nashville, Tenn. (Southern Association), in 1932, where he played for all or parts of seven seasons. He won 22 games in 1934 and again in 1936.

Released by Nashville after two contests in 1938, Speece joined the semi-pro Bona Allen Shoemakers of Buford, Ga. That August, at the National Baseball Congress semi-pro tournament in Wichita, Kan., he led the Georgia squad to a national title and earned honors as the tourney's most valuable pitcher.

During his playing days, Speece continued

to make Indiana his winter home. By 1940 he was back in organized ball, this time for a six-year stint in the Pacific Coast League that started with Portland, Ore. Joining Seattle in 1943, he went 13–9 at age 46. In 1945, with most draft-eligible players in military service for World War II, the 48-year-old Speece was part of a Seattle pitching staff that included three other hurlers over the age of 40.

Speece retired after the 1945 season and remained in Portland. Working for a local timber company in 1951, he told the *Portland Oregonian*: "It's my ambition to pitch, and win, a ball game when I'm 60, and I won't have long to wait.… I'm piling lumber these days, and will say this: Playing baseball is a lot more fun."

An avid card player, hunter and fisherman, Speece took up golf in his youth and scored his first hole-in-one at age 69 in 1966. He eventually relocated to the eastern Oregon town of Elgin to be closer to family members. He died there at age 77.

SPLITTORFF Jr., Paul William ("Split")

Born: October 8, 1946, Evansville. **Died:** May 25, 2011, Blue Springs, Missouri.
Height: 6'3". **Weight:** 205. **Batted:** left. **Threw:** left.
Debut: September 23, 1970. **Final game:** June 26, 1984.
Positions, teams, years: pitcher, Kansas City (AL) 1970–1984.
Games: 429. **Innings pitched:** 2,554.2. **Won/Lost:** 166–143. **Earned run average:** 3.81.

A big, bespectacled, blond-haired left-handed hurler with a high leg kick, stylish **Paul Splittorff** was the first player drafted by the Kansas City Royals to reach the Major Leagues.

Splittorff's family left Indiana before his first birthday, settling in the Chicago area when he was in sixth grade. He played baseball and basketball at Arlington Heights (Ill.) High School, graduating in 1964, and went to Morningside College in Sioux City, Iowa. In 1967 he pitched for the gold medal-winning USA team at the Pan American Games in Winnipeg, Manitoba. In 1968 the Royals—who would join the big leagues as an expansion team the following year—took Splittorff in the 25th round of the June draft.

Splittorff spent 1968 at Corning, N.Y., where he tied for the New York-Penn League lead with 136 strikeouts. Pitching for Omaha, Neb. (American Association), in 1969 and 1970, he helped Kansas City's top farm club to successive pennants.

After two games with Kansas City at the end of the 1970 season, Splittorff opened the 1971 campaign with a 5–2, 1.48 record in eight games for Omaha. He rejoined the Royals at the end of May, moving into the starting rotation. Not a hard thrower, he changed speed on his mid–80 mph fastball, mixing in a slider, changeup and curve. In 1973 he threw the first pitch at Kauffman Stadium (then known as Royals Stadium), and compiled a 20–11 slate, becoming the first 20-game winner in Kansas City's big-league history.

Splittorff endured a lengthy slump that began in 1974, when he went 13–19. After opening 1975 with a 1–6 start, he was banished to the bullpen in May. Eventually, he returned to the rotation and won eight of his next 12 decisions. Against the first-place Oakland Athletics on August 3, after a one-out walk and an infield single, he retired 26 consecutive batters for a 5–0 victory. He finished the year with a 9–10 record and a 3.17 ERA.

Kansas City's Opening Day pitcher in 1974, 1976, and 1977, Splittorff gave the Royals their first post-season victory with a relief win over the New York Yankees in the second game of the 1976 ALCS. He went 11–8 that year despite missing all of August due to an injured finger on his pitching hand. He helped Kansas City to another post-season berth in 1977 with a 16–6 mark, leading the AL with a .727 percentage and throwing another one-hitter on September 2, this time a 3–0 victory against the Milwaukee Brewers. He started Game 1 of the ALCS against the Yankees and got the win, but again New York bested the Royals to reach the World Series. He was 19–13 in 1978, when the Royals lost to the Yanks in the ALCS for the third consecutive year.

Splittorff posted a 15–17 record in 1979 as Kansas City slipped to second in the AL West. In 1980 he rebounded with a 14–11 mark as the Royals won their division and finally overcame the Yankees in the ALCS. He saw no action against New York and made one appearance as a reliever in the Royals' six-game World Series loss to the Philadelphia Phillies. In the strike-shortened 1981 campaign, he went 5–5. After a 10–10 record in 1982, he led Kansas City with a 13–8 slate at age 36.

By the end of May 1983 Splittorff was out of the rotation with a 1–3 mark in a dozen games. He announced his retirement on July 1, ending his 15-year career with the most wins in franchise history. Splittorff, who earned a business degree, took a job at a radio station in Blue Springs, Mo., where he broadcast high school and college football and basketball games. He joined the Royals television network in 1989 and in 1996 he became a color commentator on the team's radio network.

Splittorff was elected to the NAIA, Kansas City Royals and Evansville Sports halls of fames. In 1992 Kansas City drafted Paul's son Jamie, a right-handed pitcher, out of Blue Springs High School. Jamie Splittorff opted to attend the University of Kansas, where he became a top starting pitcher. Three years later Minnesota made Jamie its 13th-round selection, and he pitched in the Twins organization from 1995 to 1997.

Hospitalized with oral cancer and melanoma in May 2011, Paul died at age 64. He was in his 24th season as a TV analyst for Fox Sports Kansas City. "He helped put the Kansas City Royals on the map and was such a great player for so many years," Hall of Fame third baseman George Brett, Splittorff's teammate from 1973 to 1984, told *ESPN.com*. "He wasn't a real boisterous guy in the clubhouse. He just went about his work quietly and let everybody else get the headlines."

SPURGEON, Fred ("Freddy")

Born: October 9, 1901, Wabash. **Died:** November 5, 1970, Kalamazoo, Michigan.
Height: 5-11. **Weight:** 160. **Batted:** right. **Threw:** right.
Debut: September 19, 1924. **Final game:** September 3, 1927.
Positions, teams, years: second base (250), third base (56), shortstop (3), Cleveland (AL) 1924–1927.
Games: 316. **At-bats:** 1,176. **Home runs:** 1. **Average:** .285.

Before Derek Jeter emerged as a star with the New York Yankees, **Fred Spurgeon** had a claim as the finest big league shortstop from Kalamazoo, Mich.

Spurgeon's family left Indiana shortly after his birth, and he was a baseball and football standout at Kalamazoo High School. He continued to play both sports at Kalamazoo College and later for Valparaiso University.

In 1923 Spurgeon joined Dubuque, Iowa (Mississippi Valley). Under the name Fred Jackson—possibly to maintain his college eligibility—he batted .320 with 32 stolen bases as Dubuque finished first.

Still using the Jackson pseudonym in 1924, Spurgeon batted .278 as the everyday shortstop for New Orleans (Southern), and Cleveland purchased his contract toward the end of the season. Going by his real name, he saw action in three September games with the Indians.

With future Hall of Famer Joe Sewell at shortstop, Spurgeon took part in 107 games in 1925, mostly at second and third base, and batted .287. Over the winter, he stayed in shape by playing professional basketball. In 1926 he took over at second base, teaming with Sewell to give the Indians a solid keystone combination. Spurgeon batted .295, leading AL second basemen with 181 hits as Cleveland finished three games behind the pennant-winning Yankees.

In 1927 Spurgeon slumped to .257 in 57 games, losing his starting role in May to Lou Fonseca. After the season, he suffered a fractured elbow in an automobile accident in Jackson, Mich. Improperly set, the elbow had to be broken again. There was concern Spurgeon wouldn't return to baseball. "It is a pity, because Spurgeon was heading toward a high class infielder until this happened," Cleveland catcher Luke Sewell, Joe's brother, told reporters.

After sitting out the 1928 season, Spurgeon joined Kansas City (American Association) in 1929. He batted .262 for the first-place Blues, who went on to beat Rochester, N.Y. (International), in the Junior World Series. Spurgeon remained in Kansas City until 1931, when he joined Little Rock, Ark. (Southern). He retired in 1932 after helping Springfield, Mo. (Western Association), to a pennant.

Spurgeon returned to Kalamazoo, where he worked as a sales representative for Gooderham & Worts, a Canadian distillery. A respected basketball and football referee, he umpired the second College World Series at Kalamazoo in 1948. He died after a long illness at age 69.

STAHL, Charles Sylvester ("Chick")

Born: January 10, 1873, Avilla. **Died:** March 28, 1907, West Baden Springs.
Height: 5-10. **Weight:** 160. **Batted:** left. **Threw:** left.
Debut: April 19, 1897. **Final game:** October 6, 1906.
Positions, teams, years: outfield (1,295), pitcher (1), Boston (NL) 1897–1900, Boston (AL) 1901–1906.
Games: 1,304. **At-bats:** 5,069. **Home runs:** 36. **Average:** .305.
Innings pitched: 2. **Won/Lost:** 0-0. **Earned run average:** 9.00.
Manager: Boston (AL), 1906 (14-26)

Just prior to the 1907 season **Chick Stahl**, the most popular Indiana athlete of his time, ended his managing career. Three days later, he ended his life.

Stahl grew up in Fort Wayne and played for the Pilseners, a local semi-pro team. He entered organized ball with Battle Creek (Michigan) in 1894. In 1895 he joined Roanoke (Virginia), going 8–11 and batting .311 as a pitcher-outfielder. The Boston Beaneaters (today's Atlanta Braves) acquired him after he batted .337 with a league-leading 130 runs for Buffalo, N.Y. (Eastern), in 1896.

Stahl hit .359 as a rookie in 1897 and .308 in 1898 as Boston won back-to-back pennants. After two more solid seasons (.351 in 1899, .295 in 1900), he moved across town to play center field for the Boston Somersets of the fledgling AL (who later became the Red Sox). Stahl batted .323 in 1902 but dropped to .279 in 1903, when he missed nearly half the season due to illness and injury.

Boston won the 1903 AL pennant and met Pittsburgh in the first modern World Series. Healthy in time for post-season play, Stahl hit .303 as Boston beat the Pirates five games to three in a best-of-nine matchup. Boston won another pennant in 1904, with Stahl batting .295 and leading the AL with 19 triples. The NL champion New York Giants, wary of Pittsburgh's fate the previous year, refused to take part in post-season play.

Boston's fortunes tumbled after the franchise was sold at the end of the 1904 season. Player-manager Jimmy Collins frequently clashed with the new ownership. After a fourth-place finish in 1905—when Stahl's average plummeted to .258—the new owner cut player salaries. Late in the 1906 season Collins resigned as manager, with Stahl replacing him on an interim basis. The team finished last with a 49–105 record, including 26 losses in 40 games under Stahl.

Stahl was offered the managerial post on a permanent basis during the off-season, but he refused to accept without the blessings of his friend Collins. In October there were hints that Stahl, a 33-year-old bachelor, might be getting married. "'Tis said that Chick contemplates matrimony," quipped *Sporting Life*. "'Bout time." The news surprised Stahl's teammates, who had heard Chick declare that he would never marry while he was still an active player. But on November 14, 1906, Stahl married Julia Harmon of Roxbury, Mass. Returning from their honeymoon, the newlyweds visited Jimmy Collins. Stahl wasn't anxious to take his friend's job, but eventually agreed to serve as player-manager for 1907.

Stahl's Red Sox began spring training in Little Rock, Ark., in early March. By month's end the Red Sox headed north, traveling by train and playing exhibition games along the way. Boston players confided to reporters that their skipper seemed prone to "fits of melancholy and despondency."

On March 25 in Louisville, Ky., Stahl abruptly resigned. The "manifold responsibilities" of managing, explained *The Sporting News*, had caused anxieties that affected Stahl's play on the field. Boston's exhibition schedule included exhibition games in Indianapolis and Fort Wayne, and his spirits seemed to lift when the team reached the West Baden Springs Hotel.

Stahl arose early on March 28, and after breakfast he and Jimmy Collins headed up to their adjoining rooms to dress for practice. While Collins was still getting ready, Stahl walked in, stayed briefly, and then went back to his own room. A few minutes later he returned and told Collins, "I don't feel right, Jimmy." Collins asked what was wrong and the dazed Stahl said he didn't know. When he laid down on Collins' bed and began writhing in pain, Collins called for the hotel physician.

Red Sox first baseman Bob Unglaub heard Collins' cries for help and rushed into the room. Unglaub noticed the smell of carbolic acid. The poison had scalded Stahl's mouth and throat, and was rapidly shutting down his lungs and blood flow. "Why did you do this, old man?" Unglaub asked. "Boys, I couldn't help it," Stahl managed to reply. "It drove me to it."

Within minutes Stahl was dead, a suicide at 34 years of age. His teammates were stunned. In Fort Wayne, Stahl's family was overwhelmed with grief. Julia Stahl, widowed after less than twenty weeks of marriage, left Massachusetts the following day for Indiana. On March 31, in the largest funeral Fort Wayne had ever seen, Stahl was buried in Lindenwood Cemetery.

Most newspaper accounts blamed Stahl's death on job pressures, but there may have been other contributing factors. Friends revealed that Stahl had talked about killing himself as far back as his semi-pro days in Fort Wayne. Others said Chick was trying to get Collins reinstated as manager, and when it didn't happen, he decided to take his own life.

In a 1986 magazine article, author Glenn Stout claimed that Stahl had an affair with a woman in 1906 who began threatening Stahl during Spring Training in 1907, telling him she was pregnant. "Her demands were simple," Stout wrote: "either Stahl would agree to marry her or she would tell the world about their expected child."

Still another supposition holds that Stahl saw his playing career drawing to a close and decided to call it quits on his own terms. Yet judging by his 1906 performance—he played 155 games, led AL outfielders with 344 putouts, batted .286, and homered in his final at-bat of the season—Chick was far from over the hill.

Stahl was elected to the Northeast Indiana Baseball Association Hall of Fame in 1965.

STETTER, Mitchel Blake

Born: January 16, 1981, Huntingburg. **Lives:** Huntingburg.

Height: 6'5". **Weight:** 215. **Bats:** left. **Throws:** left.
Debut: September 1, 2007. **Final game:** May 14, 2011.
Positions, teams, years: pitcher, Milwaukee (NL) 2007–2011.
Games: 132. **Innings pitched:** 86. **Won/Lost:** 8–2. **Earned run average:** 4.08.

Sidearm pitcher **Mitch Stetter** compiled a 7–4 record with an 0.85 ERA in 1999 as a senior at Huntington's Southridge High School. "Mitch was a fantastic leader," Southridge coach Dave Schank told the *Evansville Courier*. "He was a quarterback in football and the main guy on the basketball team."

At Indiana State University in 2000, Stetter went 10–1 to earn Missouri Valley Conference freshman player of the year honors. "No one really had recruited him. But I believed in him," ISU coach Bob Warn told *Terre Haute Tribune-Star* sportswriter Dennis Clark. "He was left-handed and could throw three pitches for strikes."

The Milwaukee Brewers took Stetter in the 16th round of the 2003 draft and his pro career began that summer in Helena, Mont. (Pioneer). He began pitching exclusively out of the bullpen in 2005 at Huntsville, Ala. (Southern), and spent 2006 with Nashville, Tenn. (Pacific Coast). Sidelined for two months in 2006 by shoulder tendinitis, he pitched for the Brewers' rookie Arizona League affiliate and for Huntsville before returning to Nashville.

Milwaukee brought up Stetter at the end of August 2007 as a left-handed relief specialist. His first big league appearance came just thirty-six days after his former Indiana State teammate, left-hander Joe Thatcher, made his Major League debut with the San Diego Padres.

Stetter divided 2008 between Nashville (3–3, 2.48) and Milwaukee (3–1, 3.20), and during the NLCS he saw action in three games against Philadelphia. He spent all of 2009 with the Brewers, appearing in 71 games with a 4–1 mark and a 3.60 ERA. He shuttled between Milwaukee and Nashville again in 2010, pitching in nine contests for the Brewers.

A left hip injury landed Stetter on the disabled list in May 2011, and eventually he underwent surgery to correct a labrum tear. Outrighted after the season by the Brewers, he spent 2012 with Huntsville and Nashville. The

Los Angeles Angels signed him to a minor league contract for 2013, when he had a 3–1 record and 4.01 ERA in 32 games with Salt Lake (Pacific Coast).

Stetter retired after 2013 and joined the Kansas City organization as a pitching coach. He spent 2014 at Northwest Arkansas (Texas), the Royals' Double-A affiliate.

STEWART, Asa ("Ace")

Born: February 14, 1869, Terre Haute. **Died:** April 17, 1912, Terre Haute.
Height: 5–10. **Weight:** 176. **Batted:** right. **Threw:** right.
Debut: April 18, 1895. **Final game:** August 17, 1895.
Positions, teams, years: second base, Chicago (NL) 1895.
Games: 97. **At-bats:** 365. **Home runs:** 8. **Average:** .241.

During a 19-year professional baseball career, **Ace Stewart** played in 16 different cities in eight states.

Stewart learned baseball from his father, a Civil War veteran, while growing up on a farm in Terre Haute. He played for pennant–winning teams in Terre Haute (Illinois-Indiana) in 1889 and Anderson (Indiana State) in 1890. After tours of duty in Oconto and Fond du Lac (Wisconsin State) in 1891, and Oshkosh, Wis. (Michigan-Wisconsin), in 1892, he played for another first-place club in Easton (Pennsylvania State) in 1893. That season he tied for the league lead with 10 home runs.

In 1894 with Sioux City, Iowa (Western), Stewart batted .317 with 22 homers. The Washington Senators, fighting to stay out of the NL basement, tried to purchase his contract in August. But Stewart refused to sign a Washington contract, and the following month he agreed to play for Cap Anson's Chicago Colts, who would later become the Cubs.

Stewart replaced Jiggs Parrott at second base in Chicago. He enjoyed early-season success, knocking in eight runs in a game against Philadelphia on May 20, 1895. Yet Anson soured on Stewart by the end of June when, according to the *Washington Post*: "The players claim that Anson has time and again humiliated Stewart … and they do not blame him for wanting to go elsewhere."

By August, Stewart was playing for Rockford, Ill. (Western Association), where he batted .397 in 15 games. In 1896 he began a four-year stay in Indianapolis (Western), which won pennants in 1897 and 1899. In 1900 he played for three teams: Terre Haute (Central), Indianapolis and Kansas City—two teams in the American League, which would declare itself a major circuit in 1901.

Stewart spent the next three seasons back in the Western League, playing for Omaha, Neb., from 1901 to 1903. He finished the 1903 campaign with Peoria, Ill. (Western). After starting 1904 with New Orleans (Southern), he was back in Terre Haute (Central) by season's end. He split 1905 between Terre Haute and Jackson, Miss. (Cotton States), where he became the player-manager. After managing Jackson to a third-place finish in 1906, he ended his career in 1907 with stops at Meridian and Columbus, Miss., of the Cotton States League.

After leaving baseball, Stewart returned to Terre Haute. He tended bar, served on the police force and worked in the Highland mills. He was 43 when he died.

Stewart's great-great nephew, Shelbyville resident Patrick Stewart, co-authored two books with W.C. Madden: *The Western League* and *The College World Series*.

STODDARD, Timothy Paul ("Bigfoot")
Indiana Baseball Hall of Fame, 2006.
Born: January 24, 1953, East Chicago. **Lives:** Rolling Meadows, Illinois.
Height: 6'7". **Weight:** 230. **Batted:** right. **Threw:** right.
Debut: September 7, 1975. **Final game:** July 9, 1989.
Positions, teams, years: pitcher, Chicago (AL) 1975, Baltimore (AL) 1978–1983, Chicago (NL) 1984, San Diego (NL) 1985–1986, New York (AL) 1986–1988, Cleveland (AL) 1989.
Games: 485. **Innings pitched:** 729.2. **Won/Lost:** 41–35. **Earned run average:** 3.95.

A three-sport standout in high school, **Tim Stoddard** starred for East Chicago Washington's undefeated 1971 IHSAA state championship basketball team, played quarterback for the football squad, and served as captain of the baseball team. Stoddard went on to pitch for North Carolina State University, helping the Wolfpack baseball team to three consecutive Atlantic Coast Conference crowns.

He was also a starter for the basketball team alongside future ABA and NBA star David Thompson. In 1974 the Wolfpack ended UCLA's seven-year run as NCAA basketball champions, upending the Bruins in the semifinals and beating Marquette in the title game.

The White Sox made Stoddard their second-round pick in the January 1975 draft. He made one appearance for Chicago that summer. Released by the White Sox in March 1977, he signed with Baltimore and joined the Orioles bullpen in 1978. Working mainly as a middle reliever in 1979, he had a 1.71 ERA as Baltimore won the AL pennant. Stoddard was the winning pitcher in Game Four, driving in a run with a single in his first trip to the plate as a big leaguer, but the Pirates went on to win the Series in seven games.

The Orioles won another pennant in 1983 and defeated the Philadelphia Phillies in a five-game World Series. Stoddard earned a championship ring, although he didn't get a chance to pitch.

Baltimore dealt Stoddard to Oakland in December 1983, and the following March the Athletics sent him to the Cubs. After a 10–6 season in Chicago, he became a free agent and signed with San Diego for 1985. On June 18, 1986, Stoddard hit a home run against San Francisco in what would be his final Major League at-bat. The following month, the Padres traded him to the Yankees. Released by New York in August 1988, he spent part of 1989 with the Cleveland Indians before ending his playing days.

In 1994 Northwestern University hired Stoddard as its pitching coach. The year before, he took a turn at acting in the film Rookie of the Year, portraying a burly Dodgers reliever named Tregoran. "I think it was typecasting," he deadpanned.

Stoddard is one of just two men who have appeared in both the NCAA Final Four and baseball's World Series. The other is Kenny Lofton, who was also born in East Chicago and attended East Chicago Washington High School. Lofton was the University of Arizona's sixth man in the 1988 college basketball tournament. An outfielder, Lofton played in the 1995 World Series for Cleveland and in the 1992 Fall Classic for San Francisco.

In 2006 Stoddard went into the Indiana Baseball Hall of Fame. He was inducted into the Indiana Basketball Hall of Fame in 2011.

STOREN, Drew Patrick

Born: August 11, 1987, Indianapolis. **Lives:** Melbourne, Florida.
Height: 6'1". **Weight:** 195. **Bats:** both. **Throws:** right.
Debut: May 17, 2010.
Positions, teams, years: pitcher, Washington (NL) 2010–2014.
Games: 297. **Innings pitched:** 279. **Won/Lost:** 19–11. **Earned run average:** 2.94.

A first-round draft pick in 2009, **Drew Storen** reached the Major Leagues during his second pro season.

Storen played for Brownsburg Little League's state championship team in 2001, and from 2004 to 2007 he starred at Brownsburg High School. As a sophomore in 2005, he teamed with future big league pitcher Lance Lynn to lead undefeated Brownsburg (35–0) to an IHSAA Class 4A title.

The New York Yankees took Storen in the 34th round of the 2007 draft, but instead he enrolled at Stanford University. In 2008, his freshman year, he was the closer for the Cardinal team that reached the College World Series. As a draft-eligible sophomore in 2008 he went 7–1 with a 3.80 ERA. That June, the Washington Nationals had the No. 1 pick in the draft and took San Diego State University right-hander Stephen Strasburg. Washington made Storen the 10th pick overall, and this time he signed.

Storen divided the summer between low Class A Hagerstown, Md. (South Atlantic), high Class A Potomac (Carolina) and Class AA Harrisburg, Pa. (Eastern), for a combined 2–1 record with 11 saves and a 1.95 ERA. He joined the Nationals in May 2010 and supplanted Matt Capps as Washington's closer. In 2011 he went 6–3 with a 2.75 ERA and compiled 43 saves—the second highest total in franchise history.

In 2012 Storen missed the first three-and-a-half months of the season after surgery for bone chips in his elbow. He returned in July and shared the closer role with Tyler Clippard as Washington went on to win the NL East. In the NLDS the Nationals faced the St. Louis Cardinals. Storen made four relief appearances, earning a save in Game One and getting the win in Game Four (Lance Lynn, Storen's former high school teammate, took the loss). In the ninth inning of Game Five, the Cardinals scored four times to wipe out a 7–5 deficit with Storen taking the loss. "It's the best job when you're good at it," he told reporters. "It's the worst job when you fail."

Storen moved to a middle relief role in 2013, after the Nationals signed free agent Rafael Soriano and made him their closer. In late July, Storen was optioned to Syracuse (International). "We felt that he was struggling with his mechanics with his tempo, with the delivery, with his arm slot," Nationals general manager Mike Russo told the *Washington Post*. Recalled in mid–August, he finished with 4–2 record and 4.52 ERA. "I ended last season on a good note and that was key," he told Mark Ambrogi of the *Indianapolis Star*.

In 2014 the Nationals had one of baseball's best bullpens, with Storen and Clippard as setup men and Soriano as closer. When Soriano faltered after the All-Star break, Storen took over as closer and finished with 11 saves, a 2–1 record and 1.12 ERA. Washington finished first in the NL East, and met San Francisco in the NLDS. He was charged with a blown save in the Giants' 2–1, 18-inning win in Game Two. San Francisco beat Washington and went on to win the World Series.

Storen, who once served briefly as a Montreal Expos batboy, also played basketball in high school. From 2001 to 2007 he played for the Indiana Bulls traveling baseball squad. He continued to attend Stanford in the off-season, majoring in product design. His father, Mark Patrick, was the sports anchor for Indianapolis CBS affiliate WISH TV from 1990 to 1998 and later served as co-host of Baseball This Morning on MLB Network Radio.

STRINCEVICH, Nicholas ("Jumbo")

Born: March 1, 1915, Gary. **Died:** November 11, 2011, Valparaiso.
Height: 6'1". **Weight:** 180. **Batted:** right. **Threw:** right.
Debut: April 23, 1940. **Final game:** June 11, 1948.
Positions, teams, years: pitcher, Boston (NL) 1940–1941, Pittsburgh (NL) 1941–1942, 1944–1948, Philadelphia (NL) 1948.
Games: 203. **Innings pitched:** 889.2. **Won/Lost:** 46–49. **Earned run average:** 4.05.

The son of a Serbian immigrant steelworker, sidearm hurler **Nick Strincevich** was the first player from Gary to reach the Major Leagues.

Strincevich (pronounced "strink-a-vitch"), who left Lew Wallace High School to work in the steel mills, was pitching for an industrial league team in 1935 when the New York Yankees signed him. Homesick after four games with Akron, Ohio (Middle Atlantic), he returned to his mill job in Gary.

Back in baseball in 1936, Strincevich pitched for Yankee farm clubs in Butler (Pennsylvania State Association), Norfolk, Va. (Piedmont), and Newark, N.J. (International), through 1939, winning 32 games against 22 losses. In 1938 he had an 11–4 slate for pennant-winning Newark.

In 1939 New York sent Strincevich to Sacramento, Calif. (Pacific Coast), and he finished the year with a combined 3–8 slate. Hampered by arm problems for part of the year, he pitched a five-hit shutout against San Francisco in the first round of the PCL playoffs.

Strincevich, who continued to work in Gary's steel mills during the off-season, was selected by the Boston Braves in the 1939 Rule 5 draft. Alternating between the bullpen and the starting rotation that year, he went 4–8 for the Braves with a 5.53 ERA. Boston traded him to Pittsburgh in May 1941, and the Pirates optioned him to Milwaukee from the end of July to the end of August. He opened the 1942 season with Pittsburgh, and despite a 2.82 ERA in seven games, the Pirates sent him to Toronto (International). In 1942 he went 12–10 for Toronto, and his 15–7 record in 1943 helped the Maple Leafs to a first-place finish.

Exempt from World War II military service due to gastric ulcers, Strincevich rejoined Pittsburgh in 1944 and went 14–7. He posted a 16–10 record for the Pirates in 1945. In 1946 he lost his first seven decisions but managed to finish with a 10–15 record and a 3.58 ERA. He appeared in 32 games in 1947, mostly in relief, and went 1–6. The city of Gary honored Strincevich on August 31 at Chicago's Wrigley Field, presenting him with a new Pontiac.

In May 1948 Pittsburgh sent Strincevich to the Phillies. Philadelphia shipped him to Toronto in June to make room for future Hall of Famer Robin Roberts, who inherited Strincevich's roster spot, his locker and his uniform number.

After ending his baseball career with Toronto in 1950, Strincevich worked as a pressman at the Budd automotive stamping plant in Gary, retiring in 1980 as a safety inspector. One of the four original members of Gary's sports hall of fame, he lived in Portage for many years and spent his final days at an assisted living facility in Valparaiso.

Strincevich's father Luka was nicknamed "Jumbo" and, Nick explained: "Anytime friends would see my father they'd call him 'Jumbo.' Then they would take to calling me 'Little Jumbo.' I wasn't that big."

Joe Strincevich, Nick's younger brother, pitched in the minor leagues from 1941 to 1946.

STULTS, Eric William

Born: December 9, 1979, Plymouth. **Lives:** Middlebury.
Height: 6'2". **Weight:** 220. **Bats:** left. **Throws:** left.
Debut: September 5, 2006.
Positions, teams, years: pitcher, Los Angeles (NL) 2006–2009, Colorado (NL) 2011, Chicago (AL) 2012, San Diego (NL) 2012–2014.
Games: 126. **Innings pitched:** 635.2. **Won/Lost:** 35–43 **Earned run average:** 4.12.

Eric Stults grew up on a 1,200 acre farm in northern Indiana and went to Argos High School before entering Bethel College, an evangelical Christian school in Mishawaka. A member of Bethel's basketball team, Stults was also a standout pitcher and center fielder for the baseball squad. In 2002 his 10–1 record helped the Pilots win the National Christian Collegiate Athletic Association Division I baseball crown.

The Los Angeles Dodgers took Stults in the 15th round of the 2002 draft. He joined Great Falls, Mont. (Pioneer), that summer, and after a stint with Vero Beach (Florida State) he finished the year with Double-A Jacksonville, Fla. (Southern). He reached the Triple-A level with Las Vegas, Nev. (Pacific Coast), in 2005. In 2006 he went 10–11 for Las Vegas to earn a promotion to Los Angeles.

Stults shuttled between the Dodgers and the minors through 2009, compiling an 8–10 record. Prior to 2010, the Dodgers sold his contract to the Hiroshima Toyo Carp of Japan's Central League. While there were differences in the style of play, the year in Japan was "a blessing in disguise," said Stults. "My family got to travel with me on away games, which does not happen in American baseball," he told Bruce Darnell of Athletes in Action.

After a 6–10 season with Hiroshima, Stults signed with the Colorado Rockies for 2011. In 52 games at Colorado Springs (Pacific Coast)—all but 16 in relief—he went 4–4 with a 4.63 ERA. He also made six relief appearances for the Rockies.

Cut loose by Colorado after the season, Stults began the 2012 season with Charlotte, N.C. (International), the top farm club of the White Sox. Summoned to Chicago in May, he drew his release after two appearances and a 2.70 ERA. The San Diego Padres, their pitching staff ravaged by injuries, claimed him. Stults suffered a back strain and missed seven weeks, but finished the year with an 8–3 mark and a 2.92 ERA in 18 games.

Stults remained in San Diego's starting rotation for the next two years. He pitched more than 100 innings for the first time in 2013, going 11–13 with a 3.93 ERA. He helped his own cause on April 15, belting a three-run homer in a 6–3 win over the Dodgers. He struggled in 2014, finishing with an 8–17, 4.30 slate, and after the season the Padres designated him for assignment.

STURGEON, Robert Harwood ("Sturge")

Born: August 6, 1919, Clinton. **Died:** March 10, 2007, San Dimas, California.
Height: 6'0". **Weight:** 175. **Batted:** right. **Threw:** right.
Debut: April 16, 1940. **Final game:** October 3, 1948.
Positions, teams, years: shortstop (283), second base (102), third base (12), Chicago (NL) 1940–1942, 1946–1947, Boston (NL) 1948.
Games: 420. **At-bats:** 1,220. **Home runs:** 1. **Average:** .257.

Bobby Sturgeon was four years old when his family left Indiana for California, where he played high school baseball and basketball.

He was the shortstop for the Long Beach Polytechnic baseball squad that won the 1936 Southern California high school title. He also starred for the North Long Beach American Legion team.

In 1937 Sturgeon entered organized ball, sparking Albuquerque, N.M., to an Arizona-Texas League pennant with a .298 average. In 1938 he batted .297 for Columbus, Ohio, ranking among the top American Association shortstops like Pee Wee Reese of Louisville and Kansas City's Phil Rizzuto.

Sturgeon was the property of the St. Louis Cardinals when the Cubs acquired him for the 1940 season. After a seven-game stint, Chicago assigned him to Jersey City (International) for the rest of 1940. In 1941 the Cubs began the season with an all-rookie combination of Lou Stringer at second base and Sturgeon at short. Sturgeon batted .245 in 129 games.

In 1942, when he hit .247 in 63 contests, Sturgeon lost the shortstop post to Lennie Merullo. He spent the next three years in the U.S. Navy and missed the Cubs' pennant-winning 1945 season. Discharged prior to 1946, he batted .296 that year in 100 games for Chicago as a shortstop and second baseman.

After a .254 average in 87 games in 1947, the Cubs traded Sturgeon to the Boston Braves. He hit .218 for the pennant-winning Braves in 1948, but saw no action in the World Series as Boston lost in six games to the Cleveland Indians. Gone from the big leagues after '48, he continued to play in the minors through 1955. He was a player-manager at Victoria, B.C. (Western International), in 1951; Ventura (California) in 1952, and Edmonton, Alb. (Western International), in 1953–1954.

Sturgeon retired from baseball and worked as the recreation director for an airplane assembly plant in Long Beach, eventually becoming sports director for McDonnell Douglas.

SUMMERS, Oren Edgar ("Kickapoo Ed," "Chief")

Born: December 5, 1884, Ladoga. **Died:** May 12, 1953, Indianapolis.
Height: 6'2". **Weight:** 180. **Batted:** both. **Threw:** right.
Debut: April 16, 1908. **Final game:** June 1, 1912.
Positions, teams, years: pitcher, Detroit (AL) 1908–1912.
Games: 138. **Innings pitched:** 999. **Won/Lost:** 68–45. **Earned run average:** 2.42.

While he never played baseball for the Little Giants, knuckleball specialist **Eddie Summers** was the first Wabash College alumnus to play Major League baseball.

An all-around athlete, Summers was a member of the baseball, football and track teams at Ladoga High School. He entered Wabash in the winter term of 1903–1904, but before the college season began he left to play pro ball for Peoria, Ill. (Central). After stops at Springfield, Ill. (Central), in 1905, Grand Rapids, Mich. (Central), in 1906, and Indianapolis (American Association) in 1907, the Detroit Tigers acquired him for the 1908 season.

As a 23-year-old rookie, Summers turned in a brilliant 24–12 record and 1.64 ERA to help the Tigers win the 1908 AL pennant. In a doubleheader on September 25 he pitched back-to-back complete-game victories over the Philadelphia Athletics. The second game was a 10-inning two-hitter. During Detroit's five-game World Series loss to the Chicago Cubs, he lost Game One in relief and started and lost Game Four.

Detroit won a second consecutive flag in 1909 with Summers contributing a 19–9, 2.24 record. On July 16 in Washington he allowed just seven hits over 18 innings in a scoreless 0–0 tie with the Senators that was called due to darkness. He again lost twice in the World Series, starting the third and fifth contests as the Pittsburgh Pirates downed the Tigers in seven games.

In the spring of 1910 Summers went to Hot Springs, Ark., hoping to heal a knee injured by a line drive in 1908. "The bad knee, which bothered him all of last season, and half of 1908, has refused to mend," claimed the *Washington Post*.

Bothered by rheumatism throughout the 1910 season, Summers went 13–12 with a 2.53 ERA. On September 17 against the Philadelphia Athletics, he became the first 20th Century pitcher to hit two home runs in a single game. They were the only homers of his career.

Summers left Detroit's Spring Training camp in 1911 with cholera-like symptoms. Bothered by severe rheumatism, he finished the year with an 11–11, 3.66 slate. In March 1912 he suffered a shoulder injury in a train accident that limited him to a 1–1 record and a 4.86 ERA in three games. Detroit released him that July.

After several comeback attempts with Providence, R.I. (International), Summers retired in 1914 and returned to Indiana. He signed on to mentor the Wabash baseball team in 1916 while two-sport coach Paul Sheeks conducted spring football practice.

Summers eventually settled in Indianapolis and began a 32-year welding career with the Prest-O-Lite Factory in Speedway. He retired in 1950 and died at 68 after suffering a paralytic attack.

There is no evidence that Summers' ancestry was Native American. His nickname "Kickapoo" apparently stems from the name of the tribe that inhabited western Indiana.

SWARTZEL, Park B.
Born: November 21, 1865, Knightstown. **Died:** January 3, 1940, Los Angeles, California.
Height: 5'10". **Weight:** 150. **Batted:** right. **Threw:** right.
Debut: April 17, 1889. **Final game:** October 14, 1889.
Positions, teams, years: pitcher (48), outfield (4), Kansas City (American Association) 1889.
Games: 51. **Innings pitched:** 410.1. **Won/Lost:** 19–27. **Earned run average:** 4.32.
At-bats: 198. **Home runs:** 0. **Average:** .144.

Including his one year as a big leaguer, **Park Swartzel** spent four of his seven pro baseball seasons in Kansas City.

The handsome, mustachioed Swartzel broke in with Leavenworth, Kan. (Western), in 1886 and was soon considered one of the league's best hurlers. After the Leavenworth club disbanded in July 1887, he joined Lincoln, Neb. (Western), and finished the year with a league-leading 205 strikeouts. "He exercises more headwork, is cool and collected and combines wonderful control of the ball with good speed," *The Sporting News* reported in August 1887.

Pitching for the Kansas City Blues (Western Association) in 1888, Swartzel won a 16–1 no-hitter against St. Paul. He was still pitching for Kansas City in 1889, but this time for the Cowboys, who were in their second year as a Major League team in the American Association. One of four rookies on the Cowboy roster (including Billy Hamilton, who would be elected to the Hall of Fame in 1961), Swartzel went 19–27 in his lone big league campaign.

He was back in the minors with the Kansas City Blues for the next two seasons. Swartzel divided the 1892 campaign between Minneapolis (Western) and Rochester, N.Y. (Eastern), before leaving baseball.

Swartzel made his off-season home in the eastern Indiana town of Dublin for many years. After leaving baseball, he worked as the head clerk in a Cambridge City department store. In the fall of 1900 he was charged with misappropriating the store's funds and absconding with the money. He eventually returned the cash and moved to Los Angeles, where he spent 24 years as a price clerk in a retail hardware store.

Swartzel retired in 1930. The day after Christmas in 1939 he came down with influenza, which developed into bronchial pneumonia. He died eight days later at age 74.

TAYLOR, Arlas Walter ("Lefty," "Foxy")
Born: March 16, 1896, Warrick County. **Died:** September 10, 1958, Dade City, Florida.
Height: 5'11". **Weight:** unknown. **Batted:** right. **Threw:** left.
Debut: September 15, 1921. **Final game:** September 15, 1921.
Positions, teams, years: pitcher, Philadelphia (AL) 1921.
Games: 1. **Innings pitched:** 2. **Won/Lost:** 0–1. **Earned run average:** 22.50.

Toward the end of the 1921 season, Philadelphia Athletics manager Connie Mack gave spitball hurler **Foxy Taylor** a start in the first game of a doubleheader with visiting Cleveland. The first-place Indians led 5–2 after two innings en route to a 17–3 triumph. When Lena Styles batted for Taylor in the bottom of the second, Foxy's Major League career ended.

Taylor's one-game statistics included seven hits, a pair of walks, one strikeout, five runs (all earned) and the loss. The lone batter he fanned, Cleveland shortstop Joe Sewell, struck out 17 times that season. In 8,333 career plate appearances, Sewell whiffed just 114 times, making him the toughest batter in history to strike out.

Taylor served overseas with the U.S. Army during World War I. After the war he starred for the semi-pro John Millett Colonials of Hammond, Ind. With independent Harrisburg, Ill., in 1920 he pitched 50 and one-third consecutive innings without allowing a run.

After his brief stint with the Athletics, Taylor played for industrial teams in Wisconsin. In 1924 he returned to organized ball as a pitcher-outfielder for Danville, Ill. (Three-I), batting .310 and with a 4–4 record. He went 3–3 for Danville in 1925, his final season in the professional ranks.

Taylor continued to play for semi-pro teams. Returning to Hammond in 1930, he worked as a salesman for a sporting goods store while playing the outfield for a club in Aurora, Ill. He later worked as a district sales manager for a rubber company.

In 1950 Taylor purchased a home near Dade City, Fla. He was working as a real estate salesman when he suffered a heart attack and died at age 62.

TAYLOR, Benjamin Harrison

Born: April 2, 1889, Paoli. **Died:** November 3, 1946, Martin County.
Height: 5'11". **Weight:** 163. **Batted:** right. **Threw:** right.
Debut: June 28, 1912. **Final game:** July, 4, 1912.
Positions, teams, years: pitcher, Cincinnati (NL) 1912.
Games: 2. **Innings pitched:** 5.2. **Won/Lost:** 0–0. **Earned run average:** 3.18.

Ben Taylor was born less than a month after Indianapolis resident Benjamin Harrison took office as the 23rd U.S. president. Taylor, whose ancestry was Dutch and American Indian, attended elementary school in Orleans and played for amateur teams in southern Indiana.

With Saginaw (Southern Michigan) in 1910, Taylor went 6–13 in 25 games before typhoid fever ended his season. Back with Saginaw for the start of 1911, he jumped the club in June and finished the year pitching for independent teams, including the Bedford Champs. Bedford's manager was former big leaguer Bob Wicker, a native of Bono, Ind.

Taylor opened the 1912 campaign with the Cincinnati Pippins of the independent United States League, which went out of business on June 14. Two weeks later he made his big league debut with the Cincinnati Reds, who released him in mid–July. He spent 1913 pitching in the independent Federal League. He started the year with Covington, Ky., before joining the Indianapolis Hoosiers, who went on to win the pennant.

In 1914 the Federal League gained status as a third major circuit, but by then Taylor was gone from organized ball. He settled in Bedford, where he worked as an interior decorator. He was active in local boxing programs while playing for semi-pro baseball teams. Pitching for the Orleans Giants on July 6, 1913, he notched 17 strikeouts in a 3–0 no-hitter against the Bedford Welterweights.

While driving with his wife and her parents one Sunday evening, Taylor's automobile overturned not far from Shoals. All survived except for Taylor, who suffered a broken neck and died at age 57.

TAYLOR, James Harry

Born: May 20, 1919, East Glenn. **Died:** November 5, 2000, Terre Haute.
Height: 6'1". **Weight:** 175. **Batted:** right. **Threw:** right.
Debut: September 22, 1946. **Final game:** May 4, 1952.
Positions, teams, years: pitcher, Brooklyn (NL) 1946–1948, Boston (AL) 1950–1952.
Games: 90. **Innings pitched:** 357.2. **Won/Lost:** 19–21. **Earned run average:** 4.10.

Harry Taylor, a graduate of Fayetteville High School in southern Indiana, pitched in one of the most memorable World Series games in the 1947 Fall Classic. Taylor starred for Fisher-Otto Auto Sales club of Terre Haute before launching his professional career in 1938 with Tallahassee, Fla. (Georgia-Florida League).

After three mediocre minor league seasons, Taylor entered the army in 1942. He spent the next four and a half years in the service, mostly in the Pacific Theater with the 38th Infantry Division. He returned to organized ball with St. Paul in 1946, winning 15 games for a share of the American Association lead.

Taylor joined the Brooklyn Dodgers at the end of the year and pitched in four contests.

In 1947 he joined Brooklyn's starting rotation as a 28-year-old rookie. He went 10–5 for the pennant-winning Dodgers, whose rookie first baseman was Jackie Robinson, the first African-American Major Leaguer of the 20th Century. "It was difficult being on the team with the first black player," Taylor recalled. "Some of the players resented Robinson, especially at first. But then most of the Dodgers accepted him and he became just one of the boys."

A sore arm limited Taylor to just two games after August 13, but he started Game Four of the 1947 World Series against the New York Yankees. He faced four batters, departing after a first-inning, bases-loaded walk to Joe DiMaggio. The Dodgers scored in the bottom of the fifth without hitting safely. Heading into the bottom of the ninth, New York led 2–1 and Yankee pitcher Floyd Bevens hadn't given up a hit. After Bevens walked two batters, pinch-hitter Cookie Lavagetto cracked a two-out double that broke up the no-hitter and gave Brooklyn a 3–2 victory.

Stricken with appendicitis in 1948, Taylor went 2–7 in 17 games for Brooklyn. He finished the year with St. Paul and spent all of 1949 with the Saints. He had a 13–9 record for St. Paul in September 1950 when Brooklyn traded him to the Boston Red Sox. In his AL debut, Taylor pitched a two-hit shutout against the Philadelphia Athletics. He ended the year with a 2–0 record and a 1.42 ERA.

Taylor went 4–9 in 31 games for Boston in 1951 and appeared in two games in 1952 before the Red Sox shipped him to Louisville (American Association). Taylor retired after the '52 season, but made a brief comeback in 1955 with Paris, Ill. (Mississippi-Ohio Valley), before returning to Indiana to take over his father-in-law's farm near Terre Haute.

Later, Taylor worked as a millwright for the Visqueen and Bemis companies in Terre Haute before becoming a maintenance man at St. Mary-of-the-Woods College. He was 81 years old at the time of his death.

TERRELL, Charles Walter
Indiana Baseball Hall of Fame, 2005.
Born: May 11, 1958, Jeffersonville. **Lives:** Erlanger, Kentucky.

Height: 6'2". **Weight:** 205. **Batted:** left. **Threw:** right.
Debut: September 18, 1982. **Final game:** October 2, 1992.
Positions, teams, years: pitcher, New York (NL) 1982–1984, Detroit (AL) 1985–1988, San Diego (NL) 1989, New York (AL) 1989, Pittsburgh (NL) 1990, Detroit (AL) 1990–1992.
Games: 321. **Innings pitched:** 1,986.2. **Won/Lost:** 111–124. **Earned run average:** 4.22.

A durable starting pitcher, **Walt Terrell** once came within an out of pitching a no-hit game. He was also a good hitter who once clubbed two home runs in a single contest.

Terrell was a three-sport athlete at Jeffersonville High School and later at Morehead State University. His college coach, former big league pitcher Steve Hamilton, remembered Terrell as "a good athlete—point guard in basketball, a safety and tight end, an unusual combination, in football. He was a good competitor."

Drafted by the Texas Rangers in 1980, Terrell's 15 wins in 1981 for Tulsa, Okla., tied for the Texas League lead. Texas dealt him to the New York Mets in April 1982 and that September he pitched in his first big league game. A 10–1 record at Tidewater (International) in 1983 earned him a midseason promotion to the Mets rotation. In a 4–1 win over the Cubs on August 6 he homered twice off future Hall of Famer Ferguson Jenkins.

Terrell went 8–8 with a 3.57 ERA for New York in 1983. After an 11–12, 3.52 slate in 1984, the Mets traded him to Detroit. He was a mainstay in the Tigers pitching staff from 1985 to 1988. He posted win-loss records of 15–10, 15–12 and 17–10 during his first three seasons in the Motor City.

On August 20, 1986, Terrell was within one out of a no-hitter against the Angels when Wally Joyner doubled. He settled for a 3–0 one-hitter. Five days later, in a game with Oakland, he served up the first of Mark McGwire's 583 career home runs.

In 1987 Terrell helped Detroit to the LCS against Minnesota. After a 7–16, 3.97 showing in 1988, the Tigers sent him to San Diego. He had a 5–13 slate in 19 starts when the Padres traded him to the Yankees. He went 6–5 in 13 starts for New York in 1989 and signed with Pittsburgh as a free agent for 1990. Released by the Pirates in July 1990, he rejoined Detroit and won six of 10 decisions for the Tigers. He went 12–14 in 1991 and 7–10 in 1992 before leaving baseball.

Returning to Kentucky, Terrell worked for Pepsi Cola and served as baseball coach at St. Henry District High School in Erlanger, Ky. In 1995 he became head coach of the Kentucky Colonels travel team.

Terrell was elected to the Indiana Baseball Hall of Fame in 2005.

TERRY, Lancelot Yank

Born: Lancelot Terry, February 11, 1911, Huron.
Died: November 4, 1979, Bloomington.
Height: 6'1". **Weight:** 180. **Batted:** right. **Threw:** right.
Debut: August 3, 1940. **Final game:** July 20, 1945.
Positions, teams, years: pitcher, Boston (AL) 1940, 1942–1945.
Games: 93. **Innings pitched:** 457.1. **Won/Lost:** 20–28. **Earned run average:** 4.09.

The son of schoolteacher and minor league pitcher George Terry, **Yank Terry** spent his five-year big league career with the Boston Red Sox.

Terry was a member of the baseball, basketball and track squads at Bedford High School. Recruited by the University of Notre Dame, he left college after his father's death in 1931 and played for semi-pro teams in Kentucky and Indiana before joining Fort Wayne (Central) in 1934.

A 16–12 record at Terre Haute (Three I) in 1935 earned Terry a promotion to Louisville (American Association) for 1936. In 1938 he pitched a seven-inning, 3–0 no-hitter against Columbus, Ohio, but his won-loss record over five seasons with Louisville was an unimpressive 26–36.

Joining the Red Sox late in July 1940, Terry went 1–0 with a 9.00 ERA in four contests. He opened the 1941 season with San Diego (Pacific Coast) and lost six of his first 11 decisions. Cedric Durst, Terry's manager, suggested he conceal his delivery by turning his back toward batters during his windup. The advice worked wonders. "They'd get their bats around just too late or the ball would be in the catcher's glove when they started to swing," said Terry, who won 21 of his next 23 decisions. He led the league with 26 wins, 172 strikeouts and a 2.31 ERA, and won league MVP honors to earn another shot with Boston for 1942.

Exempt from World War II military service due to a heart ailment, Terry spent the next four seasons with the Red Sox. He was Boston's Opening Day starter in 1944, and that October the town of Bedford staged "Yank Terry Day" in his honor.

Before the end of the 1945 season, the Red Sox returned Terry to Louisville. His career ended the following year after a 12–15, 2.86 slate for Los Angeles (PCL). Returning to Bedford, he owned and operated Yank's Sportsman Store and later worked at the Elks Club. He died of cancer at a Bloomington hospital at the age of 68.

As a youngster, Terry didn't like his given name. According to his wife, Wilma, several younger playmates couldn't pronounce Lancelot and called him "Yankset." That led to the nickname "Yank," which Terry eventually took as his legal name.

THATCHER, Joseph Andrew ("The Throwin' Kokomoan," "Prime Minister")

Born: October 4, 1981, Indianapolis. **Lives:** Kokomo.
Height: 6'2". **Weight:** 230. **Bats:** left. **Throws:** left.
Debut: July 26, 2007.
Positions, teams, years: pitcher, San Diego (NL) 2007–2013, Arizona (NL), 2013–2014, Los Angeles (AL) 2014.
Games: 362. **Innings pitched:** 238. **Won/Lost:** 10–13. **Earned run average:** 3.40.

A basketball and baseball standout at Kokomo High School, **Joe Thatcher** went on to pitch for Indiana State University. After he went 4–8, 5.60 as a senior in 2004, Major League teams snubbed Thatcher in the draft. He signed that summer with the River City Rascals (O'Fallon, Mo.) of the independent Frontier League. In July 2005 he had a 4–2 record for the Rascals with five saves and a 1.27 ERA when the Milwaukee Brewers signed him.

Thatcher opened the 2007 campaign with Huntsville, Ala. (Southern), where an 0.55 ERA in 14 games earned him a ticket to Nashville, Tenn. (Pacific Coast). On July 25, 2007, the Brewers traded him to the Padres. The sidearm specialist joined San Diego and developed into San Diego's top left-handed reliever with a 2-2 record and a 1.29 ERA in 22 games.

In 2008 Thatcher rode the shuttle between San Diego and Portland, Ore. (Pacific Coast), going 0-4 for the Padres. He bounced back in 2009 with a 2.80 ERA in 52 games. A sore shoulder landed him on the disabled list at the start of the 2010 campaign, but he came back to post a 1.29 ERA in 65 contests. More shoulder problems and arthroscopic surgery limited him to 18 games in 2011.

Thatcher spent time on the DL in 2012 with an injured knee, but managed a 3.41 ERA in 55 contests. After the season he underwent knee surgery. Very effective against left-handed hitters, Thatcher had a 3-1 record with a 2.10 ERA in 50 games at the end of July 2013 when the Padres shipped him to Arizona.

In July 2014 Thatcher had a 2.63 ERA in 37 contests when the Diamondbacks dealt him to the Los Angeles Angels. In 16 appearances for the Angels he went 1-1 with an 8.53 ERA, spending time on the disabled list after an ankle sprain on August 3. After the season he became a free agent.

Thatcher comes from an athletic family. Phil Thatcher, his father, was a right-handed reliever for Indiana State in 1979, when coach Bob Warn won his first Missouri Valley Conference title. Joe's sister Anne played basketball for the Sycamores while another sister, Mary Kate, was a member of the Indiana State golf team. His mother, Sara, was an ISU cheerleader.

THEVENOW, Thomas Joseph ("Silent Tom")

Indiana Baseball Hall of Fame, 2001.
Born: September 6, 1903, Madison. **Died:** July 29, 1957, Madison.
Height: 5'10". **Weight:** 155. **Batted:** right. **Threw:** right.
Debut: September 4, 1924. **Final game:** October 2, 1938.
Positions, teams, years: shortstop (848), second base (188), third base (171), first base (1), St. Louis (NL) 1924-1928, Philadelphia (NL) 1929-1930, Pittsburgh (NL) 1931-1935, Cincinnati (NL) 1936, Boston (NL) 1937, Pittsburgh (NL) 1938.
Games: 1,229. **At-bats:** 4,164. **Home runs:** 2. **Average:** .247.

Light-hitting **Tommy Thevenow**, one of the top defensive shortstops of his era, was the batting star of the 1926 World Series.

Thevenow (pronounced "TEV-uh-no") played for sandlot clubs and industrial league teams in Madison before joining a semi-pro team in Centralia, Ill. He entered the professional ranks in 1923 with Joplin, Mo. (Western Association). In 1924 and 1925 he bounced back and forth between Syracuse, N.Y. (International), and the St. Louis Cardinals.

St. Louis player-manager Rogers Hornsby named Thevenow his everyday shortstop for 1926. Tommy appeared in every contest, batting .256 and playing sensational defense. The *St. Louis Post-Dispatch* described him as "a tight-lipped, silent warrior with the heart of a lion and a baby smile."

The Cardinals claimed their first pennant in 1926 and went into the Fall Classic as underdogs to the New York Yankees. But St. Louis won in seven games, led by Thevenow's 10-for-24 performance. His .417 average topped all batters, including future Hall of Famers Hornsby, Jim Bottomley, Billy Southworth and Chick Hafey of the Cardinals and New York's Babe Ruth, Lou Gehrig, Tony Lazzeri and Earle Combs. "I want to tell everybody that Tommy Thevenow is the best shortstop in baseball," proclaimed Hornsby.

In St. Louis's 6-2 victory in Game Two at Yankee Stadium, Thevenow hit a ball that eluded Babe Ruth in right field. Tommy rounded the bases and barely beat Ruth's throw to the plate for a home run. During the regular season Thevenow had two homers, also inside the park. He never hit another for the rest of his career, setting a Major League record with 3,347 consecutive at-bats without a round-tripper.

Thevenow suffered a fractured ankle in June 1927 when his spikes caught in the dirt as he slid into second base. Limited to 59 games, he batted .194. Still hampered by the injury in 1928, he hit .205 in 69 contests.

St. Louis dealt Thevenow to the Philadelphia Phillies for 1929, and the *Chicago Tribune* noted that "Tiny Tommy has been skipping around with all the skill he ever owned" before the season began. Misfortune struck again on

April 2 when Thevenow was badly injured in an automobile accident near Lakeland, Fla. After recuperating in Madison, he rejoined the Phillies in June and hit .227 in 90 games.

Playing in every game for Philadelphia in 1930, Thevenow rebounded with a .286 average. He drove in 78 runs with no homers—a record that stood until 1940 when Luke Appling of the White Sox had 79 RBI with no home runs.

The Phils traded Thevenow to Pittsburgh for 1931. A late-season surge lifted his average to .213, but on Labor Day he broke his foot sliding into home plate. He spent the next four seasons with the Pirates, mostly as a backup infielder. He played for the Cincinnati Reds in 1936 and joined the Boston Braves for 1937 before ending his career with Pittsburgh in 1938.

Thevenow was back in baseball in 1940 as player-manager for Ashland. Ky. (Mountain State), before returning to Madison. He worked in the Charlestown Powder Plant during World War II and later was an assistant manager at the Moose Home in Fairmount. He was the owner of the independent Star grocery store when he suffered a cerebral hemorrhage in 1957 and died at age 53.

Hall of Fame second baseman Frankie Frisch, Thevenow's St. Louis teammate in 1927 and 1928, said Tommy "might have developed into the greatest [shortstop] of them all" if it hadn't been for the ankle injury in 1927.

In 2001 Thevenow was posthumously inducted into the Indiana Baseball Hall of Fame.

THOMPSON, Samuel Luther ("Big Sam," "The Marvel")

National Baseball Hall of Fame, 1974. **Indiana Baseball Hall of Fame, 1979.**
Born: March 5, 1860, Danville. **Died:** November 7, 1922, Detroit, Michigan.
Height: 6'2". **Weight:** 207. **Batted:** left. **Threw:** right.
Debut: July 2, 1885. **Final game:** September 10, 1906.
Positions, teams, years: outfield (1,049), first base (1), Detroit (NL), 1885–1888, Philadelphia (NL) 1889–1898, Detroit (AL) 1906.
Games: 1,410. **At-bats:** 5,998. **Home runs:** 126. **Average:** .331.

Sam Thompson, an excellent batter who hit for power in the Deadball Era of the 19th Century, was the first Indiana-born Major League baseball star. An outstanding right fielder with an accurate, powerful throwing arm, he was also a fine baserunner. According to his Detroit teammate, catcher Charlie Bennett, "Sam took away the breath of the crowd, both hitting and fielding."

In 1884 Thompson was playing for an amateur team, the Danville Browns, when he quit his job as a carpenter and roofer to join Evansville (Northwestern). He opened the 1885 season with Indianapolis (Western). Immediately after the league disbanded in July he signed with the Detroit Wolverines of the NL. During his first big league campaign he batted .303 in 63 games.

Sporting a prodigious handlebar moustache, Thompson hit .310 for Detroit in 1886. In 1887 he became the first player to hit safely 200 times in a single season, leading the NL with 203 hits, 23 triples, a .372 average, and 166 RBI. Retroactively, this was the highest total for the 19th century ("runs batted in" didn't become an official statistic until 1920). Thompson's record stood until 1921, when Babe Ruth knocked in 171.

Detroit won the NL pennant in 1887. In a precursor of the modern World Series, the Wolverines played the St. Louis Browns, champions of the American Association, for the Dauvray Cup. Detroit won 10 of 15 games, with Thompson batting .362. During Game Eight he clubbed two homers in a 9–2 Wolverines victory.

In 1888 the *New York Clipper* described Thompson as "a big, good-natured fellow, very popular with everyone, and always plays ball to win." Hampered by an arm injury and illness that summer, he saw action in just 56 games and batted .282.

The Detroit franchise disbanded after the 1888 season and Thompson joined the Philadelphia Quakers (also known as the Phillies) for 1889. That season he became the first left-handed big league batter to hit 20 homers. Over the next six seasons, Thompson's average dipped under .300 once, and he stole 20 bases or more in all but one season. Twice he topped the NL in hits (172 in 1890; 222 in 1893) doubles (41 in 1890; 37 in 1893) and RBI (147 in 1894; 165 in 1895). In 1895 his 18 homers led the league.

Prior to the 1890 season, Thompson was one of several disgruntled NL players who signed a contract with the upstart Players League. The Phillies coaxed him back, however, by nearly doubling his annual salary. From 1891 to 1895, Thompson and two more future Hall of Fame members, Ed Delahanty and Billy Hamilton, formed one of the finest outfields of all-time. Thompson averaged .370 in 1893, .407 in 1894 (when finger surgery limited him to 99 games) and .392 in 1895. Several sources indicate Delahanty and Hamilton also batted over .400 for 1894.

Thompson had one last productive season in 1896, when he hit .298 with a dozen homers and 100 RBI despite back problems. Plagued by back and stomach woes in 1897, he missed all but three games. He retired after batting .349 in 14 games in 1898.

Making his home in Detroit, Thompson sold real estate and later worked as a U.S. marshal and as a federal court bailiff. He also played for the Detroit Athletic Club's baseball team.

At the end of the 1906 campaign the Tigers, beset by injuries, brought back the 46-year-old Thompson for eight games. Once again he manned the outfield with a pair of future Hall of Famers—Sam Crawford and 19-year-old Ty Cobb. Thompson stroked seven hits (including a triple) in 31 at-bats before retiring for a second time. He stayed involved with the Tigers as an advisor to team owner Frank Navin and continued to play for the Detroit AC until he was nearly 50.

Each autumn, Thompson returned to Danville to hunt, fish, and spend time with relatives and friends. While working as an election official in 1922, he suffered a heart attack and died at the age of 62. "His conduct was a model for the younger player," noted the *Detroit Free Press*, "and baseball is the better today for Sam Thompson having been a player."

Among 19th century players, Thompson's 126 career homers are second only to Roger Connor's 138. Yet for years, Sam received no consideration for the Hall of Fame. In *The Numbers Game*, Alan Schwarz wrote: "No one had known what a fantastic RBI man Sam Thompson had been for the 1890s Philadelphia Phillies" until the publication of *The Baseball Encyclopedia* in 1969. Statistics showed that Thompson was the game's greatest run producer of all time, driving in runs at the rate of .923 per game.

In 1974 the Veterans Committee named Thompson to the Hall of Fame. Five years later, he was one of the first players enshrined in the Indiana Baseball Hall of Fame.

A historical marker honoring Thompson was dedicated in Danville's Ellis Park in 2006.

THON, Richard William

Born: June 20, 1958, South Bend. **Lives:** Sugar Land, Texas.
Height: 5'11". **Weight:** 160. **Batted:** right. **Threw:** right.
Debut: May 22, 1979. **Final game:** October 3, 1993.
Positions, teams, years: shortstop (1,143), second base (98), third base (50), first base (1), California (AL) 1979–1980, Houston (NL) 1981–1987, San Diego (NL) 1988, Philadelphia (NL) 1989–1991, Texas (AL) 1992, Milwaukee (AL) 1993.
Games: 1,387. **At-bats:** 4,449. **Home runs:** 71. **Average:** .264.

One pitch had a dramatic effect on the promising career of **Dickie Thon**, a member of one of Puerto Rico's most prestigious baseball families.

Thon (pronounced "tahn") is the grandson of Freddie Thon, Sr., a star player in the 1940s and 1950s for the San Juan Senadores of the Puerto Rican winter league. Freddie Sr., the son of a Bavarian immigrant, also managed the Vaqueros de Bayamon in Puerto Rico and eventually founded the island's first dry-cleaning chain. Dickie's father, Freddie Thon, Jr., was a University of Notre Dame graduate whose pitching career was curtailed by arm problems. Freddie Jr. was completing his undergraduate degree when Dickie was born in South Bend. Soon afterwards the Thon family returned to Puerto Rico and settled in Rio Piedras, a district of San Juan.

Dickie, who grew up speaking Spanish, played baseball, basketball and volleyball at Rio Piedras High School. After graduation in 1975 he joined the Bayamon club. That December he signed with the California Angels and broke into organized ball in 1976 with Quad Cities (Midwest). In 1979 and 1980 Thon shuttled between Salt Lake City (Pacific Coast) and California.

On the eve of the 1981 campaign the Angels traded Thon to Houston. He took over as the Astros' everyday shortstop in 1982, batting .276 and leading the NL with 10 triples. After a 20-homer, .286 performance in 1983, San Diego Padres manager Dick Williams called Thon "the best shortstop in our league." Astros general manager Al Rosen said: "When I see Dickie Thon, I see a future Hall of Famer."

Fate intervened during a game at Houston's Astrodome on April 8, 1984, when a fastball from New York Mets pitcher Mike Torrez struck Thon in the left temple. "I was young and stubborn and crowding the plate too much," said the handsome, mustachioed Thon. The pitch fractured the orbital rim of his left eye, ending his season and threatening his career.

Relegated to a platoon player by recurring vision problems, Thon hit .251 in 84 games in 1985 and .248 in 106 contests in 1986. Optioned to Tucson (Pacific Coast) in April 1987, he rejoined the Astros and hit .212 in 32 contests. He left the team on July 3, angering Houston GM Dick Wagner, who told reporters: "We can't continue to hold a roster spot for someone who isn't sure about playing."

A free agent after the season, Thon signed with San Diego for 1988 and hit .264 as a parttimer. "I knew by then I could play," he said, "but I had to convince others that I could." After the season he requested a trade and the Padres sent him to the Philadelphia Phillies for $250,000.

Thon proved to be a bargain, hitting .271 with 15 homers in 136 games. He gave Philadelphia two more solid seasons as an everyday shortstop, batting .255 in 1990 and .252 in 1991. During his time with the Phillies, Thon received the Tony Conigliaro Award in recognition of his recovery as well as the Philadelphia Sports Writers Association's Most Courageous Player Award. He played for the Texas Rangers in 1992 and the Milwaukee Brewers in 1993 before retiring in March 1994 at age 35.

Thon subsequently coached and managed in the minor leagues. In 2003 he was inducted into the Hispanic Heritage Baseball Museum Hall of Fame. His son, shortstop Dickie Joe Thon, was the fifth-round draft pick of the Toronto Blue Jays in 2010. Frankie Thon, Dickie's younger brother, is a Major League scout and an executive with the Criollos de Caguas in the Puerto Rican winter league. Frankie's son Freddie, a first baseman, was drafted by the Texas Rangers in 2004.

THURMAN, Gary Montez

Born: November 12, 1964, Indianapolis. **Lives:** Indianapolis.
Height: 5'10". **Weight:** 170. **Batted:** right. **Threw:** right.
Debut: August 30, 1987. **Final game:** May 26, 1997.
Positions, teams, years: outfield, Kansas City (AL) 1987–1992, Detroit (AL) 1993, Seattle (AL) 1995, New York (NL) 1997.
Games: 424. **At-bats:** 798. **Home runs:** 2. **Average:** .243.

Gary Thurman has been involved in organized baseball since 1983 as a player, manager, coach and instructor.

Thurman was a baseball and football standout for North Central High School in Indianapolis, where one of his gridiron teammates was future NFL running back Lars Tate. Thurman won a gold medal in baseball at the 1982 National Sports Festival in Indianapolis. Purdue University recruited him for football and the University of Miami (Fla.) wanted him for baseball.

In June 1983 the Kansas City Royals made Thurman their top pick (21st overall) in the draft, and that summer he played for the Royals (Gulf Coast) rookie league team. He reached the majors in 1987 after hitting .293 for Omaha, Neb. (American Association). His first big league hit came on August 31, the day his daughter Brytoney was born.

After batting .296 in 27 games with Kansas City in 1987, Thurman was in the running for the Royals left field job in 1988. The job went to Bo Jackson after Thurman hit .169 in Spring Training. "The job was mine," Thurman told *Indianapolis Star* reporter Dave Garlick. "It was mine to lose … and that is exactly what I did."

Thurman opened the 1988 campaign in the minors and bounced between Omaha and Kansas City for the next two years. In 1991 he spent a full season with the Royals and batted .277 in 80 games. After a .245 season in 1992, the Royals placed him on waivers and Detroit claimed him. He played for the Tigers, Seattle Mariners and New York Mets between 1993 and 1997.

Thurman retired after dividing the 1998 season between Vancouver, B.C. (Pacific Coast), the top affiliate of the Anaheim Angels, and the independent Newark (N.J.) Bears (Atlantic).

From 1999 to 2006 Thurman managed and coached minor league clubs in the Mariners system. When John McClaren took over as Seattle's skipper in July 2007, Thurman returned to the big leagues as the Mariners first base coach. He joined the Cleveland Indians in 2008 as roving minor league baserunning instructor. In 2012 he went to Miami as the Marlins first base coach. In 2013 the Washington Nationals hired him as a minor league outfield and baserunning coordinator.

Thurman was enshrined in the North Central Hall of Fame in 1991.

TIMBERLAKE, Gary Dale

Born: August 9, 1948, Laconia. **Lives:** Louisville, Kentucky.
Height: 6'2". **Weight:** 205. **Batted:** right. **Threw:** left.
Debut: June 18, 1969. **Final game:** June 24, 1969.
Positions, teams, years: pitcher, Seattle (AL) 1969.
Games: 2. **Innings pitched:** 6. **Won/Lost:** 0–0. **Earned run average:** 7.50.

Born in the Harrison County hamlet of Laconia (population 82 in 1950) in Southern Indiana, **Gary Timberlake** spent most of his teen years across the Ohio River in Brandenburg, Ky. He threw six no-hitters for Meade County High School, where he captained the baseball and basketball teams. In 1966 the New York Yankees took him in the second round of the draft.

Timberlake showed promise at Fort Lauderdale (Florida State) in 1968 with a 5–3 record and a 1.80 ERA. That October the newly-formed Seattle Pilots took him in the expansion draft. He opened 1969 with Clinton, Iowa (Midwest), and pitched for Vancouver, B.C. (Pacific Coast), before the Pilots summoned him in June. With veteran left-hander Steve Barber shelved by shoulder problems, Timberlake started the second game of a doubleheader against the Chicago White Sox. He made one more start before going on active duty with his army reserve unit.

After the Pilots left Seattle and became the Milwaukee Brewers in 1970, Timberlake pitched for Portland, Ore. (Pacific Coast), and Jacksonville, Fla. (Southern). The following year he joined the Oakland Athletics organization and spent two seasons with Des Moines, Iowa (American Association). In 1972 three of his eight wins were shutouts. He closed out his career after pitching for Tucson, Ariz. (Pacific Coast), from 1973 to 1975.

Timberlake, who attended Western Kentucky University during his playing days, worked for the Olin Chemical Company in Brandenburg after leaving baseball.

TRAGESSER, Walter Joseph ("Trag," "Trigger")

Born: June 14, 1887, Lafayette. **Died:** December 14, 1970, Lafayette.
Height: 6'0". **Weight:** 175. **Batted:** right. **Threw:** right.
Debut: July 30, 1913. **Final game:** October 2, 1920.
Positions, teams, years: catcher, Boston (NL) 1913–1919, Philadelphia (NL) 1919–1920.
Games: 272. **At-bats:** 689. **Home runs:** 6. **Average:** .215.

A confirmed bachelor who spent his entire life in Lafayette, light-hitting **Walt Tragesser** was an excellent defensive catcher.

Tragesser lettered in baseball at Purdue University in 1908 and 1909 and in 1911 he jumped from the semi-pro ranks to organized ball with St. Paul (American Association). After batting .302 for Zanesville, Ohio (Inter-State), in 1913 he joined the Boston Braves as a backup to Bill Rariden and Bert Whaling.

Boston's "Miracle Braves" won the NL pennant in 1914, but Tragesser spent the year doing the bulk of the catching for Birmingham, Ala., which finished first in the Southern Association. He saw action in seven games for Boston in 1915, spending most of the year at Jersey City, N.J. (International).

In 1916 Tragesser was Boston's third-string receiver behind Hank Gowdy and Earl Blackburn. After America's entry into World War I in 1917, Gowdy enlisted in the army and Tragesser took over the catching duties. He hit .222 in 98 contests. That August he was declared unfit for army service due to baseball-related injuries. "He has a stiff thumb, which was broken five times while playing ball," according to the *Atlanta Constitution*. After appearing in seven games in 1918 he was reclassified fit for military service.

Tragesser entered the navy and served in Newport, R.I., as a yeoman. Discharged in time for the 1919 season, he opened the year with Boston. He was batting .175 after 20 games when the Phillies acquired him in a July trade. He hit .237 in 32 contests for Philadelphia.

Tragesser's final big league campaign was 1920, when he averaged .210 in 62 games for the Phillies. All six of his career home runs came that season. He played for Buffalo, N.Y. (International), in 1921 and spent 1922 with Reading, Pa. (International), before calling it quits.

Back in Lafayette, Tragesser went to work for the Indiana Gas Company's service department and retired as a superintendent in 1953. During the late 1920s and early 1930s, he served as an assistant to Purdue baseball coach Ward "Piggy" Lambert. Lambert also coached the Boilermakers hoops squad, and Tragesser filled in as head baseball coach until the end of the basketball season.

TRINKLE, Kenneth Wayne
Indiana Baseball Hall of Fame, 2011.
Born: December 15, 1919, Paoli. **Died:** May 10, 1976, Paoli.
Height: 6'1". **Weight:** 175. **Batted:** right. **Threw:** right.
Debut: April 25, 1943. **Final game:** October 2, 1949.
Positions, teams, years: pitcher, New York (NL) 1943, 1946–1948, Philadelphia (NL) 1949.
Games: 216. **Innings pitched:** 435.1. **Won/Lost:** 21–29. **Earned run average:** 3.74.

The son of a livestock and corn farmer, **Ken Trinkle** captained Paoli High School's basketball team and played American Legion baseball. He pitched for the Paoli Merchants, a semipro club, after graduation in 1938 and signed with Thomasville, Ga. (Georgia-Florida), for 1939. He pitched for Baltimore (International) from 1940 through 1942.

The New York Giants acquired Trinkle for 1943, and in 11 games he posted a 1–5 record with a 3.74 ERA. In mid–June the Giants shipped him to Jersey City, N.J. (International), where he went 7–11 in 23 contests.

Later that year Trinkle entered the Army. Serving with the 9th Armored Division in Europe, Trinkle headed a reconnaissance patrol and saw action in the Battle of the Bulge and received the Bronze Star medal. After Germany surrendered in 1945, he pitched for the 76th Division team, runners-up in that September's GI World Series at Nuremberg.

Trinkle rejoined New York for the 1946 season. The sidearm sinker ball specialist developed into a serviceable reliever with ERAs of 3.87 in 1946, 3.73 in 1947 and 3.18 in 1948. He topped the NL with 48 appearances in 1946 and again in 1947 with 62. "Just so long as I pitch only an inning or so a day, my arm does not tighten," Trinkle said in 1947. "But if I pitch more than two innings, I am not at my best the next day."

In 1949 New York dealt Trinkle to the Philadelphia Phillies, and in 1950 the Phils assigned him to Toronto (International). Back with Baltimore for 1951, he pitched for Baltimore and Louisville (American Association) in 1952 before retiring. Trinkle was the owner of a package store in Paoli when he suffered a fatal heart attack at age 55.

In 2011 Trinkle went into the Indiana Baseball Hall of Fame.

TROUT, Paul Howard ("Dizzy")
Indiana Baseball Hall of Fame, 1981.
Born: June 29, 1915, Sandcut. **Died:** February 28, 1972, Harvey, Illinois.
Height: 6'2". **Weight:** 195. **Batted:** right. **Threw:** right.
Debut: April 25, 1939. **Final game:** September 11, 1957.
Positions, teams, years: pitcher, Detroit (AL) 1939–1952, Boston (AL) 1952, Baltimore (AL) 1957.
Games: 521. **Innings pitched:** 2,725.2. **Won/Lost:** 170–161. **Earned run average:** 3.23.

Witty, bespectacled **Dizzy Trout**, a two-time 20-game winner, spent 14 seasons with Detroit and pitched in two World Series for the Tigers. A colorful character who became a broadcaster after his playing days, Trout borrowed his *nom de guerre* from flamboyant 1930s pitching star Dizzy Dean. "I figured if that guy can get thirty or forty thousand a year for being a screwball," Trout explained, "that's for me."

Born in the western Indiana town of Sandcut, Trout was an outstanding pitcher at Terre Haute's Otter Creek High School. He played for the North Terre Haute Grays, a local independent team, before joining a Chicago semi-pro club called the Polar Bears.

Trout signed with Terre Haute (Three-I) in 1935 and later pitched for Indianapolis and Toledo, Ohio (American Association). Dispatched to Beaumont (Texas) in 1938, Trout's 22–6, 2.12 slate earned him MVP honors and a promotion to Detroit for 1939.

From 1939 to 1942 Trout had 33 wins against 44 losses. He went 3–7 for the pennant-winning Tigers in 1940, and was the starting and losing pitcher in the fifth game of the World Series versus Cincinnati. The Reds won the Series in seven games.

Declared unfit for World War II military service due to vision and hearing impairments, Trout teamed with left-hander Hal Newhouser (classified 4-F because of a heart ailment) to give the Tigers a formidable righty-lefty combination during the war years. Between 1943 and 1945 Trout won 65 games against 41 losses. His 20 wins in 1943 topped the AL.

In 1944, when the Tigers finished one game out of first place, Trout went 27–14 and led the league with 33 complete games and 352 innings pitched. Newhouser went 29–9 and topped Trout in the MVP ballot by four votes. "I think Trout should have won it," said third baseman Mark Christman of the pennant-winning St. Louis Browns, "because Trout saved half of Newhouser's ball games."

Detroit won the pennant in 1945 with Newhouser (25–9) and Trout (18–5) leading the way. The Tigers beat the Chicago Cubs in a seven-game World Series. In Game 4 Trout went the distance in a 4–1 victory and took the loss in relief in a 12-inning, 8–7 defeat in Game 6. His ERA for the Series was 0.66. Trout had two more winning seasons for the Tigers, going 17–13 in 1946 and 13–5 in 1950, when Detroit finished three games behind the pennant-winning New York Yankees.

In June 1952 the Tigers sent Trout to the Boston Red Sox in a nine-player deal. He retired after the season and returned to Detroit, where he teamed with Van Patrick from 1953 to 1955 for Tigers radio and television broadcasts. After serving as color commentator for the Indianapolis Indians in 1956, he made an unsuccessful run for sheriff of Michigan's Wayne County.

Late in the 1957 season Trout made a brief comeback at age 42, appearing in three games for Vancouver, B.C. (Pacific Coast), and two more for the Baltimore Orioles. In 1959 he joined the Chicago White Sox as a pitching instructor and later worked in the team's public relations department. At the time of his death from stomach cancer at age 56, he was director of the White Sox speakers bureau.

A member of the Indiana Baseball Hall of Fame's Class of 1981, Trout was also a fair hitter who clubbed 20 career home runs—including two grand slams. Dizzy and his wife had ten children including Steve "Rainbow" Trout, a left-hander who pitched for four big league teams from 1978 to 1989. Steve, with Larry Names, is the author of *Home Plate: The Journey of the Most Flamboyant Father and Son Pitching Combination in Major League History*.

UNDERWOOD, Patrick John
Indiana Baseball Hall of Fame, 2005.
Born: February 9, 1957, Kokomo. **Lives:** Kokomo.
Height: 6'0". **Weight:** 175. **Batted:** left. **Threw:** left.
Debut: May 31, 1979. **Final game:** June 21, 1983.
Positions, teams, years: pitcher, Detroit (AL) 1979–1980, 1982–1983.
Games: 113. **Innings pitched:** 343.2. **Won/Lost:** 13–18. **Earned run average:** 4.43.

As a Kokomo High School junior in 1975, **Pat Underwood** threw four shutouts over a 15-day span, including three no-hit games and a two-hitter. By the time of his graduation in 1976, he owned IHSAA records for career shutouts (22) and strikeouts (637). The previous career strikeout mark belonged to Tom Underwood, his older brother.

The Detroit Tigers made Pat their first-round pick (second overall) in the 1976 draft. He broke into pro ball that summer at Lakeland (Florida State). In 1977 a 9–2, 3.38 showing in 14 games at Montgomery, Ala. (Southern), vaulted him into the Triple-A ranks at Evansville (American Association).

The following year Pat jumped from Evansville to the Tigers. His first start was against

Toronto, and the host Blue Jays countered with Tom Underwood. Before the game, Helen Marie Underwood, Pat's and Tom's mother, told reporters: "I prayed for rain, but that didn't work. Now I'm just hoping for a shutout—on both sides." In the first contest in big league history where a pitcher broke in against his brother, Pat threw eight and one-third innings of a 1–0 Detroit victory.

Pat finished the 1979 season with a 6–4 mark in 27 games, including 15 starts. After a 3–6, 3.58 record for the Tigers in 1980 (mostly out of the bullpen), he spent all of 1981 with Evansville. He rejoined Detroit for parts of 1982 and 1983 before the Tigers traded him to the Reds.

Underwood pitched for Cincinnati and Baltimore Orioles farm clubs before retiring after the 1984 season, his career curtailed by elbow problems. Returning to school, he earned an undergraduate degree from Indiana University and a master's from Indiana Wesleyan. He later worked as a product quality manager for General Motors in Kokomo.

In 2005 Pat joined his brother in the Indiana Baseball Hall of Fame.

UNDERWOOD, Thomas Gerald

Indiana Baseball Hall of Fame, 1997.
Born: December 22, 1953, Kokomo. **Died:** November 22, 2010, West Palm Beach, Florida.
Height: 5'11". **Weight:** 170. **Batted:** right. **Threw:** left.
Debut: August 19, 1974. **Final game:** September 23, 1984.
Positions, teams, years: pitcher, Philadelphia (NL) 1974–1977, St. Louis (NL) 1977, Toronto (AL) 1978–1979, New York (AL) 1980–1981, Oakland (AL) 1981–1983, Baltimore (AL) 1984.
Games: 379. **Innings pitched:** 1,586. **Won/Lost:** 86–87. **Earned run average:** 3.89.

A right-hander as a youngster, **Tom Underwood** switched to the left side at age ten. "I felt more comfortable and threw harder," he explained. At Kokomo High School he lettered in football, basketball and baseball, going 10–1 as a senior and setting an IHSAA record with 553 career strikeouts.

The Philadelphia Phillies made him their second pick in the 1972 draft. He signed that August, and in 1973 he reported to Spartanburg, S.C. (Western Carolina), where he went 13–6 with a league-leading 187 strikeouts and a 2.10 ERA.

Underwood reached the majors in 1974, his second pro season. After going 4–5 with a league-best .737 winning percentage that season for Reading, Pa. (Eastern), he pitched in seven games for the Phillies. He finished the year at Toledo (American Association). The following season he joined Philadelphia's starting rotation, going 14–13 in 1976 and 10–5 in 1977 as the Phils won back-to-back NL East Division titles.

The St. Louis Cardinals acquired Underwood in June 1977 and swapped him to Toronto that December. In two seasons with the Blue Jays, he compiled 15 wins against 30 losses for last-place teams. In November 1979 Underwood went to the Yankees in a six-player deal. His 13–9 slate in 1980 helped New York to first place in the AL East Division. Dealt to Oakland in June 1981, he served as a reliever and spot starter as the Athletics finished first in the AL West. In three years with Oakland he went 22–15 as a swingman.

A free agent after the 1983 season, Underwood pitched for the Baltimore Orioles in 1984 and retired in 1985 after spending a year in the Yankee organization. "My biggest regret in baseball is that I never played with a winning team in postseason play," he said. "I pitched in three league championship series, with three different teams, but lost each time."

Making his home in Florida, Underwood worked as a financial advisor and married Chrissy Morra, a professional golfer. He entered the Indiana Baseball Hall of Fame in 1997, and in 2000 the *Kokomo Tribune* named him Howard County's greatest athlete of the 20th Century.

Tom succumbed to pancreatic cancer at age 56. His son, right-handed pitcher J.D. Underwood, was the fifth-round draft pick of the Los Angeles Dodgers in 2013.

The 99 career wins (86 for Tom, 13 for Pat) by the Underwoods is the highest total by Indiana-born brothers.

VANRYN, Benjamin Ashley

Born: August 19, 1971, Fort Wayne. **Lives:** San Antonio, Texas.

Height: 6'5". **Weight:** 185. **Batted:** left. **Threw:** left.
Debut: May 9, 1996. **Final game:** September 26, 1998.
Positions, teams, years: pitcher, California (AL) 1996, Chicago (NL) 1998, San Diego (NL) 1998, Toronto (AL) 1998.
Games: 26. **Innings pitched:** 15.2. **Won/Lost:** 0–2. **Earned run average:** 5.74.

During his ten-year professional career, **Ben VanRyn** pitched for ten different organizations.

VanRyn (pronounced "van rin") grew up in Kendallville and starred in basketball (1,353 career points) and baseball (551 career strikeouts) at East Noble High School. He committed to the University of Texas, but instead signed with Montreal in 1990 after the Expos made him a supplemental first-round pick in the June draft.

VanRyn showed promise in 1990 with the Expos' Gulf Coast League affiliate, going 5–3 with a 1.74 ERA. After a combined 5–16 record in 1991 for two Montreal farm teams, the Expos traded him to the Los Angeles Dodgers. In 1993 at San Antonio he established himself as the Texas League's top hurler, leading the circuit with 14 wins and a 2.21 ERA.

Traded to Cincinnati in December 1994, VanRyn opened the 1995 campaign with Chattanooga, Tenn. (Southern). That May the Reds sent him to California in a waiver deal. He made the transition from starter to reliever in the Angels system and in May 1996 he reached the big leagues. A month later, California traded him to St. Louis. He spent the rest of the year with the Cardinals' top farm club in Louisville, Ky. (American Association).

The Atlanta Braves acquired VanRyn in the offseason, but released him before the start of the 1997 season. That summer he pitched in the Cubs system. He returned to the big leagues in 1998, spending time with Chicago, the San Diego Padres and the Toronto Blue Jays.

After pitching for the White Sox's top affiliate in Charlotte, N.C. (International), in 1999, VanRyn retired. He earned a degree in kinesiology from the University of Texas-San Antonio. Eventually, he became owner and president of Prospect Park Baseball Tournaments and the San Antonio Wranglers LLC, offering private baseball lessons and coaching select teams.

In 2011 VanRyn was named to the Northeast Indiana Baseball Association Hall of Fame.

VAN ZANT, Richard ("Professor")

Born: November (day unknown) 1864, Richmond.
Died: August 6, 1912, Richmond.
Height: 5'10". **Weight:** 175. **Batted:** unknown. **Threw:** unknown.
Debut: October 4, 1888. **Final game:** October 15, 1888.
Positions, teams, years: third base, Cleveland (American Association) 1888.
Games: 10. **At-bats:** 31. **Home runs:** 0. **Average:** .258.

En route to a sixth-place finish in the American Association in 1888, the Cleveland Blues got little production from their third baseman. Gus Alberts batted .206 in 49 games at the hot corner, John McGlone batted .182 in 48 contests, and Bob Gilks averaged .229 in 28 games.

Dick Van Zant, a .284 hitter that summer at Wheeling, W. Va., joined Cleveland after the end of the Tri-State League season and batted .258 in ten games. He committed eight errors for a .784 fielding percentage and, noted the *National Police Gazette:* "As a third baseman, Van Zant was a rank failure, and the Clevelands dropped him like a hot potato."

The son of Bavarian immigrants, Van Zant played for the Richmond Henleys, a powerful Indiana semi-pro team. He was a member of pennant winners in his first two professional campaigns at Duluth, Minn. (Northwest), in 1886 and Kalamazoo, Mich. (Ohio State), in 1887.

After the trial with Cleveland, Van Zant had stops at Springfield. Ill., and Burlington, Iowa (Central Inter-State), in 1889, Burlington and Tacoma, Wash. (Pacific Northwestern), in 1890, Tacoma and Spokane, Wash. (Pacific Northwestern), in 1891, and Spokane and San Francisco (California) in 1891.

After quitting baseball, Van Zant returned to Richmond and worked as a saloonkeeper. His life began to spiral downward in 1905, after his first wife Phoebe died from drinking carbolic acid. In 1907 he began acting strangely and was declared insane. Confined for a time to an asylum, he suffered a paralytic stroke in July 1911 and died 13 months later at age 47.

Van Zant's nickname has been reported as

"Foghorn," but that monicker apparently belonged to a teammate at Burlington in 1890—catcher Mike Trost, who had a booming voice. When Van Zant played for Wheeling, newspaper accounts referred to him as "Professor," and occasionally "The German Professor."

VEACH, William Walter ("Peek-A-Boo," "Peekie")

Born: June 15, 1862, Indianapolis. **Died:** November 12, 1937, Indianapolis.
Height: 6'0". **Weight:** 175. **Batted:** unknown. **Threw:** right.
Debut: August 24, 1884. **Final game:** July 25, 1890.
Positions, teams, years: first base (73), outfield (14), pitcher (13), second base (1), Kansas City (Union Association) 1884, Louisville (American Association) 1887, Cleveland (NL) 1890, Pittsburgh (NL) 1890.
Games: 100. **At-bats:** 353. **Home runs:** 3. **Average:** .215.
Innings pitched: 113. **Won/Lost:** 3–10. **Earned run average:** 2.55.

During a professional baseball career that stretched from 1884 to 1897, versatile **Peek-A-Boo Veach** played for teams in eleven states and two countries.

Orphaned at the age of 10, Veach worked as a bootblack and lamplighter in Indianapolis before joining a barnstorming team called the Indianapolis Blues. He played for semi-pro teams like the Fort Wayne Golden Eagles and the When Store club of Indianapolis before breaking into professional ball with Evansville (Northwestern) in 1884.

Before the year was out, Veach was pitching and playing the outfield for the Kansas City Cowboys of the Union Association, one of three big leagues operating that season. He went 3–9 and batted .134 for Kansas City, which won 16 times against 63 losses.

From 1885 to 1887 Veach played for six clubs, including a stop in Toronto (International) in 1886. In 1887 he had a one-game pitching appearance (a loss to Cleveland on April 26) for the big league Louisville Colonels of the American Association.

Veach played for St. Paul, Minn., and Sioux City, Iowa (Western Association), in 1888, and split 1889 between Sacramento and Oakland (California). In 1890 he spent time with Oakland and San Francisco (California) before returning to the majors with Cleveland. In 64 games at first base for the Spiders, he hit .235. Released in July, he joined the Pittsburgh Alleghenys—the NL's worst team that season with a 23–113 slate—and batted .300 in eight contests.

Despite being released by several clubs for excessive drinking, Veach continued to play minor league ball through 1897. He frequently returned to Indianapolis during the offseason to work as a railroad foreman.

When the Spanish-American War broke out in 1898, Veach joined the 2nd U.S. Volunteer Engineers and served in Cuba from November 1898 to April 1899. After his discharge, he tried unsuccessfully to return to baseball. He came back to Indianapolis where, according to the *Indianapolis Star*, he "slipped back into obscurity and loneliness in the twilight of a colorful career." He died of pneumonia at age 75 in an Indianapolis Veterans Hospital.

Veach picked up his unique nickname in 1884 while pitching for Kansas City against Cincinnati. When Veach had trouble holding runners, according to the *Star*, Kansas City manager Ted Sullivan instructed him to "Keep an eye on the bench and when my hands go up fire the ball to first." After Veach picked off a couple of baserunners, the Cincinnati players demanded Sullivan's removal from Kansas City's bench. Sullivan retreated to the stands, where he continued to send signals from behind a post. Veach kept peeking into the stands, and when he nailed another runner, "Manager Sullivan was chased from the park," noted the *Star*, "and everybody began calling Veach 'Peek-a-boo.'"

Veach's son, William Walter Veach, Jr., briefly played minor league baseball. He also was a member of the Staley Bears football team of Decatur, Ill., forerunners of the Chicago Bears of the NFL.

WACKER, Charles James ("Demon Jimmy," "Wack")

Born: December 8, 1883, Jeffersonville. **Died:** August 7, 1948, Evansville.
Height: 6'1". **Weight:** 196. **Batted:** left. **Threw:** left.
Debut: April 28, 1909. **Final Game:** April 28, 1909.
Positions, teams, years: pitcher, Pittsburgh (NL) 1909.

Games: 1. **Innings pitched:** 2. **Won/Lost:** 0-0. **Earned run average:** 0.00.

Charlie Wacker entered professional baseball in 1906, going 17–17 for Evansville (Central), where he was known as Jimmy Wacker. Local newspapers dubbed him "The Demon" or "Demon Jimmy." Sidelined for most of 1907 by appendicitis and subsequent surgery, he returned in 1908 to help Evansville win the pennant with 27 wins and a league-leading .771 percentage.

The Cincinnati Reds brought Wacker to Spring Training in 1909. On April 8 he went to the Pirates in a waiver deal. Pittsburgh's Opening Day roster included two Indiana-born rookie hurlers, Wacker and right-hander Babe Adams. Adams went 12–3 and made headlines when he beat Detroit three times in the World Series.

Wacker was long gone by then. He pitched the last two innings of an 8–2 loss at St. Louis on April 28, giving up a pair of unearned runs. His big league career ended on May 19 when Pittsburgh shipped him to Milwaukee (American Association).

That summer, Wacker compiled a 7–7 record for second-place Milwaukee. He went 12–9 for Dayton, Ohio (Central), in 1910 and split 1911 between Dayton and Fort Wayne (Central), compiling a 13–13 slate. Contemporary accounts described Wacker's "jack-knife delivery," in which he "makes two or three passes in the air, then he winds himself up, places his right foot in the air about the tip of his head and lets go."

During his early years in organized ball, Wacker spent his winters working as a butcher. In 1908 he married Pearl Elikhofer, an Evansville lady he'd met at the local ballpark. Settling in Evansville after his playing days, he worked at a flour mill. For a number of years he was employed at Bosse Field.

WADE, Cory Nathaniel

Born: May 28, 1983, Indianapolis. **Lives:** Zionsville. **Height:** 6'2". **Weight:** 185. **Bats:** right. **Throws:** right.
Debut: April 24, 2008.
Positions, teams, years: pitcher, Los Angeles (NL) 2008–2009, New York (AL) 2011–2012.
Games: 161. **Innings pitched:** 177.2. **Won/Lost:** 11–6. **Earned run average:** 3.65.

When he entered Broad Ripple High School in Indianapolis in the fall of 1997, **Cory Wade** looked like anything but a future big league pitcher. "My freshman year, I was 4-foot-11, 90 pounds," he said. "By the time I left, I was about 5-foot-9 or 5-foot-10." He had also broken the school strikeout record.

During Wade's first two years at Kentucky Wesleyan College, he added a few more inches but attracted interest from few scouts. That changed in 2004, his junior season, when he posted a 2.39 ERA with 84 strikeouts in 71⅔ innings. That June, the Los Angeles Dodgers selected him in the tenth round of the draft.

For most of his first three pro campaigns, Wade alternated between the starting rotation and the bullpen. At Inland Empire (California) in 2007, he came into his own with the help of pitching coach Charlie Hough, the winner of 116 big league contests, who helped Wade refine his curveball. Working primarily in relief, he went 7–0 with a 2.45 ERA before moving up to Jacksonville, Fla. (Southern).

In late April 2008 Wade joined Los Angeles and became the team's top setup man. He went 2–1 with a 2.27 ERA in 55 games as Los Angeles finished first in the NL West. Hampered by shoulder bursitis in 2009, he was 2–3, 5.53 in 27 appearances and finished the year in the minors.

Wade underwent shoulder surgery in March 2010. That July, Los Angeles outrighted him to Albuquerque, N.M. (Pacific Coast). Prior to 2011 he signed a minor league contract with Tampa Bay. Released by the Rays in mid-June, he joined the Yankees and went 6–1, 2.04 in 40 games as New York won the AL East title. He divided the 2012 season between New York and Scranton/Wilkes-Barre, Pa. (International).

In 2013 Wade pitched for Triple-A affiliates of the Chicago Cubs, Rays and New York Mets. He signed with Kansas City for 2014 and opened the year with Omaha, Neb. (Pacific Coast). Cut loose in April, he joined the Lancaster (Pa.) Barnstormers of the independent Atlantic League. In 19 contests, including 11 starts, he went 4–6 with a 5.45 ERA.

Without a contract at the end of the year, Wade agreed to coach the Indiana Pony Express, an Indianapolis-based travel team, for 2015.

WALLACE, Harry Clinton ("Huck," "Lefty")

Born: July 27, 1882, Richmond. **Died:** July 6, 1951, Cleveland, Ohio.
Height: 5'6". **Weight:** 160. **Batted:** left. **Threw:** left.
Debut: June 5, 1912. **Final Game:** July 1, 1912.
Positions, teams, years: pitcher, Philadelphia (NL) 1912.
Games: 4. **Innings pitched:** 4.2. **Won/Lost:** 0–0. **Earned run average:** 0.00.

Lefty Wallace, a Richmond High School alumnus, reached the Major Leagues as a 29-year-old rookie. Wallace played for semi-pro clubs in Illinois, Ohio, and Muncie, Ind., as well as minor league teams in Evansville (Central), Springfield, Ill. (Three-I), Davenport, Iowa (Three-I), and Connellsville, Pa. (Pennsylvania-West Virginia) before helping Uniontown, Pa., win the 1909 Pennsylvania-West Virginia League pennant.

Wallace pitched in the Tri-State League in 1910 and 1911. Cut loose by Reading, Pa., in May 1911, he hired on as baseball coach at the Pennington (N.J.) Seminary (known today as the Pennington School).

Philadelphia signed Wallace in April 1912. He made four relief appearances before the Phillies shipped him to Atlantic City, N.J. (Tri-State). In 1913 he pitched for York, Pa. (Tri-State), and in 1914 he moved with the franchise to Lancaster. Pa. A fair hitter, he saw action as an outfielder in 1910, 1913 and 1914.

Wallace made his home in Cleveland during his playing days. After leaving organized ball, he pitched for Standard Parts, a local semi-pro club. His teammates included former big league hurler Glen Liebhardt (a Milton, Ind., native) and George Uhle, who went on to win 200 games for the Indians, Tigers, Giants and Yankees from 1919 to 1936.

Wallace, who operated a Cleveland bowling alley for 32 years, died of congestive heart failure at age 68.

WALLACE, James Harold ("Lefty," "Slim Jim")

Born: August 12, 1921, Evansville. **Died:** July 28, 1982, Evansville.
Height: 5'11". **Weight:** 160. **Batted:** left. **Threw:** left.
Debut: May 5, 1942. **Final Game:** September 22, 1946.
Positions, teams, years: pitcher, Boston (NL) 1942, 1945–1946.
Games: 51. **Innings pitched:** 144.2. **Won/Lost:** 5–6. **Earned run average:** 4.11.

The son of a former semi-pro pitcher, **Jim Wallace** said his father "had me throwing as long as I can remember." As a senior at Evansville's Bosse High School in 1939, Wallace played the outfield and pitched, compiling an 8–1 record.

After a tryout that summer with Evansville (Three-I), manager Bob Coleman signed Wallace as a batting practice pitcher. In 1940 Coleman sent the 18-year-old left-hander to Owensboro, Ky. (Kitty), where he went 17–12 with 208 strikeouts in 262 innings. Wallace opened the 1940 season with Evansville (Three-I). After a 1–2 record in four games, Coleman sent him to Bridgeport, Conn. (Interstate), where he went 11–8 in 25 contests with a 2.84 ERA.

Manager Casey Stengel added Wallace to the Boston Braves' Opening Day roster for 1942. His first start on May 7 was a six-hit, 7–1 win over the Pirates at Pittsburgh's Forbes Field. "When we were going into the ballpark, I was between (outfielder) Paul Waner and (catcher) Ernie Lombardi and the guard at the players' gate stopped me," recalled Wallace, a baby-faced 20-year-old at the time. "He didn't think I was one of the players."

Wallace entered the U.S. Army that August after compiling a 1–3 slate in 19 appearances. Discharged due to a knee problem in November 1944, he returned to the Braves—now managed by Bob Coleman—in the spring on 1945. Eight weeks into the season, Boston optioned Wallace to Indianapolis (American Association), where he went 17–4 and topped the league in percentage (.810) and ERA (1.83). Writing for *The Sporting News*, Lester Koelling described him as a "cool, deliberate, boyish-looking figure on the mound…. He is always calm and his frigid deliberateness makes him a pitching machine."

After a 3–3 record in 27 games for the Braves in 1946, Wallace's big league days were over. Optioned to Milwaukee (American Association) for 1947, he continued to pitch in the minors until 1952. His best year came in 1950 when he had a combined 18–8 slate for Saginaw, Mich. (Central), and Birmingham, Ala. (Southern Association). His 2.05 ERA topped the Central League.

In 1953 Wallace joined the Evansville Police Department. Cited as Officer of the Year in 1973, he resigned in 1974 to become chief deputy sheriff. Wallace, who retired in 1979, was considered an expert in fingerprinting, polygraph examination, crime lab procedures, gathering evidence and criminal law. He is a member of the Evansville Sports Hall of Fame.

WARNER, John Ralph

Born: August 29, 1903, Evansville. **Died:** March 13, 1986. Mount Vernon, Illinois.
Height: 5'9". **Weight:** 165. **Batted:** right. **Threw:** right.
Debut: September 24, 1925. **Final Game:** September 30, 1933.
Positions, teams, years: third base (334), second base (71), shortstop (30), Detroit (AL) 1925–1928, Brooklyn (NL) 1929–1931, Philadelphia (NL) 1933.
Games: 478. **At-bats:** 1,546. **Home runs:** 1. **Average:** .250.

A big league infielder for eight seasons, **Jackie Warner** spent more than 60 years in organized baseball as a player, coach, manager and scout.

After graduation from Evansville High School (known today as Evansville Central), Warner joined Waynesboro, Pa. (Blue Ridge), in 1921. Released after hitting .118 in ten contests, he played for an Illinois semi-pro team in 1922 before signing with Vernon, Calif. (Pacific Coast), for 1923. Following three solid seasons with Vernon, the Detroit Tigers purchased his contract late in 1925. He was married that year in Mount Vernon, Ill., which became his permanent home.

For two seasons Warner served as Detroit's primary third baseman, batting .251 in 1926 and .267 in 1927. In 1926 he won a $25 bet when his manager, Ty Cobb—considered the fastest man in baseball during his playing days—challenged him to a footrace. On July 10, 1927, Warner hit the only home run of his Major League career off Yankees left-hander Herb Pennock in a 6–3 win over New York at Detroit's Navin Field.

Warner batted .214 in 75 games in 1928, when Marty McManus replaced him as Detroit's regular third baseman. In 1929 the Tigers shipped Warner to Toledo (American Association), where his .331 average earned him a shot with Brooklyn. Warner was a seldom-used backup infielder for the Dodgers from 1929 to 1931. Traded to the Phillies as part of a four-player deal prior to the 1933 season, he hit .224 in 107 games with Philadelphia that summer.

Warner spent the rest of his playing days in the minors, with stops at St. Paul (American Association) from 1934 to 1937; Oakland (Pacific Coast) in 1938; and San Francisco (Pacific Coast) in 1939–1940. He managed Zanesville, Ohio (Middle Atlantic), in 1941–1942 and Leaksville-Draper-Spray (Carolina) in 1945.

In 1946 Warner began a 12-year stint as a coach for the Los Angeles Angels, a Chicago Cubs farm club. He served as a West Coast scout for the Los Angeles Dodgers from 1958–1961; for the Yankees from 1962–1977 and for the Montreal Expos from 1978–82.

Warner is a member of the Evansville Sports Hall of Fame.

WATSON, Arthur Stanhope ("Watty")

Born: January 11, 1884, Jeffersonville. **Died:** May 9, 1950, Buffalo, New York.
Height: 5'10". **Weight:** 175. **Batted:** left. **Threw:** right.
Debut: May 19, 1914. **Final Game:** August 7, 1915.
Positions, teams, years: catcher (31), outfield (1), Brooklyn (Federal) 1914–1915, Buffalo (Federal) 1915.
Games: 53. **At-bats:** 95. **Home runs:** 2. **Average:** .337.

An effective pinch-hitter, **Art Watson** reached the majors as a 30-year-old rookie in 1914 when the Federal League challenged the American and National leagues as a third major circuit.

Playing for an independent team in Boonville, Ind., in 1905, Watson met a woman from Huntingburg and married her on July 10. Three months later Watson filed for divorce, alleging that his wife "went buggy riding with other men after their marriage and visited places of questionable character." She countersued, charging abandonment. After an attempt at reconciliation, the marriage was dissolved in December 1906.

Watson split 1906 between South Bend and Evansville in the Central League. While playing for Eau Claire (Wisconsin State) in 1907, he married a local lady and spent the winter there, working as a mailing clerk for a local company. Watson continued to toil in the minors from 1909 to 1913, with stops in Fond du Lac, Oshkosh and Madison (Wisconsin-Illinois), South Bend and Grand Rapids, Mich. (Central).

At the age of 30 in 1914, he caught on with the FL's Brooklyn Tip-Tops as a third-string catcher. He remained in Brooklyn during the off-season, working as a carpenter in the Ward Brothers bakery, which bankrolled the Tip-Tops. He was batting .263 after nine games for Brooklyn in 1915 when the Tip-Tops sent him to the Buffalo Blues, where he hit .467 in 22 contests. As a pinch-hitter, he was 1-for-2 in 1914 and 6-for-16 in 1915 for a career .389 average.

The Federal League ceased operations after 1915, and in 1916 Watson helped Ridgway, Pa. (Inter-State), to a first-place finish. According to the *Warren* (Pa.) *Evening Times*, he made his last at-bat a memorable one, "for he laced the pill over the fence in right field for a home run."

In 1917 Watson joined Reading, Pa. (New York State), where he was married in June for a third time. He returned to Ridgway to play for an independent team from 1920 to 1921. In 1929 he moved to Bradford, Pa., where he managed a tire shop, worked as a machinist, and later for a manufacturing company. He was also involved with the local baseball squad.

Watson had been living in Buffalo, N.Y., for three years, working as a mechanic for Chevrolet, when he died from heart disease in 1950.

WEDGE, Eric Michael ("Wedgie")

Indiana Baseball Hall of Fame, 2007.
Born: January 27, 1968, Fort Wayne. **Lives:** Mercer Island, Washington.
Height: 6'3". **Weight:** 215. **Batted:** right. **Threw:** right.
Debut: October 5, 1991. **Final Game:** July 29, 1994.
Positions, teams, years: catcher, Boston (AL) 1991–1992, Colorado (NL) 1993, Boston (AL) 1994.
Games: 39. **At-bats:** 86. **Home runs:** 5. **Average:** .233.
Manager: Cleveland (AL) 2003–2009, Seattle (AL) 2011–2013 (774–846).

Eric Wedge achieved success as a Major League manager after injuries curtailed his promising catching career at age 26.

As a high school freshman in 1983, Wedge played for Fort Wayne Northrop's state championship team. In 1989 he batted .380 to help Wichita State University to the College World Series title. That June, the Boston Red Sox made him their third-round draft pick. Between 1989 and 1991 he made stops at Elmira, N.Y. (New York-Penn), New Britain, Conn. (Eastern), Winter Haven, Fla. (Florida State), and Pawtucket, R.I. (International).

Wedge was projected as Boston's catcher of the future before undergoing the first of eight operations over a nine-year span—four on his knee, four on his elbow—in 1900. He debuted with the Red Sox as a pinch-hitter in 1991. In 1992 he hit .299 with 11 home runs in 65 games for Pawtucket. In 27 games with Boston that summer, mostly as a designated hitter, he batted .250 with five homers. In November 1992 the newly-formed Colorado Rockies claimed Wedge in the expansion draft. After spending most of 1993 in the minors, he hit .182 in nine games for the Rockies.

Released by Colorado during Spring Training in 1994, he re-signed with Boston after a chance meeting with Red Sox manager Butch Hobson at a convenience store in Natick, Mass. Wedge averaged .286 with 19 homers in 77 games for Pawtucket and saw action in two games with the Red Sox. Back in the minors for 1995, he spent 1996 in the Tigers system and played for a Phillies farm club before retiring. "I always thought I had the tools to be a good Major League catcher," said Wedge. "The only thing that got in the way was the injuries."

From 1998 to 2002 Wedge managed minor league clubs in the Cleveland Indians organization. He was the Carolina League's 1999 manager of the year. In 2001 he was the International League's top skipper and *Baseball America's* Triple-A manager of the year. *The Sporting News* named him minor league manager of the year for 2002. At age 34, he became the youngest manager in the big leagues when he took over the reins at Cleveland in 2003.

The Indians improved in each of Wedge's first three seasons and won the AL Central Division title in 2007. *USA Today's* Bob Nightengale hailed Wedge as the "best young manager in the game." Cleveland swept the Yankees in the ALDS before losing the ALCS to the Red Sox in seven games. After the season, he was named AL manager of the year and was honored by *The Sporting News* as baseball's top skipper. The Indians dropped to third in 2008 and fourth in 2009.

Wedge wasn't rehired for 2010, and agreed to manage Seattle for 2011. The Mariners finished fourth in his three years at the helm. He resigned after the 2013 season, citing differences with ownership and the front office.

A member of the Indiana Baseball Hall of Fame's Class of 2007, Wedge is also enshrined in the Northeast Indiana, Cape Cod League and Arizona Fall League halls of fame. He is co-owner of a sports complex in Danvers, Mass., and volunteers his time to a baseball camp sponsored by the Fort Wayne Sports Corporation.

WETZEL, Franklin Burton ("Dutch")

Born: July 7, 1893, Columbus. **Died:** March 5, 1942, Hollywood, California.
Height: 5'9". **Weight:** 177. **Batted:** right. **Threw:** right.
Debut: September 15, 1920. **Final Game:** October 2, 1921.
Positions, teams, years: outfield, St. Louis (AL) 1920–1921.
Games: 68. **At-bats:** 140. **Home runs:** 2. **Average:** .243.

Dutch Wetzel was involved in baseball as a player, manager and owner from 1913 to 1934.

In May 1897, Wetzel's father, a railroad engineer, died in a train accident near the Indiana town of Jonesville in Bartholomew County. His mother eventually remarried and moved to St. Louis, where Wetzel developed his baseball skills. After spending 1913 to 1915 in the minor leagues, he was out of organized ball from 1916 through 1918.

Wetzel entered the U.S. Army during World War I, serving with the 342nd Field Artillery of the 89th Division. He played for the unit's baseball team along with big league pitcher (and future Hall of Famer) Grover Cleveland Alexander. Overseas, the 89th Division saw front-line action in France.

In 1919 Wetzel returned to organized ball, and he put up monster numbers in 1920 at Flint, Mich., leading the Michigan-Ontario League in seven offensive categories and winning the triple crown (12 homers, 72 RBI, .387 average). The St. Louis Browns acquired him that September, and Wetzel batted .429 in seven contests. He spent 1921 with St. Louis, appearing in 61 games and hitting .210.

From 1922 to 1930 Wetzel played for ten teams in six different leagues. He batted .353 in 1925 and .352 in 1926 for pennant-winning teams in Des Moines, Iowa (Western), leading the league in '25 with 17 homers. At age 35 in 1928, he hit .345 for Omaha, Neb., and topped the Western League with 61 doubles. He finished up with Hollywood, Calif. (Pacific Coast), in 1930 and later managed an independent club owned by actor and baseball aficionado Joe E. Brown.

Reportedly backed by money from the estate of the late Phil Ball (who owned the Browns from 1916–1933), Wetzel purchased the Omaha franchise in February 1934. He opened the season as player-manager, batted .273 in 21 games, and sold the club in July.

Wetzel, who moved to Los Angeles in the Twenties, later worked as an electrician at RKO Pictures. His co-workers included former big leaguers Ping Bodie, Wally Rehg, and Jim Scott.

Wetzel died of heart disease at 48. Gerald "George" Wetzel, his older brother, was a minor league outfielder from 1912 to 1926.

WHALEY, William Carl ("Will")

Born: February 10, 1896, Indianapolis. **Died:** March 3, 1943, Indianapolis.
Height: 5'11". **Weight:** 178. **Batted:** right. **Threw:** right.
Debut: April 18, 1923. **Final Game:** October 6, 1923.
Positions, teams, years: outfield, St. Louis (AL) 1923.
Games: 23. **At-bats:** 50. **Home runs:** 0. **Average:** .240.

Bill Whaley, who got his start on Indianapolis sandlots with teams like the Trojans and the Merits, was a professional ballplayer from 1914 to 1931.

Whaley broke in as a pitcher-outfielder with Streator, Ill. (Illinois-Missouri), in 1914 and made stops in Waterloo, Iowa (Central), and Cedar Rapids, Iowa (Central). He was out of organized ball in 1918, when he spent five weeks in the U.S. Army. From 1919 through 1922 Whaley played for Bay City (Michigan-Ontario), batting .300 or better each year as an outfielder and part-time pitcher.

After a .341 showing in 1922, the St. Louis Browns obtained Whaley for 1923. He saw action in 23 contests as a pinch-hitter and backup outfielder. That turned out to be his lone big league campaign.

Playing for Los Angeles (Pacific Coast) over the next two years, Whaley batted .328 in 1924. He shifted to third base in 1925, when his average dipped to .258. He spent 1926 in the Southern Association, opening the year with Little Rock, Ark., and finishing the season with pennant-winning New Orleans.

Whaley briefly played for Fort Wayne (Central) in 1928, when fellow Hoosier native (and future Hall of Famer) Chuck Klein made his pro debut. Whaley enjoyed one more productive season at Lynn, Mass. (New England), in 1929, where he averaged .333 with 78 RBI.

Retiring after 1931, Whaley returned to Indianapolis and worked as a special delivery postal clerk. He was 47 years old when he died, a victim of liver disease.

WHEELER, George Harrison ("Heavy," "The Shelburn Slugger")

Born: November 10, 1881, Shelburn. **Died:** June 14, 1918, Clinton.
Height: 5'9". **Weight:** 180. **Batted:** left. **Threw:** right.
Debut: July 27, 1910. **Final Game:** August 3, 1910.
Positions, teams, years: pinch-hitter, Cincinnati (NL) 1910.
Games: 3. **At-bats:** 3. **Home runs:** 0. **Average:** .000.

George Wheeler, a star player for the local baseball team in the Southwestern Indiana town of Shelburn, played the outfield and saw occasional duty at second base over eight professional seasons.

During a brief big league career, Wheeler saw action as a pinch-hitter. He spent his first four years in the Central League, breaking in with South Bend in 1907. He ended the year with Terre Haute, where he batted .303 in 1908 and .292 in 1909. One of the team's most popular players, he was averaging .320 after 59 games when the Cincinnati Reds shelled out $1,000 for his contract in July 1910. A headline in the *Fort Wayne Sentinel* describing the transaction read: "Wail Goes Up Over Sale of George Wheeler."

Reds manager Clark Griffith used Wheeler as a pinch-hitter in a home game with Pittsburgh on July 27, and again versus the Pirates at Cincinnati on July 31. His final at-bat took place in the first game of a double-header at Boston on August 3. He struck out in two of his three turns at bat, and on August 22 the Reds released him to Jersey City, N.J. (Eastern).

In 1911 Wheeler hit .281 for Jersey City, which shipped him to Terre Haute for 1912. Wheeler was batting .343 for Terre Haute in August 1913 when Indianapolis (American Association) acquired him. He averaged a meager .209 in 13 contests and was back in Terre Haute for 1914. He closed out his playing days that summer with Dubuque, Iowa (Three-I).

Wheeler led a troubled life after leaving baseball. He returned to Shelburn, where he operated a saloon. In October 1915 he was arrested and charged with harboring two men who had robbed a coal mine company paymaster in nearby Hymera, Ind. He was arrested again that December, this time for election tampering.

Wheeler was living in Clinton, employed as a coal mine electrician, when he died of tuberculosis at age 36.

WHEELER, Harry Eugene

Born: March 3, 1858, Versailles. **Died:** October 9, 1900, Cincinnati, Ohio.
Height: 5'11". **Weight:** 165. **Batted:** right. **Threw:** right.
Debut: June 19, 1878. **Final Game:** October 15, 1884.
Positions, teams, years: outfield (237), pitcher (14), first base (12), second base (1), Providence (NL), 1878, Cincinnati (NL) 1879, Cleveland (NL) 1880, Cincinnati (NL) 1880, Cincinnati (American Association) 1882, Columbus (American Association) 1883, St. Louis (American Association) 1884, Kansas City (Union Association) 1884, Chicago/Pittsburgh (Union Association) 1884, Baltimore (Union Association) 1884. **Games:** 257. **At-bats:** 1,122. **Home runs:** 2. **Average:** .228.
Innings pitched: 97.2. **Won/Lost:** 7–6. **Earned run average:** 4.70.

Manager: Kansas City (Union Association) 1884 (0–4).

At various times in his baseball career, **Harry Wheeler** worked in three different big leagues as an infielder, outfielder, pitcher, manager and umpire. During one season, he played for teams representing five different cities.

Wheeler was tending bar in Cincinnati and playing for a semi-pro team in 1878 when he joined the NL's Providence Grays. With John Montgomery Ward handing the bulk of the pitching, Wheeler went 6–1 with a 3.48 ERA—high by the standards of the time.

Wheeler joined the Cincinnati Reds for 1879, and on May 24 he took the mound in a home game against his old club, the Grays. The result was "a disastrous defeat," according to newspaper accounts. "By way of an experiment," reported the *Chicago Tribune*, "Wheeler was substituted for W. White [Will White, Cincinnati's usual starting pitcher] and the result was ten runs scored."

Cut loose after that one appearance, Wheeler disappeared from organized baseball until 1880 when he joined the Cleveland Blues of the NL as an outfielder. He appeared in one contest for the Blues before returning to Cincinnati. He played 17 games for the Reds, batting .092, and once again drifted out of the professional ranks.

In 1882 the American Association began operations as a second major league. Wheeler umpired the Opening Day game between the Cincinnati Red Stockings and the host Pittsburgh Alleghenys. After the contest, the Red Stockings hired him as a first baseman-pitcher. On June 28, Wheeler became the second big leaguer to hit two triples in the same inning when he stroked a pair of three-base hits in the 11th inning of an 11–4 win over the Baltimore Orioles.

Cincinnati went on to win the pennant, with Wheeler appearing in 76 of the club's 80 contests. He batted .250 while compiling a 1–2 record as a pitcher. In 1883 he was back in the American Association, this time with the Cleveland Buckeyes. He started and lost one game while hitting .226 in 82 of Cleveland's 97 contests.

Wheeler opened the 1884 campaign with the American Association's St. Louis Browns. After five games, he jumped to the Union Association—a third major league—as player-manager of the Kansas City Unions. Wheeler's managerial career ended with an 0–4 record, and after 14 games he quit the club. He got into 20 games for his next team, the Chicago Browns of the Union Association, who left town on August 20 to become the Pittsburgh Stogies. He finished the year with the UA's Baltimore Monumentals

Back in the minor leagues for 1885, Wheeler played for teams in Cleveland (Western), Waterbury, Conn. (Southern New England League in 1885; Eastern League from 1886 to1887), Worcester, Mass. (New England), and Manchester, Conn. (New England). In 1887 his 84 runs and 120 hits led the Eastern League, and in 1888, his final campaign, he stole 43 bases.

Described as a "genial, warm-hearted fellow" when he played for Cincinnati, Wheeler returned there after his playing days ended. His health soon began to fail, and in August 1896 *The Sporting News* reported Wheeler was broke. Friends and fans staged a benefit that raised more than $1,000 for Wheeler, his wife and two daughters. He had been bedridden for several months when he died at 42.

WHISLER, Wesley Guy

Born: April 7, 1983, Indianapolis. **Lives:** Noblesville.
Height: 6'5". **Weight:** 240. **Batted:** left. **Threw:** left.
Debut: June 2, 2009. **Final game:** June 7, 2009.
Positions, teams, years: pitcher, Chicago (AL) 2009.
Games: 3. **Innings pitched:** 1.1. **Won/Lost:** 0–0. **Earned run average:** 13.50.

Wes Whisler was a two-sport standout at Noblesville High School. A pitcher/first baseman, he missed part of his junior season to play for Team USA at the 2000 Pan American Junior Baseball Championships in Hermosillo, Mexico.

As a senior, Whisler narrowly avoided a devastating injury during a basketball game. Undercut while going up for a shot, he landed on his neck and suffered a concussion of the head and spinal cord. The injury ended his basketball career and sidelined him for the start of the baseball season.

Whisler recovered in 2001 to win honors as Indiana's "Mr. Baseball," and in June the Chicago Cubs selected him in the 41st round of the draft. Instead he accepted a UCLA baseball scholarship. In 2002, his first year with the Bruins, he set a school freshman record with 18 home runs and ranked among the Pac-10's top pitchers and power hitters.

In 2004 *Baseball America* described Whisler as "an intriguing two-way talent." The Chicago White Sox took him as a pitcher/designated hitter in the second round of the June draft. He joined Kannapolis, N.C. (South Atlantic), taking an occasional turn at designated hitter before the White Sox made him a full-time pitcher. He played for Winston-Salem, N.C. (Carolina), and Birmingham, Ala. (Southern), before joining Charlotte, N.C. (International), for 2008, where he posted a 12–10 mark.

Whisler joined the White Sox in June 2009. In his first big league contest, he pitched an inning of shutout ball against Oakland. After two more relief appearances he was back in Charlotte.

In June 2010 the White Sox dealt Whisler to the Florida Marlins. He spent the rest of the year with New Orleans (Pacific Coast), going 3–7 with a 6.25 ERA. A free agent after the season, he re-signed with the White Sox and pitched for Chicago affiliates in 2011, 2012 and 2013.

After ten professional campaigns Whisler returned to Indiana, where he conducts baseball lessons, camps and clinics at The Strike Zone in the Indianapolis suburb of Fishers.

WHITE, John Wallace ("Johnny")

Born: January 19, 1878, Traders Point. **Died:** September 30, 1963, Indianapolis.
Height: 5'6". **Weight:** unknown. **Batted:** right. **Threw:** right.
Debut: June 26, 1904. **Final Game:** June 26, 1904.
Positions, teams, years: outfield, Boston (NL) 1904.
Games: 1. **At-bats:** 5. **Home runs:** 0. **Average:** .000.

When the Boston Beaneaters borrowed him in 1904 to fill out their lineup, career minor leaguer **Jack White** became a big league player for one day.

White's professional baseball career began in the Western Association in 1895, when he opened the year with Jacksonville, Ill., and finished the season in Quincy, Ill. He played his final game with Syracuse (New York State) in 1913.

During his first two professional campaigns, White spent time with Indianapolis (Western), where he was known as Johnny and worked as a machinist in the offseason. At Toronto (Eastern) in 1897 he batted .329 with 38 stolen bases. Prior to 1898, Toronto traded him to Buffalo, N.Y. (Eastern), for R.C. "Reddy" Grey in what the *Buffalo Courier* archly described as "a chromatic deal."

The swap broke up one of the most celebrated outfields in baseball history. In 1897, Grey had teamed with two other red-haired outfielders, Billy Clymer and Larry Gilboy. Reddy's older brother, famed author Zane Grey, wrote *The Redheaded Outfield*, a short story inspired by the trio. The setting for Grey's tale is Rochester, N.Y., and he named his characters "Ray," "Clammer" and "Gilbat."

White played all outfield and infield positions (except first base) for Buffalo in 1899, and the *Saginaw* (Mich.) *News* called him "the best utility man in the Western League." He returned to Toronto in 1902, and in 1903 he hit .320 with 36 stolen bases.

At Jersey City, N.J., on Saturday, June 25, 1904, White played left field for Toronto. The next day in Brooklyn, he played left field for Boston in a Major League contest. On Monday, June 27, he was back in left field for Toronto. That day's *Newark* (N.J.) *News* provided the explanation: "Jack White, captain of the Toronto team, played in the outfield for the Boston Nationals against Brooklyn yesterday. The Boston team was crippled, as [first baseman Fred] Tenney, [pitcher Togie] Pittinger and [pitcher Kaiser] Wilhelm do not play Sunday ball and [outfielder Dick] Cooley and [utility man] Pat Moran are ill. Manager [Al] Bruckenberger had to borrow the services of White in order to turn out nine men."

Toronto traded White to Buffalo in 1906, and he batted .286 against Columbus, Ohio, in that year's Junior World Series. Buffalo led three games to two (there was one tie) when the series abruptly ended due to a dispute over the site of the next game and distribution of the receipts.

By now White was spending winters in Toronto, where he owned a billiard parlor. He continued to play for Buffalo through 1911 and spent 1912–1913 with Syracuse.

After leaving baseball, White returned to Indianapolis, where he was self-employed. He died there at age 85.

WHITMAN, Walter Franklin ("Hooker")

Born: August 15, 1925, Marengo. **Died:** February 6, 1994, Maryville, Illinois.
Height: 6'2". **Weight:** 175. **Batted:** right. **Threw:** right.
Debut: June 30, 1946. **Final Game:** September 28, 1948.
Positions, teams, years: shortstop (7), second base (1), first base (1), Chicago (AL) 1946, 1948.
Games: 20. **At-bats:** 22. **Home runs:** 0. **Average:** .045.

Frank Whitman won 11 letters in baseball, football and basketball at Eureka (Ill.) High School, where his father was the custodian. His nickname stems from his hook shot skill on the basketball court.

The Red Sox signed Whitman to a contract in December 1941, and in 1942 he played for teams in the Boston and Cleveland Indians systems. He was in the U.S. Army from 1943 through 1945, serving as a sergeant with the 75th Infantry Division. He took part in the Battle of the Bulge and was awarded the Bronze Star.

After the war, Whitman entered Illinois Wesleyan College, where he played baseball and basketball. When he signed with the White Sox in June 1946, Chicago manager Ted Lyons called him "the best college prospect I've seen in 20 years."

Whitman appeared in 17 contests for the White Sox and got his lone Major League hit in a game with the visiting New York Yankees on July 27. Prior to an August 5 home game with the Washington Senators, fans from Eureka presented him with a radio and a razor. The White Sox won 1–0 when Whitman drew a bases-loaded walk off Early Wynn (a future Hall of Famer) in the third inning.

After spending all of 1947 in the minors, Whitman got into three games for Chicago in 1948. He divided the rest of the season between Memphis, Tenn. (Southern Association), and Muskegon, Mich. (Central), and continued to play in the minors through 1950.

Whitman coached at Bloomington (Ill.) High School before taking over as director of athletics at Canton High School in the fall of 1951. He also coached the basketball and baseball teams, and served as an assistant football coach. During a radio broadcast in January 1953, he announced his resignation as basketball coach due to "constant bickering and complaints" by Canton fans, but came back before the season ended.

Whitman remained active in baseball, pitching a three-hit shutout for Canton of the semi-pro Illinois State League in the 1954 season opener. Whitman, who also studied at Eureka College and Cornell College in Mount Vernon, Iowa, received a master's degree from Bradley University. He left Canton High after 1958 to work in the insurance and real estate business.

WICKER, Robert Kitridge

Born: May 25, 1877, Bono. **Died:** January 22, 1955, Evanston, Illinois.
Height: 6'2". **Weight:** 180. **Batted:** right. **Threw:** right.
Debut: August 11, 1901. **Final Game:** September 21, 1906.
Positions, teams, years: pitcher, St. Louis (NL) 1901–1903, Chicago (NL) 1903–1906, Cincinnati (NL) 1906.
Games: 138. **Innings pitched:** 1,036.2. **Won/Lost:** 64–52. **Earned run average:** 2.73.

A native of Lawrence County in southern Indiana, **Bob Wicker** grew up in nearby Bedford. He attended Oak Ridge Male Institute, a military prep school in North Carolina, where his father's family had lived before coming to Indiana.

Bob played for independent and semi-pro teams around Indiana and Illinois before breaking into organized ball in 1900, when he had a 22–9 record for pennant-winning Dayton, Ohio (Inter-State). In 1901 he helped coach Indiana University's baseball squad before reporting to Dayton (by now in the Western Association).

Wicker was 10–8 after 19 games with Dayton when Pittsburgh picked up his contract. But Wicker was "erratic due to ill health," according to *Sporting Life*, and without giving him a chance to pitch, the Pirates shipped him to the Cardinals. Arm trouble limited him to just one appearance with St. Louis.

Despite a mild bout with malaria in 1902, Wicker was 5-12 in 22 games for the Cardinals. After one relief appearance in 1903, St. Louis sent him to Chicago, where Wicker had a 20-9 record for the third-place Cubs.

In 1904—the first year of Chicago's famed Tinker-to-Evers-to-Chance double play combination—Wicker's 17-8 slate helped the Cubs finish second. At the Polo Grounds in New York on June 11, 1904, before a record crowd of 38,805, he beat the Giants 1-0 in 12 innings. Wicker didn't allow a hit until the tenth inning, when Sam Mertes stroked a one-out single. "The quiet Chicagoan studied out his men like so many mathematical problems," noted the *Chicago Tribune*, "seeking out their weaknesses with splendid success." Later that summer, admirers from Bedford presented him with a gold-headed cane and an Elk's button.

When the Cubs placed third in 1905, Wicker went 13-6. He was 3-5 on June 2, 1906, when Chicago dealt him to Cincinnati for Orval Overall in an exchange of right-handers. Overall was 4-5 at the time, but went 12-3 for Chicago to help the Cubs win the pennant with a jaw-dropping 116-36 record. Overall went on to help the Cubs win four pennants over the next five years, while Wicker went 6-11 for the Reds and disappeared from the majors after the 1906 season.

Wicker continued to pitch in the minors, going 14-12 in 1907 to help Columbus win the American Association pennant. He spent the next two seasons with Montreal (Eastern), going 15-11 in 1908 and 11-14 in 1909. Prior to the 1908 campaign, he once again worked with the Indiana University team.

Over the next five seasons Wicker played for semi-pro teams, including a gig with the Kokomo Red Sox as player-manager in 1914. In 1915 he was back in organized ball, managing Spokane, Wash. (Northwestern), to a third-place finish with an 81-74 slate.

Returning to Bedford in 1916, Wicker managed a local independent club. He eventually settled in Wilmette, Ill., where he worked for General Electric as a foreman. He still owned a home in Bedford, and was planning to return there when he died at age 77.

WILLIAMS, Fred ("Cy")

Born: December 21, 1887, Wadena. **Died:** April 23, 1974, Eagle River, Wisconsin.
Height: 6'2". **Weight:** 180. **Batted:** left. **Threw:** left.
Debut: July 18, 1912. **Final Game:** September 22, 1930.
Positions, teams, years: outfield, Chicago (NL) 1912-1917, Philadelphia (NL) 1918-1930.
Games: 2,002. **At-bats:** 6,780. **Home runs:** 251. **Average:** .292.

One of baseball's top power hitters of the Roaring Twenties, **Cy Williams** was the first NL player with 200 career home runs. Along the way the long, lean, left-handed slugger won or shared four league homer crowns.

The son of a farmer, Williams was a native of Wadena in northwest Indiana. In 1890 the Benton County hamlet had fewer than 100 citizens, but two of them—Williams and Otis "Doc" Crandall—went on to the Major Leagues. Both went to Wadena High School and played for a local team called the Plowboys.

In 1908 Williams entered the University of Notre Dame, where he picked up the nickname "Cy." An architecture student, he became a three-sport star for the Fighting Irish. In baseball he was the left fielder and team captain. He was a backup end (and a teammate of Knute Rockne) on the football team, and he also competed for the track squad as a high hurdler and long jumper.

Williams went straight from college to the Major Leagues in 1912, signing with the Chicago Cubs and reporting for duty on July 2. "He was called the oldest youngster in baseball," quipped a teammate, pitcher Al Demaree, "because he was bald-headed when he broke in."

In his first three big league campaigns Williams saw limited action, and in 1913 he didn't join the Cubs until June, after receiving his bachelor of science degree. When Roger Bresnahan took over as Chicago manager in 1915, he named Williams his everyday center fielder. Cy responded by hitting .257 with 13 home runs, the NL's second-highest total. His batting average climbed to .279 in 1916, when he hit 12 homers to tie for the league title.

After Williams slipped to .241 with five home runs in 1917, the Cubs traded him to Philadelphia in what turned out to be one of the best trades in Phillies history. In his first two seasons with Philadelphia, Williams batted .276 and .278. In 1920, he ripened into one of baseball's top sluggers. As the lively-ball era dawned, Williams found his stroke in Philadelphia's Baker Bowl, where the right-field wall was only 281 feet from home plate.

Williams hit better than .300 six times over the next seven seasons, including a career-high .345 in 1926. He reached double figures in home runs every year from 1920 to 1928. In 1923, when his average dipped to .293, he drove in 114 runs. His 41 homers topped the NL that year, and tied Babe Ruth for the highest total in the majors. Williams clubbed his 200th career home run that summer to eclipse Roger Connor as the NL's all-time homer king.

At age 39 in 1927 Williams became baseball's oldest homer champ, clubbing 30 home runs to equal Hack Wilson for the NL lead. On August 5 that year, he hit for the cycle against Pittsburgh. A dead-pull hitter, Williams once said: "I tried a thousand ways to hit that ball into left field, but I just couldn't make it go."

In 1920, rival teams began playing deep and to the right side of the field when he batted—22 years before Cleveland Indians manager Lou Boudreau employed a similar shift on another left-handed slugger named Williams. "Maybe Lou thought he was doing something new when he switched his whole infield over to the right for Ted Williams," Cy told reporters. "Well ... they used to do the same thing for me."

An excellent defensive player, Williams led the NL with 29 assists in 1921. Hall of Famer Joe Tinker, a Chicago teammate, praised him as "the greatest natural outfielder I ever saw." In 1928 he shared right field with rookie Chuck Klein, another native Hoosier.

Williams wrapped up his 19-year-career in 1930 at age 43 without playing for a pennant-winning team. "A World Series, to me, is only something to read about," he told *Baseball Magazine* when his career was winding down. Williams served under 14 different big league skippers. He opened 1931 as playing manager at Richmond (Eastern), but didn't last the season.

By then, Williams owned a dairy farm in Three Lakes, Wis., where he was also a bank director. He eventually formed his own construction company, and in 1966 Wisconsin governor Warren Knowles proclaimed him "The Gentleman of Baseball." Cy Williams Park was dedicated in Three Lakes that same year.

Williams, an avid outdoorsman who enjoyed hunting and fishing, died in 1974 at the age of 86.

WISE, Kendall Cole ("Casey," "K.C.," "Kick")

Born: September 8, 1932, Lafayette. **Died:** February 20, 2007, Naples, Florida.
Height: 6'0". **Weight:** 170. **Batted:** both. **Threw:** right.
Debut: April 16, 1957. **Final game:** July 3, 1960.
Positions, teams, years: second base (78), shortstop (27), third base (2), Chicago (NL) 1957, Milwaukee (NL) 1958–1959, Detroit (AL) 1960.
Games: 126. **At-bats:** 321. **Home runs:** 3. **Average:** .174.

Casey Wise, whose initials provided his nickname, grew up around ballfields. His father, Hugh Wise, played baseball for Purdue University in 1926–1927 (Casey was born while his father was there doing research work in hydraulics). The elder Wise had a cup of coffee with the Detroit Tigers in 1930 and spent half a century as a minor league player, manager, executive, and ballpark designer. Hugh Wise also scouted for the Boston and Milwaukee Braves, New York Yankees and Chicago White Sox. Casey was dubbed 'Kick' by an older brother, Hugh Jr., a minor league outfielder from 1953 to 1956.

While he was still in elementary school, Wise's family moved to Hollywood, Fla. He starred in baseball, football, basketball and track at South Broward High School and won a scholarship to the University of Texas. He later transferred to the University of Florida. Wise signed with the Chicago Cubs in 1953, even though his father was scouting for the Braves at the time. "My dad wanted me for the Braves," said Casey, "but he also wanted me to get the best deal I could."

From 1953 to 1955, Wise played for Sioux Falls, S.D. (Northern), and Des Moines, Iowa (Western). During those years, he didn't report until after his college classes ended. In

1955 he earned a mechanical engineering degree from Florida. His first full pro season was 1956, when he shifted from second base to shortstop and batted .287 to help Los Angeles win the Pacific Coast League pennant.

Wise joined the Cubs in 1957 and hit .179 in 43 games. Traded to Milwaukee for 1958, he batted .197 in 31 contests. In the World Series—won by the Yankees in seven games—he saw action in two games as a pinch-hitter and pinch-runner.

In 1959 Wise was one of several players who subbed for Red Schoendienst after the Braves second baseman was sidelined with tuberculosis. In 22 games Wise hit .171, and after the season Milwaukee sent him to Detroit in a five-player deal. He batted .147 in 30 games for the Tigers in 1960, and that July he was gone from the majors for good. Out of baseball in 1961, he returned with Jacksonville, Fla. (International), in 1962. After the death of manager Ben Geraghty in June 1963, Wise took over as skipper.

By then Wise was a graduate student at the University of Tennessee, where he earned degrees in dentistry and orthodontics. From 1968 to 1991 he had an orthodontics practice in Naples, Fla., where he was a community activist as well as a boating enthusiast, scuba diver and tennis player.

Wise died of complications following heart surgery when he was 74.

WOEHR, Andrew Emil

Born: February 4, 1896, Fort Wayne. **Died:** July 24, 1990, Fort Wayne.
Height: 5'11". **Weight:** 165. **Batted:** right. **Threw:** right.
Debut: September 15, 1923. **Final game:** September 23, 1924.
Positions, teams, years: third base (57), second base (1), Philadelphia (NL) 1923–1924.
Games: 63. **At-bats:** 193. **Home runs:** 0. **Average:** .274.

A significant figure in Fort Wayne baseball history, **Andy Woehr** played for the Western Gas Company team in the city's Shop League starting in 1915. After World War I military service, he broke into organized ball in 1920 with Grand Rapids, Mich. (Central), and played for Bloomington, Ill. (Three-I), in 1921. He opened 1922 with Ludington, Mich. (Central), taking over as manager in mid-season. His .316 average helped Ludington to a first-place finish.

In 1923 Woehr (pronounced "ware") batted .310 for Williamsport, Pa. (New York-Penn). When the season ended he joined the Philadelphia Phillies and hit .341 in 13 games. He spent all of 1924 with Philadelphia, hitting .217 in 50 games. He was back in the minors in 1925, this time with Beaumont (Texas), where he became the second of two managers for a last-place team. He opened the 1926 season with Beaumont and finished the year with Shreveport, La. (Texas). He remained with Shreveport through 1929, and before the summer was out he was back in Indiana, playing for the semi-pro Indianapolis Kautskys.

Returning to Fort Wayne, Woehr went to work for International Harvester. He continued to play for independent teams, including the Pennsylvania Railroad squad, where he took over as playing manager in 1931. When International Harvester formed a club in 1938, he served as player-manager. He later played for the Lincoln National Life Insurance team.

After quitting baseball, Woehr enjoyed bowling and golf, usually shooting in the 70s for 18 holes. He retired from International Harvester in 1964, and was inducted into the Northeast Indiana Baseball Association Hall of Fame that year along with two other ex-big leaguers, Pinky Hargrave and Butch Henline.

Woehr, who died at age 94, was the father of Richard Woehr, an infielder for Columbia, S.C. (South Atlantic), in 1942.

WOODS, Clarence Cofield

Born: June 11, 1892, Woods Ridge. **Died:** July 2, 1969, Rising Sun.
Height: 6'5". **Weight:** 230. **Batted:** right. **Threw:** right.
Debut: August 8, 1914. **Final game:** August 16, 1914.
Positions, teams, years: pitcher, Indianapolis (Federal) 1914.
Games: 2. **Innings pitched:** 2. **Won/Lost:** 0–0. **Earned run average:** 4.50.

In the summer of 1914 **Clarence Woods**, a real-life Walter Mitty, left his home in Rising Sun and showed up at Federal League Park in Indianapolis to request a tryout with the Indianapolis Hoosiers. "Lean, lank and gawky, but possessing all the earmarks of being a diamond in the rough, Clarence Wood (sic) ... came to town Saturday—came unheralded—for a tryout with the Hoosier Feds," according to the *Indianapolis News*.

"[Indianapolis manager] Bill Phillips watched Clarence warm up for a few minutes and saw that there were a few points that he had overlooked in the pitching art," the *News* continued. "He did see, however, that Clarence had a world of speed and a wide breaking curve, and sent him to the mound for an opportunity to show his stuff against the Baltimore Terrapins in the ninth."

It was the second game of a doubleheader, and Baltimore had an 8-0 lead. "The Terrapins laughed and chortled with glee at Clarence out there getting ready to pitch, but the sight was not so funny after all," the *News* noted. "[Hack] Simmons, the first man up, walked and pilfered his way to third, but Runt Walsh fanned the breeze. Clarence then made the mistake of throwing [Mickey] Doolan out on his sacrifice when he had plenty of time to trap Simmons on the line, and the error of judgment cost a run."

Prior to that day—August 8, 1914—there is no record of Woods in organized ball. "Just how a promising young pitcher could arise to the towering hight [sic] of more than six feet on the settlement around Rising Sun, and escape the eagle eye of Tom Brolley [author of a bill that allowed Sunday baseball in Indiana], is rather hard to comprehend, but such is the case," opined the *News*. "With a little seasoning," the newspaper concluded, "Wood [sic] gives promise of becoming a regular pitcher."

Woods made one more relief appearance, tossing a scoreless inning in the Hoosiers' 21-6 home win over the Pittsburgh Rebels on August 16. And that was the end of his professional baseball career.

Except for a hitch in the U.S. Army during World War I, Woods spent the rest of his life in Ohio County. He worked as a rural mail carrier for 35 years, was active in community affairs and was a charter member of the Ohio County Historical Society. In 1954 he and his wife opened a real estate business in Rising Sun. An outdoorsman, Woods was active in trap shooting and field trials and served as president of Ohio County's Fish and Game Protection Association. He was 77 at the time of his death.

WRIGHT, Robert Cassius

Born: December 13, 1891, Decatur County. **Died:** July 30, 1993, Carmichael, California.
Height: 6'1". **Weight:** 175. **Batted:** right. **Threw:** right.
Debut: September 21, 1915. **Final Game:** September 24, 1915.
Positions, teams, years: pitcher, Chicago (NL) 1915.
Games: 2. **Innings pitched:** 4. **Won/Lost:** 0-0. **Earned run average:** 2.25.

Born in a log house on a farm near the southeastern Indiana town of Westport, **Bob Wright** pitched for Westport High School's baseball team and later for a local semi-pro club. In 1912 the Indianapolis Indians (American Association) signed the spitball specialist and sent him to Newark (Ohio State) for seasoning. After ten games and a 3-4 record, he became homesick and quit the team. In 1913 he was back in organized ball with Kankakee, Ill. (Illinois-Missouri), and in 1914 he pitched for Virginia, Minn. (Northern).

Wright's 19-13 slate for Virginia in 1915 caught the attention of the Chicago Cubs, who bought his contract in September. He debuted in a 5-4 loss to the New York Giants in the first game of a doubleheader at Chicago's West Side Park. In 1988 Wright described his big league debut in an interview with the *Associated Press*: "I came in with the bases loaded. I struck out the first guy. The next guy hit a grounder to Heinie Zimmerman at third and I hollered 'throw it home.' Heinie threw to the second baseman who threw to first. Double play and the inning was over."

Before the season ended, Wright made one more relief appearance. In 1916 he went to Spring Training with the Cubs, but Chicago had an abundance of pitchers after the breakup of the Federal League. "They didn't carry me very long," said Wright. "After that I went back to the minors, and it broke my heart."

Wright toiled for four teams in three different leagues between 1916 and 1917. Out of baseball in 1918 due to World War I military service, he returned in 1921 with Toledo, Ohio (American Association).

After the 1923 season, Wright left Toledo to take a job with Nash Motors in Kenosha, Wis., where he played for the company's industrial league team. "In organized baseball, I never came close to making the money I made with that team," he said.

Wright eventually returned to Indiana, where he owned a farm and worked as chief of the Gross Revenue Division for the State of Indiana. In his late 1970s he moved to California, and in 1989 he returned to Chicago for Wrigley Field's 75th anniversary celebration. He threw out the ceremonial first pitch—a spitball, of course. Wright was the oldest ex-big league player when he died at 101 in 1993.

WYATT, Loral John ("Joe," "L.J.")

Born: April 6, 1900, Petersburg. **Died:** December 5, 1970, Oblong, Illinois.
Height: 6'1". **Weight:** 175. **Batted:** right. **Threw:** right.
Debut: September 11, 1924. **Final game:** September 13, 1924.
Positions, teams, years: outfield, Cleveland (AL) 1924.
Games: 4. **At-bats:** 12. **Home runs:** 0. **Average:** .167.

After World War I military service in 1918, **Joe Wyatt** was a four-year letterman at Wabash College. As a senior in 1924 he was the center fielder and team captain while his brother Fred played first base. At the outset of the 1924 season, *The Bachelor*, Wabash's school paper, observed: "[Joe] Wyatt is the hardest hitter on the team, cracking the pill last season for the total average of .491 besides stealing 15 bases and making only one error in 38 chances."

After graduation, the Cleveland Indians signed Wyatt and assigned him to Terre Haute (Three-I). He hit .306 in 61 games and joined the Indians toward the end of the season. He started both ends of a September 11 doubleheader against St. Louis Browns, going 1-for-2 in the first game and 1-for-5 in the nightcap. Over the next two days he started two more contests, going hitless in five at-bats.

Wyatt spent the 1925 season with Terre Haute, batting .308. He started the 1926 season with Indianapolis (American Association), which loaned him to Columbus, Ohio (American Association). He finished the year with a .308 average. Back with Indianapolis in 1927, Wyatt was hitting .329 after 25 games when New Orleans (Southern Association) acquired him. He batted .255 in 52 games and retired after the season. "I didn't want to let my college education go to waste by playing in the minors," he said in a 1970 interview. "There isn't any money in those leagues and it just wasn't worth it at that time."

Wyatt went to work for Firestone Rubber, managing a company store in Vincennes and organizing Firestone's industrial league baseball club. Later, he was a dealer for Texaco gasoline. He retired from J&N Beverages, a beer distributorship in Vincennes, where he spent his final years. Wyatt was on a hunting trip in Illinois when he suffered a fatal heart attack at age 70.

YOUNG, Harlan Edward ("Cy the Third")

Born: September 28, 1883, Portland. **Died:** March 26, 1975, Jacksonville, Florida.
Height: 6'2". **Weight:** 190. **Batted:** right. **Threw:** right.
Debut: April 21, 1908. **Final game:** July 4, 1908.
Positions, teams, years: pitcher, Pittsburgh (NL) 1908, Boston (NL) 1908.
Games: 14. **Innings pitched:** 75.2. **Won/Lost:** 0–3. **Earned run average:** 2.62.

Denton True "Cy" Young was already a baseball legend by the first decade of the 20th Century. Pitchers who shared his last name inevitably inherited Cy's nickname.

Irving Melrose Young reached the big leagues in 1905 and was known as "Young Cy" Young. When shine ball specialist **Harley Young** arrived in 1908, he was dubbed "Cy the Third," or "Cy Young III."

Indiana's Cy Young spent his early years in the Jay County town of Portland in the eastern part of the state. His family relocated to Oklahoma City, and he appears in photographs of the 1904 and 1905 Oklahoma City High School baseball teams. He entered organized ball in 1905 with Pittsburg, Kan. (Missouri Valley), where he went 18–3.

In the spring of 1906 Young failed a tryout with the St. Louis Browns and spent the year at Springfield, Mo. (Western Association), where he compiled a 24-17 slate. In 1907 he went 29-4 at Wichita, Kan. (Western Association), leading the league in wins and percentage (.879).

The Pittsburgh Pirates bought Young's contract on August 3, 1907, and he opened the 1908 season in the big leagues. He was 0-2 with a 2.25 ERA after eight appearances when Pittsburgh traded him to the Boston Doves (today's Atlanta Braves) in return for Irv "Young Cy" Young. In six games with Boston, Harley had an 0-1 record with a 3.33 ERA and the Doves shipped him to Jersey City, N.J. (Eastern).

Young never returned to the Major Leagues. In 1909 he joined Oklahoma City (Texas), going 17-10 despite losing a month due to an arm injury. Sent to Topeka, Kan. (Western), for 1910, he held out for two months before reporting. In late July, Topeka shipped Young back to Oklahoma City, where he went 3-8.

After an 18-17 mark with 245 strikeouts for Oklahoma City in 1911, Young was back in the Western League for 1912. He started the season with Topeka and finished up in Sioux City, S.D. He compiled an 11-15 record, and in August the Detroit Tigers acquired him.

Once again, Young failed to make the big club. He spent the 1913 season with Sioux City, going 8-12. He was out of organized baseball from 1914 to 1916, when he worked as superintendent of a Florida citrus plantation.

Young made a comeback in 1917 with Tulsa, Okla. (Western Association), going 22-15 and finishing the year as manager. In 1918 he pitched for Shreveport, La. (Texas), and Seattle (Pacific Coast International), and in 1919 he had an 0-1 record for Tulsa. His last year in organized ball was 1920, when he pitched for Victoria, B.C. (Pacific Coast International), and Petersburg (Virginia).

Young eventually returned to Florida, where he owned and managed a golf course. He later worked as an accountant and operated an apartment complex. He was 91 when he died of a heart attack.

Often mistaken for Irv Young, the man he was traded for in 1908, Harley is also frequently confused with William "Cy" Young, a University of Wisconsin pitcher who defeated Notre Dame (and future Major League hurler Ed Reulbach) in a game at South Bend in April 1904.

ZEIDER, Rollie Hubert ("Bunions," "Polly," "Hook")

Born: November 16, 1883, Hoover. **Died:** September 12, 1967, Garrett.
Height: 5'10". **Weight:** 162. **Batted:** right. **Threw:** right.
Debut: April 14, 1910. **Final game:** August 29, 1918.
Positions, teams, years: second base (335), third base (307), shortstop (162), first base (106), outfield (8), Chicago (AL) 1910-1913, New York (AL) 1913, Chicago (Federal) 1914-1915, Chicago (NL) 1917-1918.
Games: 941. **At-bats:** 3,210. **Home runs:** 5. **Average:** .240.

During a nine-year career, **Rollie Zeider** played for three Chicago teams in three different leagues and saw action at all four infield positions and the outfield.

Zeider, who started out as a pitcher, grew up in Auburn and played for the town baseball team. His pro career began in 1905 with Crookston, Minn. (Northern), and before the year ended he joined Winnipeg, Manitoba (Northern Copper Country). In 1907 he went from Winnipeg to San Francisco (Pacific Coast). He stole 93 bases for San Francisco in 1908, and in 1909 he manned third base for the pennant-bound Seals, leading the league in steals (93) and runs (141).

Zeider joined the Chicago White Sox in 1910, and in March he came down with typhoid fever. After recovering, he hit .217 and stole 49 bases—an AL rookie record that would last until 1986. In 1910 he was the Sox's main second baseman, and in 1912 he was their primary first baseman. Nicknamed "Bunions" by now because of his abnormally swollen toes (as well as "Hook" and "Polly" due to a prominent nose), Zeider was popular with Chicago fans—"cheered lustily by the Windy City fans every time he steps to the plate," according to a contemporary newspaper account.

On June 1, 1913, the White Sox traded Zeider and first baseman Babe Borton to the New York Yankees for Hal Chase, New York's star first sacker. *New York Globe* sportswriter Mark Roth groused that the Yanks had given up Chase "for a bunion and an onion." The trade was a bust for both teams. Chase, a controversial figure, was eventually banned from baseball. The prickly Borton (hence the "onion" label) was gone from New York before the year was out, and injuries limited Zeider to just 29 games.

Rollie quit the Yanks to sign with the Chicago Whales in 1914, when the Federal League claimed big league status. He batted .274 that year as the ChiFeds finished third. With Zeidler handling most of the second base chores in 1915, Chicago won the pennant. The Federal League went under after the season, and in 1916 Zeider went to a third Chicago team in yet another loop, joining the Cubs. A valuable backup during his first two seasons on the Northside, he was Chicago's primary second baseman in 1918 when they won the NL flag. The Cubs lost the World Series in six games to the Boston Red Sox, with Zeider making two appearances at third base and drawing a pair of walks.

Zeider left Chicago in 1919 to become playing manager at Toledo, Ohio (American Association), but he resigned in July and joined an independent club in La Porte, Ind. He returned to organized ball in 1920 and continued to play in the minors through 1924.

Back in Indiana, he operated Polly's Tavern in Garrett for many years and moved to Orland in 1959. In 1965 Zeider was inducted into the Northeast Indiana Baseball Association Hall of Fame. He died from stomach cancer at the age of 83.

Bibliography

Books

General History

Abrams, Roger. *The First World Series and the Baseball Fanatics of 1903*. Boston: Northeastern University Press, 2003.

Alexander, Charles. *Our Game*. New York: Henry Holt, 1991.

Allen, Lee. *The American League Story*. New York: Hill & Wang, 1962.

_____. *The National League Story*. New York: Hill & Wang, 1961.

_____. *100 Years of Baseball*. New York: Bartholomew House, 1951.

Anton, Todd, and Bill Nowlin. *When Baseball Went to War*. Chicago: Triumph, 2008.

Asinof, Eliot. *Eight Men Out*. Evanston, Ill.: Holtzman Press, 1963.

Aylesworth, Thomas, Benton Minks, and John Bowman. *The Encyclopedia of Baseball Managers*. New York: Crescent, 1990.

Bailey, Bob. *History of the Junior World Series*. Lanham, Md.: Scarecrow, 2004.

The Baseball Encyclopedia, 1st–11th eds. New York: Macmillan. 1969–2000.

Batesel, Paul. *Major League Baseball Players of 1884*. Jefferson, N.C.: McFarland, 2011.

_____. *Major League Baseball Players of 1916*. Jefferson, N.C.: McFarland, 2007.

_____. *Players and Teams of the National Association, 1871–1875*. Jefferson, N.C.: McFarland, 2012.

Bauer, Carlos. *The Coast League Cyclopedia: Vols.1–3*. San Diego: Baseball Press, 2003.

Bauer, Carlos, Bob McConnell, and John Benesch, Jr., eds. *SABR Guide to Minor League Statistics*. 3d ed. Cleveland: Society for American Baseball Research, 2007.

Beverage, Richard. *The Angels*. Placentia, Calif.: Deacon Press, 1981.

_____. *The Hollywood Stars*. Placentia, Calif.: Deacon Press, 1984.

Bjarkman, Peter. *The Encyclopedia of Major League Baseball Team Histories: The American League*. Westport, Conn.: Meckler, 1991.

_____. *The Encyclopedia of Major League Baseball Team Histories: The National League*. Westport, Conn.: Meckler, 1991.

Bodenhamer, David, and Robert Barrows, eds. *The Encyclopedia of Indianapolis*. Bloomington: Indiana University Press, 1994.

Bouton, Jim. *Ball Four*. New York: World, 1970.

Bowman, Larry. *Before the World Series*. DeKalb: Northern Illinois University Press, 2003.

Brucato, Thomas. *Baseball Skippers and Their Crews*. Haworth, N.J.: St. Johann Press, 2007.

Buckley, James. *Perfect: The Inside Story of Baseball's Sixteen Perfect Games*. Chicago: Triumph, 2002.

Byrd, Cecil, and Ward Moore. *Varsity Sports at Indiana University*. Bloomington: Indiana University Press, 1991.

Caillaut, Jean-Pierre. *The Complete New York Clipper Baseball Biographies: Vols. 1–2*. Jefferson, N.C.: McFarland, 2009.

_____. *A Tale of Four Cities*. Jefferson, N.C.: McFarland, 2003.

Carmichael, John. *My Greatest Day in Baseball*. New York: Grossett & Dunlap, 1945.

Charlton, Jim. *The Baseball Chronology*. New York: Macmillan, 1991.

Chrisman, David. *The History of the International League, 1919–1960 (Part 1)*. Self-published, 1981.

_____. *The History of the Piedmont League (1920–1955)*. Bend, Ore.: Maverick, 1986.

_____. *The History of the Virginia League (1900–1928; 1939–1951)*. Bend, Ore.: Maverick, 1988.

Clark, Dick, and Larry Lester. *The Negro Leagues Book*. Cleveland: SABR, 1994.

Cleve, Craig. *Hardball on the Home Front*. Jefferson, N.C.: McFarland, 2004.

Cobb, Ty. *Busting 'Em and Other Big League Stories*. Jefferson, N.C.: McFarland, 2003.

Coberly, Rich. *The No-Hit Hall of Fame*. Newport Beach, Calif.: Triple Play, 1985.

Coffey, Michael. *27 Men Out: Baseball's Perfect Games*. New York: Atria Books, 2004.

Cohen, Richard, David Neft, and Jordan Deutsch.

The World Series: Complete Play-by-Play of Every Game, 1903–1968. New York: Dial Press, 1979.
Cook, William. *The 1919 World Series: What Really Happened?* Jefferson, N.C.: McFarland, 2001.
Creamer, Robert. *Baseball in '41.* New York: Penguin, 1991.
Crissey, Kit. *Athletes Away.* Philadelphia: Archway Press, 1984.
_____. *Teenagers, Graybeards and 4-F's—Vols. I–II.* Trenton, N.J.: White Eagle, 1981.
Cuicchi, Richard. *Family Ties.* Self-published, 2012.
Daley, Arthur. *Inside Baseball.* New York: Grosset & Dunlap, 1950.
Darnell, Tim. *The Crackers: Early Days of Atlanta Baseball.* Athens, Ga.: Hill Street Press, 2005.
_____. *Southern Yankees: The Story of the Atlanta Crackers.* Self-published, 1995.
Davis, Mac. *The Lore and Legend of Baseball.* New York: Lantern Press, 1953.
DiPrimio, Pete. *Hoosier Hitmen: Indiana University Baseball.* Charleston, S.C.: Arcadia, 2003.
Dittmar, Joseph. *Baseball's Benchmark Boxscores.* Jefferson, N.C.: McFarland, 1990.
Dobbins, Dick. *The Grand Minor League: An Oral History of the Old Pacific Coast League.* Emoryville, Calif.: Woodford Press, 1999.
Dobbins, Dick, and Jon Twichell. *Nuggets on the Diamond: Professional Baseball in the Bay Area From the Gold Rush to the Present.* San Francisco: Woodford Press, 1994.
Dowling, John. *The I-I-I League, 1901–1961.* Watseka, Ill.: Self-published, 1992.
Eidson, William. *State Champs: The Final Four in Indiana Baseball.* Hagerstown, Ind.: Exponent Publishers, 1991.
Ekin, Larry. *Baseball Fathers, Baseball Sons.* White Hall, Va.: Betterway Publications, 1992.
Elfers, James. *The Tour to End All Tours: The Story of Major League Baseball's 1913–1914 World Tour.* Lincoln: University of Nebraska Press, 2003.
Elston, Gene. *A Stitch in Time: A Baseball Chronology, 1845–2000.* Houston: Halcyon Press, 2001.
The Encyclopedia of Indiana, 2d ed. New York: Somerset Publishers, 1993.
Enright, Jim. *Trade Him! 100 Years of Baseball's Greatest Deals.* Chicago: Follett, 1976.
Erskine, Carl, and Burton Rocks. *What I Learned From Jackie Robinson.* New York: McGraw-Hill, 2005.
Felber, Bill. *A Game of Brawl: The Orioles, the Beaneaters and the Battle for the 1897 Pennant.* Lincoln: University of Nebraska Press, 2007.
_____. *Under Pallor, Under Shadow: The 1920 American League Pennant Race That Rattled and Rebuilt Baseball.* Lincoln: University of Nebraska Press, 2011.
Filichia, Peter. *Professional Baseball Franchises.* New York: Facts on File, 1993.
Finoli, David. *For the Good of the Country: World War II Baseball in the Major and Minor Leagues.* Jefferson, N.C.: McFarland, 2002.
Finoli, David, and Bill Ranier. *When Cobb met Wagner: The Seven-Game World Series of 1909.* Jefferson, N.C.: McFarland, 2010.
Fleitz, David. *Ghosts in the Gallery at Cooperstown: Sixteen Little-Known Members of the Hall of Fame.* Jefferson, N.C.: McFarland, 2004.
_____. *More Ghosts in the Gallery: Another Sixteen Little-Known Greats at Cooperstown.* Jefferson, N.C.: McFarland, 2007.
_____. *Silver Bats and Automobiles.* Jefferson, N.C.: McFarland, 2011.
Fleming, G.H. *The Dizziest Season.* New York: William Morrow, 1984.
_____. *The Unforgettable Season.* New York: Penguin, 1982.
Freedman, Lew. *The Day All the Stars Came Out.* Jefferson, N.C.: McFarland, 2010.
Freese, Mel. *Charmed Circle: Twenty-Game-Winning Pitchers in Baseball's 20th Century.* Jefferson, N.C.: McFarland, 1997.
Friederich, Marty. *The Iron Men of Baseball.* Jefferson, N.C.: McFarland, 2006.
Gagnon, Cappy. *Notre Dame Baseball Greats: From Anson to Yaz.* Charleston S.C.: Arcadia, 2004.
Gilbert, Bill. *They Also Served: Baseball and the Home Front, 1941–1945.* New York: Crown, 1992.
Ginter, John. *Baseball at Ball State.* Charleston, S.C.: Arcadia, 2002.
Gladstone, Douglas. *A Bitter Cup of Coffee: How MLB and the Players Association Threw 874 Retirees a Curve.* Tarentum, Pa.: Word Association Publishers, 2010.
Godin, Roger. *The 1922 St. Louis Browns.* Jefferson, N.C.: McFarland, 1991.
Goldstein, Richard. *Spartan Seasons.* New York: Macmillan, 1980.
Golenbock, Peter. *Forever Boys.* New York: Birch Lane Press, 1991.
Good, Howard. *Diamonds in the Dark: America, Baseball and the Movies.* Lanham, Md.: Scarecrow, 1997.
Gramling, Chad. *Baseball in Fort Wayne.* Charleston, S.C.: Arcadia, 2007.
Green, Jerry. *Year of the Tiger: The Diary of Detroit's World Champions.* New York: Coward-McCann, 1969.
Gutman, Bill. *The Golden Age of Baseball: 1941–*

1964. Greenwich, Conn.: Brompton Books, 1989.
Hammel, Bob, and Kit Klingelhoffer. *Glory of Old IU: 100 Years of Indiana Athletics*. Champaign, Ill.: Sports Publishing, 1999.
Hart, Stan. *Scouting Reports: The Original Reviews of Some of Baseball's Greatest Stars*. New York: Macmillan, 1995.
Heidenry, John, and Brett Topel. *The Boys Who Were Left Behind: The 1944 World Series Between the Hapless St. Louis Browns & the Legendary St. Louis Cardinals*. Lincoln: University of Nebraska Press, 2006.
Hetrick, Thomas. *Misfits! The Cleveland Spiders in 1899*. Jefferson, N.C.: McFarland, 1991.
Hodges, Gil, and Frank Slocum. *The Game of Baseball*. New York: Crown, 1969.
Honig, Donald. *The American League*. New York: Crown, 1983.
_____. *The National League*. New York: Crown, 1983.
Huhn, Rick. *The Chalmers Race: Ty Cobb, Napoleon Lajoie, and the Controversial 1910 Batting Title That Became a National Obsession*. Lincoln: University of Nebraska Press, 2014.
Ivor-Campbell, Fred, Robert L. Tiemann, and Mark Rucker, eds. *Baseball's First Stars*. Cleveland: Society for American Baseball Research, 1996.
Jacobson, Steve. *Carrying Jackie's Torch: The Players Who Integrated Baseball—And America*. Chicago: Lawrence Hill Books, 2007.
James, Bill. *The Bill James Guide to Baseball Managers From 1870 to Today*. New York: Scribner, 1997.
_____. *The Bill James Historical Baseball Abstract*. New York: Villard, 1986.
_____. *The New Bill James Historical Baseball Abstract*. New York: The Free Press, 2001.
_____. *This Time Let's Not Eat the Bones*. New York: Villard, 1989.
James, Bill, and Rob Neyer. *The Neyer/James Guide to Pitchers*. New York: Fireside, 2006.
Jensen, Chris. *Baseball State by State: Major and Negro League Players, Ballparks, Museums and Historical Sites*. Jefferson, N.C.: McFarland, 2012.
Johnson, Daniel. *Japanese Baseball: A Statistical Handbook*. Jefferson, N.C.: McFarland, 1999.
Johnson, Lloyd. *The Minor League Register*. Durham: Baseball America, 1994.
_____. *Baseball's Dream Teams*. New York: Crescent Books, 1990.
Johnson, Lloyd, and Brenda Ward. *Who's Who in Baseball History*. New York: Barnes & Noble, 1994.
Johnson, Lloyd, and Miles Wolff. *The Encyclopedia of Minor League Baseball: Third Edition*. Durham: Baseball America, 2007.
Jones, David, ed. *Deadball Stars of the American League*. Dulles, Va.: Potomac, 2006.
Kahn, Roger. *The Era 1947–1957: When the Yankees, Dodgers and Giants Ruled the World*. New York: Ticknor & Fields, 1993.
Karst, Gene, and Martin Jones. *Who's Who in Professional Baseball*. New Rochelle, N.Y.: Arlington House, 1973.
Kaufman, Alan, and James Kaufman. *The Worst Baseball Pitchers of All Time*. Jefferson, N.C.: McFarland, 1993.
Keene, Kerry. *1960: The Last Pure Season*. Champaign, Ill.: Sports Publishing, 2000.
Kelley, Brent. *Baseball Stars of the 1950s*. Jefferson, N.C.: McFarland, 1993.
_____. *Baseball's Biggest Blunder: The Bonus Rule of 1953–1957*. Lanham, Md.: Scarecrow, 1997.
_____. *The Case for Those Overlooked by the Baseball Hall of Fame*. Jefferson, N.C.: McFarland, 1992.
_____. *The Early All-Stars*. Jefferson, N.C.: McFarland, 1997.
_____. *In the Shadow of the Babe: Interviews With Baseball Players Who Played With or Against Babe Ruth*. Jefferson, N.C.: McFarland, 1995.
_____. *100 Greatest Pitchers*. New York: Crescent Books, 1988.
_____. *The Pastime in Turbulence*. Jefferson, N.C.: McFarland, 2001.
Kellman, Howard. *61 Humorous & Inspiring Lessons I Learned from Baseball*. Bloomington, Ind.: AuthorHouse, 2010.
Kelly, Robert. *Baseball's Offensive Greats of the Deadball Era*. Jefferson, N.C.: McFarland, 2009.
Kerr, Don. *Opening Day: All Major League Baseball Season Opening Games, 1876–1998*. Jefferson, N.C.: McFarland, 1999.
Kiernan, Thomas. *The Miracle at Coogan's Bluff*. New York: Thomas Y. Crowell, 1975.
Kiser, Brett. *Baseball's War Roster: A Biographical Dictionary of Major and Negro League Players Who Served, 1861 to the Present*. Jefferson, N.C.: McFarland, 2012.
Koppett, Leonard. *Koppett's Concise History of Major League Baseball*. Philadelphia: Temple University Press, 1998.
Koszarek, Ed. *The Players League: History, Clubs, Ballparks and Statistics*. Jefferson, N.C.: McFarland, 2006.
Kovach, John. *Benders! Tales From South Bend's*

Baseball Past. South Bend, Ind.: Green Stocking Press, 1991.

Krah, Steve. *Hitting and Hurling in the Heartland: A Look at Indiana High School Baseball*. Elkhart, Ind.: Self-published, 2002.

Krueger, Joseph. *Baseball's Greatest Drama*. Milwaukee: Self-published, 1945.

Kubik, Richard. *Baseball Trades and Acquisitions, 1950–1979*. Smithtown, N.Y.: Exposition Press, 1981.

Lamster, Mark. *Spalding's World Tour*. New York: PublicAffairs, 2006.

Lanigan, Ernest. *Baseball Cyclopedia*. New York: Baseball Magazine Co., 1922.

Langford, Walter. *Legends of Baseball: An Oral History of the Game's Golden Age*. South Bend, Ind.: Diamond Communications, 1987.

Lansche, Jerry. *The Forgotten Championships: Postseason Baseball, 1882–1981*. Jefferson, N.C.: McFarland, 1989.

_____. *Glory Fades Away: The Nineteenth-Century World Series Rediscovered*. Dallas: Taylor, 1991.

Larsen, Don, and Mark Shaw. *The Perfect Yankee*. Champaign, Ill.: Sagamore, 1996.

Leary, Edward. *Indianapolis: The Story of a City*. Indianapolis: Bobbs-Merrill, 1971.

Lee, Bill. *The Baseball Necrology*. Jefferson, N.C.: McFarland, 2003.

Leeke, Jim. *Ballplayers in the Great War: Newspaper Accounts of Major Leaguers in World War I Military Service*. Jefferson, N.C.: McFarland, 2003.

Lenburg, Jeff. *Baseball's All-Star Game: A Game-by-Game Guide*. Jefferson, N.C.: McFarland, 1986.

Levenson, Barry. *The Seventh Game: The 35 World Series That Have Gone the Distance*. New York: McGraw-Hill, 2004.

Levine, Peter. *Baseball History: An Annual of Original Baseball Research*. Vols. 1–4. Westport, Conn.: Meckler, 1989–1991.

Levitt, Daniel. *The Battle That Forged Modern Baseball: The Federal League Challenge and Its Legacy*. Chicago: Ivan R. Dee, 2012.

Lewin, Josh. *You Never Forget Your First: Ballplayers Recall Their Big League Debuts*. Washington, D.C.: Potomac Books, 2005.

Lieb, Fred. *Baseball as I Have Known It*. New York: Coward, McCann & Geoghegan, 1997.

_____. *The Baseball Story*. New York: G.P. Putnam's Sons, 1950.

_____. *The Story of the World Series*. New York: G.P. Putnam's Sons, 1949.

Lingo, Will. *Baseball America Draft Almanac: A Complete Listing of Every Player Ever Drafted, 1965–2009*. Durham: Baseball America, 2009.

Linkugel, Will, and Edward Pappas. *They Tasted Glory: Among the Missing at the Baseball Hall of Fame*. Jefferson, N.C.: McFarland, 1998.

Mackey, Scott. *Barbary Baseball: The Pacific Coast League of the 1920's*. Jefferson, N.C.: McFarland, 1995.

Madden, W.C. *Baseball in Indianapolis*. Charleston, S.C.: Arcadia, 2003.

_____. *Baseball's First-Year Player Draft*. Jefferson, N.C.: McFarland, 2001.

_____. *The Hoosiers of Summer*. Indianapolis: Madden, 1994.

Madden, W.C., and Patrick Stewart. *The Western League: A Baseball History, 1885 Through 1999*. Jefferson, N.C.: McFarland, 2002.

Madison, James. *The Indiana Way: A State History*. Bloomington: Indiana University Press, 1986.

Mandelaro, Jim, and Scott Pitoniak. *Silver Seasons: The Story of the Red Wings*. Syracuse: Syracuse University Press, 1996.

Marazzi, Rich, and Len Fiorito. *Aaron to Zipfel*. New York: Avon Books, 1985.

_____. *Aaron to Zuverink: Baseball Players of the 1950s: a Biographical Dictionary of All 1,560 Major Leaguers*. New York: Stein and Day, 1982.

Marshall, William. *Baseball's Pivotal Era: 1945–1951*. Lexington: University Press of Kentucky, 1999.

Masterson, Dave, and Timm Boyle. *Baseball's Best: The MVP's*. Chicago: Contemporary Books, 1985.

Masur, Louis. *Autumn Glory: Baseball's First World Series*. New York: Hill & Wang, 2003.

Mathews, Garret. *Can't Find a Dry Ball: The Evansville Otters ... On the Lowest Rung of Baseball*. Tampa: Albion Press, 2002.

Mathewson, Christy. *Pitching in a Pinch*. New York: G.P. Putnam's Sons, 1912.

Mayer, Ronald. *Perfect! 14 Pitchers of "Perfect" Games*. Jefferson, N.C.: McFarland, 1991.

McCombs, Wayne. *Let's Goooooooooo Tulsa! The History and Record Book of Professional Baseball in Tulsa, Oklahoma, 1905–1989*. Tulsa: Self-published, 1990.

McConnell, Bob. *Going for the Fences: The Minor League Home Run Book*. Cleveland: Society for American Baseball Research, 2009.

McConnell, Bob, and David Vincent. *The Home Run Encyclopedia*. New York: Macmillan, 1996.

McCullough, Bob. *My Greatest Day in Baseball: 1946–1997*. Dallas: Taylor, 1998.

McGee, Ryan. *The Road to Omaha: Hits, Hopes and History at the College World Series.* New York: Thomas Dunne, 2009.

McGuire, Mark, and Michael Gormley. *Moments in the Sun: Baseball's Briefly Famous.* Jefferson, N.C.: McFarland, 1999.

McKenna, Brian. *Early Exits: The Premature Endings of Baseball Careers.* Lanham, Md.: Scarecrow, 2007.

Mead, William. *Even the Browns.* Chicago: Contemporary Books, 1978.

Meany, Tom. *Baseball's Greatest Pitchers.* New York: A.S. Barnes, 1951.

_____. *Baseball's Greatest Players.* New York: Grosset & Dunlap, 1953.

_____. *Baseball's Greatest Teams.* New York: Bantam, 1949.

Mercurio, John. *Chronology of Major League Baseball Records.* New York: Harper & Row, 1989.

Moffi, Larry. *This Side of Cooperstown: An Oral History of Major League Baseball in the 1950s.* Iowa City: University of Iowa Press, 1996.

Moffi, Larry, and Jonathan Kronstadt. *Crossing the Line: Black Major Leaguers, 1947–1959.* Jefferson, N.C.: McFarland, 1994.

Morales, Bill. *Farewell to the Last Golden Era: The Yankees, the Pirates and the 1960 Baseball Season.* Jefferson, N.C.: McFarland, 2011.

Morris, Peter. *A Game of Inches: The Stories Behind the Innovations That Shaped Baseball—The Game on the Field.* Chicago: Ivan R. Dee, 2006.

Murdock, Eugene. *Baseball Between the Wars: Memories of the Game by the Men Who Played It.* Westport, Conn.: Meckler, 1992.

_____. *Baseball Players and Their Times: a History of the Major Leagues.* Westport, Conn.: Meckler, 1991.

Murphy, Cait. *Crazy '08.* New York: Smithsonian Books, 2007.

Neft, David, and Richard Cohen. *The World Series: Complete Play-by-Play of Every Game, 1903–1989.* New York: St. Martin's Press, 1990.

Neft, David, Richard Cohen, and Michael Neft. *The Sports Encyclopedia: Baseball.* New York: St. Martin's-Griffin, 2005.

Nemec, David. *The Beer and Whisky League: The Illustrated History of the American Association–Baseball's Renegade Major League.* Guilford, Conn.: Lyons Press, 2004.

_____. *The Great American Baseball Team Book.* New York: Penguin, 1992.

_____. *The Great Encyclopedia of 19th Century Major League Baseball.* New York: Donald I. Fine Books, 1997.

_____. *Major League Baseball Profiles 1871–1900: The Ballplayers who Built the Game—Vol. 1 and 2.* Lincoln: University of Nebraska Press, 2011.

_____. *The Rank and File of 19th Century Major League Baseball: Biographies of 1,084 Players, Owners, Managers and Umpires.* Jefferson, N.C.: McFarland, 2012.

Nemec, David, and Dave Zeman. *The Baseball Rookies Encyclopedia.* Dulles, Va.: Brassey's, 2004.

Neyer, Rob. *Rob Neyer's Big Book of Baseball Legends.* New York: Simon & Schuster, 2008.

_____. *Rob Neyer's Big Book of Baseball Lineups.* New York: Fireside, 2003.

Neyer, Rob, and Eddie Epstein. *Baseball Dynasties: The Greatest Teams of All Time.* New York: W.W. Norton, 2000.

Nogowski, John. *Last Time Out: Big League Farewells of Baseball's Greats.* Lanham, Md.: Taylor Trade, 2005.

Oakley, Ronald. *Baseball's Last Golden Age, 1946–1960.* Jefferson, N.C.: McFarland, 1994.

O'Brien, John, Jerry Debruin and John Husman. *Mud Hen Memories.* Perrysburg, Ohio: BWD Publishing, 2001.

Ogden, Dale. *Hoosier Sports Heroes.* Indianapolis: Guild Press of Indiana, 1990.

Okkonen, Marc. *Baseball Memories 1900–1909.* New York: Sterling, 1992.

_____. *Baseball Memories 1930–1939.* New York: Sterling, 1994.

_____. *Baseball Memories 1950–1959.* New York: Sterling, 1993.

_____. *Federal League of 1914–1915: Baseball's Third Major League.* Garrett Park, MD: Society for American Baseball Research, 1989.

Olderman, Murray. *Nelson's 20th Century Encyclopedia of Baseball.* New York: Thomas Nelson & Sons, 1963.

Oliphant, Thomas. *Praying for Gil Hodges.* New York: Thomas Dunne Books, 2005.

O'Neal, Bill. *The American Association: A Baseball History 1902–1991.* Austin: Eakin Press, 1991.

_____. *The International League: A Baseball History 1884–1991.* Austin: Eakin Press, 1992.

_____. *The Pacific Coast League 1903–1988.* Austin: Eakin Press, 1990.

_____. *The Southern League: Baseball in Dixie, 1885–1994.* Austin: Eakin Press, 1994.

_____. *The Texas League.* Austin: Eakin Press, 1987.

Palmer, Pete, and Gary Gillette. *ESPN Baseball Encyclopedia.* New York: Sterling, 2005.

Paper, Lew. *Perfect: Don Larsen's Perfect Game and the Men Who Made It Happen.* New York: New American Library, 2009.

Pearson, Daniel. *Baseball in 1889*. Bowling Green, Ohio: Popular Press, 1993.

Peary, Danny. *Cult Baseball Players*. New York: Simon & Schuster, 1990.

_____. *We Played the Game: 65 Players Remember Baseball's Greatest Era, 1947–1964*. New York: Hyperion, 1994.

Pepe, Phil. *Talkin' Baseball: An Oral History of Baseball in the 1970s*. New York: Ballantine, 1998.

Phillips, John. *The Fall Classics of the 1890s*. Cabin John, Md.: Capital, 1989.

Pietrusza, David. *Major Leagues: The Formation, Sometimes Absorption and Mostly Inevitable Demise of 18 Professional Baseball Organizations, 1871 to Present*. Jefferson, N.C.: McFarland, 1991.

Pietrusza, David, Matthew Silverman, and Michael Gershman. *Baseball: The Biographical Encyclopedia*. New York: Total Sports Illustrated, 2000.

Pope, Edwin. *Baseball's Greatest Managers*. Garden City, N.Y.: Doubleday, 1960.

Porter, David, ed. *Biographical Dictionary of American Sports: Baseball A-F*. Westport, Conn.: Greenwood, 2000.

_____. *Biographical Dictionary of American Sports: Baseball G-P*. Westport, Conn.: Greenwood, 2000.

_____. *Biographical Dictionary of American Sports: Baseball Q-Z*. Westport, Conn.: Greenwood, 2000.

Powers, Jimmy. *Baseball Personalities: Vivid Stories of More Than 50 of the Most Colorful Ballplayers of All Time*. New York: Rudolph Field, 1949.

Price, Nelson. *Indiana Legends: Famous Hoosiers from Johnny Appleseed to David Letterman*. Carmel: Guild Press of Indiana, 1997.

Quigley, Martin. *The Crooked Pitch*. Chapel Hill: Algonquin Books, 1984.

Rader, Benjamin. *Baseball: A History of America's Game*. Urbana: University of Illinois Press, 1992.

Raterman, Dale. *The Big Ten: A Century of Excellence*. Champaign, Ill.: Sagamore, 1996.

Reddick, David, and Kim Rogers. *The Magic of Indians Baseball: 1887–1987*. Indianapolis: Indians, 1988.

Reichler, Joseph. *The Baseball Trade Register*. New York: Collier Books, 1984.

_____. *Baseball's Great Moments*, updated 1981 edition. New York: Rutledge Book, 1987.

Reichler, Joseph, and Ken Samelson. *The Great All-Time Baseball Record Book*. New York: Macmillan, 1981 (additional material, 1993).

Reidenbaugh, Lowell. *Baseball's 50 Greatest Games*. St. Louis: The Sporting News, 1986.

_____. *Baseball's 25 Greatest Pennant Races*. St. Louis: The Sporting News, 1987.

Reisler, Jim. *The Best Game Ever: Pirates vs. Yankees, October 13, 1960*. Cambridge: Carroll & Graf, 2007.

Ribowsky, Mark. *A Complete History of the Negro Leagues, 1884–1955*. New York: Birch Lane Press, 1995.

Riley, James. *The Biographical Encyclopedia of the Negro Baseball Leagues*. New York: Carroll & Graf, 1994.

Ritter, Lawrence. *The Glory of Their Times*. Toronto: Macmillan, 1966.

Ritter, Lawrence, and Donald Honig. *The 100 Greatest Baseball Players of All Time*. New York: Crown, 1986.

Robbins, Mike. *Ninety Feet From Fame: Close Calls With Baseball Immortality*. New York: Carroll & Graf, 2004.

Robertson, John. *The Babe Chases 60: That Fabulous 1927 Season, Home Run by Home Run*. Jefferson, N.C.: McFarland, 1999.

Rosenthal, Harold. *The 10 Best Years of Baseball*. New York: Van Nostrand Reinhold, 1981.

Rossi, John. *A Whole New Game: Off the Field Changes in Baseball, 1946–1960*. Jefferson, N.C.: McFarland, 1999.

Russo, Frank, and Gene Racz. *Bury My Heart at Cooperstown: Salacious, Sad and Surreal Deaths in the History of Baseball*. Chicago: Triumph, 2006.

Schiffer, Don. *World Series Encyclopedia*. New York: Thomas Nelson & Sons, 1961.

Schlossberg, Dan. *Barons of the Bullpen*. New York: Tempo Books, 1975.

Schott, Arthur. *70 Years with the Pelicans*. New Orleans: Self-published, 1975.

Schulz, Charles. *Sandlot Peanuts*. New York: Holt, Rinehart and Winston, 1977.

Schwarz, Alan. *The Numbers Game: Baseball's Lifelong Fascination with Statistics*. New York: Thomas Dunne, 2004.

Seaver, Tom, and Marty Appel. *Great Moments in Baseball*. New York: Birch Lane Press, 1992.

Selko, Jamie. *Minor League All-Star Teams, 1922–1962*. Jefferson, N.C.: McFarland, 2007.

Selzer, Jack. *Baseball in the Nineteenth Century: An Overview*. Cleveland: Society for American Baseball Research, 1986.

Seymour, Harold. *Baseball: The Early Years*. New York: Oxford University Press, 1960.

_____. *Baseball: The Golden Age*. New York: Oxford University Press, 1971.

_____. *Baseball: The People's Game*. New York: Oxford University Press, 1990.

Shalin, Mike, and Neil Shalin. *Out by a Step: The

100 Best Players Not in the Baseball Hall of Fame. Lanham, Md.: Diamond Communications, 2002.

Shatzkin, Mike. *The Ballplayers: Baseball's Ultimate Biographical Reference.* New York: Arbor House, 1990.

Shiffert, John. *Base Ball in Philadelphia: A History of the Early Game, 1831–1900.* Jefferson, N.C.: McFarland, 2006.

Skipper, James. *Baseball Nicknames: A Dictionary of Origins and Meanings.* Jefferson, N.C.: McFarland, 1992.

Skipper, John. *A Biographical Dictionary of the Baseball Hall of Fame.* Jefferson, N.C.: McFarland, 2000.

_____. *A Biographical Dictionary of Major League Baseball Managers.* Jefferson, N.C.: McFarland, 2003.

_____. *Inside Pitch: Classic Baseball Moments.* Jefferson, N.C.: McFarland, 1996.

Smith, Burge. *The 1945 Detroit Tigers.* Jefferson, N.C.: McFarland, 2010.

Smith, Ira. *Baseball's Famous Pitchers.* New York: A.S. Barnes, 1954.

Smith, Myron. *Baseball: A Comprehensive Bibliography.* Jefferson, N.C.: McFarland, 1986.

_____. *Baseball: A Comprehensive Bibliography: Supplement 1 (1985–May 1992).* Jefferson, N.C.: McFarland, 1993.

_____. *Baseball: A Comprehensive Bibliography: Supplement 2 (1992–1997).* Jefferson, N.C.: McFarland, 1998.

Smith, Robert. *Baseball: The Game, the Men Who Played It, and Its Place in American Life.* New York: Simon & Schuster, 1947.

_____. *Baseball in the Afternoon: Tales from a Bygone Era.* New York: Simon & Schuster, 1993.

_____. *Baseball in America.* New York: Holt, Rinehart & Winston, 1961.

Smith, Red. *To Absent Friends From Red Smith.* New York: Plume, 1982.

Smith, Ron, ed. *The Sporting News Chronicle of Baseball.* St. Louis: The Sporting News, 1993.

Snelling, Dennis. *A Glimpse of Fame: Brilliant but Fleeting Major League Careers.* Jefferson, N.C.: McFarland, 1993.

_____. *The Greatest Minor League: A History of the Pacific Coast League, 1903–1957.* Jefferson, N.C.: McFarland, 2012.

_____. *The Pacific Coast League: A Statistical History, 1903–1957.* Jefferson, N.C.: McFarland, 1995.

Solomon, Burt. *The Baseball Timeline: The Day-by-Day History of Baseball, From Valley Forge to the Present Day.* New York: Avon Books, 1997.

Sowell, Mike. *July 2, 1903.* New York: Macmillan, 1992.

_____. *The Pitch that Killed.* New York: Macmillan, 1989.

Spalding, A.G. *Baseball: America's National Game.* San Francisco: Halo Books, 1991.

Spalding, John. *Pacific Coast League Stars Vol. I.* Manhattan, Kan.: Ag Press, 1994.

_____. *Pacific Coast League Stars Vol. II.* Manhattan, Kan.: Ag Press, 1997.

_____. *Sacramento Senators and Solons.* Manhattan, Kan.: Ag Press, 1995.

Spink, Alfred. *The National Game.* Carbondale: Southern Illinois University Press, 2000.

Stein, Fred. *And the Skipper Bats Cleanup: A History of the Baseball Player-Manager, with 42 Biographies of Men Who Filled the Dual Role.* Jefferson, N.C.: McFarland, 2002.

Sugar, Bert. *Baseball's 50 Greatest Games.* New York: Exeter Books, 1986.

Swaine, Rick. *Beating the Breaks: Major League Ballplayers Who Overcame Disabilities.* Jefferson, N.C.: McFarland, 2006.

_____. *The Black Stars Who Made Baseball Whole.* Jefferson, N.C.: McFarland, 2004.

_____. *The Integration of Major League Baseball: A Team by Team History.* Jefferson, N.C.: McFarland, 2009.

Szalontai, James. *Teenager on First, Geezer at Bat, 4-F on Deck: Major League Baseball in 1945.* Jefferson, N.C.: McFarland, 2009.

Tellis, Richard. *Once Around the Bases: Bittersweet Memories of Only One Game in the Majors.* Chicago: Triumph, 1998.

Thorn, John, and Pete Palmer with David Reuther. *Total Baseball*, 1st and 2d eds. New York: Warner, 1989 and 1991.

Thorn, John, and Pete Palmer with Michael Gershman. *Total Baseball*, 3d ed. New York: HarperPerennial, 1993.

_____. *Total Baseball*, 4th ed. New York: Viking, 1995.

Thorn, John, Pete Palmer, Michael Gershman, and David Pietrusza. *Total Baseball*, 5th ed. New York: Viking, 1997.

_____. *Total Baseball*, 6th ed. New York: Total Sports, 1999.

Thorn, John, Pete Palmer, and Michael Gershman. *Total Baseball*, 7th ed. Kingston, N.Y.: Total Sports, 2001.

Thornley, Stew. *On to Nicollet: The Glory and Fame of the Minneapolis Millers.* Minneapolis: Nodin Press, 1988.

Tiemann, Robert L., and Mark Rucker, eds. *Nineteenth Century Stars.* Cleveland: Society for American Baseball Research, 1989.

Tomlinson, Gerald. *Baseball Research Handbook.* Cooperstown, NY: Society for American Baseball Research, 1987.

Torres, John. *Home Run Hitters: Heroes of the Four-Home Run Game.* New York: Macmillan, 1995.

Treto Cisneros, Pedro. *The Mexican League: Comprehensive Player Statistics, 1937–2001.* Jefferson, N.C.: McFarland, 2002.

Trucks, Rob. *A Cup of Coffee: The Very Short Careers of Eighteen Major League Pitchers.* New York: Smallmouth Press, 2002.

Turner, Fredrick. *When the Boys Came Back: Baseball and 1946.* New York: Henry Holt, 1996.

Usereau, Alain. *The Expos in Their Prime: The Short-Lived Glory of Montreal's Team, 1977–1984.* Jefferson, N.C.: McFarland, 2013.

Vaccaro, Mike. *The First Fall Classic: The Red Sox, the Giants and the Cast of Players, Pugs and Politicos Who Reinvented the World Series in 1912.* New York: Doubleday, 2009.

Van Blair, Rick. *Dugout to Foxhole: Interviews With Baseball Players Whose Careers Were Affected by World War Two.* Jefferson, N.C.: McFarland, 1994.

Van Hyning, Thomas. *Puerto Rico's Winter League.* Jefferson, N.C.: McFarland, 1995.

_____. *The Santurce Crabbers.* Jefferson, N.C.: McFarland, 1999.

Van Lindt, Carson. *The Seattle Pilots Story.* New York: Marabou, 1993.

Vincent, David, Lyle Spatz, and David Smith. *The Midsummer Classic: The Complete History of Baseball's All-Star Game.* Lincoln: University of Nebraska Press, 2000.

Vincent, Fay. *We Would Have Played for Nothing: Baseball Stars of the 1950s and 1960s Talk About the Game They Love.* New York: Simon & Schuster, 2008.

Voigt, David Q. *American Baseball, Vol. I: From the Gentleman's Sport to the Commissioner System.* University Park: Penn State Press, 1983.

_____. *American Baseball, Vol. II: From the Commissioners to Continental Expansion.* University Park: Penn State Press, 1983.

_____. *American Baseball, Vol. III: From Postwar Expansion to the Electronic Age.* University Park: Penn State Press, 1983.

Von Borries, Philip. *Louisville Diamonds: The Louisville Major League Reader, 1876–1899.* Paducah, Ky.: Turner, 1996.

Votano, Paul. *Late and Close: A History of Relief Pitching.* Jefferson, N.C.: McFarland, 2002.

Waterman, Ty, and Mel Springer. *The Year the Red Sox Won the Series: A Chronicle of the 1918 Championship Season.* Boston: Northeastern University Press, 1999.

Weisberger, Bernard. *When Chicago Ruled Baseball: The Cubs-White Sox World Series of 1906.* New York: William Morrow, 2006.

Wells, Donald. *Baseball's Western Front: The Pacific Coast League During World War II.* Jefferson, N.C.: McFarland, 2004.

_____. *The Race for the Governor's Cup: The Pacific Coast League Playoff, 1936–1954.* Jefferson, N.C.: McFarland, 2000.

_____. *Splendor on the Diamond: Interviews With 35 Stars of Baseball's Past.* Gainesville: University Press of Florida, 2000.

Westcott, Rich, and Allen Lewis. *No-Hitters: The 225 Games, 1893–1999.* Jefferson, N.C.: McFarland, 2001.

Westcott, Rich, and Rich Bilovsky. *The New Phillies Encyclopedia.* Philadelphia: Temple University Press, 1993.

Wiggins, Robert. *The Federal League of Base Ball Clubs: The History of an Outlaw Major League, 1914–1915.* Jefferson, N.C.: McFarland, 2009.

Wilbert, Warren. *Baseball's Iconic 1–0 Games.* Lanham, Md.: Scarecrow, 2013.

_____. *A Cunning Kind of Play: The Cubs-Giants Rivalry, 1876–1932.* Jefferson, N.C.: McFarland, 2002.

_____. *Rookies Rated: Baseball's Finest Freshman Seasons.* Jefferson, N.C.: McFarland, 2000.

_____. *The Greatest World Series Games.* Jefferson, N.C.: McFarland, 2005.

Wilbert, Warren, and William Hageman. *The 1917 White Sox: Their World Championship Season.* Jefferson, N.C.: McFarland, 2004.

Williams, Peter. *The Joe Williams Baseball Reader.* Chapel Hill: Algonquin, 1989.

Wolter, Tim. *POW Baseball in World War II: The National Pastime Behind Barbed Wire.* Jefferson, N.C.: McFarland, 2002.

Wright, Marshall. *The American Association: Year-by-Year Statistics for the Baseball Minor League. 1920–1952.* Jefferson, N.C.: McFarland, 1997.

_____. *The Eastern League in Baseball: A Statistical History, 1923–2005. Vols. 1 and 2.* Jefferson, N.C.: McFarland, 2007.

_____. *The International League: Year-by-Year Statistics, 1884–1953.* Jefferson, N.C.: McFarland, 2005.

_____. *The National Association of Baseball Players, 1857–1870.* Jefferson, N.C.: McFarland, 2000.

_____. *Nineteenth Century Baseball: Year-by-Year Statistics for the Major League Teams—*

1871 Through 1900. Jefferson, N.C.: McFarland, 2009.
_____. *The South Atlantic League, 1904–1963: A Year-by-Year Statistical History.* Jefferson, N.C.: McFarland, 2009.
_____. *The Southern Association in Baseball, 1885–1961.* Jefferson, N.C.: McFarland, 2002.
_____. *The Texas League in Baseball, 1888–1958.* Jefferson, N.C.: McFarland, 2004.
Zardetto, Ray. *'30: Major League Baseball's Year of the Batter.* Jefferson, N.C.: McFarland, 2008.
Zingg, Paul, and Mark Medeiros. *Runs, Hits and an Era: The Pacific Coast League, 1903–58.* Urbana: University of Illinois Press, 1994.
Zinn, Paul, and John Zinn. *The Major League Pennant Races of 1916.* Jefferson, N.C.: McFarland, 2009.
Zucker, Harvey, and Lawrence Babich. *Sports Films: A Complete Reference.* Jefferson, N.C.: McFarland, 1987.

Autobiographies/Biographies

Alexander, Charles. *John McGraw.* New York: Viking, 1988.
_____. *Ty Cobb.* New York: Oxford University Press, 1989.
Amoruso, Marino. *Gil Hodges: The Quiet Man.* Middlebury, Vt.: Paul S. Eriksson, 1991.
Anson, Adrian. *A Ball Player's Career.* Mattituck, N.Y.: Amereon House, 1900.
Axelson, G.W. *Commy.* Chicago: The Reilly & Lee Co., 1919.
Barrow, Ed, and James Kahn. *My Fifty Years in Baseball.* New York: Coward-McCann, 1951.
Bevis, Charlie. *Jimmy Collins: A Baseball Biography.* Jefferson, N.C.: McFarland, 2012.
Bogen, Gil. *Tinker, Evers and Chance: A Triple Biography.* Jefferson, N.C.: McFarland, 2003.
Bragan, Bobby, and Jeff Guinn. *You Can't Hit the Ball with the Bat on Your Shoulder.* Fort Worth: The Summit Group, 1992.
Browning, Reed. *Cy Young: A Baseball Life.* Amherst: University of Massachusetts Press, 2000.
Bruns, Roger. *Preacher: Billy Sunday and Big-Time American Evangelism.* New York: W.W. Norton, 1992.
Carroll, Jeff. *Sam Rice.* Jefferson, N.C.: McFarland, 2008.
Clark, Jerry, and Martha Webb. *Alexander the Great: The Story of Grover Cleveland Alexander.* Omaha: Making History, 1993.
Clavin, Tom, and Danny Peary. *Gil Hodges.* New York: New American Library, 2012.
Cobb, Ty, and Al Stump. *My Life in Baseball.* Garden City, N.Y.: Doubleday, 1961.
Cobb, William. *Honus Wagner on His Life and Baseball.* Ann Arbor: Sports Media Group, 2006.
Cooper, Brian. *Ray Schalk.* Jefferson, N.C.: McFarland, 2009.
Dellinger, Susan. *Red Legs and Black Sox: Edd Roush and the Untold Story of the 1919 World Series.* Cincinnati: Emmis Books, 2006.
DeValeria, Dennis, and Jean DeValeria. *Honus Wagner: A Biography.* New York: Henry Holt, 1996.
Dorsett, Lyle. *Billy Sunday and the Redemption of Urban America.* Grand Rapids: William B. Eerdmans, 1991.
Durso, Joseph. *The Days of Mr. McGraw.* Englewood Cliffs, N.J.: Prentice-Hall, 1969.
Evers, John, and Hugh Fullerton. *Touching Second.* Jefferson, N.C.: McFarland, 2005.
Fleitz, David. *Cap Anson: The Grand Old Man of Baseball.* Jefferson, N.C.: McFarland, 2005.
_____. *Napoleon Lajoie: King of Ballplayers.* Jefferson, N.C.: McFarland, 2013.
Flood, Curt, and Richard Carter. *The Way It Is.* New York: Pocket Books, 1972.
Frick, Ford. *Games, Asterisks and People.* New York: Crown, 1973.
Gough, David. *Burt Shotton, Dodgers Manager: A Baseball Biography.* Jefferson, N.C.: McFarland, 1994.
Graham, Frank. *McGraw of the Giants.* New York: G.P. Putnam & Sons, 1944.
Hageman, William. *Honus: The Life and Times of a Baseball Hero.* Champaign, Ill.: Sagamore, 1996.
Hartley, Michael. *Christy Mathewson: A Biography.* Jefferson, N.C.: McFarland, 2004.
Hettinger, Dan. *Welcome to the Big Leagues: The Darrel Chaney Story.* New York: Morgan James, 2013.
Hittner, Arthur. *Honus Wagner: The Life of Baseball's "Flying Dutchman."* Jefferson, N.C.: McFarland, 1996.
Howard, Arlene, and Ralph Wimbish. *Elston and Me.* Columbia: University of Missouri Press, 2001.
Hroncich, Colleen. *The Whistling Irishman: Danny Murtaugh Remembered.* Philadelphia: Sports Challenge Network, 2010.
John, Tommy, and Sally John. *The Sally and Tommy John Story: Our Life in Baseball.* New York: Macmillan, 1983.
John, Tommy, and Sally John with Joe Musser. *The Tommy John Story.* Old Tappan, N.J.: Fleming H. Revell, 1978.

John, Tommy, and Dan Valenti. *TJ: My 26 Years in Baseball*. New York: Bantam, 1991.

Jordan, David. *A Tiger in His Time: Hal Newhouser and the Burden of Wartime Baseball*. South Bend, Ind.: Diamond Communications, 1990.

Kavanagh, Jack. *Ol' Pete: The Grover Cleveland Alexander Story*. South Bend, Ind.: Diamond Communications, 1996.

Kemmerer, Russ, and W.C. Madden. *Ted Williams: "Hey, Kid, Just Get it Over the Plate!"* Fishers, Ind.: Madden, 2002.

Knickerbocker, Wendy. *Sunday at the Ballpark: Billy Sunday's Professional Baseball Career 1883–1890*. Lanham, Md.: Scarecrow, 2000.

Lanctot, Neil. *Campy: The Two Lives of Roy Campanella*. New York: Simon & Schuster, 2011.

Leavengood, Ted. *Clark Griffith: The Old Fox of Washington Baseball*. Jefferson, N.C.: McFarland, 2011.

Leavy, Jane. *The Last Boy: Mickey Mantle and the End of America's Childhood*. New York: Harper, 2010.

Lieb, Fred. *Connie Mack: Grand Old Man of Baseball*. New York: G.P. Putnam's Sons, 1945.

Linn, Ed. *Hitter: The Life and Turmoils of Ted Williams*. New York: Harcourt Brace, 1993.

Lowenfish, Lee. *Branch Rickey: Baseball's Ferocious Gentleman*. Lincoln: University of Nebraska Press, 2007.

Macht, Norman. *Connie Mack and the Early Years of Baseball*. Lincoln: University of Nebraska Press, 2007.

_____. *Connie Mack: The Turbulent and Triumphant Years, 1915–1931*. Lincoln: University of Nebraska Press, 2012.

Mack, Connie. *My 66 Years in the Big Leagues*. Philadelphia: John C. Winston, 1950.

Mayer, Ronald. *Christy Mathewson: A Game-by-Game Profile of a Legendary Pitcher*. Jefferson, N.C.: McFarland, 1993.

McGraw, John. *My Thirty Years in Baseball*. Lincoln: University of Nebraska Press, 1995.

McKeon, Jack, and Tom Friend. *Jack of All Trades*. Chicago: Contemporary Books, 1988.

McKeon, Jack, and Kevin Kernan. *I'm Just Getting Started*. Chicago: Triumph, 2005.

Montville, Leigh. *Ted Williams: The Biography of an American Hero*. New York: Random House, 2004.

Pinelli, Babe. *Mr. Ump*. Philadelphia: Westminster Press, 1953.

Plaschke, Bill, and Tommy Lasorda. *I Live for This! Baseball's Last True Believer*. Boston: Houghton Mifflin, 2007.

Roberts, Robin, and Paul Rogers. *My Life in Baseball*. Chicago: Triumph, 2003.

Robinson, Frank, and Al Silverman. *My Life Is Baseball*. Garden City, N.Y.: Doubleday, 1968.

Robinson, Frank, and Berry Stainback. *Extra Innings*. New York: McGraw-Hill, 1988.

Robinson, Jackie. *I Never Had It Made*. New York: G.P. Putnam's Sons, 1972.

Robinson, Jackie, and Wendell Smith. *Jackie Robinson: My Own Story*. New York: Greenberg, 1948.

Robinson, Ray. *Matty: An American Hero*. New York: Oxford University Press, 1993.

Seib, Philip. *The Player: Christy Mathewson, Baseball and the American Century*. New York: Four Walls Eight Windows, 2003.

Seidel, Michael. *Ted Williams: A Baseball Life*. Chicago: Contemporary Books, 1991.

Shalin, Mike. *Donnie Baseball: The Definitive Biography of Don Mattingly*. Chicago, Triumph, 2011.

Smelser, Marshall. *The Life That Ruth Built*. New York: Quadrangle, 1975.

Snider, Duke, and Bill Gilbert. *The Duke of Flatbush*. New York: Zebra Books, 1988.

Stinson, Mitchell. *Edd Roush: A Biography of the Cincinnati Reds Star*. Jefferson, N.C.: McFarland, 2010.

Thomson, Cindy, and Scott Brown. *Three Finger: The Mordecai Brown Story*. Lincoln: University of Nebraska Press, 2006.

Torre, Joe, and Tom Verducci. *The Yankee Years*. New York: Doubleday, 2009.

Tygiel, Jules. *Baseball's Great Experiment*. New York: Oxford University Press, 1983.

Waldo, Ronald. *Fred Clarke: A Biography of the Baseball Hall of Fame Player-Manager*. Jefferson, N.C.: McFarland, 2010.

Williams, Dick, and Bill Plaschke. *No More Mr. Nice Guy*. New York: Harcourt Brace Jovanovich, 1990.

Williams, Ted, and John Underwood. *My Turn at Bat*. New York: Simon & Schuster, 1969.

Yastrzemski, Carl, and Gerald Eskenazi. *Yaz: Baseball, the Wall and Me*. New York: Doubleday, 1990.

TEAM HISTORIES

Allen, Lee. *The Cincinnati Reds*. New York: G.P. Putnam's Sons, 1948.

Anderson, William. *The Detroit Tigers*. South Bend, Ind.: Diamond Communications, 1990.

Billington, Charles. *Wrigley Field's Last World Series*. Chicago: Lake Claremont Press, 2005.

Borst, Bill. *Ables to Zoldak Vols. I–III*. St. Louis: Krank Press, 1988.

_____. *Still Last in the American League*. West

Bloomfield, Mich.: Altwerger and Mandel, 1992.

Broeg, Bob, and Jerry Vickery. *The St. Louis Cardinals Encyclopedia*. Chicago: Masters Press, 1998.

Brown, Warren. *The Chicago Cubs*. New York: G.P. Putnam's Sons, 1946.

_____. *The Chicago White Sox*. New York: G.P. Putnam's Sons, 1952.

Buege, Bob. *The Milwaukee Braves: A Baseball Eulogy*. Milwaukee: Douglas American Sports, 1988.

Cantor, George. *The Tigers of '68*. Dallas: Taylor, 1997.

Carney, Gene. *Burying the Black Sox*. Washington, D.C.: Potomac Books, 2006.

Caruso, Gary. *The Braves Encyclopedia*. Philadelphia: Temple University Press, 1995.

Cava, Pete. *Tales From the Cubs Dugout*. Champaign, Ill.: Sports Publishing, 2000.

Deveaux, Tom. *The Washington Senators, 1901–1971*. Jefferson, N.C.: McFarland, 2001.

Eckhouse, Morris. *Legends of the Tribe: An Illustrated History of the Cleveland Indians*. Dallas: Taylor, 2000.

Ehrgott, Roberts. *Mr. Wrigley's Ball Club*. Lincoln: University of Nebraska Press, 2013.

Ellard, Harry. *Baseball in Cincinnati: A History*. Cincinnati: Self-published, 1907.

Erskine, Carl. *Tales from the Dodger Dugout*. Champaign, Ill.: Sports Publishing, 2000.

Falls, Joe. *The Detroit Tigers*. New York: Walker & Co., 1989.

Feldmann, Doug. *September Streak: The 1935 Chicago Cubs Chase the Pennant*. Jefferson, N.C.: McFarland, 2003.

Finoli, David, and Bill Ranier. *The Pittsburgh Pirates Encyclopedia*. Champaign, Ill.: Sports Publishing, 2003.

Fitzgerald, Ed. *The Story of the Brooklyn Dodgers*. New York: Bantam, 1949.

Ford, Whitey, and Phil Pepe. *Few and Chosen: Defining Yankee Greatness Across the Eras*. Chicago: Triumph, 2001.

Frommer, Frederic. *The Washington Nationals*. Lanham, Md.: Taylor Trade, 2006.

Frommer, Harvey. *The New York Yankee Encyclopedia*. New York: Macmillan, 1997.

Gallagher, Danny, and Bill Young. *Remembering the Montreal Expos*. Toronto: Scoop Press, 2007.

Gallagher, Mark. *The Yankees Encyclopedia*. New York: Leisure Press, 1982.

Gentile, Derek. *The Complete Chicago Cubs: The Total Encyclopedia of the Team*. New York: Black Dog & Leventhal, 2002.

_____. *The Complete New York Yankees: The Total Encyclopedia of the Team*. New York: Black Dog & Leventhal, 2001.

Gesker, Mike. *The Orioles Encyclopedia*. Baltimore: Johns Hopkins University Press, 2009.

Gold, Eddie, and Art Ahrens. *The Golden Era Cubs 1876–1940*. Chicago: Bonus Books, 1985.

_____. *The New Era Cubs 1941–1985*. Chicago: Bonus Books, 1985.

_____. *The Renewal Era Cubs 1985–1990*. Chicago: Bonus Books, 1990.

Golenbock, Peter. *Amazin': The Miraculous History of New York's Most Beloved Baseball Team*. New York: St. Martin's, 2002.

_____. *Bums: An Oral History of the Brooklyn Dodgers*. New York: G.P. Putnam's Sons, 1984.

_____. *Dynasty: The New York Yankees, 1949–1964*. Englewood Cliffs, N.J.: Prentice-Hall, 1975.

_____. *Fenway: An Unexpurgated History of the Boston Red Sox*. New York: G.P. Putnam's Sons, 1992.

_____. *The Spirit of St. Louis: A History of the St. Louis Cardinals and Browns*. New York: Avon Books, 2000.

_____. *Wrigleyville: A Magical History Tour of the Chicago Cubs*. New York: St. Martin's Press, 1996.

Graham, Frank. *The Brooklyn Dodgers*. New York: G.P. Putnam's Sons, 1945.

_____. *The New York Giants*. New York: G.P. Putnam's Sons, 1952.

_____. *The New York Yankees*. New York: G.P. Putnam's Sons, 1943.

Hardy, James. *The New York Giants Baseball Club 1870 to 1900*. Jefferson, N.C.: McFarland, 1996.

Hartley, James. *Washington's Expansion Senators (1961–1971)*. Germantown, Md.: Corduroy Press, 1997.

Hawkins, Jim, and Dan Ewald. *The Detroit Tigers Encyclopedia*. Champaign, Ill.: Sports Publishing, 2003.

Hertzel, Bob. *The Big Red Machine*. Englewood Cliffs, N.J.: Prentice-Hall, 1976.

Hogan, Kenneth. *The 1969 Seattle Pilots*. Jefferson, N.C.: McFarland, 2007.

Holmes, Tommy. *The Dodgers*. New York: Rutledge Books, 1975.

Holtzman, Jerome, and George Vass. *The Chicago Cubs Encyclopedia*. Philadelphia: Temple University Press, 1997.

Hood, Robert *The Gashouse Gang*. New York: William Morrow, 1976.

Hynd, Noel. *The Giants of the Polo Grounds*. New York: Doubleday, 1988.

Jensen, Brian. *Where Have All Our Yankees Gone?*

Past the Pinstripes. Lanham, Md.: Taylor Trade, 2004.
Jordan, David. *The Athletics of Philadelphia: Connie Mack's White Elephants, 1901–1954*. Jefferson, N.C.: McFarland, 1999.
_____. *Occasional Glory: A History of the Philadelphia Phillies*. Jefferson, N.C.: McFarland, 2002.
Kaese, Harold. *The Boston Braves, 1871–1953*. Boston: Northeastern University Press, 2004.
Kahn, Roger. *The Boys of Summer*. New York: Harper & Row, 1971.
Kelley, Brent. *They Too Wore Pinstripes: Interviews With 20 Glory-Days New York Yankees*. Jefferson, N.C.: McFarland, 1998.
Kittle, Ron, and Bob Logan. *Ron Kittle's Tales from the White Sox Dugout*. Champaign, Ill.: Sports Publishing, 2005.
Klapisch, Bob, and Pete Van Wieren. *The World Champion Braves: An Illustrated History of America's Team, 1871–1995*. Atlanta: Turner, 1995.
Klima, John. *Bushville Wins!* New York: Thomas Dunne Books, 2014.
Klumpe, Jack, and Kevin Grace. *The Cincinnati Reds 1950–1985*. Charleston, S.C.: Arcadia, 2004.
Koppett, Leonard. *The New York Mets*. New York: Collier Books, 1970.
Lang, Jack, and Peter Simon. *The New York Mets*. New York: Henry Holt, 1986.
Langford, Jim. *The Game is Never Over: An Appreciative History of the Chicago Cubs*. South Bend, Ind.: Icarus Press, 1980.
Lawson, Earl. *Cincinnati Seasons*. South Bend, Ind.: Diamond Communications, 1987.
Lewis, Franklin. *The Cleveland Indians*. New York: G.P. Putnam's Sons, 1949.
Lieb, Fred. *The Baltimore Orioles*. Carbondale: Southern Illinois University Press, 2005.
_____. *The Boston Red Sox*. New York: G.P. Putnam's Sons, 1947.
_____. *The Detroit Tigers*. New York, G.P. Putnam's Sons, 1946.
_____. *The Pittsburgh Pirates*. Carbondale: Southern Illinois University Press, 2003.
_____. *The St. Louis Cardinals*. New York: G.P. Putnam's Sons, 1944.
Lieb, Fred, and Stan Baumgartner. *The Philadelphia Phillies*. Kent, Ohio: Kent State University Press, 2009.
Lindberg, Rich. *The White Sox Encyclopedia*. Philadelphia: Temple University Press, 1997.
_____. *Who's on Third?* South Bend, Ind.: Icarus Press, 1983.
Logan, Bob. *More Tales from the Cubs Dugout*. Champaign, Ill.: Sports Publishing, 2003.
Luisi, Vincent. *New York Yankees: The First 25 Years*. Charleston, S.C.: Arcadia, 2002.
Mandelaro, Jim, and Scott Pitoniak. *Silver Seasons and a New Frontier: The Story of the Rochester Red Wings*. Syracuse: Syracuse University Press, 1995.
Marzano, Rudy. *The Brooklyn Dodgers in the 1940s*. Jefferson, N.C.: McFarland, 2005.
_____. *The Last Years of the Brooklyn Dodgers*. Jefferson, N.C.: McFarland, 2008.
Matthews, Gary, and Phil Pepe. *Few and Chosen: Defining Phillies Greatness Across the Eras*. Syracuse: Syracuse University Press, 2010.
Matthews, George. *When the Cubs Won It All: The 1908 Championship Season*. Chicago: Triumph, 2012.
Mayer, Ronald. *The 1923 New York Yankees: A History of Their First World Championship Season*. Jefferson, N.C.: McFarland, 2010.
McCarver, Tim, and Phil Pepe. *Few and Chosen: Defining Cardinal Greatness Across the Eras*. Chicago: Triumph, 2003.
McCollister, John. *The Bucs! The Story of the Pittsburgh Pirates*. Lenexa, Kan.: Addax, 1998.
McNeil, William. *The Dodgers Encyclopedia*. Champaign, Ill.: Sports Publishing, 1997.
Meany, Tom. *The Magnificent Yankees*. New York: Grosset & Dunlap, 1952.
Mercurio, John. *Chronology of New York Yankees Records*. New York: Harper & Row, 1989.
Mitchell, Fred. *Cubs: Where Have You Gone?* Champaign, Ill.: Sports Publishing, 2004.
Mumau, Thad. *An Indian Summer: The 1957 Milwaukee Braves, Champions of Baseball*. Jefferson, N.C.: McFarland, 2007.
Nowlin, Bill, ed. *When Boston Still Had the Babe: The 1918 World Champion Red Sox*. Burlington, Mass.: Rounder Books, 2008.
O'Brien, Jim. *Maz and the '60 Bucs: When Pittsburgh and the Pirates Went All the Way*. Pittsburgh: Self-published, 1993.
Overfield, Joseph. *The 100 Seasons of Buffalo Baseball*. Kenmore, N.Y.: Partners' Press, 1985.
Pajot, Dennis. *Baseball's Heartland War 1902–1903: The Western League and American Association Vie for Turf, Players and Profits*. Jefferson, N.C.: McFarland, 2011.
_____. *The Rise of Milwaukee Baseball: The Cream City From Midwestern Outpost to the Major Leagues, 1859–1901*. Jefferson, N.C.: McFarland, 2011.
Peterson, John. *The Kansas City Athletics: A Baseball History 1954–1967*. Jefferson, N.C.: McFarland, 2003.
Phalen, Rich. *Our Chicago Cubs*. South Bend, Ind.: Diamond Communications, 1992.

Phillips, John. *Bill Hinchman's Boner and the 1908 Naps*. Cabin John, Md.: Capital, 1990.
_____. *Buck Ewing and the 1893 Cleveland Spiders*. Cabin John, Md.: Capital, 1992.
_____. *Cleveland Baseball: The 1894 Spiders*. Cabin John, Md.: Capital, 1991.
_____. *Cleveland Baseball: Who Was Who in 1911–1919*. Cabin John, Md.: Capital, 1990.
_____. *Cleveland Baseball: Who Was Who in the Twenties*. Cabin John, Md.: Capital, 1990.
_____. *The Cleveland Baseball Winners: Who Was Who in 1946–56*. Cabin John, Md.: Capital, 1987.
_____. *Cleveland Blues*. Cabin John, Md.: Capital, 1991.
_____. *The 1895 Cleveland Spiders: Temple Cup Champions*. Cabin John, Md.: Capital, 1990.
_____. *The '99 Spiders: The Story of the Worst Baseball Team Ever to Play in the Major Leagues*. Cabin John, Md.: Capital, 1988.
_____. *The 1903 Naps*. Cabin John, Md.: Capital, 1989.
_____. *The 1920 Indians*. Cabin John, Md.: Capital, 1989.
_____. *The Spiders: Who Was Who*. Cabin John, Md.: Capital, 1991.
_____. *When Lajoie Came to Town: Cleveland Blues 1902*. Cabin John, Md.: Capital, 1988.
_____. *Who Was Who in Cleveland Baseball in 1901–1910*. Cabin John, Md.: Capital, 1989.
Pluto, Terry. *The Curse of Rocky Colavito*. New York: Simon & Schuster, 1994.
_____. *Our Tribe: A Baseball Memoir*. New York: Simon & Schuster, 1999.
Podoll, Brian. *The Minor League Milwaukee Brewers, 1859–1952*. Jefferson, N.C.: McFarland, 2003.
Porter, David, and Joe Naiman. *The San Diego Padres Encyclopedia*. Champaign, Ill.: Sports Publishing, 2002.
Posnanski, Joe. *The Machine: A Hot Team, a Legendary Season, and a Heart-Stopping World Series—The Story of the 1975 Cincinnati Reds*. New York: William Morrow, 2009.
Povich, Shirley. *The Washington Senators*. New York: G.P. Putnam's Sons, 1954.
Prince, Carl. *Brooklyn's Dodgers: The Bums, the Borough and the Best of Baseball*. New York: Oxford University Press, 1996.
Rains, Rob. *Cardinals, Where Have You Gone?* Champaign, Ill.: Sports Publishing, 2005.
_____. *The St. Louis Cardinals*. New York: St. Martin's Press, 1992.
Raley, Dan. *Pitchers of Beer: The Story of the Seattle Rainiers*. Lincoln: University of Nebraska Press, 2011.
Ranier, Bill, and David Finoli. *When the Bucs Won It All: The 1979 World Champion Pittsburgh Pirates*. Jefferson, N.C.: McFarland, 2005.
Redmount, Robert. *The Red Sox Encyclopedia*. Champaign, Ill.: Sports Publishing, 1998.
Reed, Robert. *Colt .45s—A Six-Gun Salute: An Illustrated History of the Houston Colt .45s*. Houston: Lone Star Press, 1999.
Reisler, Jim. *Before They Were Bombers: The New York Yankees' Early Years, 1903–1915*. Jefferson, N.C.: McFarland, 2002.
Rhodes, Greg, and John Erardi. *Big Red Dynasty: How Bob Howsam and Sparky Anderson Built the Big Red Machine*. Cincinnati: Road West Publishing, 1997.
Rhodes, Greg, and John Snyder. *Redleg Journal: Year by Year and Day by Day with the Cincinnati Reds Since 1866*. Cincinnati: Road West Publishing, 2006.
Roberts, Randy, and Carson Cunningham. *Before the Curse: The Chicago Cubs Glory Years, 1870–1945*. Urbana: University of Chicago Press, 2012.
Romanowski, Rev. Jerome. *The Mackmen*. Upper Darby, Pa.: Self-published, 1979.
Ryan, Bob. *When Boston Won the World Series: A Chronicle of Boston's Remarkable Victory in the First Modern World Series of 1903*. Philadelphia: Running Press, 2003.
Ryczek, William. *The Amazin' Mets, 1962–1969*. Jefferson, N.C.: McFarland, 2008.
Schneider, Russell. *The Cleveland Indians Encyclopedia*. Philadelphia: Temple University Press, 1996.
Schott, Tom, and Nick Peters. *The Giants Encyclopedia*. Champaign, Ill.: Sports Publishing, 1999.
Shafer, Ronald. *When the Dodgers Were Bridegrooms*. Jefferson, N.C.: McFarland, 2011.
Shropshire, Mike. *Seasons in Hell*. New York: Donald I. Fine, 1996.
Silverman, Matthew, and Ken Samelson. *The Miracle Has Landed: The Amazin' Story of How the 1969 Mets Shocked the World*. Hanover, Mass.: Maple Street Press, 2009.
Skipper, John. *The Cubs Win the Pennant*. Jefferson, N.C.: McFarland, 2004.
_____. *Take Me Out to the Cubs Game*. Jefferson, N.C.: McFarland, 2000.
Smith, Fred. *Cub Tales and Trivia*. West Bloomfield, Mich.: Altwerger and Mandel, 1991.
_____. *Tiger Tales and Trivia*. Lathrup Village, Mich.: Self-Published, 1988.
Smizik, Bob. *The Pittsburgh Pirates*. New York: Walker & Co., 1990.
Snider, Duke, and Phil Pepe. *Few and Chosen: Defining Dodgers Greatness Across the Eras*. Chicago: Triumph, 2006.
Spatz, Lyle, and Steve Steinberg. *1921: The Yan-

kees, the Giants and the Battle for Baseball Supremacy in New York. Lincoln: University of Nebraska Press, 2010.
Staub, Rusty, and Phil Pepe. *Few and Chosen: Defining Mets Greatness Across the Eras.* Chicago: Triumph, 2009.
Stout, Glenn, and Richard A. Johnson. *The Dodgers: 120 Years of Dodgers Baseball.* Boston: Houghton Mifflin, 2004.
_____. *Red Sox Century: One Hundred Years of Red Sox Baseball.* Boston: Houghton Mifflin, 2000.
_____. *Yankees Century: 100 Years of New York Yankees Baseball.* Boston: Houghton Mifflin, 2002.
Swank, Bill. *Echoes From Lane Field: A History of the San Diego Padres 1916–1957.* Paducah, Ky.: Turner, 1997.
Tofel, Richard. *A Legend in the Making: The New York Yankees in 1939.* Chicago: Ivan R. Dee, 2002.
Turner, Dan. *The Expos Inside Out.* Toronto: The Canadian Publishers, 1983.
Waldo, Ronald. *The Battling Bucs of 1925.* Jefferson, N.C.: McFarland, 2012.
Weintraub, Robert. *The House that Ruth Built: A New Stadium, the First Yankee Championship, and the Redemption of 1923.* New York: Little, Brown, 2011.
Westcott, Rich. *Philadelphia's Top 50 Baseball Players.* Lincoln: University of Nebraska Press, 2013.
Whalen, Thomas. *When the Red Sox Ruled: Baseball's First Dynasty, 1912–1918.* Chicago: Ivan R. Dee, 2011.
White, Gaylon. *The Bilko Athletic Club: The Story of the 1956 Los Angeles Angels.* Lanham, Md.: Rowman & Littlefield, 2014.
Williams, Peter. *When the Giants Were Giants: Bill Terry and the Golden Age of New York Baseball.* Chapel Hill: Algonquin Books, 1994.
Zimmerman, Paul, and Dick Schaap. *The Year the Mets Lost Last Place.* New York: World, 1969.
Zimniuch, Fran. *Phillies, Where Have You Gone?* Champaign, Ill.: Sports Publishing, 2009.

Periodicals

ANNUALS

American Association on Parade
American Association Sketchbook
American League Redbook
Baseball America Almanac
Baseball America Directory
Baseball America Prospect Handbook
Baseball American Super Register
Baseball Weekly Almanac
Bill James Baseball Abstract
Bill James Major League Handbook
Elias Baseball Analyst
International League of Professional Baseball Clubs Record Book
Japan Pro Baseball Fan Handbook and Media Guide
Mutual Baseball Almanac
National League Green Book
Pacific Coast League Thumbnail Sketches
Players National League Guide
Reach Baseball Guide
The Scouting Report
The Sporting News Baseball Register
The Sporting News Daguerreotypes
The Sporting News Famous Sluggers
The Sporting News Official Baseball Guide
The Sporting News Record Book
Stats: The Scouting Notebook
Who's Who in the American Association
Who's Who in Baseball
Who's Who in the Major Leagues
Yankees Magazine

MEDIA GUIDES

Anaheim/California/Los Angeles Angels
Atlanta Braves
Baltimore Orioles
Buffalo Bisons
Charlotte Knights
Chicago Cubs
Chicago White Sox
Cincinnati Reds
Cleveland Indians
Colorado Rockies
Columbus Clippers
Columbus Jets
Detroit Tigers
Durham Bulls
Florida Marlins
Houston Astros
Indianapolis Indians
Kansas City Royals
Lehigh Valley Iron Pigs
Los Angeles Dodgers
Louisville Bats
Louisville River Bats
Milwaukee Brewers
Minnesota Twins
Montreal Expos
New York Mets
New York Yankees

Norfolk Tides
Oakland Athletics
Omaha Royals
Ottawa Lynx
Pawtucket Red Sox
Philadelphia Phillies
Pittsburgh Pirates
Rochester Red Wings
Sacramento River Cats
St. Louis Cardinals
San Diego Padres
San Francisco Giants
Scranton/Wilkes-Barre Red Barons
Scranton/Wilkes-Barre Yankees
Seattle Mariners
Syracuse Sky Chiefs/Syracuse Chiefs
Tampa Bay Devil Rays/Tampa Bay Rays
Texas Rangers
Toledo Mud Hens
Toronto Blue Jays
Trenton Thunder

NEWSPAPERS

Akron Beacon Journal
Anderson (Ind.) *Herald Bulletin*
Atlanta Journal-Constitution
Baltimore Sun
Bloomington (Ind.) *Herald-Times*
Bluffton (Ind.) *News-Banner*
Boston Globe
Boston Herald
Boston Post
Brazil (Ind.) *Times*
Brooklyn Eagle
Buffalo News
Champaign (Ill.) *News-Gazette*
Charlotte (N.C.) *Observer*
Chicago Defender
Chicago Sun-Times
Chicago Tribune
Cincinnati Enquirer
Cincinnati Post
Cleveland Plain-Dealer
Columbia City (Ind.) *Post & Mail*
Columbus (Ohio) *Dispatch*
Columbus (Ind.) *Republic*
Crawfordville (Ind.) *Journal-Review*
Dallas Morning News
Dayton (Ohio) *Daily News*
Denver Post
Des Moines Register
Detroit Free Press
Detroit News
Durham (N.C.) *Herald Sun*
Elkhart (Ind.) *Truth*

Evansville Courier
Evansville Press
Fort Wayne Journal-Gazette
Fort Wayne News-Sentinel
Fort Worth Star-Telegram
Frankfort (Ind.) *Times*
Gary Post-Tribune
Grand Rapids (Mich.) *Press*
Greencastle (Ind.) *Banner-Graphic*
Greensburg (Ind.) *Daily News*
Greenville (S.C.) *News*
Hartford (Conn.) *Courant*
Hartford City (Ind.) *News-Times*
Huntington (Ind.) *Herald-Press*
Indianapolis Journal
Indianapolis News
Indianapolis Star
Indianapolis Times
Jasper (Ind.) *Herald*
Jeffersonville (Ind.) *Evening News*
Kalamazoo (Mich.) *Gazette*
Kankakee (Ill.) *Journal*
Kansas City Star
Knoxville News-Sentinel
Kokomo Tribune
La Porte (Ind.) *Herald-Argus*
Lafayette (Ind.) *Journal & Courier*
Lebanon (Ind.) *Reporter*
Lexington (Ky.) *Herald-Leader*
Logansport (Ind.) *Pharos-Tribune*
Los Angeles Herald-Examiner
Los Angeles Times
Louisville Courier-Journal
Madison (Ind.) *Courier*
Marion (Ind.) *Chronicle-Tribune*
Michigan City (Ind.) *News-Dispatch*
Milwaukee Journal-Sentinel
Minneapolis Star-Tribune
Muncie Star-Press
Munster (Ind.) *Times*
Nashville Banner
Nashville Tennessean
New Albany (Ind.) *Tribune*
New Castle (Ind.) *Courier-Times*
New Orleans Times-Picayune
New York Daily News
New York Herald-Tribune
New York Journal-American
New York Times
New York World, Telegram & Sun
Noblesville (Ind.) *Ledger*
Oklahoma City Daily Oklahoman
Omaha World-Herald
Peoria (Ill.) *Journal-Star*
Peru (Ind.) *Tribune*
Philadelphia Enquirer

Bibliography—Periodicals

Pittsburgh Post-Gazette
Portland Oregonian
Princeton (Ind.) *Daily Clarion*
Raleigh (N.C.) *News & Observer*
Richmond (Ind.) *Palladium-Item*
Richmond (Va.) *Times Dispatch*
Rochester (N.Y.) *Democrat Chronicle*
Rushville (Ind.) *Republican*
St. Louis Globe-Democrat
St. Louis Post-Dispatch
St. Paul Pioneer Press
Salt Lake City Deseret News
San Antonio Express-News
San Diego Union-Tribune
San Francisco Chronicle
San Francisco Examiner
Seattle Post-Intelligencer
Seymour (Ind.) *Tribune*
Shelbyville (Ind.) *News*
Shreveport (La.) *Times*
South Bend Tribune
Spokane (Wash.) *Spokesman-Review*
Staten Island Advance
Syracuse (N.Y.) *Herald-Journal*
Syracuse (N.Y.) *Post-Standard*
Terre Haute Tribune-Star
Tipton (Ind.) *Tribune*
Topeka (Kan.) *Capital-Journal*
Tulsa (Okla.) *World*
USA Today
Valparaiso (Ind.) *Vidette-Times*
Wabash (Ind.) *Plain Dealer*
Washington (Ind.) *Times-Herald*
Washington Post
Wichita Eagle

Journals and Magazines

Baseball America
Baseball Digest
Baseball History
Baseball Magazine
Baseball Research Journal
Elysian Fields Quarterly
Inside Sports
Memories & Dreams
Minneapolis Review of Baseball
The National Pastime
New York Clipper
Reach Guide
SABR Minor League History Journal, Vols. 1 and 2.
Saturday Evening Post
Spalding's Official Baseball Guide
Spitball
Sport Magazine
Sporting Life
The Sporting News
Sports Collectors Digest
Sports Illustrated
Traces of Indiana and Midwestern History
USA Today Sports Weekly

Index

Aaron, Hank 68, 137, 158
Adams, Babe 3–4, 138, 210
Adcock, Joe 46
Aguilera, Rick 71
Akers, Jerry 4
Alberts, Gus 208
Aldridge, Vic 4–5
Alexander, Grover Cleveland "Pete" 26, 214
Allen, Bernie 125
Allen, Dick 99
Allen, Frank 17
Allen, Lee 184
Allensworth, Jermaine 5–6
Allison, Mack 22
Ambrogi, Mark 193
Amoruso, Marino 93
Anderson, Bob 6–7
Andres, Ernie 7, 103
Andriole, Rich 96
Anson, Cap 9, 61, 75, 123, 183, 191
Appling, Luke 201
Arndt, Harry 7–8
Arnold, Billy 137
Averill, Earl 40
Aydelott, Jake 8

Baker, Harold 107
Baker, Kirt 8–9
Ball, Artie 9
Ball, Phil 44, 214
Ballew, Bill 158
Banister, Jeff 21
Banks, Ernie 6
Barber, Steve 204
Barker, Al 9–10
Barmes, Bruce 10
Barmes, Clint 10–11
Barnhart, Tucker 11
Barnhart, Vic 74
Barrett, Aaron 11–12
Barrett, Kewpie 154
Barrett, Tim 12
Bateman, Harry 51
Baum, Spider 154
Baumann, Paddy 12–13
Beachy, Brandon 13
Beck, George 13–14
Beckett, Josh 31
Bejma, Lou "Shorty" 14
Bejma, Ollie 14
Bell, Jay 105

Bench, Johnny 124
Benes, Adam 16
Benes, Alan 14–15, 16, 34
Benes, Andy 15–16, 28, 123
Benes, Drew 16
Bennett, Charlie 201
Bennett, Dennis 88
Benton, Rube 156–157
Benz, Joe 16
Berg, Moe 46
Bergman, Al 16–17
Bergman, Art 17
Bergman, Joe 17
Berra, Yogi 17, 122
Berry, Claude 17, 101
Berry, Tyrus 17
Berryhill, Damon 53
Bevens, Floyd 198
Beville, Monte 17–18
Bigbie, Larry 18
Biggs, Charlie 18–19
Bildilli, Emil 19
Billiard, Pre 19
Bird, Larry 101
Bissonette, Del 38
Blackburn, Earl 204
Blackley, Travis 146
Blaemire, Rae 20
Blake, Casey 34
Blemker, Ray 20
Bluege, Ossie 35, 133
Blyleven, Bert 146
Bodie, Ping 214
Boehler, George 20–21
Bogar, Tim 21
Bolin, Bob 52
Bonds, Barry 68
Bonin, Luther 21–22
Bonura, Zeke 106
Boone, Bob 63
Bootcheck, Chris 22–23
Bootcheck, Dan 22
Borton, Babe 224–225
Bottomley, Jim 200
Boudreau, Lou 97, 220
Bourn, Michael 94
Bowen, Cy 23
Boyd, Brenda 125
Boyd, Ray 23–24
Boyer, Ken 166
Bradley, Phil 24
Bragan, Bobby 110
Brands, Edgar 66
Brandt, Bill 24–25

Brenly, Bob 42
Bresnahan, Roger 118, 219
Brett, George 188
Bridges, Tommy 38
Bridwell Al 41
Brolley, Tom 222
Brown, Charlie 25
Brown, Elmer 25–26
Brown, Kevin 26
"Brown, Roy" 154
Brown, Scott 27
Brown, Three-Finger 26–27, 44, 64
Browning, Pete 86
Bruckenberger, Al 217
Bruntlett, Eric 27–28, 169
Brush, John T. 17
Bryan, William Jennings 88
Buckingham, Ashley 163
Buente, Jay 28
Bullington, Bryan 28–29
Bullington, Larry 29
Bumbry, Al 24, 38
Bunning, Jim 50
Burkett, Jesse 25
Burnside, Sheldon 29
Bush, Donie 29–30, 50, 68
Butera, Drew 30–31
Butera, Sal 31
Butland, Bill 31
Butler, Brett 48
Byers, Bill 31–32

Cabrera, Miguel 127
Callahan, Wes 32
Campanella, Roy 93
Campaneris, Bert 178
Campau, Charles "Count" 182
Campbell, Dave 32–33
Canseco, Jose 59
Cantillon, Joe 36
Capps, Matt 192
Carey, Evangeline 23
Carey, Max 33–34, 138, 172
Carey, Scoops 34
Carey, Skip 36
Carlton, Steve 24, 137
Carmichael, Chet 34
Carroll, Jamie 34–35
Carroll, Jeff 162
Carroll, Wes 35

Cary, Scott 35
Casey, Sean 15
Cash, Norm 145
Castillo, Luis 28
Castle, Don 35
Cates, Eli 36
Caylor, O.P. 169
Cespedes, Yoenis 78
Chance, Frank 51, 134
Chandler, A.B. "Happy" 60
Chaney, Darrel 36
Chaney, Keith 36
Chapman, Pete 36–37
Chase, Hal 224–225
Christenson, Larry 70
Christman, Mark 206
Cicotte, Eddie 4, 102
Cissell, Bill 121
"Clammer" 217
Clark, Bob 161
Clark, Dennis 190
Clarke, Fred 3, 4, 33, 69, 181
Clavin, Tom 93
Clemens, Roger 24
Clemente, Roberto 124
Cleveland, Grover 83
Cline, Monk 169
Clippard, Tyler 192
Clymer, Billy 217
Closser, JD 37
Cobb, Ty 3, 12–13, 17, 30, 33, 41, 50, 79, 161, 202, 212
Coggins, Rich 37–38
Coleman, Bob 38–39, 118, 211
Collier, Gene 70
Collier, Phil 129
Collins, Bill 39–40
Collins, Eddie 156
Collins, Jimmy 189–190
Collins, Orth 39
Combs, Earle 39, 122, 200
Comiskey, Charles 16
Concepcion, Davey 36
Cone, David 113
Connor, Roger 202, 220
Cooley, Dick 217
Coombs, Jack 89
Corhan, Roy 40
Coridan, Phil 40–41
Corriden, Johnny 41
Corriden, Red 41–42

243

Index

Cottier, Chuck 24
Counsell, Craig 42–43
Counsell, John 43
Coveleski, Stan 66, 186
Covington, Wes 38
Cramer, Bill 43
Crandall, Arnold 43
Crandall, Del 38
Crandall, Doc 43–44, 63, 219
Crandall, Jim 44
Crandall, Karl 43
Crawford, Ken 44
Crawford, Sam 50, 202
Criger, Elmer 45
Criger, Lou 8, 44–45
Cronin, Joe 31
Crouse, Buck 45–46
Crowder, Enoch 89
Crowe, George 46–47
Crowe, Ray 47
Crume, Levi 97
Cuppy, Nig 47
Curtis, Chad 47–48
Cuyler, KiKi 33

Dale, Carl 48–49
Dalton, Jack 51
Daniels, Cheri 89
Daniels, Mitch 89
Daringer, Cliff 49, 184
Daringer, Howard 49, 181, 184
Daringer, Rolla "Rollie" 49, 184
Dark, Alvin 6
Darling, Ron 71
Darnell, Bruce 194
Dauss, George 50
Dauss, Ray "Bud" 50
Davenport, Dave 84
Davidson, Bill 50–51
Dean, Dizzy 66, 205
Dean, Everett 63
DeBusschere, Dave 158
Dedeaux, Rod 110
DeKever, Pete 66
Delahanty, Ed 87, 202
Delahanty, Jim 36
Dellinger, Dr. Susan 168
Delmore, Vic 6
Demaree, Al 219
Dempsey, Jack 59
Devaney, John 93
Devlin, Art 174
Dexter, Charlie 51
Dickey, Bill 17, 81
Dietz, Dick 52
DiMaggio, Dom 67
DiMaggio, Joe 39, 40, 54, 91, 122, 198
Dinneen, Bill 45
Distel, Dutch 52–53
Dixon, Leo 82
Doby, Larry 82
Donica, Harry 143
Donica, Nellie 143
Donna, Gary 103
Donovan, Dick 38
Donovan, Patsy 164

Doolan, Mickey 222
Dorais, Gus 17
Dorsett, Brandon 53
Dorsett, Brian 53
Doster, David 53–54
Dowling, William Worth 75
Downey, Red 54
Driscoll, Doug 165
Drysdale, Don 52, 66
Dudley, Bruce 112
Duffy, Frank 63
Duggan, Elmer 54–55
Duggan, Johnny 5
Dumoulin, Dan 55
Dumoulin, Joan 55
Dunne, Mike 55–56
Dunwoody, Todd 56, 169
Durocher, Leo 42, 142
Durst, Cedric 199

Earl, Scott 56–57
East, Hugh 20
Eckersley, Dennis 152
Edgerton, Bill 57
Edington, Stump 57–58
Edwards, Harry P. 116
Eggleston, Edward 5
Elikhoffer, Pearl 210
Eller, Hod 58
Elliott, Rowdy 58–59
Ellsbury, Jacoby 160
Englehardt, Gordon 173
Eppard, Jim 59
Erb, Cindy 33
Erskine, Carl 59–61, 131
Erskine, Gary 60
Erskine, Jimmy 60
Escalera, Nino 83
Eskew, Alan 139
Esposito, Sammy 7
Eubank, John 61
Evans, Steve 119
Everitt, Bill 61–62
Evers, Johnny 73, 134–135
Ewing, Buck 168

Farmer, Howard 62, 63
Farmer, Mike 62–63
Farrell, Duke 129
Feezle, Stan 131
Fehring, Dutch 63
Feller, Bob 7
Ferguson, Cecil 63–64, 182
Fernandez, Sid 71
Ferrell, Rick 67
Finch, David 64
Finch, Joel 64
"Fine, Charlie" 82
Fisher, Chauncey 64–65
Fisher, Maury 65
Fisher, Tom 65
Fitts, Robert 91
Fitzsimmons, Fred 66
Fodge, Gene 66–67
Fogel, Horace 98
Fonseca, Lou 188
Ford, John 94
Fossas, Tony 140

Fox, Allison 68
Fox, Pete 38, 67–68
Fox, Don 67
Fox, Jake 68
Fox, James 68
Fox, Terry 68
Franco, Julio 84
Francoeur, Jeff 28
Francona, Terry 21
Franks, Herman 176
Frascatore, John 15
Frazee, Harry 175
Freedman, Andrew 23, 169
Freitas, Tony 154
French, Charlie 68
Freund, Lentz 69
Frick, Ford 97
Friend, Bob 69–70
Friend, Paul 69
Frisch, Frankie 201
Fritz, Larry 70–71
Fullerton, Hugh 30
Furcal, Rafael 34

Gaff, Brent 71
Gagnon, Cappy 85
Galvin, Pud 77
Gandil, Chick 4
Garlick, Dave 203
Garms, Debs 18
Gates, Joe 71
Gehrig, Lou 121, 122, 123, 175, 200
Geraghty, Ben 221
Gibbon, Joe 35
Gibson, Bob 137
Gibson, George 180
Gibson, Kyle 72
Gibson, Norwood 144
Gibson, Sam 79
Gick, George 72–73
"Gilbat" 217
Gilboy, Larry 217
Gilks, Bob 208
Gill, Doc 73
Gill, Roy 73
Gillenwater, Claral 73–74
Gilmore, Len 74
Gionfriddo, Al 74
Gladstone, Doug 57
Glenalvin, Bob 74–75, 126
Glenn, Harry 75–76
Goar, Jot 76
Golenbock, Peter 88
Gomez, Lefty 40, 66
Gonzalez, Luis 42
Gooden, Dwight 71
Goodwin, Danny 59
Gordon, Jeff 120
Gowdy, Hank 204
Graman, Alex 76
Grant, Mudcat 124
Gray, Charlie 77
Gray, Susan 164
Green, Jerry 158
Green, Paul 70
Greenberg, Hank 38
Greene, Mark 37

Greenwood, Chuck 152
Grey, R.C. "Reddy" 217
Grey, Zane 217
Griffin, A.J. 146
Griffith, Calvin 103
Griffith, Clark 35, 215
Grill, Lauren 120
Grimes, Burleigh 5
Grossman, Harley 77
Grossman, Keith 77
Grossman, Kim 77
Grott, Matt 77–78
Grove, Bob "Lefty" 140 147
Grube, Jarrett 78
Guinn, Jeff 110
Gullette, Florence 178

Hack, Stan 111
Hafey, Chick 200
Hagen, Paul 166
Haines, Jesse 66
Hamilton, Billy 196, 202
Hamilton, Steve 198
Hankins, Don 78
Hanlon, Ned 97
Hannah, Truck 21
Hanski, Don 79
Hanyzewski, Ed 79–80
Harder, Mel 50
Hardy, Jack 185
Hargan, Steve 80–81
Hargrave, Bubbles 81, 82
Hargrave, Pinky 81–82, 221
Harmon, Chuck 82–83
Harrison, Benjamin 197
Hartley, Grover 83–84, 100, 221
Hawkins, LaTroy 84–85
Hayward, Gordon 11
Heilman, Aaron 85–86
Heilman, Joe 86
Heilman, Michelle 86
Heimach, Fred 178
Heinzman, Jack 86
Heinzman, Jon 86
Helton, Todd 10
Hendrickson, Don 86–87
Henline, Butch 87
Henning, Pete 87–88
Herman, Billy 41, 88–89, 94
Herman, Billy, Jr. 89
Herrmann, Ed 89
Herrmann, Garry 84
Herrmann, Marty 89
Herzog, Whitey 176
Hettinger, Dan 36
Hicks, Jim 24, 89–90
Higgins, Bob 172
Hildebrand, Oral 90, 107
Hillman, Eric 90–91
Hillman, Heather 91
Hillman, Tim 157
Hisner, Jim 91–92
Hobson, Butch 213
Hockett, Oris 92
Hodges, Bob 93
Hodges, Gil 34, 92–94

Index

Hodges, Gil, Jr. 93–94, 131
Hofferth, Stew 94
Hofferth, Ted 94
Hoffman, John C. 42
Holke, Walter 157
Holt, Tyler 94–95
Hoose, Phillip 113
Hornsby, Rogers 5, 40, 81, 88, 200
Hough, Charlie 210
Houseman, Frank 51
Houtz, Fred 95
Howard, Elston 17
Howard, Harrison 176
Hubbell, Carl 66, 107
Huggins, Miller 175
Hughes, Tom 45
Huhn, Hap 95–96
Hunter, Bob 130–131
Hunter, Tommy 96
Hurley, Mary 35
Hutchinson, Wild Bill 123

Inks, Bert 96–97
Inks, Will 97
Irelan, Hal 97

Jackson, Bo 157, 203
"Jackson, Fred" 188
Jackson, Henry 98
Jackson, Joe 16, 50, 114
James, Jeff 98
Javier, Stan 59
Jenkins, Ferguson 50, 198
Jessup, Clarence 12
Jeter, Derek 168, 188
Jimenez, Elvio 105
Jobe, Dr. Frank 99
John, Tommy 98–100
John, Tommy III 99
Johns, Doug 100
Johnson, Ban 41
Johnson, Charles 37
Johnson, Dave 181
Johnson, Elmer 100
Johnson, Ernie 36
Johnson, Josh 28
Johnson, Otis 100–101
Johnson, Randy 42, 91, 170
Johnson, Wallace 101–102
Johnson, Walter 5, 16, 118, 140
Jones, Barry 102
Jordan, Stacia 57
Joyner, Wally 198
Justis, Walt 102

Kahle, Bob 102–103
Kearns, Doc 59
Kearns, Helen 59
Keeley, Burt 144
Keller, Jason 104
Keller, Ron 7, 103–104
Kendall, Jason 127
Kennedy, Brian 169
Kerins, Jack 104, 155
Kessinger, Don 177
Keuster, Ivan 77
Kiermayer, Kevin 104–105

Kiley, Mike 24
Kilroy, Matt 155
King, Clyde 176
King, Jack 105
King, Jeff 28, 105
King, Jim 105
Kinzer, Lee 106
Kinzer, Matt 106
Kinzer, Taylor 106
Kirke, Jay 42
Kittle, Ron 106–107
Klein, Chuck 90, 107–108, 109, 130, 215, 220
Klem, Bill 87
Kline, Jake 158
Kluszewski, Ted 46
Knepper, Charlie 108
Knoll, Punch 109–110, 181
Knoll, Thelma 181
Knolls, Hub 109
Knowles, Warren 220
Koelling, Lester 211
Koerner, Dave 167
Konopka, Bruno 109–110
Koufax, Sandy 66
Kraft, Big Boy 58, 110–111
Krah, Steve 84
Kraly, Steve 111

Lackey, John 3
Lajoie, Nap 16, 41
Lally, Bud 69
LaMaster, Dorothy 112
LaMaster, Wayne 111–112
Lambert, Ward "Piggy" 205
Landis, Doc 169
Landis, Kenesaw Mountain 44, 94
Lane, F.C. 175
Larmore, Bob 112
Larsen, Don 112–113
LaRussa, Tony 166
Lavagetto, Cookie 198
LaValliere, Mike 55
Lazar, Danny 113–114
Lazzeri, Tony 200
Leflore, Ron 176
Leiber, Hank 140
Leibold, Nemo 114
Lemon, Bob 66
Lennox, Ed 135
Leppert, Don 114–115
Leppert, Steve 115
Leppert, Tim 115
Lewis, Larry 115
Lewis, Richie 115
Liebhardt, Glenn 115–116, 211
Liebhardt, Glenn Ignatius 116
Liebhardt, Terry 116
Lind, Adam 116
Lindblom, Josh 117
Lindeman, Jim 55
Liriano, Francisco 30
"Little Nemo in Slumberland" 114
Lofton, Kenny 117–118, 192

Logan, Bob 107
Logan, Johnny 38
Loggins, Josh 169
Lombardi, Ernie 81, 211
Lombardi, Joan 93
Lowdermilk, Grover 15, 118–119
Lowdermilk, Lou 15, 119
Lowe, Bobby 156
Lusk, Janet 138
Lynn, Lance 11, 119–120, 192–193
Lyons, Curt 120
Lyons, Ted 50, 218

Maceo, Antonio 47
Mack, Connie 17, 76, 110, 120, 163, 178, 196
Madden, W.C. 191
Maggert, Harl 120–121
Maggert, Harl Warren 121
Mann, Johnny 121
Mann, Raymond "Pete" 121
Mannelly, Pat 100
Mantilla, Felix 38
Mantle, Mickey 39, 111, 122, 168
Maranville, Rabbit 12
Maris, Roger 113, 124
Martin, Billy 35
Mascari, Gina 53
Mathewson, Christy 27, 43, 63, 168
Mattingly, Don 34, 121–123, 173
Mattingly, Preston 123
Mattingly, Randy 123
Mattingly, Taylor 123
Mauck, Al 123
Mauer, Joe 30
Maurer, Rob 123
May, Milt 124–125
May, Milt, Jr. 125
May, Pinky 123–124
Mays, Willie 33, 137, 168
McBride, George 36
McCabe, Joe 125
McCarthy, Joe 42
McCarthy, Tom 125–126, 182
McCarthy, Tommy 104
McCauley, Al 126
McCauliffe, Dick 145
McClaren, John 204
McClendon, Bo 127
McClendon, Lloyd 6, 126–127
McCool, Billy 127–128, 165
McCormack, Barry 167
McCormick, Mike 141
McCracken, Branch 7
McCurdy, Harry 46
McDonald, Dave 128
McDonald, Les 128
McDowell, Roger 71
McElroy, Jim 184
McGann, Dan 164
McGill, Willie 123

McGinnity, Joe 63
McGlone, John 208
McGraw, John 9, 43, 66, 84, 88, 133, 167
McGraw, Tug 156
McGwire, Mark 100, 198
McIntyre, Harry 50
McKechnie, Bill 4, 33
McKinney, Frank 30
McLean, Larry 100
McManus, Marty 212
McRae, Hal 124
Meadows, Lee 133
Meekin, James 129
Meekin, Jouett 128–129, 168
Mercer, Jordy 11
Mercer, Sid 100
Merkle, Fred 73
Mertes, Sam 219
Merullo, Lennie 195
Mesoraco, Devin 11
Metzger, Butch 129–130
Meusel, Irish 21, 87
Meyers, Chief 83, 100
Middleton, Jimmy 130
Milan, Clyde 179
Miles, Don 130–131
Miles, Jim 35
Miller, Bruce 7, 131
Miller, Doggie 9
Miller, Dyar 131–132
Miller, Ralph 132–133
Miller, Roscoe 133–134
Miller, Speedy 132
Miller, Walt 134
Milone, Tommy 146
Moffi, Larry 93
Monday, Rick 103
Moore, Charley 134–135
Moore, Earl 154
Moran, Pat 217
Moran, Roy 135
Morandini, Mickey 54, 105
More, Forrest 135, 182
Morgan, James "Red" 144
Morgan, Joe 36, 71
Morra, Chrissy 207
Morris, Jack 137
Morrison, Johnny 136
Morrison, Phil 136
Moss, Mal 136–137
Mowe, Ray 137
Muffett, Billy 137–138
Munson, Thurman 17
Munzel, Edgar 113, 142
Murdock, Eugene 14
Murphy, Daniel 28
Murphy, Leo 138
Musgraves, Dennis 138–139
Musgraves, Wilson 139
Musial, Stan 6, 137
Muskat, Carrie 151
Musser, Joe 99
Musser, Neal 139
Myers, Henry 169
Myers, Wil 105
Myers, Randy 71

Index

Names, Larry 206
Navin, Frank 202
Nehf, Art 139–140
Nelson, Billy 140–141
Nelson, Rob 59
Neun, Johnny 79
Newhouser, Hal 66, 206
Newkirk, Floyd 141
Newkirk, Joel 141
Newlin, Maurice 141–142
Newman, Ray 142
Newton, Doc 142–143
Nicholson, Ovid 143
Niehaus, Dick 32
Nightengale, Dave 214
Nill, Dr. John 144
Nill, Rabbit 143–144
Nixon, Russ 124

O'Connor, Jack 17, 41
O'Connor, Louise 131
O'Connor, Tom 131
O'Day, Hank 73
O'Doul, Lefty 40
Olerud, John 100
Oliphant, Thomas 93
Oliver, Joe 53
Olson, Lute 117
O'Neill, Peaches 144
Onslow, Jack 42
Ontiveros, Steve 131
Ordonez, Magglio 127
Orme, George 144–145
Orosco, Jesse 152
Osburn, Pat 125
Ott, Mel 20
Overall, Orval 219
Oyler, Ray 145
Ozark, Danny 158

Pactwa, Joe 145–146
Paige, Satchel 85
Paine, Essie 65
Parker, Jarrod 146–147
Parker, Justin 147
Parks, Bob 95
Parrett, Jeff 147
Parrott, Jiggs 191
Pascual, Camilo 103
Patrick, Mark 193
Patrick, Van 206
Patterson, Robert 179
Peary, Danny 93
Peckinpaugh, Roger 133
Peitz, Heinie 144
Pena, Tony 55
Penner, Ken 147–148
Pennington, Brad 148
Pennock, Herb 212
Perini, Lou 38
Perranoski, Ron 149
Perrotto, John 170
Perry, Gaylord 52
Perzanowski, Stan 148–149
Peterek, Jeff 149
Pfeffer, Fred 75
Phegley, Josh 150–151, 171
Phillips, Bill 222
Phillips, Heath 150–151

Pieratt, Marty Ford 83
Pierce, Billy 106
Pierce, Flora 23
Pignatiello, Carmen 151
Pilarcik, Al 151
Pinckney, George 175
Pinson, Vada 46
Pishkur, Dave 152
Pittenger, Togie 217
Plesac, Dan 152
Plesac, Joe 152
Polonia, Luis 59
"Porter, J. James" 153
Porter, Odie 152–153, 180
Posada, Jorge 17
Powers, Mike 142
Prough, Clint 153–154
Pruiett, Tex 154
Puckett, Troy 154

Rader, Don 155–156
Ramsdell, Willard 60
Ramsey, Toad 104, 155–156
Ransdell, Herb 125
Rapoport, Ron 146
Rapp, Vern 130
Rariden, Bill 156–157, 182, 204
Rauch, Jon 91
"Ray" 217
Ray, Larry 157
Reed, Ron 157–158
Reese, John "Bonesetter" 47
Reese, Pee Wee 93, 195
Rehg, Wally 214
Reiger, Frank 96
Reis, Tom 111
Reising, Charlie 158–159
Reith, Brian 159
Repko, Jason 159–160
Replogle, Andy 160
Reulbach, Ed 224
Reynolds, Candace 48
Reynolds, Charlie 160–161
Rice, John 152
Rice, Sam 161–162
Richard, Clayton 162–163
Richards, Duane 163
Richards, Paul 42
Richardson, Ken 163–164
Richardson, Will 164
Rickey, Branch 70
Ritter, Lawrence 58, 167
Rizzuto, Phil 195
Roach, Roxy 42
Robbins, Bruce 164–165
Robbins, Leroy 165
Roberts, Robin 194
Robinson, Frank DeHaas 47
Robinson, Glenn 84
Robinson, Jackie 61, 198
Robinson, Ron 101
Robinson, Wilbert 89
Rockne, Knute 17, 219
Rocks, Burton 61
Rodgers, Bill 74

Roesler, Mike 165
Rogers, Phil 101
Rolen, Scott 124, 165–167
Rolfe, Red 124
Rose, Don 63
Rose, Pete 35, 69
Roseman, Chief 104
Rosen, Al 203
Roth, Mark 101
Roush, Edd 58, 167–168
Ruel, Muddy 82
Runyon, Damon 43
Ruppert, Jim 177
Rusie, Amos 23, 103, 137, 168–169
Russ, John 169
Russo, Mike 193
Ruth, Babe 44, 79, 122, 168, 175, 200, 201, 220
Ryan, Nolan 24, 77, 103, 137, 157, 173

Sabel, Erik 169–170
Samardzija, Jeff 150, 170–171
Samardzija, Sam 171
Samardzija, Sam, Jr. 171
Samson 108
Sanguillen, Manny 124
Santiago, Benito 53, 56
Schafer, David 171
Schafer, Jordan 171
Schafly, Larry 22
Schalk, Ray 45
Schang, Wally 82
Schank, Dave 190
Scheeren, Fritz 138, 171–172
Scheeren, Tillman 171
Schellhase, Al 172
Schellhase, Dave 172
Schellhase, Greg 172
Schilling, Curt 42
Schlei, George 144, 158
Schmidt, Mike 166
Schneider, Dan 172–173
Schoendienst, Red 221
Schreiber, Ken 22
Schulman, Bill 70
Schulz, Charles 14
Schulz, Jeff 171–172
Schurr, Wayne 174
Schwarz, Alan 202
Schwind, Art 174–175
Scott, Everett 175
Scott, Jim 214
Scott, Rodney 175–176
Seaver, Tom 24, 93, 127, 137, 168
Sellers, Ruby 157
Sember, Mike 177
Senteney, Karina 177
Senteney, Monica 177
Senteney, Steve 177
Sewell, Joe 188, 196–197
Sewell, Luke 188
Shanner, Bill 177–178
Shapiro, Milton 93
Shaughnessy, Frank 174
Shaw, Mark 113

Sheeks, Paul 196
Sheldon, Scott 178
Shepard, Bert 178–179
Shepherd, Keith 180
Shomberg, Otto 98
Show, Eric 183
Shy, Don 38
Shy, Les 38
Simmons, Hack 222
Simon, Mike 189–181
Simon, Syl 181–182
Siner, Hosea 182
Skinner, Bob 98
Slagle, John 182
Slocum, Frank 93
Slusarski, Joe 182–183
Smith, Carr 186
Smith, Charles N. "Pacer" 184
Smith, Clifford 184
Smith, Ed 184–185
Smith, George 39
Smith, Happy 51
Smith, Harry 183–184
Smith, Joseph 184
Smith, Mayo 145
Smith, Red 140
Smith, Tony 50
Smith, Zeke 185
"Snoopy" 14
Somerlott, Jack 185–186
Soriano, Rafael 193
Southworth, Billy 200
Sowders, Len 126
Spahn, Warren 38
Spalding, Al 183
Speece, By 186
Spence, Harry 98
Spilman, Harry 77
Splittorff, Jamie 188
Splittorff, Paul 187–188
Spudic, Kevin 85
Spurgeon, Fred 188–189
Stahl, Chick 45, 189–190
Stahl, Julia Harmon 189–190
Staley, Harry 77
Stallings, George 13
Stanley, Mickey 145
Statz, Jigger 21
Stengel, Casey 33, 37, 38, 57, 74, 88, 111, 186, 211
Stetter, Mitch 190–191
Stevens, Howard 94
Stewart, Ace 191
Stewart, James 72
Stewart, Patrick 191
Stinson, Mitchell 168
Stoddard, Tom 191–192
Storen, Drew 11, 120, 192–193
Stottlemyre, Mel 138
Stout, Glenn 190
Straily, Dan 146
Strasburg, Steve 192
Stratton, Monty 72
Strincevich, Joe 194
Strincevich, Luka 194
Strincevich, Nick 193–194
Stringer, Lou 195

Index

Stults, Eric 194
Sturgeon, Bobby 194–195
Styles, Lena 196
Sullivan, Ted 209
Summers, Eddie 195–196
Sunday, Billy 9
Swallow, Essie 168
Swartzel, Park 196

Tate, Lars 203
Taylor, Ben 197
Taylor, Foxy 196
Taylor, Harry 197
Taylor, Sammy 6
Taylor, Tony 6
Tebbetts, Birdie 38
Tebeau, Patsy 25, 47
Tellis, Richard 65
Tenney, Fred 217
Terrell, Walt 71, 198–199
Terry, Bill 20
Terry, George 199
Terry, Yank 199
Thatcher, Anne 200
Thatcher, Joe 190, 199–200
Thatcher, Mary Kate 200
Thatcher, Phil 200
Thatcher, Sara 200
Thevenow, Tommy 53, 200–201
Thigpen, Bobby 102
Thompson, David 192
Thompson, Sam 126, 201–202
Thompson, Tommy 123
Thomson, Cindy 27
Thon, Dickie 202–203
Thon, Dickie Joe 203
Thon, Frankie 203
Thon, Freddie, Jr. 202
Thon, Freddie, Sr. 202
Thon, Freddie III 203
Thornton, Matt 12
Thurman, Allen G. 83

Thurman, Brytoney 203
Thurman, Gary 203–204
Timberlake, Gary 204
Tinker, Joe 44, 134–135, 220
Tinker-to-Evers-to-Chance 27, 109, 219
Toney, Fred 95
Torgeson, Earl 46
Torre, Joe 122
Torrez, Mike 203
Tovar, Cesar 178
Tragesser, Walt 204
"Tregoran" 192
Trinkle, Ken 206
Trost, Mike "Foghorn" 208
Trout, Dizzy 205–206
Trout, Steve "Rainbow" 206
Tucker, Michael 15
Tulowitzki, Troy 11
Turner, Dan 176

Uhle, George 211
Underwood, J.D. 207
Underwood, Marie 207
Underwood, Pat 206–207
Underwood, Tom 55, 206–207
Unglaub, Bob 190

Valenti, Dan 99
Valentine, Bobby 21, 91
Vance, Dazzy 66
VanRyn, Ben 207–208
Van Slyke, Andy 55
Van Wieren, Pete 36
Van Zant, Dick 208–209
Van Zant, Phoebe 208
Vaughan, Manning 114
Vaughn, Jim 95
Veach, Peek-A-Boo 209
Veach, William Walter, Jr. 209

Velarde, Randy 122
Visner, Joe 161
Von der Ahe, Chris 156

Wacker, Charlie 209–210
Waddell, Rube 140
Wade, Cory 210–211
Wagner, Dick 203
Wagner, Honus 57, 180
Wallace, Jim 211–212
Wallace, Lefty 210
Walsh, Runt 222
Waner, Paul 33, 40, 211
Warn, Bob 190, 200
Warner, Jackie 212
Washington, Ron 21
Waters, Sylvia 181
Watson, Art 212–213
Watson, Bob 124
Wayne, John 94
Weaver, Earl 38
Wedge, Eric 213–214
Weeghman, Charles 44
Wells, David 84
Wendlestedt, Harry 52
Wetzel, Dutch 214
Wetzel, Gerald "George" 214
Wexelberg, Roger 71
Whaley, Bill 214–215
Whaling, Bert 204
Wheat, Zach 51, 54, 167
Wheeler, George 215
Wheeler, Harry 215–216
Whisler, Wes 216–217
Whitaker, Lou 56–57
Whitcomb, Edgar 49
White, Jack 217–218
White, Will 216
Whitman, Frank 218
Wicker, Bob 197, 218–219
Wilhelm, Hoyt 152
Wilhelm, Kaiser 217
Williams, Bernie 39
Williams, Cy 43, 219–221

Williams, Dick 176, 203
Williams, Joe 33
Williams, Mitch "Wild Thing" 148
Williams, Ted 14, 31, 67, 137, 151, 220
Wilson, Art 59, 83
Wilson, Hack 220
Wilson, Phillip B. 115
Wiltse, Hooks 129
Wingo, Ivy 157
Winkles, Bobby 176
Wise, Casey 220–221
Wise, Hugh 220
Wise, Hugh, Jr. 220
Woehr, Andy 221
Woehr, Richard 221
Woods, Clarence 221–222
"Woodstock" 14
Woodward, Woody 36
Worrell, Josh 13
Worrell, Todd 13
Wright, Bob 222–223
Wright, Harry 9
Wrightstone, Russ 133
Wyatt, Fred 223
Wyatt, Joe 223
Wyatt, Whit 14, 38
Wynn, Early 218

Youmans, Matt 159
Young, Cy 36, 45, 47
Young, Harley "Cy the Third" 223–224
Young, Irv "Young Cy" 223–224
Young, Nick 129
Young, William "Cy" 224

Zachary, Tom 140
Zachry, Pat 129
Zeider, Rollie 224–225
Zimmerman, Heinie 156–157, 222